D0773609

CYBER FORENSICS

OTHER INFORMATION SECURITY BOOKS FROM AUERBACH

802.1X Port-Based Authentication
Edwin Lyle Brown
ISBN: 1-4200-4464-8

Audit and Trace Log Management: Consolidation and Analysis
Phillip Q. Maier
ISBN: 0-8493-2725-3

The CISO Handbook: A Practical Guide to Securing Your Company
Michael Gentile, Ron Collette and Thomas D. August
ISBN: 0-8493-1952-8

Complete Guide to Security and Privacy Metrics: Measuring Regulatory Compliance, Operational Resilience, and ROI
Debra S. Herrmann
ISBN: 0-8493-5402-1

Crisis Management Planning and Execution
Edward S. Devlin
ISBN: 0-8493-2244-8

Computer Forensics: Evidence Collection and Management
Robert C. Newman
ISBN: 0-8493-0561-6

Curing the Patch Management Headache
Felicia M Nicastro
ISBN: 0-8493-2854-3

Cyber Crime Investigator's Field Guide, Second Edition
Bruce Middleton
ISBN: 0-8493-2768-7

Database and Applications Security: Integrating Information Security and Data Management
Bhavani Thuraisingham
ISBN: 0-8493-2224-3

Guide to Optimal Operational Risk and BASEL II
Ioannis S. Akkizidis and Vivianne Bouchereau
ISBN: 0-8493-3813-1

How to Achieve 27001 Certification: An Example of Applied Compliance Management
Sigurjon Thor Arnason and Keith D. Willett
ISBN: 0-8493-3648-1

Information Security: Design, Implementation, Measurement, and Compliance
Timothy P. Layton
ISBN: 0-8493-7087-6

Information Security Architecture: An Integrated Approach to Security in the Organization, Second Edition
Jan Killmeyer
ISBN: 0-8493-1549-2

Information Security Cost Management
Ioana V. Bazavan and Ian Lim
ISBN: 0-8493-9275-6

Information Security Fundamentals
Thomas R. Peltier, Justin Peltier, and John A. Blackley
ISBN: 0-8493-1957-9

Information Security Management Handbook, Sixth Edition
Harold F. Tipton and Micki Krause
ISBN: 0-8493-7495-2

Information Security Risk Analysis, Second Edition
Thomas R. Peltier
ISBN: 0-8493-3346-6

Investigations in the Workplace
Eugene F. Ferraro
ISBN: 0-8493-1648-0

IT Security Governance Guidebook with Security Program Metrics on CD-ROM
Fred Cohen
ISBN: 0-8493-8435-4

Managing an Information Security and Privacy Awareness and Training Program
Rebecca Herold
ISBN: 0-8493-2963-9

Mechanics of User Identification and Authentication: Fundamentals of Identity Management
Dobromir Todorov
ISBN: 1-4200-5219-5

Practical Hacking Techniques and Countermeasures
Mark D. Spivey
ISBN: 0-8493-7057-4

Securing Converged IP Networks
Tyson Macaulay
ISBN: 0-8493-7580-0

The Security Risk Assessment Handbook: A Complete Guide for Performing Security Risk Assessments
Douglas J. Landoll
ISBN: 0-8493-2998-1

Testing Code Security
Maura A. van der Linden
ISBN: 0-8493-9251-9

Wireless Crime and Forensic Investigation
Gregory Kipper
ISBN: 0-8493-3188-9

AUERBACH PUBLICATIONS
www.auerbach-publications.com
To Order Call: 1-800-272-7737 • Fax: 1-800-374-3401
E-mail: orders@crcpress.com

CYBER FORENSICS

A Field Manual for Collecting, Examining, and
Preserving Evidence of Computer Crimes

Second Edition

Albert J. Marcella, Jr.
Doug Menendez

 Auerbach Publications
Taylor & Francis Group
New York   London

CRC Press is an imprint of the
Taylor & Francis Group, an **informa** business

Auerbach Publications
Taylor & Francis Group
6000 Broken Sound Parkway NW, Suite 300
Boca Raton, FL 33487-2742

© 2008 by Taylor & Francis Group, LLC
Auerbach is an imprint of Taylor & Francis Group, an Informa business

No claim to original U.S. Government works
Printed in the United States of America on acid-free paper
10 9 8 7 6 5 4 3 2 1

International Standard Book Number-13: 978-0-8493-8328-1 (Hardcover)

This book contains information obtained from authentic and highly regarded sources. Reprinted material is quoted with permission, and sources are indicated. A wide variety of references are listed. Reasonable efforts have been made to publish reliable data and information, but the author and the publisher cannot assume responsibility for the validity of all materials or for the consequences of their use.

No part of this book may be reprinted, reproduced, transmitted, or utilized in any form by any electronic, mechanical, or other means, now known or hereafter invented, including photocopying, microfilming, and recording, or in any information storage or retrieval system, without written permission from the publishers.

For permission to photocopy or use material electronically from this work, please access www.copyright.com (http://www.copyright.com/) or contact the Copyright Clearance Center, Inc. (CCC) 222 Rosewood Drive, Danvers, MA 01923, 978-750-8400. CCC is a not-for-profit organization that provides licenses and registration for a variety of users. For organizations that have been granted a photocopy license by the CCC, a separate system of payment has been arranged.

Trademark Notice: Product or corporate names may be trademarks or registered trademarks, and are used only for identification and explanation without intent to infringe.

Library of Congress Cataloging-in-Publication Data

Cyber forensics : a field manual for collecting, examining, and preserving evidence of computer crimes / Albert J. Marcella and Doug Menendez. -- 2nd ed.
    p. cm.
Includes bibliographical references and index.
ISBN 978-0-8493-8328-1 (alk. paper)
    1. Computer crimes--Investigation--Handbooks, manuals, etc. I. Marcella, Albert J. II. Menendez, Doug.

HV8079.C65C93 2008
363.25'968--dc22   2007029431

Visit the Taylor & Francis Web site at
http://www.taylorandfrancis.com

and the Auerbach Web site at
http://www.auerbach-publications.com

Disclaimer

As always with any book of this nature, here is the disclaimer....

The information contained within this book is intended to be used as a reference and not as an endorsement, of the included providers, vendors, and informational resources. Reference herein to any specific commercial product, process, or service by trade name, trademark, service mark, manufacturer, or otherwise does not constitute or imply endorsement, recommendation, or favoring by the authors or the publisher.

As such, users of this information are advised and encouraged to confirm specific claims for product performance as necessary and appropriate.

The legal or financial materials and information that are available for reference through this book are not intended as a substitute for legal or financial advice and representation obtained through legal or financial counsel. It is advisable to seek the advice and representation of legal or financial counsel as may be appropriate for any matters to which the legal or financial materials and information may pertain.

Web sites included in this book are intended to provide current and accurate information, neither the authors, publisher, nor any of its employees, agencies, and officers can warranty the information contained on the sites and shall not be held liable for any losses caused on the reliance of information provided. Relying on information contained on these sites is done at one's own risk. Use of such information is voluntary, and reliance on it should only be undertaken after an independent review of its accuracy, completeness, efficacy, and timeliness.

Throughout this book, reference "links" to other Internet addresses have been included. Such external Internet addresses contain information created, published, maintained, or otherwise posted by institutions or organizations independent of the authors and the publisher. The authors and the publisher do not endorse, approve, certify, or control these external Internet addresses and do not guarantee the accuracy, completeness, efficacy, timeliness, or correct sequencing of information located at such addresses. Use of such information is voluntary, and reliance on it should only be undertaken after an independent review of its accuracy, completeness, efficacy, and timeliness.

Any mention of commercial products or reference to commercial organizations is for information only; it does not imply recommendation or endorsement by the authors, publisher, reviewers, contributors, or representatives nor does it imply that the products mentioned are necessarily the best available for the purpose.

Dedication

Given that a dedication's main objective is to honor the person, place, or event to which the author has a deep emotional connection, this book is dedicated to my family, which has had such a profound effect on my life in so many wonderful, beautiful ways.

Searching for the words to capture the emotions, the feelings, I have borrowed from universal proverbs, from cultures rich and varied, young and ancient. Proverbs, which speak from the heart, which speak words of truth and thought.

In the years to come, always know that Kristina, Erienne, Andy and Diane, you have always been my greatest source of inspiration, pride, joy and love.

Kristina   There is nothing noble in being superior to some other person. The true nobility is in being superior to your previous self.

Erienne   You already possess everything necessary to become great.

Andy   When you were born, you cried and the world rejoiced. Live your life so that when you die, the world cries and you rejoice.

Diane   All the flowers of all our tomorrows are in the seeds of today. Thank you for all the beauty that you have sown.

We will be known forever by the tracks we leave.
The Dakota

Al Marcella

Dedication

Dedication

Thanks to my family: Marcene, Emily and Matt, for their love and support throughout this project. Also, thanks to Al Marcella for the opportunity to co-author this book and for his friendship over the years.

Douglas A. Menendez

Contents

Foreword

This text will not make you a cyber forensics investigator or technician, if you are not one already! This text is designed to provide the reader with an introduction and overview of the field of cyber forensics, and the policies, legal ramifications and implications, procedures and methodologies of a cyber forensic investigation, from both a theoretical and practical perspective.

Without having the necessary skills and training, you should not attempt to investigate, for litigious purposes, the contents of or recover data from a computer (e.g., do not touch the keyboard or click the mouse) or any other electronic device.

Both practice and experience are good teachers, however, do not practice on a computer, cell phone or other electronic device capable of storing data that is part of a pending or ongoing civil or criminal investigation, doing so may critically jeopardize the ability to submit any data gathered as evidential matter in a court of law. Doing so may also jeopardize your professional career and expose you to potential legal and financial liability.

> Facts do not cease to exist because they are ignored.
>
> **Aldous Huxley**

This text will guide the reader through the various steps of basic cyber forensic investigations, with the objective of preparing the reader to participate with trained cyber forensic professionals, and to forensically evaluate a suspect machine. The reader is cautioned against using this material as the sole source of education and training and not to attempt to seize or evaluate a suspect machine without undergoing extensive and certified forensic education and field-level training.

The reader will be presented with information that will provide a platform for establishing a stronger understanding of the forensic process and its relationship to and dependency on technology, and its codependency on the legal and legislative process. The reader is taken on an in-depth examination of just how someone may manipulate the dark side of technology in an attempt to conceal illegal activities and how cyber forensics can be utilized to uncover these activities.

Additional critical topics to be addressed in the pages that you are about to read include defining cyber forensics; explaining the rules of evidence and chain of custody in maintaining electronic evidence; how to begin an investigation, the investigative methodology to employ as well as an examination of the steps in a cyber forensics investigation. Added to that, discussions on topics and issues such as establishing standard operating procedures for a cyber forensic laboratory, conducting a cyber forensic investigation while working within the legal framework at both the local and federal levels, and the current data security and integrity exposure of multifunctional devices are presented to the reader.

Further details describing the forensic process; how to take control of a suspect computer and its "operating" environment, along with potential exposures will be addressed as well.

The reader will find that a wealth of additional information has been included in the ample Appendices which can be found at the end of this text. The reader is encouraged to review these Appendices, which have been developed and compiled to supplement and add value to the material contained in the body of this text.

Sit back, relax and turn now to Chapter 1 and begin your journey into the exciting, professional arena of cyber forensic investigations.

Acknowledgments

We have relied upon professionals from varied walks of life, to share with us their knowledge, information, expertise, concerns, fears, experiences, and best practices. Without these resources, without the willingness of these individuals to share their secrets, sometimes private information, this book would not have met its objective.

The following dedicated professionals, some personal contacts and colleagues, have provided the authors with a wealth of knowledge, the breadth and depths of their experience, contributed content for inclusion in this book, and over the past year have unfailingly answered a barrage of questions. Each deserves our genuine and humblest thanks and deepest gratitude for their contributions to this text.

> Kent Mortimore, attorney and consultant providing training and technical legal advice to prosecutors, judges and professors, for his expertise and insights in developing the material for Chapter 12, Cyber Forensics and the Changing Face of Investigating Criminal Behavior. Kent currently lives and works in the Middle East. Prior to his overseas assignment, he served for 20 years as a prosecutor in Oregon.
>
> Vincent Liu, Managing Director, Stach and Liu, LLC for sharing his technical expertise in the area of antiforensics and antiforensic tools, for his insightful replies to the author's interview questions regarding the impact of antiforensic tools on the field of cyber forensics and for his untiring professionalism in answering a stream of seemingly unending questions.
>
> The Forensic Black Bag, Chapter 9, a peek inside a cyber forensic first responder's field bag, and Chapter 6, Standard Operating Procedures: Digital Forensic Laboratory Accreditation Standards were written by John Minotti, Managing Director, at Acquisition Data. The authors are grateful to John for his extensive contributions to this text and for providing superior field-level, practical advice through both his insights and extensive experience in the field of cyber forensics.
>
> Rick Sarre, Professor of Law and Criminal Justice, School of Commerce, Division of Business, University of South Australia, for his unique perspective on the fusion between the concept of privacy and privacy rights with the discipline of cyber forensics. Read Dr. Sarre's thoughts on this critical interrelationship in Chapter 8, Privacy and Cyber Forensics: An Australian Perspective.

The authors wish to acknowledge and thank the following individuals and organizations for their support in providing valuable information and in many cases, permission to reprint materials, which were critical to the timeliness and success of the research, supporting this text. To each of these individuals and organizations, our deepest thanks.

Atif Ahmad, Senior Tutor, Department of Information Systems, University of Melbourne

Illena Armstrong, Editor-in-Chief, *SC Magazine*

Wesley Augur, CTO, Oxona Corporation

Richard Braman, Executive Director, The Sedona Conference

Thomas Bruce, Research Associate and Director, Legal Information Institute, Cornell Law School

CNET Networks Inc., publishers of TechRepublic.com

Fulbright & Jaworski, LLP

Information Systems Audit and Control Association

International Journal of Digital Evidence

Barbara Churchill, IBM Program Director of Risk, Governance and Compliance

Peter Cybuck, Associate Director Solution and Security Business Development, Sharp Electronics Corporation

Matthew Drake, attorney and colleague

Matthew Geiger, CERT Software Engineering Institute, Carnegie Mellon University

Greg Gerritzen, District Sales Manager, Sharp Electronics

Steve Grimm, Officer, Webster Groves Police Department, Regional Computer Crimes Education and Enforcement Group

Jim Hadfield, President, CEO, Acquisition Data

Steve Hailey, President, CEO, CyberSecurity Institute

Chet Hosmer, President, CEO, WetStone Technologies, Inc.

Internet Security Systems, Inc.

Jim Kaplan, CEO, AuditNet

Orin Kerr, Associate Professor of Law, The George Washington University Law School

Gary Kessler, Associate Professor, Director of Computer & Digital Forensics, Information Technology & Sciences Division, Director, Center for Digital Investigation, Champlain College

Marc Kirby, Senior Lecturer in Forensic Computing at Cranfield University, U.K.

John J. Knoll, Assistant City Attorney/Police Legal Advisor, City of Topeka, Kansas

Charles Kozierok, Editor and Developer, *The PC Guide*

Eddy Kurms, CEO, LSoft Technologies, Inc.

Omar Leeman, Executive Vice President, AccessData

Gregory Miles, President, CFO, Principal Security Consultant, Security Horizon, Inc.

Brian Mize, Detective, Chesterfield Police Department, Regional Computer Crimes Education and Enforcement Group

Andre Moenssens, Douglas Stripp Missouri Professor of Law Emeritus, University of Missouri at Kansas City

Peter L. Murray, Edward R. Johnston Lecturer on Law, Robert Braucher Visiting Professor of Law from Practice, Harvard Law School

Brian O'Neil, President, Confidential Computers

Charles R. Nesson, Weld Professor of Law, Harvard Law School

New Technologies, Inc.

Mark Powell, OIT Data Security, University of Minnesota
Marc Rogers, Associate Professor Computer Technology, Purdue University
RSA Security, Inc.
Justin Ryburn, CEO, Ryburn Consulting
Dennis Waldron, President, DEW Associates Corporation
Ziff Davis Media

Finally, albeit not without great appreciation, the authors wish to thank Sam Fitzgerald, Director of Academic Affairs for the St. Louis campuses of the University of Phoenix for her assistance in compiling the survey responses and preparing the corresponding data analysis for Chapter 14.

To each individual, organization, corporation, and association, we thank you for your time, contribution, dedication, commitment, spirit, and support. This book is a better product as a result of your involvement.

Our deepest thanks and words of appreciation to Melissa LaMonica and Nicolas Indelicato who assisted us in incalculable ways by providing countless hours of their personal time in the overall project management of this research and writing effort, lent their artistic talents in photography and graphic design to produce many of the photos and graphics found throughout this text, and ensured that each completed chapter met the publisher's stringent editorial guidelines. Thank you Melissa and Nic, this text could not have been completed so successfully without your diligent and conscientious efforts, oversight, and personal involvement.

Al Marcella, PhD, CISA

Douglas A. Menendez, CIA, CISA

About the Authors

Albert J. Marcella Jr, PhD, CISA is president of Business Automation Consultants, LLC a global information technology and management consulting firm providing IT management consulting and IT audit and security reviews and training for an international clientele. Dr. Marcella is an internationally recognized public speaker, researcher, and seminar leader with 30 years of experience in IT audit, security and assessing internal controls, and an author of numerous articles and 28 books on various audit- and security-related subjects. Prior to the formation of his own firm in 1984, Dr. Marcella was employed by Dun & Bradstreet Corporation where he established and formalized that organization's IT audit function.

Dr. Marcella's additional professional experiences include providing internal systems consulting services to the Hartford Insurance Group, and the design and execution of operational, financial, and information technology audits for the Uniroyal Corporation, both in the United States and abroad.

Dr. Marcella is the Institute of Internal Auditors' Leon R. Radde Educator of the Year, 2000, Award recipient. Dr. Marcella has taught IT audit seminar courses for the Institute of Internal Auditors, and has been recognized by the IIA as a Distinguished Adjunct Faculty Member. Dr. Marcella also leads IT audit seminars for the Information Systems Audit and Control Association.

Douglas A. Menendez, CIA, CISA, MBA has over 26 years of financial, operational and information technology auditing experience in a variety of industries, including the Federal Reserve Bank, Citicorp Mortgage, Ralston Purina, Venture Stores, Express Scripts, and Enterprise Rent-A-Car.

Doug has presented seminars at local, national and international conferences. Previous presentations include the ISACA CACS Conference, the ISSA International Conference, and the CA World Conference.

He has written several articles for audit and security publications, including the IIA's *Internal Auditor* and Auerbach's *EDPACS*. He was also a module reviewer for the IIA's Systems Auditability and Control (SAC) project.

Doug is a CISA (Certified Information Systems Auditor), a CIA (Certified Internal Auditor), and earned an MBA from Saint Louis University. He is also a past president of the St. Louis chapter of the Information Systems Audit and Control Association (ISACA) and the Institute of Internal Auditors (IIA).

Doug was the IT Audit Program Committee Chairman for the 1990 IIA International Conference held in St. Louis, Missouri.

Chapter 1

Introduction

Although technology in general and computers specifically, since their introduction and dissemination into mainstream society, have benefited society, there is also a sinister, dark side to this technology when it is abused. In recent years, society has seen the rise in abuse of various kinds—personal or private and corporate, conducted with, through or by technology.

These abuses usually have as their objective, the misappropriation of assets (financial or otherwise), disruption of commerce, theft of personally identifiable information, the exploitation of innocent individuals, destabilization of governmental infrastructure, outright terrorism (political, cyber, and religious), theft of intellectual property and the suppression of generally outright illegal activities conducted in the safety of one's home or office, thousands of miles removed from the victim's geographical location, cloaked in the secrecy of a virtual world. A world that exists solely as electronic bits and bytes, where one's actions and activities, illegal or not, can exist for a fleeting picosecond or be captured and archived, saved for perpetuity.

The existence of data in electronic form, representative of one's activities while working, living, and playing in a virtual environment, creates electronic footprints and an electronic trail of our daily lives and activities. The necessity and ability to identify, capture, recreate, display, and store these electronic footprints, enable those professionals charged with protecting personal, corporate and governmental security and safety, to perform their assigned responsibilities and to pursue those individuals, organizations and nation states who utilize the dark side of technology to engage in illegal activities.

> As computers become more advanced, so do criminal activities. Therefore, the computer forensics niche is in constant progression along with the technological advancements of computers.

> **Frederick Gallegos**

1

Technology Abuses Affecting Corporate and Personal Securities

Headlines ripped straight from the daily news send waves of terror through the executive level and boardrooms of today's global organizations. The impact on earnings, the threat of loss of customer confidence, the specter of potential jail time for corporate executives are very real, and sentencing outcomes of recent litigation bear witness to the validity of these exposures. How will organizations affected by these (or comparable) acts, by similar failures in information security, employee integrity and outright fraud, defend themselves legally, and in the court of public opinion?

■ May 22, 2006—The Department of Veterans Affairs (VA) learned that an employee—a data analyst, took home electronic data from VA, which he was not authorized to do. This data included names, social security numbers, dates of birth, some disability ratings for up to 26.5 million veterans and some spouses, personal information on as many as 1.1 million military members on active duty, 430,000 members of the National Guard, and 645,000 members of the Reserves. Importantly, the affected data did not include any of VA's electronic health records or any financial information. The employee's home was burglarized and this data was stolen [1].

■ April 20, 2006—A U.S. district court judge ordered an invention promotion operation to pay $26 million in consumer redress and to permanently halt the bogus claims that the company used to recruit customers. The court also ordered that in future dealings with consumers, the company make specific and detailed disclosures about their track record in helping inventors market their ideas [2].

■ February 28, 2006—Kenneth J. Flury, was sentenced to 32 months in prison, to be followed by three years of supervised release, as a result of Flury's recent convictions for bank fraud and conspiracy. Flury was charged with one count of bank fraud, arising from Flury's scheme to defraud CitiBank that occurred between April 15, 2004 and May 4, 2004, and involved Flury obtaining stolen CitiBank debit card account numbers, personal identification numbers, and personal identifiable information of the true account holders which Flury fraudulently encoded onto blank automatic teller machine (ATM) cards. After encoding blank cards with the stolen account information, Flury used the counterfeit ATM to obtain cash advances, to withdraw cash and obtain cash advances totaling over $384,000 (USD) from ATM machines located in the Greater Cleveland area over a three-week period. After Flury fraudulently obtained the funds, he transferred approximately $167,000 of the fraud proceeds via Western Union money transfer to the individuals supplying the stolen CitiBank account information located in Europe and Asia. Law enforcement officers seized approximately $157,080 in cash from Flurry on May 5, 2004, and also intercepted an additional $32,345 Flury had attempted to transfer via Western Union to Russia on or about May 4, 2004 [3].

■ November 17, 2005—Six men who administered and operated the "Shadowcrew.com" Web site—one of the largest online centers for trafficking in stolen credit and bankcard numbers and identity information, were sentenced. The one-stop online marketplace operated by the defendants was taken down in October 2004 by the U.S. Secret Service, closing an illicit business that trafficked in at least 1.5 million stolen credit and bankcard numbers that resulted in losses in excess of $4 million. Shadowcrew members sent and received payment for illicit merchandise and services via Western Union money transfer and digital currencies such as E-Gold and Web Money. In addition, it was determined that in September 2004, members of this organization illegally acquired via computer, approximately 18 million e-mail accounts with associated usernames, passwords, dates of birth, and other personally identifying information—approximately 60,000 of which included first and last name, gender, address, city, state, country, and telephone number [4].

- August 12, 2005—Scott Levine was found guilty of 120 counts of unauthorized access of a protected computer, two counts of access device fraud and one count of obstruction of justice. He and some of his coworkers at e-mail distributor Snipermail stole more than one billion records containing personal information from business partner and data management firm Acxiom [5].
- July 14, 2005—Allan Eric Carlson was convicted of 79 counts of computer and identity fraud and sentenced to 48 months in jail. An unhappy baseball fan, he spoofed e-mails complaining about the poor performance of the Philadelphia Phillies from writers at area newspapers, Fox Sports, ESPN, and other media [5].
- February 28, 2005—Juju Jiang was sentenced to 27 months in prison for installing key loggers on computers at various Kinko's locations throughout Manhattan. He collected confidential information that gave him access to individuals' bank accounts [5].

An ability to prove, to attest to the viability of internal control structures within the procedures, the systems and the applications of an organization, beyond a shadow of a doubt, will increasingly become the challenge of organizations that are faced with the need to demonstrate that the exposures, the loss of information, the breech of security, or the unauthorized release of information was not a breakdown of the corporate entity but, the misguided acts of individuals, working independently, for personal gain.

Computers can be used in a variety of roles in the commitment of a crime. Each of these roles can raise novel investigative and prosecutorial issues because of the unique attributes of computers and the electronic evidence they hold. Today, the need for organizations to implement a vigilant cyber forensic program with appropriate personnel training, engagement policies, and applicable procedures has never been more critical.

Now that the Sarbanes–Oxley Act and other laws dictate that companies not destroy data records, e-mails and even instant messages are being used increasingly as evidence in high-profile court cases. Technology managers must get at their data fast and vouch for its completeness. Those who cannot produce what the courts require on a timely basis put their companies at risk for fines or punishments.

Across industries, big companies are scrapping with judges and regulators over data.

A U.S. District Court judge in Washington, D.C. ordered Philip Morris USA to pay $2.75 million in fines when it came out during federal tobacco litigation in 2004 that 11 managers did not save printouts of their e-mail messages, as per company policy. As an added punishment, those managers were barred from testifying at trial, according to the order from U.S. District Court Judge Gladys Kessler.

Bank of America Securities, a brokerage arm of Bank of America, "repeatedly failed promptly to furnish" e-mail, compliance reviews and stock-trading records during a preliminary investigation in 2001, the Securities and Exchange Commission (SEC) said. The brokerage also gave "misinformation" about its records and provided incomplete, unreliable data—some of it 15 months after first requests. In a 2004 settlement between the brokerage and the SEC, the SEC found the brokerage violated two Exchange Act sections and Bank of America agreed to pay a $10 million fine.

Last year, in a lengthy sex discrimination case against UBS Warburg filed in 2002, a U.S. District Court judge in New York found that the company deleted e-mail in violation of a court order and could not produce backup tapes. The judge told the jury they could "infer that the [missing] evidence would have been unfavorable to UBS." The jury decided against the bank and awarded plaintiff Laura Zubulake $29.3 million. Although UBS Warburg denied discriminating against her and said it would appeal, the bank settled the case last September for an undisclosed sum.

What happened at Morgan Stanley last year, however, stands apart because of the huge judgment levied against it in a Florida state court. The investment bank repeatedly failed to turn over data related to a fraud suit last year brought by Coleman Holdings Inc., the owner of camping gear maker Coleman Co., according to an order written by the judge in the case, Elizabeth T. Maass. One of Morgan Stanley's technology workers concealed knowledge of 1423 backup tapes, later found in Brooklyn, NY, when he certified that the bank had produced all its evidence, according to court documents. At least three other times, the judge said, the bank lost or mislaid backup tapes.

Fed up, Maass took dramatic action. She read a three-page statement to the jury detailing the missteps—which included overwriting e-mails and using flawed search software that hampered searches of Lotus Notes messages. She told the jury to assume the bank acted with "malice or evil intent" unless it could prove otherwise.

Morgan Stanley lost the case, big: The jury awarded Coleman $1.6 billion. The bank is appealing.

In December 2006, new amendments to the Federal Rules of Civil Procedure (FRCP) went into effect. The new rules require lawers to know enough about their clients' information systems to disclose all sources of electronic information relevant to a case. That includes sources where data is not "reasonably accessible" because it is costly or hard to produce. Dusty and perhaps forgotten backup tapes are a prime example. If one side wants hard-to-get information, the other side has the burden to show why they cannot have it.

If, during an audit or lawsuit, the company is unable to produce data that its policy says it should have on hand, it risks repercussions. They range from admonishments from a judge or regulatory body to multimillion-dollar fines, as happened to Bank of America Securities and Philip Morris, USA [6].

> These "cyber-crimes" are not necessarily new crimes, but rather classic crimes exploiting computing power and accessibility to information. They are a consequence of excessive availability and user proficiency of computer systems in unethical hands. To catch and prosecute criminals involved with digital crime, investigators must employ consistent and well-defined forensic procedures. [7]

Defining Cyber Forensics

The technological perspective versus a medical or financial perspective of forensics as discussed throughout this text will dominate the discipline of cyber forensic investigation. Thus beginning with a workable definition of cyber forensics seems to be a logical starting point. Logical, yes and easy, no.

The world of cyber forensic investigation is relatively new and evolving and as such, long-term standards, protocols, definitions, policies, and procedures are emerging as well. They are being defined and redefined; therefore, agreeing upon a single name for the process has not been globally standardized.

Cyber forensics, e-discovery (electronic evidence discovery), digital forensics, computer forensics, all relevant, each meaning relatively the same thing, and depending on whom you speak with, each meaning something very different, yet none has emerged as a de facto standard. Therefore, as this profession, this art, science continues to develop, emerge and be defined, we present here a selected few "working" definitions of cyber forensics, taken from a sampling of practitioners, authors, and governmental sources to help set the stage for the discussions to follow and as a starting point for further discussion of the information to be presented throughout this book.

Working Definitions for the Advancement of the Profession

Computer forensics is the science of locating, extracting, and analyzing types of data from difference devices, which specialists then interpret to serve as legal evidence [8].

E-discovery is the preservation, processing, review, and production of computer evidence in response to civil litigation discovery requirements [9].

Computer forensics is the discipline that combines elements of law and computer science to collect and analyze data from computer systems, networks, wireless communications, and storage devices in a way that is admissible as evidence in a court of law [10].

Computer forensics is the science of locating, extracting, analyzing, and protecting types of data from difference devices, which specialists then interpret to serve as legal evidence [11].

E-discovery refers to the discovery of electronic documents and data. Electronic documents include e-mail, Web pages, word processing files, computer databases, and virtually anything that is stored on a computer. Technically, documents and data are "electronic" if they exist in a medium that can be read only through the use of computers. Such media include cache memory, magnetic disks (such as computer hard drives or floppy disks), optical disks (such as DVDs or CDs), and magnetic tapes. E-discovery is often distinguished from "paper discovery," which refers to the discovery of writings on paper that can be read without the aid of some devices [12].

Cyber Forensic Investigation Process

In general, the process of cyber forensic investigation consists of (policies and procedures do vary slightly among organizations) the following steps:

1. Identification—documentation
2. Collection or extraction—documentation
3. Preservation—documentation
4. Interpretation or analysis—documentation
5. Communication

The preservation of the integrity of the electronic evidence collected is tightly coupled to ensuring that there is in place a solid documentation process. The documentation process should be designed to authenticate and substantiate each step taken to identify, collect (extract) preserve, and interpret or analyze, the electronic evidence as well as each individual who may have in any way, interacted with (handled) the electronic evidence.

Greater emphasis cannot be placed on the importance of documenting the cyber forensic process, as such; it is shown here as a sub-step of the first four steps in the cyber forensic process. These four steps should not be initiated, conducted or completed without extensive, clear, and detailed documentation. The documentation process typically begins with a sound chain of custody process (explained in greater detail later in this chapter).

Identification requires the investigator along with organizational management or potentially external assistance (e.g., witnesses, law enforcement professionals, etc.) to make a determination as to exactly what might be a source of evidence (electronic or manual) [i.e., personal digital assistants (PDAs), pagers, files, laptops, hard drives, storage area networks (SANs), etc.]. The physical housing containing the technology is not electronic evidence, although the physical housing may provide additional evidence of a non-electronic type (e.g., fingerprints, serial numbers, etc.), the housing is merely a receptacle for the electronic evidence, which resides stored on drives, or in files. The cyber forensic investigator must determine and must identify what and where the electronic evidence is to be collected.

Collection or extraction is the process of physically gathering the electronic evidence, which will eventually be copied several times (typically making three forensic copies), using specialty software and hardware along with backup methods designed to document and preserve the original data. These copying and backup processes allow the investigator to work on and examine an identical, forensically sound, yet duplicate copy of the original electronic evidence (data). This is the preservation step of the cyber forensic process.

Preservation is performed so that (a) the electronic evidence collected will be preserved in its original, unaltered form; (b) the cyber forensic investigator can examine the electronic evidence utilizing special analysis tools without fear of damaging, destroying or altering the original electronic evidence source, and (c) in the unlikely event that a copy of the electronic evidence is unusable or damaged in some manner, the cyber forensic investigator can resort to making another copy from a still existing, untouched backup copy. The originally collected electronic evidence, once duplicated, is sealed and securely locked away.

Finding electronic evidence is fairly easy, making sense out of what is found and determining its integrity, feasibility, usefulness, to provide an opinion on the relevance of the electronic evidence to the case at hand, however, is another matter. Interpretation or analysis—results of the cyber forensic examination requires sound cyber forensics training and many years experience—to correctly interpret the findings. The ramifications of incorrectly interpreting the examined electronic evidence or in failing to identify evidence altogether could very well mean significant financial loss and legal liability for an organization as well as professional liability for the cyber forensic investigator.

Communicating the findings of a cyber forensic investigation may well be dictated by circumstance. Was the investigation initiated by a private, internal corporate request (e.g., internal audit)? As a result of a law enforcement warrant? In response to a legal action taken against a current or former employee, contractor or third-party? Depending on who initiated the investigation or the circumstances leading to the cyber forensic investigation, communicating the results may require the cyber forensic investigator to appear in court or before a corporate Board of Directors.

Regardless of the final setting, the investigator's final report should be considered proprietary, confidential and disclosed to only those individuals with the appropriate need to know clearances and authorizations. The detail, content and design of the final report may vary among organizations and departments; in general, however, the report should provide a clear timeline and substantiated documentation of the steps, actions, findings, and conclusions of cyber forensic investigator. It is imperative that the investigator makes adequate copies of this final report, retaining, however, distribution control of all copies.

Illegal Activities Warranting Cyber Forensic Investigation

Each of the following potential exposures, depending on their impact on internal control structures and relevance to organizational information technology (IT) systems, would possibly warrant an organization mobilizing and initiating a forensic investigation.

- Fraud audits
- Identity theft
- Hacking
- Embezzlement
- Instances of homicide
- Drug and embezzlement record keeping
- Child pornography
- Civil litigation in cases of divorce, age or race discrimination, sexual harassment, wrongful dismissal, termination.
- Compromise customer privacy data stored electronically
- Peer-to-peer file sharing

- Leak or unauthorized disclosure of internal and confidential information
- Theft of trade secrets, intellectual property
- Unlawful access to company computers
- Use of company computers or technology for personal gain (running auction sites, shopping, E-bay, fantasy sports leagues, etc.)
- Violation of company acceptable use policies (downloading music and movies, accessing adult Web site, etc.)
- Launching denial of service attacks against a competitor

Additional examples of various exposures to corporate, government and private data, and operations, which may benefit from a cyber forensic investigation include, but are not limited to: the theft of 40 million records at Card Systems (a third party processor for payment card transactions); Broadcom Corporation's prosecution of former employees for the theft of intellectual property; the loss of untold number of debit card information at Citibank, Bank of America, Washington Mutual, and Wells Fargo; loss of laptops at a Fidelity Investments, Ford Motor Company, Ameriprise, The Providence Health Care Hospital, Verizon, and FBI, and more routine activities such as inadvertently posting of private information online.

> Many organizations are placing enterprise computer forensics in their core security and controls processes, including, the detection and investigation of intellectual property (IP) theft.
>
> **John Patzakis**

Cyber Forensics: Thwarting Corporate Risk

Plaintiff Four Seasons Hotels sued its licensee for computer fraud, copyright infringement and misappropriation of customer profile, proprietary information valued at over $2 million. The plaintiff's expert established that the defendant had hacked into plaintiff's Open Reach virtual private computer network and management's e-mail accounts, downloaded proprietary data onto backup tapes, fabricated electronic evidence and engaged in spoliation by deleting files and overwriting data with 525 megabytes of files on a computer hard drive shortly before its production.

The court found that the "only possible reason for creating files of that large a size on the day before a computer was scheduled to be turned over for inspection would be to prevent subsequent examination of the space where that data was stored." The court found the defendant in violation of the federal Computer Fraud and Abuse Act on multiple occasions and awarded the defendant $2,118,000 (the value of the information plus $28,000 in expert expenses). The court also entered judgment for the defendant under the Electronic Communications Privacy Act but could not determine the damages and so awarded attorneys fees and costs on this count [Four Seasons Hotels and Resorts B.V. V. Consorcio Barr, S.A., 16 Fla. L. Weekly Fed. D389 (S.D. Fla. 2003)].

According to Brian Ingram—author of the article *"Locate Smoking Guns Electronically,"* more than 90 percent of new corporate data is created electronically, and 40 percent of that data is never converted to paper [13]. This deluge of corporate data raises serious issues about storage, accessibility, and legal compliance.

The problem is not just then the tremendous volume of electronic data accumulated and retained by organizations, the problem becomes determining exactly which data is valuable, critical or necessary in the defense of a client, or corporation.

Ingram goes on to state, "Numerous examples exist of cases won or lost on the discovery of a single word or phrase that resided in an old e-mail system."

In another case, after accepting a position with a competing company, the defendant, a former employee of the plaintiff company, copied numerous files from his work computer. The defendant asserted that he wanted to remove personal files from his computer and did not know how to do so without copying the entire "My Documents" folder. Computer forensic examination, however, discovered that certain files that the defendant copied were not part of the "My Documents" folder. Additionally, forensic examination revealed the defendant's attempts to cover evidence of the downloads [*LeJeune v. Coin Acceptors, Inc.*, 2004 Md. LEXIS 251 (Md. Ct. App. May 13, 2004)].

The risks faced by management only increases as technology becomes more sophisticated. Individuals intent on misusing technology realize that their ability to do so becomes easier as management's ability to deter them becomes exponentially more challenging and more difficult.

The International Data Corporation predicts that the total number of e-mail messages sent daily is expected to exceed 60 billion worldwide, up from 31 billion in 2002. Slightly more than half of these messages will be person-to-person e-mails. This means that approximately 25 billion messages will be business-related e-mails. These e-mails may some day become part and parcel to litigation, regulatory, and compliance-related electronic discovery. This expansion of the demand for electronic data is a key factor in the continuing growth of the e-discovery industry [14].

Fraud, embezzlement, theft of IP, accusations of sexual harassment, wrongful termination—words that strike fear in the hearts of management. How to prove or better yet disprove such allegations is even a bigger fear.

Allegations brought by an employer against an employee or an employee against his or her employer require proof and evidence. Evidence that can be brought to court, evidence that can ultimately withstand the rigors of a legal system that has stringent rules, which guide and govern the admissibility of evidence, which may exist solely in an electronic state.

In an employment dispute, the employee obtained an order allowing her forensics expert to have full access to search the employer's e-mail server, central server, and individual work stations after the employer had denied the existence of any documents and her computer forensic expert showed numerous references to the "active space" on the employer's computers and in deleted files [*Tilberg v. Next Management*, 2005 WL 2759860 (S.D.N.Y. Oct. 24, 2005)].

Any investigation, whether it leads to a company taking action against an employee or the successful prosecution of a suspected industrial spy, requires irrefutable proof.

Trends: The Increasing Need for Proactive Cyber Forensic Investigative Abilities

The collapse of Enron and Arthur Andersen, and the legislative response to these events, including the Sarbanes–Oxley Act of 2002, confirmed the importance of handling electronic document production in a defensible manner. (The Sedona Conference Working Group Steering Committee on Electronic Document Production, July 2005 [15].)

Fulbright and Jaworski commissioned an independent survey of corporate General Counsel, from 311 companies headquartered in 29 states to participate in what has become one of the largest polls of corporate counsel on litigation issues. In addition to U.S. respondents, Fulbright surveyed law departments in 22 other countries, including the United Kingdom, Canada, Mexico, Japan, Brazil, and elsewhere in Asia, Europe, and Latin America.

The 354 conducted interviews, including 50 participants in the United Kingdom, again made this a statistically significant survey sample and likely the largest survey of corporate litigation trends ever conducted. The Fulbright survey found that U.S. companies face an average of 305 pending lawsuits internationally. For large U.S. companies—those with $1 billion or more in annual gross revenue—the number of lawsuits soared to 556 cases, with an average of 50 new disputes emerging each year for close to half of them.

Billion-dollar + companies carry the biggest litigation burden, fielding 556 cases on average, almost half facing 50 new suits annually; 40 percent of large companies expect number of actions to increase in coming year; insurers are the litigation Olympians, confronting an average of 1696 lawsuits, followed by retailers and energy firms.

Litigation has its effect, with 63 percent of United States companies launching internal investigations requiring outside counsel in the past year; foreign companies cite high legal costs, punitive damages as prime anxieties about litigating in the United States; despite recent options backdating woes, labor or employment and contract disputes top list of litigation concern. Businesses give as well as they get—70 percent of U.S. companies have brought actions as plaintiffs in past year. Vast majority of reporting businesses say they are not prepared to handle an e-discovery challenge.

The average litigation expenditure for the 311 U.S. companies participating in the Fulbright study was $12 million—an amount that does not include ultimate case settlement or judgment payments. That figure looms larger considering that it represents more than 70 percent of overall legal spending by the average American business. For a number of industries, the costs associated with litigation—everything from attorneys' fees to document production, court filings, and jury consultants—were considerably steeper.

The ability to handle difficult e-discovery matters is a source of concern for most organizations surveyed. Just 19 percent of respondents consider their companies to be well-prepared for e-discovery issues while the vast majority (81 percent) report being not at all prepared to only somewhat prepared.

More than a third of the United Kingdom contingent (35 percent) felt "not at all" or "poorly prepared," while 23 percent of the United States respondents fell into this category. Even the largest companies demonstrated little confidence in their preparedness with just 19 percent feeling well-prepared. No one feels completely prepared.

When asked about the resources they use for e-discovery assistance, the majority start with their in-house, general IT resources (61 percent), and supplement them with others, most frequently outside e-discovery vendors (31 percent). Law firms with e-discovery expertise are part of the mix for 25 percent of the respondents, and 13 percent also rely to some extent on in-house e-discovery teams. This practice is more widely used in the United Kingdom and internationally than in the United States.

Despite the growing concern in legal circles over the potential impact of e-discovery, most companies do not appear to have had their discovery protocols and procedures tested in court. A 70 percent majority of U.S. counsel said that e-discovery issues had rarely or never been the subjects of a motion, hearing or ruling in even one of their cases over the past year. Only four percent indicated they faced an e-discovery challenge with any frequency.

For now, technology or communications companies feel the greatest heat from e-discovery contests—43 percent reported litigating e-discovery disputes with a high degree of frequency in the past year. The only other sectors showing a meaningful blip in the number of e-discovery contests were health care (14 percent) and manufacturing (8 percent).

Should a wave of e-discovery problems wash over American business, as some observers have predicted, companies may have to scramble to get ready. Only 15 percent of U.S. counsel surveyed by Fulbright said their companies were well-prepared to handle a difficult e-discovery challenge as part of a contested civil matter or regulatory investigation.

However, with the amended federal rules concerning e-discovery, companies may face more court tests of their e-discovery preparedness in cases where the meet-and-confer process does not effectively resolve e-discovery disputes. Amendments to the Civil Procedure Rules in England and Wales are likely to have a similar effect.

Since the collapse of Arthur Andersen in 2002, "document retention" has become a watchword for many corporate law departments alert to the dangers of improper purging of company information.

The 2006 survey shows that corporate counsels are indeed heeding the importance of document preservation procedures in the face of a lawsuit or investigation. Seventy-nine percent of respondents said their companies had a written records retention policy in accordance with applicable statutes and regulations. Of the minority remaining, two-thirds said they were planning to adopt a records policy in the coming year.

At the same time, 80 percent of counsel indicated their companies had procedures in place for issuing a "litigation hold"—precise instructions for document retention in the event of a civil suit or enforcement action. Approximately half of those without a litigation hold policy said they expected to implement one in the next 12 months. Larger companies appear more advanced in this area—around 90 percent of billion-dollar firms reported having both retention and litigation hold protocols in place, whereas for companies under $100 million, the averages were about six in ten. Implementation of retention and litigation hold protocols remains an open question, as 64 percent of respondents indicated they had not yet conducted any employee training in these related areas.

In 2005, 37 percent of respondents said they had plans to adopt or revise their litigation hold policy in the coming year; in 2006, 42 percent had plans to do so. Banking or financial services companies show the greatest increase (21 percent in 2005, 57 percent in 2006), reflecting the ongoing effects of the Sarbanes–Oxley Act and other regulatory requirements in the United States.

The number of respondents in the United Kingdom who plan to adopt or revise litigation hold procedures has dropped from 31 percent in 2005 to 23 percent in 2006. This decrease may reflect the fact that regulatory issues are becoming a primary concern for the United Kingdom companies and therefore most have already adopted or recently revised such policies [15].

The results of the 2005 Socha–Gelbmann e-discovery survey report, which covered the calendar year 2004, estimated that 2004 domestic commercial e-discovery revenues were in the range of $832 million—a 94 percent increase from 2003 [16]. This finding is significant to both the firms that provide services in the form e-discovery, business is only bound to get better, to increase, to those organizations that may need to acquire these specialized services. Failing to have an internal cyber forensic investigative function capable of leading internal investigations and the collection and preservation of electronic evidence could prove financially expensive.

The cost of designing and ultimately implementing a viable internal cyber forensic investigative team may be less in the long run than sourcing that responsibility to an external third-party. Additionally, the ability to keep internal sensitive materials, policies, procedures, and data secure, and away from external view, during an investigation, may be a greater corporate incentive for the development of an internal cyber forensic investigative team.

Knowing how to identify, collect, preserve, and present the evidence collected as a result of the e-discovery effort is critical to successfully protecting a company's digital assets (IP) and even its public reputation.

The art, the science of identifying, collecting, preserving and presenting that evidence when it exists solely as electronic bit and bytes, when it is locked away in the hard drive of a PC, laptop, or hidden in a server, is the evolving discipline of cyber forensics. Peeking under the hood, rooting out the electronic evidence in a manner that will satisfy your legal staff, your HR Director, the external legal system, and comply with existing legal statutes requires a precise methodology, part art; part science; and the skills of a cyber forensic investigator.

The legal system gives everyone benefit of the doubt. You are innocent until proven guilty. In today's technically dominated society, the ability to abuse and misuse technology, places even the innocent at risk—at risk from the inability to gather the evidence necessary to make a conviction or secure and acquittal.

As the legal system presses organizations, with increasing legal rigor, to provide evidence, electronic evidence of current or historical transactional activities, in a timely fashion, an inability to do so will result in organizations facing legal and financial liabilities.

The Sedona Principles for Electronic Document Production stipulate 14 best practice principles and recommendations for addressing electronic document production. These best practices are also valuable in determining policy and procedure for retention of electronic documents which one-day may become evidence [17].

Selected from the list of 14 best practices, the following should give every reader pause for reflection and a personal assessment of his or her organization's internal procedures and preparedness to meet the electronic evidence requirements of the 21st century:

- Electronic data and documents are potentially discoverable under Fed. R. Civ. P. 34 or its state law equivalents. Organizations must properly preserve electronic data and documents that can reasonably be anticipated to be relevant to litigation.
- Sanctions, including spoliation findings, should only be considered by the court if, upon a showing of a clear duty to preserve, the court finds that there was an intentional or reckless failure to preserve and produce relevant electronic data and that there is a reasonable probability that the loss of the evidence has materially prejudiced the adverse party.
- The reader interested in reviewing the complete list of 14 best practices along with the Committee's complete report will find this document at www.thesedonaconference.org/dlt.

Evidence: Separating the Wheat from the Chaff

But just what is evidence, how is it identified, justified, collected, preserved, and finally formatted, according to governing laws, to enable a company to pursue legal remedies for illegal use, access, and/or dissemination of its most valuable asset, its data?

Evidence in its purest form is information presented in testimony or in documents that is used to persuade the fact finder (judge or jury) to decide the case for one side or the other.

Electronic evidence is information and data of investigative value that is stored on or transmitted by an electronic device. Such evidence is acquired when data or physical items are collected and stored for examination purposes.

Electronic evidence is often latent in the same sense as fingerprints or DNA evidence. Electronic evidence:

- Can transcend borders with ease and speed
- Is fragile and can be easily altered, damaged, or destroyed
- Is sometimes time-sensitive [18]

Evidence must have a margin of error associated with it and the output must always be verified. A first responder (auditor, law enforcement professional, human resource director, etc.) may be responsible for the recognition, collection, preservation, transportation, or storage of electronic evidence.

Thus knowledge of even the rudimentary rules governing the collection, preservation, and safeguarding of evidence is critical. A greater in-depth knowledge of the rules of evidence is highly recommended for any professional engaged in or considering cyber forensic investigations.

Handling electronic evidence normally consists of the following steps:

- Recognition and identification of the evidence
- Documentation of the site of evidence collection
- Collection and preservation of the evidence
- Packaging and transportation of the evidence

The courts may closely scrutinize actions that have the potential to alter, damage, or destroy original evidence. Within the legal system, such uncontrolled destruction of potential evidence is referred to as spoliation. Spoliation can be defined as the destruction or material alteration of evidence or to the failure to preserve property for another's use as evidence in pending or reasonably foreseeable litigation.

Twentieth century forensic scientist Edmond Locard postulated the Locard exchange principle, also known as Locard's theory. Locard was the director of the very first crime laboratory in existence, located in Lyon, France. Locard's exchange principle states that "with contact between two items, there will be an exchange" [19].

Essentially Locard's principle is applied to crime scenes in which the perpetrator(s) of a crime comes into contact with the scene, so he will both bring something into the scene and leave with something from the scene. Every contact leaves a trace. Cyber forensic investigations are no different. Managers have the responsibility of ensuring that personnel under their direction are adequately trained and equipped to properly handle and protect any electronic evidence, which may have been obtained as part of a cyber forensic investigation, to preserve the environment from which the electronic evidence was collected.

One cannot speak about evidence in a literal vacuum, and must therefore also address the additional critical element that supports the collection of evidence and the eventual use and acceptability of that evidence, that being—chain of custody.

The "chain of custody" is a concept in jurisprudence that applies to the handling of evidence and its integrity. "Chain of custody" also refers to the document or paper trail showing the seizure, custody, control, transfer, analysis, and disposition of physical and electronic evidence.

Because evidence can be used in court to convict persons of crimes, it must be handled in a scrupulously careful manner to avoid later allegations of tampering or misconduct, which can compromise the case of the prosecution toward acquittal or to overturning a guilty verdict upon appeal. Establishing the chain of custody is especially important when the evidence consists of fungible goods. In practice this most often applies to illegal drugs which have been seized by law enforcement personnel, however, increasingly this concept is being applied to data, electronic evidence that is fragile, exists as simple bits and bytes and can easily be altered or destroyed if not collected and secured properly.

An identifiable person must always have the physical custody of a piece of evidence. In law enforcement, this means that a police officer or detective will take charge of a piece of evidence, document its collection, and hand it over to an evidence clerk for storage in a secure place. In the corporate world, a similar responsible individual will need to be identified and will be required to assume similar responsibilities as his or her law enforcement counterpart. It will become imperative that the corporate cyber forensic investigator maintain and adhere to the same stringent rules of collecting, preserving, handling, and storing evidence as followed by law enforcement professionals. This is especially true if the corporation wishes to ultimately use the collected evidence in the legal pursuit of wrongdoing by an employee, contractor, trading partner or other third party.

These transactions, and every succeeding transaction between the collection of the evidence and its appearance in court, should be completely documented chronologically to withstand legal challenges to the authenticity of the evidence. Documentation should include the conditions under which the evidence is gathered, the identity of all evidence handlers, duration of evidence custody, security conditions while handling or storing the evidence, and the manner in which evidence is transferred to subsequent custodians each time such a transfer occurs [20].

Ultimately, rules of evidence must be established and maintained and the chain of custody must be preserved for all evidence that may be potentially or eventually used in court. This chain in part insures the integrity of the evidence. In practice, the person responsible for maintaining custody of the evidence can testify that the evidence was not altered (or if it was how it was altered).

The reader interested in a further examination and discussion of the legalities surrounding evidence collection and preservation is directed to Chapter 11, Law 201: Legal Considerations for IT Managers.

The professional and competent practice of cyber forensics, undertaken with full knowledge of existing, associated laws pertaining to identification, collection, preservation, custody, and transportation of electronic evidence, is critical to organizations competing and operating in the 21st century.

Who Should Be Aware of or Knowledgeable of Cyber Forensics?

Today, the individual professionals who must be made aware of and continue to keep abreast of, both the laws affecting (potential) forensic activity within their organization, the basics of cyber forensic investigations, include but, are not limited to:

- Members of Organization Board of Directors
- Chief Financial Officers, whose responsibilities include among many others, adherence to multiple legislative acts (SoX, HIPAA, GLB, Basel II, etc.)
- Chief Operating Officers
- Chief Information Officers
- Chief Security Officers
- Chief Internal Auditors
- Directors of Human Resources
- Business professionals responsible for business continuity and incident management planning

The breadth of those individuals who will need to become increasingly aware of the potential negative impact resulting from being unprepared to address or implement a successful cyber forensic investigation will only broaden, and begin to infiltrate even the second and tertiary levels of organizational infrastructure.

■ Information security (InfoSec) professionals whose responsibilities include implementation, monitoring and maintenance of enterprisewide security such as firewalls, intrusion detection systems (IDS), proxies, etc.
■ Law enforcement personnel who in the course of investigating a crime may seize technology present at a crime scene. Technology as defined here can range in simplicity from a suspect's cell phone or pager to a laptop computer, which may contain hundreds or thousands of files.
■ System administrators with oversight responsibilities for day-to-day operations and network tasks.
■ Business managers responsible for establishing internal procedures for data retention, backup, and recovery. Such procedures and their results, may affect the integrity of data, which may ultimately affect its admissibility as evidential matter.
■ Corporate professionals responsible for grievance and compliance. New laws are being proposed and passed at an increasing rate that require organizations to demonstrate its ability to protect and safeguard the privacy of personal data and the accuracy of financial data presented for public consumption.

Legislation such as SoX, GLB, HIPAA, California SB1386, etc. makes it imperative that organizations are able to substantiate their compliance not only to these legislative acts but to accepted industry security best practices as well.

Why Employ Cyber Forensic Analysis?

Within the past several years, there has been a flood of legislative action at the state and federal level, which has made the need to have a forensically sound assessment process of organizational information technologies (IT) in place and verifiable. There is no operation in today's 21st century organization that is not touched in some way, in some manner, by technology.

The legislative requirement to attest to the accuracy, the integrity, and the validity of those data that comprise the organization's published financial statements, which investors may rely upon, demand that an organization have the ability to assess and where appropriate and necessary, identify and prevent manipulation of those data, which by failing to do so, may lead to financial fraud.

As organizations move further into the 21st century, increasingly dependent upon technology, with no alternative plan possible, the single most important asset held by any global organization may no longer be the Euros, Dollars, Dirhams, or Yen, held in corporate treasury accounts but, the electronic bits and bytes, when logically pulled together, represent the lifeblood of the organization—its data!

The ability to identify potential or actual misuse of these data will drive the need for organizations to implement and sustain cyber forensically sound internal control strategies, policies, and procedures. A cry from those most affected by the ease and ability by which such critical data may be manipulated or misused has already been heard and global legislation has already begun the process of holding corporate executives accountable.

The ability (many will say the need) to prove culpability beyond the corporate boardroom, in cases involving the theft of, the misuse of corporate assets will become the greatest challenge of those professionals charged with protecting this asset (e.g., internal, external auditors, information security professionals, etc.).

There are many compliance and governance issues now that involve an organization's electronic record archives (and transactional, historical data) that stem from relatively new legislation (enacted within the past two to three years) that an organization may not be aware of, yet pose potential liabilities (financial and legal) if not properly addressed. Such issues as:

- Information systems internal control assessment and auditing
- Risk management
- Lawsuit investigations
- Performance management
- Investigations and management reporting
- Data retention policies, archiving, and storage

The following briefly summarizes the primary legislative actions that have made the ability to identify and to mitigate fraudulent activity via forensically sound procedures a corporate necessity in the 21st century.

Driving Force behind Implementing Corporate Cyber Forensic Capabilities

Sarbanes–Oxley Act of 2002 (SoX)

The SoX Act of 2002 ("the Act") sought, among other things, to improve the U.S. system of financial reporting by reinforcing the checks and balances that are critical to investor confidence. Additionally, the U.S. Congress recognized that questions remain, regarding the approach by which accounting standards are established.

The Act requires changes in many facets of the financial reporting by and analysis of companies. Some of the important changes being implemented and studies being undertaken under the direction of the Act are: (1) required certification of information by company CEOs and CFOs, (2) empowerment of audit committees to engage and approve the services provided by independent auditors, (3) more stringent auditor independence standards, (4) greater oversight of auditors through the establishment of the Public Company Accounting Oversight Board, (5) a study of whether investment banks played a role in the manipulation of earnings by some public companies, and (6) greater independence for the accounting standard setter.

The following sections of SoX contain the three rules that affect the management of electronic records.

The first rule deals with destruction, alteration, or falsification of records.

> Sec. 802(a) "Whoever knowingly alters, destroys, mutilates, conceals, covers up, falsifies, or makes a false entry in any record, document, or tangible object with the intent to impede, obstruct, or influence the investigation or proper administration of any matter within the jurisdiction of any department or agency of the United States or any case filed under title 11, or in relation to or contemplation of any such matter or case, shall be fined under this title, imprisoned not more than 20 years, or both."

The second rule defines the retention period for records storage. Best practices indicate that corporations securely store all business records using the same guidelines set for public accountants.

Sec. 802(a)(1) "Any accountant who conducts an audit of an issuer of securities to which Section 10A(a) of the Securities Exchange Act of 1934 [(15 U.S.C 78j-1(a)] applies, shall maintain all audit or review work papers for a period of 5 years from the end of the fiscal period in which the audit or review was concluded."

This third rule refers to the type of business records that need to be stored, including all business records and communications, including electronic communications.

Sec. 802(a)(2) "The Securities and Exchange Commission shall promulgate, within 180 days, such rules and regulations, as are reasonably necessary, relating to the retention of relevant records such as work papers, documents that form the basis of an audit or review, memoranda, correspondence, communications, other documents, and records (including electronic records) which are created, sent, or received in connection with an audit or review and contain conclusions, opinions, analyses, or financial data relating to such an audit or review [21]."

Gramm–Leach–Bliley Act (GLBA)

The Gramm–Leach–Bliley Act (GLBA) represents the culmination of more than 30 years of U.S. Congressional efforts aimed at reforming the regulation of financial services. The GLBA changed federal statutes governing the scope of permissible activities and the supervision of banks, bank holding companies, and their affiliates. The GLBA lowers (although does not altogether eliminate) barriers between the banking and securities industries erected by the Banking Act of 1933 (popularly known as the "Glass-Steagall Act") and between the banking and the insurance industries erected by the 1982 amendments to the Bank Holding Company Act of 1956 (the "Bank Holding Company Act").

When Congress enacted the Exchange Act in 1934, it completely exempted banks from the regulatory scheme provided for brokers and dealers. Over the past 60 years, however, evolution of the financial markets driven by competition and technology eroded the separation that previously existed between banks, insurance companies, and securities firms. Regulators responded to these changes with interpretations that increasingly sought to accommodate the market changes.

The Commission long supported modernizing the legal framework governing financial services, so long as it was consistent with a system of functional regulation to ensure that investors purchasing securities through banks received the same protections as those when they purchased securities from registered broker-dealers. The GLBA is the product of many years of U.S. Congressional deliberation and reflects a careful balance between providing investors with the same protections wherever they purchase securities, while not unnecessarily disturbing certain bank securities activities.

The GLBA repealed certain provisions of the Glass–Steagall Act and other restrictions applicable to banks and bank holding companies. As a result, banks are able to affiliate with securities firms and insurance companies within the same financial holding company.

The GLBA codified the concept of functional regulation—that is, regulation of the same functions, or activities, by the same expert regulator, regardless of the type of entity engaging in those activities. The U.S. Congress believed that, given the expansion of the activities and affiliations in the financial marketplace, functional regulation was important to building a coherent financial regulatory scheme.

The U.S. federal securities laws provide a comprehensive and coordinated system of regulation of securities activities. They are specifically and uniquely designed to assure the protection of investors through full disclosure concerning securities and the prevention of unfair and inequitable practices in the securities markets [22].

California Security Breach Information Act (SB 1386)

This bill went into effect on July 1, 2003, and requires a state agency, or a person or business that conducts business in California, that owns or licenses computerized data that includes personal information, to disclose in specified ways, any breach of the security of those data, to any resident of California whose unencrypted personal information was, or is reasonably believed to have been, acquired by an unauthorized person.

The bill requires an agency, person, or business that maintains computerized data that includes personal information owned by another to notify the owner or licensee of the information of any breach of security of the data.

> Section 2. Section 1798.29 of SB 1386 was modified to read: (a) Any agency that owns or licenses computerized data that includes personal information shall disclose any breach of the security of the system following discovery or notification of the breach in the security of the data to any resident of California whose unencrypted personal information was, or is reasonably believed to have been, acquired by an unauthorized person.
>
> The disclosure shall be made in the most expedient time possible and without unreasonable delay, consistent with the legitimate needs of law enforcement, to determine the scope of the breach and restore the reasonable integrity of the data system. Any agency that maintains computerized data that includes personal information that the agency does not own shall notify the owner or licensee of the information of any breach of the security of the data immediately following discovery, if the personal information was, or is reasonably believed to have been, acquired by an unauthorized person.
>
> Section 3. Section 1798.82 of the Civil Code goes on to state, that (a) any customer injured by a violation of this title may institute a civil action to recover damages. Any business that violates, proposes to violate, or has violated this title may be enjoined.
>
> Section 4. Section 1798.82 is added to the Civil Code, to read: (a) Any person or business that conducts business in California, and that owns or licenses computerized data that includes personal information, shall disclose any breach of the security of the system following discovery or notification of the breach in the security of the data to any resident of California whose unencrypted personal information was, or is reasonably believed to have been, acquired by an unauthorized person.
>
> The disclosure shall be made in the most expedient time possible and without unreasonable delay, consistent with the legitimate needs of law enforcement, [and to take] any measures necessary to determine the scope of the breach and restore the reasonable integrity of the data system.

"Breach of the security of the system" means unauthorized acquisition of computerized data that compromises the security, confidentiality, or integrity of personal information maintained by the agency [23].

Health Insurance Portability and Accountability Act (HIPAA) of 1996

The Standards for Privacy of Individually Identifiable Health Information ("Privacy Rule") establishes, for the first time, a set of national standards for the protection of certain health information. The U.S. Department of Health and Human Services (HHS) issued the Privacy Rule to implement the requirement of the HIPAA of 1996. The Privacy Rule standards address the use and disclosure of individuals' health information—called "protected health information" by organizations subject to the Privacy Rule—called "covered entities," as well as standards for individuals' privacy rights to understand and control how their health information is used. Within HHS, the Office for Civil Rights (OCR) has responsibility for implementing and enforcing the Privacy Rule with respect to voluntary compliance activities and civil money penalties.

A major goal of the Privacy Rule is to assure that individuals' health information is properly protected while allowing the flow of health information needed to provide and promote high quality health care and to protect the public's health and well being. The rule strikes a balance that permits important uses of information, while protecting the privacy of people who seek care and healing.

The Privacy Rule applies to health plans, health care clearinghouses, and to any health care provider who transmits health information in electronic form in connection with transactions for which the Secretary of HHS has adopted standards under HIPAA.

The Privacy Rule protects all "individually identifiable health information" held or transmitted by a covered entity or its business associate, in any form or media, whether electronic, paper, or oral.

"Individually identifiable health information" is information, including demographic data, that relates to:

- The individual's past, present, or future physical or mental health or condition,
- The provision of health care to the individual, or
- The past, present, or future payment for the provision of health care to the individual, and that identifies the individual or for which there is a reasonable basis to believe can be used to identify the individual. Individually identifiable health information includes many common identifiers (e.g., name, address, birth date, Social Security Number) [24].

Basel II Capital Accord

Basel II is an effort by international banking supervisors to update the original international bank capital accord (Basel I), which has been in effect since 1988. The Basel Committee on Banking Supervision, on which the United States serves as a participating member, developed the current proposals. They aim to improve the consistency of capital regulations internationally, make regulatory capital more risk sensitive, and promote enhanced risk-management practices among large, internationally active banking organizations [25].

Basel II ruling requires the largest internationally active banks to enhance the measurement and management of their risks, including credit risk and operational risk. It also requires these banks to have rigorous processes for assessing overall capital adequacy in relation to their total risk profile and to publicly disclose information regarding their risk profile and capital adequacy [26].

The Basel Committee on Banking Supervision is a committee of banking supervisory authorities that was established by the central bank governors of the Group of Ten countries in 1975. It consists of senior representatives of bank supervisory authorities and central banks from Belgium, Canada, France, Germany, Italy, Japan, Luxembourg, the Netherlands, Spain, Sweden, Switzerland, the United Kingdom, and the United States. It usually meets at the Bank for International Settlements in Basel, where its permanent Secretariat is located [27].

USA PATRIOT and Terrorism Prevention Reauthorization Act of 2005 (HR 3199)

The Uniting and Strengthening America by Providing Appropriate Tools Required to Intercept and Obstruct Terrorism (USA PATRIOT) Act of 2001 (Public Law 107-56), the Intelligence Reform and Terrorism Prevention Act of 2004 (Public Law 108-458), expanded the powers of federal law enforcement and intelligence agencies to investigate and prosecute terrorist acts. HR 3199 permanently authorized certain provisions of the 2001 act, many of which would have expired on December 31, 2005.

No Electronic Theft ("NET") Act

One of the key provisions of NET is the creation of a criminal offense to cover the unauthorized distribution or reproduction of copyrighted materials, regardless of whether the distributor was trying to profit from the activity. The provision covers a gap in the current criminal statute that was exposed by the District Court's dismissal of an indictment in the *United States v. LaMacchia*, 871 F. Supp. 535 (D. Mass. 1994).

Thus, the Act made it a crime to do what was prohibited in the Wire Fraud Act even though the defendant did not gain financially. Therefore, hackers that allow others to download software for free, but do not gain financially are still committing a crime.

Economic Espionage Act

The U.S. Congress, recognizing the importance of the protection of IP and trade secrets to the economic health and security of the United States, enacted the Economic Espionage Act of 1996, Pub.L. 104-294, 110 Stat. 3489 (October 11, 1996) ("EEA"), to address the growing problem of theft of trade secrets. The EEA contains two separate provisions that criminalize the theft or misappropriation of trade secrets. The first provision, codified at 18 U.S.C. § 1831, is directed toward foreign economic espionage and requires that the theft of the trade secret be done to benefit a foreign government, instrumentality or agent. The second provision makes criminal the more common commercial theft of trade secrets, regardless of who benefits (18 U.S.C. § 1832).

There are a number of important features to the EEA, including a provision for the criminal forfeiture of any property or proceeds derived from a violation of the EEA (18 U.S.C. § 1834). The EEA also permits the Attorney General to institute civil enforcement actions and obtain appropriate injunctive relief for violations (18 U.S.C. § 1836). Further, because of the recognized difficulty of maintaining the secrecy of a trade secret during litigation, the EEA requires that courts take actions, as necessary, to preserve the confidentiality of the trade secret (18 U.S.C. § 1835). The EEA also covers conduct occurring outside the United States where the offender is a citizen or permanent resident alien of the United States, or an act in furtherance of the offense was committed in the United States (18 U.S.C. § 1837).

Rounding Out the Field

There are a multitude of legislative acts, which by their very nature, make a strong case for the development and integration of a highly viable and pro-active cyber forensic initiative be incorporated into the control, audit and attestation infrastructure of every organization.

Consider whether your organization would have the ability to identify, collect, document, safeguard, and submit electronic evidence in a court of law, if your organization were faced with the requirement of complying with any of these existing laws.

Consider your organization's ability if the organization had to defend itself (or an employee) of accusations brought against the organization or the employee, under guidelines or stipulations of any of these laws, when the only evidence available may exist solely as electronic bits and bytes. Consider the impact on your organization!

Child Pornography Prevention Act (2005)

To enhance prosecution of child pornography and obscenity by strengthening Section 2257 of Title 18, the United States Code, to ensure that children are not exploited in the production of pornography, prohibiting distribution of child pornography used as evidence in prosecutions, authorizing assets forfeiture in child pornography and obscenity cases, expanding administrative subpoena power to cover obscenity cases, and prohibiting the production of obscenity, its transportation, distribution, and sale, and for other purposes (www.govtrack.us/congress/bill.xpd?bill=h109-3726).

Local Law Enforcement Hate Crimes Prevention Act (2001)

Authorizes the Attorney General to provide technical, forensic, prosecutorial, or other assistance in the criminal investigation or prosecution of any crime that: (1) constitutes a crime of violence under federal law or a felony under State or Indian tribal law; and (2) is motivated by prejudice based on the race, color, religion, national origin, gender, sexual orientation, or disability of the victim or is a violation of the hate crime laws of the state or tribe. Directs the Attorney General to give priority for assistance to crimes committed by offenders who have committed crimes in more than one state and to rural jurisdictions that have difficulty covering the extraordinary investigation or prosecution expenses (http://thomas.loc.gov/cgi-bin/bdquery/z?d107:HR01343:@@@ D&summ2=m&).

Computer Fraud and Abuse Act (2001)

Has as its intent, the mitigation of abuse and reduction of "hacking" into federal computer systems. In addition, the Computer Fraud and Abuse Act provides for civil remedies that employers may be able to sue employees or ex-employees under less stringent requirements than more traditional claims.

In November 2005, the 3rd U.S. Circuit Court of Appeals issued its opinion in *P.C. Yonkers vs. Celebrations The Party and Seasonal Superstore*. The decision was the 3rd Circuit's first interpretation of the scope of remedies available under the federal Computer Fraud and Abuse Act (CFAA). It should be particularly significant to employers because it applies the CFAA's civil remedies in the context of a claim against a former employee.

The 3rd Circuit's decision in Yonkers is significant because, by expressly holding that a civil claim can be asserted under the CFAA, the court has given employers a new weapon to use against employees who access a computer without authorization. Historically, many employers who discovered the theft of computerized information asserted a variety of common law claims, including misappropriation of trade secrets, conversion of property, unfair competition or breach of fiduciary duty (www.usdoj.gov/criminal/cybercrime/1030_new.html).

Digital Millennium Copyright Act (1998)

Makes it a criminal act to circumvent any technology or product that is designed to prevent unauthorized access to copyrighted material (www.copyright.gov/legislation/dmca.pdf).

Identity Theft and Assumption Deterrence Act (1998)

According to the Act, is illegal to knowingly transfer without lawful authority, a means of identification of another person with intent to commit, or aid and abet, any unlawful activity that constitutes a violation under federal law (www.ftc.gov/os/statutes/itada/itadact.htm).

Children's Online Protection Act (1998)

The primary goal of the act and the rule is to place parents in control over what information is collected from their children online. The rule is designed to be strong, yet flexible, to protect children while recognizing the dynamic nature of the Internet (www.ftc.gov/ogc/coppa1.htm).

Wire Fraud Act (1997)

Made it a crime to do what was prohibited in the Wire Fraud Act even though the defendant did not gain financially. Thus hackers that allow others to download software for free, but do not gain financially are still committing a crime. To be guilty under the Wire Fraud Act it must be shown that something of value was taken (www.usdoj.gov/criminal/cybercrime/18usc1343.htm).

National Information Infrastructure Protection Act (1996)

Revises federal criminal code provisions regarding fraud and related activity in connection with computers. Sets penalties with respect to anyone who having knowingly accessed a computer without authorization or exceeding authorized access, obtains specified restricted information or data and, with reason to believe that such information could be used to the injury of the United States or to the advantage of any foreign nation, willfully communicates, delivers, or transmits it to any person not entitled to receive it (or causes or attempts such communication) or willfully retains it and fails to deliver it to the U.S. officer or employee entitled to receive it (http://thomas.loc.gov).

Computer Security Act (1987)

Directs the National Bureau of Standards to establish a computer standards program for federal computer systems, including guidelines for the security of such systems. Sets forth authorities of the Bureau in implementing such standards. Requires the Bureau to draw upon computer system technical security guidelines developed by the National Security Agency regarding protecting sensitive information (http://thomas.loc.gov).

Electronic Communication Privacy Act (1986)

Makes it illegal to intercept any wire, oral, or electronic communication. Included in the interpretation of this law are e-mail, other computer generated transmissions, and cell phone conversations (http://floridalawfirm.com/privacy.html).

Auditing vs. Cyber Forensic Investigation

Table 1.1 briefly summarizes the differences albeit subtle between auditing which can include financial, operational and even fraud auditing and a cyber forensic investigation. A cyber forensic investigation as Table 1.1 details is distinct and unique, and should not be confused with or merged into the common lexicon of audit types—as cyber forensic investigation is not auditing, and auditing is not a cyber forensic investigation.

Table 1.1 Auditing vs. Cyber Forensic Investigation

Elements	Audit	Cyber Forensic Investigation
Definition	Auditing is simply examining information and operations for mathematical accuracy, legality, and propriety. Internal Audit reports risk and makes recommendations to promote sound operating practices. Items and areas of examination generally include: ■ documents; ■ records; ■ reports; ■ systems of internal control; ■ accounting procedures; and ■ actual operations.	The process of extracting information and data from computer storage media and guaranteeing its accuracy and reliability.
Objective	To determine whether all transactions are properly recorded in the accounts, and appropriately reflected in the organization's statements and reports.	To identify digital evidence using scientifically derived and proven methods that can be used to facilitate or further the reconstruction of events in an investigation. Secondary: To identify the responsible person and the seriousness of the misconduct.
Scope	Refers to the activities covered by an audit. Audit scope includes, where appropriate: ■ Audit objectives ■ Risk assessment ■ Nature and extent of auditing procedures performed ■ Time period audited ■ Related activities not audited to delineate the boundaries of the audit ■ Reliance on previous audits.	The use of scientifically derived and proven methods toward the identification, collection, analysis, validation, interpretation, preservation, documentation, and presentation of electronic evidence derived from digital sources for the purpose of facilitating or furthering the restoration of actions found to be unlawful.

continued

Table 1.1 (continued)

Timing	Several factors influence the scheduling of audits, including: the degree of risk or exposure to loss, type of audit, and the current and planned work in other audit projects requiring substantial time commitments. Audits can be regularly scheduled, may be conducted on a period basis, or they may also be initiated as the result of a special request.	Conducted when: ■ Mandated to investigate (compliance to local, state, federal law) ■ Required to determine liability ■ Stopping violations of policy or procedure ■ Gaining control to mitigate damages ■ Avoiding general or civil liability ■ Complaint, grievance or anonymous tip or report is made ■ Unexplained changes in behavior, morale, or productivity of personnel ■ Constructive knowledge of misconduct ■ Property misuse or damage is identified ■ Acts of workplace violence are reported ■ Violation of policy or law ■ External administrative charge ■ Notice of lawsuit ■ Theft of corporate asset (financial or data).
Methodology	Typically follows generally accepted accounting principles (GAAP). Additionally, audits may be conducted in accordance with Generally Accepted Government Auditing Standards (GAGAS), standards and guidelines established by The Auditing Standards Board (ASB) of the AICPA, and The International Standards for the Professional Practice of Internal Auditing as set forth by the Institute of Internal Auditors. (Other methodologies, standards, and guidelines exist and may be followed at the discretion of the organization or as dictated by local legislation.)	Review the complaint Establish a basis or justification for action Determine impact of the incident Determine the feasibility of conducting an investigation Get approval to proceed Gather the evidence Compile a list of witnesses, subjects, targets Correlate the evidence—file a report.

continued

Table 1.1 (continued)

Reporting	Generally the results of an audit are communicated via a written report to management. The "look and feel" as well as the distribution of the final report may vary by organization, ranging from a formal; audit report with distribution to all levels of management and external stakeholders, to a general letter of comment, distributed solely to the immediate management of the entity being audited.	The report will be submitted to the investigator, prosecutor, law enforcement, organizational management, and others (dependent on circumstances which initiated the investigation). Departmental policy may dictate report-writing specifics, such as its order and contents. The report may also consist of a brief summary of the results of the examinations performed on the items submitted for analysis.
Impact	Typically conducted in a non-confrontational manner, with generally helpful assistance afforded the auditor by the auditee.	May be adversarial. Each investigation is independent and unique.

Summary

This initial chapter opens the door and sheds some additional light on the evolving and emerging profession of cyber forensics and the roles and responsibilities of those professionals actively working as cyber forensic investigators and those seeking to pursue a career in this field.

Cyber forensics as was discussed can be defined many ways, some with only slight differences, evidence to a discipline, a field—part art, part science, which is still developing, emerging, and establishing itself as a legitimate profession, rightfully so, among the existing audit and associated forensic disciplines, with skilled and dedicated professionals capable of performing detailed analysis and examinations of the digital breadcrumbs, the bits and bytes which make up our virtual world, all in the pursuit of mitigating unlawful activity, while securing and protecting data assets.

Existing laws have forced organizations of all sizes and financial stability to take a hard look at their ability to examine internal control exposures, identify unsecured IT operations and determine sources of potential liability to the organization both internally and externally. No organization operating in the 21st century can afford to turn a blind eye to the eventual need for qualified cyber forensic talent, whether employed as internal professional staff or retained through an external third-party arrangement. It is not a case of if but when.

The basic steps in performing a cyber forensic investigation along with a discussion on the basic element of evidence and the important concept of chain of custody were reviewed, with a more extensive and detailed discussion of the legal issues facing management to be addressed in Chapter 11.

The multitude of various transactions, actions, and events taking place daily in organizations, departments, agencies, companies, and subsidiaries creates conditions for the willful and unlawful use of organizational technologies and the potential to use those technologies in the commission of illegal activities. The continued development of technology, the growth in organizational dependence on these technologies and the potential for misuse of these technologies warrants a proactive position by organizations to augment their existing cyber forensic capabilities or establish them immediately.

Chapter 2 will provide the reader with a review of the cyber forensic tools and utilities that are most commonly encountered in the field and which should be included in every cyber forensic investigator's toolkit.

There are literally hundreds of specific and unique application software packages, which could qualify as a cyber forensic tool. Add to that, the hundreds of utilities available for the same task, the job of identifying and examining the best and most utilized tool is daunting and overwhelming to say the least.

Chapter 2 will help sort through this exhaustive list and provide a succinct overview of the most useful and appropriate cyber forensic tools for the 21st century cyber forensic investigator.

References

1. Department of Veterans Affairs Statement Announcing the Loss of Veterans' Personal Information, May 22, http://www1.va.gov/opa/data/docs/initann.doc, 2006, retrieved June 2006.
2. Court Halts Bogus Invention Promotion Claims Orders $26 Million in Redress For Consumers; USPTO's Director Jon Dudas Praises Court Decision, Federal Trade Commission News, Office of Public Affairs, Press Release, www.ftc.gov, retrieved June 2006, www.uspto.gov/main/homepagenews/bak2006fapr20.htm.
3. Cleveland, Ohio Man Sentenced to Prison for Bank Fraud and Conspiracy, U.S. Department of Justice, Northern District of Ohio, www.usdoj.gov/criminal/cybercrime/flurySent.htm, retrieved June 2006.
4. Six Defendants Plead Guilty in Internet Identity Theft and Credit Card Fraud Conspiracy, Department Of Justice, CRM, www.usdoj.gov/criminal/cybercrime/mantovaniPlea.htm, retrieved June 2006.
5. Harris, S. (December 2005), To Catch a Thief, Information Security, http://informationsecurity.techtarget.com/magLogin/1,291245,sid42_gci1147990,00.html, retrieved June 2006.
6. Nash, K., Gage, D. (August 2, 2006), E-Mail Retention: The High Cost of Digging Up Data. Reprinted from www.baselinemag.com, [www.baselinemag.com/article2/0,1540,1998110,00.asp], August 2, 2006, with permission. Copyright © 2006 Ziff Davis Publishing Holdings Inc. All Rights Reserved.
7. Reith, M., Clint Carr, and Gregg Gunsch (2002), An Examination of Digital Forensic Models, *International Journal of Digital Evidence* Fall 2002, 1, 3.
8. Gallegos, F. (2005) Computer Forensics: An Overview, *Information Systems Control Journal*, 6, 13–16.
9. Patzakis, J. (February 2006), Why the eDiscovery Revolution is important to Infosec, *The ISSA Journal*, 7.
10. Computer Forensics, US-CERT, 2005.
11. Pianich, R (fall 2004), An Investigation of Computer Forensics, *Information Systems Control Journal*, 3, 47.
12. The Sedona Conference Working Group on Electronic Document Production, July 2005, www.thesedonaconference.org.
13. Ingram, B. (September 9, 2003), Locate Smoking Guns Electronically, Law Technology News, http://www.law.com/special/supplement/e_discovery/smoking_gun.shtml, retrieved July 2006.
14. Reissner, H. (January, 2005), Electronic Discovery Growing in Epic Proportions: Should law firms bring electronic discovery in-house? www.planetds.com/docs/PD%206-05%20eDiscGrow.pdf, retrieved July 2006.

15. Study Pursuant to Section 108(d) of the Sarbanes-Oxley Act of 2002 on the Adoption by the United States Financial Reporting System of a Principles-Based Accounting System. Submitted to Committee on Banking, Housing, and Urban Affairs of the United States Senate and Committee on Financial Services of the United States House of Representatives, Office of the Chief Accountant, Office of Economic Analysis, United States Securities and Exchange Commission, www.sec.gov/news/studies/principlesbasedstand.htm#executive, retrieved June 2006.

16. Fulbright (October 2006), Third Annual Litigation Trends Survey Findings, Fulbright & Jaworski, Fulbright Tower, 1301 McKinney, Suite 5100, Houston, TX 77010-3095, (713) 651 5151, www.fullbright.com, retrieved October 2006, used with permission.

17. Socha (2004), The 2005 Socha-Gelbmann Electronic Discovery Survey Results, www.sochaconsulting.com/2005surveyresults.htm, retrieved June 2006.

18. The Sedona Principles: Best Practices Recommendations & Principles for Addressing Electronic Document Production (July 2005), The Sedona Conference, 180 Broken Arrow Way South, Sedona, AZ 86351-8998, (928)284-2698, [Fax: (928) 284-4240], tsc@sedona.net, retrieved July 2006, used with permission.

19. United States Department of Justice, (July 2001), Electronic Crime Scene Investigation: A Guide for First Responders, NCJ 187736, NIJ Guide, Office of Justice Programs, National Institute of Justice, www.ojp.usdoj.gov/nij, 810 Seventh Street N.W., Washington, DC 20531, retrieved July 2006.

20. Locard, 2006, Locard's exchange principle, In Wikipedia, The Free Encyclopedia. http://en.wikipedia.org/w/index.php?title=Locard%27s_exchange_principle&oldid=63946537, retrieved July 16, 2006.

21. Chain of custody (2006), In Wikipedia, The Free Encyclopedia. http://en.wikipedia.org/w/index.php?title=Chain_of_custody&oldid=62538181, retrieved July 2006.

22. Definition of Terms in and Specific Exemptions for Banks, Savings Associations, and Savings Banks Under Sections 3(a)(4) and 3(a)(5) of the Securities Exchange Act of 1934, Securities And Exchange Commission, www.sec.gov/rules/final/34-44291.htm#secxii, retrieved June 2006.

23. California Security Breach Information Act, Bill Number: SB 1386, Chaptered, Bill Text http://info.sen.ca.gov/pub/01-02/bill/sen/sb_1351-1400/sb_1386_bill_20020926_chaptered.html, retrieved June 2006.

24. Summary Of The HIPAA Privacy Rule, The U.S. Department of Health and Human Services, the Office for Civil Rights, www.hhs.gov/ocr/privacysummary.pdf, retrieved June 2006.

25. Basel II Capital Accord, Federal Reserve Bank, www.federalreserve.gov/generalinfo/basel2/default.htm, retrieved June 2006.

26. Notice of proposed rulemaking to implement Basel II risk-based capital requirements in the United States for large, internationally active banking organizations, March 30, 2006, www.federalreserve.gov/boarddocs/press/bcreg/2006/20060330/default.htm, retrieved June 2006.

Chapter 2

Cyber Forensic Tools and Utilities

Introduction

Today's cyber forensic investigator has literally hundreds of specific and unique application software packages and hardware devices that could qualify as cyber forensic tools. Added to that, the hundreds of utilities available for the same task, the job of identifying and examining the best and most utilized tools are daunting and overwhelming to say the least.

The information contained within this chapter is intended to be used as a reference and not as an endorsement, of the included providers, vendors, and informational resources. Reference herein to any specific commercial product, process, or service by trade name, trademark, service mark, manufacturer, or otherwise does not constitute or imply endorsement, recommendation, or favoring by the authors or the publisher, nor does it imply that the products mentioned are necessarily the best available for the purpose.

Web sites included in this chapter are intended to provide current and accurate information; however, it is impossible for anyone (read authors, publisher, etc.) to warrant that the information contained on the sites is accurate or timely.

Relying on information contained on these sites is done at one's own risk. Use of such information is voluntary, and reliance on it should only be undertaken after an independent review of its accuracy, completeness, efficacy, and timeliness. As such, users of this information are advised and encouraged to confirm specific claims for product performance as necessary and appropriate.

It is worth noting that no single text, guideline or reference book can adequately and definitively state which cyber forensic tool should be used when and under which circumstances and conditions. It is the responsibility of the cyber forensic investigator to (a) have a thorough understanding of the environment and case specifics of the investigation to be performed and (b) to assess and know the specific limitations of each tool before placing unfretted reliance on any single piece of software or hardware.

Failing to heed these precautions, and to assess one's skill and abilities in utilizing the tools reviewed here, is both unethical and places everyone involved in the investigation at risk.

Good! Now that, that has been said, this chapter will help the reader sort thought this exhaustive list and provide a succinct overview of the host of cyber forensic tools available for the 21st century cyber forensic investigator.

Examining a Breadth of Products

Given the wealth of resources available that list, categorize, analyze, and assess cyber forensics tools, rather than re-performing and replicating previous and validated surveys of cyber forensic products, the authors obtained permission from *SC Magazine*, published by Haymarket Media, to reprint a July 2006 survey of forensic tools complied by Peter Stephenson, Associate Program Director MSIA, Norwich University, an internationally recognized writer, consultant, researcher, and lecturer on theoretical and experimental information assurance [1].

A summary of Dr. Stephenson's findings as to the most applicable or "best of breed" forensic tool is presented throughout the following pages.

These tools are available to "public" users. Many of the more sophisticated tools are classified and restricted to government and law enforcement personnel only, and not available for purchase "over the counter". Remember that no one tool or suite of tools is right for all situations that you may encounter as a cyber forensic investigator. The key is having the right tool or tools for the job.

Cyber Forensic Tools

Managing security incidents is essentially a problem of forensics. Dr. Stephenson approached the assessment of appropriate forensic tools from the perspective of incident response.

Essentially, incident management is a forensic problem. We want to know what might be on various computer media as well as what has traveled over the network, what the configurations of various networked devices are, and how all the disk images, network logs, and other valuable data hooks together. That challenge demands a serious toolkit of computer forensic, network-enabled forensic, network forensic, and analytical tools.

Dr. Stephenson examined the leading commercial and open source computer forensic tools, network enabled tools and auditing software, network forensic or log analysis tools, and the market leader in link analysis tools. Selections were grouped into three incident-response toolkits based on price and because of the wide range of products reviewed; three "best of breed" products were identified.

An amazing number of excellent open source tools for various forensic tasks are available and, for those organizations that cannot afford big price tags or which simply want a second tool, these are excellent.

In the world of information technology (IT) forensics, expert digital forensic analysts generally recommend multiple tools as a best practice. Analysis of results from various forensic tools was inconsistent across tools. One would expect agreement from tool to tool but, for a variety of reasons, this is not often the case. The case for using multiple tools is clear—you do not want to miss important evidence just because your tool has a glitch.

A standard image was created with several glitches in it to determine the analysis and acquisition capabilities of the computer forensics tools; this was the "test bed" against which the forensics tools discussed here were tested. These included a restored operating system on top of a different, larger operating system (OS) without deleting the original OS.

Each tool in the survey was used to image the disk both in the tool's native imaging format and, where available, dd. The image was then analyzed looking for certain artifacts. Finally, Dr. Stephenson analyzed a standardized dd image using those tools that could take a dd file as input. (dd is a common UNIX program used for copying files.)

Also tested were the log aggregators or analyzers using a standard set of snort logs compiled over an 18-month period. Roughly six month's worth of data was collected and those data were used as the test case. Each tool was examined for ease of import, number of file source types the device could handle, whether it needed security logs or could take anything, and ease of set-up and configuration.

A last test conducted exported data from each tool to the link analyzer and attempted to build a case that could explain various events using link analysis. Virtually all the products tested were capable of generating an output that was useful to the link analyzer. A link analyzer tool is used to analyze the outbound and inbound links of any given page. Link analyzers are not used widely by IT professionals, but they should be. If used properly, they can cut weeks off the chore of making sense out of large amounts of information.

Metadata from the computer forensics tools can provide input for the link analyzer, and logs can provide network analysis input. As a result, using the link analyzer, the investigator can "connect the dots" and get a much better understanding of the interactions that caused the incident. If you use a link analyzer once for an incident investigation, you will never want to be without one.

The bottom line for the forensic connection to incident response is that your ability to clear an incident, get back to production, recover lost or damaged data, and arrive at an explanation will probably depend on your successful use of the types of tools reviewed here.

Tools recommended for their strong capabilities that were demonstrated throughout the battery of testing included:

1. AccessData's Forensic Toolkit, for its completeness, affordable price, and excellent court track record;
2. Mandiant First Response, as a first-response tool for gathering a snapshot of the network with very limited intrusiveness prior to a detailed forensic examination; and
3. The Sleuth Kit & Autopsy Browser, as a great second forensic tool for those users who are comfortable in the UNIX or Linux environments.

Good, Better, Best: What's the Right Incident Response Tool for Your Organization?

Selecting the appropriate incident response and post mortem toolkit depends on several factors— the size and type of your organization, your network architecture, your budget, and human resources. All of these make a real difference in the tool set you choose. See Table 2.1.

There are, however, some rules of thumb that most forensics experts point out as being important for all organizations that do their own forensic investigations. Forensics is an important part of incident response, so that should include most organizations. First, it is a good idea to have more

Table 2.1 Specifications for Forensics Tools Tested

Product	Coroner's Toolkit	Encase Forensic	Forensic Toolkit	i2Analyst's Notebook	LogLogic LX2000	Mandiant First Response	NetWitness	ProDiscover Incident Response	Sleuth Kit/ Autopsy Browser
Supplier	Open source	Guidance Software	AccessData	i2 Inc.	LogLogic	Mandiant	Man Tech Intl.	Technology Partners	Open source
UNIX/Linux platform	Yes	No	No	No	Yes	No	Yes	No	Yes
Windows platform	No	Yes	Yes	Yes	No	Yes	No	Yes	No
Analyzes W = Windows U = UNIX/Linux	U	W,U	W,U	—	—	W	—	W,U	W,U
Remote capture	No	No	No	—	Yes	Yes	—	Yes	No
GUI	No	Yes	Yes	Yes	Yes	Yes	No	Yes	Yes
Requires remote agents	No	No	No	No	No	Yes	No	No	No
Pre-forensics audit	No	Yes	Yes	No	No	Yes	No	Yes	No

than one computer forensics tool. This allows the verification of findings and, to some extent, confidence that all data on disks being analyzed has been found.

A second rule is that information on logs can be fragile depending on your organization's log recycling process. If you turn logs over every 24 hours, you are at risk of losing critical information. The logs need to be captured and retained regularly.

Finally, you should select the tool set that fits your organization's needs most closely and ensure that your employees are well-trained on those tools. To help you select, the best of the products tested were placed into three tool sets—good, better, and best. These tool sets are, roughly, consistent with the resource availabilities of companies or other organizations of small to medium, medium to large, and large to very large companies respectively.

The largest organizations might be expected to have widely distributed enterprises. Hence, in the tool groupings there are products that address widespread networks. At the other end of the spectrum, smaller organizations have smaller budgets, fewer trained employees, and much smaller enterprises to support.

The following are Dr. Stephenson's suggested tool sets, broken down by category classification:

- Good—these tools are appropriate for small- to medium-sized companies whose networks tend to be small and concentrated:
  - Computer forensics primary: AccessData FTK
  - Computer forensics secondary: The Sleuth Kit or Autopsy (you will need someone familiar with Linux or other UNIX)
  - Network forensics: NetWitness
  - Pre-forensics audit: Mandiant First Response
  - Optional: i2 Analyst's Notebook
- Better—this tool set would be appropriate for medium to large organizations which have geographically disbursed networks, but a limited number of sites:
  - Computer forensics primary: ProDiscover Incident Response
  - Computer forensics secondary: AccessData FTK
  - Network forensics: LogLogic LX 2000
  - Pre-forensics audit: Mandiant First Response
  - Analysis: i2 Analyst's Notebook
  - Optional: The Sleuth Kit or Autopsy for organizations with a significant UNIX or Linux presence
- Best—this tool set is appropriate for the largest organizations with widely disbursed networks:
  - Computer forensics primary: ProDiscover Incident Response
  - Computer forensics secondary: AccessData FTK
  - The Sleuth Kit or Autopsy and Coroner's Toolkit for UNIX or Linux support
  - Network forensics: LogLogic LX 2000 with ST 3000
  - Pre-forensics audit: Mandiant First Response
  - Analysis: i2 Analyst's Notebook

Tool Review

The following pages contain specific observations from Dr. Stephenson's in-depth review of forensic tools. We have retained, to the best of our ability, the original format and layout of the collected data.

Each review provides the product's name, release or version, the vendor's name, cost as of July 2006, and URL contact information. The products as listed here are in no specific order and the reader should not infer any superiority or inferiority of any product simply due to the order in which it appears in the following pages.

It is worth repeating thus we will … It is the responsibility of the cyber forensic investigator to (a) have a thorough understanding of the environment and case specifics of the investigation to be performed and (b) to assess and know the specific limitations of each tool before placing unfretted reliance on any single piece of software or hardware.

Coroner's Toolkit

Version:	1.16
Supplier:	Open source or Dan Farmer and Wietse Venema
Price:	Free
Contact:	www.porcupine.org

The Coroner's Toolkit (TCT), is an open source set of forensic tools for performing post-mortem analysis on UNIX systems. Written by Dan Farmer and Wietse Venema, both very well known in security circles for such programs as SATAN, TCT is not an easy product to use. A serious knowledge of UNIX is a prerequisite for success, but if you can manage it, this is an extremely powerful set of tools.

This is not a GUI-based product. It is a collection of command line tools designed for the experienced UNIX engineer. In that context we found that the TCT has everything we needed to analyze a Linux disk. Using a command line forensics program can be difficult, although forensic analysts who have used the older NTI Tools will feel at home. Our grade of four stars for features comes with the caveat that this is a UNIX-only tool and that the user is well versed in UNIX. It is the same story with the Toolkit's high performance rating. It has no trouble taking an image and using the individual tools to perform analyses of various kinds.

Table 2.2 Overall Product Rating—Coroner's Toolkit

Features	Δ	Δ	Δ	Δ	Δ
Ease of use	Δ	Δ	Δ	Δ	Δ
Performance	Δ	Δ	Δ	Δ	Δ
Documentation	Δ	Δ	Δ	Δ	Δ
Support	Δ	Δ	Δ	Δ	Δ
Value of money	Δ	Δ	Δ	Δ	Δ
Overall rating	Δ	Δ	Δ	Δ	Δ

Note: Pros: extremely powerful UNIX forensic tool in the right hands; freeware. Cons: not for the faint-hearted—it is difficult to use and requires a significant knowledge of UNIX to use it successfully; virtually no documentation. Verdict: very useful collection of tools, but a high barrier to entry.

Documentation is skimpy, but there is a complete set of slides from a class taught on TCT in 1999. We found them both useful and interesting. Also, since this product is intended for experienced UNIX users, there is an implied understanding of common UNIX functions and conventions, make files, main pages, utilities, and so on.

There is, essentially, no support for this product. Typical of many open source products, users are left to their own devices. There is a mail list supported by the developers and, also typical of the UNIX open source community, help can be found there. But the bottom line is: if you want to use TCT, you are on your own.

If you know UNIX and you use UNIX, TCT is an excellent second product to back-up your primary IT forensic tool. The developers are extremely proficient in UNIX and the UNIX file system, so TCT is reliable and useful in the right hands and for its intended purpose. And as far as freeware goes, the price certainly is right.

EnCase Forensic

Version:	5.0
Supplier:	Guidance Software
Price:	$3000
Contact:	www.guidancesoftware.com

This new version of EnCase shows its pedigree as the oldest of the GUI-based IT forensic tools. The testers found it very simple to operate and use.

The interface is much like other IT forensic tools, but slightly more intuitive and comfortable to use. Moving around is quick and easy and all evidence data is organized by case and is simple to access.

EnCase Forensic is first and foremost a computer forensic tool, but it includes other useful features including the ability to preview and acquire disks through many types of connections, such as direct network crossover cable, parallel connection, and direct disk-to-disk.

Table 2.3 Overall Product Rating—EnCase Forensic

Features	Δ	Δ	Δ	Δ	Δ
Ease of use	Δ	Δ	Δ	Δ	Δ
Performance	Δ	Δ	Δ	Δ	Δ
Documentation	Δ	Δ	Δ	Δ	Δ
Support	Δ	Δ	Δ	Δ	Δ
Value of money	Δ	Δ	Δ	Δ	Δ
Overall rating	Δ	Δ	Δ	Δ	Δ

Note: Pros: easy to use, its intuitive interface makes acquiring, analyzing and viewing evidence simple and reliable; long and honorable track record in the courts. Cons: expensive! Competent, but not significantly superior to its competitors. Verdict: still on top, but the gap is narrowing.

There is an organized user interface that makes viewing media contents straightforward. These views include a gallery of picture and image evidence and hex and file tree views. EnCase Forensic can also acquire many different media, including Palm Pilots and most types of removable media.

The product performed well under the testing parameters. It had a reasonable acquisition time and the testers were able to gather most of the data on the test disk. But it did miss some hidden or deleted data in unformatted sections of the test disk.

The program comes with plenty of documentation—a large paper manual and PDF manual that are clear, organized, easy to read, and include a lot of screenshots and illustrations. The Web site has a wealth of applications, legal notes and other useful information, such as hash sets and scripts for its enScript scripting language.

The Guidance Software Web site is loaded with support options for EnCase. Support is available for both customer service and technical help and includes both phone and e-mail support. There are also support videos and articles available on the Web site.

This product is a useful tool, at a cost of around $3000 (almost three times that of its major competitor), the cost seems to be inflated out of proportion with the market.

The testers found that this tool does not perform significantly better than most of its competitors, but is much more costly. It is a trend the testers have noticed with Guidance Software—raising prices to the point that only the largest organizations can afford the products.

Forensic Toolkit

Version:	1.61
Supplier:	AccessData
Price:	$1095
Contact:	www.accessdata.com

The Forensic Toolkit (FTK) is very powerful and comes loaded with features, although it is naturally difficult to make such a powerful tool completely simple to use. The program interface can

Table 2.4   Overall Product Rating—Forensic Toolkit

Features	Δ	Δ	Δ	Δ	Δ
Ease of use	Δ	Δ	Δ	Δ	Δ
Performance	Δ	Δ	Δ	Δ	Δ
Documentation	Δ	Δ	Δ	Δ	Δ
Support	Δ	Δ	Δ	Δ	Δ
Value of money	Δ	Δ	Δ	Δ	Δ
Overall rating	Δ	Δ	Δ	Δ	Δ

Note: Pros: extensive features beyond basic forensics. Cons: documentation can be vague at certain points, especially in the more complex areas of the program. Verdict: very powerful program with tons of great features at an affordable price.

overwhelm at first glance, with all its different features and options, but after reading the documentation and getting to know the program, it becomes much more intuitive. As a basic IT forensic tool, it includes features such as a registry viewer, in-depth easy-to-read logging, an easy-to-use standalone disk imager, and direct e-mail and zip file analysis.

The testers found this program to be an excellent and comprehensive forensic toolkit. And with its extended features—such as the password recovery feature, for gaining access to protected files to search for evidence, and the powerful Distributed Network Attack feature, which can be used to crack encrypted files over a network—the testers felt that its performance as an incident response tool was formidable.

FTK performed excellent in all tests. The easy-to-read logs and information screens made it simple for the testers to acquire the test disk and draw in-depth conclusions from the collected data.

Documentation for this product is quite good. The manual is a PDF file included on the software CD and it contains all installation and user information for the program. Testers found the documentation fairly easy to read and quite easy to navigate. However, the testers did find the documentation was not very specific in some of the more complex areas of the product's features, which is where manuals are most useful.

The AccessData support center has several ways in which to find technical and product support. The first is offered both by phone and e-mail. For additional product support, the site includes a forum, customer service phone number, and customer service e-mail.

AccessData makes owning FTK easy. It is powerful and loaded with features for very little cost, and is both a great IT forensic tool and very cost-effective. For example, as long as users have an active dongle (a hardware device that plugs into a parallel or a USB port, acting as copy protection for a particular software application), they can download updates and new product versions straight from the Web site.

i2 Analyst's Notebook

Version: 6.0.55
Supplier: i2, Inc.
Price: $3652, includes one year's support
Contact: www.i2inc.com

This is a very different type of analysis tool from those information security professionals are used to. Link analysis, a crucial aspect of incident response, is usually done manually or by trying to use log correlators. This is a true link analyzer with a long pedigree in analyzing complex crimes and security incidents. The application does all the installation work, after which come example charts and a superb help system to quickly move you from installation to production.

Within the first two hours, the testers had imported and analyzed metadata from EnCase for a detailed analysis of data on a hard disk, put in hacker profiles to analyze interrelationships between hackers and hacks, and analyzed a 65,000 record intrusion detection system (IDS instru) log for links between attacks and attackers.

Link analysis is applied to incident response post mortem. Logs, events and other data feed the link analyzer's analysis process. The easiest way to input data is by importing it from a spreadsheet using a CSV file. This allows users to import logs of virtually any kind into the analyzer, and then the tool sets up the relationships and displays them in various formats.

Table 2.5   Overall Product Rating—i2 Analyst's Notebook

Features	Δ	Δ	Δ	Δ	Δ
Ease of use	Δ	Δ	Δ	Δ	Δ
Performance	Δ	Δ	Δ	Δ	Δ
Documentation	Δ	Δ	Δ	Δ	Δ
Support	Δ	Δ	Δ	Δ	Δ
Value of money	Δ	Δ	Δ	Δ	Δ
Overall rating	Δ	Δ	Δ	Δ	Δ

Note: Pros: superb link analyzer with a stellar pedigree. Cons: not targeted directly at IT security incidents in its training, icon sets or application notes. Verdict: intuitive, powerful analysis tool for complex incidents.

Once data is organized, viewing relationships is intuitive. Analyst's Notebook is part of a suite of products that allow very large, complex logs to be analyzed and subtle connections to be found in extensive distributed enterprises.

Most documentation is in the help file, which testers found to be helpful, while directories are created with extensive PDF files and examples, as well as a paper Quick Start Guide and a Guide to Power2, the core technology in the product.

Support is extensive, with online and phone support and consulting teams available to assist. The product is priced in the range of most forensic tools and far lower than typical log analysis appliances. The product will also reduce significantly the analysis time for an incident, so it can be resolved, production restored, and large amounts of data analyzed.

Rather than replacing log correlators, Analyst's Notebook leverages existing investment in expensive tools. The cost of the product and user training will be amortized in the first incident upon which it is used.

LogLogic's LX 2000

Supplier:	LogLogic, Inc.
Price:	$49,999
Contact:	www.loglogic.com

LogLogic's LX 2000 is an excellent log analysis tool. It is powerful, can be distributed, and is a mature and useful product. But it is not for the faint-hearted. While its user interface is excellent, it has many hidden capabilities that require some time to understand.

The testers had wanted to feed the product to their log test set, but found that challenging since the LX 2000 is intended to analyze logs in near real-time. While it is quite capable of batch analysis, it takes an effort to import the logs for analysis, although once imported, analysis is intuitive and the user has a large variety of options. Some of these depend on the type of log, and the

Table 2.6 Overall Product Rating—LogLogic's LX 2000

Features	Δ	Δ	Δ	Δ	Δ
Ease of use	Δ	Δ	Δ	Δ	Δ
Performance	Δ	Δ	Δ	Δ	Δ
Documentation	Δ	Δ	Δ	Δ	Δ
Support	Δ	Δ	Δ	Δ	Δ
Value of money	Δ	Δ	Δ	Δ	Δ
Overall rating	Δ	Δ	Δ	Δ	Δ

Note: Pros: excellent log analysis features. Cons: quite pricey; can be complex to set up under certain conditions. Verdict: high-powered; generally intuitive operation and high functionality.

LX 2000 offers an immediately available chart for every type of log that specifies what analysis features the log type supports.

The LX 2000 is as feature-rich as anyone could wish. Its displays are straightforward and one can perform a wide variety of analyses with relative ease. Coupled with the ST 3000 large-scale storage appliance, the LX 2000 becomes an extremely powerful tool for managing, analyzing, and archiving huge amounts of data.

Documentation comes as a set of PDF files on a CD. The manuals are clear and comprehensive, with all the detail needed for most tasks. Specialized tasks need to be referred to LogLogic support, and testers found support for the LX 2000 to be first rate.

It does not come cheap, although given the high-end environment for which it is intended, the price is reasonable.

A product such as the LX 2000, as well as being an important network forensic analysis tool, is a key ingredient in managing the overall security of all sizes of networks. The LX 2000 alone is suitable for small- to mid-sized enterprises, while the addition of other LogLogic family products allows scaling to virtually any size.

Mandiant First Response

Version: 1.1
Supplier: Mandiant
Price: Free
Contact: www.mandiant.com

First Response is a freeware audit tool and is a little difficult to use in the beginning. The interface, deploying agents and gathering data can also be a little awkward at first, but this program can be very useful once the user has a grasp on what it does and what it is capable of. Testers found that after working with this product for a while, the information it gathers is reported in an organized and simple-to-read fashion.

Table 2.7 Overall Product Rating—Mandiant First Response

Features	Δ	Δ	Δ	Δ	Δ
Ease of use	Δ	Δ	Δ	Δ	Δ
Performance	Δ	Δ	Δ	Δ	Δ
Documentation	Δ	Δ	Δ	Δ	Δ
Support	Δ	Δ	Δ	Δ	Δ
Value of money	Δ	Δ	Δ	Δ	Δ
Overall rating	Δ	Δ	Δ	Δ	Δ

Note: Pros: strong audit features. Cons: limited support and limited documentation. Verdict: free audit tool that deploys agents across network computers to gather a snap shot before evidence is gathered.

This product has features that make it a great addition to any set of forensic and incident response toolkits. First Response is less a forensic tool and more of an audit tool. It has a console that deploys on a single computer on a network, with agents deployed across the network to gather information from connected computers.

The information gathered includes system information, current processes, services, tasks, files, issues, and registry information. After all the data has been gathered, it then can all be put into a central report to provide a nice snapshot of a network before any additional forensic evidence is acquired. The agents this program deploys leave a small footprint.

Once installed initially the testers had no trouble deploying First Response agents on the test network and gathering information on network computers. They found this program to perform quite well and they were able to gather and analyze data in a fairly short period of time.

First Response has fairly comprehensive documentation, which is quite good for a freeware program. The user guide is a combination of a program overview and a light guide to program features. The manual does a good job of explaining the program, but is fuzzy as to how to do certain things such as deploying agents and using some program features.

Since this is a program that Mandiant offers as freeware, its only support is limited to e-mail. But being free, the program is an excellent addition to any forensic toolkit. This program is recommended for all three levels of incident response kits.

NetWitness

Version: 6.0
Supplier: ManTech International Corp.
Price: $30,000
Contact: www.netwitness.com

NetWitness is a network traffic security analyzer that the vendor describes as a "security intelligence" tool. Set-up is simplified by its new installation wizard that worked correctly the first time,

Table 2.8   Overall Product Rating—NetWitness

Features	Δ	Δ	Δ	Δ	Δ
Ease of use	Δ	Δ	Δ	Δ	Δ
Performance	Δ	Δ	Δ	Δ	Δ
Documentation	Δ	Δ	Δ	Δ	Δ
Support	Δ	Δ	Δ	Δ	Δ
Value of money	Δ	Δ	Δ	Δ	Δ
Overall rating	Δ	Δ	Δ	Δ	Δ

Note: Pros: easy to use; very good user interface. Cons: scalability and documentation. Verdict: a strong network forensics product that could be a winner with a little work.

and was a breeze. The testers fed it a set of snort packet logs that it accepted without complaint, and were able to begin analysis within an hour.

NetWitness presents standard intrusion detection packet logs in a comprehensive format for analysis. But one of its most promising features, the packet miner, is only available for Cisco IPS 4200 sensors.

Basically, it helps to automate the IDS analysis process, a valuable function in an incident, and NetWitness should have it available for other IDS products. As it stands, the appliance can collect logs from other systems, but it is left to the analyst to make sense of them.

One additional key feature is the ability to identify such things as credit card numbers and Social Security numbers—a very strong feature in the area of compliance.

NetWitness behaved well in the test suite. Testers had no difficulty feeding it a set of pre-collected logs and it is expected that it will also behave well in production.

While the testers did not test data throughput (the amount of work that a computer can do in a given time period), based on user comments it is expected that volume of data flow is not likely to be a problem. But one possible challenge is the need to add additional storage for large enterprises. This scalability problem is matched by the apparent lack of an explicit distributed configuration for appliances in a large geographically disbursed enterprise.

Documentation, by all accounts significantly improved on the previous version, is divided into separate, focused manuals for administration, best practices, installation, and user guide. But although very well produced, the manuals are a bit skimpy. They seem to assume best case for everything and, if one gets into trouble, offer only limited help.

Support is limited to web-based and e-mail-based contact from registered users. Escalation to a live engineer on the phone is available, as is a training program, and there is also a registered user section of the Web site with a range of information. However, the testers were surprised that the apparent level of support seems so limited.

NetWitness is appropriately priced for the market, but lacks some features that would make it a truly strong competitor in the very large enterprise arena. What it does, it does very well and, in fact, has one of the best user interfaces among the products tested.

ProDiscover Incident Response

Version: 4.55
Supplier: Technology Pathways
Price: $7995
Contact: www.techpathways.com

ProDiscover Incident Response (IR) is a complete IT forensic tool that can access computers over the network (with agents installed) to enable media analysis, image acquisition and network behavior analysis.

Other capabilities include the remote analysis of running processes, open files, open ports and services, and other network-based functions. This is an invaluable capability in an incident.

ProDiscover IR is fairly easy to use. Its complexity and granularity mean the user must have some experience of working with a program of this nature, but the testers quickly found themselves moving through it with little trouble. The user interface is laid-out much like other products in this category, and testers could navigate around it with barely any trouble at all.

The product combines features for computer forensics with tools for complete incident response. It features all the basic IT forensic capabilities—full disk imaging, an ability to find hidden data, file metadata information, and hash keeping, as well as gather data on disks across an entire network. All its features are built into one main interface that is quite task-efficient with all functionality in one place.

The program performed well under all tests. Once the testers became familiar with the layout of the interface, they found it was a powerful tool—able to fully image both the disk on their forensics test disk and a disk on a computer on their network. They also found that it was efficient with fast and accurate imaging.

Documentation is well laid-out with clear explanations of all the program features. Technology Pathways offers in-depth support on its Web site, including how to contact support via phone and e-mail as well as an online forum.

Table 2.9   Overall Product Rating—ProDiscover IR

Features	Δ	Δ	Δ	Δ	Δ
Ease of use	Δ	Δ	Δ	Δ	Δ
Performance	Δ	Δ	Δ	Δ	Δ
Documentation	Δ	Δ	Δ	Δ	Δ
Support	Δ	Δ	Δ	Δ	Δ
Value of money	Δ	Δ	Δ	Δ	Δ
Overall rating	Δ	Δ	Δ	Δ	Δ

Note: Pros: all the basic forensic tools plus incident response. Cons: requires some experience with tools of this nature to get the full benefit. Verdict: fully functional network-based IT forensics tool with the ability to gather evidence remotely across a network at and attractive price.

This product is an excellent value—comparable products are far more expensive. The features of a fully capable network-based computer forensics tool, along with the ability to gather evidence remotely make it an excellent value. Testers rated this product as their Best Buy in the computer forensics product class.

Sleuth Kit and Autopsy Browser

Version:	The Sleuth Kit 2.04; Autopsy Browser 2.07
Supplier:	Open Source or Brian Carrier
Price:	Free
Contact:	www.sleuthkit.org

The Sleuth Kit and Autopsy Browser are excellent examples of what happens when a talented developer builds on good prior work. These products, used together, are freeware, open source computer forensic tools built on the Coroner's Toolkit. But the developer, Brian Carrier, has taken his considerable expertise in file systems of all kinds and applied it here.

The products are straightforward to use and will feel familiar to anyone comfortable in UNIX file systems. However, the products can analyze non-UNIX file systems with ease. Both The Sleuth Kit and the browser run in UNIX or Linux and the browser can run on any HTML environment and connect to the Autopsy server.

Because the underlying tool set is solid, the resulting Sleuth Kit is, likewise, highly competent. However, the developer has added significant functionality to the original Coroner's Toolkit and the further addition of the browser brings this product set very close to commercial quality. Indeed, the features for analysis and case management are just what one would expect from a competent commercial computer forensic tool.

The Sleuth Kit performed in every respect as expected. It is more difficult to use than many commercial products, but once the user has become comfortable with operating in a UNIX environment, performance is quite acceptable.

Table 2.10   Overall Product Rating—Sleuth Kit and Autopsy Browser

Features	Δ	Δ	Δ	Δ	Δ
Ease of use	Δ	Δ	Δ	Δ	Δ
Performance	Δ	Δ	Δ	Δ	Δ
Documentation	Δ	Δ	Δ	Δ	Δ
Support	Δ	Δ	Δ	Δ	Δ
Value of money	Δ	Δ	Δ	Δ	Δ
Overall rating	Δ	Δ	Δ	Δ	Δ

Note: Pros: surprisingly good documentation and support. Cons: bring UNIX-based, it requires some special skills from users. Verdict: solid, well-crafted and supported freeware computer forensic tool.

For an open source tool, Sleuth Kit or Autopsy sports remarkable documentation. As well as the expected UNIX manual pages, there are application notes (Sleuth Kit Implementation Notes or "SKINs"), mail lists, reference documents and a bi-monthly newsletter called *The Sleuth Kit Informer.*

Support is better than is typical of open source tools. Although there is no direct support, the developer makes his e-mail address available and there is a forum specifically for support issues. The products are well-supported in terms of ongoing upgrades and bug fixes. It is clear that the developer intends The Sleuth Kit to be an acceptable and accepted computer forensic tool.

The Sleuth Kit is a solid product with a well-known and respected developer behind it. More importantly, it has become firmly accepted in the computer forensic community, adding to its value.

Best Buy or Recommended

Dr. Stephenson rated i2's Analyst's Notebook the Best Buy in the analysis class for its powerful analytic capabilities, ease of use and its acceptable pricing. LogLogic's LX 2000 was rated Best Buy in the network forensics class for its high power, scalability and overall reasonable cost of ownership and return on investment beyond initial purchase. And ProDiscover Incident Response received Best Buy honors in the computer forensics class for its powerful capabilities at a very reasonable price.

Additional Tools for the Investigator's Tool Bag

The following cyber forensics tools were not included among the products tested by Dr. Stephenson and his team, and featured in the *SC Magazine* article but, are presented here by the authors as additional forensic tools which are available for the reader to evaluate and consider for inclusion in the cyber forensic investigator's "tool bag."

The following product information was complied and summarized directly from the vendor's Web sites. Once again, readers are reminded that relying on information contained on these sites is done at one's own risk. Use of such information is voluntary, and reliance on it should only be undertaken after an independent review of its accuracy, completeness, efficacy and timeliness, and a complete examination of the product to ensure its compatibility to the investigator's specific forensic needs. As such, users of this information are advised and encouraged to confirm specific claims for product performance as necessary and appropriate.

ComputerCOP (www.computercop.com)

ComputerCOP Forensic is engineered to be used by detectives, investigators, agents, and computer forensic professionals of law enforcement agencies. Ease of use, speed and built-in crime categories allow the average investigator to perform computer searches at the time of a search warrant execution.

The seizure or down time associated with taking business computers for hard drive mirroring and examination has resulted in successful litigation. Because of this, some courts are issuing warrants that require that a suspect computer be searched on site, and not seized without a demonstration that evidence exists on the computer.

ComputerCOP Forensic uses a new, parallel interface to search a suspect computer at an effective rate that is more than 200 times the speed of the traditional LapLink cable currently in use. ComputerCOP Forensic is installed on the investigator's laptop and searches the suspect computer via a proprietary parallel link at the effective rate of nearly 400 megabytes per minute, at a speed five times faster than a 10BaseT local area network connection.

The suspect computer is started from a DOS boot disk and ComputerCOP's memory resident server software enables the suspect computer to be accessed from the investigator's computer at LAN speeds, without any chance of the suspect computer being modified during the search. The search and review processes are run from an installed version of ComputerCOP Forensic on the investigator's machine.

ComputerCOP Forensic can provide an MD5 hash value for each of the computer's hard drives both prior to and after the examination, demonstrating that the examined drive was not adulterated. ComputerCOP Forensic examines all the suspect computer's local drives for files, deleted files, hidden, and zipped files. The product is also able to search and allow the investigator to review both the "file slack" and "RAM slack" remotely via the parallel connection.

ComputerCOP Forensic makes use of a "multi view image review" and "word category directory tree," both of which assist the investigator in the computer review process after the search of the suspect machine. After the review process is completed, the investigator may print as many of the selected pictures per page as he or she wishes.

ComputerCOP Forensic offers law enforcement professionals extensive image and word search options. The Image Options include file type selection, file header examination and file size range. The Word Options includes the ability to customize a search using nearly 7500 words and phrases that are categorized by crime types. They include categories such as controlled substances and drug paraphernalia, burglary and robbery, sex crimes, terrorism, and gambling. The examiner may add specific words to be searched for; those words may be searched alone or in conjunction with the specific word categories. Additionally, the examiner may add to the search word list a set of words stored on the examiner's machine or on a floppy disk.

ComputerCOP Forensic allows the examiner to copy any file, image or word, from the suspect computer to any storage media attached to the examiner's computer (e.g., floppy drive, Jaz drive, Zip drive, or mapped network drives). The text and images are saved in an evidence folder for review and or for printing at a later time. A click on the "SECURE IN EVIDENCE FOLDER" button and the file is copied to the evidence folder along with its MD5 hash signature and all available file metadata. A window opens and the investigator types in a description of the evidence. The file description is recorded on an "evidence log" that resides in the evidence folder along with the directory path of the evidence.

ComputerCOP Forensic's ability to detect graphic files by file header, as well as by file type, insures that the examiner will not fail to review renamed image files. The product is able to find images and text files that have been added to a zip file, even if the file has been compressed multiple times.

ComputerCOP's "word category directory tree" allows the examiner to obtain an overview of suspect word usage in: existing files, deleted files, unallocated disk space, "file slack" and "ram slack" on the computer being examined. The ability to look at unallocated disk sectors and "file slack" allows users to review portions of deleted files containing questionable text. All suspect text files found are documented in an expanding directory tree structure. The examiner has the option of listing the suspect words by crime category or by word usage in descending order of occurrence. This feature allows the examiner to get a complete overview of the suspect computers textual content from a single screen of information and significantly improves the investigator's ability to review text usage in a timelier manner.

At the conclusion of the examination, opening the "Case Manager" reveals the case number and the computer serial numbers of each examined computer in the case. With a click on a serial number, the examiner is presented with the print options of: The Report Cover Page, The Audit Trail that demonstrates the activity during the examination, the individual pieces of evidence with all the relevant data and description, The Evidence Log, The Evidence receipt, and Search Warrant Court Return. The "Case Manager" enables the investigator to easily document the evidence collected in such a way as to help obtain a quick plea bargain or a conviction.

The audit trail details every step of the search. The Cover Page and Evidence Log document all of the information that was collected during the search of the suspect computer. The Evidence report shows each piece of evidence along with specific information about each one.

From the Evidence Report, the user may open the piece of evidence in its associated application (i.e., .doc in Word, .gif in a browser, .xls in Excel). In order show the evidence in the associated application, a copy of the evidence is made and the associated application accesses the copy.

The latest version of ComputerCOP Forensic provides a report of the directory structure of the suspect machine. In the Case Manager the directory structure may be viewed as if the MS Explorer was displaying it. The directory may be printed fully expanded or at any level of expansion the investigator chooses.

Throughout the entire Evidence Management process the integrity of the evidence is maintained with an MD5 hash signature that is derived before the evidence is secured. Every time the evidence is accessed, the MD5 hash signature is verified. Cases are able to be archived on removable media or network drives and may be restored for examination later.

It should be noted in the Case Manager Report tree that the time and date has been added to the serial number. This is done by ComputerCOP and enables the same computer to be examined multiple times as part of the same case.

ComputerCOP Forensic makes use of the Windows operating system on the examiner's machine and DOS on the suspect machine, nothing is installed on the suspect machine and it is impossible to detect that Forensic has been run on the computer.

Mares and Company (www.dmares.com)

Maresware: Computer Forensics software provides an essential set of tools for investigating computer records and securing private information. It is highly flexible to meet the needs of all types of investigators including: law enforcement, intelligence agency, private investigator, corporate security officers, and human resources personnel.

Used within a forensic paradigm, the software enables discovery of evidence for use in criminal or civil legal proceedings. Internal investigators can develop documentation to support disciplinary actions, yet do so non-invasively, to preserve evidence that could end up in court.

IT managers can quickly wipe drives to DOD standards for reuse, retirement, or for compliance with HIPAA and other privacy of information regulations.

- MSome frequently used functions of Maresware: Computer Forensics
  - Discovery of "hidden" files (such as NTFS Alternate Data Streams)
  - For incident response purposes

- Evaluation of timelines
- Powerful file key word searching and comparing
- Files verification
- Drive wiping for information privacy and security
- Keyboard locking
- Diskette imaging
- File reformatting
- Documenting all the examiner's steps and procedures

■ Four programs of special interest from Maresware: Computer Forensics
  - Declassify a disk wiping program that overwrites a physical hard drive to DoD standards. Prepare drives for reuse or retirement; secure the privacy of information to meet HIPAA and other regulatory requirements.
  - Brandit used to brand ownership information on a hard disk drive. Useful in tracing stolen hard drives.
  - Bates_no a program for adding identifying numbers to filenames in e-documents to prepare records for evidentiary use. Or simply use as a records management tool.
  - Upcopy a copy program. Copies source files (directories) to a destination (directory), while maintaining full path and meta-information (file dates or times). Excellent for maintenance purposes, or evidence discovery.

■ Key Features of Maresware: Computer Forensics
  - Speed and High capacity: Extremely rapid processing of files of virtually unlimited size (a design feature engineered through the use of highly-efficient C-programming and by the development of non-integrated, highly-targeted individual programs).
  - User Control: By selecting which program(s) to use, the user—not the software—determines each step of the analysis and specifies his preferred output format. All programs use similar command line options.
  - Flexibility: Do streamlined single-step tasks or use any combination and sequence of programs for multi-step operations. Automate for unattended processing. Simplify repetitive tasks with familiar batch-file procedures.
  - Documentation of examiner's procedures: Document a complete history of your procedures and findings at every step. Provide proof of the authenticity and integrity of the evidence.

New Technologies, Inc. (NTI)

Computer Incident Response Suite (www.forensics-intl.com)

NTI has compiled a suite of tools to aid corporate and government computer specialist's deal with realized and potential computer risks associated with accidents, malicious acts, criminal acts and corporate policy abuses. The Computer Incident Response Suite can be purchased with or without training.

The Computer Incident Response Suite includes the following:

■ Copy QM—A U.S. DoD tested and certified floppy diskette duplication tool that is used to create duplicates of frequently used floppy diskettes in incident responses.
■ CRCMd5—A CRC file hashing program that validates the contents of one or more files.

- DiskScrub—A U.S. DoD tested and certified hard disk drive scrubbing utility used to securely eliminate all data.
- DiskSig Pro—A CRC hashing tool that is used to validate mirror image backup accuracy. This tool is also used to inventory all of the partitions or operating systems on a computer hard disk drive.
- FileList Pro—A hard disk and floppy diskette cataloging tool used to evaluate computer usage time lines.
- Filter_G—A patented intelligent fuzzy logic filter used with windows swap or page files and other ambient data sources to identify English language communications.
- Filter_I—A forensic filter used to eliminate binary data and control characters from ambient data sources.
- Filter_N—An intelligent fuzzy logic filter used to identify data patterns associated with credit card numbers, social security numbers, phone numbers and bank account numbers.
- GetFree—A U. S. DoD tested and certified ambient data collection tool used to capture unallocated (erased file) data.
- GetHTML—An intelligent fuzzy logic filter that is used to quickly identify patterns of HTML in ambient data sources.
- GetSlack—A U. S. DoD tested and certified ambient data collection tool used to capture file slack for analysis.
- GetTime—A program used to document the CMOS system time and date on a computer seized as evidence.
- Graphics Image File Extractor—An ambient data collection tool which quickly and automatically reconstructs previously BMP, GIF, and JPG files in cases involving the inappropriate (or illegal) download or viewing of pornography on the Internet.
- HexSearch—A forensic hex search utility that is used to find binary data patterns associated with file headers and foreign language data patterns.
- NTA Stealth—A patented forensic software tool which is used to quickly identify Internet account uses and abuses.
- NTA Viewer—An analysis and reporting tool for use with NTI's patented Net Threat Analyzer software.
- M-Sweep—A U. S. DoD tested and certified ambient data security scrubbing utility.
- SafeBack 3.0—A program which is used to create an evidence grade bit stream backup of a computer hard disk drive, zip disk or flash memory card.
- Seized—A program used to lock and secure evidence computers.
- TextSearch Plus—A U. S. DoD tested and certified text search utility which is used to conduct searches on DOS, Windows 95 and Windows 98-based computer systems. This tool is used in computer-related investigations and in computer security risk reviews.
- TextSearch NT—A U. S. DoD tested and certified text search utility which is used to conduct searches on Windows NT, Windows 2000 and Windows XP-based computer systems. This tool is used in computer-related investigations and in computer security risk reviews.

Web Sites for Additional Forensic Tool Information and Products

Table 2.11 lists several Web sites and their URL references that the cyber forensic investigator is encouraged to visit and to examine and test within the confines of his or her own lab, utilizing test

Table 2.11 Web Sites for Additional Forensic Tools

Product Name	URL Reference
TUCOFS—The Ultimate Collection of Forensic Software	www.tucofs.com
The Electronic Evidence Information Center	www.e-evidence.info
Talisker Security Wizardry Portal	www.networkintrusion.co.uk
Computer Forensics World	www.computerforensicsworld.com
Computer Forensics Community	www.computerforensics.99er.net
Computer Forensics, Cybercrime and Steganography Resources	www.forensics.nl or www.forensix.org
CERIAS – Digital Forensics	www.cerias.purdue.edu/research/forensics
Computer Forensics Toolkit	www.computer-forensics.privacyresources.org

data and under typical forensic investigation conditions, the tools offered by these various vendors and collaborative sites.

Only by continually seeking out, identifying, examining, and testing the growing market of cyber forensic tools, will the cyber forensic investigator be prepared for the variety and multitude of investigative situations which he or she may be presented with on any given day.

The material as presented in this chapter is designed to assist the reader by providing a perspective of the multitude of cyber forensic products currently on the market and to do so with an air of neutrality, as well as completeness. The authors realize, as should the reader, that no review can ever been 100 percent complete at any time. The introduction of new methods and procedures forces older products to re-design themselves or to disappear, and for new products to appear and to replace outdated technologies.

The authors hope that they have helped the reader sort through some of the most useful and most appropriate cyber forensics tools available on the market at this writing, and have helped to shorten the research cycle time typically needed to establish a "short list" of viable cyber forensic tools. A final note, once again, be advised and appropriately aware, that no one tool or suite of tools is right for all situations that a cyber forensics investigator may encounter. The key is having the right tool or tools for the job.

Final Note

The authors again wish to acknowledge and to thank the editors at *SC Magazine*, and the staff at Haymarket Media, for granting permission to reprint material from Dr. Peter Stephenson's review of forensic tools, which appeared in the magazine's July 2006 issue.

Chapter 3 provides an in depth examination of the varied ways in which a suspect may attempt to criminally conceal inappropriate activities utilizing technology and the techniques that a cyber forensics investigator should be aware of in an effort to expose these criminal activities.

Postscript

As this text was in its final stages of development Dr. Stephenson released an update of his July 2006 Forensic Tools report. This report appeared in the *SC Magazine* April 2007 issue (www.scmagazine.com/us/grouptest/details/e7d1bb8e-fc93-2f33-0bb1-49fb952f6f78/forensic-tools-2007/).

This updated report reviewed such forensic tools as Gargoyle Investigator, LiveWire Investigator v.3.1.1c, Device Seizure v.1.1, Forensic Tool Kit v1.70, EnCase Forensic v.6, and LR1000 v.3.5, among others.

Readers interested in further information on these and all of the products reviewed by Dr. Stephenson should reference the above URL or obtain a copy of the April 2007 issue (page 56) of *SC Magazine*.

Reference

1. Stephenson, P. (July 2006), Group Test: Forensic Tools, *SC Magazine*, pages 58–64, www.scmagazine.com.

Chapter 3

Concealment Techniques

You Cannot Find What You Cannot Investigate

Of the many issues facing the cyber forensic investigator one initial issue is determining where evidence may be found and where to actually begin to look for the electronic evidence. Even more pressing an issue however, is determining where evidence may be hidden.

Many an investigator will begin by examining the more obvious places where electronic evidence is to be found, such as slack space, swap files, drive slack, etc. However, as technology evolves, so do the opportunities for new and innovative ways and methods for concealing potential evidence, by those individuals who may be engaged in unlawful activities or seeking to hide malicious actions.

The speed, at which new technologies enter the market and subsequently can be abused or misused for ill gain, makes it almost impossible for the cyber forensic investigator to keep abreast with or even ahead of the bad guys. The cyber forensic investigator must remain vigilant, keep informed, and continually hone his or her technical skills via active training and continuing education.

Spoliation

Spoliation refers to the destruction or material alteration of evidence or the failure to preserve property for another's use as evidence in a pending or reasonably foreseeable litigation. In some courts, the failure to suspend a document destruction policy when litigation is anticipated may constitute spoliation.

Although there are different expressions of the rule, spoliation customarily has three component parts.

1. The alleged spoliator must have possession of the evidence and an obligation to preserve it at the time the evidence was destroyed.
2. The evidence destroyed also must have been "relevant" to the issues in the case.
3. Finally, all courts have some form of "culpability" requirement [1].

Spoliation can be inadvertent or intentional, either of which may not be immediately clear at the time of an initial investigation, and either if undertaken by an individual or organization, in the face of pending litigation may result in the destruction or manipulation of critical electronic evidence.

As for technical complexity, spoliation could easily run the gamut from a simplistic shredding of incriminating correspondences to the use of sophisticated software, specifically designed to electronically shred digital information, stored in an organization's information technology (IT) system.

The objective of this chapter is to present an overview examination of various technologies which can be used to delete, obliterate, conceal, or alter potential electronic evidence, as well as altering or concealing the identity of the perpetrator. Cyber forensic investigators should be aware of the technologies, as these may be encountered during the course of an investigation.

Several of the technologies discussed here have existed for many years and their use pre-dates the evolution of cyber crime as we currently know it. Several of the technologies which will be reviewed were never intended to be used as virtual decoys by individuals attempting to hide themselves and their actions from the harsh light of day and public scrutiny—but their use as such has grown exponentially in recent years. While the remainder are tools and techniques which are just emerging and their use in cloaking the illegal actions of cyber criminals, dishonest employees, cyber stalkers and others are only just being fully examined and realized.

The cyber forensic investigator must wear many hats, play many roles and remain technically competent on many diverse fronts, most often following a pre-determined investigation methodology that ensures not only the investigator's safety, but also the reliability, integrity, and ultimately the admissibility of the data (evidence) which the cyber forensic investigator collects and extracts from the suspect desktop systems, drives, files, laptops, PDAs, and so on.

Beyond skill building, training, and reading journals, the application of field experience plays a pivotal role in a cyber investigator's ability to find and collect the electronic evidence which may break a case or prove the innocence or guilt of a suspect. One way to keep that experience edge is by following the old adage "to catch a thief, you have to think like a thief."

As new technologies emerge and are incorporated into the mainstream of society and into the daily operations of organizations, the cyber forensic investigator should evaluate and assess these technologies from a perspective of how the technologies can be used to undermine good internal controls, bypass security, hide or conceal an individual's actions or even the individual him or herself. Almost any technology has the potential to be used in a manner foreign to its original intended purpose.

An awareness of following technologies, their intended uses and their ability to be misused, will help to guide a cyber forensic investigator to a more successful investigation.

Cryptography—An Old Workhorse

As the field of cryptography has advanced, the dividing lines for what is and what is not cryptography have become blurred. Cryptography today might be summed up as the study of techniques and applications that depend on the existence of difficult problems. Cryptanalysis is the study of how to compromise (defeat) cryptographic mechanisms, and cryptology (from the Greek kryptós lógos, meaning "hidden word") is the discipline of cryptography and cryptanalysis combined. To most people, cryptography is concerned with keeping communications private. Indeed, the protection of sensitive communications has been the emphasis of cryptography throughout much of its history [Kah67]. However, this is only one part of today's cryptography.

Encryption is the transformation of data into a form that is as close to impossible as possible to read without the appropriate knowledge (a key; see below). Its purpose is to ensure privacy by keeping information hidden from anyone for whom it is not intended, even those who have access to the encrypted data. Decryption is the reverse of encryption; it is the transformation of encrypted data back into an intelligible form.

Encryption and decryption generally require the use of some secret information, referred to as a key. For some encryption mechanisms, the same key is used for both encryption and decryption; for other mechanisms, the keys used for encryption and decryption are different.

Today's cryptography is more than encryption and decryption. Authentication is as fundamentally a part of our lives as privacy. We use authentication throughout our everyday lives—when we sign our name to some document for instance—and, as we move to a world where our decisions and agreements are communicated electronically, we need to have electronic techniques for providing authentication.

Cryptography is extremely useful; there is a multitude of applications, many of which are currently in use. A typical application of cryptography is a system built out of the basic techniques. Such systems can be of various levels of complexity. Some of the more simple applications are secure communication, identification, authentication, and secret sharing. More complicated applications include systems for electronic commerce, certification, secure electronic mail, key recovery, and secure computer access.

Secret Sharing

Another application of cryptography, called secret sharing, allows the trust of a secret to be distributed among a group of people. For example, in a (k, n)–threshold scheme, information about a secret is distributed in such a way that any "k" out of the "n" people (k £ n) have enough information to determine the secret, but any set of k-1 people do not. In any secret sharing scheme, there are designated sets of people whose cumulative information suffices to determine the secret. In some implementations of secret sharing schemes, each participant receives the secret after it has been generated. In other implementations, the actual secret is never made visible to the participants, although the purpose for which they sought the secret (for example, access to a building or permission to execute a process) is allowed.

Cryptography allows people to carry over the confidence found in the physical world to the electronic world, thus allowing people to do business electronically without worries of deceit and deception. Everyday thousands of people interact electronically, whether it is through e-mail, e-commerce (business conducted over the Internet), ATM machines, or cellular phones. The perpetual increase of information transmitted electronically has lead to an increased reliance on cryptography [2].

Types of Cryptographic Algorithms

There are several ways of classifying cryptographic algorithms. For purposes of this text, they will be categorized based on the number of keys that are employed for encryption and decryption, and further defined by their application and use. The three types of algorithms that will be discussed are (Figure 3.1):

- Secret Key Cryptography (SKC): Uses a single key for both encryption and decryption
- Public Key Cryptography (PKC): Uses one key for encryption and another for decryption
- Hash Functions: Uses a mathematical transformation to irreversibly "encrypt" information

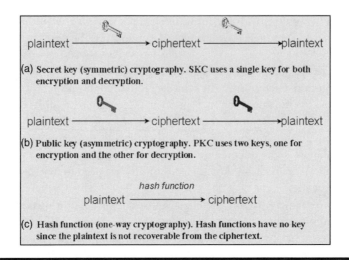

FIGURE 3.1   Three types of cryptography: secret-key, public key, and hash function.

Secret Key Cryptography

With SKC, a single key is used for both encryption and decryption. The sender uses the key (or some set of rules) to encrypt the plaintext and sends the ciphertext to the receiver. The receiver applies the same key (or the rule set) to decrypt the message and recover the plaintext. Because a single key is used for both functions, secret key cryptography is also called symmetric encryption.

With this form of cryptography, it is obvious that the key must be known to both the sender and the receiver; that, in fact, is the secret. The biggest difficulty with this approach, of course, is the distribution of the key.

Secret key cryptography schemes are generally categorized as being either stream ciphers or block ciphers. Stream ciphers operate on a single bit at a time and implement some form of feedback mechanism so that the key is constantly changing. A block cipher is so called because the scheme encrypts one block of data at a time using the same key on each block. In general, the same plaintext block will always encrypt to the same ciphertext when using the same key in a block cipher whereas the same plaintext will encrypt to different ciphertext in a stream cipher. Stream ciphers come in several flavors but two are worth mentioning here. Self-synchronizing stream ciphers calculate each bit in the keystream as a function of the previous n bits in the keystream. It is termed "self-synchronizing" because the decryption process can stay synchronized with the encryption process merely by knowing how far into the n-bit keystream it is. One problem is error propagation; a garbled bit in transmission will result in n garbled bits at the receiving side. Synchronous stream ciphers generate the keystream in a fashion independent of the message stream but by using the same keystream generation function at sender and receiver. Although stream ciphers do not propagate transmission errors, they are, by their nature, periodic so that the keystream will eventually repeat.

Block ciphers can operate in one of several modes; the following four are the most important:

- Electronic Codebook (ECB) mode is the simplest and most obvious application. The secret key is used to encrypt the plaintext block to form a ciphertext block. Two identical plaintext blocks, then, will always generate the same ciphertext block. Although, this is the most common mode of block ciphers, it is susceptible to a variety of brute-force attacks.

▪ Cipher Block Chaining (CBC) mode adds a feedback mechanism to the encryption scheme. In CBC, the plaintext is exclusively–ORed (XORed) with the previous ciphertext block prior to encryption. In this mode, two identical blocks of plaintext never encrypt to the same ciphertext.

▪ Cipher Feedback (CFB) mode is a block cipher implementation as a self-synchronizing stream cipher. CFB mode allows data to be encrypted in units smaller than the block size, which might be useful in some applications such as encrypting interactive terminal input. If we were using 1-byte CFB mode, for example, each incoming character is placed into a shift register the same size as the block, encrypted, and the block is transmitted. At the receiving side, the ciphertext is decrypted and the extra bits in the block (i.e., everything above and beyond the one byte) are discarded.

▪ Output Feedback (OFB) mode is a block cipher implementation conceptually similar to a synchronous stream cipher. OFB prevents the same plaintext block from generating the same ciphertext block by using an internal feedback mechanism that is independent of both the plaintext and ciphertext bitstreams.

Secret key cryptography algorithms that are in use today include:

▪ Data Encryption Standard (DES): The most common SKC scheme used today, DES, was designed by IBM in the 1970s and adopted by the National Bureau of Standards (NBS) [now the National Institute for Standards and Technology (NIST)] in 1977 for commercial and unclassified government applications. DES is a blockcipher employing a 56-bit key that operates on 64-bit blocks. DES has a complex set of rules and transformations that were designed specifically to yield fast hardware implementations and slow software implementations, although this latter point is becoming less significant today, because the speed of computer processors is several orders of magnitude faster today than twenty years ago. IBM also proposed a 112-bit key for DES, which was rejected at the time by the government; the use of 112-bit keys was considered in the 1990s, however, conversion was never seriously considered.

DES is defined in American National Standard X3.92 and three Federal Information Processing Standards (FIPS):

    – FIPS 46-3: DES [http://csrc. nist. gov/publications/fips/fips46-3/fips46-3.pdf]

    – FIPS 74: Guidelines for Implementing and Using the NBS Data Encryption Standard [www.itl.nist.gov/fipspubs/fip74.htm]

    – FIPS 81: DES Modes of Operation [www.itl.nist.gov/fipspubs/fip81.htm]

Information about vulnerabilities of DES can be obtained from the Electronic Frontier Foundation [www.eff.org//Privacy/Crypto_misc/DES_Cracking]

Two important variants that strengthen DES are:

    – Triple-DES (3DES): A variant of DES that employs up to three 56-bit keys and makes three encryption or decryption passes over the block; 3DES is also described in FIPS 46-3 and is the recommended replacement to DES.

    – DESX: A variant devised by Ron Rivest, by combining 64 additional key bits to the plaintext prior to encryption, effectively increases the key length to 120 bits.

▪ Advanced Encryption Standard (AES): In 1997, NIST initiated a very public, 4-1/2 year process to develop a new secure cryptosystem for U. S. government applications. As a result, the AES, became the official successor to DES in December 2001. AES uses an SKC scheme called Rijndael, a block cipher designed by Belgian cryptographers, Joan Daemen and Vincent Rijmen. The algorithm can use a variable block length and key length; the latest specification allowed any combination of keys lengths of 128, 192, or 256 bits and blocks of length 128, 192, or 256 bits. NIST initially selected Rijndael in October 2000 and formal adoption as the AES standard came in December 2001. FIPS PUB 197 [http://csrc.nist.gov/publications/fips/fips197/fips-197.pdf]describes a 128-bit block cipher employing a 128-, 192-, or 256-bit key.

- CAST-128/256: CAST-128, is a DES–like substitution-permutation crypto algorithm, employing a 128-bit key operating on a 64-bit block. CAST-256 is an extension of CAST-128, using a 128-bit block size and a variable length (128, 160, 192, 224, or 256 bit) key. CAST is named for its developers, Carlisle Adams and Stafford Tavares and is available internationally. CAST-256 was one of the Round 1 algorithms in the AES process.
- International Data Encryption Algorithm (IDEA): "Secret-key cryptosystem" written by Xuejia Lai and James Massey, in 1992 and patented by Ascom, a 64-bit SKC block cipher using a 128-bit key, is also available internationally.
- Rivest Ciphers (aka Ron's Code): Named for Ron Rivest, a series of SKC algorithms.
  - RC1: Designed on paper but never implemented.
  - RC2: A 64-bit block cipher using variable-sized keys designed to replace DES. Its code has not been made public, although many companies have licensed RC2 for use in their products.
  - RC3: Found to be breakable during development.
  - RC4: A stream cipher using variable-sized keys; it is widely used in commercial cryptography products, although it can only be exported using keys that are 40 bits or less in length.
  - RC5: A block cipher supporting a variety of block sizes, key sizes, and number of encryption passes over the data.
  - RC6: An improvement over RC5, RC6 was one of the AES Round 2 algorithms.
- Blowfish: A symmetric 64-bit block cipher invented by Bruce Schneier; optimized for 32-bit processors with large data caches, it is significantly faster than DES on a Pentium or Power PC-class machine. Key lengths can vary from 32 to 448 bits in length. Blowfish, available freely and intended as a substitute for DES or IDEA, is in use in over 80 products.
- Twofish: A 128-bit block cipher using 128-, 192-, or 256-bit keys. Designed to be highly secure and highly flexible, well-suited for large microprocessors, 8-bit smart card microprocessors, and dedicated hardware. Designed by a team led by Bruce Schneier and was one of the Round 2 algorithms in the AES process.
- Camellia: A secret-key, block-cipher crypto algorithm developed jointly by Nippon Telegraph and Telephone (NTT) Corp. and Mitsubishi Electric Corporation (MEC) in 2000. Camellia has some characteristics in common with AES: a 128-bit block size, support for 128-, 192-, and 256-bit key lengths, and suitability for both software and hardware implementations on common 32-bit processors as well as 8-bit processors (e.g., smart cards, cryptographic hardware, and embedded systems).
- MISTY1: Developed at Mitsubishi Electric Corp., a block cipher using a 128-bit key and 64-bit block, and a variable number of rounds. Designed for hardware and software implementations, and is resistant to differential and linear cryptanalysis.
- Secure and Fast Encryption Routine (SAFER): Secret-key crypto scheme designed for implementation in software. Versions have been defined for 40-, 64-, and 128-bit keys.

- KASUMI: A block cipher using a 128-bit key that is part of the Third-Generation Partnership Project (3gpp), formerly known as the Universal Mobile Telecommunications System (UMTS). KASUMI is the intended confidentiality and integrity algorithm for both message content and signaling data for emerging mobile communications systems.
- SEED: A block cipher using 128-bit blocks and 128-bit keys. Developed by the Korea Information Security Agency (KISA) and adopted as a national standard encryption algorithm in South Korea.
- Skipjack: SKC scheme proposed for Capstone. Although the details of the algorithm were never made public, Skipjack was a block cipher using an 80-bit key and 32 iteration cycles per 64-bit block.

Public-Key Cryptography

Public-key cryptography has been said to be the most significant new development in cryptography in the last 300–400 years. Modern PKC was first described publicly by Stanford University professor Martin Hellman and graduate student Whitfield Diffie in 1976. Their paper described a two-key crypto system in which two parties could engage in a secure communication over a nonsecure communications channel without having to share a secret key.

PKC depends upon the existence of so-called one-way functions, or mathematical functions that are easy to compute whereas their inverse function is relatively difficult to compute.

Generic PKC employs two keys that are mathematically related although knowledge of one key does not allow someone to easily determine the other key. One key is used to encrypt the plaintext and the other key is used to decrypt the ciphertext. The important point here is that, it *does not matter which key is applied first*, but that both keys are required for the process to work. Because a pair of key is required, this approach is also called asymmetric cryptography.

In PKC, one of the keys is designated the public key and may be advertised as widely as the owner wants. The other key is designated the private key and is never revealed to another party. It is straight forward to send messages under this scheme. Suppose Alice wants to send Bob a message, then Alice encrypts some information using Bob's public key; Bob decrypts the ciphertext using his private key. This method could be also used to prove who sent a message; Alice, for example, could encrypt some plaintext with her private key; when Bob decrypts using Alice's public key, he knows that Alice sent the message and Alice cannot deny having sent the message (non-repudiation).

Public-key cryptography algorithms that are in use today for key exchange or digital signatures include:

- RSA: The first, and still most common, PKC implementation, named after the three MIT mathematicians who developed it—Ronald Rivest, Adi Shamir, and Leonard Adleman. RSA today is used in hundreds of software products and can be used for key exchange, digital signatures, or encryption of small blocks of data. RSA uses a variable size encryption block and a variable size key. The keypair is derived from a very large number, "n," that is the product of two prime numbers chosen according to special rules; these primes may be 100 or more digits in length each, yielding an n with roughly twice as many digits as the prime factors. The public key information includes n and a derivative of one of the factors of n; an attacker cannot determine the prime factors of n (and, therefore, the private key) from this information alone and that is what makes the RSA algorithm so secure. (Some descriptions of PKC erroneously state that RSA's safety is due to the difficulty in factoring large prime numbers. In fact, large prime numbers, like small prime numbers, only have two factors!) The ability for computers to factor large numbers, and therefore, attack schemes such as RSA, is rapidly improving and systems today can find the prime factors of numbers with more than 140 digits. The presumed protection of RSA, however, is that users can easily increase the key size to always stay ahead of the computer processing curve. As an aside, the patent for RSA expired in September 2000 which does not appear to have affected RSA's popularity one way or the other.

■ Diffie-Hellman: After the RSA algorithm was published, Diffie and Hellman came up with their own algorithm. D-H is used for secret-key key exchange only, and not for authentication or digital signatures.
■ Digital Signature Algorithm (DSA): The algorithm specified in NIST's Digital Signature Standard (DSS), provides digital signature capability for the authentication of messages.
■ ElGamal: Designed by Taher Elgamal, a PKC system similar to Diffie-Hellman and used for key exchange.
■ Elliptic Curve Cryptography (ECC): A PKC algorithm based upon elliptic curves. ECC can offer levels of security with small keys comparable to RSA and other PKC methods. It was designed for devices with limited compute power or memory, such as smartcards and PDAs.
■ Public-Key Cryptography Standards (PKCS): A set of interoperable standards and guidelines for PKC, designed by RSA Data Security Inc.
■ Cramer-Shoup: A public-key cryptosystem proposed by R. Cramer and V. Shoup of IBM in 1998.
■ Key Exchange Algorithm (KEA): A variation on Diffie-Hellman; proposed as the key exchange method for Capstone.
■ LUC: A public-key cryptosystem designed by P. J. Smith and based on Lucas sequences. Can be used for encryption and signatures, using integer factoring.

Hash Functions

Hash functions, also called message digests and one-way encryption, are algorithms that, in some sense, use no key. Instead, a fixed-length hash value is computed based upon the plaintext that makes it impossible for either the contents or length of the plaintext to be recovered. Hash algorithms are typically used to provide a digital fingerprint of a file's contents, often used to ensure that the file has not been altered by an intruder or virus. Hash functions are also commonly employed by many operating systems to encrypt passwords. Hash functions, then, provide a measure of the integrity of a file.

Hash algorithms that are in common use today include:

■ Message Digest (MD) algorithms: A series of byte-oriented algorithms that produce a 128-bit hash value from an arbitrary-length message.
  - MD2—Designed for systems with limited memory, such as smart cards.
  - MD4—Developed by Rivest, similar to MD2 but designed specifically for fast processing in software.
  - MD5—Also developed by Rivest after potential weaknesses were reported in MD4; this scheme is similar to MD4 but is slower because more manipulation is made to the

original data. MD5 has been implemented in a large number of products although several weaknesses in the algorithm were demonstrated by German cryptographer Hans Dobbertin in 1996.

Secure Hash Algorithm (SHA): Algorithm for NIST's Secure Hash Standard (SHS). SHA-1 produces a 160-bit hash value and was originally published as FIPS 180-1 and RFC 3174. FIPS 180-2 describes five algorithms in the SHS: SHA-1 plus SHA-224, SHA-256, SHA-384, and SHA-512 which can produce hash values that are 224, 256, 384, or 512 bits in length, respectively.

RIPEMD: A series of message digests that initially came from the RIPE (RACE Integrity Primitives Evaluation) project. RIPEMD-160 was designed by Hans Dobbertin, Antoon Bosselaers, and Bart Preneel, and optimized for 32-bit processors to replace the then-current 128-bit hash functions. Other versions include, RIPEMD-256, RIPEMD-320, and RIPEMD-128.

HAVAL (HAsh of VAriable Length): Designed by Y. Zheng, J. Pieprzyk, and J. Seberry, a hash algorithm with many levels of security. HAVAL can create hash values that are 128, 160, 192, 224, or 256 bits in length.

Whirlpool: A relatively new hash function, designed by V. Rijmen and P. S. L. M. Barreto. Whirlpool operates on messages less than 2^{256} bits in length, and produces a message digest of 512 bits. The design of this hash function is very different than that of MD5 and SHA-1, making it immune to the same attacks as on those hashes.

Hash functions are sometimes misunderstood and some sources claim that no two files can have the same hash value. This is, in fact, not correct. Consider a hash function that provides a 128-bit hash value. There are, obviously, 2^{128} possible hash values. But there are a lot more than 2^{128} possible files. Therefore, there have to be multiple files—in fact, there have to be an infinite number of files—that can have the same 128-bit hash value.

The difficulty is finding two files with the same hash! What is, indeed, very hard to do is to try to create a file that has a given hash value so as to force a hash value collision—which is the reason that hash functions are used extensively for information security and computer forensics applications. Alas, researchers in 2004 found that practical collision attacks could be launched on MD5, SHA-1, and other hash algorithms. At this time, there is no obvious successor to MD5 and SHA-1 that could be put into use quickly; there are so many products using these hash functions that it could take many years to flush out all use of 128- and 160-bit hashes [3].

Cryptography: The Untold Story

This brief introduction, overview of cryptography has only scratched the surface of what is an extensive science and involves hundreds of specific elements which have not been discussed here yet, but are of critical importance to the successful application of cryptography to keeping secrets secret.

Block ciphers, stream ciphers, message authentication codes, elliptic curve cryptosystems, probabilistic encryption, blind signature schemes, digital timestamping, key recovery, covert channels, biometric techniques, tamper-resistant hardware, random number generators, key generation, key establishment, digital signatures, the list is almost endless.

These technologies and many more support and exist within the world of cryptography, so the cyber forensic investigator must attempt to keep abreast of or at least be aware of the entire spectrum of cryptography and the implications which this technology has on the ability to render potential electronic evidence inaccessible.

A time will come (again not if but when) the investigator will encounter electronic evidence which has been encrypted. Knowledge of basic encryption techniques and encryption methodologies will help the forensic investigator to better assess the situation and possibly help to identify which tools may enable the investigator to both unlock and unscramble potential electronic evidence.

Yes, there is room for stealth in the Enterprise world.

John Pescatore
Gartner Group

Spoofing

Criminals have long employed the tactic of masking their true identity, from disguises to aliases to caller-id blocking. It should come as no surprise then that criminals who conduct their nefarious activities on networks and computers should employ such techniques. Internet Protocol (IP) spoofing is one of the most common forms of online camouflage. In IP spoofing, an attacker gains unauthorized access to a computer or a network by making it appear that a malicious message has come from a trusted machine by "spoofing" the IP address of that machine [4].

Internet Protocol

The function or purpose of IP is to move datagrams through an interconnected set of networks. This is done by passing the datagrams from one Internet module to another until the destination is reached. The Internet modules reside in hosts and gateways in the Internet system. The datagrams are routed from one Internet module to another through individual networks based on the interpretation of an Internet address. Thus, one important mechanism of the Internet protocol is the Internet address.

The Internet protocol implements two basic functions: addressing and fragmentation.

The Internet modules use the addresses carried in the Internet header to transmit Internet datagrams toward their destinations. The selection of a path for transmission is called routing. The Internet modules use fields in the Internet header to fragment and reassemble Internet datagrams when necessary for transmission through "small packet" networks.

The model of operation is that an Internet module resides in each host engaged in Internet communication and in each gateway that interconnects networks. These modules share common rules for interpreting address fields and for fragmenting and assembling Internet datagrams. In addition, these modules (especially in gateways) have procedures for making routing decisions and other functions [5].

Transmission Control Protocol

Transmission Control Protocol (TCP) is a connection-oriented, end-to-end reliable protocol designed to fit into a layered hierarchy of protocols which supports multi-network applications. The TCP provides for reliable interprocess communication between pairs of processes in host computers attached to distinct but interconnected computer communication networks. Very few assumptions are made as to the reliability of the communication protocols below the TCP layer.

TCP assumes that it can obtain a simple, potentially unreliable datagram service from the lower level protocols. In principle, the TCP should be able to operate above a wide spectrum of communication systems ranging from hard-wired connections to packet-switched or circuit-switched networks [6].

Spoofing is the creation of TCP/IP packets using somebody else's IP address. Routers use the "destination IP" address to forward packets through the Internet, but ignore the "source IP" address. That address is only used by the destination machine when it responds back to the source.

A common misconception is that "IP spoofing" can be used to hide your IP address when surfing the Internet, chatting online, sending e-mail, and so forth, which is generally not true. Forging the source IP address causes the responses to be misdirected, meaning you cannot create a normal network connection. However, IP spoofing is an integral part of many network attacks that do not need to see responses (blind spoofing).

Examples of spoofing:

- Man-in-the-middle: packet sniffs on link between the two end points, and can therefore pretend to be one end of the connection.
- Routing redirect: redirects routing information from the original host to the hacker's host (this is another form of man-in-the-middle attack).
- Source routing: redirects individual packets by hackers host.
- Blind spoofing: predicts responses from a host, allowing commands to be sent, but cannot get immediate feedback.
- Flooding: SYN flood fills up receive queue from random source addresses; smurf or fraggle spoofs victim's address, causing everyone to respond to the victim [7].

Hijacked Session Attacks

A second clandestine activity similar to spoofing and designed to hide the original source of access or identity, involves the use of a tool called "tap" to take over existing login sessions on a system.

This tool allows an intruder with root access to gain control of any other session currently active on the system, executing commands as if they had been typed by the owner of the session. If the user session has previously performed a telnet or login to another system, then the intruder may gain access to the remote system as well, bypassing any authentication normally required for access.

Currently, the tap tool is only known to affect SunOS 4.1.x systems, although the system features that allow the attack are not unique to Sun systems [8].

Given that both spoofing and session hacking techniques, utilized and undertaken by knowledgeable individuals, may result in a deception of the original source of attack or penetration of IP address, cyber forensic investigators should be both aware of these methods of concealment and examine for such potentialities when investigating an E-crimes scene. The documented source of a suspect's potentially incredulous (or suspicious) e-mail while forensically sound, may in fact not be the logical, original source of the e-mail, if the suspect's system has been compromised to the point where a third party may have had the opportunity to re-route or manipulate the suspect's machine.

As Matthew Tanase states in his article *IP Spoofing: An Introduction* [4], "Obviously, it's very easy to mask a source address by manipulating an IP header," an investigator must establish beyond reasonable doubt that the e-evidence collected from the suspect's machine was, in fact, generated from the suspect's machine and not via an external source.

Polymorphism

In general, polymorphism describes multiple possible states for a single property (it is said to be polymorphic or polymorphous). In computer terminology, polymorphic code is code that mutates although keeping the original algorithm intact. This technique is sometimes used by computer viruses, shellcodes and computer worms to hide their presence.

Most anti-virus software and intrusion detection systems attempt to locate malicious code by searching through computer files and data packets sent over a computer network. If the security software finds patterns that correspond to known computer viruses or worms, it takes appropriate steps to neutralize the threat. Polymorphic algorithms make it difficult for such software to locate the offending code as it constantly mutates.

Encryption is the most commonly used method of achieving polymorphism in code. However, not all of the code can be encrypted as it would be completely unusable. A small portion of it is left unencrypted and used to jumpstart the encrypted software. Anti-virus software targets this small unencrypted portion of code.

Malicious programmers have sought to protect their polymorphic code from this strategy by rewriting the unencrypted decryption engine each time the virus or worm is propagated. Sophisticated pattern analysis is used by anti-virus software to find underlying patterns within the different mutations of the decryption engine in hopes of reliably detecting such malware [9].

"Malware" is short for malicious software and is typically used as a catch-all term to refer to any software designed to cause damage to a single computer, server, or computer network, whether its a virus, spyware, et al. [10]. Malware is sometimes known as a computer contaminant.

"Computer contaminant" means a computer program designed to modify, damage, destroy, disable, deny, or degrade access to, allow unauthorized access to, functionally impair, record, or transmit information within a computer, computer system, or computer network without the express or implied consent of the owner. Computer contaminants include, but are not limited to:

1. A group of computer programs commonly known as "viruses" and "worms" that are self-replicating or self-propagating, and that are designed to contaminate other computer programs, compromise computer security, consume computer resources, modify, destroy, record, or transmit data, or disrupt the normal operation of the computer, computer system, or computer network
2. A group of computer programs commonly known as "Trojans" or "Trojan horses" that are not self-replicating or self-propagating, and that are designed to compromise computer security, consume computer resources, modify, destroy, record, or transmit data, or disrupt the normal operation of the computer, computer system, or computer network
3. A group of computer programs commonly known as "zombies" that are designed to use a computer without the knowledge and consent of the appropriate principal, and that are designed to send large quantities of data to a targeted computer network for the purpose of degrading the targeted computer's or network's performance, or denying access through the network to the targeted computer or network, resulting in what is commonly know as "Denial of Service" or "Distributed Denial of Service" attacks

4. A group of computer programs commonly know as "trap doors," "back doors," or "root kits" that are designed to bypass standard authentication software, and that are designed to allow access to or use of a computer without the knowledge or consent of the appropriate principal [11]

Polymorphism is briefly discussed and included here to alert investigators that what may initially seem to be benign, or unimportant files or programs, may indeed be legitimate electronic evidence and may have been altered from its original state, (e.g., the insertion of a virus or Trojan by a suspect into the suspect's employer's IT infrastructure) and should be fully investigated. All software and programs that do not appear on an approved list should be collected, examined, and investigated as potential evidence.

Steganography

Steganography is the art of covered or hidden writing. The purpose of steganography is covert communication to hide a message from a third party. This differs from cryptography, the art of secret writing, which is intended to make a message unreadable by a third party but does not hide the existence of the secret communication. Although, steganography is separate and distinct from cryptography, there are many analogies between the two, and some authors categorize steganography as a form of cryptography as hidden communication is a form of secret writing [12].

Encryption is used to keep the contents of information private or confidential, and only those holding the proper keys can extract the secret contents. The sole purpose for the use of steganography, on the other hand, is to hide the fact that the secret message, (possibly containing incriminating evidence) even exists. The military calls this "covert communication," and the path for this communication is called a "covert channel."

There are many techniques used for hiding secret messages in images. The common denominator among them is that they combine a carrier file with a secret message to produce a resulting binary file containing the hidden message. The process hides the data in such a way that the changes are indiscernible to the human eye (or ear in the case of audio). The methodologies vary widely from simple least significant bit (LSB) modification to sophisticated JPEG and MP3 transform modifications.

The increase in availability, sophistication, and popularity of steganography programs increases the potential opportunities for industrial espionage, trade secret theft, cyber weapon exchange, and criminal coordination and communication [13].

Steganography hides the covert message but not the fact that two parties are communicating with each other. The steganography process generally involves placing a hidden message in some transport medium, called the carrier. The secret message is embedded in the carrier to form the steganography medium. The use of a steganography key may be employed for encryption of the hidden message or for randomization in the steganographic scheme.

On computers and networks, steganography applications allow for someone to hide any type of binary file in any other binary file, although image and audio files are today's most common carriers.

Although conceptually similar to steganography, digital watermarking usually has different technical goals. Generally, only a small amount of repetitive information is inserted into the carrier, it is not necessary to hide the watermarking information, and it is useful for the watermark to be able to be removed while maintaining the integrity of the carrier [14].

What threat does this technology pose to organizations, and why is knowledge of this concealment methodology important for cyber forensic investigators?

First, the use of steganography provides the ability to smuggle sensitive information out of an organization by a disgruntled or angry employee. This can be accomplished by hiding the information via steganographic techniques inside an innocuous looking attachment to an e-mail message.

Second, the use of steganography allows someone to hide criminal or unethical information on corporate resources. A quick scan of a departing user's desktop might reveal digital photos from the company picnic, family outings, or a collection of clipart used for building slide presentations. These all will appear completely harmless and innocuous, when in fact they may contain potentially incriminating information that had been hidden from view.

Finally, the use of steganography allows for the utilization of corporate resources to communicate criminal or terrorist information. Most companies are diligent in their awareness regarding the content of their corporate Web sites and public facing information. However, every image on that corporate Web site is a potential carrier of hidden information if exploited. Many of these images float around the organization and originate from many sources, providing the opportunity for insertion of secret or covert content [13].

Derivatives of this concealment method come in many flavors and designs. Although it may be close to impossible to stay ahead of the rapidly changing technology that encompasses the world of steganography, it is important to have at least a familiarity, an understanding of steganography's offspring. These various mutations include:

- Covert channels [www.rsasecurity.com/rsalabs/node.asp?id=2351]
- File appending [www.pageresource.com/cgirec/ptut15.htm]
- Steganalysis [www.jjtc.com/Steganalysis/]
- Watermarking [www.watermarkingworld.org/] and
- Word substitution [www.public.asu.edu/~droussi/text4.pdf]

What may appear to be unimportant photos of Aunt Esther, screen saver images downloaded from ESPN.com, or the latest Dilbert cartoon, may actually be hiding copies of classified documents, intellectual property, or pornographic images. Technology continues to provide a variety of opportunities for individuals to engage in criminal activity, thus it is increasingly important that the cyber forensic investigator keep abreast of the advances in the ancient art of deception—hiding in plain sight—steganography.

Reversing the Steganographic Process

There are many steganographic software packages available in the marketplace today; however, the available software packages vary by large degrees in their ability to consistently provide the highest level of steganographic security often sought by users. This is either a good or bad, depending on the reasons you have for attempting to conceal data.

A loose classification scheme for assigning taxonomy to steganography software by the method in which data was inserted into the carrier file was formulated by Janvier Guillermito. In his assessment and reverse engineering of many steganographic software packages, Mr. Guillermito provided an educational analysis and examination of the steganographic software's ability to "do its job," at a detailed level far beyond the intended scope of this book.

For the cyber forensic investigator interested in learning more about the technical "inner workings" of steganographic software, the good, the bad, and yes the ugly, a more detailed review and examination of following the steganographic software is highly recommended.

The "Guillermito classification" categorizes steganographic software as follows:

1. A few thoughts about steganography
   - http://www.guillermito2.net/stegano/ideas.html
2. Adding data at the end of the carrier file:
   - Camouflage [www.guillermito2.net/stegano/camouflage/index.html]
   - JpegX [www.guillermito2.net/stegano/jpegx/index.html]
   - SecurEngine for JPG [http://securengine.isecurelabs.com/]
   - Safe&Quick [www.guillermito2.net/stegano/sqfilehide/index.html]
   - Steganography 1.50 [www.guillermito2.net/stegano/steganography/index.html]
3. Inserting data in some junk or comment field in the header of the file structure:
   - Invisible Secrets 2002 for JPG and PNG [www.guillermito2.net/stegano/invisiblesecrets/index.html]
4. Embedding data in the carrier byte stream, in a linear, sequential, and fixed way:
   - InPlainView [www.guillermito2.net/stegano/inplainview/index.html]
   - InThePicture [www.guillermito2.net/stegano/inthepicture/index.html]
   - ImageHide [www.guillermito2.net/stegano/imagehide/index.html]
   - JSteg [www.securityfocus.com/tools/1434]
5. Embedding data in the carrier byte stream, in a pseudorandom way depending on a password:
   - CryptArkan [www.kuskov.com/cryptarkan/]
   - JPHide [http://linux01.gwdg.de/~alatham/stego.html]
6. Embedding data in the carrier byte stream, in a pseudorandom way depending on a password, and changing other bits of the carrier file to compensate for the modifications induced by the hidden data, to avoid modifying statistical properties of the carrier file:
   - Outguess [www.outguess.org/detection.php]
   - F5 [www.rn.inf.tu-dresden.de/~westfeld/f5.html]

StegHide [http://steghide.sourceforge.net/] is a steganographic program that is able to hide data in various kinds of image- and audio-files. The color and respectively sample-frequencies are not changed thus making the embedding resistant against first order statistical tests. The current version is 0.5.1. features:

- Compression of embedded data
- Encryption of embedded data
- Embedding of a checksum to verify the integrity of the extracted data
- Support for JPEG, BMP, WAV, and AU files

JSteg shell [http://www.tiac.net/users/korejwa/jstegshella.zip] is a Win95/98/NT interface to run JSteg DOS, a program by Derek Upham, which hides data in the ever popular JPG image format. Version 1.0 has a number of new improvements, including 40 bit RC4 encryption, determination of the amount of data a JPG can hide beforehand, and user-selectable JPG options (i.e., degree of compression). JSteg Shell has a slick, easy to use interface that makes using JSteg DOS a snap.

AppendX [www.unet.univie.ac.at/~a9900470/appendX/], Version: v0. 2b, is a steganographic tool, which simply appends data to other files (like JPEGs or PNGs) to hide it. It supports PGP header stripping.

Stego Suite [www.wetstonetech.com/catalog/item/1104418/619451.htm] is a tool that identifies the presence of steganography without prior knowledge of the steganographic algorithm that might have been used against the targeted file and is known as "blind steganography detection" (www.guillermito2.net/stegano/jsteg/index.html, retrieved July 2006).

Counter- or Anti-Forensics

Digital forensic analysts may find their task complicated by any of more than a dozen commercial software packages designed to irretrievably erase files and records of computer activity. These counter-forensic tools have been used to eliminate evidence in criminal and civil legal proceedings and represent an area of continuing concern for forensic investigators.

User awareness has grown that "deleting" files does not mean obliterating the information they contain—an awareness heightened by a string of headlines, from the 1986 resurrection of erased Iran-Contra records on Oliver North's computer to the recovery of files and e-mail communications in the Enron Corp. investigation. This awareness has spawned demand for counter-forensic software, which developers market as guarding users' privacy or protecting them from being penalized for activity on the computer.

Commercial tools claim to expunge all traces of information about specific computer usage, including documents and other files created, records of Web sites visited, images viewed, and files downloaded. To do this, counter-forensic tools must locate activity records scattered across the filesystem and erase them irretrievably, while leaving the rest of the operating system intact.

Forensic reviews of digital media often include an assessment of whether or not such counter-forensic tools were used, and it has been suggested that these tools should be banned by corporate policies [15].

Deleted files are also a source of potential evidence. The process of recovering deleted files is usually not difficult or time consuming. However, it can be made very difficult and time consuming by using scrubbing tools and shredding software, which are programs designed to destroy information.

They wipe clean the targeted space by writing over clusters several times. In some cases, even after the clusters are overwritten several times, the data or at least part of it can be recovered; however, the time spent in data recovery increases greatly. So, to avoid unnecessary delays and costs for the recovery of deleted files, it is advisable for the company to prohibit the use of this kind of software [16].

Courts have grappled with how to treat the use of these tools. Indeed, courts have ruled that the use of such software implies intent to conceal evidence and have sanctioned the users. Several specific cases reflect the growing trend of courts to sanction use of these counter-forensic tools:

- *U.S. v. H. Marc Watzman*, 2003
  - Agents from the living room of the Watzman Residence also recovered a Sony Vaio laptop computer. During surveillance conducted on or about October 7, 2003, federal agents observed WATZMAN with what appeared to be this same computer at XXXXX Hospital in XXXXXX, Illinois. A preliminary forensic examination of this laptop revealed, among other items, a computer program called "Evidence Eliminator" used to erase, among other things, images that were received or stored on computers. In addition, the preliminary forensic examination revealed approximately 3,000–5,000 images stored in various directories. On or about October 11, 2003, agents intercepted a parcel

from Germany that was addressed to WATZMAN. The parcel was inspected, and was found to contain encryption software commonly used to hide pictures within pictures, to hide text within pictures, and to encrypt computer files (www.usdoj.gov/usao/iln/indict/2003/watzman.pdf#search=%22%22H.%20Marc%20Watzman%22%22, retrieved August, 2006).

■ *Kucala Enterprises v. Auto Wax Co.*, 2003
- *Kucala Enterprises v. Auto Wax Co., Inc.*, "Kucala VII," 2004 U.S. Dist. LEXIS 22271 (N.D.Ill. Nov. 2, 2004). This case highlights the disastrous results that can befall a litigant that uses a wiping program such as Evidence Eliminator. In this patent infringement case in federal court in Illinois, the district court, in response to a discovery request by the defendant, had ordered the inspection of a computer used by the plaintiff. The defendant then hired an experienced forensic investigator to use EnCase to create a forensic image and analyze the plaintiff's computer.
- On February 28th, the investigator imaged the subject computer. His analysis revealed that the plaintiff had employed Evidence Eliminator on his computer between midnight and 4 a. m. on February 28th to delete and overwrite over 12,000 files, and that an additional 3,000 files had been deleted and overwritten three days earlier. In addressing the proprietary of the plaintiff's use of Evidence Eliminator, the Court stated "Any reasonable person can deduce, if not from the name of the product itself, then by reading the Web site, that Evidence Eliminator is a product used to circumvent discovery. Especially telling is that the product claims to be able to defeat EnCase ..." (emphasis added).
- The Court described the plaintiff's actions as "egregious conduct" that was wholly unreasonable, and found the plaintiff at fault for not preserving evidence that it had a duty to maintain. As a result, the Magistrate Judge recommended to the district court that the plaintiff's case be dismissed with prejudice, and that the plaintiff be ordered to pay the defendant's attorney fees and costs incurred with respect to the issue of sanctions (Case summary courtesy of Guidance Software, Inc., retrieved from www.forensics.com/html/trng_edu_case_must_read.html, August 2006).

■ *U.K. v. Timothy Pickup*, 2004
- Pickup was arrested in 2003 during investigations into an international Internet pedophile ring called the Shadows Brotherhood. He was jailed in June. Pickup admitted in a police interview that he was the administrator of a bulletin board used by members to distribute indecent images of children.
- He was only caught in possession of the type treated by the criminal justice system as less serious, although police suspected he had cleaned his computer with software that can destroy evidence (http://news.bbc.co.uk/2/hi/uk_news/england/west_yorkshire/4076237.stm retrieved August 2006).

■ *U.S. v. Robert Johnson*, 2005
- According to the indictment and JOHNSON's guilty plea, JOHNSON, the former Chief Executive Officer of a publicly traded company headquartered in New York City (the Company), knowingly possessed sexually explicit photographs of children on a computer owned by the Company. JOHNSON had obtained the illegal images by purchasing membership rights to Web sites that sold child pornography.
- According to the Indictment and JOHNSON's statement in court, prior to May 3, 2004, ICE agents learned that ROBERT JOHNSON, using the Internet aliases "robjob714" and "jobobo55," had purchased memberships in Web sites believed to contain and distribute child pornography and had done so through a computer that the agents

traced to the Company. On May 4, 2004, an ICE agent spoke to two executives of the Company and informed them that ICE was investigating usage of a Company computer to access Internet Web sites believed to contain and distribute child pornography but did not tell the Company executives that ICE was investigating ROBERT JOHNSON. On May 4, 2004, one of the executives told JOHNSON, in substance, that the Company had received an inquiry from federal authorities concerning use of a Company computer to access Internet Web sites that contain and distribute child pornography.

- According to the Indictment and JOHNSON's statement in court, on May 5 and 6, 2004, after learning about the federal investigation into the use of a Company computer to access child pornography, JOHNSON used a computer program called "Evidence Eliminator" to destroy and obliterate more than 12,000 files from the hard disk drive of the desktop and laptop computers assigned to him by the Company.
- In his plea allocution in court, JOHNSON acknowledged that he had possessed at least two images of child pornography that he had downloaded from an Internet Web site and he had used the "Evidence Eliminator" program to destroy computer files from his desktop and laptop computers after he learned of the federal investigation.
- JOHNSON faces a maximum of 10 years in prison on the charge of possession of child pornography and a maximum of 20 years in prison on the charge of destruction of documents in connection with a federal investigation. The latter charge was brought pursuant to a statute enacted as part of the Sarbanes–Oxley Act of 2002 (www.ice.gov/pi/news/newsreleases/articles/060804ny.htm, retrieved August, 2006).

■ *State of Missouri v. Zacheriah Tripp*, 2005
- Zacheriah Tripp appeals his convictions of first degree murder, kidnapping, and forcible rape. He raises three points of error on appeal. In his second point, Tripp argues that the trial court plainly erred in permitting testimony regarding the contents of his laptop, claiming that the testimony was legally irrelevant, with its prejudicial effect outweighing any probative value it might have had.
- The evidence presented at trial established that Tripp once had the Microsoft Office Suite installed on the computer, had used the computer for word processing, and had deleted the Office Suite on the night of Sarah's disappearance. There was also evidence of a substantial amount of empty space on the computer and a reference to "wipeinfo.exe" in the computer's swap file (which is used to temporarily hold data from the computer's active memory).
- Even accepting the testimony that a wipe utility had been used on portions of the computer's hard drive, the testimony stopped short of any indication that the primary use of such a utility would be to conceal information. Nor does it appear that such a conclusion could be inferred from the testimony in the record (Opinion Missouri Court of Appeals Western District, www.courts.mo.gov/courts/pubopinions.nsf/e53581bdd14e64858625661f004bc8fd/a146c42d2b4a0e6486257018005e0edd?OpenDocument).

On modern personal computer systems, two broad factors complicate the task of eliminating user files and activity records. One is the creation of arbitrary temporary files and cached data streams by common user applications, such as Microsoft Corp's Office Suite or Internet Explorer Web browser. Identifying and locating all the sensitive temporary data written to disk by user applications under varying circumstances is nontrivial. These temporary files are often deleted by the applications that created them, significantly increasing the difficulty of locating the data subsequently to securely wipe it.

At the same time, modern filesystems and the operating systems that govern them employ redundancy and performance-enhancing techniques that can propagate sensitive data onto arbitrary areas of storage media. These techniques include "swapping" data from RAM to a temporary file on the disk to better manage system memory usage, and creating a file to store the contents of RAM and system state information to support a hibernate function. Journaling file systems such as NTFS, ext3, and Reiser also record fractional changes to files in separate journal structures to allow filesystem records to be rebuilt more swiftly and consistently after a system crash [17].

Anti-Forensics: A View from the Edge

In an effort to shed more light on the emerging, albeit slowly and most oftentimes hidden world of anti-forensics, the authors interviewed Vincent Liu, Managing Director, Stach & Liu, LLC, a leading authority on anti-forensics. The following is an excerpt from that interview:

Authors (A.M.)	What is your definition of anti-forensics?
Vincent Liu (V.L.)	In the strictest interpretation, anti-forensics is the application of the scientific method to digital media to invalidate factual information for judicial review. More practically, anti-forensics is not getting caught.
A.M.	Is anti-forensics a set of tools or products a process or a methodology?
V.L.	Anti-forensics is a combination of people, process, and tools. In each situation, a person must evaluate the circumstances and choose to utilize the appropriate anti-forensics technique. These techniques are captured in processes and tools, which aide in the performance of each technique.
A.M.	Why should an organization seek to either own or have a working knowledge of these tools/products?
V.L.	Organization must seek to understand the mindset, skill set, and capabilities of those employing anti-forensics techniques. This is similar to the situation where organizations realize that the best way to understand the threat posed to their information systems is by viewing it from an attacker's perspective.
	Properly understood, this knowledge allows an organization to mitigate the effects of these techniques when they are applied against their information systems.
A.M.	Can such tools be seen as lurking on the dark side? Could anti-forensic tools be considered equally black hat and white hat "tools"? Trying to subvert mainstream corporate environs?
V.L.	Absolutely. Most tools in the security space have two edges. Every network administrator has a copy of nmap in their toolkit, which they use to gain a better understanding of their network. In this case, the network administrator may seek to identify and remediate potential security issues.
	On the other hand, malicious attackers can also utilize nmap to gain a better understanding of the network. In this case, however, the attacker seeks to identify and exploit the potential security issues. In both instances, nmap is used to assist in the identification of the issue.

Anti-forensics tools can be viewed in a similar fashion. A tool such as timestomp may permit an attacker to subvert file times to corrupt a forensic analysis, but it can also be used to validate various forensics tools for reliability.

Network routers are subjected to load tests to determine their ability to handle traffic under extreme conditions. Forensics tools can now be subjected to tests to determine their ability to provide valid information that could potentially be submitted in court.

A.M.   What is your working definition of Disk Configuration Overlay (DCO), and what is its role in concealing potential digital evidence?

V.L.   DCO is an extension of the Advanced Technology Attachment (ATA) command set. From a practical point of view, it results in a hidden partition similar to Host Protected Areas (HPA).

A.M.   What is the benefit of having a tool such as Self-Monitoring, Analysis and Reporting Tool (SMART)?

V.L.   SMART is an extended feature set that's built into most hard drives today to permit for performance and diagnostics. An extremely paranoid or extremely advanced malicious attacker might attempt to monitor the statistics, that is, Power_Cycle_Count, to determine whether a particular machine has been rebooted and thus forensically acquired.

A.M.   You stated in your presentation, ["Bleeding-Edge Anti-Forensics," InfoSec World Conference and Expo, Orlando, FL, April 2006], that "… Forensics takes time. Time is money. Make the investigation cost as much as possible (i.e., pick the largest drives, RAID, leave a mess on as many systems as possible). Businesses will have to make a judgment call of when to stop analysis and just image and rebuild."

What other ways could an individual attempt to either delay or throw off an investigation into a suspect system, without outright physical damage or destruction of the technology in question?

V.L.   Conventional thinking would suggest that the attacker will attempt to leave as little evidence as possible. Viewed from a different perspective, however, there are significant advantages to an attacker for creating extraneous evidence.

The first is that "forensics takes time and time is money." Multi-system compromises against enterprise networks result in a non-linear increase in the amount of effort required to accurately analyze the suspect systems. In situations where an extraordinary number of machines are under suspicion, businesses can rarely afford to perform a full analysis of these machines.

Businesses must make business decisions. When a compromise occurs, a business will only analyze machines until it become economically inefficient to do so. In these instances, the decision must be made to continue analysis or just image the drives, wipe them clean, and restore the data. When this choice is made, potential evidence is never examined. Thus, an attacker who can "make the investigation cost as much as possible" can actually create a business case against in-depth forensic analysis.

A.M.   You discuss various anti-forensic tactics in your presentations … beyond the technical aspects … could you discuss one of these?

V.L.   The technological aspect of anti-forensics is only one approach to prevent an effective analysis from being performed. Attacking weaknesses in analyst mentality and training is another very effective means of non-conventional anti-forensics. First, it is important to understand the mentality taken by 99 percent of investigators.

The best quote I have ever heard that truly captures this was provided by an audience member at ToorCon 7 in San Diego. The individual commenting was a very well respected forensics expert, and he stated that forensics is "a lot like looking for your lost keys. Once you find them, you stop looking."

The second piece of information to leverage against an analyst, is knowing what [are] an analyst's goals during an investigation. Most often, the investigator is looking to understand (1) how the break-in occurred and (2) how far did they get?

Combining the mentality and goals of the analyst, we know that if a malicious attacker were to plant easily identifiable, fake evidence to answer the two questions above, the investigator would cease looking and would miss the true nature of the attack.

A.M.   How would an individual attempt to conceal data in MFT Slack Space?

V.L.   There are two things that we are talking about here. For very small files, NTFS will attempt to store the data within the MFT record itself instead of pointing the $DATA attribute to clusters on disk. When these small files are stored in the MFT, the $DATA attribute is a fixed length, which means that if it is not full, there will be unused space behind it.

After I mentioned this technique as a potential future direction, two researchers from Lockheed Martin developed a tool, FragFS, that does exactly that. They have a couple of BlackHat presentations, which detail the techniques to do so.

The other slack space hiding technique would be the one I developed a tool to perform. It takes advantage of a implementation oddity within NTFS. For performance reasons, files are allocated in clusters, which are composed of smaller sectors. For example's sake, let's say that a particular file we have requires one cluster (or eight sectors). Using the standard NTFS settings, a cluster is 4096 bytes, which makes the sector 512 bytes. If a file were only 3500 bytes long, then there would be 596 bytes of unused space at the end of the cluster.

The oddity in NTFS is that when the file is saved, NTFS zeros out the data behind the file, but only up to the end of the last used sector. This means that the first seven sectors, 3584 bytes, would be filled with the file data, which was 3500 bytes. This leaves 84 bytes that are zeroed out by NTFS.

However, this means that there is one additional sector at the end of the cluster which has been allocated, but not used and not cleared with zeros. An attacker could programmatically leverage the standard Win32 file system API to write data into that last sector.

Because the sector is allocated but unassociated with the normal file, it is hidden from normal view. Even when viewed during forensics analysis, basic encryption or simple obfuscation can be employed to hide the data.

A.M.   You referenced "Packers" in your presentation; can you explain further how this particular process (tool) works and how one might counteract its application?

V.L.   Packers have been plaguing forensics experts since the beginning of time. They were originally designed to create smaller executables by compressing the original executable and pre-pending the decompression routine. The various compression methods and decompression routines is what differentiates the various packers.

When a packed executable is run, it loads the compressed executable into memory then enters into the decompression routine which decompresses the original executable into memory and then passes control to the original executable.

One primary job duty of a forensic analyst is to understand the state of the system being examined, which often involves understand the behavior of suspicious executables.

When a malicious executable is packed, the executable content becomes obfuscated and it becomes very difficult for an analyst to take apart the program to analyze its behavior.

A.M.   On your Web site [www.stachliu.com], you refer to various tools such as timestomp, slacker, transmogrify, and SAM juicer. Will you please provide a brief overview of these particular tools and how each may be used to circumvent forensic analysis? Why do they fall into the category of anti-forensic tools?

As equally as interesting, would you provide a counter action that an individual or forensic professional might employ to either prevent disruptive action via these tools or to reverse the affect on potential digital evidence through the use of these tools?

V.L.   TimeStomp

This tool leverages a series of Win32 system calls to modify the Last Modified (M), Last Accessed (A), Creation Date (C), and Entry Modified (E), together referred to as the MACE, values stored within the each MFT record for each file.

During a forensic analysis, the examiner will use these values to attempt to piece together a timeline of events. If an attacker is able to undetectably modify these entries then the examiner can no longer rely on timestamps to create a timeline. A glitch in the Windows API also results in a blank value being displayed when the time values are set below a certain threshold. One popular forensic analysis tool, EnCase, relies on the Windows API to perform the timestamp translation. As a result, it cannot display low values properly, and an examiner cannot see these values.

An examiner looking at a system would be advised to examine not only the MACE values stored within the Standard Information attribute of the

MFT record but also the Filename attribute, which stores a separate copy. Although the MACE values in the Filename attribute are not updated as regularly as the SI attribute values, comparison of the two values may allow an examiner to flag any potentially suspicious files.

Slacker

This tool leverages an NTFS implementation oddity where it only zeros out the file slack space up to the end of the last used sector. This means that any sectors in an allocated cluster beyond the last used sector can be used to safely hide data.

By performing a series of standard Win32 function calls, an attacker can place data into the end of the cluster. A subsequent series of function calls permits an attacker to retrieve the stored data. This tool allows a malicious user to hide information on a system that may not be immediately distinguished from other random slack space information.

Little can be done to examine hidden slack space information that has been properly obfuscated or encrypted. The only recommendation that would prevent this from occurring would be to routinely clear disk slack space.

Transmogrify

This tool is a simple search and replace engine that allows for file signatures to be changed between various types. For example, an attacker might change a JPG file to show up as a Window Executable. Because popular forensic tools only perform the most basic pattern matching and file extension examination to identify a file's type, an examiner relying on these tools will most certainly misidentify the file type and allow it to go unexamined.

More thorough automated analysis of the file types must be performed by the tools. Ultimately, the only way to tell if a file is a JPG would be to open it, and the only way to tell if a file is an EXE would be to execute it. This is because a JPG hidden as an EXE would never run, and an EXE hidden as a JPG would never display.

SAM Juicer

Although the previous tools have focused on changing, hiding, or planting misleading evidence, this tool was designed to highlight the ability for advanced attackers to prevent evidence from ever being created.

The SAM Juicer tool was released as an add-on to the Meterpreter payload available from the Metasploit Project. This tool is used post-compromise in conjunction with the Meterpreter payload. When a machine has been exploited and the Meterpreter payload has been passed into the memory of the target machine, the SAM Juicer add-on is sent to the memory-resident Meterpreter module.

Meterpreter then loads SAM Juicer directly into memory and avoids leaving any evidence on disk. SAM Juicer extracts all the Windows password hashes directly from memory and passes it back to the attacker over the network.

Again, no evidence ever hits disk, so a post-mortem forensic analysis of the disk will not reveal any clues as to how the compromise occurred or how extensive the attacker's control was over the system. There is no easy solution to prevent SAM Juicer from running once a machine has been compromised [17].

A.M.   Thank you, Mr. Liu, for your time.

Windows XP Command Line Program Cipher

Cipher is automatically included with Windows XP and Windows 2000. Used with the "/w" it will hex wipe the free space on the selected drive. This functions the same as other hex wiping tools, but is built into Windows. It completely wipes any data beyond recovery, therefore, EnCase cannot see or retrieve it. However, the very fact that the action has been carried out raises suspicion so other media may have to be taken into account. It also takes quite some time to complete, so it may not be as big a concern if the user starts it at time of seizure (www.guidancesoftware. com/support/esolutiondetail. asp?ID=590GS&strSearch=wiping+program+).

Cloaking Techniques: Data Hide and Seek

Swap Files

A swap file allows an operating system to use hard disk space to simulate extra memory. When the system runs low on memory, it swaps a section of RAM that an idle program is using onto the hard disk to free up memory for other programs. Then when you go back to the swapped out program, it changes places with another program in RAM. This causes a large amount of hard disk reading and writing that slows down your computer considerably.

This combination of RAM and swap files is known as virtual memory. The use of virtual memory allows your computer to run more programs than it could run in RAM alone.

The way swap files are implemented depends on the operating system. Some operating systems such as Windows, can be configured to use temporary swap files that they create when necessary. The disk space is then released when it is no longer needed. Other operating systems, such as Linux and UNIX, set aside a permanent swap space that reserves a certain portion of your hard disk.

Permanent swap files take a contiguous section of your hard disk while some temporary swap files can use fragmented hard disk space. This means that using a permanent swap file will usually be faster than using a temporary one. Temporary swap files are more useful if you are low on disk space because they do not permanently reserve part of your hard disk [18].

Microsoft Windows-based computer operating systems utilize a special file as a "scratch pad" to write data when additional random access memory is needed. In Windows, Windows 95, and Windows 98, these are called Windows swap files. In Windows NT, Windows 2000, and Windows XP they are called Windows page files but they have essentially the same characteristics as Windows swap files.

Windows swap or page files are huge and most computer users are unaware of their existence. The size of these files can range from 100 million bytes to over a gigabyte and the potential exists for these huge files to contain remnants of word processing, e-mail messages, Internet browsing activity, database entries and almost any other work that may have occurred during past Windows work sessions.

This situation creates a significant security problem because the potential exists for data to be transparently stored within the Windows swap file without the knowledge of the computer user.

This can occur even if the work product was stored on a computer network server. The result is a significant computer security weakness that can be of benefit to the computer forensics specialist. Windows swap files can actually provide the computer forensics specialist with investigative leads that might not otherwise be discovered.

Windows swap files are relied upon by Windows, Windows 95, and Windows 98 to create "virtual memory"; that is, using a portion of the hard disk drive for memory operations. The storage area is important to the computer forensics specialist for the same reason that file slack and unallocated space are important, that is, large volumes of data exist for which the computer user likely has no knowledge. Windows swap files can be temporary or permanent, depending on the version of Windows involved and settings selected by the computer user. Permanent swap files are of more interest to a computer forensics specialist because they normally store larger amounts of information for much longer periods of time.

Large permanent swap files can hold vast quantities of data and they should be targeted early in the examination by the computer forensics specialist to identify leads relative to past uses of the subject computer [19].

File Slack

Depending on their contents, files are created in different lengths. On DOS, Windows, and Windows NT-based computers, files are stored in clusters, which are fixed blocks of data. Because the size of a cluster hardly ever exactly matches the size of a file, extra data storage space exists from the end of the file to the end of the last cluster assigned to the file. This space is known as "file slack."

For example, if you create and save a long document that fills up 75 percent of a cluster, and then you delete it with a standard delete command, the data will still be available in those 75 percent of the cluster, but the cluster itself will be available for future reuse.

If you then create and save a short document that fills up only 50 percent of that same cluster, the 25 percent left over from the old, deleted document will still remain in the cluster. The slack data is invisible to simple windows file editors (Notepad, MS Word, and etc.) but it is easy to read it with any special utility. So it is important to wipe file slacks to get a complete confidence that all your data were deleted from the disk [20].

File slack can exist on floppy disks, hard disks, zip disks, and other computer storage media.

Whenever slack space exists, the computer tries to fill up the space using RAM or drive data. RAM slack is randomly selected data from the memory of the computer. It may contain information that was created, viewed, modified, downloaded, or copied since the computer was last booted. Drive slack contains information that is not currently in use by the computer—data that may have remnants of previously deleted files or data from the format pattern associated with the original disk configuration.

In DOS, Windows, Windows 95, Windows 98, and Windows NT/2000/XP systems, file slack is automatically created each time a file is saved to a disk. When a file is deleted, the drive slack remains in the last cluster at the end of the deleted file. Until the data is overwritten be a new file, the clusters will stay on the disk in the form of unallocated storage space (currently unused space). Depending on the cluster size on the drive, quite a bit of data may remain. Unlike other unallocated space, slack space will remain as long as the file that has allocated the particular cluster remains. It is quite possible to find file slack space from events taking place years earlier.

File slack can help uncover lost or hidden data or help identify network logon names, passwords, and other sensitive information. File slack can also contain e-mail and word processing document fragments. A thorough computer forensic investigation can help uncover file slack data and more, helping you determine the "who, what, when, where, and how" of computer related activity in your case [21].

Renaming Files

Potential system abusers and suspects may attempt to conceal their actions (e.g., uploading unauthorized files or programs) or even hide data by altering the file extensions of illegal or unauthorized files (e.g., changing the file extension .EXE or .JPG to .DLL).

A dynamic link library (DLL) is a collection of small programs, any of which can be called when needed by a larger program that is running in the computer. The small program that lets the larger program communicate with a specific device such as a printer or scanner is often packaged as a DLL program (usually referred to as a DLL file). DLL files that support specific device operation are known as device drivers.

The advantage of DLL files is that, they do not get loaded into random access memory (RAM) together with the main program, space is saved in RAM. When and if a DLL file is needed, then it is loaded and run. For example, as long as a user of Microsoft Word is editing a document, the printer DLL file does not need to be loaded into RAM. If the user decides to print the document, then the Word application causes the printer DLL file to be loaded and run.

A DLL file is often given a ".dll" file name suffix .DLL files are dynamically linked with the program that uses them during program execution rather than being compiled with the main program. The set of such files (or the DLL) is somewhat comparable to the library routines provided with programming languages such as C and C++.

DLLs can also contain just data. DLL files usually end with the extension .dll, .exe, .drv, or .fon.

If a suspect simply wishes to conceal data, images, or unauthorized programs, changing the file extension to .dll, for example, will cause the unauthorized data, image, or program to figuratively fade into the background and with luck the suspect hopes it will be "lost" among all of the other operating system programs. When the suspect wishes to view the files or run the program, simply renaming the file with the appropriate file extension will allow the suspect to then view the file's contents or execute (run) the program.

File Name Modification

File name extensions are used to include meaningful extensions on the file, which you create, to distinguish word-processing files from plain text files and other types of files.

With today's technology, the application of file name extensions is typically taken care of automatically by the application software. Even when you do not want it to—for an example:

- *.PPT for Power Point files
- *.EXE Program files; they actually run a particular program
- *.DOC for MS Word documents
- *.TXT for text files usually created by Windows Notepad

- *.PAR which are permanent swap files for Windows
- *.MID typical sound files that contain musical notes
- *.TTF for true type fonts, and so on.

Application programs take advantage of Windows use of file name extensions. Most application programs which utilize Windows place their unique file extensions onto a file when you issue the file save command.

For instance, the Windows Media Player program uses a .AVI extension for all files created when using Windows Media Player, while Microsoft Power Point for example, applies a .PPT file extension when a "save" command is executed. These unique extensions serve two purposes:

1. They let Windows determine what program was used to create a particular file, and
2. They allow the user to determine the type of file created simply from viewing the file name extension.

When a file name extension is associated with a particular program, Windows will open the file and its corresponding program. Just double click the file's icon in the File Manager.

Using File Manager, you can change the associations between files and extensions, which is a helpful feature if you use your own system of file name extensions. This could also be a handy way of manipulating file extensions in an effort to conceal illegal or inappropriate files from view by others.

Legitimately for instance, if an individual were to use say the file extension .PHT as the extension for all of his or her digital photos (say instead of the application issued .JPG extension), then one could associate all .PHT extension files with the user's photo processing program.

The ability of Windows to use file name extensions and to associate file name extensions with a particular application is very helpful when opening new files from within a program. Instead of reading every file in a particular directory, most Windows programs automatically restrict the listing of files only to those with extensions matching the program's associations.

Thus, if a user has opened the Power Point application, Windows automatically displays only those files within the directory that match the known Power Point file extension (.PPT), no other files, even though they may be in the same Power Point directory, will be displayed as available to access, open, and use.

Therefore, it is extremely easy for an individual to attempt to conceal inappropriate or illegal files almost within plain sight by altering the file name extension. When a particular file type is being sought say .PIX (graphics files.), .MPG (movie files), .GIF (graphics and picture files in a compressed format), or .JPG (picture files), if the investigator is simply scanning to know file extension types, of the target file, there may be a very good chance that the scan will turn up negative, with no hits on a particular file extension type.

It is important to examine the entire contents of a suspect data source (e.g., hard drive) and to sort the directory contents by file type and to review each file type or extension. Asking, for example, the logical questions:

1. Are the file extension types identified reasonable and typical for this directory? Meaning, for example, files in a folder called Performance Reviews, which might typically only contain .DOC files that are labeled .SCR or .VOC.
2. Are the file sizes appropriate for the type of data supposedly contained in the files? A file with a .DOC extension, named Annual Report, with a file size of 61KB, should be suspect (unless of course maybe if the organization experienced a very poor financial year).

Alternatively, an .XLS file labeled Tulsa Expense Report, with a file size of 893KB, should raise some suspicion.

The process whereby a suspect may alter a file's extension in an attempt to conceal its location or even existence, let alone its content is fairly straightforward and nontechnical.

The steps to accomplish this transformation are as follows (Figures 3.2 through 3.8):

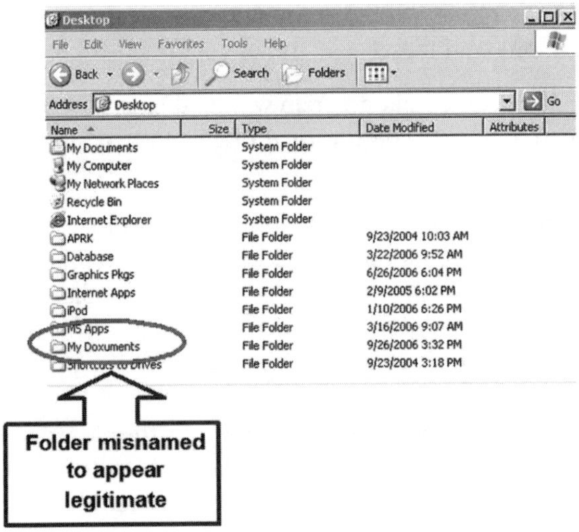

Figure 3.2 Step 1 changing a file name extension.

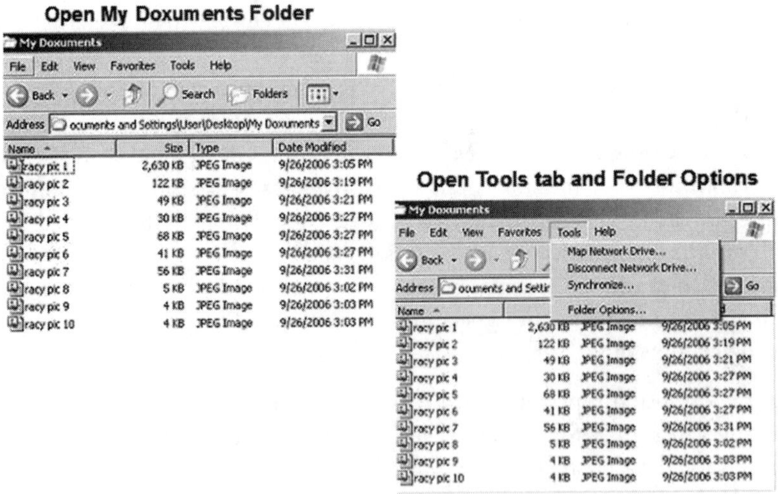

Figure 3.3 Step 2 changing a file name extension.

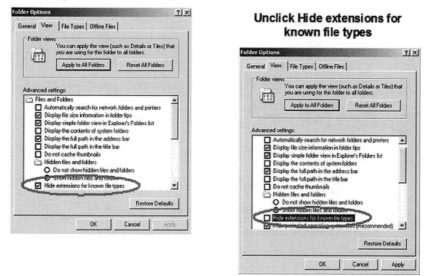

Figure 3.4   Step 3 changing a file name extension.

File extension is revealed

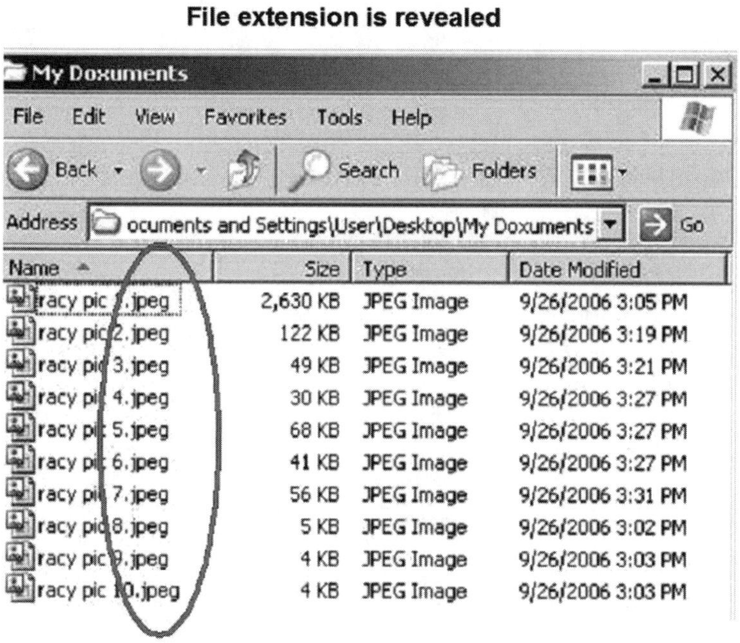

Figure 3.5   Step 4 changing a file name extension.

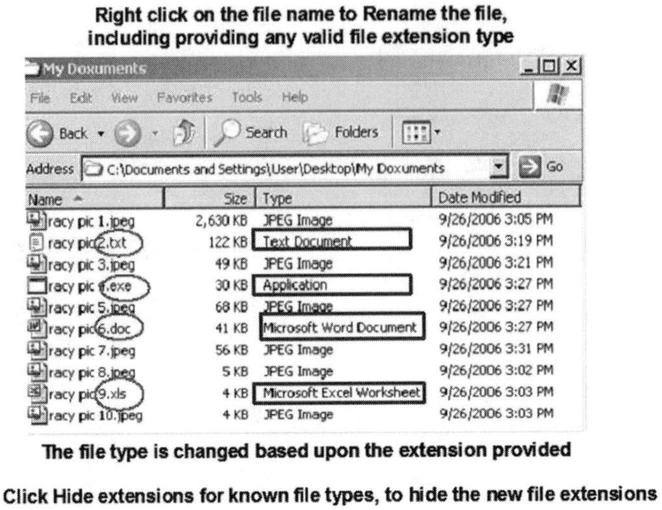

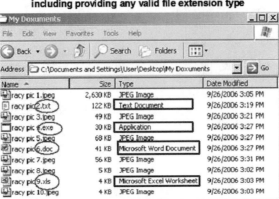

Figure 3.6 Step 5 changing a file name extension.

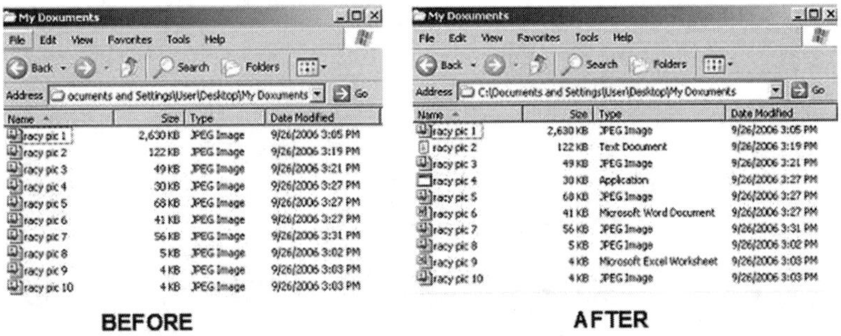

Figure 3.7 Step 6 changing a file name extension.

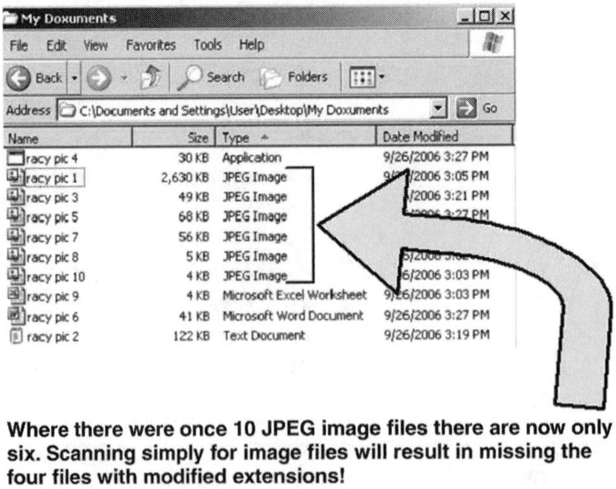

Figure 3.8 Step 7 changing a file name extension.

Playing with Attributes–Hiding Files in Plain Sight

The ability to completely hide folders and files within a directory, so that their existence is not displayed at all, raises the stakes in the game of hiding data in plain sight. Hidden files neither appear in My Computer or Windows Explorer, nor do they show up when using the operating system's search utility.

The steps for hiding the file Hide File 1.doc in plain sight from view are as follows (Figures 3.9 through 3.14):

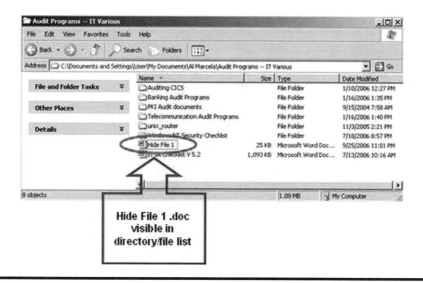

Figure 3.9   Step 1 hiding files in plain sight.

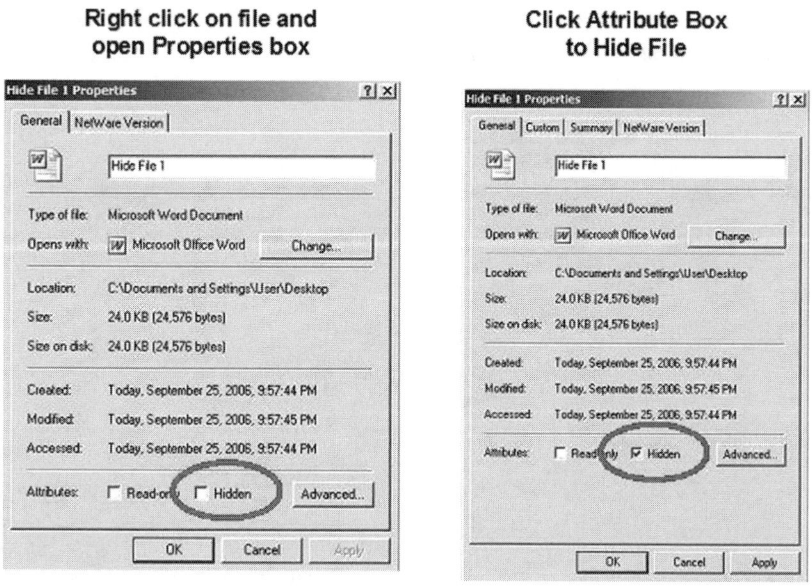

Figure 3.10   Step 2 hiding files in plain sight.

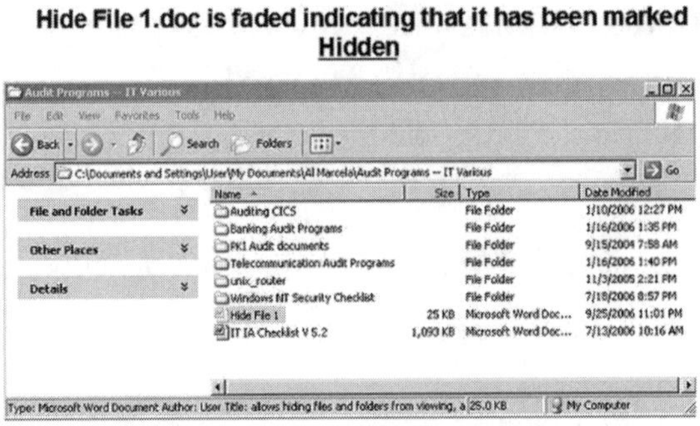

Hide File 1.doc is faded indicating that it has been marked Hidden

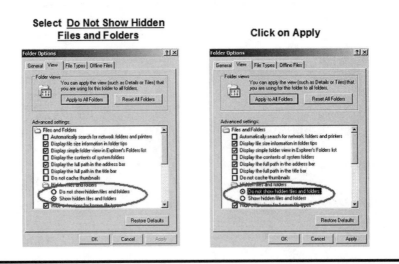

Figure 3.11   Step 3 hiding files in plain sight.

To hide the file, open the Folder Options dialog box, and select the View tab

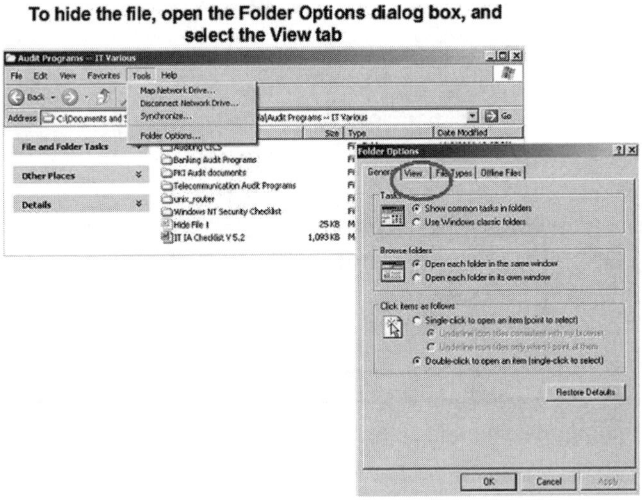

Figure 3.12   Step 4 hiding files in plain sight.

Select Do Not Show Hidden Files and Folders

Click on Apply

Figure 3.13   Step 5 hiding files in plain sight.

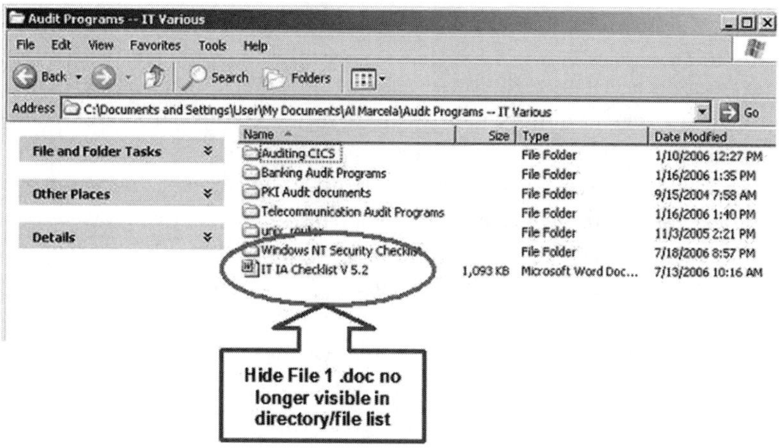

Figure 3.14 Step 6 hiding files in plain sight.

Although specific forensic tools do exist that are capable of detecting hidden files, not all investigators, or all organizations may have access to these automated tools. Thus the cyber forensics investigator must be aware of this routine procedure for hiding files and folders and be able to reverse engineer the process as part of the initial analysis and data gathering phase of an investigation.

Ghosting

Ghosting can have different meanings: From the general:

- Ghosting (television), a double image when receiving a distorted or multi-path input signal in analog television broadcasting.
- Ghosting (identity theft), a form of identity theft, whereby a person takes on the role of a deceased person.
- A technique used in online games, usually team-based "last man standing" first-person shooters, where dead players inform their team mates who are still alive of the whereabouts of the enemy: this is frowned upon in many communities.
- A technique used in preparing proposals for government contracts in which the weaknesses of a competitor are indirectly referenced to improve the proposer's position.

To the artistic:

- Ghosting, a Gothic Music band from Germany. Formed in 1989, this band released seven full length albums, before its members retired in 2003.
- Ghosting, a noise band from Portland, Oregon.

To the technical:

- The act of creating a completely identical copy, or a ghost image, of a hard disk using backup software such as Ghost, on to removable media or a network drive to be used as a backup copy of a PC in case a restore of that PC is required.

- Printing white letters on a white background, or black letters on a black background.
- A problem in LCD screens when tiny pixels creating the image take time to switch on and off and cannot do it fast enough. The problem, widely recognized as the main drawback of LCD screens, is apparent in fast moving objects such as tennis balls, but even slower moving images get fuzzy. Most modern LCD screens no longer have this problem.
- A printing problem where the effect of lack of ink replenishment on a printing press caused by the printing of an ink-intensive design on a page, or by chemical solvent contamination.
- When a person (on AOL) seems as though they signed off, but in fact they are online. All they have done is change their settings to block all users from seeing them [22].

For our discussions here, we will concentrate on the ability of a suspect to disguise the contents of a file by simply changing the following:

1. Color of the default font (e.g., from black to white) resulting in the appearance of a blank page within a document or a file that contains no data.
2. Background color of the default document (e.g., from white to black). This may be a less successful and more obvious attempt to cloak text or data, as an investigator that encounters a document which contains a series of black pages (or even blank pages), would (should) logically investigate further by manipulating application features that are associated with font and background settings.

Sensitive data, intellectual property, private communiqué can all be successfully hidden in plain sight by combining and manipulating both font colors and background color settings of application software.

These manipulations are not limited to word processing applications but extend to such applications as presentation managers, data base management packages, spreadsheet software, (e.g., Microsoft's suite of office applications), any application that allows the end user direct access and ability to modify default application settings, with respect to how information is displayed or printed.

This is not a technical ploy; in fact it is so simplistic that some investigators may overlook the possibility. Applying logic to your investigation and assessing the suspect's technical capabilities is a prudent first step of the investigation process. It does not take any technical prowess to change the font color to white thus concealing text on a page. Looking at the contents of a document that is multiple pages in length and finding only blank pages, should send up red flags and prompt the investigator to probe deeper, asking the logical question "why so many blank pages in a document saved to the suspects storage device?"

Compressed Files

In today's online environment a suspect may attempt to move copy or download files from online sources, between computers or to external storage devices (e.g., CDs, USB drives, etc.). In an attempt to conceal his or her activities and to reduce the possibility of tripping an internal control mechanism designed to identify movement (onto or off of the suspect's computer), the suspect may utilize file compression. File compression is also known as "packing" or "archiving."

File compression works via a complicated mathematical equation to scan a file for repeating patterns in the data. File compression replaces reoccurring data patterns with smaller coded data that overall reduces the size of a file, thus reducing the time it takes to download, copy or move a particular file. File compression changes the original size of the file thus, making it easier to potentially hide (large graphic files naturally have large file sizes, take up more space, and may be more easily spotted or scanned), or reduce the amount of file space necessary to store the file.

For example, one way compression software's work is to replace repeating text characters with a code that also notes the locations of those characters in the data. With a graphic image, for example, it would find all of the flesh tone pieces, and replace them with a code. One of the most basic such tricks in file compression, is to remove redundant data. Instead of storing a piece of data for every flesh-colored pixel in a photo, for instance, a file compression program (or archive as these programs are sometimes referred to), might store one flesh-tone pixel and a digital note to repeat that pixel as needed throughout the image.

A compatible file decompression program specifically designed to read these codes is required to reverse engineer the process and to convert these codes back into their original state.

However, many individuals select to compress one or many files for the following very legitimate reasons:

1. Storage—Compressed files take up less space.
2. Speed or efficiency—In many cases smaller files can be executed or read in less time.
3. Bandwidth or transfer time—Smaller files take less time to download or upload.

The majority of file types that investigators will encounter will include:

- Graphics:
  - Bmp—Bitmap Image
  - Pcx—Paintbrush Bitmap Image
  - Tif—Tagged Image File Format
  - Png—Portable Network Graphic and
  - Cgm—Computer Graphics Metafile
- Image:
  - JPEG (JPG)—Joint Photographic Experts Group [JPEG], The shorter JPG (without the E) extension or version is usually only used in association with PC platform files; and
  - GIF—Graphical Interchange Format
- Audio and Video:
  - aac—A newer MPEG sound format.
  - ac3—A Dolby-Digital encoded audio file. Used primarily in DVDs. Needs proprietary codec to play.
  - aif, aiff—Audio Interchange File. The Mac equivalent of wav, but it is cross platform as well.
  - asf—Advanced Streaming Format. The original file extension for Windows Media files, this extension refers to both audio and video files. The confusion this caused lead to Microsoft abandoning this extension in favor of wma and wmv.
  - avi—Audio-Video Interleaved. One of the most common video files.
  - divx—Some DivX encoders and applications give the option of using the divx file extension for DivX encoded files. The files are exactly the same as those with the avi extension, with the only difference being that they have substantially worse compatibility (many applications that can play and import DivX encoded avis do not work with files that have the divx extension). Needless to say, the extension is pointless and you should not use it.
  - dv—Raw DV stream. Not commonly used, because most raw DV streams use an avi or mov extension.

- m1v—An elementary MPEG-1 video stream. Cannot contain audio.
- m2p—MPEG-2 program stream.
- m2v—An elementary MPEG-2 video stream. Cannot contain audio. Requires MPEG-2 codec (commonly acquired with DVD player software) to playback. Most professional DVD authoring packages require m2v files.
- mov, moov—Quicktime movie.
- mpa—An elementary MPEG-2 audio stream.
- mpg, mpeg—A multiplexed (audio and video combined) MPEG-1 or MPEG-2 file (although most commonly MPEG-1).
- mp1—MPEG audio, layer 1.
- mp2—MPEG audio, layer 2.
- mp3—The ubiquitous audio format that we all know and love. It is actually called "MPEG audio, layer 3" and, as the name implies, intended to encode the audio portion of MPEG-1 movies.
- mp4—MPEG-4 movie (although MPEG-4 movies can also be avi or mov). Some people claim that mp4 is a new version of mp3.
- mpv—See m2v.
- ogg—Ogg Vorbis audio file.
- ogm—Ogg Vorbis video file.
- omf—Open Media Format, a video format developed by and used primarily by Avid editing systems, but has been adopted by other professional video applications and has become a high-end standard. Usually, these files are not playable from the desktop but rather only inside the applications that use them.
- qt—Quicktime movie.
- rm—Real video file.
- ram—Real audio file.
- swf—Macromedia Flash animation file.
- vob—Video object file. Used in DVDs. Contains MPEG-2 video and several possible audio formats, as well as menus and interactivity.
- wav—Microsoft wave audio file. PCM (pulse code modulation) audio, usually uncompressed.
- wma—Windows Media audio file.
- wmv—Windows Media video file.

The reader interested in knowing more about the multitude of file types currently available or an investigator attempting to identify a suspect file type, is encouraged to review the excellent reference library of existing file type with appropriate definitions and explanations as to their use, at Santa Ana College's Academic Computing Center Web site, at http://sacacc.sac.edu/webscout/Computer_Info/File_Extensions/index.htm.

Some of the file types that an investigator will encounter may be compressed, while other file types may not be. As technology advances with rapid progress, those individuals intent on subversion and illegal activities will always find new and even novel ways to accomplish their goals and objectives.

The ability for data to be "hidden," interlaced between musical notes, concealed behind shifting color pixels or infused into the hiss of white noise, has already been attempted—successfully. The methodology behind such technology is not the focus of this chapter or of this text. It is safe to say that the cyber forensic investigator will need to continually remain abreast of the changes in technology and how those changes may be employed counter productively and used to engage in and to commit illegal acts.

The most common compressed files are those with extensions such as .zip (Zipped File), and .sit (Stuffit Archive), used originally on the MAC now available cross-platform).

Additional compression file formats that the investigator may encounter, again depending on the age of the technology under review include:

- .ace—WinAce Compressed File.
- .ape—Monkey's Audio Lossless Audio File.
- .arc—This DOS format uses ARC, ARCE, or LHARC for decompression.
- .arj—Compressed file archive using Robert Jung compression.
- .bh—BlakHole Archive or group of files compressed with BlakHole compression, a ZipTV algorithm.
- .binhex—BinHex is a format which is used to both encode and compress files.
- .cab—Windows Cabinet File.
- .cpt—This Mac format uses Compact Pro for decompression.
- .gz—This is gnu's Unix compression method.
- .hqx—This Mac format requires BinHex for decompression.
- .jar—Java Archive File.
- .lha—Compressed Archive.
- .lzh—Compressed File. A File or archive compressed using Lempel–Ziv and Haruyasu compression algorithm.
- .mpeg—MPEG is short for Moving Pictures Expert Group. MPEG is actually used to refer to several standards for various types of files, including video (MPEG) and Audio (MPEG Layer 3, or MP3).
- .ogg—Ogg Vorbis digitally encoded music or audio file.
- .pit—This Mac format uses StuffIt or PackIt.
- .rar—WinRAR Compressed Archive. Compressed file or group of files; uses a higher compression ratio than typical ZIP compression.
- .sea—A Mac self-extracting archive (.sea) file.
- .shar—This Unix format uses the unshar command for decompression.
- .sit—This Mac format uses StuffIt for decompression.
- .tar—tape archive–used primarily with tape drives. A "tarred" file is often further compressed with the .z method. Such files end with .tar.z. They must first be uncompressed.
- .tgz—Compressed file archive created by TAR and GNUzip.
- .uue—Uuencoded File. A file encoded by Unix uuencode.
- .war—Web application archive.
- .xxe—Compressed file ASCII archive created by XXENCODE.
- .z—This is a Unix compression method.
- .zip—A DOS or Windows compression utility. A Macintosh version called Zipit creates files that are compatible with the Windows or DOS version of PKZip.
- .zoo—This is a Unix and MS-DOS format that requires a program called zoo for decompression.

Sometimes software is compressed into a Self-Extracting Archive file (with a file extension of .exe on PC and .sea on an Apple). These applications can be a file with the decompression scheme built into the file's internal code, so all one has to do is 'double click' it for decompression to begin, or the program may simply spawn an install routine. If this is the case, you do not need to proceed any further, just double-click and run, and the file is automatically decompressed.

As stated previously, a file compression program is required to compress files into smaller footprints, taking up less storage room or taking less time to send from point "a" to point "b." Depending on how the files were originally compressed, some files will not decompress or decode if the extension is removed.

File compression is also know as or referred to as:

- Decompression Software
- Text Compression Software
- Uncompression Software
- gzip Utility
- Unzipping
- Compression Software
- Unzip File Utility
- Data Compression Software, and
- Zip File Utility

File compression is the art of minimizing the size in bytes of a graphics file without degrading the quality of the image to an unacceptable level. The reduction in file size allows more images to be stored in a given amount of disk or memory space. It also reduces the time required for images to be sent over the Internet or downloaded from Web pages.

A ZIP file is created to package one or more files into a single file in a compressed format. The ZIP format was originally intended primarily for use on a PC. However, it is now widely used and can be decompressed on most operating systems.

There are many options available for decompressing ZIP files on a PC. For machines which the investigator encounters that are running Microsoft Windows, WinZip is a popular program—once installed, you can double-click on the ZIP file name and the program will launch. Windows XP comes with an unZIP program already built in; if you double click on the ZIP file you can choose to "expand" (decompress) it.

Decompressing a ZIP file on a Apple [use StuffIt file format (.sit)] or on a Unix or Linux machine [use PKZIP] is relatively easy to do. Some Unix or Linux operating systems (OS) already have unZIP software built into the OS. Various unpacking utilities and supported file types are shown in Table 3.1.

Bottom line, by packing, zipping, archiving, etc., an individual intent on manipulating file sizes and their content has multiple ways in which to attempt to hide data. Taking large graphic files and compressing the file size would enable an individual to:

- Hide the graphic in a file by changing the file's extension and type, and renaming the file. The smaller sized file may avoid detection. Conversely, a large Microsoft Word document (zipped and renamed from an illegal downloaded graphics file) may go unnoticed.
- Transport files outside the organization, a quicker transfer rate may help the suspect avoid detection or tripping an exception report designed to track outgoing e-mail containing attachments over a certain file size.
- Utilize the double compression feature of some software to hide data within data.
- Conceal illegal images or documents by simply reducing the file's data footprint (i.e., file size).

Table 3.1 Unpacking Utilities and Supported File Types

Utility	File Types Current Versions Can Unpack
Stufflt Expander	ARC, BinHex, BZIP, CAB, GZ, HQX, LHA, MIME, RAR, SIT, SITX, TAR, ZIP, others
UnRAR	RAR (command line utility)
WinAce	ACE, ARC, ARJ, CAB, GZ, JAR, LHA, RAR, TAR, ZIP (64-bit), ZOO
WinRAR	ACE, ARJ, BZ2, CAB, GZ, LZH, RAR, TAR, TAR. BZ2, TAR. GZ, ZIP (64-bit), others
WinZip	BinHex, CAB, GZ, MIME, TAR, TGZ, TAZ, UUE, XXE, Z, ZIP (64-bit)
ZipGenius	ACE, CAB, CZIP, EAR, JAR, RAR, RPM, SQX, TAR, WAR, XPI, ZIP, 7z, others

Source: File Decompression Utilities (chart) Appearing in the article *"Crack Open that Compressed File,"* PC Today, April 2007, Vol. 5 Issue 4, page(s) 71–72, Sandhills Publishing Company, www.pctoday.com/compressedfile. With permission.

Manipulating File Systems

A file system is a part of the operating system that determines how files are named, stored, and organized on a volume. A file system manages files and folders, and the information needed to locate and access these items by local and remote users. Some earlier Microsoft Windows operating systems, as well as removable disks and floppy disks, support only the FAT file system.

File Allocation Table

A file system used by MS-DOS and other Windows-based operating systems to organize and manage files. The file allocation table (FAT) is a data structure that Windows creates when you format a volume by using the FAT or FAT32 file systems. Windows stores information about each file in the FAT so that it can retrieve the file later.

The FAT stores information about the clusters on the disk in a table. There are three different varieties of this file allocation table, which vary based on the maximize size of the table. The system utility that you use to partition the disk will normally choose the correct type of FAT for the volume you are using, but sometimes you will be given a choice of which you want to use.

Because each cluster has one entry in the FAT, and these entries are used to hold the cluster number of the next cluster used by the file, the size of the FAT is the limiting factor on how many clusters any disk volume can contain.

The following are the three different FAT versions which you may encounter:

FAT12. The oldest type of FAT uses a 12-bit binary number to hold the cluster number. A volume formatted using FAT12 can hold a maximum of 4,086 clusters, which is 2^{12} minus a few values (to allow for reserved values to be used in the FAT). FAT12 is therefore most suitable for very small volumes, and is used on floppy disks and hard disk partitions smaller than about 16MB (the latter being rare today).

FAT16. The FAT used for most older systems, and for small partitions on modern systems, uses a 16-bit binary number to hold cluster numbers. When you see someone refer to a "FAT" volume generically, they are usually referring to FAT16, because it is the de facto standard for hard disks, even with FAT32 now more popular than FAT16. A volume using FAT16 can hold a maximum of 65,526 clusters, which is 2^{16} less a few values (again for reserved values in the FAT). FAT16 is used for hard disk volumes ranging in size from 16 MB to 2,048 MB. VFAT is a variant of FAT16.

FAT32. A derivative of the FAT file system. FAT32 supports smaller cluster sizes and larger volumes than FAT, which results in more efficient space allocation on FAT32 volumes.

Here's a summary table showing how the three types of FAT compare (Table 3.2):

Table 3.2   File Allocation Table Attributes

Attribute	FAT12	FAT16	FAT32
Used for	Floppies and very small hard disk volumes	Small to moderate-sized hard disk volumes	Medium-sized to very large hard disk volumes
Size of each FAT entry	12 bits	16 bits	28 bits
Maximum number of clusters	4,086	65,526	~268,435,456
Cluster size used	0.5 KB to 4 KB	2 KB to 32 KB	4 KB to 32 KB
Maximum volume size	16,736,256	2,147,123,200	about 2^{14}

It is named FAT32 because it uses 32-bit numbers to represent clusters, instead of the 16-bit numbers used by FAT16. FAT32 allows single partitions of very large size to be created, where FAT16 was limited to partitions of about 2 GB. It also saves wasted space due to slack when compared to FAT16 partitions, because it uses much smaller cluster sizes than FAT16 does [23].

NTFS File System

An advanced file system that provides performance, security, reliability, and advanced features that are not found in any version of FAT. For example, NTFS guarantees volume consistency by using standard transaction logging and recovery techniques. If a system fails, NTFS uses its log file and checkpoint information to restore the consistency of the file system. In Windows 2000 and Windows XP, NTFS also provides advanced features such as file and folder permissions, encryption, disk quotas, compression, and support for volumes up to 256 terabytes in size (www.microsoft.com/technet/prodtechnol/winxppro/maintain/convertfat.mspx).

NTFS is a much more complex and capable file system than any of the FAT family of file systems. It was designed with the corporate and business environment in mind; it is built for networking and with the goals of security, reliability, and efficiency. It includes many features, including file-by-file compression, full permissions control and attribute settings, support for very large files, and transaction-based operation (www.pcguide.com/ref/hdd/file/fileNTFS-c.html).

The Windows NT file system (NTFS) provides a combination of performance, reliability, and compatibility not found in the FAT file system. It is designed to quickly perform standard file operations such as read, write, and search - and even advanced operations such as file-system recovery—on very large hard disks.

Formatting a volume with the NTFS file system results in the creation of several system files and the Master File Table (MFT), which contains information about all the files and folders on the NTFS volume.

The first information on an NTFS volume is the Partition Boot Sector, which starts at sector 0 and can be up to 16 sectors long. The first file on an NTFS volume is the MFT.

The NTFS file system has a simple, yet very powerful design. Basically, everything on the volume is a file and everything in a file is an attribute, from the data attribute, to the security attribute, to the file name attribute. Every sector on an NTFS volume that is allocated belongs to some file. Even the file system metadata (information that describes the file system itself) is part of a file [24].

File Storage Hardware and Disk Organization

A hard disk is a sealed unit containing a number of platters in a stack (Figure 3.15). Hard disks may be mounted in a horizontal or a vertical position. Electromagnetic read or write heads are positioned above and below each platter. As the platters spin, the drive heads move in toward the center surface and out toward the edge. In this way, the drive heads can reach the entire surface of each platter.

On a hard disk, data is stored in thin, concentric bands. A drive head, while in one position can read or write a circular ring, or band called a track. There can be more than a thousand tracks on a 3.5-inch hard disk. Sections within each track are called sectors. A sector is the smallest physical storage unit on a disk, and is almost always 512 bytes (0.5 KB) in size.

To the operating system of a computer, tracks are logical rather than physical in structure, and are established when the disk is low-level formatted. Tracks are numbered, starting at 0 (the outermost edge of the disk), and going up to the highest numbered track, typically 1,023 (close to the center). Similarly, there are 1,024 cylinders (numbered from 0 to 1,023) on a hard disk.

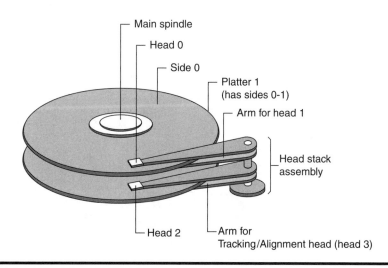

Figure 3.15   Hard disk components.

Sectors and Clusters

A sector (Figure 3.16), being the smallest physical storage unit on the disk, is almost always 512 bytes in size because 512 is a power of 2 (2 to the power of 9). The number 2 is used because there are two states in the most basic of computer languages—on and off.

Each disk sector is labeled using the factory track-positioning data. Sector identification data is written to the area immediately before the contents of the sector and identifies the starting address of the sector.

The optimal method of storing a file on a disk is in a contiguous series, that is, all data in a stream stored end-to-end in a single line. As many files are larger than 512 bytes, it is up to the file system to allocate sectors to store the file's data. For example, if the file size is 800 bytes, two 512 k sectors are allocated for the file. A cluster is typically the same size as a sector (Figure 3.16). These two sectors with 800 bytes of data are called two clusters.

They are called clusters because the space is reserved for the data contents. This process protects the stored data from being over-written. Later, if data is appended to the file and its size grows to 1,600 bytes, another two clusters are allocated, storing the entire file within four clusters.

If contiguous clusters are not available (clusters that are adjacent to each other on the disk), the second two clusters may be written elsewhere on the same disk or within the same cylinder or on a different cylinder—wherever the file system finds two sectors available. A file stored in this non-contiguous manner is considered to be fragmented.

Cluster size can be changed to optimize file storage. A larger cluster size reduces the potential for fragmentation, but increases the likelihood that clusters will have unused space (i.e., slack). Using clusters larger than one sector reduces fragmentation, and reduces the amount of disk space needed to store the information about the used and unused areas on the disk [25].

Slack Space—Forensic Nirvana

Wasted space, optimization, fragmentation, defragmentation, and slack. Terms that not too long ago had little or no meaningful relationship to computers, let alone hard drives, or any type of drive for that matter. File fragmentation, one of the vagaries of the FAT file system, has garnered

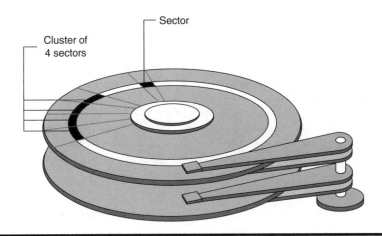

Figure 3.16 Disk sector and clusters.

considerably more attention in recent years with the advent of hard drives above 1 GB in size. When hard drives were in the range of 40 MB to 1 GB, no one had a clue that their drives had wasted space.

As a matter of fact, most were enthralled at the release of a 1 GB hard drive. It was not until the mid-1990s, when hard drives began climbing above 2 GB, did we realize that there was something wrong, yet we had no idea just what it was. Hard drives were not being divided into multiple partitions at that time, and after a period of continued use, users began noticing that large amounts disk space seemed to literally disappear. Although on smaller drives, those below 1 GB, this was barely noticeable, but on larger drives approaching 2 GB, this amounted to hundreds of megabytes. As file fragmentation was more fully understood, and defragmentation tools began to develop, users finally understood the "why" behind the disappearing disk space.

Shortly, after the release of the FAT32 file system, the issue of fragmentation became less critical. Now, however, as hard drive sizes climb above the 80 GB range, we begin revisiting the old terms such as wasted space, optimization, fragmented, defragmentation, and add a new one, "slack." As long as hard drives remained below the 30 GB range, FAT32 tended to keep everything cleaned up, but as we passed the 40 GB mark, even FAT32 has its problems controlling slack.

Obviously, this missing drive space is not really gone, unless we are talking about damaged or lost clusters, at which point this missing drive space is actually unusable portions of the hard drive that need to be recovered with the appropriate disk utility. However, we are not discussing that aspect of missing drive space, we are discussing slack. This slack space is simply space wasted as a result of the cluster system that FAT file system uses. A cluster is the minimum amount of space that can be assigned to a file, and no file can use merely a part or piece of a cluster and a separate file use the remainder under the FAT file system.

Essentially, when a file is assigned to a cluster, even if it were merely a single byte of data, the space assigned would be rounded to an integer multiple equal to the cluster size itself. If you add to that file, gradually the entire cluster would be used until you reach the maximum size of that cluster. As soon as the file becomes larger than the capacity of that single cluster, even by a single byte, the additional byte is then allocated to another cluster, and the file's space usage will double, even though the file only increased in size by one byte.

Given that files are allocated entire clusters regardless of the file size, as drive sizes grow and along with them cluster sizes grow, the more space that will be wasted. As an example, if you had 200 files, each of which had a single byte of data occupying a cluster, the amount of wasted space, or slack, would be enormous. In essence, by doubling the cluster size of the disk, you are doubling the amount of disk space that is wasted. The space left at the end of the last cluster allocated to the file, is commonly called slack.

As every user's situation is unique, most of the projections or examples of wasted space or slack that are provided on the Internet are presented in theoretical form. The reality, however, is far worse. No, scare tactics here, just hard facts. If files sizes were truly random, meaning that you had as many large files as you did small ones, then the problem would not be as bad. However, the reality is that most files on a system are small in size, and if you doubt that, take a look at your cache directory. A hard disk that uses more small files will result in far more space being wasted.

Let's put all of this into perspective. Consider a hard disk volume that is using 32 kiB (32,768 bytes) clusters, and there are 15,000 files on a single partition. Let's presume for the moment that each of those 15,000 files creates 15,000 end clusters, each of which contains slack equal to one-half its size, or 16 kiB of space per file (16,384 bytes). If you multiply the 15,000 files by the slack of 16kiB, or 16,384 bytes, you have 245.8 MiB of wasted space (240MB).

Let's take this a step further. If we were to make the further assumption that most of the files are smaller, and that the true space consumed is more like 25 percent, the slack jumps to an amazing 368.8 MiB or 360 MB. Translating this to disk sizes, if this were a 1.2 GB disk using 32 kiB clusters, the slack space would be approximately 30 percent. If the disk were 2.1 GB in size, the slack space would be approximately 17 percent. Whether you use Mebibyte (MiB) or Megabyte (MB) to define the disk size, it's still allot of wasted space!

Obviously, you can draw the same conclusions that we do, the larger the cluster size you use, the more of the disk space you will waste due to slack. Hence, it is better to use smaller cluster sizes whenever possible. Unfortunately though, doing this is not always easy. The number of clusters that you use is limited by the design of the FAT file system, and there are performance issues to consider when using smaller cluster sizes. There are two principle methods to avoid some of these slack issues.

One is to use FAT32 as opposed to FAT16, and the other is to use the NTFS file system. Both have their own caveats though. On very large hard drives with large partitions even FAT32 uses extremely large cluster sizes. If you decide to use the NTFS file system, and you are using Windows 95 or 98 or Windows ME, you will have to upgrade to Windows 2000 or Windows XP [26].

Hiding Data in Filesystem Slack Space with Bmap

Bmap is a Linux utility which uses filesystem slack space to hide data on unused hard disk blocks. Bmap was written for use with the ext2 filesystem, but very few professionals use ext2 on modern Linux boxes. Luckily, ext3 uses identical on-disk data structures as ext2 but adds journaling for improved performance. As a result, bmap can be used on more common ext3 partitions making it a much more useful tool.

Informed usage of bmap first requires basic knowledge of hard disks and filesystems. The filesystem views the disk as a contiguous series of blocks, which are the smallest addressable unit. On the ext2 filesystem, blocks are 1024, 2048 or 4096 bytes. A file's inode contains a blockmap of the possibly non-contiguous blocks where the file resides. As is expected, internal fragmentation occurs when the file does not fill an entire block. The free space between the end of the file and the end of the block is known as slack space. It is technically reserved for the file, but unused; furthermore, it is non-addressable by the kernel. As a result, data can be reliably hidden in this slack space.

Hiding data in slack space, like most things, has advantages and disadvantages. Advantages include the fact that the filesystem appears unchanged from the kernel's perspective. File sizes, timestamps, and even file hashes such as md5 remain unchanged. The hidden data will be invisible to the kernel and the only known ways to view the data are via bmap or a thorough forensic evaluation.

Disadvantages include the fact that the data can still be found by a competent forensic analyst so if you do not want to get caught, encrypt your data before storing it in slack space. And lastly, data hidden in slack space can be corrupted under certain circumstances, namely when someone tries to grow a file and it overwrites the slack space. As a result, it is wise to use slack space around infrequently modified files.

There are several other interesting options accepted by bmap including the ability to list the blocks a file uses, extract raw blocks from disk, and wipe raw blocks from disk. These options can come in handy while doing advanced analysis of your hard disk for whatever reason.

Bmap seems useful, but what do you do when the file you want to hide is bigger than the slack space available on a file, which has an absolute maximum of 4,096 bytes. Luckily, there is a companion tool called 'slacker,' which operates on entire directory trees to store large files [27].

Data Hiding on NTFS with Alternate Data Streams

Microsoft Windows NTFS supports a little known feature called Alternate Data Streams (ADS). ADS were introduced in Windows NT 3.1 to provide compatibility with the Macintosh Hierarchical Filesystem and it allows arbitrary attributes (i.e., files) to be attached to files or directories. ADS are manipulated from the command line and no graphical tools recognize their existence including Windows Explorer. Furthermore, many antivirus checkers, IDS, and other security tools also overlook ADS.

One can view ADS for example, as hidden files that are appended to the visible ones. The primary reason they are potentially dangerous from a security perspective is that most users are unaware of their existence they are for the most part, generally hidden to the user, and that there are few security programs that can identify them.

Fortunately, there is a tool known as List Alternate Data Streams (LADS) [www.heysoft.de/nt/ep-lads.htm], which can search NTFS partitions for ADS. It should also be noted that while ADS are unlikely to be found by users or system administrators, a thorough forensic evaluation would certainly uncover them [28]. Readers may also wish to examine CrucialADS [www.crucialsecurity.com/downloads.html], as a secondary, alternative program for identifying ADS.

One thing you cannot do on an NTFS Windows computer is turn off alternate data streams. Not only do a lot of applications use ADS; so does Windows itself. There is neither a way to disable ADS the way you can disable many unneeded Windows services, nor can you simply delete an alternate data stream without deleting the file to which it is attached. In fact, you cannot use the Windows delete command to get rid of an ADS attached to a root directory.

Some ADS detection utilities will automatically delete alternate data streams. However, many of them simply notify you of the existence of alternate data streams.

If your detection utility does not delete alternate data streams, you need to get creative. The great weakness of alternate data streams is that they are only supported on NTFS. The older FAT filesystems do not recognize ADS. If you copy a file from an NTFS drive to a FAT drive, any attached ADS will be eliminated. If you are on an ADS hunt, it might be worthwhile to set up a FAT partition on your system simply to wash files through. These days, most Windows systems use NTFS and are not installed with any FAT partitions [29].

Augur suggests an even quicker way to prune a single ADS, which is to essentially use the UNIX "cat" command, which concatenates files, as ADS are not concatenated with the base file.

Note: Alternate data streams are strictly a feature of the NTFS file system and may not be supported in future file systems. However, NTFS will be supported in future versions of Windows NT (http://support.microsoft.com/kb/105763, July 2004).

The reader who may be interested in a further analysis of ADS, which goes beyond the scope of this text, can find such sources at the following:

■ Alternate Data Streams in NTFS [www.heysoft.de/nt/ntfs-ads.htm]
■ Alternate Data Streams and Windows XP Test [www.girlgeekette.net]
■ Windows Alternate Data Streams [www.bleepingcomputer.com/tutorials/tutorial25.html]

Additional Ways in Which Data May Be Concealed from Investigators

Camouflaged files are those that are placed in large often unseen directories such as /dev or files that have camouflaged names. In particular, the filename "." (<period><space>) is popular as it very often goes unnoticed [28].

Host-Protected Areas and Disk Configuration Overlay

The Host Protected Area (HPA) as defined is a reserved area on a Hard Disk Drive (HDD). It was designed to store information in such a way that it cannot be easily modified, changed, or accessed by the user, BIOS, or the OS. This area can contain information ranging from HDD utilities, to diagnostic tools, as well as boot sector code.

An additional hidden area on many of today's HDDs is the Device Configuration Overlay (DCO). The DCO allows system vendors to purchase HDDs from different manufacturers with potentially different sizes, and then configure all HDDs to have the same number of sectors. An example of this would be using DCO to make an 80 GB HDD appear as a 60 GB HDD to both the OS and the BIOS.

Usually, when information is stored in either the DCO or HPA area, it is not accessible by the BIOS, OS, or the user. However, certain tools can be used to modify the HPA or DCO. Given the potential to place data in these hidden areas, this is an area of concern for computer forensics investigators. An additional issue for forensic investigators is imaging the HDD that has the HPA or DCO on it. Although certain vendors claim that their tools are able to both properly detect and image the HPA, they are either silent on the handling of the DCO or indicate that this is beyond the capabilities of their tool.

These areas can be problematic for computer forensic investigators, because many of the common industry tools cannot detect the presence of the HPA and DCO. A review of the ATA specifications indicate that these areas can be accessed, modified, and written to by end users using specific open source and freely available tools, allowing data to be stored or hidden in these areas. This greatly increases the risk that image acquisitions may not be a true copy of the physical drive in question. This also could result in the obfuscation of data, leading to incomplete or erroneous investigative conclusions [30].

Author Note—[ATA refers to AT Attachment storage interface utilized as the disk drive interface on most personal and mobile computers today].

Hiding in File or Slack Space

- The area between the end of a file and the end of the disk cluster it is stored in. This is a naturally occurring event in IT as data rarely fill completely the fixed storage locations they are assigned. Residual data occurs when a smaller file is written to a cluster that had a previous larger file.
- Hiding data in the space between allocated and actual bytes in a file.
- Hidden data usually indistinguishable from old, overwritten files in slack.
- See discussion above.

Wiping Tools (aka Destroying Data)

- Eraser—Eraser is an advanced security tool (for Windows), which allows you to completely remove sensitive data from your hard drive by overwriting it several times with carefully selected patterns. Works with Windows 95, 98, ME, NT, 2000, XP, Windows 2003 Server, and DOS. Eraser is free software and its source code is released under General Public License (GNU) (www.heidi.ie/eraser).

■ The Defiler's Toolkit is a set of programs that is designed to prevent forensics investigators from identifying what activities were performed by a hacker by limiting the quality and quantity of forensic evidence left behind. The current Toolkit targets the Linux Ext2fs filesystem. The Toolkit allows hackers to hide data or destroy data while making it difficult to determine that these actions have taken place.

■ Data hiding occurs when the attacker associates good blocks with the bad block inode to store data by marking a section of the host's hard drive as being bad. Normally, the bad blocks inode identifies blocks that do not function properly, so the Coroner's toolkit (a forensics tool used to recover deleted files and examine deleted directory entries) will not look in the bad blocks. The only clue to the forensic investigator that something has happened is that the drive appears smaller than before, but it is difficult to determine what has been stored on the hard drive. Data can also be stored in the ext3 journal file and in directory files. Such techniques can be used to store virtually any kind of data a hacker desires.

■ Two programs are included in the toolkit to facilitate data destruction. Normally, when a file is deleted, only the data is removed, leaving the metadata (inodes and directory entries) intact. Directory entries normally make it possible for a forensics investigator to identify deleted filenames and their sizes. Necrofile uses deletion time criteria to remove the metadata from the inodes, making it more difficult for a forensic investigator to determine that a file has been deleted. Klismafile identifies directory entries for deleted filenames and eliminates them. Through combined use of these two programs, the hacker removes the obvious evidence that data has been deleted, making the forensic investigator's job much more difficult.

■ Examining blocks of hard drives that are marked bad is also an important step when trying to identify hacker activities. Hidden data can provide leads regarding the hacker's identity and objectives (wonko-ga, http://answers.google.com/answers/threadview?id=345604).

■ In investigations, do not forget to look in blocks marked bad! There could be some very useful data hidden in there.

More on Data Wiping Tools

The following tables summarize a variety (albeit not every) of products available that are designed to wipe, erase, delete, shred, and obliterate data, each making the cyber forensic investigators job even more challenging. The products have been grouped by operating systems Windows (Table 3.3), Macintosh (Table 3.4), and UNIX (Table 3.5).

The information in Tables 3.3, 3.4, and 3.5 was derived from the University of Minnesota, Office of Information Technology's Web site, Destroying Data, www.umn.edu/oit/security/assureddelete.html, 2007, and used with permission, Regents of the University of Minnesota.

Rootkits

■ A rootkit is a collection of tools (programs) that enable administrator-level access to a computer or computer network. Typically, a cracker installs a rootkit on a computer after first obtaining user-level access, either by exploiting a known vulnerability or cracking a password. Once the rootkit is installed, it allows the attacker to mask intrusion and gain root or privileged access to the computer and, possibly, to the other machines on the network.

Table 3.3   Windows

Product	Windows Platforms	Options	Web Site
BC wipe	95, 98, ME, NT, XP, 2000 and 2003	Free trial, purchase	www.jetico.com/download.htm
Darik's boot & Nuke	95, 98, ME, NT, XP and 2000	Free	http://dban.sourceforge.net/
Data eraser	All IBM compatible PC's on all operating systems	Purchase	www.ontrack.com/dataeraser/
Eraser	95, 98, NT, 2000, XP and DOS	Free	www.heidi.ie/eraser/
PGP wipe utility & wipe free space	95, 98, ME, NT, XP and 2000	Free trial or purchase	www.pgp.com/products/ desktop/index.html
R-wipe & clean*	98, ME, NT4.0, 2000, XP	Free trial or purchase	www.r-wipe.com/
WinPT wipe file utility	95, 98, ME, NT, XP and 2000	Free	http://winpt.sourceforge.net/en/ a front-end for www.gnupg.org
Tracks eraser pro 6. 0	95/98/ME/NT/2000/ XP compatible	Purchase	www.acesoft.net/index.html

*All users should select Tools and Customize and uncheck "event logs" and "firewall logs" under the system heading so that there important logs are always left alone. Also, some users may want to uncheck "recent documents" or they can unckeck each time they use the program.

Table 3.4   Macintosh

Product	Macintosh Platforms	Options	Web Site
Secure Empty Trash	Macintosh (10.3 or newer)	Built into the Mac Operating System	Shreds specific files. Move the file to the Trash, and then the "Secure Empty Trash" is accessed from the Finder menu.
Burn	OS 8.5 and the new Mac OS HFS + file system	Free	http://www.thenextwave.com/burnHP. html
Eraser pro	Minimum OS 7	Free	http://users.libero.it/yellowsoft/ theeraser.html
ShredIt	Minimum OS 8	Purchase	http://www.mireth.com/text/shredit_sp.html
PGP wipe utility & wipe free space	OS X 10.3.9 ("Panther"), 10.4.0 through 10.4.4 ("Tiger")	Free trial or purchase	http://www.pgp.com/products/desktop/ index.html

Table 3.5   Unix

Product	Platforms	Options	Web Site
BC wipe	Various platforms	Free trial, purchase	http://www.jetico.com/download.htm
Darik's boot & nuke	Various platforms	Free	http://dban.sourceforge.net/
Secure delete	Various platforms	Free	http://freshmeat.net/projects/securedelete/?topic_id=43
uniShred	Various platforms	Purchase	http://ftp.lat.com/usp_main.htm
Wipe	Various platforms	Free	http://wipe.sourceforge.net/

- A rootkit may consist of spy ware and other programs that: monitor traffic and keystrokes; create a "backdoor" into the system for the hacker's use; alter log files; attack other machines on the network; and alter existing system tools to escape detection (http://searchsecurity. techtarget.com/sDefinition/0,sid14_gci547279,00.html).

- The rootkit itself does not typically cause deliberate damage. Its purpose is to hide software. But rootkits are used to hide malicious code. A virus, worm, backdoor, or spy ware program could remain active and undetected in a system for a long time if it uses a rootkit (www. f-secure.com/blacklight/rootkit.html).

- Given the technical implications of masking an intrusion and gaining root or privileged access to a host computer and, then possibly other end user machines on the network, investigating for the presence of such rootkit programs may be essential in determining or identifying both a logical access path and audit trail, on a machine under investigation as well as determining if a third party may have had potential access to the subject machine, raising issue of a potential external compromise. The use of rootkits to install suspect programs raise issue with the potential for theft of intellectual property and theft of technology assets on the compromised machine or machines connected across networks.

Several vendors make products that will detect installed rootkits (Table 3.6).

Forensic Eavesdropping: Analyzing Voice Over IP

One of the many technologies becoming more widely used is Voice Over IP (VoIP). This technology allows the user to place voice calls over an IP network. Providers like Vonage (www.vonage. com), Skype (www.skype.com), and Free World Dialup(www.freeworlddialup.com) all offer a user the ability to send and receive calls to any telephone number through the Internet.

This can be accomplished using software on a computer or using a regular phone connected to a hardware device that converts voice audio into IP packets. There are also instant messaging clients like iChat, AOL Instant Messenger (AIM), Yahoo, and others that allow users to do audio and video chats using VoIP technology.

Table 3.6   Rootkit Products by Platform

Rootkit Products	Windows Platforms	Options	Web Site
F-Secure blacklight	Windows 2000 or later (32 bit only)	Purchase	www.f-secure.com/blacklight/rootkit.html
RootkitRevealer v1. 71	Windows NT 4 and higher	Free	www.microsoft.com/technet/sysinternals/ utilities/RootkitRevealer.mspx
Microsoft® Windows® Malicious Software Removal Tool v1. 23	Windows XP, Windows 2000, and Windows Server 2003 computers	Free	www.microsoft.com/downloads/details. aspx?FamilyId=AD724AE0-E72D-4F54-9AB3-75B8EB148356&displaylang=en
RootKit Hook Analyzer 2. 0	Windows XP, 2000 and 2003 Server on both 32 and 64 bit editions	Free	www.resplendence.com/hookanalyzer
Chkrootkit 0. 47	Linux 2.0.x, 2.2.x, 2.4.x and 2.6.x FreeBSD 2.2.x, 3.x, 4.x and 5.x OpenBSD 2.x and 3.x. NetBSD 1.6.x Solaris 2.5.1, 2.6, 8.0 and 9.0 HP-UX 11 Tru64 BSDI and Mac OS X	Free	www.chkrootkit.org/
Strider	Windows 2000 or later (32 bit only)	Free	http://research.microsoft.com/rootkit
IceSword	Windows NT 4 and higher	Free	http://xfocus.net/tools/200509/1085.html

VoIP calls are accomplished by using two main protocols: Session Initiation Protocol (SIP) and Real-time Transport Protocol (RTP). The SIP protocol, as the name implies, is used to initiate the session between the two users wishing to setup a VoIP call. SIP packets will contain information about where the call is coming from, where it is going, and what voice compression will be used. You can think of SIP as the addresses on the outside of an envelope.

The RTP protocol is used to carry the actual audio stream of the voice conversation, which cannot take place until the call has been setup via SIP. You can think of RTP as the letter inside an envelope. It contains the actual message being delivered but could not get where it is going without the envelope.

Because these calls are using IP packets to transmit the voice stream, IP packet capturing software can be used to listen to them. This is a three-step process that involves capturing the packets, reassembling them into a stream, and then playing them back with an audio player capable of handling RTP stream audio. There are many software packages that can be used to accomplish this but this example will show the use of Ethereal (www.ethereal.com/), Sun Java Media Framework (http://java.sun.com/products/java-media/jmf/), and RTP Tools (www.cs. columbia.edu/IRT/software/rtptools/).

First, we need to capture the packets using Ethereal. Once you have launched Ethereal, you can start a new capture by selecting "Capture" → "Options" from the menus. You should get a screen that looks like Figure 3.17.

Make sure that the field labeled "Interface": is displaying the interface on which you wish to capture packets. Keep in mind that this interface will need to have access to packets containing the RTP stream.

If you want to be able to see the packets as they are being captured, make sure that you select "Update list of packets in real time" and "Automatic scrolling in live capture." Once you have made these changes, click on "Start" to begin your capture. Your capture should look something like Figure 3.18.

Once you have captured all of the packets from the call you are wishing to hear, you can click on "Stop" to stop the packet capture. If you look in the protocol field, you should have some packets that are labeled as RTP protocol packets. These packets contain the actual voice conversation you are trying to capture!

Next, we want to export the RTP packets to a file. Click on "Statistics" → "RTP" → "Show All Streams" to get to a screen that looks like Figure 3.19.

Notice that there is a separate stream for each direction of the conversation. If you want to hear both sides of the conversation, you will have to export both streams. Click on the conversation stream you wish to hear and click the "Save As" button (Figure 3.20). Give the file a name that you can remember.

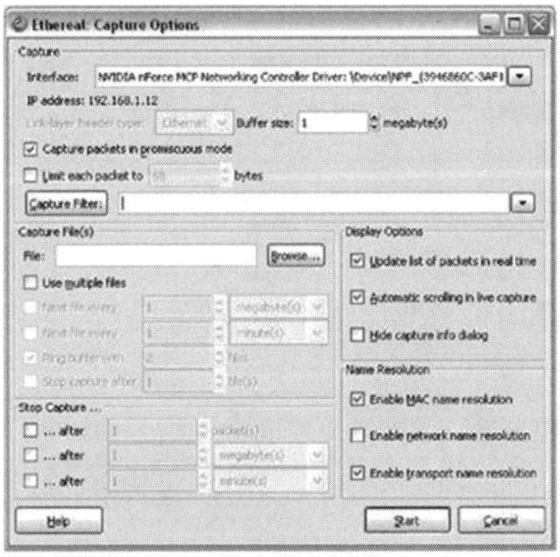

Figure 3.17   Ethereal screen shot: capture options.

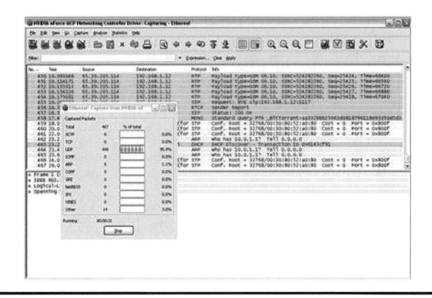

Figure 3.18   Ethereal screen shot: packet capturing.

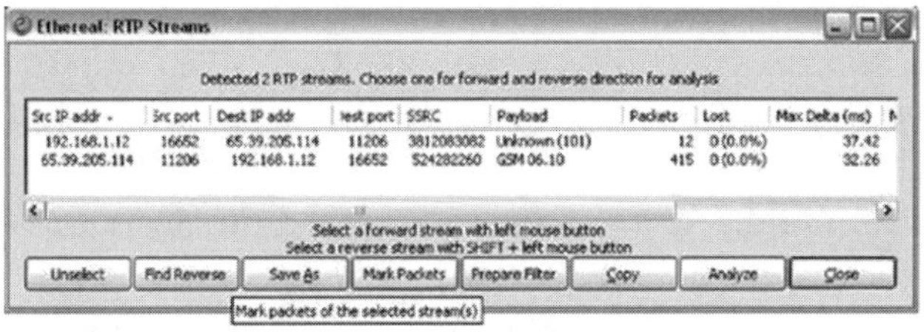

Figure 3.19   Ethereal screen shot: RTP streams.

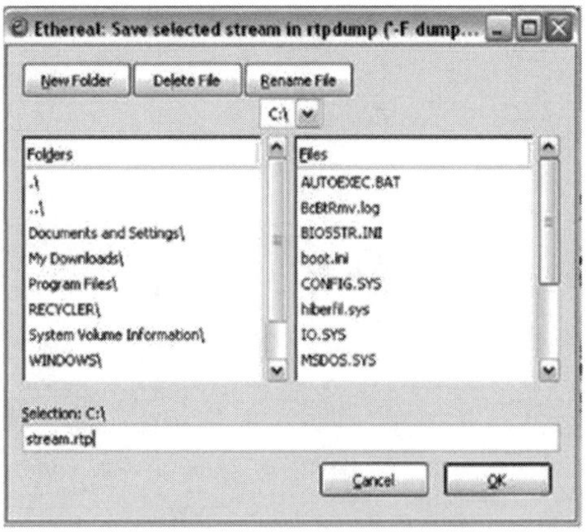

Figure 3.20   Ethereal screen shot: save selected stream.

Figure 3.21 JMStudio screen shot: upon RTP session.

Now that we have the RTP stream saved to a file, we need to setup JMStudio to play our audio stream. To do this, launch JMStudio and click "File" → "Open RTP Session…" (Figure 3.21).

This should bring up a screen with options that looks like Figure 3.22.

In the field labeled "Address:" you want to enter your own IP address. The other settings can be left as the defaults.

Once you have setup JMStudio to accept the stream, you need to send a stream to it by using rtpplay that comes with RTP Tools.

The filename "stream. rtp" should be replaced with the name and location of the file that you saved from Ethereal when you exported the RTP stream. Once this command has been entered, you should hear the audio of the phone conversation played back over your computer speakers (Figure 3.23).

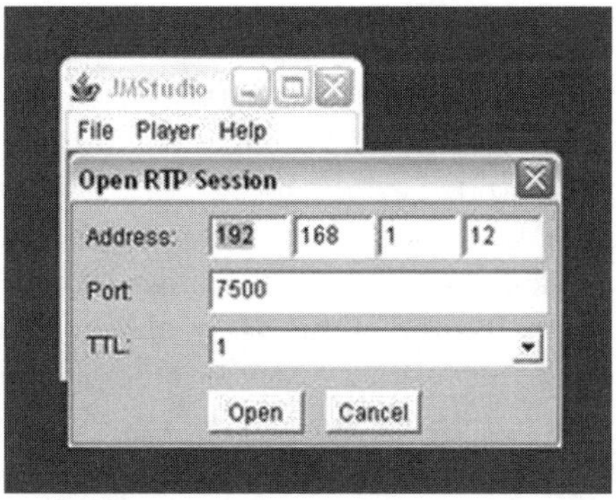

Figure 3.22 JMStudio screen shot: enter IP address.

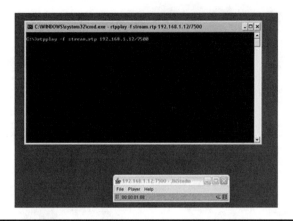

Figure 3.23 JMStudio screen shot: audio playback.

If you have more than one stream, you will need to setup JMStudio again for each stream and then use rtpplay to play the file back.

There are a few other things that should be mentioned with respect to capturing VoIP calls:

1. Packets can only be captured while the conversation is in place. If the situation makes it infeasible for a person to setup an Ethereal capture at the exact moment the call will be placed, a capture can be setup that saves the packets to a file. The settings to do this in Ethereal are very straightforward. Once the packets are captured, the export and playback can be done at a later time.
2. With the proper legal permission, it may be possible to contact the VoIP provider and request that they record all conversations associated with a given account.
3. Finally, if the VoIP call is taking place over an encrypted connection, it will be impossible to play back the audio stream. Typically Ethereal will see UDP packets instead of RTP packets as in Figure 3.24 below, which captures packets from a Skype conversation.

Capturing RTP packets is a very useful technique for listening in on VoIP conversations [31]. Anyone conducting data forensic analysis should be aware of this procedure.

Making Sure Security Logs Exhibit Accurate Time with NTP

It is vital that organizations take steps to synchronize the time on their network and devices, but it is even more important to make sure the logs produced by security devices reflect the accurate time. To do so, many use the Network Time Protocol (NTP), which is designed to synchronize the clocks of computers over a network, NTP has been around for a long time.

However, this synchronization takes on even more significance when it comes to security devices on your network. It is important that the logs produced by these security devices reflect accurate time. When you are dealing with a heavy volume of traffic, it can be impossible to correlate log files from different sources if the times does not match up.

Your security correlation tool will be utterly useless if the time on your log files does not correspond. An unsynchronized network can mean spending a great deal of time tracking events

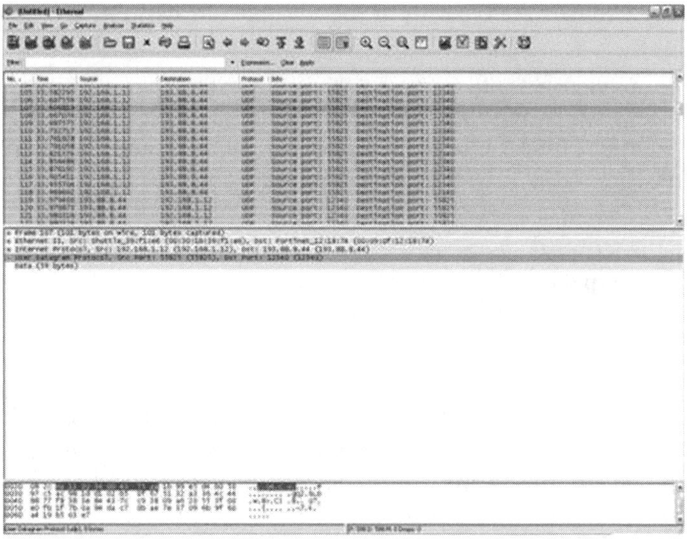

Figure 3.24   Ethereal screen shot: encrypted VoIP packets.

manually. Let us look at how you can synchronize your network and make sure your security logs exhibit accurate time.

Find the Time

When it comes to synchronizing your network, the first step is using a reliable time source to provide a consistent time to your network devices. Known as a stratum, this time source comes in four categories. Lets look at your options:

1. Stratum 0: This is the U. S. Naval Observatory (USNO) or a GPS (Global Positioning System) clock.
2. Stratum 1: This is a radio receiver that obtains the time from Stratum 0.
3. Stratum 2: This is a client that receives the time over a network connection from a Stratum 1 clock.
4. Stratum 3: This is a client that obtains the time from Stratum 2.

If you are not sure where to start, the Network Time Protocol project (www.ntp.org) maintains a large list of both public and private time sources. So if your company does not possess an internal time source to synchronize your network with, this list is a good resource to turn to. Using it, you can find a primary and secondary time server in your geographical area.

Coordinate the Time

Your next step is actually synchronizing the network. From all of your network devices, pick two routers that will receive the time from the outside world and distribute that time to the rest of the network. These routers are typically at the edge of your network and connect directly to the Internet.

Lets look at an example. We will detail the necessary steps to specify an NTP server for two Cisco routers and update their software clocks.

After you have found a time source that's in your geographical area, log in to the routers with administrative privileges. Then, issue the following commands:

- Router# Config terminal
- Router(config)# ntp server TimeServerOne prefer
- Router(config)# ntp server TimeServerTwo
- Router(config)# ntp update-calendar

These commands set TimeServerOne (which you would replace with the IP address of the selected time server) as the primary time server. And, of course, replace TimeServerTwo with the IP address of the secondary time server. The update-calendar command configures the router to update its hardware clock from the software clock.

Next, configure the rest of your network devices to draw time from these routers. Here is an example:

- Router# Config terminal
- Router(config)# ntp server RouterOne
- Router(config)# ntp server RouterTwo
- Router(config)# ntp update-calendar

Make the Time Secure

By default, all interfaces disable NTP services until you issue the first NTP command. To ensure security, its a good idea to prevent devices from receiving or transmitting NTP packets—you do not want to become a timing source for the entire Internet.

You can accomplish this for a specific interface by issuing the following command in Interface Configuration Mode. This turns off NTP on a given interface.

- Router(config-if)# ntp disable

For more information on configuring NTP on Cisco routers, check out the Cisco IOS Configuration Fundamentals Configuration Guide (www.cisco.com/en/US/products/ps6350/products_configuration_guide_book09186a0080430ee6.html) for the IOS version you are currently running.

Making Time

When it comes to security, the time of occurrence can mean everything. If your logs become evidence in a court case, it is imperative that you are able to illustrate a smooth progression of events as they transpired through your network—and you need to do so in an understandable, non-technical approach. Time might be the only thing the jury or judge that understands.

Failing to properly synchronize your network could mean the difference between a conviction and an acquittal. That's one more reason why you should set up a reliable time source for your network today [32].

Synchronize a Cisco Router's Clock with Network Time Protocol

It is critical that all devices on an organization's network display the accurate time and date. If they do not, things can go wrong in a hurry.

Whether you are working with a server, router, switch, firewall, or PC, it's imperative that all devices on your organization's network exhibit the correct time and date. If this critical information is not accurate, a variety of things can go wrong.

That means event logs and firewall logs can be incorrect, you might not be able to tell when your router rebooted, or Windows devices may not be able to log in to the domain. The fact that Microsoft has integrated the Windows Time Service into its products only underscores the importance of proper time synchronization.

Cisco routers have embraced the Network Time Protocol (NTP), a protocol designed to synchronize the clocks of computers over a network, for many years. NTP Version 3 is a standard—formalized in RFC 1305 (www.faqs.org/rfcs/rfc1305.html)—that uses the User Datagram Protocol (UDP) and port 123.

Unlike PCs or servers, Cisco network devices specifically need to run NTP to synchronize the time and date. That's because most Cisco devices do not have an internal clock.

For example, when a Cisco 2600 or 3600 series router loses power or the network administrator needs to reload it, the time and date are lost. Consequently, all log files, time-based access lists, or any other configuration based on time or date will either be incorrect or not work at all.

An NTP client synchronizes the time and date with an NTP server. The NTP server should be a reliable source, such as a time server on the Internet. A number of free public Internet time servers are available.

One example is the National Institute of Standards and Technology (NIST) Internet Time Service (http://tf.nist.gov/service/its.htm), which bases its time on an atomic clock. The NIST Web site also provides a list of the publicly available NIST Internet Time Servers on the Internet (http://tf.nist.gov/service/time-servers.html). In fact, you'll even find Microsoft on this list. The software giant runs its own free Internet time server—time-nw. nist. gov with an IP address of 131.107.1.10.

Known as stratum-1 time servers, these public Internet time servers obtain their time directly from a stratum-0 device, a reference clock that cannot be an NTP server on the network (such as an atomic clock). The greater the stratum of the server, the greater the distance between that server and the reliable time source.

To ensure that your network devices display the most accurate time, you need to configure the NTP protocol and link your devices to a reliable time source. To do so, you have a couple of options.

You could purchase a hardware time device that obtains the time via GPS or some other method. In effect, you're essentially creating your own stratum-1 time server. However, for most small to midsize companies, a better alternative is to opt for a free Internet time server.

In my organization, we use UNIX scripts that depend on the proper router date. We receive a morning e-mail that lists all router events that occurred the previous day. The scripts go to each router and use a command similar to "*show logging | include May 16*" to gather the date, combine it in a file, and e-mail it to all network administrators.

So, when a router reboots, if no one has configured NTP, then the command will find no data from that router. Nor is the command likely to ever retrieve data again because the router reverts back to its default date of February or March 1993.

Because of such possibilities, it's easy to see why it's imperative to configure NTP on your routers and switches. Configuring NTP on a Cisco IOS device is a relatively easy process.

Follow these steps:

1. Choose the NTP server your devices will use.
2. Find out the IP address for this server. It could be an external source such as NIST, or it could be an internal device that offers NTP services (such as a hardware device or software server from Symmetricom) (www.ntp-systems.com).
3. Enter the following commands on the IOS device:
   - Router# configure terminal
   - Router(config)# ntp server <IP address of NTP Server>
4. Verify the association with the server using the show ntp status and show ntp associations commands. Exhibit 3.1 offers an example of the output of these commands.

Before you get started, I would like to point out a couple of things to keep in mind:

■ NTP is a slow protocol, and the formation of NTP associations can take a long time. So, do not expect anything to happen fast. You can keep an eye on it using the debug ntp <option> set of commands.
■ If you decide to use an Internet NTP server, make sure you open UDP port 123 inbound on your firewall to your NTP client.

For more information, as well as detailed instructions for the options you can enable with NTP, check out Cisco's "Configuring NTP" documentation (www.cisco.com/univercd/cc/td/doc/product/software/ios122/122cgcr/ffun_c/fcfprt3/fcf012.htm#wp1001170) [33].

```
Router# show ntp status
Clock is synchronized, stratum 3, reference is 10.1.1.1
nominal freq is 250.0000 Hz, actual freq is 249.9939 Hz, precision is
2**18
reference time is C634CA99.AF41F140 (14:55:05.684 CDT Tue May 17
2005)
clock offset is -6.2157 msec, root delay is 31.97 msec
root dispersion is 75.50 msec, peer dispersion is 0.92 msec


Router# show ntp associations

    address      ref clock     st when poll reach delay offset   disp
'~10.1.1.1     132.163.4.102    2   0   64  377   0.9   9.35   15.1
 ' master (synced), # master (unsynced), + selected, - candidate, ~
configured
Router#
```

Exhibit 3.1   Output of configuring NTP on a Cisco IOS device.

Rootkits

By definition, a rootkit is a hacker security tool that captures passwords and message traffic to and from a computer. A collection of tools that allows a hacker to provide a backdoor into a system, collect information on the network, mask the fact that the system is compromised, and much more. Rootkits is a classic example of Trojan horse software. Rootkit is available for a wide range of operating systems.

Generally, Windows rootkits have the ability to hide:

- Processes,
- Files (.txt, .exe, .jpg, .sys, etc.) and folders,
- Registry entries,
- Services and drivers,
- Ports and connections,
- Any other code or software included or added in the package like backdoors, key loggers, sniffers, virus, and so on.

Rootkits can be used legally or not, with or without a physical access to a machine. For:

- Personal research, education, for antirootkits development,
- Hiding files from others users (porn pictures etc.),
- Increasing the stealth abilities of a spy software (a basic keylogger hidden by a rootkit can be more stealth than some "invisible keyloggers"),
- Advanced criminal attackers for criminal goals (like cyber extortions), and by
- People involved in wars and piracy (hiding files on servers),
- Private and government security agencies for spying firms for patent, sensitive, and promising technologies or potential terrorists and activists (http://kareldjag.over-blog.com/article-895476.html).

In order for a rootkit to alter the normal execution path of the operating system, one of the techniques it may employ is "hooking." In modern operating systems, there are many places to hook because the system was designed to be flexible, extendable, and backward compatible. By using a hook, a rootkit can alter the information that the original operating system function would have returned. There are many tables in the Windows operating system that can be hooked by a rootkit [34].

FU

The FU rootkit can hide processes, elevate process privileges, and fake out the Windows Event Viewer so that forensics is impossible, and even hide device drivers, all this without any hooking. It does all this by Direct Kernel Object Manipulation, and no hooking!

Hacker Defender

Hacker Defender is the rootkit, which is the most widely used.

Hacker Defender or HxDef is the favorite rootkit of Script-Kiddies for many reasons:

- It is "light" (199k for the zip, 315k for the entire package);
- An exhaustive package which already integrates a backdoor;

- Highly configurable (INI file);
- Ready to use with a simple command line;
- Does not require advanced skill; and
- Can be installed remotely.

BIOS Rootkits

Advanced Configuration and Power Interface (ACPI) is an open industry specification co-developed by Hewlett-Packard, Intel, Microsoft, Phoenix, and Toshiba.

ACPI establishes industry-standard interfaces enabling OS-directed configuration, power management, and thermal management of mobile, desktop, and server platforms.

When first published in 1999, ACPI evolved an existing collection of power management BIOS code, Advanced Power Management (APM) application programming interfaces (APIs), PNPBIOS APIs, and Multiprocessor Specification (MPS) tables into a well-defined power management and configuration interface specification.

The specification enables new power management technologies to evolve independently in operating systems and hardware while ensuring that they continue to work together.

ACPI, which as stated above, is used by the power-management services in operating systems, could be subverted to hide a rootkit in the flash memory used by the BIOS.

The BIOS is a particularly potent means of attacking a computer, because code in the BIOS will survive hard disk reformats and operating system reinstallations. Malware present in the BIOS is difficult to detect and even more difficult to remove [35].

The forensics potential here is interesting. What if instead of injecting malware into the BIOS, an individual decided to hide a snippet of stolen proprietary code, data or text? What if the suspect (possibly a disgruntled employee), under investigation, was intent on causing a technology disruption with his or her employer's operations? Corruption or misuse of the ACPI via the BIOS may be a logic attack point.

The potential for someone with the appropriate level of access and knowledge to manipulate this sensitive and hard to detect area within the operating system platform, presents a viable exposure worth investigating—under the proper circumstances (when the suspect's knowledge of technology and the means with which to exploit these technologies appears to be beyond "entry level," when the suspect's position within the organization affords the suspect the potential opportunity to abuse these technologies) and as the case situation warrants.

Knowledge of an individual's potential to conceal either intellectual property or destructive malware in this sensitive area is an important consideration for the cyber forensic investigator.

Hooking

The term Hooking represents a fundamental technique of getting control over a particular piece of code execution. It provides a straightforward mechanism that can easily alter the operating system's behavior as well as third party products, without having their source code available. By injecting hooks one can provide an easy way to change and extend existing module functionalities. For example many third party products sometimes do not meet specific security requirements and have to be adjusted to meet specific needs. Spying of applications allows developers to add sophisticated pre- and post-processing around the original API functions. This ability is an extremely useful for altering the behavior of the already compiled code [36].

Knowledge of this operation is important for a cyber forensic investigator to consider when attempting to determine (a) the validity of compiled code under review, (b) that no unauthorized access to the API functions had been attempted, and (c) any action aimed at manipulating electronic, system evidence.

Usually, a Hook system is composed at least two parts—a Hook Server and a Driver. The Hook Server is responsible for injecting the Driver into targeted processes at the appropriate moment. It also administers the driver and optionally can receive information from the Driver about its activities whereas the Driver module that performs the actual interception [36].

Hooking is done by altering the Import Address Table. In computer programming, every win32 executable application has an Import Address Table (IAT) residing inside the program. The IAT is used as a lookup table when the application is calling a windows API function. If you look at the Windows System directory, typically \Windows\System under Window 95/98 and \Winnt\ System32 under Windows NT, you will find a number of Dynamic Link Library (.DLL) files. These files contain functions that are used to run the operating system and to ensure a consistent user interface and operating environment. These files make up the Windows API.

API Hooking

Any time you are trying to intercept some function, imported from an external DLL library for some purpose, you are concerned with an API Hooking problem.

IAT Hooking

IAT hooking involves overwriting Import Address Table entries and gives an individual the power to snoop, change, and control thus, providing added concern for the cyber forensic investigator to more closely examine all electronic evidence for apparent and not so apparent signs of tampering. Tampering may ultimately lead to invalidating any electronic evidence gathered as part of an investigation.

Inline Hooking (aka Detouring—aka Jmp Hooking)

One of the most widely used techniques. The hooking code is inserted into a running process by techniques seen only in user-mode root kits. Kernel-mode inline hooking is not however well documented. User-mode and other techniques have been effective enough; however, they will probably change in the future. Inline hooking involves overwriting the first part of a function to jump to another function.

The technique is called inline because the first bytes of a function are altered. That is why this method is really efficient, you can call a function directly or with a table system, the hook will always work.

Direct Kernel Object Manipulation

Direct Kernel Object Manipulation (DKOM) relies upon the fact that the operating system creates kernel objects to do bookkeeping and auditing. If a rootkit modifies these kernel objects, then it will subvert what the operating system believes exists on the system. By modifying a token object, the rootkit can alter who the operating system believes performed a certain action, thereby subverting any logging [34].

This potential for subversion should be investigated and could be critical if an investigator is attempting to determine who may have had access to, or has previously accessed a machine which is under investigation. Any attempt to manipulate log entries may result in the deletion or alteration of potential electronic evidence, evidence which may be essential to the successful prosecution of a suspect, and the litigation of a case.

A cyber forensics investigator should be knowledgeable of the existence of these tools and methodologies, which may be used to alter or conceal data (evidence); as such, knowledge may be beneficial in justifying the examiner's need to expand the investigation to include a more detailed review of the seized technology, to determine if intentional modification or destruction of evidence has occurred.

Hash Collisions

In its basic form, hashing is the process (typically via complex mathematical algorithms) of taking "digital fingerprints" of data to validate authenticity. The production of a "hash value" is generated to ensure that duplicated data derived from original, source data is protected against tampering. A hash value is created using a specific formula that can be used at a later time (for e.g., by an independent third party) to ensure that the duplicated data is the same as when the hash value was created from the source, original data. One of the advantages of utilizing hashing is in the ability to detect data tampering.

Collisions can be a problem for systems that involve signed code. In particular, a collision attack can enable adversaries to construct an innocuous program and a malicious program with the same hash. For example, a trusted compiler or verifier might accept and sign the innocuous program, which could then be substituted for the malicious one. Collision attacks do not allow tampering with arbitrary programs; this would require a preimage attack.

A preimage attack would enable someone to find an input message that causes a hash function to produce a particular output. In contrast, a collision attack finds two messages with the same hash, but the attacker cannot pick what the hash will be.

Collisions can be a problem for systems that involve signed code. In particular, a collision attack can enable adversaries to construct an innocuous program and a malicious program with the same hash (www.cryptography. com/cnews/hash.html, retrieved January 2007).

The "classical" threat induced by hash collisions is the following: If someone was able to create two documents having identical hash values and if he could persuade a person to sign one of these documents digitally (employing that hash function) he would at the same time obtain a valid signature for the second document. Clearly, this could cause a serious problem for the signer. Similarly, a dishonest signer could create two such documents, sign the first and later claim that he signed the second one, for example, in case of liability, to discredit a signature system. Of course, signature schemes should exclude such attacks regardless whether they are viewed as realistic under real world conditions, that is, with respect to actual signature laws and practice. That is, the used hash function should not only have the one-way-property but also be collision resistant [37].

The implications of this potentially lethal technology is that, if successfully ported to the cyber forensics field, it may well call into question the cyber forensic examiner's ability to validate and to ensure, beyond question, that the file (or an entire disk drive), which was examined and presented as evidence, was indeed an exact, identical copy of the file or drive acquired in the field.

Knowledge of hashing, hashing techniques, hashes which have been broken to date, and the potential to undermine the credibility of currently secure hashes add another dimension to the growing information base required of 21st century cyber forensic examiners. The cyber forensic investigator will be required to ensure that any hash routine used during an investigation is verified, validated, cross checked, and that the hash routine used to validate the examination files could not be compromised.

Readers interested in learning more on hashing and collision attacks are directed to the following:

- Lenstra, A., Wang, X., and Weger, B. (October 23, 2006), "Colliding X. 509 Certificates," www.win.tue.nl/~bdeweger/CollidingCertificates
- Biham, E., Chen, R., et al. (May 2005), "Collisions of SHA-0 and Reduced SHA-1," http://cat.inist.fr/?aModele=afficheN&cpsidt=17026978
- Wang, X. and Yu, H., (Eurocrypt 2005), "How to break MD5 and other hash functions," www.infosec.sdu.edu.cn/paper/md5-attack.pdf
- McGlinn, J., "Password Hashing," http://phpsec.org/articles/2005/password-hashing.html
- Kaminski, D. (December 6, 2004), "MD5 to be considered harmful someday," http://209.85.165.104/search?q=cache:TduHJN-ML50J:www.doxpara.com/md5_someday.pdf+%22MD5+to+be+considered+harmful+someday+%22&hl=en&gl=us&ct=clnk&cd=1
- Mikle, O. (December 2, 2004), "Practical Attacks on Digital Signatures using MD5 message digest," Cryptology ePrint Archive, Report 2004/356, http://eprint.iacr. org/2004/356

Social Engineering

Theft of sensitive or classified information, economic terrorism, industrial espionage, loss of intellectual property, violation of contractual non-compete or non-disclosure terms, and so on, are all emerging and growing crimes of the 21st century and of organizational reliance on technology and trust in personnel to safeguard and manage that technology. A cyber forensic investigator may be called upon to investigate these activities as well as many others, as global organizations move to an increasing dependency on technology and as the cost of developing or legally acquiring that technology continues to escalate.

Most people think computer break-ins are purely technical, the result of technical flaws in computer systems that the intruders are able to exploit. The truth is, however, that social engineering often plays a big part in helping an attacker slip through the initial security barriers. Lack of security awareness or gullibility of computer users often provides an easy stepping stone into the protected system in cases when the attacker has no authorized access to the system at all [38].

This method of concealment or diversion is possibly the least technical yet probably the most dangerous. Concealing (or altering) one's virtual identity as well as manipulating another's non-virtual identity is by far the fastest growing non-technical ploy used by persons to engage in an illegal activities, whether these activities employ technology or rely on time proven deception techniques.

Social engineering relies on attacking the weakest link in any technology based environment—people. An individual who desires to engage in illegal activities either within his or her own organization or within a third-party's operation will begin by amassing as much information about their intended target as possible, via all possible sources, private as well as public.

An individual's ability to portray himself or herself as someone else, in an effort to gather valuable information which may by essential and necessary to perpetrate a crime, provides the potential criminal with the ideal disguise and cover. It is possible for a hacker to forge e-mail for example (see spoofing) making it look like it came from somebody the recipient knows to say a supervisor or trusted colleague.

If an individual were able to portray himself or herself as say a system administrator or the manager of accounts payable, the potential for a breech in system integrity and the misuse of technology is highly probable.

Thus, as stated, humans and human-centric controls are the weakest link in most security protocols, and as such, represent a valid exposure which a potential criminal may seek to exploit in an effort to gain access to or manipulate organizational systems (technological, financial, automated and manual).

Typically, an attacker, or potential criminal will attempt to get an employee to comply with their wishes by performing a task which is typically either beyond or outside of, the employee's level of responsibility, or into breaking normal security protocol. Because every (to this author's knowledge) computer system requires human interaction to function (at some, even basic level), every computer system is vulnerable to potential abuse via a well planned, well researched and well executed social engineering attack.

The most common and growing use of social engineering today, is in the area of identity theft. Identity theft is much more than misuse of a Social Security number—it can also include credit card and mail fraud. ID Theft Clearinghouse [www.consumer.gov/idtheft/pdf/clearinghouse_2005.pdf] reported 686,683, cases of identity thefts in the U.S. as of December 31, 2005.

The ability to become someone else, especially in a virtual, unseen environment, provides excellent cover to a potential criminal intent on misusing or stealing an organization's assets (i.e., financial or technical). The cyber forensic investigator must be aware of the potential breech of security risks that are associated with the art of social engineering and investigate all potential opportunities a suspect may have utilized in an attempt to undermine established internal controls and established procedures.

Activities associated with the broader area of social engineering and each of which is capable of contributing to undermining system security and integrity and allowing a potential criminal to obtain critical information which can be used to potentially conceal the suspect's activities and movements within an organization's IT systems.

The cyber forensics investigator should remain abreast of the following methodologies, which support social engineering as these methods, tools, and techniques change constantly with the ever evolving IT marketplace and advances in technology:

- Brute force cracking (http://searchsecurity.techtarget.com/sDefinition/0,290660,sid14_gci499494,00.html)
- Buffer overflow (www.windowsecurity.com/articles/Analysis_of_Buffer_Overflow_Attacks.html)
- Phishing (www.antiphishing.org/)
- Rootkit (http://searchsecurity.techtarget.com/sDefinition/0,290660,sid14_gci547279,00.html)
- Pharming (http://reviews.cnet.com/4520-3513_7-5670780-1.html)

Summary

This chapter has examined many different and varied tools and techniques that can be employed by someone intent on hiding or attempting to hide unauthorized or illegal acts conducted via information technology systems.

The tools and techniques examined in this chapter run the gamut from very simplistic requiring little if no technology expertise to very complex, and requiring the user to possess a fairly sophisticated level of technology understanding to successfully deploy or implement these techniques.

One important step, which the cyber forensic examiner should perform prior to beginning a detailed investigation is to first evaluate the technical proficiency of the suspected offender.

Is the suspected offender technically capable of employing first any of the tools or techniques examined in this chapter? Does the individual have access to the technology necessary to deploy such cloaking or data alteration techniques?

If the suspect appears to have some level of technical proficiency, what is this level? Determining this level of proficiency will help the investigator to determine which technical ploys he or she should specifically be looking for and which can be eliminated as being too advanced for the suspect to utilize. Knowing this information in advance will help the investigator to narrow his or her investigation, focusing on just those potential means which a suspect may have used to cloak, hide, shred, or destroy unauthorized, illegal or inappropriate cyber activities.

Having now examined potential ways in which someone may attempt to conceal their cyber activities, Chapter 4 provides a closer look behind the scenes and "beneath the hood" of typical IT hardware that an investigator may encounter in the course of routine cyber forensic investigations.

Web Sites

Analyzing steganography softwares
http://www.guillermito2.net/stegano/index.html
International Association for Cryptologic Research:
www.iacr.org
The Waterloo Crypto Centre:
www.cacr.math.uwaterloo.ca/
The Handbook Online:
www.cacr.math.uwaterloo.ca/hac
RSA Laboratories:
www.rsasecurity.com/rsalabs/
Cryptography.com:
www.cryptography.com/
Certicom Research:
www.certicom.com/research.html
Hewlett-Packard Research:
www.hpl.hp.com/research/index.html
The Advanced Encryption Standard Homepage:
csrc. nist. gov/encryption/aes/
The web page of the AES algorithm Rijndael by the designers of the algorithm is at www.esat.kuleuven. ac.be/~rijmen/rijndael/
NIPC and other CERTS
www.nipc.gov
www.cert.org
www.fedcirc.gov
www.sans.org

References

1. Dalrymple, B. and Harshman, D. (October 27, 2004), Electronic Discovery: What You Need to Know and What It May Cost If You Don't, www.nixonpeabody.com/publications_detail3.asp?Type=P&PAID=0&ID=771&Bro=&Hot=&NLID=0, retrieved January 2007.
2. RSA (2004), RSA Laboratories' Frequently Asked Questions About Today's Cryptography, Version 4.1, www.rsasecurity.com/rsalabs/node.asp?id=2152, RSA Security Inc., 174 & 176 Middlesex Turnpike, Bedford, MA 01730, (781) 515-6212, retrieved July 2006, used with permission.

3. Kessler, G. (April 13, 2006), An Overview of Cryptography, www.garykessler.net/library/crypto.html, www.garykessler.net, retrieved July 2006, used with permission.

4. Tanase, M. (March 11, 2003), IP Spoofing: An Introduction, www.securityfocus.com/infocus/1674, retrieved August 2006.

5. DARPA, 1981a. Internet Program, Protocol Specification, September 1981, prepared for, Defense Advanced Research Projects Agency, Information Processing Techniques Office, 1400 Wilson Boulevard, Arlington, Virginia22209, Information Sciences Institute University of Southern California, 4676 Admiralty Way, Marina del Rey, California90291, September 1981, www.faqs.org/rfcs/rfc791.html, retrieved August 2006.

6. DARPA, 1981b, Transmission Control Protocol (TCP), DARPA Internet Program, Protocol Specification, September 1981, prepared for, Defense Advanced Research Projects Agency, Information Processing Techniques Office, 1400 Wilson Boulevard, Arlington, Virginia22209, Information Sciences Institute University of Southern California, 4676 Admiralty Way, Marina del Rey, California90291, September 1981, www.faqs.org/rfcs/rfc791.html, retrieved August 2006.

7. ISS, 2006 Spoofing www.iss.net/security_center/advice/Underground/Hacking/Methods/Technical/Spoofing/default.htm, Internet Security Systems, Inc., 6303 Barfield Road, Atlanta, GA 30328, retrieved August 2006, used with permission.

8. Computer Incident Advisory Committee (CIAC) (1995). Advisory Notice F-08 Internet Spoofing and Hijacked Session Attacks. [On-line], Available: http://ciac.llnl.gov/ciac/bulletins/f-08/shtml, retrieved August 2006.

9. Polymorphic Code (July 19, 2006). In Wikipedia, The Free Encyclopedia. http://en.wikipedia.org/w/index.php?title=Polymorphic_code&oldid=64589128.retrieved 14:34, August 4, 2006.

10. Moir, R. (2003), Defining Malware, FAQ, Published: October 1, 2003, Microsoft Corporation, One Microsoft Way, Redmond, Washington 98052-6399 U. S. A, www.microsoft.com/info/cpyright.mspx, retrieved August 2006.

11. South Carolina Code of Laws, 2005. Title 16 - Crimes and Offenses, Chapter 16, Computer Crime Act, Section 16-16-10. Definitions, www.scstatehouse.net/code/t16c016.htm, retrieved August 2006.

12. Bauer, F. L. Decrypted Secrets: Methods and Maxims of Cryptology, 3rd ed. Springer-Verlag, New York, 2002.

13. Hosmer, C. and Hyde, C. (2003), Discovering Covert Digital Evidence, WetStone Technologies, Inc., chet@wetstonetech.com, Digital Forensic Research Workshop, 2003, http://www.dfrws.org/2003/presentations/Paper-Hosmer-digitalevidence.pdf, retrieved August 2006, used with permission.

14. Kessler, G. (July 2004), An Overview of Steganography for the Computer Forensics Examiner, Forensic Science Communications, Volume 6, Number 3, www.fbi.gov/hq/lab/fsc/backissu/july2004/research/2004_03_research01.htm, retrieved August 2006, used with permission.

15. Geiger, M. (2005). Evaluating Commercial Counter-Forensic Tools, Carnegie Mellon University, Pittsburgh, PA, mgeiger@cmu.edu, 2005 Digital Forensic Research Workshop (DFRWS) 11, New Orleans, LA, www.dfrws.org/2005/proceedings/geiger_couterforensics.pdf, retrieved August 2006.

16. Yasinsac, A. and Manzano, Y. (2001), Policies to Enhance Computer and Network Forensics. Proceedings of the 2001 IEEE Workshop on Information Assurance and Security, United States Military Academy, West Point, New York, 5–6 June, 2001. www.itoc.usma.edu/Workshop/2001/Authors/Submitted_Abstracts/paperW2B3(37).pdf, retrieved August 2006.

17. Liu, V. (2006), Managing Director, Stach & Liu, LLC, Phoenix, AZ, personal interview via phone and e-mail, September 2006.

18. Indiana University (2006), Technology Services, What is a swap file? http://kb.iu.edu/data/aagb.html, retrieved September 2006.

19. NTI (2006), Windows Swap/Page File Defined, www.forensics-intl.com/def7.html, retrieved September 2006, Armor Forensics, 13386 International Parkway, Jacksonville, FL 32218, (800) 852-0300, info@forensics-intl.com

20. Jetico (2006), What is a slack file and is it okay to delete? www.jetico.com/index.htm#/bcwipe_faq. htm, retrieved September 2006, Jetico, Inc., Innopoli 2, Tekniikantie 14, 02150 Espoo, Finland, +358-9-251 73030.

21. Lange, M. C. S. (2004), Technology You Should Know: Using File Slack to Track Down Electronic Data, www.krollontrack.com/newsletters/cybercrime/jun04.html, Kroll Ontrack, 9023 Columbine Road, Eden Prairie, MN 55347, (800) 347-6105, retrieved September 2006.

22. Ghosting. Wikipedia, The Free Encyclopedia. 20 September 2006, 21:26 UTC. Wikimedia Foundation, Inc. 27 September 2006, http://en.wikipedia.org/w/index.php?title=Ghosting&oldid=76863876

23. Kozierok, C. (2004), PC File Systems, www.pcguide.com/ref/hdd/file/file_FAT32.htm, The PC Guide, www.PCGuide.com, retrieved October 2006, used with permission.

24. NTFS (2006b), NTFS The Basics, www.ntfs.com/hard-disk-basics.htm, reprinted with permission of LSoft Technologies, LSoft Technologies Inc., 2550 Argentia Road, Suite 218, Mississauga Ontario, CANADA L5N 5R1, (877) 477-3553, www.NTFS.com, retrieved October, 2006.

25. NTFS (2006a), File Storage Hardware and Disk Organization, www.ntfs.com/hard-disk-basics.htm, reprinted with permission of LSoft Technologies, LSoft Technologies Inc., 2550 Argentia Road, Suite 218, Mississauga Ontario, CANADA L5N 5R1, (877) 477–3553, www.NTFS.com, retrieved October 2006.

26. Waldron, D. (2006), Cutting the Slack: (or maybe the Fat!), DEW Associates Corporation, 1 Ridge Circle, Sussex, NJ 07461, (973) 702-0545, www.dewassoc.com/kbase/hard_drives/fat_slack.htm, retrieved November 2006, used with permission.

27. Augur, W. (December 2, 2004b), Hiding Data in Filesystem Slack Space with BMAP, http://users. ece.gatech.edu/~owen/Academic/ECE4112/Fall2004/fall2004.htm, used with permission, retrieved October 2006.

28. Augur, W. (December 2, 2004a), Data Hiding on NTFS with Alternate Data Streams, http://users. ece.gatech.edu/~owen/Academic/ECE4112/Fall2004/fall2004.htm, used with permission, retrieved October 2006.

29. Cook, R. (September 16, 2005), Alternate Data Streams: Threat or Menace? www.informit.com/articles/article.asp?p=413685&seqNum=6&rl=1, retrieved October 2006.

30. Gupta, M. Hoeschele, M., and Rogers, M. (Fall 2006), Hidden Disk Areas: HPA and DCO, International Journal of Digital Evidence, Volume 5, Issue 1, www.utica.edu/academic/institutes/ecii/publications/articles/EFE36584-D13F-2962-67BEB146864A2671.pdf, retrieved January 2007, used with permission.

31. Ryburn, J. (2007), Forensic Eavesdropping: Analyzing Voice Over IP.

32. Mullins, M. (February 9, 2006), How do I. Make sure security logs exhibit accurate time with NTP? TechRepublic, http://articles.techrepublic.com.com/5100-1009_11-6034571.html, retrieved January 2007. Used with permission from CNET Networks, Inc., Copyright 2007. All rights reserved.

33. Davis, D. (May 26, 2005), Synchronize a Cisco router's clock with Network Time Protocol (NTP), TechRepublic, http://articles.techrepublic.com.com/5100-1035_11-5712046.html, retrieved January 2007. Used with permission from CNET Networks, Inc., Copyright 2007. All rights reserved.

34. Butler, J. and Sparks, S. (November 11, 2004), Windows rootkits of 2005, part one, www.securityfocus.com/infocus/1850, retrieved January 2007.

35. Taylor, G. (January 30, 2006), Motherboard chips latest target for rootkit hackers, www.contractoruk. com/news/002490.html, retrieved January 2007.

36. Ivanov, I. (April 6, 2002), API Hooking Revealed, www.codeproject.com/system/hooksys.asp.

37. Gebhardt, M., Illies, G., and Schindler, W. (October 31, 2005), A Note on the Practical Value of Single Hash Collisions for Special File Formats, Bundesamt für Sicherheit in der Informationstechnik, (BSI) Godesberger Allee 185–189, 53175 Bonn, Germany, http://csrc.nist.gov/pki/HashWorkshop/2005/Oct31_Presentations/Illies_NIST_05.pdf, retrieved January 2007.

38. DSS (2006), Social Engineering, www.dss.mil/training/csg/security/V1comput/Social.htm, Defense Security Service (DSS) developed by the Defense Personnel Security Research Center (PERSEREC), retrieved August 2006.

Bibliography

Delp. E. (2005), Security, Steganography, and Watermarking of Multimedia Contents VII (Proceedings of SPIE), SPIE Society of Photo-Optical Instrumentation Engineering, ISBN: 819456543.

Dunin, E. (2006), *The Mammoth Book of Secret Codes and Cryptograms*, Carroll & Graf Publishers, ISBN: 786717262.

Ferguson, N. (2003), *Practical Cryptography*, John Wiley & Sons Inc., ISBN: 471223573.

Petitcolas, F. (1999), *Information Hiding Techniques for Steganography and Digital Watermarking*, Artech House, ISBN:1580530354.

Stinson, D. (2005), *Cryptography Theory and Practice*, Chapman & Hall/CRC, ISBN: 584885084.

Wayner, P. (2002), Disappearing Cryptography: Information Hiding—Steganography and Watermarking (The Morgan Kaufmann Series in Software Engineering and Programming), ISBN:1558607692.

Chapter 4

Hardware: Model System Platforms

Introduction

In recent years computer technology has taken quantum leaps making computers smaller, faster, more user friendly and capable of storing large amounts of data. Computers of the 21st century are also coming in different forms, shapes, and sizes. There are desktops, laptops, tablets, PDAs, and even cell phones today are fully equipped, capable of being classified as mini computers.

A vast majority of people uses at least one of these data storage or manipulation devices, and many others use more than one and on a daily basis. But using a computer and understanding how it works are two very different things. In today's world most people have at least a basic knowledge of how to use a computer. However what most people do not have is an understanding of how a computer works—on the inside.

This chapter is designed to provide the reader with a basic understanding and insight into the various hardware components, which the reader would expect to see (find), when actually opening the exterior shell of most typical, common computing devices available on the market today, and which the cyber forensic investigator may encounter in the normal course of an investigation.

Remember, any device capable of recording and storing digital, audio, and video data, represents a device, which may contain evidential information, that the cyber forensic investigator may elect to examine. Knowledge of what these devices are and how they work and are put together will aid the cyber forensic investigator in deciding upon a proper, safe, and forensically prudent investigative path.

Computers

The first step in knowing, where to look for information is to determine, what exactly you are looking at. And yes, the inside of a computer can be a little scary. There are a lot of wires, boards,

Figure 4.1a   End user work station with tower.

and things that you just are not sure what they do. It is confusing, intimidating and frustrating—and that is ok.

But once you start to break it down and take it apart, literally, it is easier than you think to understand, and most of the mystery disappears.

Let us start with the basics. Most desktop computers have what is called a tower that holds the insides of a computer and looks like Figures 4.1a and 4.1b.

Figure 4.1b   Desktop computer tower.

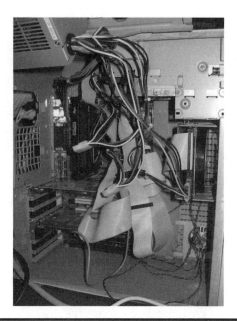

Figure 4.2   Components of the computer.

Within the tower are all of the pieces that make the computer run. When you take off the side cover of the tower you can see all the components of the computer (see Figure 4.2).

Again, a confusing mass of electronics, but it gets easier. The starting point for this tower is called the motherboard. By itself it looks like Figure 4.3.

The motherboard alone is not so intimidating. Think of it as a room with a bunch of power outlets. Each "outlet" has been designated for a certain "appliance" in the computer. The appliances

Figure 4.3   Computer motherboard.

Figure 4.4   Expansion slots.

attached to the motherboard can include a variety of devices and cards, such as sound cards, Network Interface Controller Cards (NIC cards) floppy drives, CD or DVD drives, etc.

The appliances that fall into the card category: sound cards, video cards, network cards, etc., are inserted into what are called expansion slots. These expansion slots do exactly that, they expand the computer's capabilities (Figure 4.4).

In most of today's computers, audio, video, networking, Universal Serial Bus (USB), and firewire are all frequently built into the motherboard. This allows the motherboard to have free expansion slots that can be used for other cards. The reason these expansion slots are valuable is because of their ability to allow cards to be swapped out or replaced (Figure 4.5). You can actually see the card's port through the back of the computer. For additional information, see Appendix J.

Floppy drives, zip drives, CD ROM or DVD drives all attach to the motherboard using what are called IDE cables (Figure 4.6). IDE stands for Integrated Drive Electronics. These cables resemble flat pieces of ribbon and they go between the motherboard and the drive. Since these drives are not directly connected to the motherboard, these cables allow the drives to be placed away from the motherboard, and in the front of the tower case where they are accessible to the user.

Figure 4.5   Expansion card in slot on motherboard.

Figure 4.6   IDE cable.

Power Supply

To make all of this work, you need power. The power supply is also attached to the motherboard through its own outlet and is located near the back of the tower casing. You can see where the power supply is on a computer if you look at the back of the tower.

On the back of the machine, there is a fan vent near a power inlet. That is the power supply. Inside the tower, the power supply is usually a metal box, and is directly attached to the incoming power cord from the back of the computer, which is plugged into the outlet of the home or office.

From the power supply there are colorful wires that run to each of the computer's internal parts requiring power, like the motherboard (Figure 4.7). Anything connected to the motherboard using IDE cables does not get their power from the motherboard but instead are directly connected to the power supply, which is why the power box has multiple cords (Figure 4.8).

One of the most important "appliances" plugged into the motherboard's outlet is the hard drive.

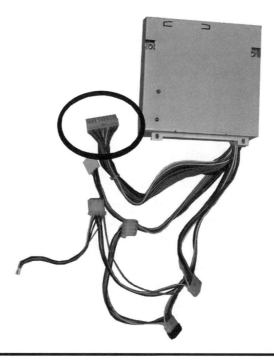

Figure 4.7   Power supply.

Figure 4.8   Power supply connected to motherboard.

Hard Drive

In the computer the hard drive has a protective covering. But once it is removed, a computer's hard drive has a striking resemblance to a record player (see Figures 4.9a–c).

What looks like the needle is, what is called the read or write head and does exactly that. It writes the information that you save to the "record" or platter as it is called.

From the side view you can tell that there are multiple layers of platters. It can also "play" or read the data that has been written to it. A hard drive is permanent storage space on your computer.

To give an example of how it works, say you write a letter in a text editor such as Microsoft Word. You finish the letter but are not interested in printing at the moment so you save it. While you have been working on your letter it was stored in RAM, which again is the temporary storage area for things you have open and are working on (any time you open a program and are working on something it is temporarily saved in RAM, there will be more detail on that later).

When you are finished with the letter and you go to file SAVE AS and you save your letter, unless you have decided to save it to an external storage device (we will get to those in a minute), the letter will be written to the hard drive. Whether you are saving it to the desktop, the My Documents folder, or anywhere else, it is still on the hard drive.

The hard drive can store different amounts of memory just depending on how big or small a drive the user decides to have installed in his or her computer. The drive actually looks like a metal box. The back of the hard drive has a few connectors that need to be explained.

In Figure 4.10 you can see the four pins that accept a power cord from the power supply. There will also be 40 pins on the back of the hard drive that will accept the IDE cable to link to the

Figure 4.9a   Hard drive protective covering.

motherboard. This cable will be the cable that transports the data to and from the drive and the motherboard.

On the back of the drive will also be a series of pins that are jumper-setting pins. These are the pins that control how the motherboard and its BIOS, basic input output system, treat the drive.

Depending upon the placement of the jumper (see Figure 4.11), which is a small piece of plastic lined with metal that is used to connect two of the pins, the drive can be set to a number of different options, such as master, slave, and cable select. Usually when a hard drive fails to boot in a system, an error has been made in the placement of the jumper. Since there are multiple devices that require placement on IDE cables, the jumper placement on these devices is vital. Commonly there

Figure 4.9b   Hard drive–side view.

Figure 4.9c   Hard drive–top view.

are two devices that use the same cable to connect to the motherboard. For example, if two hard drives are on the same IDE cable, the one whose jumper pins have been set to master will be the boot drive. The other hard drive, therefore, cannot be set as master and must subsequently be set as a slave device.

CD-ROM, DVD-ROM, floppy, and zip drives all have similar connections to those of the hard drive. The backs of these drives will contain a four-pin area that is used to connect the power source to the drive; those colorful cables come into play again. The drive will also have a grouping of 40 pins that are used to connect the IDE cable to the drive.

Jumper pins will also be present on the back of the drive and perform the same tasks as described in the hard drive section. The drives also have a group of pins that give audio output to the soundcard. This audio output may also run to the motherboard, as some motherboards have onboard sound cards.

Figure 4.10   Hard drive–back view.

Figure 4.11   Jumper.

Motherboard

There are a few things that come attached to the motherboard and are necessary for the computer to work. The CPU, RAM memory, and ROM memory are some examples. The CPU is commonly known as "the brain" of the computer and stands for Central Processing Unit (Figure 4.12).

This is where all the processing, is done. It takes all the information that the user gives it then reacts by following the instructions, doing mathematical equations, etc. The CPU is a very important part of the computer; actually the computer could not function without it. It would be like a human trying to function without their brain (hence calling the CPU "the brain" of the computer).

Figure 4.12   Motherboard–showing CPU.

For an example, if someone asked you to write something your brain tells your hand to pick up a pen and piece of paper. If a user wants to print something, the CPU takes that request from the user and tells the printer to print the page.

When people talk about how fast their computer is, they are usually referring to the CPU, which is measured in MegaHertz. It can be found on the motherboard and looks deceptively small. But remember, big things come in small packages.

Random access memory is also attached to the motherboard and is visible as small boards.

A computer itself will store data in RAM or Random Access Memory or in ROM, Read Only Memory. RAM is a temporary storage area and this temporary storage area will be deleted once the computer has been shut off or it has lost its power source, like after you have been working on something for two hours have not saved it yet and then you accidentally kick the cord out of the socket shutting the computer down.

ROM however is read only memory and contains instructions that cannot be modified and are used to run the computer itself. These instructions tell the CPU what to do once the computer is turned on, this will be further explained below.

For all the things that RAM does it is very small and is about the width of a ruler and about six inches long (see Figure 4.13).

An example of ROM can be found on the motherboard and is used to control the Basic Input Output System of the computer, or BIOS.

The BIOS is a software component that is placed in the ROM of the motherboard to protect memory from any potential crashes that the computer may suffer (Figure 4.14). The BIOS of the computer is the system programs, that start the computer and which performs the routine checks that ensure that the required accessories, like the keyboard, RAM, the monitor, and the hard drive, are installed and functional.

The BIOS also examines the RAM of the system and actually iterates through each address of memory to test its functionality. Although the BIOS is stored in ROM, it is possible to update the BIOS with new features or updates to allow it to support newer hardware components. This is done through a process called flashing, allowing certain parts of the BIOS to be updated while other parts of the BIOS cannot be changed—to guard against the possibility of destroying the ability of the computer to boot.

Laptops

Most laptops do not have the floppy disk drives that desktops have, but they do have USB ports, hard drives, and many come standard with CD drives or even DVD writers and readers. Some are even configured with digital camera card readers.

Figure 4.13 RAM.

Figure 4.14 Motherboard–showing BIOS.

Figure 4.15a Laptop computer.

Figure 4.15b   Lifting keyboard to access laptop components.

Figure 4.15c   Laptop keyboard–lifted to show components.

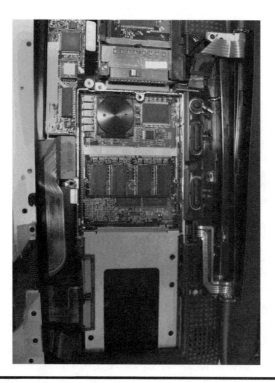

Figure 4.15d   Laptop motherboard.

As mentioned before laptops or notebooks as they are sometimes called, have all the components of a desktop computer just on a smaller scale. In addition, they are completely portable, can run on AC power or off batteries for a period of time, allowing people to use them on planes, in coffee shops, at school, work, home, anywhere.

Laptops can weigh between four to ten pounds, given their size and configuration as selected by the user. Typically lighter weight laptops are selected by users who travel frequently or are working

Figure 4.15e   Laptop RAM.

Figure 4.16 5¼ inch floppy disk.

from a mobile platform, not restricted to the typical office environment, and who want the connivance of portability, and are willing to forgo some of the luxuries found in a full-blown desktop or tower model.

There will be the hard drive and then most of the rest of the storage will be external, either through USB drives, external hard drives, CDs, DVDs, etc. See the following figures for a look at the inside of a laptop (Figures 4.15b–4.15e).

Figure 4.17 3½ inch floppy disk.

Figure 4.18   USB drive.

Tablets

A tablet PC is basically an ordinary laptop, only it has the ability for the user to write directly upon the screen, or monitor. The accompanying software and hardware configuration of a tablet PC then translates that written information into digital data.

To write upon the screen, the user writes with a stylus that is very similar to a pen or pencil, only the instrument does not contain any ink or marking abilities. Tablet computers give the user, the ability to either use the keyboard and the mouse to provide input, or use the stylus to operate the computer. Many of these computers have the ability to perform character recognition and can therefore take the user's writing and transform it into text, which the computer can read and understand. Tablet computers also give the user the ability to operate an onscreen keyboard that can be operated just like the normal keyboard, only with a stylus.

External Storage

External storage devices are used for extra space, portability, and convenience. These are devices separate and are detachable from the computer and they can contain data and information. If you

Figure 4.19   External hard drive.

are familiar with computers more than likely you have come across one or more type of external storage such as floppy disks.

Originally, floppy disks were the first form of external storage and were 5¼-inches and literally floppy, as they were made out of flexible plastic (Figure 4.16). Currently "floppy" disks are 3½-inches and made out of a harder plastic that does not bend (Figure 4.17). However, these disks have only about 1.44 megabytes of storage, which is not much anymore, and are being quickly replaced with USB drives. "Floppy" disks are so called because of the floppy magnetic medium inside of the plastic 5¼ or 3½-inch protective case.

The USB drive holds several times the amount of storage capacity of floppy disks, are less than half the size and are extremely portable. The USB drives also go by such names as jump drives, flash drives and keys (Figure 4.18). It is common to see people carry the USB drives on their keychain or possibly even around their necks, especially in a business or educational atmosphere.

An additional characteristic of the USB drive is that it can be used on both Macintosh and PC computers, which comes in handy when working between the two different kinds of computers.

An external hard drive is another external storage device, which is exactly what it sounds like (Figure 4.19). A computer's internal hard drive that we discussed earlier (which is a standard feature on every computer) can hold ever increasing amount of data.

An external hard drive works the same and connects to the computer in the way the USB drive does, through the USB ports, or it can also be connected via firewire (firewire is a wire used to transfer data from a digital device to the computer at a high rate of speed. It works with such things as external hard drives, scanners, digital cameras, and digital video cameras (see Figure 4.20).

External hard drives also work in the same way as they can store various amounts of data depending on the size of the magnetic platters on the inside.

In addition to these devices, Compact Discs (CDs) and Digital Video Discs or Digital Versatile Discs (DVDs) can be used (Figure 4.21). CDs can have a storage capacity of 650 or 700 megabytes. There are two types of CDs that can have data written to them:

CD writable disks (CD-Rs)
CD rewritable disks (CD-RWs)

CD-Rs have the ability to have data written on them one time only. This only means that data may not be erased once it is written. CD-Rs can, however, be written to multiple times.

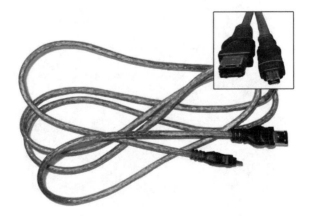

Figure 4.20 Firewire.

Figure 4.21 CD/DVD.

It is possible, for example, to write data to the CD–R and then write more data to it in the future, as long as the CD–R was not "finalized," which is the process that prevents any further data to be written to the CD–R. CD–RWs, on the other hand, have the ability to be rewritten thousands of times. CD–RWs can be utilized in the same format as a floppy disk, with the ability to have data written, changed, and then rewritten.

Similar to CDs, DVDs exist in several different varieties. The different types of DVDs include:

DVD–R
DVD+R
DVD–RW
DVD+RW
DVD–RAM

DVD–R and DVD+R are similar to the CD–R in the sense that they can only be written on one time, with differences between the "plus" and "minus" formats being minimal.

DVD–RW, DVD+RW, and DVD–RAM are all versions of DVDs that can be written and rewritten more than once and are similar to the CD–RWs described above.

The differences in storage capacities are found in the attributes of the disk; whether the disk has one or two layers or one or two sides. Standard single layered, single sided DVDs have a capacity of 4.7 gigabytes. Dual layered, single sided DVDs have a capacity of 8.5 gigabytes. Dual sided, single layered DVDs have a capacity of 9.4 gigabytes. Dual sided, dual layered DVDs have a capacity of 17 gigabytes.

Zip disks are also available for storage. These disks look similar to floppies but hold more data (Figure 4.22).

On average while the floppy holds only 1.44 megabytes of data, the zip disk can hold 100 to 250 megabytes of data. The drives for these disks can be internal (as previously discussed) or they can be an external addition to a computer.

Figure 4.22   ZIP disk.

All of these external storage devices are highly sensitive to magnetic fields and care should be taken to make sure that these external media are protected from accidental or intentional destruction, manipulation or misuse and mishandling, any of which may permanently invalidate any data collected from further forensic analysis and use as evidence.

Servers

Servers do not differ greatly from the desktop computers commonly found throughout offices. A server is basically a centralized computer located within an environment, connected to one or many client computers.

A client computer is any computer that connects to another computer to use the services the host (or server) provides. For example, the use of your computer and its corresponding web browser to retrieve information from a Web site would constitute a client or server relationship, with your computer being the client and the web server of the site being the server. Servers can have many purposes and are used to control applications, databases, and web services.

The inner components of servers are very similar to those of desktop computers, but may have a few subtle differences. Since servers are usually very processing intensive, servers may contain significantly larger amounts of Random Access Memory than desktop computers along with significantly larger storage space, i.e., hard disk drives.

Servers may also house multiple CPUs to perform their specialized tasks. Servers can be used to store and run applications that are then made available to the client computers. Servers can also be used to hold database software and storage. Servers housing database software can contain a wealth of information hidden behind tables, primary keys, and relationships.

Although these data are technically not hidden in the sense that they are invisible, the ability to decipher these data may not be intuitive to the casual observer without prior database knowledge or expertise. Depending on the purpose of the designated server, it can provide a variety of tasks to its client computers as described above, and process that information for the client computers to interpret. Depending upon the needs and requirements of the server or servers, certain components within the server may be upgraded from the standard hardware used in client side machines. In fact, the hardware available for and in use in desktops today, surpass the hardware that was used only a few decades ago costing millions of dollars and taking up multiple rooms.

iPods®

Nonessential devices, such as the portable audio players that are very popular, come equipped with either flash memory or hard disk drives. These devices are very similar to USB drives and hard disk drives. Portable audio players, such as the iPod, come in both formats and include operating systems conducive to the sorting and playing of music and very little else.

Devices such as the above have the ability to store large amounts of data and could be used to store data either in a music format or a considerable amount of other data that is usually found in personal information managers. In addition to being a portable music player, devices like the iPod are a form of personal information manager and can store calendars, contact numbers, photos, and videos—all potential electronic evidence (see Figure 4.23).

Figure 4.23   iPod.

Figure 4.24   Personal digital assistant.

PDAs

Personal digital assistants, or PDAs as they are more commonly known, are a breed of small computers. These little computers have the ability to be extremely portable, more so than a laptop and are becoming increasingly smaller (Figure 4.24).

PDAs have gained popularity in recent years and in addition to becoming smaller, they are also becoming less expensive. These devices, with the ability to house a vast array of information, can help to divulge even some of the most intimate details of someone's life.

PDAs are a form of personal information management tools that can include phone, e-mail or address contact lists, calendars, e-mail messages, and documents (Figure 4.25).

The role of the PDA is to collect, maintain, and provide useful information about events or people in someone's life. A PDA is a great source of information, quite literally capable of providing a detailed description, albeit electronically, of someone's life, relationships, habits, and activities.

Mobile phones are beginning to take the form of personal information managers, as they no longer contain only the capacity to store phone numbers. Mobile phones are gaining processing power and memory capacity so that they are more capable and able to provide such features as calendars, web browsers, contact lists, cameras, and files such as music files.

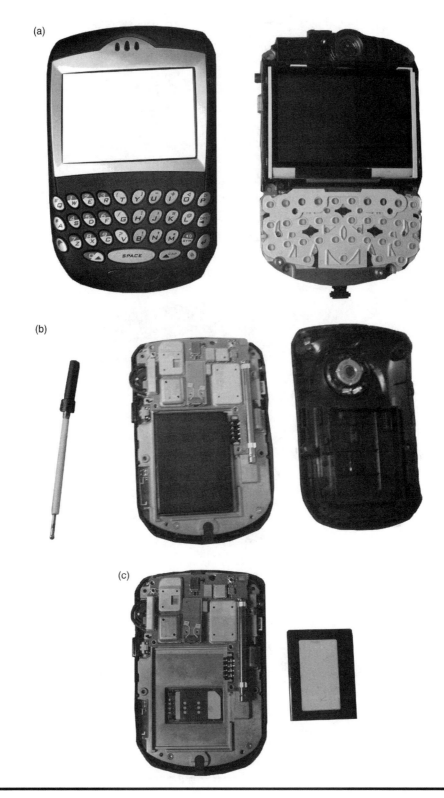

Figure 4.25 PDA components and SIM card.

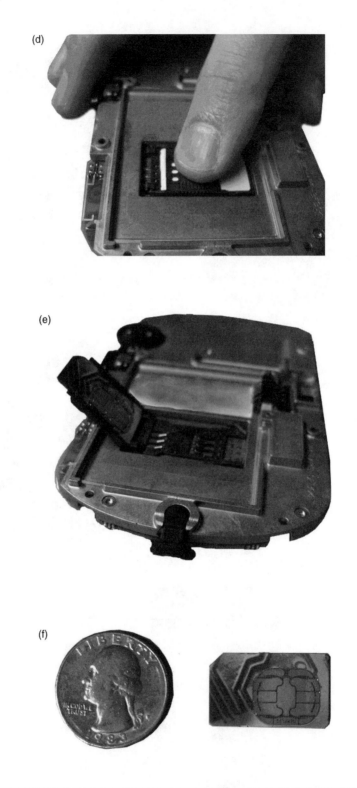

Figure 4.25 (Continued).

Figure 4.26a   Mobile phone.

Most of this information is stored on the mobile phone's internal flash memory. There is, however, a limited amount of storage capacity available on a mobile phone's SIM card. The SIM card is a Subscriber Identity Module that is actually a small piece of a smart card. A smart card is about the same size as a credit card and is similar to credit cards in the sense that they both have the ability to store data. The smart card, however, is able to store more data than the credit card and does so in a small metallic chip embedded in the front of the card.

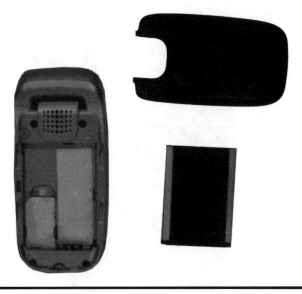

Figure 4.26b   Mobile phone components.

Figure 4.26c   Mobile phone SIM card.

The SIM card of the mobile phone, which is usually found underneath the battery pack of the phone (see Figure 4.26c), stores information about the subscriber's network, the subscriber's phone number, and the subscriber's phone book among other things, and may utilize some security in the form of a PIN number that could be necessary to access the SIM card's data or allow the card to operate in a mobile phone.

Although the SIM card may not be found on every mobile phone, as it is dependent upon the configuration and technology of the mobile network, it is becoming more popular as the global system for mobile communication, or GSM, gains acceptance throughout the world. The use of a SIM card, for example, allows the holder of the SIM card to place the card in any phone capable of accepting SIM cards and permits the phone to assume the telephone number of the SIM card.

This is contingent on the assumption that the phone accepting the SIM card is able to use the network band the card operates on and the provider of the cellular service.

Recent developments in technology have now given mobile phone networks the ability to transfer data wirelessly to devices. This technology has made it possible for mobile phones to connect to the Internet and transmit data. The ability of phones to connect to the Internet allows mobile phone users the ability to search for data through their phone, in addition to being able to send e-mail and instant messages from the same phone.

Many mobile phones now come equipped with high quality six to eight mega pixel cameras that have the ability to capture pictures and even video clips with audio. These pictures or video clips can then be sent to e-mail addresses or other mobile phones. Such data capture represents potential evidence, which the cyber forensic investigator must be prepared to analyze, if it is determined that such devices contain electronic data, which may be of value or interest pertaining to the investigation under way.

Summary

Data written to any medium discussed in this chapter can typically be recovered. The cyber forensic investigator should take great care in the collection and preservation of data on any device, since devices that seemingly have no identifiable data can have their file structures rewritten and "lost" or deleted data made accessible and viewable.

The deletion of any file off of any device, for example a hard disk drive, does not permanently delete the file. The deletion of the file only erases the pointers to the actual file or its pieces. The deletion of files or the reformatting of a hard drive will leave the actual files within the device but free up the space that was allocated to them.

Therefore, the installation or saving of additional files on the device, after files have been deleted, could result in the reallocation of the space that was once occupied by the deleted file. This means that it is especially important that the computer system be left as it had been found.

There are programs, however, that claim to make it impossible to recover deleted data. There is only one flaw with this belief: these programs that claim to completely erase the data without a trace, must write over the data according to some predefined algorithm. The discovery of this algorithm will allow one to undelete the overwritten files and recover the data stored within the device.

As discussed in Chapter 3, there are many ways in which a potential suspect may attempt to conceal illegal activities or attempt to hide data; Chapter 4 has provided a glimpse into where those data may reside, from the physical nature of the computer's hardware architecture.

Chapter 5 will provide the reader with information that describes what a "typical" software application environment might look like, and what software a cyber forensic investigator may typically encounter during an investigation. The reader will be presented, in Chapter 5, with a basic introduction to the typical system and application software which he or she may encounter as they conduct their forensic examination, and how they should maneuver their way through these various types of software.

Chapter 5

Software: Operating Systems, Network Traffic, and Applications

Introduction

In Chapter 4, the authors examined the various hardware components that the cyber forensics investigator might encounter. The information contained within this chapter is intended as a reference and to provide an overview of the various software components that the cyber forensic investigator should have familiarity with. These software components are divided into three distinct categories: operating systems, network traffic, and applications.

Web sites included in this chapter are intended to provide current and accurate information; however, it is impossible for anyone (read authors, publisher, etc.) to warrant that the information contained on the sites is accurate or timely.

Relying on information contained on these sites is done at one's own risk. Use of such information is voluntary, and reliance on it should only be undertaken after an independent review of its accuracy, completeness, efficacy, and timeliness. As such, users of this information are advised and encouraged to confirm specific claims for product performance as necessary and appropriate.

Any mention of commercial products or reference to commercial organizations is for information only; it does not imply recommendation or endorsement by the authors, publisher, reviewers, contributors, or representatives nor does it imply that the products mentioned are necessarily the best available for the purpose.

It is worth noting; that no single text, guideline, or reference book can adequately and definitively cover all of the various operating systems, network components, and software applications. It is the responsibility of the cyber forensic investigator to (a) have a thorough understanding of the environment and case specifics of the investigation to be performed and (b) to assess and know the specifics of the software components that will be investigated.

Failing to heed these precautions and to assess one's skills and abilities in utilizing the tools reviewed here, is both unethical and places everyone involved in the investigation at risk.

Good! Now that, that has been said, let's begin our review of software, operating systems, network traffic and applications.

National Institute of Standards and Technology (NIST)

From automated teller machines and atomic clocks to mammograms and semiconductors, innumerable products and services rely in some way on technology, measurement, and standards provided by the NIST.

To that end, NIST is a federal technology agency that develops and promotes measurement, standards, and technology.

Material in this chapter was synthesized from an outstanding and rather lengthy (121 pages) NIST document published in August 2006, entitled Guide to Integrating Forensic Techniques into Incident Response. In some circles this document is known by a more subdued title, simply Special Publication 800-86. NIST developed this document in furtherance of its statutory responsibilities under the Federal Information Security Management Act (FISMA) of 2002, Public Law 107-347.

While use of NIST material by nongovernmental organizations is done so on a voluntary basis and is not subject to copyright, the authors wish to thank and to acknowledge here Karen Kent, Suzanne Chevalier, Tim Grance, and Hung Dang, the individuals who researched, compiled, and crafted Special Publication 800-86 into its final form. The authors wish to thank these professionals for their contribution both to the larger field of cyber forensics, and specifically assisting in providing you the reader with a better understanding of the various software components that the 21st century cyber forensic investigator may encounter on any given day, on any given investigation.

Those interested in reviewing the entire NIST document are referred to the following URL: http://csrc.nist.gov/publications/nistpubs/800-86/SP800-86.pdf.

Using Data from Operating Systems

An operating system is a program that runs on a computer and provides a software platform on which other programs can run. In addition, an operating system is responsible for processing input commands from a user, sending output to a display, interacting with storage devices to store and retrieve data, and controlling peripheral devices such as printers and modems.

Some common operating systems for workstations or servers include various versions of Windows, Linux, UNIX, and Mac operating system. Some network devices, such as routers, have their own proprietary operating systems (e.g., Cisco Internetwork Operating System). PDAs often run specialized operating systems, including PalmOS and Windows CE. Many embedded systems, such as cellular phones, digital cameras, and audio players, also use operating systems.

This chapter discusses the components of an operating system that might be relevant to the cyber forensic investigator and provides guidance on collecting, examining, and analyzing data from common workstation and server operating systems.

Operating System Basics

Operating system data exists in both non-volatile and volatile states. Non-volatile data refers to data that persists even after a computer is powered down, such as a file system stored on a hard drive. Volatile data refers to data on a live system that is lost after a computer is powered down, such as the current network connections to and from the system. Many types of non-volatile and volatile data may be of interest from a cyber forensics perspective.

Non-Volatile Data

The primary source of non-volatile data within an operating system is the file system. The file system is also usually the largest and richest source of data within the operating system, containing most of the information recovered during a typical forensic event. The file system provides storage for the operating system on one or more media. A file system typically contains many types of files, each of which may be of value to cyber forensic investigators in different situations. In addition, important residual data can be recovered from unused file system space. Several types of data that are commonly found within operating system file systems are as follows:

■ Configuration Files—The operating system may use configuration files to store operating system and application settings. On Widows systems, many configuration settings reside in a set of special files know as the registry. For more information on the Windows registry, see Microsoft Knowledge Base article 256986, "Description of the Microsoft Windows Registry," available at: http://support.microsoft.com/?id=256986.

For example, configuration files could list the services to be started automatically after system boot, and specify the location of log files and temporary files. Users might also have individual operating system and application configuration files that contain user-specific information and preferences, such as hardware-related settings (e.g., screen resolution, printer settings) and file associations. Configuration files of particular interest include:

- Users and Groups—The operating system keeps a record of its user accounts and groups. Account information may include group membership, account name and description, account permissions, account status (e.g., active, disabled), and the path to the account's home directory.
- Password Files—The operating system may store password hashes in data files. Various password-cracking utilities may be used to convert a password hash to its clear text equivalent for certain operating systems.
- Scheduled Jobs—The operating system maintains a list of scheduled tasks that are to be performed automatically at a certain time (e.g., perform a virus scan every week). Information that can be gleaned from this include the task name, the program used to perform the task, command line switches and arguments, and the days and times when the task is to be performed.
- Logs—Operating system log files contain information about various operating system events, and may also hold application-specific event information. Depending on the operating system, logs may be stored in text files, proprietary-format binary files, or databases. Some operating systems write log entries to two or more separate files. The types of information typically found in operating system logs are as follows:
  - System Events—System events are operational actions performed by operating system components, such as shutting down the system or starting a service. Typically, failed events and the most significant successful events are logged, but many operating systems permit system administrators to specify which types of events will be logged. The details logged for each event also vary widely. Each event is usually time stamped; other supporting information could include event codes, status codes, and username.

- ● Audit Records—Audit records contain security event information such as successful and failed authentication attempts and security policy changes. Operating systems typically permit system administrators to specify which types of events should be audited. Administrators also can configure some operating systems to log successful, failed, or all attempts to perform certain actions.
- ● Application Events—Application events are significant operational actions performed by applications, such as application startup and shutdown, application failures, and major application configuration changes.
- ● Command History—Some operating systems have separate log files (typically for each user) that contain a history of the operating system commands performed by each user.
- ● Recently Accessed Files—An operating system might log the most recent file accesses or other usage, creating a list of the most recently accessed files.

- ■ Application Files—Applications can be composed many types of files, including executables, scripts, documentation, configuration files, log files, history files, graphics, sounds, and icons.
- ■ Data Files—Data files store information for applications. Examples of common data files are text files, word processing documents, spreadsheets, databases, audio files, and graphics files. In addition, when data is printed, most operating systems create one or more temporary print files that contain the print-ready version of the data.
- ■ Swap Files—Most operating systems use swap files in conjunction with RAM to provide temporary storage for data often used by applications. Swap files essentially extend the amount of memory available to a program by allowing pages (or segments) of data to be swapped in and out of RAM. Swap files may contain a broad range of operating system and application information, such as usernames, password hashes, and contact information.
- ■ Dump Files—Some operating systems have the ability to store the contents of memory automatically during an error condition to assist in subsequent troubleshooting. The file that holds the stored memory contents is known as a dump file.
- ■ Hibernation Files—A hibernation file is created to preserve the current state of a system (typically a laptop) by recording memory and open files before shutting off the system. When the system is next turned on, the state of the system is restored.
- ■ Temporary Files—During the installation of an operating system, application, or operating system or application updates and upgrades, temporary files are often created. Although such files are typically deleted at the end of the installation process, this does not always occur. In addition, temporary files are created when many applications are run; again, such files are usually deleted when the application is terminated, but this does not always happen. Temporary files could contain copies of other files on the system, application data, or other information.

Basic Input or Output System (BIOS)

Although file systems are the primary source of non-volatile data, another source of interest is the BIOS. The BIOS contains many types of hardware-related information, such as the attached devices (e.g., CD-ROM drives, hard drives), the types of connections and interrupt request line (IRQ) assignments (e.g., serial, USB, network card), motherboard components (e.g., processor type and speed, cache size, memory information), system security settings, and hot keys.

The BIOS also communicates with RAID drivers [Redundant Array of Inexpensive (or Independent) Drives (or Disks)] and displays the information provided by the drivers. For example, the BIOS views a hardware RAID as a single drive and a software RAID as multiple drives.

The BIOS typically permits the user to set passwords, which restrict access to the BIOS settings and may prevent the system from booting if the password is not supplied. The BIOS also holds the system date and time.

Volatile Data

Operating systems execute within the RAM of a system. While the operating system is functioning, the contents of RAM are constantly changing. At any given time, RAM might contain many types of data and information that could be of interest. For example, RAM often contains frequently and recently accessed data, such as data files, password hashes, and recent commands. In addition, like file systems, RAM can contain residual data in slack and free space, as follows:

- Slack Space—Memory slack space is much less deterministic than file slack space. For example, an operating system generally manages memory in units known as pages or blocks, and allocates them to requesting applications. Sometimes, although an application might not request an entire unit, it is given one anyway. Residual data could therefore reside in the unit of memory allocated to an application, although it might not be addressable by the application. For performance and efficiency, some operating systems vary the size of the units they allocate, which tends to result in smaller memory slack spaces.
- Free Space—Memory pages are allocated and reallocated much like file clusters. When they are not allocated, memory pages are often collected into a common pool of available pages— a process often referred to as garbage collection. It is not uncommon for residual data to reside in these reusable memory pages, which are analogous to unallocated file clusters.

Both of these "volatile data" as discussed in Chapter 3, provide an excellent starting point for forensic examination, simply due to the residual "data" that the investigator may uncover, which may be very relevant to the investigation underway.

Some other significant types of volatile data that might exist within an operating system include:

- Network Configuration—Although many elements of networking, such as network interface card (NIC) drivers and configuration settings, are typically stored in the file system, networking is dynamic in nature. For example, many hosts are assigned Internet Protocol (IP) addresses dynamically by another host, meaning that their IP addresses are not part of the stored configuration. Many hosts also have multiple network interfaces defined, such as wired, wireless, virtual private network (VPN), and modem; the current network configuration indicates which interfaces are currently in use. Users also may be able to alter network interface configurations from the defaults, such as manually changing IP addresses. Accordingly, cyber forensic investigators should use the current network configuration, not the stored configuration, whenever possible.
- Network Connections—The operating system facilitates connections between the system and other systems. Most operating systems can provide a list of current incoming and outgoing network connections, and some operating systems can list recent connections as well.

For incoming connections, the operating system typically indicates which resources are being used, such as file shares and printers. Most operating systems can also provide a list of the ports and IP addresses at which the system is listening for connections.

■ Running Processes—Processes are the programs that are currently executing on a computer. Processes include services offered by the operating system and applications run by administrators and users. Most operating systems offer ways to view a list of the currently running processes. This list can be studied to determine the services that are active on the system, such as a Web server, and the programs that individual users are running (e.g., encryption utility, word processor, e-mail client). Process lists may also indicate which command options were used. Identifying the running processes is also helpful for identifying programs that should be running but have been disabled or removed, such as antivirus software and firewalls.

■ Open Files—Operating systems may maintain a list of open files, which typically includes the user or process that opened each file.

■ Login Sessions—Operating systems typically maintain information about currently logged-in users (and the start time and duration of each session); previous successful and failed logons, and privileged usage. However, login session information might be available only if the computer has been configured to audit logon attempts. Logon records can help to determine a user's computer usage habits and confirm whether a user account was active when a given event occurred.

■ Operating System Time—The operating system maintains the current time and stores daylight savings time and time zone information. This information can be useful when building a timeline of events or correlating events among different systems. Cyber forensic investigators should be aware that the time presented by the operating system might differ from that presented by the BIOS because of operating system-specific settings, such as time zone.

Collecting Operating System Data

As described previously, operating system data exists in both non-volatile and volatile states. Non-volatile operating system data such as file system data can be collected by performing logical backups and bit stream imaging. Volatile operating system data should be collected before the computer is powered down. Below are recommendations for collecting volatile and non-volatile operating system data, respectively.

Collecting Volatile Operating System Data

Volatile operating system data involving an event can be collected only from a live system that has not been rebooted or shut down since the event occurred. Every action performed on the system, whether initiated by a person or by the operating system itself, will almost certainly alter the volatile operating system data in some way. Therefore, cyber forensic investigators should decide as quickly as possible whether the volatile operating system data should be preserved.

Ideally, the criteria for making this decision should have been documented in advance so that the cyber forensic investigator can make the best decision immediately. The importance of this decision cannot be stressed enough, because powering off the system or even disconnecting it from a network can eliminate the opportunity to collect potentially important information. For example, if a user recently ran encryption tools to secure data, the computers RAM might contain password hashes, which could be used to determine the passwords.

On the other hand, collecting volatile operating system data from a running computer has inherent risks. For instance, the possibility always exists that files on the computer might change and other volatile operating system data might be altered. In addition, a malicious party might have installed root kits designed to return false information, delete files, or perform other malicious acts.

In deciding whether to collect volatile data, the risks associated with such collection should be weighed against the potential for recovering important information. If evidence may be needed, the cyber forensic investigator should fully document what is seen on the screen before touching the system. If a live system is in sleep mode or has visible password protection, cyber forensic investigators should also decide whether to alter the state of the system by waking it from sleep mode or attempting to crack or bypass the password protection so that cyber forensic investigators can attempt to collect volatile data. If the effort needed to collect the volatile data is not merited, cyber forensic investigators might instead decide to perform a shutdown.

The following section describes how forensic tools should be compiled in preparation for collecting volatile operating system data. Next, we discuss several types of data and mention categories of tools or specific operating system tools that are effective in collecting each type of data. Finally, we explain the need to identify the types of volatile operating system data that are most likely to be valuable in a particular situation and then to prioritize the collection of data based on importance and relative volatility.

Types of Volatile Operating System Data

The following list shows several types of volatile operating system data and explains how forensic tools can be used in collecting each type of data:

- Contents of Memory—There are several utilities that can copy the contents of RAM to a data file and assist in subsequent analysis of the data. On most systems, it is not possible to avoid alteration of RAM when running a utility that attempts to make a copy of RAM. Instead, the goal is to perform the copying with as small a footprint as possible to minimize the disruption of RAM.
- Network Configuration—Most operating systems include a utility that displays the current network configuration, such as ifconfig on UNIX systems and ipconfig on Windows systems. Information that can be provided through network configuration utilities includes the host name, the physical and logical network interfaces, and configuration information for each interface [e.g., IP address, Media Access Control (MAC) address, current status].
- Network Connections—Operating systems typically provide a method for displaying a list of the current network connections. Both Windows and UNIX-based systems usually include the netstat program, which lists network connections by source and destination IP addresses and ports, and also lists which ports are open on each interface. Third-party utilities are available that can display port assignments for each program. Most operating systems also can display a list of remotely mounted file systems, which provides more detailed information than a network connection list.
- Running Processes—All UNIX-based systems offer the ps command for displaying currently running processes. Although Windows offers a graphical user interface (GUI) based process list utility, the Task Manager, it is usually preferable to have a text-based listing. Third-party utilities can be used to generate a text list of running processes for Windows systems.

- Open Files—All UNIX-based systems offer the lsof command for displaying a list of open files. Third-party utilities can be used to generate text lists of open files for Windows systems.
- Login Sessions—Some operating systems have built-in commands for listing the currently logged on users, such as the w command for UNIX systems, which also lists the source address of each user and when the user logged onto the system. Third-party utilities are available that can list currently connected users on Windows systems.
- Operating System Time—There are several utilities available for retrieving the current system time, time zone information, and daylight savings time settings. On UNIX systems, the date command can be used to retrieve this information. On Windows systems, the date, time, and nlsinfo commands can be used collectively to retrieve this information.

In addition to the tools in the preceding list, it is often useful to include some general purpose tools in the forensic toolkit, such as the following:

- Operating System Command Prompt—This utility provides an operating system command prompt through which the other tools in the toolkit can be executed, such as cmd on Windows systems.
- SHA-1 Checksum—A utility that can compute the SHA-1 message digest of data files is helpful in file verification. It may also be useful to include in the toolkit a list of SHA-1 message digests for system data files associated with the target operating system to assist in file verification. Utilities are available for various operating systems for this purpose.
- Directory List—A utility for listing the contents of directories should be included for navigating a file system and seeing its contents. Practically all operating systems include such a utility; for example, the ls command is used on UNIX systems, whereas on Windows systems, the dir command is used.
- String Search—A utility for performing a text string search can be useful in identifying data files of interest. UNIX systems offer the grep command for performing text string searches, and a third-party grep utility is also available on Windows systems.
- Text Editor—A simple text editor can be useful for viewing text files or composing notes. Numerous text editors are available, such as Notepad on Windows systems and vi on UNIX systems.

In addition to these tools, Chapter 2 contains a further examination and comparison of cyber forensic tools that the investigator may wish to consider adding to his or her tool kit.

Prioritizing Data Collection

The types of volatile data that may be collected with the toolkit depend on the specific need. For instance, if a network intrusion is suspected, it might be useful to collect network configuration information, network connections, login sessions, and running processes to determine how someone gained access to a system. If an investigation concerns identity theft, for example, then the contents of RAM, the list of running processes, the list of open files, network configuration information, and network connections might reveal social security and credit card numbers, programs used to obtain or encrypt data, password hashes, and methods that might have been used to obtain the information over a network. When in doubt, it is usually a good idea to collect as much volatile data as possible because all opportunities to collect such volatile data will be lost once the computer is powered down. Later, a determination can be made as to which collected volatile data should be examined.

An automated script on a toolkit CD can be used for consistency in collecting volatile data. The script can include ways to transfer the collected information to local storage media, such as a thumb drive, and to networked drive locations.

Because volatile data has a propensity to change over time, the order and timeliness with which volatile data is collected is important. In most cases, cyber forensic investigators should first collect information on network connections and login sessions, because network connections may time out or be disconnected and the list of users connected to a system at any single time may vary. Volatile data that is less likely to change, such as network configuration information, should be collected later. The recommended order, in which volatile data generally should be collected, from first to last, is as follows:

1. Network connections
2. Login sessions
3. Contents of memory
4. Running processes
5. Open files
6. Network configuration
7. Operating system time

Collecting Non-Volatile Operating System Data

After obtaining volatile operating system data, cyber forensic investigators often should collect non-volatile operating system data. To do so, the cyber forensic investigator first should decide whether the system should be shut down. Shutting down the system not only affects the ability to perform bit stream imaging and many logical backups, but can also change which operating system data is preserved. Most systems can be shut down through two methods:

■ Perform a graceful operating system shutdown—Nearly every operating system offers a shutdown option. This causes the operating system to perform cleanup activities, such as closing open files, deleting temporary files, and possibly clearing the swap file, before shutting down the system. A graceful shutdown can also trigger removal of malicious material; for example, memory-resident root kits may disappear, and Trojan horses may remove evidence of their malicious activity. The operating system is typically shut down from the account of the administrator or the current user of the system (if the current user has sufficient privileges).

■ Remove power from the system—Disconnecting the power cord from the back of the computer (and removing the batteries on a laptop or other portable device) can preserve swap files, temporary data files, and other information that might be altered or deleted during a graceful shutdown. Unfortunately, a sudden loss of power can cause some operating systems to corrupt data, such as open files. In addition, for some consumer devices, such as PDAs and cell phones, removing battery power can cause a loss of data.

Some tools are able to perform collection actions on running systems without any problems, while other tools are best run on systems that have been shut down. In the latter case, cyber forensic investigators should be aware of the characteristics of each operating system and choose a shutdown method based on the typical behavior of the operating system and the types of data that need to be preserved.

For example, DOS and Windows 95/98 systems generally do not corrupt data when power is removed suddenly, so removing power should preserve data.

Table 5.1 provides a summary of action to be taken when determining whether to pull the plug or not.

If the operating system cannot be easily determined, pulling the plug will suffice. When pulling the plug, however, make sure that you pull the lead out from the computer unit itself. This is because if the computer is connected to an uninterruptible power supply and the power to this is turned off, the power to the computer will remain operational.

Shutting the computer down by the correct method is critical if certain data that is normally stored only in memory is to be committed back to disk when the machine is powered off. Shutting down computers, which do not normally store data in memory (such as Windows XP) by the usual method, may result in possible changes to the data on the hard drive.

Other operating systems might corrupt data, such as open files or files that were being accessed at the time, if there is a loss of power. In these cases, a graceful shutdown is generally best unless swap files or temporary data files are of particular interest or the system might contain root kits, Trojan horses, or other malicious programs that might be triggered by a graceful shutdown. After performing a shutdown (if needed), the cyber forensic investigator should acquire file system data from the system's storage media.

After the computer has been powered off, all components, storage devices, media, and peripheral devices connected to the computer should be inventoried and labeled if they are needed as evidence. Whenever possible, the inventory should include the model number, serial number, and description

Table 5.1 Summary of Action

Operating System	Action Taken
DOS	Pull the plug
Windows 3.1	Pull the plug
Windows 95	Pull the plug
Windows 98	Pull the plug
Windows NT	Pull the plug
Windows NT Server	Shut down
Windows 2000	Pull the plug
Windows 2000 Server	Shut down
Windows XP	Shut down
Linux	Shut down
Unix	Shut down
Macintosh OS 9 and older	Pull the plug
Macintosh OS X	Shut down

of the item. In addition, information about how each item is connected to the outside or inside of the computer (e.g., cable connections, jumper settings) should be documented and photographed. This will help the cyber forensics investigator to recreate the user's computer setup.

Assuming that the evidence can be legally seized, each item should be handled using antistatic bracelets, guarded against electrostatic discharges that can damage the item, sealed properly (i.e., a box that is taped shut), and packed securely for transport (consider sealing the package with tamper-proof evidence tape). Handlers should wear antistatic bracelets when handling sensitive media and protect media with antistatic bags and other special packing materials.

Once the file system data has been collected, tools can be used to acquire specific types of data from the file system. Acquiring regular files, such as data, application, and configuration files, is relatively straightforward. The following list describes several other types of non-volatile operating system data and explains how tools can be useful in acquiring each type from the file system:

- Users and Groups—Operating systems maintain a list of users and groups that have access to the system. On UNIX systems, users and groups are listed in /etc/passwd and /etc/groups, respectively. In addition, the groups and users commands can be used to identify users who have logged onto the system and the groups to which they belong. On Windows systems, the net user and net group commands can be used to enumerate the users and groups on a system.
- Passwords—Most operating systems maintain password hashes for users' passwords on disk. On Windows systems, third-party utilities can be used to dump password hashes from the Security Account Manager (SAM) database. On UNIX systems, password hashes are usually in the /etc/passwd or /etc/shadow file. Password cracking programs can be used to extract passwords from their hashes.
- Network Shares—A system may enable local resources to be shared across a network. On Windows systems, the SrvCheck utility can be used to list network shares. Third-party utilities can provide similar information for other operating systems.
- Logs—Logs that are not stored in text files might necessitate use of log extraction utilities. For example, specialized utilities can retrieve information about recent successful and failed logon attempts on Windows systems, which are stored in binary format logs. Most log entries on UNIX systems are stored in text files by syslog or in the /var/log directory, so special utilities are not needed to acquire information from the logs. Searching for filenames ending in .log should identify most log files.

Occasionally, cyber forensic investigators may need to collect data from the BIOS, such as system date and time or processor type and speed. Because the BIOS primarily contains information related to the system's hardware configuration, BIOS data collection is most likely to be needed when a system administrator is troubleshooting operational issues. Typically, cyber forensic investigators who need BIOS data first collect any needed volatile data and file systems, then reboot the system and press the appropriate function key (generally specified in the initial screen during boot) to display the BIOS settings.

If the BIOS password is set, the cyber forensic investigator might not be able to gain access to the BIOS settings easily and might have to attempt to guess default passwords or circumvent the password protection. A variety of methods can be used to bypass BIOS passwords, including finding the appropriate manufacturer backdoor password, using a password cracker, moving the appropriate jumper on the motherboard, or removing the Complementary Metal Oxide Semiconductor (CMOS) battery (if possible). Systems vary, so cyber forensic investigators should first research the particular characteristics of the system they are analyzing, as described in mother-board documentation, to avoid harming a system unnecessarily (see Chapter 4 for more information on hardware systems).

Examining and Analyzing Operating System Data

Various tools and techniques can be used to support the examination process. Many of the tools and techniques used for examining collected data files can also be used with collected operating system data. In addition, security applications, such as file integrity checkers and host IDSs, can be very helpful in identifying malicious activity against operating systems. For instance, file integrity checkers can be used to compute the message digests of operating system files and compare them against databases of known message digests to determine whether any files have been compromised. If intrusion detection software is installed on the computer, it might contain logs that indicate the actions performed against the operating system.

Another issue that cyber forensic investigators face is the examination of swap files and RAM dumps, which are large binary data files containing unstructured data. Hex editors (also called a binary file editor or byte editor, is a type of program that allows a user to view and edit the raw and exact contents of files, that is, at the byte level, in contrast to the higher level interpretations of the same contents that are provided by other, higher level application programs) can be used to open these files and examine their contents; however, on large files, manually trying to locate intelligible data using a hex editor can be a time-consuming process. Filtering tools automate the process of examining swap and RAM dump files by identifying text patterns and numerical values that might represent phone numbers, names of people, e-mail addresses, Web addresses, and other types of critical information.

Cyber forensic investigators often want to gather additional information about a particular program running on a system, such as the process's purpose and manufacturer. After obtaining a list of the processes currently running on a system, cyber forensic investigators can look up the process name to obtain such additional information. However, users might change the names of programs to conceal their functions, such as naming a Trojan program calculator.exe. Therefore, process name lookups should be performed only after verifying the identity of the process's files by computing and comparing their message digests. Similar lookups can be performed on library files, such as DLLs on Windows systems, to determine which libraries are loaded and what their typical purposes are.

As described earlier, cyber forensic investigators may collect many different types of operating system data, including multiple file systems. Trying to sift through each type of data to find relevant information can be a time-intensive process. Cyber forensic investigators generally find it useful to identify a few data sources to review initially, and then find other likely sources of important information on the basis of that review. In addition, in many cases, analysis can involve data from other types of sources, such as network traffic or applications.

Recommendations for Using Data from Operating Systems

Recommendations for using data from operating systems are as follows.
Cyber forensic investigators should:

■ Act appropriately to preserve volatile operating system data: The criteria for determining whether volatile operating system data must be preserved should be documented in advance so that cyber forensic investigators can make informed decisions as quickly as possible.

To determine whether the effort required to collect volatile operating system data is warranted, the risks associated with such collection should be weighed against the potential for recovering important information.

■ Consider the use of a forensic toolkit for collecting volatile operating system data: Use of a forensic toolkit enables accurate operating system data to be collected while minimizing the disturbance to the system and protecting the tools from changes. The cyber forensic investigator should know how each tool is likely to affect or alter the system during collection of data.

■ Investigate and select the most appropriate shutdown method for each system: Each method of shutting down a particular operating system can cause different types of data to be preserved or corrupted; cyber forensic investigators should be aware of the typical shutdown behavior of each operating system.

Using Data from Network Traffic

Cyber forensic investigators can use data from network traffic to reconstruct and analyze network-based attacks and inappropriate network usage, as well as to troubleshoot various types of operational problems. The content of communications carried over networks, such as e-mail messages or audio, might also be collected in support of an investigation. The term network traffic refers to computer network communications that are carried over wired or wireless networks between hosts.

This section provides an introduction to network traffic, including descriptions of major sources of network traffic data (e.g., intrusion detection software, firewalls). In addition, it discusses techniques for collecting data from these sources and points out the potential legal and technical issues in such data collection. The remainder of the section focuses on the techniques and tools for examining and analyzing data from network traffic. The section begins with an overview of Transmission Control Protocol or Internet Protocol (TCP or IP). A basic knowledge of TCP or IP is necessary to understand the data, tools, and methodologies presented in this section.

TCP or IP Basics

TCP or IP is widely used throughout the world to provide network communications. TCP or IP communications are composed of four layers that work together. When a user wants to transfer data across networks, the data is passed from the highest layer through intermediate layers to the lowest layer, with each layer adding additional information.

The lowest layer sends the accumulated data through the physical network; the data is then passed up through the layers to its destination. Essentially, the data produced by a layer is encapsulated in a larger container by the layer below it.

The four TCP or IP layers work together to transfer data between hosts. Readers interested in further additional detail information on TCP or IP are encouraged to visit the following Web site www.uga.edu/~ucns/lans/tcpipsem.

The four TCP or IP layers, of interest to the cyber forensics investigator are:

1. Application Layer—This layer sends and receives data for particular applications, such as Domain Name System (DNS), Hypertext Transfer Protocol (HTTP), and Simple Mail Transfer Protocol (SMTP).

2. Transport Layer—This layer provides connection-oriented or connectionless services for transporting application layer services between networks. The transport layer can optionally ensure the reliability of communications. Transmission Control Protocol (TCP) and User Datagram Protocol (UDP) are commonly used transport layer protocols.
3. Internet Protocol Layer (also known as Network Layer)—This layer routes packets across networks. IP is the fundamental network layer protocol for TCP or IP. Other commonly used protocols at the network layer are Internet Control Message Protocol (ICMP) and Internet Group Management Protocol (IGMP).
4. Hardware Layer (also known as Data Link Layer)—This layer handles communications on the physical network components. The best known data link layer protocol is Ethernet.

Layers' Significance in Network Forensics

Each of the four layers of the TCP or IP protocol suite contains important information. The hardware layer provides information about physical components, while other layers describe logical aspects. For events within a network, a cyber forensic investigator can map an IP address (logical identifier at the IP layer) to the MAC address. A MAC address, short for Media Access Control, is a unique code assigned to most forms of networking hardware. The address is permanently assigned to the hardware, so limiting a wireless network's access to hardware—such as wireless cards—is a security feature employed by closed wireless networks. But an experienced hacker—armed with the proper tools—can still figure out an authorized MAC address, masquerade as a legitimate address and access a closed network of a particular NIC (physical identifier at the physical layer), thereby identifying a host of interest.

A network interface card (NIC) is a computer circuit board or card that is installed in a computer so that it can be connected to a network. Personal computers and workstations on a local area network (LAN) typically contain a network interface card specifically designed for the LAN transmission technology, such as Ethernet. Network interface cards provide a dedicated, full-time connection to a network.

The combination of the IP protocol number (IP layer field) and port numbers (transport layer fields) can tell a cyber forensic investigator which application was most likely being used or targeted. This can be verified by examining the application layer data.

Network forensic analysis relies on all of the layers. When cyber forensic investigators begin to examine data, they typically have limited information—most likely an IP address of interest and perhaps protocol and port information. Nevertheless, this is enough information to support searching common data sources for more information. In most cases, the application layer contains the actual activity of interest—most attacks are against vulnerabilities in applications (including services), and nearly all misuse involves misuse of applications.

Analysts need IP addresses so that they can identify the hosts that may have been involved in the activity. The hosts may also contain additional data that would be of use in analyzing the activity. Although some events of interest may not have relevant application-level data (e.g., a distributed denial of service attack designed to consume all network bandwidth), most do; network forensics provide important support to the analysis of application-layer activities.

Network Traffic Data Sources

Organizations typically have several types of information sources concerning network traffic that might be useful for network forensics. These sources collectively capture important data from all four TCP or IP layers. The following subsections highlight the major categories of network traffic data sources—firewalls and routers, packet sniffers and protocol analyzers, IDSs, remote access, security event management software, and network forensic analysis tools, as well as several other types of data sources. The subsections explain the purpose of each source described and the type of data that is typically collected and can potentially be collected.

Firewalls and Routers

Network-based devices such as firewalls and routers, and host-based devices such as personal firewalls, examine network traffic and permit or deny it based on a set of rules. Firewalls and routers are usually configured to log basic information for most or all denied connection attempts and connectionless packets; some log every packet. Information logged typically includes the date and time the packet was processed, the source and destination IP addresses, the transport layer protocol (e.g., TCP, UDP, ICMP), and basic protocol information (e.g., TCP or UDP port numbers, ICMP type and code). The content of packets is usually not recorded.

Network-based firewalls and routers that perform network address translation (NAT) may contain additional valuable data regarding network traffic. NAT is the process of mapping addresses on one network to addresses on another network; this is most often accomplished by mapping private addresses from an internal network to one or more public addresses on a network that is connected to the Internet. NAT differentiates multiple internal addresses that are mapped to a single external address by assigning a different source port number to the external address for each internal address. The NAT device typically records each NAT address and port mapping.

Some firewalls also act as proxies. A proxy receives a request from a client, and then sends a request on the client's behalf to the desired destination. When a proxy is used, each successful connection attempt actually results in the creation of two separate connections: one between the client and the proxy server, and another between the proxy server and the true destination. Proxy servers may log basic information about each connection. Many proxies are application-specific, and some actually perform some analysis and validation of application protocols, such as HTTP. The proxy may reject client requests that appear to be invalid and log information regarding these requests.

In addition to providing NAT and proxy services, firewalls and routers may perform such other functions as intrusion detection and maintaining a VPN [a virtual private network (VPN) is a private data network that makes use of the public telecommunication infrastructure, maintaining privacy through the use of a tunneling protocol and security procedures. The idea of the VPN is to give the company the same capabilities at much lower cost by using the shared public infrastructure rather than a private one].

Packet Sniffers and Protocol Analyzers

Packet sniffers are designed to monitor network traffic on wired or wireless networks and capture packets. Normally, a NIC accepts only the incoming packets that are specifically intended for it. But when a NIC is placed in promiscuous mode, it accepts all incoming packets that it sees, regardless of their intended destinations. Packet sniffers generally work by placing the NIC in promiscuous mode; the user then configures the sniffer to capture all packets or only those with particular characteristics (e.g., certain TCP ports, certain source or destination IP addresses).

Packet sniffers are commonly used to capture a particular type of traffic for troubleshooting or investigative purposes. For example, if IDS alerts indicate unusual network activity between two hosts, a packet sniffer could record all of the packets traveling between the hosts, potentially providing additional information for cyber forensic investigators.

Most packet sniffers are also protocol analyzers, which mean that they can reassemble streams from individual packets and decode communications that use any of hundreds or thousands of different protocols. Protocol analyzers usually can process not only live network traffic, but also packets that have been recorded previously in capture files by packet sniffers. Protocol analyzers are extremely valuable in displaying raw packet data in an understandable format.

Intrusion Detection Systems (IDS)

Network IDSs perform packet sniffing and analyze network traffic to identify suspicious activity and record relevant information. Host IDSs monitor characteristics of a particular system and events occurring within the system, which can include network traffic. Unlike network IDS sensors, which can monitor all network traffic on a particular network segment, host IDS software is intended to monitor network traffic only for the host on which it is installed for each suspicious event, IDS software typically records the same basic event characteristics that firewalls and routers record (e.g., date and time, source and destination IP addresses, protocol, basic protocol characteristics), as well as application-specific information (e.g., username, filename, command, status code). IDS software also records information that indicates the possible intent of the activity. Examples include the type of attack (e.g., buffer overflow), the targeted vulnerability, the apparent success or failure of the attack, and pointers to more information about the attack.

Some IDSs can be configured to capture packets related to suspicious activity. This can range from recording only the packet that triggered the IDS to label the activity suspicious, to recording the rest of the session. Some IDSs even have the ability to store all sessions for a short period of time so that if something suspicious is detected, the previous activity in the same session can be preserved. The packets are captured primarily so that intrusion detection cyber forensic investigators can review them when validating IDS alerts and investigating suspicious activity. Some IDSs also have intrusion prevention capabilities, which mean that they actively attempt to stop attacks in progress. Any use of intrusion prevention features should be indicated in the IDS logs.

Remote Access

Remote access servers are devices such as VPN gateways and modem servers that facilitate connections between networks. This often involves external systems connecting to internal systems through the remote access server but could also include internal systems connecting to external or internal systems. Remote access servers typically record the origin of each connection and might also indicate which user account was authenticated for each session.

If the remote access server assigns an IP address to the remote user, this is also likely to be logged. Some remote access servers also provide packet filtering functions, which typically perform logging similar to that provided by firewalls and routers. Remote access servers typically work at a network level, supporting the use of many different applications. Because the servers have no understanding of the application's functions, they usually do not record any application-specific data.

In addition to remote access servers, organizations typically use multiple applications that are specifically designed to provide remote access to a particular host's operating system. Examples include secure shell (SSH), telnet, terminal servers, and remote control software. Such applications can typically be configured to log basic information for each connection, including source IP address and user account. Organizations also typically use many applications that are accessed remotely, such as client or server applications. Some of these applications also log basic information for connections.

Although most remote access-related logging occurs on the remote access server or the application server, in some cases the client also logs information related to the connection.

Security Event Management Software

Security event management (SEM) software is capable of importing security event information from various network traffic-related security event data sources (e.g., IDS logs, firewall logs) and correlating events among the sources. It generally works by receiving copies of logs from various data sources over secure channels, normalizing the logs into a standard format, then identifying related events by matching IP addresses, timestamps, and other characteristics.

SEM products usually do not generate original event data; instead, they generate meta-events based on imported event data. Many SEM products not only can identify malicious activity, such as attacks and virus infections, but also can detect misuse and inappropriate usage of systems and networks. SEM software can be helpful in making many sources of network traffic information accessible through a single interface.

Because SEM products can handle nearly any security event data source, such as operating system logs, antivirus software alerts, and physical security device logs, SEM products may contain a wide variety of information regarding events. However, it is typical for only some data fields to be brought over. For example, if an IDS records packets, the packets may not be transferred to the SEM because of bandwidth and storage limitations. In addition, because most data sources record information in different formats, SEM products typically normalize the data-converting each data field to a standard format and labeling the data consistently.

Although this is beneficial for analysis, the normalization process occasionally introduces errors in the data or causes some data to be lost. Fortunately, SEM products typically do not alter the original data sources, so cyber forensic investigators should retain copies of the original logs and use them to verify the accuracy of the data if needed.

Network Forensic Analysis Tools

Network forensic analysis tools (NFAT) typically provide the same functionality as packet sniffers, protocol analyzers, and SEM software in a single product, whereas SEM software concentrates on correlating events among existing data sources (which typically include multiple network traffic-related sources), NFAT software focuses primarily on collecting, examining, and analyzing network traffic.

NFAT software also offers additional features that further facilitate network forensics, such as the following:

- Reconstructing events by replaying network traffic within the tool, ranging from an individual session [e.g., instant messaging (IM) between two users] to all sessions during a particular time period. The speed of the replaying can typically be adjusted as needed.
- Visualizing the traffic flows and the relationships among hosts. Some tools can even tie IP addresses, domain names, or other data to physical locations and produce a geographic map of the activity.

- Building profiles of typical activity and identifying significant deviations.
- Searching application content for keywords (e.g., "confidential," "proprietary").

Additional network forensic analysis tools are examined in further detail in Chapter 2.

Other Sources

Most organizations have other sources of network traffic information that can be of use for forensics in some capacity, including the following:

- Dynamic Host Configuration Protocol Servers—The DHCP service assigns IP addresses to hosts on a network as needed. Some hosts might have static IP addresses, which mean that they always receive the same IP address assignment; however, most hosts typically receive dynamic assignments. This means that the hosts are required to renew their IP address assignments regularly and that there is no guarantee that they will be assigned the same addresses. DHCP servers may contain assignment logs that include the MAC address, the IP address assigned to that MAC address, and the time the assignment occurred.
- Network Monitoring Software—Network monitoring software is designed to observe network traffic and gather statistics about it. For example, it may record high-level information about traffic flows for a particular network segment, such as the amount of bandwidth typically consumed by various protocols. Network monitoring software may also collect more detailed information about network activity, such as the payload size and the source and destination IP addresses and ports for each packet. Some managed switches and other network devices offer basic network monitoring capabilities, such as collecting statistics concerning bandwidth usage.
- Internet Service Provider (ISP) Records—ISPs may collect network traffic-related data as part of their normal operations and when investigating unusual activity, such as extremely high volumes of traffic or an apparent attack. Usual ISP records often might be kept only for days or hours. With the emergence of new legislation aimed directly at records retention, especially electronic information or records, organizations are rethinking their policies and retaining records for much longer periods of time, if not in perpetuity.
- Client or Server Applications—Some client or server applications used over networks may record information regarding successful and failed usage attempts, which could include connection-related data such as the client's IP address and port. The data fields recorded (if any) vary widely among applications.
- Hosts' Network Configurations and Connections—Network information can be collected from individual hosts, including the TCP and UDP ports at which a host is listening.

Collecting Network Traffic Data

Organizations typically have network traffic data recorded in many places during normal operations. Organizations also use the same data recording mechanisms to collect additional data on an as needed basis when investigating incidents or troubleshooting problems. For example, a network administrator or incident handler might deploy a packet sniffer to examine unusual packets sent by a host.

Network traffic data is usually recorded to a log or stored in a packet capture file. In most cases, collecting the data is as simple as collecting the logs and packet capture files. If data is not stored in a file (e.g., traffic flow map displayed graphically, data displayed on the console screen only), screen captures or photographs of the screen might be needed. Although collecting network traffic data is typically straightforward, there are several important legal and technical issues that can make data collection more complicated. The reader is advised to spend some time reading Chapter 11, which addresses some of these important legal issues.

Examining and Analyzing Network Traffic Data

When an event of interest has been identified, cyber forensic investigators assess, extract, and analyze network traffic data with the goal of determining what has happened and how the organization's systems and networks have been affected. This process might be as simple as reviewing a few log entries on a single data source and determining that the event was a false alarm, or as complex as sequentially examining and analyzing dozens of sources (most of which might contain no relevant data), manually correlating data among several sources, then analyzing the collective data to determine the probable intent and significance of the event. However, even the relatively simple case of validating a few log entries can be surprisingly involved and time consuming.

Although current tools (e.g., SEM software, NFAT software) can be helpful in gathering and presenting network traffic data, such tools have rather limited analysis abilities and can be used effectively only by well-trained, experienced cyber forensic investigators. In addition to understanding the tools, cyber forensic investigators should also have reasonably comprehensive knowledge of networking principles, common network and application protocols, network and application security products, and network-based threats and attack methods. It is also very important that cyber forensic investigators have knowledge of the organization's environment, such as the Network architecture and the IP addresses used by critical assets (e.g., firewalls, publicly accessible servers), as well as knowledge of the information supporting the applications and operating systems used by the organization.

If cyber forensic investigators understand the organization's normal computing baseline, such as typical patterns of usage on systems and networks across the enterprise, they should be able to perform their work easier and faster. Analysts should also have a firm understanding of each of the network traffic data sources, as well as access to supporting materials, such as intrusion detection signature documentation. Analysts should understand the characteristics and relative value of each data source so that they can locate the relevant data quickly.

Given the potential complexities of the analysis process and the extensive knowledge of networking and information security required for analyzing network traffic data effectively, a full description of techniques needed for analyzing data and drawing conclusions in complex situations is beyond the scope of this chapter. Instead, the section focuses on the basic steps of the examination and analysis processes and highlights some significant technical issues that cyber forensic investigators should consider.

Identify an Event of Interest

The first step in the examination process is the identification of an event of interest. Typically, this identification is made through one of two methods:

- Someone within the organization (e.g., help desk agent, system administrator, security administrator) receives an indication, such as an automated alert or a user complaint, that there is a security or operational-related issue. The cyber forensic investigator is asked to research the corresponding activity.

■ During a review of security event data (e.g., IDS monitoring, network monitoring, firewall log review), which is part of the cyber forensic investigator's regular duties; the cyber forensic investigator identifies an event of interest and determines that it should be researched further.

When an event of interest has been identified, the cyber forensic investigator needs to know some basic information about the event as a basis for research. In most cases, the event will have been detected through a network traffic data source, such as an IDS sensor or a firewall, so the cyber forensic investigator can simply be pointed to that data source for more information.

However, in some cases, such as a user complaint, it might not be apparent which data sources (if any) contain relevant information or which hosts or networks might be involved. Therefore, cyber forensic investigators might need to rely on more general information—for example, reports that several systems on the fourth floor have been rebooting themselves. Although data examination is easier if the event information is specific (e.g., IP addresses of affected systems), even general information provides the cyber forensic investigator with a starting point for finding the relevant data sources.

Examine Data Sources

Organizations may have many sources of network traffic-related data. A single event of interest could be noted by many of these data sources, but it may be inefficient or impractical to check each source individually. For initial event data examination, cyber forensic investigators typically rely on a few primary data sources, such as an IDS console that displays alerts from all IDS sensors, or SEM or NFAT software that consolidates many other data sources and organizes the data. Not only is this an efficient solution, but also in most cases the event of interest will be identified by an alert from one of these primary data sources.

For each data source examined, cyber forensic investigators should consider its fidelity. In general, cyber forensic investigators should have more confidence in original data sources than in data sources that receive normalized (modified) data from other sources. In addition, cyber forensic investigators should validate data that is based on interpretation, such as IDS and SEM alerts. No tool for identifying malicious activity is completely accurate; they produce both false positives (incorrectly reporting benign activity as malicious) and false negatives (incorrectly classifying malicious activity as benign).

Tools such as NFAT and IDS might also produce inaccurate alerts if they do not process all packets within a connection. Validation should be based on an analysis of additional data (e.g., raw packets, supporting information captured by other sources), a review of available information on alert validity (e.g., vendor comments on known false positives), and past experience with the tool in question. In many cases, an experienced investigator can quickly examine the supporting data and determine that an alert is a false positive and does not need further investigation.

Cyber forensic investigators may also need to examine secondary network traffic data sources, such as host-based firewall logs and packet captures, and non-network traffic data sources, such as host operating system audit logs and antivirus software logs. The most common reasons for doing this are as follows:

■ No Data on Primary Sources—In some cases, the typical primary network traffic data sources do not contain evidence of the activity. For example, an attack might have occurred between two hosts on an internal network segment that is not monitored or controlled by network security devices. In these cases, investigators should identify other likely data sources and examine them for evidence.

■ Insufficient or Invalidated Data on Primary Sources—Investigators might need to examine secondary data sources if primary data sources do not contain sufficient information or cyber forensic investigators need to validate the data. After reviewing one or more primary data sources, cyber forensic investigators should query the appropriate secondary data sources based on the pertinent data from the primary data sources. For example, if IDS records indicate an attack against the system at IP address 216.239.51.100 with an apparent origin of IP address 165.113.245.2, querying other data sources using one or both IP addresses might uncover additional data regarding the activity. Analysts also use timestamps, protocols, port numbers, and other common data fields to narrow their search as necessary.

■ Best Source of Data Elsewhere—Occasionally, the best sources of network traffic data is located on a particular host, such as host-based firewall and IDS logs on a system that was attacked. Although such data sources can be very helpful, their data may be altered or destroyed during a successful attack.

If additional data is needed but cannot be located and the suspicious activity is still occurring, cyber forensic investigators might need to perform more data collection activities. For example, a cyber forensic investigator could perform packet captures at an appropriate point on the network to gather more information. Other ways to collect more information include configuring firewalls or routers to log more information on certain activity, setting an IDS signature to capture packets for the activity, and writing a custom IDS signature that alerts when a specific activity occurs. Collecting additional data may be helpful if the activity is ongoing or intermittent; if the activity has ended, there is no opportunity to collect additional data.

Data Source Value

Organizations typically have many different sources of network traffic data. Because the information collected by these sources varies, the sources may have different value to the cyber forensic investigator, both in general and for specific cases. The following items describe the typical value of the most common data sources in network forensics:

■ IDS Software—IDS data is often the starting point for examining suspicious activity. Not only do IDSs typically attempt to identify malicious network traffic at all TCP or IP layers, but also they log many data fields (and sometimes raw packets) that can be useful in validating events and correlating them with other data sources. Nevertheless, as noted previously, IDS software does produce false positives, so IDS alerts should be validated. The extent to which this can be done depends on the amount of data recorded related to the alert and the information available to the cyber forensic investigator about the signature characteristics or anomaly detection method that triggered the alert.

■ SEM Software—Ideally, SEM can be extremely useful for forensics because it can automatically correlate events among several data sources, then extract the relevant information and present it to the user. However, because SEM software functions by bringing in data from many other sources, the value of SEM depends on which data sources are fed into it, how reliable each data source is, and how well the software can normalize the data and correlate events.

- NFAT Software: NFAT software is designed specifically to aid in network traffic analysis, so it is valuable if it has monitored an event of interest. NFAT software usually offers features that support analysis, such as traffic reconstruction and visualization.

- Firewalls, Routers, Proxy Servers, and Remote Access Servers—By itself, data from these sources is usually of little value. Analyzing the data over time can indicate overall trends, such as an increase in blocked connection attempts. However, because these sources typically record little information about each event, the data provides little insight into the nature of the events. Also, many events might be logged each day, so the sheer volume of data can be overwhelming. The primary value of the data is to correlate events recorded by other sources.

  For example, if a host is compromised and a network IDS sensor detected the attack, querying the firewall logs for events involving the apparent attacking IP address might confirm where the attack entered the network and might indicate other hosts that the attacker attempted to compromise. In addition, address mapping (e.g., NAT) performed by these devices is important for network forensics because the apparent IP address of an attacker or a victim might actually have been used by hundreds or thousands of hosts. Fortunately, cyber forensic investigators usually can review the logs to determine which internal address was in use.

- Dynamic Host Configuration Protocol (DHCP) Servers—DHCP servers typically can be configured to log each IP address assignment and the associated MAC address, along with a timestamp. This information can be helpful to investigators in identifying which host performed an activity using a particular IP address. However, investigators should be mindful of the possibility that attackers on an organization's internal networks falsified their MAC addresses or IP addresses, a practice known as spoofing.

- Packet Sniffers—Of all the network traffic data sources, packet sniffers can collect the most information on network activity. However, sniffers might capture huge volumes of benign data as well—millions or billions of packets—and typically provide no indication as to which packets might contain malicious activity. In most cases, packet sniffers are best used to provide more data on events that other devices or software has identified as possibly malicious. Some organizations record most or all packets for some period of time so that when an incident occurs, the raw network data is available for examination and analysis. Packet sniffer data is best reviewed with a protocol analyzer, which interprets the data for the cyber forensic investigator based on knowledge of protocol standards and common implementations.

- Network Monitoring—Network monitoring software is helpful in identifying significant deviations from normal traffic flows, such as those caused by a distributed denial-of-service (DDoS) system attacks, during which, hundreds or thousands of systems launch simultaneous attacks against particular hosts or networks. On the Internet, a DDoS is one in which a multitude of compromised systems attack a single target, thereby causing denial of service for users of the targeted system. The flood of incoming messages to the target system essentially forces it to shut down, thereby denying service to the system to legitimate users. The more common attacks use built-in "features" of the TCP or IP protocol to create exponential amounts of network traffic.

  Network monitoring software can document the impact of these attacks on network bandwidth and availability, as well as providing information about the apparent targets. Traffic flow data can also be helpful in investigating suspicious activity identified by other sources. For example, it might indicate whether a particular communications pattern has occurred in the preceding days or weeks.

- ISP Records—Information from an ISP is primarily of value in tracing an attack back to its source, particularly when the attack uses spoofed IP addresses.

Examination and Analysis Tools

Because network forensics can be performed for many purposes with dozens of data source types, cyber forensic investigators may use several different tools on a regular basis, each well suited to certain situations. Investigators should be aware of the possible approaches to examining and analyzing network traffic data and should select the best tools for each case, rather than applying the same tool to every situation. Analysts should also be mindful of the shortcomings of tools; for example, a particular protocol analyzer might not be able to translate a certain protocol or handle unexpected protocol data (e.g., illegal data field value). It can be helpful to have an alternate tool available that might not have the same deficiency.

Tools are often helpful in filtering data. For example, a cyber forensic investigator might need to search data without any concrete information that could narrow the search. This is most likely to occur when the investigator is responsible for performing periodic or ongoing reviews of security event data logs and alerts. If the volume of log entries and alerts is low, reviewing the data is relatively easy, but in some cases, there may be many thousands of events listed per day.

When a manual data review is not possible or practical, cyber forensic investigators should use an automated solution that filters the events and presents the cyber forensic investigators with only the events that are most likely to be of interest. One effective review technique is to import the logs into a database and run queries against them, either eliminating types of activity highly likely to be benign and reviewing the rest, or focusing on the types of activity most likely to be malicious. For example, if the initial suspicion is that the server was compromised through HTTP activity, and then log filtering might start by eliminating everything except HTTP activity from consideration.

A cyber forensic investigator who is very familiar with a particular data source can generally perform a blind search on it relatively quickly, but, on unfamiliar data sources, blind searches can take an extremely long time, because there might be little or no basis for eliminating certain types of activity from consideration.

Another analysis option is to use a visualization tool. These tools present security event data in a graphical format. This is most often used to represent network traffic flows visually, which can be very helpful in troubleshooting operational issues and identifying misuse. For example, attackers might use covert channels, using protocols in unintended ways to secretly communicate information (e.g., setting certain values in network protocol headers or application payloads). The use of covert channels is generally hard to detect, but one useful method is identifying deviations in expected network traffic flows.

Visualization tools are often included in NFAT software. Some visualization tools can perform traffic reconstruction, by using timestamp and sequential data fields, the tools can determine the sequence of events and graphically display how the packets traversed the organization's networks. Some visualization tools can also be used to display other types of security event data. For example, a cyber forensic investigator could import intrusion detection records into a visualization tool, which would then display the data according to several different characteristics, such as source or destination IP address or port. A cyber forensic investigator could then suppress the display of known good activity so that only unknown events are shown.

Although visualization tools can be very effective for analyzing certain types of data, cyber forensic investigators typically experience a steep learning curve with such tools. Importing data into the tool and displaying it is usually relatively straightforward, but learning how to use the tool efficiently to reduce large datasets to a few events of interest can take considerable effort. Traffic reconstruction can also be performed by protocol analyzers. Although these tools generally lack visualization capabilities, they can turn individual packets into data streams and provide sequential context for activities.

Chapter 2 provides a further and more extensive review of cyber forensic tools.

Draw Conclusions

One of the most challenging aspects of network forensics is that the available data is typically not comprehensive. In many cases, if not most, some network traffic data has not been recorded and consequently has been lost. Generally, cyber forensic investigators should think of the analysis process as a methodical approach that develops conclusions based on the data that is available and assumptions regarding the missing data (which should be based on technical knowledge and expertise).

Although cyber forensic investigators should strive to locate and examine all available data regarding an event, this is not practical in some cases, particularly when there are many redundant data sources. The investigator should eventually locate, validate, and analyze enough data to be able to reconstruct the event, understand its significance, and determine its impact. In many cases, additional data is available from sources other than network traffic-related sources (e.g., data files or host operating systems).

Generally, investigators should focus on identifying the most important characteristics of the activity and assessing the negative impact it has caused or may cause the organization. Other actions, such as determining the identity of an external attacker, are typically time-intensive and difficult to accomplish, and do not aid the organization in correcting the operational issues or security weaknesses. Determining the intent of an attacker is also very difficult; for example, an unusual connection attempt could be caused by an attacker, malicious code, misconfigured software, or an incorrect keystroke, among other causes. Although understanding intent is important in some cases, the negative impact of the event should be the primary concern.

Establishing the identity of the attacker might be important to the organization, particularly when criminal activity has occurred, but in other cases it should be weighed against other important goals to put it into perspective. The focus of the investigation should be determined at the onset by the appropriate parties, who should decide if learning the identity of the attacker is vital. It is particularly important to seek the advice of legal counsel when developing policies and procedures related to making such decisions, as well as when guidance is needed for a particular situation.

Organizations should be interested not only in analyzing real events, but also in understanding the causes of false alarms. For example, investigators are often well positioned to identify the root causes of IDS false positives. As merited, cyber forensic investigators should recommend changes to security event data sources that improve detection accuracy.

Attacker Identification

When analyzing most attacks, identifying the attacker is not an immediate, primary concern, but ensuring that the attack is stopped and recovering systems and data are the main interests. If an attack is ongoing, such as an extended denial of service attack, organizations might want to identify the IP address used by the attacker so that the attack can be stopped. Unfortunately, this is often not as simple as it sounds. The following items explain potential issues involving the IP addresses apparently used to conduct an attack:

■ Spoofed IP Addresses—Many attacks use spoofed IP addresses. Spoofing is far more difficult to perform successfully for attacks that require connections to be established, so it is most commonly used in cases where connections are not needed. When packets are spoofed, usually the attacker has no interest in seeing the response. This is not always true—attackers could spoof an address from a subnet that they monitor, so that when the response goes to that system, they can sniff it from the network. Sometimes spoofing occurs by accident, such as an attacker misconfiguring a tool and accidentally using internal NAT addresses. Sometimes an attacker spoofs a particular address on purpose—for example, the spoofed address might be the actual intended target of the attack, and the organization seeing the activity might simply be a middleman.

■ Many Source IP Addresses—Some attacks appear to use hundreds or thousands of different source IP addresses. Sometimes this appearance reflects reality—for example, DDoS attacks typically rely on large numbers of compromised machines performing a coordinated attack. Sometimes this appearance is illusory—an attack might not require the use of real source IP addresses, so the attacker generates many different fake IP addresses to add confusion. Sometimes attackers will use one real IP address and many fake ones; in that case, it might be possible to identify the real IP address by looking for other network activity occurring before or after the attack that uses any of the same IP addresses. Finding a match does not confirm that it was the attacker's address; the attacker could have inadvertently or purposely spoofed a legitimate IP address that happened to be interacting with the organization.

■ Validity of the IP Address—Because IP addresses are often assigned dynamically, the system currently at a particular IP address might not be the same system that was there when the attack occurred. In addition, many IP addresses do not belong to end-user systems, but instead to network infrastructure components that substitute their IP address for the actual source address, such as a firewall performing NAT. Some attackers use anonymizers (e.g., onion routing www.onion-router.net, or crowds (http://avirubin.com/crowds.pdf), which are intermediate servers that perform activity on a user's behalf to preserve the user's privacy.

Several ways of validating the identity of a suspicious host are as follows:

■ Contact the IP Address Owner—The Regional Internet Registries, such as the American Registry for Internet Numbers (ARIN), provide WHOIS query mechanisms on their Web sites for identifying the organization or person who owns—is responsible for a particular IP address. This information can be helpful in analyzing some attacks, such as seeing that three different IP addresses generating suspicious activity are all registered to the same owner. However, in most cases, cyber forensic investigators should not contact the owner directly; instead, they should provide information about the owner to the management and legal advisors of the cyber forensic investigator's organization, who can initiate contact with the organization or give the cyber forensic investigator approval to do so if needed. This caution is primarily related to concerns about sharing information with external organizations; also, the owner of an IP address could be the person attacking the organization.

■ Send Network Traffic to the IP Address—Organizations should not send network traffic to an apparent attacking IP address to validate its identity. Any response that is generated cannot conclusively confirm the identity of the attacking host. Moreover, if the IP address is for the attacker's system, the attacker might see the traffic and react by destroying evidence or attacking the host sending the traffic. If the IP address is spoofed, sending unsolicited network traffic to the system could be interpreted as unauthorized use or an attack. Under no circumstances should investigators attempt to gain access to others' systems without permission.

■ Seek ISP Assistance: ISPs generally require a court order before providing any information to an organization about suspicious network activity. Accordingly, ISP assistance is generally an option during only the most serious network-based attacks. This assistance is particularly useful in relation to attacks that involve IP address spoofing. ISPs have the ability to trace ongoing attacks back to their source, whether the IP addresses are spoofed or not.

■ Research the History of the IP Address: Analysts can look for previous suspicious activity associated with the same IP address or IP address block. The organization's own network traffic data archives and incident tracking databases might show previous activity. Possible external sources include Internet search engines and online incident databases that allow searches by IP address.

■ Look for Clues in Application Content: Application data packets related to an attack might contain clues to the attacker's identity. In addition to IP addresses, valuable information could include an e-mail address or an Internet relay chat (IRC) nickname.

In most cases, organizations do not need to positively identify the IP address used for an attack.

Recommendations for Using Data from Network Traffic

Organizations should:

■ Have policies regarding privacy and sensitive information—The use of forensic tools and techniques might inadvertently disclose sensitive information to investigators and others involved in forensic activities (see Chapter 8). Also, long-term storage of sensitive information inadvertently captured by forensic tools might violate data retention policies. Policies should also address the monitoring of networks, as well as requiring warning banners on systems that indicate activity may be monitored.

■ Provide adequate storage for network activity-related logs—Organizations should estimate typical and peak log usage, determine how many hours or days worth of data should be retained based on the organization's policies, and ensure that systems and applications have sufficient storage available. Logs related to computer security incidents might need to be kept for a substantially longer period of time than other logs.

■ Configure data sources to improve the collection of information—Over time, operational experience should be used to improve the organization's forensic analysis capabilities. Organizations should periodically review and adjust the configuration settings of data sources to optimize capture of relevant information.

Cyber forensic investigators should:

■ Have reasonably comprehensive technical knowledge—Because current tools have rather limited analysis abilities, investigators should be well-trained, experienced, and knowledgeable in networking principles, common network and application protocols, network and application security products, and network-based threats and attack methods.

■ Consider the fidelity and value of each data source—Investigators should have more confidence in original data sources than in data sources that receive normalized data from other sources. Investigators should validate any unusual or unexpected data that is based on interpretation of data, such as IDS and SEM alerts.

■ Generally focus on the characteristics and impact of the event—Determining the identity of an attacker and other similar actions are typically time-intensive and difficult to accomplish, and do not aid the organization in correcting operational issues or security weaknesses. Establishing the identity and intent of an attacker may be important, especially if a criminal investigation will ensue, but should be weighed against other important goals, such as stopping an attack and recovering systems and data.

Using Data from Applications

Applications such as e-mail, Web browsers, and word processors are what make computers valuable to users. Operating systems, files, and networks are all needed to support applications: operating systems to run the applications, networks to send application data between systems, and files to store application data, configuration settings, and logs. From a forensic perspective, applications bring together files, operating systems, and networks. This section describes application architectures—the components that typically make up applications and provide insights into the types of applications that are most often the focus of forensics. The section also provides guidance on collecting, examining, and analyzing application data.

Application Components

All applications contain code in the form of executable files (and related files, such as shared code libraries) or scripts. In addition to code, many applications have one or more of the following components: configuration settings, authentication, logs, data, and supporting files.

Configuration Settings

Most applications allow users or administrators to customize certain aspects of the application's behavior by altering configuration settings. From a forensics perspective, many settings are trivial (e.g., specifying background colors), but others might be very important, such as the host and directory where data files and logs are stored or the default username. Configuration settings may be temporary, set dynamically during a particular application session or permanent. Many applications have some settings that apply to all users, and also support some user-specific settings. Configuration settings may be stored in several ways, including the following:

■ Configuration File—Applications may store settings in a text file or a file with a proprietary binary format. Some applications require the configuration file to be on the same host as the application, whereas other applications allow configuration files to be located on other hosts. For example, an application might be installed on a workstation, but the configuration file for a particular user could be stored on the user's home directory on a file server.

■ Runtime Options—Some applications permit certain configuration settings to be specified at runtime through the use of command-line options. For example, the UNIX e-mail client mutt has options for specifying the location of the mailbox to open and the location of the configuration file. Identification of the options being used for an active session is operating system and application-specific; possible identification methods include reviewing the list of active operating system processes, examining an operating system history file, and reviewing an application log. Runtime options can also be specified in icons, startup files, batch files, and other ways.

■ Added to Source Code—Some applications that make source code available (e.g., open source applications, scripts, etc.) actually place user or administrator-specified configuration settings directly into the source code. If the application is then compiled (e.g., converted from human-readable code to a binary, machine-readable format), the configuration settings may actually be contained within executable files, potentially making the settings far more difficult to access than if they were specified in configuration files or as runtime options. In some cases, the settings can be found by searching for text strings within the executable files.

Authentication

Some applications verify the identity of each user attempting to run the application. Although this is usually done to prevent unauthorized access to the application, it may also be done when access is not a concern so that the application can be customized based on the user's identity. Common authentication methods include the following:

■ External Authentication—The application may use an external authentication service, such as a directory server. Although the application may contain some records related to authentication, the external authentication service is likely to contain more detailed authentication information.

■ Proprietary Authentication—The application may have its own authentication mechanism, such as user accounts and passwords that are part of the application, not the operating system.

■ Pass-Through Authentication—Pass-through authentication refers to passing operating system credentials (typically, username and password) unencrypted from the operating system to the application.

■ Host or User Environment—Within a controlled environment (e.g., managed workstations and servers within an organization) some applications may be able to rely on previous authentication performed by the operating system. For example, if all hosts using an application are part of the same Windows domain and each user has already been authenticated by the domain, then the application can extract the operating system-authenticated identity from each workstation's environment. The application can then restrict access to the application by tracking which users are permitted to have access and comparing the operating system-authenticated identity to the authorized user list. This technique is effective only if users cannot alter the user identity in the workstation environment.

Authentication implementations vary widely among environments and applications. The details of such implementations are beyond the scope of this document. However, cyber forensic investigators should be aware that there are many ways in which users can be authenticated and that, accordingly, the sources of user authentication records might vary greatly among applications and application implementations. Analysts should also know that some applications use access control (typically enforced by the operating system) to restrict access to certain types of information or application functions. This knowledge can be helpful in determining what a particular application user could have done. In addition, some applications record information related to access control, such as failed attempts to perform sensitive actions or access restricted data.

Logs

Although some applications (primarily very simple ones) do not record any information to logs, most applications perform some type of logging. An application may record log entries to an operating system-specific log (e.g., syslog on UNIX systems, event logs on Windows systems), a text file, a database, or a proprietary file format. Some applications record different types of events to different logs. Common types of log entries are as follows:

- Event—Event log entries typically list actions that were performed, the date and time each action occurred, and the result of each action. Examples of actions that might be recorded are establishing a connection to another system and issuing administrator-level commands. Event log entries might also include supporting information, such as what username was used to perform each action and what status code was returned (which provides more information about the result than a simple successful or failed status).
- Audit—Audit log entries, also known as security log entries, contain information pertaining to audited activities, such as successful and failed logon attempts, security policy changes, file access, and process execution. Applications may use audit capabilities built into the operating system or may provide their own auditing capabilities.
- Error—Some applications create error logs, which record information regarding application errors, typically with timestamps. Error logs are helpful in troubleshooting both operational issues and attacks. Error messages can be helpful in determining when an event of interest occurred and in identifying some characteristics of the event.
- Installation—An application may create a separate installation log file that records information pertinent to the initial installation and subsequent updates of that application. Information recorded in an installation log varies widely but is likely to include the status of various phases of the installation. The log may also indicate the source of the installation files, the locations where the application components were placed, and options involving the application's configuration.
- Debugging—Some applications can be run in a debugging mode, which means that they log far more information than usual regarding the operation of the application. Debugging records are often very cryptic and may have meaning only to the software's creator, who can decipher error codes and other facets of the records. If an application offers a debugging capability, typically it is enabled only if administrators or developers need to resolve a specific operational problem.

Data

Nearly every application is specifically designed to handle data in one or more ways, such as creating, displaying, transmitting, receiving, modifying, deleting, protecting, and storing data. For example, an e-mail client allows a user to create an e-mail message and to send it to someone, as well as to receive, view, and delete an e-mail message from someone else. Application data often resides temporarily in memory, and temporarily or permanently in files. The format of a file containing application data may be generic (e.g., text files, bitmap graphics) or proprietary.

Data may also be stored in databases, which are highly structured collections of files and data specifications. Some applications create temporary files during a session, which may contain application data. If an application fails to shut down gracefully, it may leave temporary files on media. Most operating systems have a directory designated for temporary files; however, some applications have their own temporary directory, and other applications place temporary files in the same directory where data is stored. Applications may also contain data file templates and sample data files (e.g., databases, documents).

Supporting Files

Applications often include one or more types of supporting files, such as documentation and graphics. Supporting files tend to be static, but that does not mean that they are not of value for forensics. Types of supporting files include the following:

- Documentation—This may include administrator and user manuals, help files, and licensing information. Documentation can be helpful to cyber forensic investigators in many ways, such as explaining what the application does, how the application works, and what components the application has. Documentation also typically contains contact information for the vendor of the application; the vendor might be able to answer questions and provide other assistance in understanding the application.
- Links—Also known as shortcuts, links are simply pointers to something else, such as an executable (a statement or procedural step in a programming language that calls for processing action by the computer, e.g., performing arithmetic, reading data from an external medium, making a decision, etc. An executable file is a file with its mode is set to executable, making it a file that performs a process rather than simply holding data). Links are most frequently used on Windows systems; for example, the items listed on the Start menu are really links to programs. By examining the properties of a link, an investigator can determine what program the link runs, where the program is, and what options (if any) are set.
- Graphics—These files may include standalone graphics used by the application, as well as graphics for icons. Although application graphics are typically of little interest to an investigator, icon graphics may be of interest for identifying which executable was running.

Types of Applications

Applications exist for nearly every purpose imaginable. Although forensic techniques can be applied to any application, certain types of applications are more likely to be the focus of forensic analysis, including e-mail, Web usage, interactive messaging, file sharing, document usage, security applications, and data concealment tools. Nearly every computer has at least a few applications installed from these categories. The following sections describe each of these types of applications in more detail.

E-Mail

E-mail has become the predominant means for people to communicate electronically. Each e-mail message consists of a header and a body. The body of the e-mail contains the actual content of the message, such as a memorandum or a personal letter. The header of the e-mail includes various pieces of information regarding the e-mail. By default, most e-mail client applications display only a few header fields for each message: the sender's and recipient's e-mail addresses, the date and time the message was sent, and the subject of the message. However, the header typically includes several other fields, including the following:

- Message ID
- Type of e-mail client used to create the message
- Importance of the message, as indicated by the sender (e.g., low, normal, high)
- Routing information: which e-mail servers the message passed through in transit and when each server received it
- Message content type, which indicates whether the e-mail content simply consists of a text body or also has file attachments, embedded graphics, etc.

E-mail client applications are used to receive, store, read, compose, and send e-mails. Most e-mail clients also provide an address book that can hold contact information, such as e-mail addresses, names, and phone numbers. Encryption programs are sometimes used in conjunction with e-mail clients to encrypt an e-mail's body or attachments.

When a user sends an e-mail, it is transferred from the e-mail client to the server using SMTP [Simple Mail Transfer Protocol is a protocol used to send and receive email]. If the sender and recipient of the e-mail use different e-mail servers, the e-mail is then routed using SMTP through additional e-mail servers until it reaches the recipient's server. Typically, the recipient uses an e-mail client on a separate system to retrieve the e-mail using Post Office Protocol 3 (POP3) or Internet Message Access Protocol (IMAP); in some cases, the e-mail client may be on the destination server (e.g., a multi-user UNIX system).

The destination server often performs checks on the e-mails before making them available for retrieval, such as blocking messages with inappropriate content (e.g., spam, virus). From end to end, information regarding a single e-mail message may be recorded in several places—the sender's system, each e-mail server that handles the message, and the recipient's system, as well as antivirus, spam, and content filtering servers.

Web Usage

Through Web browsers, people access Web servers that contain nearly every type of data imaginable. Many applications also offer Web-based interfaces, which are also accessed through Web browsers. Because they can be used for so many purposes, Web browsers are one of the most commonly used applications.

The basic standard for Web communications is Hypertext Transfer Protocol (HTTP). HTTP is the set of rules for exchanging files (text, graphic images, sound, video, and other multimedia files) on the World Wide Web. Relative to the TCP or IP suite of protocols (which are the basis for information exchange on the Internet), HTTP is an application protocol; however, HTTP can contain many types of data in a variety of standard and proprietary formats. HTTP is essentially the mechanism for transferring data between the Web browsers and the Web servers.

Typically, the richest sources of information regarding Web usage are the hosts running the Web browsers. Information that may be retrieved from Web browsers include a list of favorite Web sites, a history (with timestamps) of Web sites visited, cached Web data files, and cookies (including their creation and expiration dates). Another good source of Web usage information are Web servers, which typically keep logs of the requests they receive. Data that is often logged by Web servers for each request includes a timestamp; the IP address, Web browser version, and operating system of the host making the request; the type of request (e.g., read data, write data); the resource requested; and the status code.

The response to each request includes a three-digit status code that indicates the success or failure of the request. For successful requests, the status code explains what action was performed; for failures, the status code explains why the request failed.

Several other types of devices and software, in addition to Web browsers and servers, might also log related information. For example, Web proxy servers and application proxy firewalls might perform detailed logging of HTTP activity, with a level of detail similar to that of Web server logs. Routers, non-proxy firewalls, and other network devices might log the basic aspects of HTTP network connections, such as source and destination IP addresses and ports. Organizations that use Web content monitoring and filtering services might find useful data in the services' logs, particularly regarding denied Web requests.

Interactive Communications

Unlike e-mail messages, which may typically take minutes to go from sender to recipient, interactive communications services provide real-time (or near-real-time) communications. Types of applications commonly used for interactive communications include the following:

- Blogs—A frequent, chronological publication of personal thoughts and Web links. A blog is often a mixture of what is happening in a person's life and what is happening on the Web, a kind of hybrid diary or guide site, although there are as many unique types of blogs as there are people. People maintained blogs long before the term was coined, but the trend gained momentum with the introduction of automated published systems, most notably Blogger at blogger.com.
- Group Chat—Group chat applications provide virtual meeting spaces where many users can share messages at once. Group chat applications typically use a Client or Server architecture. The most popular group chat protocol, Internet Relay Chat (IRC), is a standard protocol that uses relatively simple text-based communications. IRC also provides a mechanism for users to send and receive files.
- Instant Messaging (IM) Applications—IM applications are either peer-to-peer, allowing users to send text messages and files directly to each other, or client or server, passing messages and files through a centralized server. IM application configuration settings may contain user information, lists of users that the user has communicated with, file transfer information, and archived messages or chat sessions. There are several major Internet-based IM services, each of which uses its own proprietary communications protocols. Several companies also offer enterprise IM products that are run within an organization. Such products are often integrated to some extent with the organization's e-mail services and can be used only by authenticated e-mail users.

■ Audio and Video—As the capacity of networks continues to increase, conducting real-time video and audio communications across systems computer networks also becomes more common. Technologies such as Voice over IP (VoIP) permit people to conduct telephone conversations over networks such as the Internet. Some audio implementations provide computer-based service from end to end, whereas others are only partially computer-based, with an intermediate server converting the communications between computer networks and standard phone networks. Many audio technologies are primarily peer-to-peer applications. Video technologies can be used to hold teleconferences or to have "video phone" communications between two individuals. Commonly used protocols for audio and video communications include H.323 [ITU (International Telecommunications Union) standard for videoconferencing over local area networks and packet-switched networks generally. It is based on a recognized real-time standard and is commonly used with video over the Internet to ensure that users can communicate with each other, as long as they are using videoconferencing software which complies with the standard, for example, Microsoft NetMeeting, Netscape Conference. The standard applies both to one-to-one and multi-party videoconferences] and Session Initiation Protocol (SIP).

Document Usage

Many users spend much of their time working with documents, such as letters, reports, and charts. Documents may contain any type of data, so they are often of interest to cyber forensic investigators. The class of software used for creating, viewing, and editing such documents is known as office productivity applications. This includes word processor, spreadsheet, presentation, and personal database software. Documents often have user or system information embedded in them, such as the name or username of the person who created or most recently edited the document, or the license number of the software or the MAC address of the system used to create the document.

Security Applications

Hosts often run one or more security applications that attempt to protect the host from misuse and abuse occurring through commonly used applications, such as e-mail clients and Web browsers. Some commonly used security applications are antivirus software, spy ware detection and removal utilities, content filtering (e.g., anti-spam measures), and host-based intrusion detection software. The logs of security applications may contain detailed records of suspicious activity and may also indicate whether a security compromise occurred or was prevented. If the security application is part of an enterprise deployment, such as centrally managed and controlled antivirus software, logs may be available both on individual hosts and on a centralized application log.

Data Concealment Tools

Some people use tools that conceal data from others. This might be done for benign purposes, such as protecting the confidentiality and integrity of data against access by unauthorized parties, or for malicious purposes, such as concealing evidence of improper activities. Examples of data concealment tools include file encryption utilities, steganographic tools, and system cleanup tools. System cleanup tools are special-purpose software that removes data pertaining to particular applications, such as Web browsers, as well as data in general locations, such as temporary directories. The use of most data concealment tools is unlikely to be captured in logs. Analysts should be aware of the capabilities of these tools so that they can identify such tools on a system and recognize the tools' effects. See Chapter 3 for a further in-depth discussion and review of Data Concealment Techniques.

Collecting Application Data

Application-related data may be located within file systems, volatile operating system data, and network traffic. The types of application data that these sources may contain are as follows:

- File systems—File systems may contain many types of files related to applications, including executable files and scripts, configuration files, supporting files (e.g., documentation), logs, and data files.
- Volatile operating system data—Volatile operating system data may contain information about network connections used by applications, the application processes running on a system and the command line arguments used for each process, and the files held open by applications, as well as other types of supporting information.
- Network traffic—The most relevant network traffic data involves user connections to a remote application and communications between application components on different systems. Other network traffic records might also provide supporting information, such as network connections for remote printing from an application, and DNS lookups by the application client or other components to resolve application components' domain names to IP addresses.

Cyber forensics investigators often face a major challenge in determining which data should be collected. In many cases, the investigator must first decide which application is of interest. For example, it is common to have multiple Web browsers and e-mail clients installed on a single system. If investigators are asked to collect data regarding an individual's use of the organization's e-mail services, they need to be mindful of all the ways in which the individual could have accessed those services.

The user's computer could contain three different e-mail clients and two Web browsers that could be used to access a Web-based e-mail client provided by the organization. For the user's computer, investigators could simply collect all data from the computer and then determine during the examination process which clients were actually used for e-mail.

However, there are many potential data sources aside from the user's computer, and these sources might vary based on the client that was used. For example, use of the Web-based client might have been recorded in Web server, firewall, IDS, and content monitoring software logs, as well as in Web browser history files, Web browser caches, cookies, and personal firewall logs. In some situations, collecting the necessary data might involve identifying all components of the application, deciding which were most likely to be of interest (based on the details of the situation and the need), finding the location of each component, and collecting data from those components.

Examining and Analyzing Application Data

Examining and analyzing application data largely consists of looking at specific portions of application data—file systems, volatile operating system data, and network traffic. Examination and analysis might be hindered if the application were custom, such as a program written by the user; the cyber forensic investigator is unlikely to have any knowledge of such an application. Another possible issue in examination involves use of application-based security controls, such as data encryption and passwords. Many applications use such security controls to thwart unauthorized access to sensitive data by authorized users.

In some cases, cyber forensic investigators bring together pertinent application data from several varied application data sources; this is largely a manual process. Detailed analysis of application-related events and event reconstruction usually require a skilled and knowledgeable cyber forensic investigator who understands the information presented by all the sources. The cyber forensic investigator can review the results of the examination and analysis of individual application data sources and see how the information fits together. Tools that may be helpful to cyber forensic investigators include security event management software, which can correlate some application-related events among multiple data sources, and log analysis software (including some types of host-based intrusion detection software), which can be run against certain types of logs to identify suspicious activity.

Recommendations for Using Data from Applications

Cyber forensics investigators should:

- Consider all possible application data sources—Application events might be recorded by many different data sources. In addition, applications might be used through multiple mechanisms, such as multiple client programs installed on a system and Web-based client interfaces. In such situations, investigators should identify all application components, decide which are most likely to be of interest, find the location of each component of interest, and collect the data.
- Bring together application data from various sources—The investigator should review the results of the examination and analysis of individual application data sources and determine how the information fits together, to perform a detailed analysis of application-related events and event reconstruction.

Conclusion

The material presented in this chapter is designed to assist the reader by providing an introduction and basic understanding of the data available from operating systems, network traffic and basic desktop applications.

The authors realize, as should the reader, that no single chapter, review or article can ever been 100 percent complete at any time, the introduction of new versions of software forces older products to redesign themselves or to disappear, and for new products to appear and to replace outdated technologies.

The authors hope that they have helped the reader gain an understating of the various types of data that are available from operating systems, network traffic and applications, and by doing so have assisted the cyber forensic investigator in expanding his or her knowledge base and have increased everyone's overall comfort level in dealing with this element of a cyber forensic investigation.

Reference

1. Kent, K., Chevalier, S., Grance, T. and Dang, H. (August 2006), Guide to Integrating Forensic Techniques into Incident Response, Special Publication 800-86, National Institute of Standards and Technology, Computer Security Division, Information Technology Laboratory, Gaithersburg, MD 20899–8930, http://csrc.nist.gov/publications/nistpubs/800-86/SP800-86.pdf, retrieved April 2007.

Chapter 6

Standard Operating Procedures: Digital Forensic Laboratory Accreditation Standards

Introduction

In 2005, the Texas State Legislature was going to require that all digital forensics labs be accredited if they were going to continue to present computer evidence in Texas criminal court cases. At that time, the only accreditation process available was through the American Society of Crime Laboratory Directors Laboratory Accreditation Board (ASCLD or LAB), which was cost prohibitive for most digital forensic labs. In response to the Texas Department of Public Safety Special Crimes Division's request for an accreditation process that addressed digital forensic labs, Acquisition Data (www.acquisitiondata.com) formed a nonprofit organization to develop best practices and recommended Standard Operational Procedures for such laboratories.

The Digital Forensic Laboratory Standard Operational Procedures and Accreditation Program is open to any digital forensic crime laboratory that strives to demonstrate that its management, operations, personnel, procedures, equipment, physical location, security, and health and safety procedures meet established standards. The accreditation process also includes proficiency testing, continuing education, and other programs designed to assist the digital forensic crime laboratory to provide better overall service to the criminal justice system. The program is managed by, select industry professionals from state, federal and private digital forensic laboratories. To assist requesting digital forensics laboratories in this accreditation process, the following Standard Operating Procedures were developed.

Digital Forensic Laboratory Accreditation Standards

Grading Criteria

Each section is graded with two ratings: Mandatory (M) or Recommended (R). The laboratory under review will be graded Yes or No if they have met the listed standard.

- Mandatory is an item that contains a component that effects the overall operation of the laboratory and the forensic work related to the integrity of the examination on the evidence. All items listed as the aforementioned are included.
- Recommended is an item that would enhance the laboratory and could indirectly provide the laboratory in a more professional appearance. It is denoted with an (*), and has been integrated into the checklist.

The laboratory must achieve 100 percent of the Mandatory and 50 percent of the Recommended. Following review, the digital forensic laboratory will meet the required accreditation standards.

Standard Operating Procedures Checklist

The Standard Operating Procedures are intended to be a guide to the uniform process of conducting digital forensic examination in a precise and accurate manner.

The Standard Operating Procedures should be a set of documents that are generally accepted in the technical community and the digital forensics field. For job assignments, one person can be assigned to one or more positions in the laboratory.

Standard Operating Procedures Checklist

1.1	Does the laboratory have a written set of Standard Operating Procedures? *Comments:*	Yes	No
1.2	Are all of the laboratory personnel furnished with copies of the objectives and understand them? *Comments:*	Yes	No
1.3	Do the Standard Operating Procedures address personnel, assignments, and qualifications? *Comments:*	Yes	No
1.4	Do the Standard Operating Procedures address laboratory security? *Comments:*	Yes	No
1.5	Do the Standard Operating Procedures address evidence handling to maintain its integrity? *Comments:*	Yes	No
1.6	Do the Standard Operating Procedures address security and storage of examination reports? *Comments:*	Yes	No

1.7	Do the Standard Operating Procedures address how equipment is maintained and verified? *Comments:*	Yes	No
1.8	Are the procedures accepted in the digital forensics field with regards to preserving, analyzing, and reporting? *Comments:*	Yes	No
1.9	Is there a policy in place to verify or audit records on file? *Comments:*	Yes	No
1.10	Do the Standard Operating Procedures address proficiency examinations and the required time to complete the exams? *Comments:*	Yes	No
1.11	Do the Standard Operating Procedures address record retention of personnel records, training records, equipment records, etc.? *Comments:*	Yes	No
1.12	Are personnel assignments, duties, and responsibilities clearly stated in the Standard Operating Procedures? *Comments:*	Yes	No

Date: _____/_____/_____   Location: _____

Inspector: (Please print) _____

Inspector: (Signature) _____

Laboratory Manager Checklist

The laboratory manager should have a minimum of a baccalaureate degree in Criminal Justice, Organizational Management or Leadership, or Computer Science. The laboratory manager should have the knowledge related to digital forensics, and should have experience in conducting forensic examinations of digital evidence.

Laboratory Manager Checklist

2.1*	Does the laboratory manager possess a baccalaureate degree in Criminal Justice, Organizational Management or Leadership, or Computer Science or equivalent experience in computer forensics? *Comments:*	Yes	No
2.2*	Does the laboratory manager have experience in management? *Comments:*	Yes	No
2.3*	Does the laboratory manager have the knowledge related to digital forensics and have experience in conducting forensic examinations of digital evidence? *Comments:*	Yes	No

2.4*	Is the laboratory manager's responsibility and authority well defined? *Comments:*	Yes	No
2.5*	Is there a policy in place to allow for delegation of duties? *Comments:*	Yes	No
2.6*	Does the laboratory manager regularly review laboratory personnel, activities, and records? *Comments:*	Yes	No
2.7*	Does the laboratory manager hold meetings to go over laboratory policies and procedures on a regular basis? *Comments:*	Yes	No
2.8	Are the procedures accepted in the digital forensics field with regards to preserving, analyzing, and reporting? *Comments:*	Yes	No
2.9	Are the personnel files on previous laboratory managers maintained in the laboratory for a minimum of five years? *Comments:*	Yes	No
2.10	Does the laboratory manager maintain files of all previously assigned personnel for a minimum of five years? *Comments:*	Yes	No

Date: _____/_____/_____   Location: _____

Inspector: (Please print) _____

Inspector: (Signature) _____

Digital Forensic Examiner Checklist

Examiners should have the education, experience, and training to be able to examine evidence and produce factual results.

Training should be received from a nationally recognized training facility or an individual certified as an instructor by the training center to provide instruction (i.e., Guidance Software, EnCase, FLETC, FBI, Access Data, etc.).

Proficiency testing can be completed internally if resources exist or from an outside organization that is knowledgeable in computer forensics.

Digital Forensic Examiner Checklist

3.1	Does each examiner have a minimum of a high school diploma or equivalent education certification? *Comments:*	Yes	No
3.2	Does each examiner have a minimum of eighty-hours of digital forensic training? *Comments:*	Yes	No

3.3	Is all formal training received from a person approved as an instructor in the discipline being taught? *Comments:*	Yes	No
3.4	Are training syllabi or certification of completion maintained on file for each class attended? *Comments:*	Yes	No
3.5*	Does each examiner hold an industry recognized certification in digital forensics? *Comments:*	Yes	No
3.6	Has each examiner successfully completed, at a minimum an annual or semi-annual proficiency exam? *Comments:*	Yes	No
3.7	Is each examiner knowledgeable in the use of the examination equipment, software, and the procedures used in conducting examinations? *Comments:*	Yes	No

Date: _____/_____/_____   Location: _____

Inspector: (Please print) _____

Inspector: (Signature) _____

Technician or Assistant Checklist

The Technician or Assistant is a person who assists examiners, but does not conduct forensic examinations.

Proficiency or competency testing can be completed internally if resources exist or from an outside organization that is knowledgeable in computer forensics.

Technician or Assistant Checklist

4.1	Does each technician or assistant meet the requirements to their job classification as stated in the Standard Operating Procedures? *Comments:*	Yes	No
4.2*	Is there a competency test for technician or assistant personnel appropriate for their duties? *Comments:*	Yes	No
4.3	Did all technician or assistant personnel successfully complete the competency test? *Comments:*	Yes	No
4.4*	Are technician or assistants required to complete an annual or semi-annual competency test? *Comments:*	Yes	No

4.5	Are records maintained on current and past technician or assistants in the laboratory for review for a minimum of five years? *Comments:*	Yes	No
4.6	Is there a policy in place to describe who can issue the competency testing? *Comments:*	Yes	No

Date: _____/_____/_____   Location: _____

Inspector: (Please print) _____

Inspector: (Signature) _____

Budget Checklist

The laboratory should have an adequate budget or resources to permit it to operate and maintain it standards. The budget should allow for the laboratory to meet its goals and objectives as set out in the Standard Operating Procedures.

If no formal budget is in place, the laboratory should have a document on file explaining how the organization will provide financial support.

Budget Checklist

5.1*	Does the laboratory have a formal, adequate budget? *Comments:*	Yes	No
5.2*	Does the budget adequately address the needs of the laboratory? *Comments:*	Yes	No

Date: _____/_____/_____   Location: _____

Inspector: (Please print) _____

Inspector: (Signature) _____

Training and Testing Checklist

Education and continue training is extremely important in the digital forensic field. The ever-changing hardware and software issues create a challenge for examiners.

Training should be received from a nationally recognized training facility or an individual certified as an instructor by the training center to provide instruction (i.e., Guidance Software, EnCase, FLETC, FBI, Access Data, etc.).

Proficiency testing can be completed internally if resources exist or from an outside organization that is knowledgeable in computer forensics.

Training and Testing Checklist

6.1	Does the laboratory have a well-documented training program for examiners? *Comments:*	Yes	No

6.2	Does the laboratory maintain the training syllabi or completion for each person for each training class? *Comments:*	Yes	No
6.3	Is the type of training applicable for each employee's job description? *Comments:*	Yes	No
6.4	Are the training classes received from a nationally recognized training center or by qualified or approved trainers? *Comments:*	Yes	No
6.5	Does the training program address remedial training? *Comments:*	Yes	No
6.6	Does the laboratory have a proficiency testing procedure? *Comments:*	Yes	No
6.7	Are all training records maintained on current and former employees of the laboratory for a minimum of five years? *Comments:*	Yes	No
6.8	Are all personnel supplied with copies of the documented training program? *Comments:*	Yes	No
6.9	Do all forensic examiners maintain a minimum of 80 hours of job related training every two years from a nationally recognized training center or by approved trainers? *Comments:*	Yes	No

Date: ____/____/_____ Location: _____

Inspector: (Please print) _____

Inspector: (Signature) _____

Evidence Control Checklist

The forensic laboratory must have a policy in place that ensures the integrity of the evidence. A policy should include recording when evidence is submitted and when the evidence is released. This should be in a written or electronic format.

Evidence Control Checklist

7.1	Is there a written policy in place in regards to the chain of custody of all evidence submitted to the laboratory? *Comments:*	Yes	No
7.2	Is all of the evidence submitted to the laboratory marked for identification that is visible? *Comments:*	Yes	No

7.3	Is the evidence maintained in a secure area pending examination and is this area restricted to authorized personnel only? *Comments:*	Yes	No
7.4	Is the evidence maintained in a way to insure proper control and protected from loss or tampering? *Comments:*	Yes	No
7.5	Is there a tracking system in place to show where evidence is at all times? Do you have a confidentiality agreement? *Comments:*	Yes	No
7.6	Have all employees been trained in the proper chain of custody procedures and this information placed in their personnel files? *Comments:*	Yes	No

Date: ____/____/_____ Location: _____

Inspector: (Please print) _____

Inspector: (Signature) _____

Quality Assurance Checklist

The Quality Assurance program is a set of protocols and procedures implemented to meet expected standards of quality needed to fulfill objectives. Quality assurance is the process of evaluating the overall performance of the lab on a regular basis and to provide confidence in the result.

The duties of the Quality Assurance Manager can be assigned to anyone in addition to other duties in the laboratory. The Quality Assurance Manager should be trained and have experience over all aspects of digital forensics.

With regards to removing equipment from service, the policy should address the issue of hard drives. Unless the drive is wiped or physically destroyed, residual data may exist that could be related to an investigation.

Audits of the unit can be conducted internally or by an external organization that is familiar with computer forensic procedures.

Quality Assurance Checklist

8.1	Does the laboratory have a Quality Assurance Manager? *Comments:*	Yes	No
8.2	Does the Quality Assurance Manager have training and experience to address the needs of the laboratory? *Comments:*	Yes	No
8.3	Does the laboratory have a clearly written Quality Assurance manual? *Comments:*	Yes	No
8.4	Does the laboratory conduct annual audits of operations and document the review results? *Comments:*	Yes	No

8.5	Are new procedures and equipment tested and validated before being used in examinations and are these test results documented? How? *Comments:*	Yes	No
8.6	Are all personnel supplied with copies of the Quality Assurance Manual? *Comments:*	Yes	No
8.7	Is there a policy of random review of case reports on examinations by the examiners supervisor, lab manager, or equivalent personnel? *Comments:*	Yes	No
8.8	Does the laboratory have a policy to review the testimony of examiners in legal proceedings on a random basis? *Comments:*	Yes	No
8.9	Does the laboratory have a policy in place that addresses corrective action for defective equipment when needed? *Comments:*	Yes	No
8.10	Does the laboratory have an information system in place to track case assignments, case status, and evidence tracking? *Comments:*	Yes	No
8.11	Is there a policy in place to allow the Quality Assurance Manager to address problems above the Laboratory Manager? *Comments:*	Yes	No
8.12	Are internal audits developed to address all current systems, programs, personnel qualifications, records, etc.? *Comments:*	Yes	No
8.13*	Is there a policy in place for an audit of the quality assurance program? *Comments:*	Yes	No
8.14	Are auditors specially trained to conduct internal audits of the laboratory's quality assurance procedures? *Comments:*	Yes	No
8.15	Are annual audit results documented with nonconformances and the corrective action that was taken? *Comments:*	Yes	No
8.16	Are all previous audit reports maintained on file for a minimum of five years? *Comments:*	Yes	No

Date: _____/_____/_____   Location: _____

Inspector: (Please print) _____

Inspector: (Signature) _____

Equipment Checklist

The equipment used for examinations must be adequate for the task and should be maintained in good working order. With regards to removing equipment from service, the policy should address the issue of hard drives. Unless the drive is wiped or physically destroyed, residual data may exist that could be related to an investigation.

Licensing of the operating system software and the forensic software being utilized is not only important but required by law.

Equipment Checklist

9.1	Is the equipment used for examinations adequate for the tasks assigned? *Comments:*	Yes	No
9.2	Is all equipment tested or evaluated before being placed into use? *Comments:*	Yes	No
9.3	Is the equipment used for examinations maintained in proper working order? *Comments:*	Yes	No
9.4	Is there a maintenance program in place to assure that equipment is maintained and functional? *Comments:*	Yes	No
9.5	Are logs maintained on examination equipment and are these logs up to date? *Comments:*	Yes	No
9.6*	Does the laboratory have a procedure in place to check the reliability of the examination equipment (Diagnostics Software)? *Comments:*	Yes	No
9.7*	Is backup equipment available if the primary equipment is no longer functional? *Comments:*	Yes	No
9.8*	Is there a policy in place to upgrade software, hardware, and other equipment? *Comments:*	Yes	No
9.9	Are all copies of the computers operating system and forensic software licensed for use within the guidelines of the manufacturer? *Comments:*	Yes	No
9.10	Are policies in place to remove and repair equipment from service if found defective? *Comments:*	Yes	No

Date: _____/_____/_____   Location: _____

Inspector: (Please print) _____

Inspector: (Signature) _____

Health and Safety Checklist

The position of the Health and Safety Manager is to focus on the safety and health of the laboratory personnel by ensuring that local, state, and federal regulations are being met.

The laboratory must be maintained in a manner that does not create a hazardous working condition. Review of the health and safety program can be completed by the laboratory manager or by an outside individual that is knowledgeable with health and safety issues.

Health and Safety Checklist

10.1	Does the laboratory have an individual assigned as a Health and Safety Manager? *Comments:*	Yes	No
10.2	Is there a documented health and safety program? *Comments:*	Yes	No
10.3*	Are laboratory personnel issued copies of the health and safety document or is it available for review? *Comments:*	Yes	No
10.4*	Is the Health and Safety program reviewed annually and modified as needed? *Comments:*	Yes	No
10.5*	Are all personnel trained in Health and Safety issues and is this training documented? *Comments:*	Yes	No
10.6*	Does the laboratory maintain or have immediate access to first aid kits? *Comments:*	Yes	No
10.7*	Is the laboratory maintained in a clean and organized manner *Comments:*	Yes	No

Date: _____/_____/_____   Location: _____

Inspector: (Please print) _____

Inspector: (Signature) _____

Laboratory Facilities Checklist

The digital laboratory must maintain a secure and healthy environment so that the examiners can efficiently conduct examinations. The proper design of the laboratory can facilitate the operation of the laboratories functions and activities. Security of the laboratory is of paramount importance to the integrity of the evidence and the examination results.

If the laboratory does not have an alarm, monitored security must be provided. This can be accomplished by having a security officer or a designated person that can physically observe the laboratory or have a monitored CCTV system observing the laboratory's entry and exit points.

Laboratory Facilities Checklist

11.1	Does the laboratory have adequate workspace for each employee to complete their examinations and complete reports? *Comments:*	Yes	No
11.2	Does the Quality Assurance Manager have training and experience to address the needs of the laboratory? *Comments:*	Yes	No
11.3	Does the laboratory have adequate ventilation, heating, and cooling for personnel and equipment and do they meet equipment specifications? *Comments:*	Yes	No
11.4	Is access to evidence limited and controlled to authorized personnel? *Comments:*	Yes	No
11.5	Is access to the laboratory limited and controlled to authorized personnel only? *Comments:*	Yes	No
11.6	Do all access points into the laboratory have adequate entry locking controls? *Comments:*	Yes	No
11.7	Does the laboratory maintain a distribution log of personnel assigned keys, lock codes, magnetic cards, etc.? *Comments:*	Yes	No
11.8*	Does the laboratory have an unsecured area for meetings with officers submitting evidence, attorneys, or other individuals not authorized entry into the lab? *Comments:*	Yes	No
11.9	Does the laboratory have a monitored alarm system or security officer? *Comments:*	Yes	No
11.10	Does the laboratory have adequate power and wiring for equipment? *Comments:*	Yes	No
11.11*	Is there a plan in place to address backup power such as a backup generator or backup power supplies for examination equipment? *Comments:*	Yes	No
11.12	Does the laboratory maintain a visitor's Log? *Comments:*	Yes	No
11.13*	Does the laboratory have a fire detection system? *Comments:*	Yes	No

11.14	Does the laboratory have class C fire extinguishers accessible to all personnel? *Comments:*	Yes	No
11.15*	Does the laboratory have a technical library that contains current books, journals, and other literature addressing digital forensics? *Comments:*	Yes	No
11.16*	Is the technical library accessible by all assigned laboratory personnel? *Comments:*	Yes	No

Date: _____/_____/_____   Location: _____

Inspector: (Please print) _____

Inspector: (Signature) _____

Additional Comments:

Date: _____/_____/_____   Location: _____

Inspector: (Please print) _____

Inspector: (Signature) _____

Conclusion

The standard operating procedures for assessing the eventual accreditation of a digital forensic laboratory as presented in this chapter provides the reader with a blueprint, a road map for the overall quality assessment and operational audit of an existing digital forensic lab.

These checklists may also be used proactively as baselines or best practice statements for individuals tasked with either developing operational standards for a digital forensic lab yet to be placed into operation or as an assessment tool for auditors charged with the audit and assessment of an existing digital forensic lab.

The reader is advised to use these checklists as guidelines and note that specific alterations, additions and enhancements may be required to account for local, state or federal legislation in the jurisdiction where the lab is to operate, the potential impact of international law, that may dictate the lab's operations and procedures.

As always when performing an assessment of this nature, in this type of technical environment, one should first determine what impact, if any, local cultural and ethnic differences, requirements and nuances may have on the implementation of any individual and exact control objectives and the overall operational functioning of any one specific lab.

These checklists and the areas which they assess should not be applied universally without first assessing the operational environment under, which the digital forensic laboratory is designed to function.

The authors are indebted to John Minotti, Managing Director of Acquisition Data, for granting permission to include theses standard operating procedures here in this text.

These standard operating procedures have withstood the test of actual implementation and daily use in digital forensic laboratories around the world, laboratories that faithfully follow guidelines established and developed by John and Acquisition Data. Readers interested in further information on these standard operating procedures are invited to contact John at Acquisition Data, jminotti@acquisitiondata.com or at jminotti@gmail.com, or visit the firm's web site at www.acquisitiondata.com.

Chapter 7

Performing a Cyber Forensic Investigation: Flowchart for the Seizure of Electronic Evidence and Associated Internal Control Questionnaires

Introduction

Chapter seven presents the reader with a structured approach, in the form of a procedures flowchart, for a critical step in the performance for a cyber forensic investigation, the seizure of electronic evidence. Additionally, this chapter provides introductory, foundation material through an internal control questionnaire (ICQ) designed to assist the reader in beginning an assessment of his or her organization's preparedness to mitigate the exposures resulting from cyber crime and providing a methodology to investigate these crimes via cyber forensic analysis.

Charting Your Way through an Investigation

The following flowchart (Figure 7.1) is offered here to provide assistance and direction to the reader as one prepares to undertake a cyber forensic investigation, and the critical step, the seizure of electronic evidence.

The continued and rapid growth of information technology presents the cyber forensic investigator with an ever increasing field of devices capable of storing and transmitting electronic data and ultimately electronic evidence. Potential evidence may be found on many varied devices,

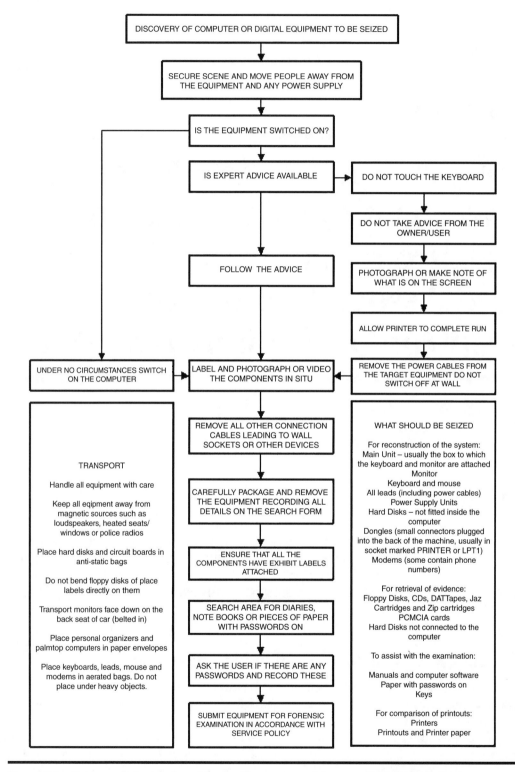

Figure 7.1 Seizure of electronic evidence. (From www.nhtcu.org. With permission.)

even devices that one might not have traditionally considered examining. One such device is the personal digital assistant (PDA). For an overview of the steps a cyber forensic investigator may take in the seizure of such a device, the reader is directed to Appendix G, which presents a Flowchart for the Seizure of a Personal Digital Assistant.

What Is an Internal Control?

The Committee of the Sponsoring Organizations (COSO) of the Treadway Commission defines internal controls as "a process, effected by an entity's board of directors, management and other personnel, designed to provide reasonable assurance regarding the achievement of objectives in the following categories:

- Effectiveness and efficiency of operations
- Reliability of financial reporting
- Compliance with applicable laws and regulations"

With key concepts supporting this definition to be:

- Internal control is a process. It is a means to an end, not an end in itself.
- Internal control is affected by people. It's not merely policy manuals and forms, but people at every level of an organization.
- Internal control can be expected to provide only reasonable assurance, not absolute assurance, to an entity's management and board.
- Internal control is geared to the achievement of objectives in one or more separate but overlapping categories (www.coso.org).

Cyber Forensic Investigation and Internal Auditing

Cyber forensics involves the identification, extraction, documentation, interpretation, and preservation of electronic data, whose eventual disposition maybe used as evidentiary material in a court of law.

In general terms, a cyber forensic investigator will use specific tools in an effort to gather specific data from an information system, which may be a single computer, a network of computers, or any device capable of storing and transmitting electronic data, in such a manner as to not alter, those data identified on a system under investigation.

Internal auditing is an independent appraisal function established within an organization to examine and evaluate the organization's activities as a service to the organization. The objective of internal auditing is to assist members of the organization in the effective discharge of their responsibilities. To this end, internal auditing furnishes them with analyses, appraisals, recommendations, counsel, and information concerning the activities reviewed. The audit objective includes promoting effective control at reasonable cost.

An internal auditor is a professional within an organization's internal auditing department who is assigned the responsibility of performing internal auditing functions, and who provides information to the organization's management, stakeholders and board of directors.

With respect to the audit of technology, the information technology (IT) auditor is a member of an integrated audit team of professionals who deliver services in the most efficient and effective means possible, while the IT auditor is specifically charged with assessing business risk as it relates to an organization's use and misuse of information technology assets.

Although seemingly different on initial examination, the roles and responsibilities of both professionals, the cyber forensic investigator and the IT auditor, are more closely related than one would realize. Both are tasked with investigating, examining, assessing and reporting on how technology has been used legally or illegally, in the performance of daily operations whether by individuals acting on their own or as employees of multi-national corporations.

Each utilizes a wealth of experience to establish a procedure, a methodology, and an approach, which enables the professional to acquire the proof necessary to substantiate the existence of inappropriate activities perpetrated through the application of information technologies.

The cyber forensic investigator as does the IT auditor gathers substantiating and corroborating evidence, of inappropriate activity, through many varied means. The starting point in either an audit or investigation is—to gather information by asking questions, lots of questions. Both professionals do so to better assist in defining the breadth, depth and scope of their eventual investigation or audit. The more information gathered at the onset, will prove invaluable to the eventual success of either the investigation or the audit.

One means of gathering information and assessing the potential for IT risk, exposure and abuse is through the use of an internal control questionnaire. Although such a tool may more heavily favor the objectives of the IT auditor, cyber forensic investigators may also benefit from incorporating such data gathering and assessment tools into their professional arsenal as well.

Internal Control Questionnaire (ICQ)

ICQ is a tool used by the auditor to conduct an internal control review. The ICQ should contain a list of key control questions that the auditor can use to assess how effectively a particular activity under review is controlled.

The ICQ should be constructed so that "yes" responses indicate good control practices and "no" responses represent potential vulnerabilities. The auditor should become familiar with the questions on the ICQ and then conduct sufficient interviews, investigation and examination to determine the answers.

A not applicable (N/A) column should also be provided on the ICQ for areas that are not appropriate for the specific activity under review. In addition, a comments column should be used by the auditor to explain, for example, for each "no" response, why the auditor does not believe the controls over this area to be adequate. The auditor should also use the comments column to indicate potential areas for audit testing (www.auditnet.org/pgms_frm.htm, retrieved February 2007).

The cyber forensic investigator should customize the ICQs to define each specific organization's constraints, policies and practices as well as specific goals of the audit or investigation.

Cyber Crime: Incident Response and Digital Forensics— Internal Control Questionnaire

Purpose

The general incident response questionnaires were created to help those responding to an incident protect mission-critical systems and assets from internal and cyberthreats. The specific questionnaires provide guidelines for five specific types of incidents, including:

■ Intrusions
■ Denial-of-service attacks

Table 7.1   Questionnaire Template (Questions Used are Examples)

Question	Response	Comments
How many computers were affected?	12	All computers in the second floor office.
Is the intranet affected?	Yes	It has been verified that the intranet has been affected.
Did the incident happen internally or externally?	Externally	

- Malicious code
- Malicious communication
- Misuse of resources

The audiences for the questionnaires are practitioners including IT security officers, members of the IRT (Incident Response Team) and IT auditors. Prior to completing these questionnaires, users should familiarize themselves with the overall cyber response methodology. During the use of these questionnaires, users should communicate effectively with the IRT and management to minimize damage and recovery within the acceptable time frame. After recovering from the incident, users should debrief the IRT and management and implement steps to minimize the risk of future incidents.

Author's Note: For our purposes we are only showing the questions rather than the entire questionnaire. However, we are providing the reader with a basic template that can be filled in, using the appropriate questions for your situation, along with the response and comments. Please see Table 7.1 for the template.

General Incident Response Questionnaire

The purpose of the incident response questionnaire is to provide an approach for reacting efficiently and quickly to information security-related incidents, so the current situation can be resolved and future problems can be prevented. The questionnaire presents a basic methodology for responding to incidents and provides the user with a consistent way in which to operate and document activity during an incident.

The incident response questionnaire has the following objectives, as shown in Figure 7.2.

- They facilitate a common understanding of the problem
- They provide a framework to define and assess the problem
- They provide an efficient approach to respond to incidents

Each type of incident is broken down into six steps that need to be executed (Table 7.2). These steps include:

- Preincident
- Immediate action
- Secondary action

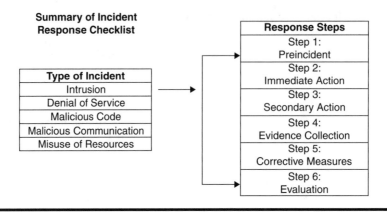

Figure 7.2   Incident response questionnaires.

Table 7.2   General Incident Response Progression Questionnaire

1. Preincident Steps—These steps are designed for planning activities that occur prior to an incident.
a. Develop and disseminate policies on incidence response.
b. Establish an internal incident notification tree to include out-of-band communication methods and redundant alternatives.
c. Establish incident response team points of contact.
d. Write and disseminate incident handling procedures and guides.
e. Provide appropriate training.
f. Know the background, authority level and expertise level of IRT members and all other personnel involved in an incident.
g. Review preincident response processes and steps on a regular basis.
2. Immediate Action—These steps are designed to be taken as soon as an incident occurs to generate a quick assessment of the situation. An incident can progress quickly and collecting the first pieces of information is critical.
a. Document all actions including the: ■ Names ■ Dates ■ Times ■ Places ■ Technical events associated with the first critical response actions
b. Contact the enterprise IRT and, if possible, provide a single individual as the primary point of contact for the incident and multiple methods of contacting that individual.
c. Verify the validity of the incident as well as the type of incident—extremely important in the initial assessment.

d. Notify the appropriate technical personnel and personnel from any other area needed to act on the incident.
e. Determine whether the incident is actively occurring or if activity has ceased.
f. Establish and define the scope of the incident.
g. Assess the immediate risk.
3. Secondary Action—These steps are designed to contain damages and set the stage for the ensuing investigation.
a. Evaluate and implement temporary defensive measures. These actions may include taking systems offline and implementing additional perimeter security controls, such as modifying firewall or e-mail filters.
b. Ensure that evidence is preserved as securely as possible. Although this is not necessarily the evidence collection phase, this step ensures that evidence is not destroyed before it can be safely collected and stored.
4. Evidence Collection—This step is designed to collect, record and transmit evidence. Evidence collection during an incident may involve more than just computer or network evidence.
a. Determine whether any paper files and records, badge logs, facility or building security tapes or logs, personnel, telephone, and other access records need to be collected.
5. Corrective Measures—These steps are designed to evaluate and improve corrective measures.
a. Evaluate the stopgap defensive measures implemented in secondary actions.
b. Verify that solutions implemented at this stage have been well researched, tested and designed as long-term solutions.
6. Evaluation—Lessons learned from live incidents are invaluable and the opportunity for improvement should not be missed.
a. Evaluate the effectiveness of the components of the incident response process.
b. Identify problem areas and implement improvements.
c. Assess all aspects of the incident, including the technical solutions, communications among team members, incident resolution and preventive strategies.

- Evidence collection
- Corrective measures
- Evaluation

Specific Incident Response Questionnaire

The following questionnaires document the steps that can help the user react quickly and efficiently to specific types of incidents. The questionnaires in Tables 7.3 through 7.7 identify five broad types or categories of incidents. Each incident questionnaire includes a description, related vulnerabilities and risks. The level of criticality is based on the level of risk combined with a lack of action to correct the vulnerability. The incident types include:

- Intrusion
- Denial of service
- Malicious code
- Malicious communication
- Misuse of resources

The incident response questionnaires represent and contain both the incident types and the execution steps. The questionnaires are designed to provide a quick view of the actions needed to be taken during the course of an incident. The scope of the questionnaires is meant to serve as a basic approach for responding to specified types of incidents in a timely and efficient manner. They do not address all the issues involved with incident handling nor do they address every type of incident.

Incident response progression provides an explanation based on the chronology and criticality of an incident. Each incident is discovered and handled in a different manner; however, there are some basic components that exist across all incidents.

Intrusion Incident Response Questionnaire

Table 7.3 shows the basic steps for handling intrusion incidents when an unauthorized user gains access or root privileges through some means of intrusion and is able to use and modify the system in the same way as a legitimate user. Some attacks in this category exploit weaknesses in operating system security and do not require the attacker to knock at the door; the door opens itself for them. Possible means of detection include:

- Unauthorized modifications discovered to system software and configuration files
- Discovery of unknown files, directories and tools installed on networks (e.g., sniffer)
- Discovery of an unknown IP address connecting to system
- Unusual activity (e.g., after-hours logins, weekend activity)

Denial-of-Service Incident Response Questionnaire

Table 7.4 lists the questions to ask in a denial-of-service incident. An incident falls into this category when an attack seeks to deny access to or use of provided services, applications or systems. Possible means of detection include:

- Users complain about not being able to access an application, a host computer or a network
- The system administrator receives multiple alerts of excessive attempts into a host computer or network

Malicious Code Incident Response Questionnaire

Table 7.5 describes procedural steps for responding to a malicious code incident. Malicious code is any code or computer program that embeds itself in other code and replicates or is intentionally

Table 7.3   Incident Response Questionnaire for Intrusion Incidents

Immediate Actions
A. Document all actions.
1. Record all system events (audit records). Documenting all details related to the incident provides valuable information to determine the course of events.
2. Document all actions taken (time-stamped). Documenting an incident helps when a final assessment of damage is done and provides the basis for a follow-up analysis.
3. Document all phone conversations including the: ■ Name of the person with whom spoken ■ Date and time ■ Content of the conversation
4. Document as if gathering evidence for a court case as it is often infeasible to determine at this time whether prosecution is viable.
B. Contact the IRT.
1. Contact the IRT: ■ During business hours (insert contact data) ■ During nonbusiness hours, weekends and holidays. If page is not returned in 15 minutes, contact the network control center or 24-hour technical assistance (insert contact data).
2. If possible, provide a single primary point of contact for the incident and provide multiple methods of contacting this individual.
C. Verify the incident.
1. Upon learning of a possible security incident, take steps to verify that the incident actually does exist.
2. If the source of the incident information is unfamiliar or not trusted, verify the source, especially if the source has identified him or herself as a representative of a legal or investigative agency.
3. Verify the incident, firsthand if possible, to ensure that the incident is not a harmless misunderstanding or a hoax.
4. Be aware of false alarms and other activities that may resemble something more serious.
D. Notify the appropriate personnel.
1. Notify the proper personnel to prepare them to deal with the issues. Often the following methods can be combined: ■ Technical personnel from the organization or the IRT will be part-time members who work the incident. ■ Additional team members for a specific incident can be pulled from different departments if necessary.
2. Ensure that IRT has representatives from information systems security, public affairs, legal, corporate security and human resources and also has access to management in other areas.

continued

Table 7.3 (continued)

3. Ensure that each member of the team has a solid understanding of the organization's policies and procedures.
4. Ensure that only the appropriate personnel are kept informed as the incident progresses.
E. Determine whether the incident is actively occurring.
1. Decide what (if any) temporary defensive measures should be taken based on whether the incident is actively occurring.
F. Establish the scope of the incident.
1. Once the incident is verified, determine its scope. Determining the scope includes asking the following questions: ■ Did the incident affect an isolated computer or many? ■ How many systems are affected? What types? ■ Did the incident affect a single network segment or multiple segments? ■ Is the intranet affected? ■ Did the incident happen internally or externally? ■ In the case of an e-mail incident, is there any pattern to the affected e-mail addresses?
2. Determine who should be notified. Although the real scope of the incident may not be apparent at this stage, knowing whether it affects other parts of the organization assists in determining who to notify.
3. Decide whether a system should be: ■ Shut down entirely ■ Disconnected from the network ■ Allowed to continue to run in a monitored state
4. Assess the scope of the business and human effects. Although the technical system may have suffered a certain type and scope of consequence, the human or business fallout from the incident may be significantly different yet no less important.
G. Assess the immediate risk.
1. Determine the immediate risk, which may include more than just analyzing what took place technically. In some situations, people or facilities may be affected. The following questions may help in the decision process: ■ Did the incident affect the safety or security of any employees? ■ Did the incident reveal any vulnerability in the technical or physical security of the company? ■ Did the incident disclose any financial data? ■ Did the incident disclose any salary or personnel data? ■ Did the incident affect research and development, corporate secrets, intellectual property or the confidentiality of any closely held organizational information? ■ Did the incident affect the reputation of the company? ■ Is the company in a legally vulnerable situation? ■ Are files being destroyed? ■ Are corporate systems being used to launch attacks against other systems? ■ Is it prudent to follow and track the intruder's activity, or must these actions be stopped as soon as possible?

H. Determine whether to sanitize and restore the affected systems or to investigate the source of the attack and person(s) responsible.

1. Conduct an investigation. Typical investigation activities include the need to:
   - Examine data
   - Gather information from those involved with the incident
   - Look for the perpetrator

2. Carefully obtain and manage information obtained in an investigation. Any information that is gathered could conceivably become evidence in a court or administrative hearing.

3. The protection of personnel and assets takes priority in most cases. However, note that isolating and sanitizing systems quickly may prevent analysts from determining the nature and motive of the attack. Even if the systems are backed up, it is not always apparent what method the intruder used to enter the system initially, which vulnerabilities were exploited, or whether the intruder was an outsider or an employee. The decision-making capability and communication among the organization's IRT members determine how successfully the incident is handled.

Secondary Actions

I. Evaluate and implement temporary defensive measures.

1. Evaluate the temporary defensive measures implemented and consider alternatives.

2. Investigate identified solutions to ensure that they are:
   - Well researched
   - Tested
   - Designed as long-term solutions

3. Implement any selected corrective measures in accordance with the site's change control procedure.

J. Ensure that evidence is preserved.

1. Identify and locate possible sources of evidence to ensure that evidence is preserved.

2. The possible evidence in an e-mail incident includes (but is not limited to):
   - E-mail messages, including full headers and attachments
   - E-mail server logs
   - Perimeter security device logs
   - Network monitoring system logs (especially useful when showing a denial-of-service condition)
   - Other systems and logs, as appropriate. (e.g., a desktop system that may have been used in an e-mail attack should be secured for later analysis.)

Evidence Collection

K. Document the chain of custody.

1. Ensure that the evidence chain of custody is protected and well documented during all phases of evidence collection. Remember that entire sources of evidence can be invalid in a legal proceeding if the evidence chain of custody is faulty.

continued

Table 7.3 (continued)

2. Note that evidence may need to be referred to in cases of corporate policy violation.
L. Collect and store evidence.
1. Collect evidence, which may consist of: ■ Hard disk drives ■ Floppy drives ■ A backup ■ Other storage media ■ Printouts ■ E-mail messages ■ Logs ■ Other files in paper or electronic format
2. Ensure that evidence is stored securely to prevent accidental or intentional modification or destruction of evidence.
M. Check the audit or log files for unusual or unknown activity.
1. To help determine the cause of the incident, use: ■ System logs ■ Network and router logs ■ Files placed or modified on the system
2. Note that many attackers attempt to delete or overwrite system or security logs. The absence of logs or missing time periods in logs are clues regarding the source of an attack.
N. Set up monitoring of system if necessary.
1. Notify the IRT's core team legal counsel members soon after it is established that an incident is in progress.
2. Consult with the IRT's core team legal staff for guidance on monitoring systems and check to see how security policies address monitoring. Liabilities due to monitoring could make the organization vulnerable to a lawsuit if users at the site or elsewhere discover that account activity is being monitored. At a minimum, legal counsel needs to be involved to protect the legal and financial interests of the organization.
Corrective Measures
O. Disconnect from the network or Internet (copy system audit or log files first).
1. When starting an investigation, do not copy logs or do anything on the system, because that may cause changes. Many times, when accessing logs, the date and times will be changed; this could possibly hamper an investigation. If the investigation turns up evidence that is to be used in a court of law, the evidence must be traceable.
2. Consult with the IRT to determine operational priorities.

3. Establish a notification chain.
4. Discuss evidence collection and communicate other pertinent details relevant to the incident.
P. Never log into a compromised system as root.
1. Take the system offline. A compromised system could have Trojan programs and sniffers running that could capture the root password or exploit other administrative privileges and thus possibly make matters worse.
2. Examine the media as read-only on a trusted operating system.
Q. Check for tools that the intruder left behind.
1. If no investigation is to take place, and the system is left connected to the network check for all tools that the intruder left behind (e.g., tools to capture user IDs and passwords). This indicates what back doors the attacker might have placed for further exploitation. The discovery of hacker files or hacker tools may indicate whether user accounts are compromised.
R. Check for modifications to the system files.
1. Check for modifications to the system files and make sure that the modifications are corrected. The intruder often modifies system files to make further exploitation easier. Modifications could include: ■ Changing permissions on files and directories ■ Creating hidden directories and files ■ Trojan programs
2. One way to check for file modifications or Trojans is to run a hash algorithm against the files and compare them to hashes from known clean files.
S. Transmit evidence to the IRT.
1. Transmit evidence to the IRT in a manner commensurate with the physical nature and security sensitivity of the evidence.
2. Use F-Secure to encrypt files being sent, or coordinate sender and recipient input to determine the most effective and secure methods of evidence transmission.
T. Identify, evaluate, test and implement corrective measures.
1.Evaluate the temporary defensive measures implemented and consider alternatives.
2. Investigate identified solutions to ensure that they are: ■ Well researched ■ Tested ■ Designed as long-term solutions.
3. Implement any selected corrective measures in accordance with the site change control procedure.

continued

Table 7.3   (continued)

U. Consider a complete rebuild of the system from original media.
1. Consider conducting a complete rebuild of the system to make sure that all the intruder's tools, back doors and Trojan programs are completely negated. Consider this especially when there is evidence of root kit.
V. Install security patches if needed (e.g., vendor patches).
1. Install the proper security patches to prevent future exploitation by the same vulnerability. Many times systems are exploited because the operating systems and other applications are not properly patched.
2. Always test patches on a test server before installing on the production system, unless the incident makes it infeasible.
W. Reconfigure firewalls if needed.
1. If it is discovered that the firewalls are not configured properly, reconfigure them and install any patches that may be needed. Most vulnerabilities in firewalls are from improper configurations that leave holes for possible exploitation. Proper configurations and installation of security patches prevent future exploitation by the discovered vulnerabilities.
2. Always test patches before installing on the production system, unless the incident makes it infeasible.
X. Change compromised passwords.
1. If the system is compromised, change all passwords to mitigate further exploitation.
2. This is also a good opportunity to run a crack-type program on systems to see if users are using easily crackable programs.
Evaluation
Y. Assess performance and implement improvements.
1. Evaluate the effectiveness and operation of the various incident response components during the incident and identify problem areas.
2. Consider and implement improvements as appropriate, in accordance with the site change control procedure.

Table 7.4   Incident Response Questionnaire for DoS Incidents

Immediate Actions
A. Document all actions.
1. Record all system events (audit records). Documenting all details related to the incident provides valuable information to determine the course of events.
2. Document all actions taken (time- stamped). Documenting an incident helps when a final assessment of damage is done and provides the basis for a follow-up analysis.
3. Document all telephone conversations including the: ■ Name of the person with whom spoken ■ Date and time ■ Content of the conversation
4. Document as if gathering evidence for a court case as it is often infeasible to determine at this time whether prosecution is viable.
B. Contact the IRT
1. Contact the IRT: ■ During business hours (insert contact data) ■ During nonbusiness hours, weekends and holidays. If page is not returned in 15 minutes, contact the network control center or 24-hour technical assistance (insert contact data).
2. If possible, provide a single primary point of contact for the incident and provide multiple methods of contacting this individual.
C. Verify the incident.
1. Upon learning of a possible security incident, take steps to verify that the incident actually does exist.
2. If the source of the incident information is unfamiliar or not trusted, verify the source, especially if the source has identified him/herself as a representative of a legal or investigative agency.
3. Verify the incident, firsthand if possible, to ensure that the incident is not a harmless misunderstanding or a hoax.
4. Be aware of false alarms and other activities that may resemble something more serious.
D. Notify the appropriate personnel.
1. Notify the proper personnel to prepare them to deal with the issues. Often the following methods can be combined: ■ Technical personnel either from the organization or IRT will be part-time members who work the incident. ■ Additional team members for a specific incident can be pulled from different departments if necessary.
1. Ensure that IRT has representatives from information systems security, public affairs, legal, corporate security and human resources, as well as access to management in other areas.

continued

Table 7.4 (continued)

2. Ensure that each member of the team has a solid understanding of the company's policies and procedures.
3. Ensure that only the appropriate personnel are kept informed as the incident progresses.
E. Determine whether the incident is actively occurring.
1. Decide what (if any) temporary defensive measures should be taken based on whether the incident is actively occurring.
F. Establish the scope of the incident.
1. Once the incident is verified, determine its scope. Determining the scope may include asking the following questions: ■ Did the incident affect an isolated computer or many? ■ How many systems are affected? What types? ■ Did the incident affect a single network segment or multiple segments? ■ Is the intranet affected? ■ Did the incident happen internally or externally? ■ In the case of an e-mail incident, is there any pattern to the affected e-mail addresses?
2. Determine who should be notified. While the real scope of the incident may not be apparent at this stage, knowing whether it affects other parts of the organization assists in determining who to notify.
3. Decide whether a system should be: ■ Shut down entirely ■ Disconnected from the network ■ Allowed to continue to run in a monitored state
4. Assess the scope of the business and human effects. Although the technical system may have suffered a certain type and scope of consequence, the human or business fallout from the incident may be significantly different, yet no less important.
G. Assess the immediate risk.
1. Determine the immediate risk, which may include more than just analyzing what took place technically. In some situations, people or facilities may be affected. The following questions may help in the decision process: ■ Did the incident affect the safety or security of any employees? ■ Did the incident reveal any vulnerability in the technical or physical security of the company? ■ Did the incident disclose any financial data? ■ Did the incident disclose any salary or personnel data? ■ Did the incident affect research and development, corporate secrets, intellectual property, or the confidentiality of any closely held organizational information? ■ Did the incident affect the reputation of the company? ■ Is the company in a legally vulnerable situation? ■ Are files being destroyed? ■ Are corporate systems being used to launch attacks against other systems? ■ Is it prudent to follow and track the intruder's activity, or must these actions be stopped as soon as possible?

H. Determine whether to sanitize and restore the affected systems or to investigate the source of the attack and person(s) responsible.

1. Conduct an investigation. Typical investigation activities include the need to:
   ■ Examine data
   ■ Gather information from those involved with the incident
   ■ Look for the perpetrator

2. Carefully obtain and manage information obtained in an investigation. Any information that is gathered could conceivably become evidence in court or in an administrative hearing.

3. The protection of personnel and assets takes priority in most cases. However, note that isolating and sanitizing systems quickly may prevent analysts from determining the nature and motive of the attack. Even if the systems are backed up, it is not always apparent what method the intruder used to enter the system initially, which vulnerabilities were exploited, or whether the intruder was an outsider or an employee. The decision-making capability and communication among the organization's IRT members determine how successfully the incident is handled.

Secondary Actions

I. Evaluate and implement temporary defensive measures.

1. Identify temporary defensive measures, based on the status of the incident and the identified risk. Many defensive measures may be instituted, depending upon the attack type.

2. In an e-mail incident, defensive measures may include:
   ■ Filters on e-mail servers
   ■ Filters on perimeter security devices
   ■ Disabling e-mail servers
   ■ Disconnecting the network

Secondary Actions

J. Ensure that evidence is preserved.

1. Identify and locate possible sources of evidence to ensure that evidence is preserved.

2. The possible evidence in an e-mail incident includes (but is not limited to):
   ■ E-mail messages, including full headers and attachments
   ■ E-mail server logs
   ■ Perimeter security device logs
   ■ Network monitoring system logs (especially useful when showing a denial-of-service condition)
   ■ Other systems and logs, as appropriate. For example, a desktop system that may have been used in an e-mail attack should be secured for later analysis.

K. Check to see if the application or network has been inadvertently taken offline or if system maintenance is causing the problem.

continued

Table 7.4   (continued)

1. Check the following possible causes before concluding that an intentional DoS is occurring: ■ A system was taken offline ■ New hardware was installed ■ New software was installed ■ An application was misconfigured
L. Check to see how many users are having problems with this service or system and what symptoms were noticed.
1. To narrow the pool of causes concerning a DoS attack, check how many users are affected by the incident. The combination of these components may assist in identifying the cause of the attack as well as some possible solutions.
2. Assess the symptoms of the attack.
Evidence Collection
M. Document the chain of custody.
1. Ensure that the evidence chain of custody is protected and well documented during all phases of evidence collection. Remember that entire sources of evidence can be invalid in a legal proceeding if the evidence chain of custody is faulty.
2. Note that evidence may need to be referred to in cases of corporate policy violation.
N. Collect and store evidence.
1. Collect evidence, which may consist of: ■ Hard disk drives ■ Floppy drives ■ A backup ■ Other storage media ■ Printouts ■ E-mail messages ■ Logs ■ Other files in paper or electronic format
2. Ensure that evidence is stored securely to prevent accidental or intentional modification or destruction of evidence.
O. Check binaries and configuration files for any modifications that might lead to the system outage.
1. Check for modifications to system binaries and configuration files as another possibility for causing DoS in a system.
P. Check firewall event logs for any unauthorized access.
1. To help determine the cause of the incident, check: ■ System logs ■ Network logs ■ Router logs ■ Files placed or modified on the system. These logs help determine if the DoS is occurring from outside the company's domain

2. Determine whether the intruder is internal or external to the organization.
Q. Have the IRT contact the legal staff for investigation advice.
1. Involve the IRT core team legal counsel members to protect the legal and financial interests of the organization. Some of the legal and practical issues include: ■ Reputation damage—Is the organization willing to risk negative publicity or exposure to cooperate with legal prosecution efforts? ■ Liability considerations—If a compromised system is left up and running so it can be monitored and another system is damaged because the attack originated from the system, the organization may be liable for damages incurred. ■ Disclosure of information—If the organization discloses information about an attack in which another company may be involved or information on a vulnerability in a product that may affect the marketing of that product, it may be liable for any damages (including damage of reputation). ■ Liabilities due to monitoring—The organization could be vulnerable to a lawsuit if users at its site or elsewhere discover that account activity is being monitored.
R. Set up monitoring of the system if necessary.
1. Ensure that the IRT notifies its core team legal counsel members soon after it is established that an incident is in progress.
2. Ensure that the IRT consults with the core team legal staff for guidance on monitoring systems and checks to see how security policies address monitoring. Liabilities due to monitoring could make the organization vulnerable to a lawsuit if users at the site or elsewhere discover that account activity is being monitored. At a minimum, legal counsel needs to be involved to protect the legal and financial interests of the organization.
Corrective Measures
S. Transmit evidence to the IRT.
1. Transmit evidence to IRT in a manner commensurate with the physical nature and security sensitivity of the evidence.
2. Use F-Secure to encrypt files being sent or coordinate sender and recipient input to determine the most effective and secure methods of evidence transmission.
T. Identify, evaluate, test and implement corrective measures.
1. Evaluate the temporary defensive measures implemented and consider alternatives.
2. Investigate solutions to ensure that they are: ■ Well researched ■ Tested ■ Designed as long-term solutions
3. Implement any corrective measures selected in accordance with the site change control procedure.
U. Do not run servers at a level too close to capacity.
1. Consider reducing the risk of a DoS attack by not running the company servers at too high capacity, if appropriate.

continued

Table 7.4   (continued)

V. Use packet filtering to prevent obviously forged packets from entering into the network address space.
1. Prevent forged packets from entering the network by using packet filtering, thus reducing the risk of a DoS attack.
W. Keep up to date on security-related patches.
1. Keep up to date on security-related patches for the designated operating systems to help reduce the risk of a DoS attack.
Evaluation
X. Assess performance and implement improvements.
1. Evaluate the effectiveness and operation of the various incident response components during the incident and identify problem areas.
2. Consider improvements and implement as appropriate, in accordance with the site's change control procedure.

Table 7.5   Incident Response Questionnaire for Malicious Code Incidents

Immediate Actions
A. Document all actions.
1. Record all system events (audit records). Documenting all details related to the incident provides valuable information to determine the course of events.
2. Document all actions taken (time stamped). Documenting an incident helps when a final assessment of damage is done and provides the basis for a follow-up analysis.

3. Document all telephone conversations including:
    ■ Name of the person with whom spoken
    ■ Date and time
    ■ Content of the conversation

4. Document as if gathering evidence for a court case as it is often infeasible to determine at this time whether prosecution is viable.
B. Contact the IRT.

1. Contact the IRT:
    ■ During business hours, (insert contact data)
    ■ During nonbusiness hours, weekends and holidays. If page is not returned in 15 minutes, contact the network control center or 24-hour technical assistance (insert contact data).

2. If possible, provide a single primary point of contact for the incident and multiple methods of contacting this individual.

Table 7.5   (continued)

C. Notify the antivirus team.
1. If the organization currently has an antivirus team in place, report any virus activity to the antivirus team and the IRT.
D. Verify the incident.
1. Upon learning of a possible security incident, take steps to verify that the incident actually does exist.
2. If the source of the incident information is unfamiliar or not trusted, verify the source, especially if the source has identified him or herself as a representative of a legal or investigative agency.
3. Verify the incident, firsthand if possible, to ensure that the incident is not a harmless misunderstanding or a hoax.
4. Be aware of false alarms and other activities that may only resemble something more serious.
E. Notify the appropriate personnel.
1. Notify the proper personnel to prepare them to deal with the issues. Often the following methods can be combined: ■ Technical personnel either from the enterprise or the IRT will be part-time members who work the incident. ■ Additional team members for a specific incident can be pulled from different departments if necessary.
F. Ensure that IRT has representatives from information systems security, public affairs, legal, corporate security and human resources, as well as access to management in other areas.
2. Ensure that each member of the team has a solid understanding of the company's policies and procedures.
3. Ensure that only the appropriate personnel are kept informed as the incident progresses.
G. Determine whether the incident is actively occurring.
1. Decide what (if any) temporary defensive measures should be taken based on whether the incident is actively occurring.
H. Establish the scope of the incident.
1. Once the incident is verified, determine its scope. Determining the scope includes asking the following questions: ■ Did the incident affect an isolated computer or many? ■ How many systems are affected? What types? ■ Did the incident affect a single network segment or multiple segments? ■ Is the intranet affected? ■ Did the incident happen internally or externally? ■ In the case of an e-mail incident, is there any pattern to the affected e-mail addresses?

continued

Table 7.5   (continued)

2. Determine who should be notified. Although the real scope of the incident may not be apparent at this stage, knowing whether it affects other parts of the organization assists in determining who to notify.
3. Decide whether a system should be: ■ Shut down entirely ■ Disconnected from the network ■ Allowed to continue to run in a monitored state
4. Assess the scope of the business and human effects. Although the technical system may have suffered a certain type and scope of consequence, the human or business fallout from the incident may be significantly different, yet no less important.
I. Assess the immediate risk.
1. Determine the immediate risk, which may include more than just analyzing what took place technically. In some situations, people or facilities may be affected. The following questions may help in the decision process: ■ Did the incident affect the safety or security of any employees? ■ Did the incident reveal any vulnerability in the technical or physical security of the company? ■ Did the incident disclose any financial data? ■ Did the incident disclose any salary or personnel data? ■ Did the incident affect research and development, corporate secrets, intellectual property, or the confidentiality of any closely held organizational information? ■ Did the incident affect the reputation of the company? ■ Is the company in a legally vulnerable situation? ■ Are files being destroyed? ■ Are corporate systems being used to launch attacks against other systems? ■ Is it prudent to follow and track the intruder's activity, or must these actions be stopped as soon as possible?
J. Run disinfecting program on all diskettes and systems, checking for any virus infection.
1. Run the disinfecting program on all diskettes and systems to help reduce the risk of future infection by the virus program.
Evaluation
K. Assess performance and implement improvements.
1. Evaluate the effectiveness and operation of the incident response components during the incident and identify problem areas.
2. Consider improvements and implement as appropriate, in accordance with the site's change control procedure.

included in a system for an unauthorized purpose. Once active, it takes unwanted and unexpected actions that can result in either destructive or nondestructive outcomes (e.g., Trojan horse, virus)

Malicious Communication Incident Response Questionnaire

Table 7.6 describes procedural steps for responding to malicious communication incidents that can result from a variety of behaviors, including:

- Employee posting cyberthreats
- Spamming
- Threatening or harassing e-mail
- Phreaking

Table 7.6   Incident Response Questionnaire for Malicious Communication Incidents

Immediate actions
A. Document all actions.
1. Record all system events (audit records). Documenting all details related to the incident provides valuable information to determine the course of events.
2. Document all actions taken (time-stamped). Documenting an incident helps when a final assessment of damage is done and provides the basis for a follow-up analysis.
3. Document all telephone conversations including the: ■ Name of the person with whom spoken ■ Date and time ■ Content of the conversation
4. Document as if gathering evidence for a court case as it is often infeasible to determine at this time whether prosecution is viable.
B. Contact the IRT.
1. Contact the IRT: ■ During business hours (insert contact data) ■ During nonbusiness hours, weekends and holidays. If page is not returned in 15 minutes, contact the network control center or 24-hour technical assistance (insert contact data).
2. If possible, provide a single primary point of contact for the incident and multiple methods of contacting this individual.
C. Verify the incident.
1. Upon learning of a possible security incident, take steps to verify that the incident actually does exist.
2. If the source of the incident information is unfamiliar or not trusted, verify the source, especially if the source has identified him or herself as a representative of a legal or investigative agency.

continued

Table 7.6   (continued)

3. Verify the incident, firsthand if possible, to ensure that the incident is not a harmless misunderstanding or a hoax.
4. Be aware of false alarms and other activities that may resemble something more serious.
D. Notify the appropriate personnel.
1. Notify the proper personnel to prepare them to deal with the issues. Often the following methods can be combined: ■ Technical personnel either from the enterprise or IRT will be part-time members who work the incident. ■ Additional team members for a specific incident can be pulled from different departments if necessary. Ensure that IRT has representatives from information systems security, public affairs, legal, corporate security and human resources, as well as access to management in other areas.
2. Ensure that each member of the team has a solid understanding of the company's policies and procedures.
3. Ensure that only the appropriate personnel are kept informed as the incident progresses.
E. Determine whether the incident is actively occurring.
1. Decide what (if any) temporary defensive measures should be taken based on the knowledge of whether the incident is actively occurring.
F. Establish the scope of the incident.
1. Once the incident is verified, determine its scope. Determining the scope includes asking the following questions: ■ Did the incident affect an isolated computer or many? ■ How many systems are affected? What types? ■ Did the incident affect a single network segment or multiple segments? ■ Is the intranet affected? ■ Did the incident happen internally or externally? ■ In the case of an e-mail incident, is there any pattern to the affected e-mail addresses?
2. Determine who should be notified. Although the real scope of the incident may not be apparent at this stage, knowing whether it affects other parts of the organization assists in determining who to notify.
3. Decide whether a system is: ■ Shut down entirely ■ Disconnected from the network ■ Allowed to continue to run in a monitored state
4. Assess the scope of the business and human effects. Although the technical system may have suffered a certain type and scope of consequence, the human or business fallout from the incident may be significantly different, yet no less important.

G. Assess the immediate risk.
1. Determine the immediate risk, which may include more than just analyzing what took place technically. In some situations, people or facilities may be affected. The following questions may help in the decision process: ■ Did the incident affect the safety or security of any employees? ■ Did the incident reveal any vulnerability in the technical or physical security of the company? ■ Did the incident disclose any financial data? ■ Did the incident disclose any salary or personnel data? ■ Did the incident affect research and development, corporate secrets, intellectual property, or the confidentiality of any closely held organizational information? ■ Did the incident affect the reputation of the company? ■ Is the company in a legally vulnerable situation? ■ Are files being destroyed? ■ Are corporate systems being used to launch attacks against other systems? ■ Is it prudent to follow and track the intruder's activity, or must these actions be stopped as soon as possible?
Secondary Actions
H. Evaluate and implement temporary defensive measures.
1. Identify temporary defensive measures, based on the status of the incident and the identified risk. Many defensive measures may be instituted, depending upon the attack type.
2. In an e-mail incident, defensive measures may include: ■ Filters on e-mail servers ■ Filters on perimeter security devices ■ Disabling e-mail servers ■ Disconnecting the network
I. Ensure that evidence is preserved.
1. Identify and locate possible sources of evidence to ensure that evidence is preserved.
2. The possible evidence in an e-mail incident includes (but is not limited to): ■ E-mail messages, including full headers and attachments ■ E-mail server logs ■ Perimeter security device logs ■ Network monitoring system logs (especially useful when showing a denial-of-service condition) ■ Other systems and logs, as appropriate. For example, a desktop system that may have been used in an e-mail attack should be secured for later analysis
Evidence Collection
J. Document the chain of custody.
1. Ensure that the evidence chain of custody is protected and well documented during all phases of evidence collection. Remember that entire sources of evidence can be invalid in a legal proceeding if the evidence chain of custody is faulty.

continued

Table 7.6 (continued)

2. Note that evidence may need to be referred to in cases of corporate policy violation.
K. Collect and store evidence.
1. Collect and securely store evidence including: ■ Hard disk drives ■ Floppy drives ■ A backup ■ Other storage media ■ Printouts ■ E-mail messages ■ Logs ■ Other files in paper or electronic format
2. Ensure that evidence is stored securely to prevent accidental or intentional modification or destruction of evidence.
Corrective Measures
L. Transmit evidence to the IRT.
1. Transmit evidence to the IRT in a manner commensurate with the physical nature and security sensitivity of the evidence.
2. Use F-Secure to encrypt files being sent, or coordinate sender and recipient input to determine the most effective and secure method of evidence transmission.
M. Identify, evaluate, test and implement corrective measures.
1. Evaluate the temporary defense measures implemented and consider alternatives.
2. Investigate identified solutions to ensure that they are: ■ Well researched ■ Tested ■ Designed as long-term solutions
3. Implement any corrective measures in accordance with the site's change control procedure.
Evaluation
N. Assess performance and implement improvements.
1. Evaluate the effectiveness and operation of the incident response components during the incident and identify problem areas.
2. Consider and implement improvements as appropriate, in accordance with the site's change control procedure.

Misuse of Resources Incident Response Questionnaire

Table 7.7 describes procedural steps for responding to a misuse of resources incident, which covers a wide range of behavior and activities. Behavior or activity of this type includes but is notlimited to:

- Excessive use of system administrator privileges
- Sabotage
- Stealing of passwords
- Use of unauthorized or pirated software
- Pornography
- Use of company equipment to attack another system
- Theft of services

Table 7.7   Incident Response Questionnaire for Misuse of Resources Incidents

Immediate Action
A. Document all actions.
1. Record all system events (audit records). Documenting all details related to the incident provides valuable information to determine the course of events.
2. Document all actions taken (time-stamped). Documenting an incident helps when a final assessment of damage is done and provides the basis for a follow-up analysis.

3. Document all telephone conversations including:
  ■ Name of the person with whom spoken
  ■ Date and time
  ■ Content of the conversation

4. Document as if gathering evidence for a court case, as it is often infeasible to determine at this time whether prosecution is viable.
B. Contact the IRT.

1. Contact IRT:
  ■ During business hours (insert contact data).
  ■ During nonbusiness hours, weekends and holidays. If page is not returned in 15 minutes, contact the network control center or 24-hour technical assistance (insert contact data).

2. If possible, provide a single primary point of contact for the incident and multiple methods of contacting this individual.
C. Verify the incident.
1. Upon learning of a possible security incident, take steps to verify that the incident actually does exist.
2. If the source of the incident information is unfamiliar or not trusted, verify the source, especially if the source has identified him or herself as a representative of a legal or investigative agency.

continued

Table 7.7   (continued)

3. Verify the incident, firsthand if possible, to ensure that the incident is not a harmless misunderstanding or a hoax.
4. Be aware of false alarms and other activities that may resemble something more serious.
D. Notify the appropriate personnel.
1. Notify the proper personnel to prepare them to deal with the issues. Often the following methods can be combined: ■ Technical personnel either from the enterprise or IRT will be part-time members who work the incident. ■ Additional team members for a specific incident can be pulled from different departments if necessary. Ensure that IRT has representatives from information systems security, public affairs, legal, corporate security and human resources, as well as access to management in other areas.
2. Ensure that each member of the team has a solid understanding of the company's policies and procedures.
3. Ensure that only the appropriate personnel are kept informed as the incident progresses.
E. Determine whether the incident is actively occurring.
1. Decide what (if any) temporary defensive measures should be taken, based on the knowledge of whether the incident is actively occurring.
F. Establish the scope of the incident.
1. Once the incident is verified, determine its scope. Determining the scope includes asking the following questions: ■ Did the incident affect an isolated computer or many? ■ How many systems are affected? What types? ■ Did the incident affect a single network segment or multiple segments? ■ Is the intranet affected? ■ Did the incident happen internally or externally? ■ In the case of an e-mail incident, is there any pattern to the affected e-mail addresses?
2. Determine who should be notified. Although the real scope of the incident may not be apparent at this stage, knowing whether it affects other parts of the organization assists in determining who to notify.
3. Decide whether a system should be: ■ Shut down entirely ■ Disconnected from the network ■ Allowed to continue to run in a monitored state
4. Assess the scope of the business and human effects. Although the technical system may have suffered a certain type and scope of consequence, the human or business fallout from the incident may be significantly different, yet no less important.
G. Assess the immediate risk.

Table 7.7   (continued)

1. Determine the immediate risk, which may include more than just analyzing what took place technically. In some situations, people or facilities may be affected. The following questions may help in the decision process: ■ Did the incident affect the safety or security of any employees? ■ Did the incident reveal any vulnerability in the technical or physical security of the company? ■ Did the incident disclose any financial data? ■ Did the incident disclose any salary or personnel data? ■ Did the incident affect research and development, corporate secrets, intellectual property, or the confidentiality of any closely held organizational information? ■ Did the incident affect the reputation of the company? ■ Is the company in a legally vulnerable situation? ■ Are files being destroyed? ■ Are corporate systems being used to launch attacks against other systems? ■ Is it prudent to follow and track the intruder's activity, or must these actions be stopped as soon as possible?
Secondary Actions
H. Evaluate and implement temporary defensive measures.
1. Identify temporary defensive measures, based on the status of the incident and the identified risk. Many defensive measures may be instituted, depending upon the attack type.
2. In an e-mail incident, defensive measures may include: ■ Filters on e-mail servers ■ Filters on perimeter security devices ■ Disabling e-mail servers ■ Disconnecting the network
I. Ensure that evidence is preserved.
1. Identify and locate possible sources of evidence to ensure that evidence is preserved.
2. The possible evidence in an e-mail incident includes (but is not limited to): ■ E-mail messages, including full headers and attachments ■ E-mail server logs ■ Perimeter security device logs ■ Network monitoring system logs (especially useful when showing a denial-of-service condition) ■ Other systems and logs, as appropriate. For example, a desktop system that may have been used in an e-mail attack should be secured for later analysis.
Evidence Collection
J. Document the chain of custody.
1. Ensure that the evidence chain of custody is protected and well documented during all phases of evidence collection. Remember that entire sources of evidence can be invalid in a legal proceeding if the evidence chain of custody is faulty.

continued

Table 7.7   (continued)

2. Note that evidence may need to be referred to in cases of corporate policy violation.
K. Collect and store evidence.
1. Collect and securely store evidence, including: ■ Hard disk drives ■ Floppy drives ■ A backup ■ Other storage media ■ Printouts ■ E-mail messages ■ Logs ■ Other files in paper or electronic format
2. Ensure that evidence is stored securely to prevent accidental or intentional modification or destruction of evidence.
L. Set up monitoring of system if necessary.
1. The IRT notifies its core team legal counsel members soon after an incident is established as in progress.
2. The IRT consults with the core team legal staff for guidance on monitoring systems and how security policies address monitoring. Liabilities due to monitoring could make the organization vulnerable to a lawsuit if users at the site or elsewhere discover that account activity is being monitored. At a minimum, legal counsel needs to be involved to protect the legal and financial interests of the organization.
Corrective Measures
M. Transmit evidence to the IRT.
1. Transmit evidence to the IRT in a manner commensurate with the physical nature and security sensitivity of the evidence.
2. Use F-Secure to encrypt files being sent, or coordinate sender and recipient input to determine the most effective and secure methods of evidence transmission.
N. Identify, evaluate, test and implement corrective measures.
1. Evaluate the temporary defensive measures implemented and consider alternatives.
2. Investigate identified solutions to ensure that they are: ■ Well researched ■ Tested ■ Designed as long-term solutions
3. Implement any selected corrective measures in accordance with the site's change control procedure.
O. The IRT consults with core team members from legal and human resources regarding acceptable use policy, if one exists.

Table 7.7 (continued)

1. Review the acceptable use policy, which covers a wide range of behavior and activities. A good, acceptable use policy describes what an organization allows employees to do with company-owned assets and information, and documents the penalties for deviating from acceptable uses.
2. Consult with the legal staff and human resources staff before confronting any employee in question of violating the acceptable use policy.
Evaluation
P. Assess performance and implement improvements.
1. Evaluate the effectiveness and operation of the incident response components during the incident, and identify problem areas.
2. Implement improvements as appropriate, in accordance with the site's change control procedure.

Virus-Related Incident Questionnaire

The audiences for the questionnaire are practitioners, including IT security officers, members of the VRT (Virus Response Team) and IT auditors. Prior to completing the questionnaire, users should familiarize themselves with the overall virus response methodology. Although using this questionnaire, users should communicate effectively with the VRT and management to minimize damage and recover within the acceptable time frame. After recovering from the incidents, users should debrief the VRT and management and implement steps to minimize the risk of future incidents.

Virus Reporting Questionnaire

Table 7.8 consists of security questions to assist with the reporting of a virus-related incident. These questions are usually asked during the initial communication.

The following virus reporting descriptions provide guidelines for specific types of incidents. These descriptions are not intended to be all-inclusive, but rather to supplement existing policies and the information provided elsewhere in this document and in the comprehensive incident response questionnaire in Table 7.2.

Virus Discovered on Network Server

Means of detection:

■ Determine whether virus software alerts were sent to inform the system administrator that a virus had been found on the network
■ Determine whether user complaints were received that executable files on system were not functioning
■ Determine whether user complaints were received that the network was not accessible

Table 7.8 Virus-Related Incident Questionnaire

1. Determine whether antivirus software is being used. If yes, find out what message the antivirus software gave.
2. Determine the name of the antivirus software and the date of its last update.
3. Determine whether it is known how the virus was obtained, via: ■ Diskette ■ File downloaded ■ New software ■ E-mail ■ Other
4. Determine the name of the virus.
5. Determine the type of virus.
6. Determine whether other viruses have been experienced.
7. Determine whether anyone else in the organization is infected with the same virus. ■ Determine how many others are infected ■ Determine whether anyone is infected with a different virus
8. Determine whether any of the following symptoms were noticed: ■ Change in file sizes ■ Reassignment of system resources ■ Unaccounted use or reduction of RAM ■ Slower disk activity ■ Strange hardware behavior ■ Strange messages, music or graphical displays
9. Determine how many systems or users are affected.
10. Determine the operating system.
11. Determine whether the system is on a network.
12. Determine what has been done thus far to mitigate or identify the incident.

Reactions to the incident:

■ Obtain user assistance in identifying the virus and eradicating it from the systems.
■ Boot system from a clean diskette.
■ Run disinfecting program on all diskettes and systems, checking for any virus infections.
■ Check all diskettes for viruses.

Virus Detected on Workstations

Means of detection:

■ Determine whether virus software alerts were sent to inform the user that a file may be infected with a virus

- Determine whether user complaints were received that executable files on system were not functioning

Reactions to the incident:

- Obtain user assistance in identifying the virus and eradicating it from the systems
- Boot system from a clean diskette
- Run disinfecting program on all diskettes and systems, checking for any virus infections
- Check all diskettes for viruses

Organizational Questionnaire

Table 7.9 focuses on organizational aspects of the intrusion or incident that may not be covered in the technical portions of the incident response checklist. These questions assist the enterprise IRT with ascertaining the source of the incident and assessing organizational impact.

Table 7.9   Organizational Questionnaire

1. Determine geographically the point of entry or point of origination of the incident
2. Determine whether the incident was contained to one office or location
3. Determine the potential for the incident to spread to other locations
4. Determine whether the intrusion or incident occurred in a public or secured location
5. Determine how many people had access to that location
6. Determine how many people have knowledge of the targeted system, server or file location of the targeted data
7. Determine whether the intruder must have special knowledge or access
8. Determine who now knows about the incident
9. Determine the level of technical sophistication the intruder would need to conduct the attack
10. Determine how many people or groups are affected at the enterprise. Determine whether the effects of the incident, by nature, make the incident public. If appropriate, determine what steps have been taken to inform people
11. Determine the sensitivity level of the compromised data or system
12. Determine the nature or content of the compromised data
13. Determine what recent changes occurred in the overall organization or the targeted organization. Determine whether there are any: ■ Management changes ■ Reorganizations ■ Location changes ■ Layoffs

continued

Table 7.9 (continued)

14. Determine whether the incident included:
  ■ Message or text
  ■ E-mail messages
  ■ Internet postings
  ■ Chat room dialog

15. Determine whether anyone or anything was threatened. If so, determine:
  ■ How the threat was made
  ■ To whom the threat was made
  ■ When the threat was issued
  ■ What physical security measures were taken. Whether this type of incident occurred prior to this instance

16. Determine whether there is a recognizable pattern
17. Determine what types of incidents have occurred prior to this one
18. Determine whether the organization is the source of the incident or the target of the incident
19. Determine whether the organization was targeted and attacked
20. Determine whether the attack or incident originated from within the organization
21. Determine who discovered the incident or intrusion. Was this a technical person? What alerted this person to the incident?
22. Determine to whom and how the discovery was reported. Was the incident reported to management, the enterprise IRT or someone else? How long did it take before the enterprise IRT was alerted? Was the incident reported in verbal or written form? Was the incident reported anonymously?
23. Determine whether there were any precursory events to the incident. Were there any stolen laptops or computer equipment, or compromised passwords?
24. Determine how many employees were recently terminated. Were any terminations considered hostile?
25. Determine whether there was any unusual or atypical activity at the incident site. Were there any visitors or new contractors onsite at conferences? Any other observations?
26. Determine whether any other departments have been contacted (i.e., human resources, legal, physical security, public relations)

The audiences for the questionnaire are practitioners, including IT security officers, members of the IRT and IT auditors. Prior to completing the questionnaire, users should familiarize themselves with the overall cyberresponse methodology. While using this questionnaire, users should communicate effectively with the IRT and management to minimize damage and recover within the acceptable time frame. After recovering from the incidents, users should debrief the IRT and management and implement steps to minimize the risk of future incidents.

Post-Incident Questionnaire

The incident should be reviewed chronologically for specific occurrences that illustrate actions that went right or wrong. All persons involved in the incident should have input, because perceptions of the same event may differ from person to person. Some of the basic issues the enterprise may want to track are listed in the questionnaire in Table 7.10.

Table 7.10 Postincident Questionnaire

Actions and Assessment
1. Determine whether incident preparation was adequate
2. Determine whether incident detection took place promptly
3. Identify who detected the incident. Was that the right person or should another group or organization have detected it earlier?
4. Determine whether additional tools or techniques could have assisted in detecting the problem sooner
5. Determine whether the incident was sufficiently contained
6. Determine whether the emergency contact process worked well internally and externally
7. Determine whether there was effective communication among team members
8. Determine whether there was effective communication between team members and other enterprise organizations
9. Determine whether there was effective communication between team members and outside organizations, such as law enforcement agencies
10. Determine the cost of the incident (including the cost of recovery)
11. Determine whether the backup process worked well
12. Determine whether the restoration process was adequate
13. Identify the most difficult issue
14. Identify what would be done differently in a second chance to address this incident
15. Identify how this incident affected the organization
16. Determine whether there was anything that could have prevented this incident from happening
17. Determine whether this could be prevented from happening again
Recommendations and Improvements
1. Determine whether the recommendation is appropriate. Does it meet the needs of the enterprise without underestimating or overestimating threats and risk? Is it cost-effective given the risk level?

continued

Table 7.10 (continued)

2. Determine whether the recommendation is applicable. Does it actually solve the issue without creating other vulnerabilities?
3. Determine whether the recommendation is flexible. Does it meet the needs of the enterprise with respect to providing technology or security changes that integrate well with business operations?
4. Determine whether the recommendation is implemented in a timely fashion
5. Determine whether the recommendation is the most current solution. Does it reflect the recent technological and other developments in security?
6. Determine whether the recommendation is practical. Does it create unreasonable restrictions on users, customers or business operations?
7. Determine whether the recommendation integration is ready. Does it supplement and integrate well with the enterprise's existing policies and infrastructure?

The audiences for the questionnaire are practitioners, including IT security officers, members of the IRT and IT auditors. After recovering from the incidents, users should use this questionnaire, debrief the IRT and management and implement steps to minimize the risk of future incidents.

Additional Questions

Readers interested in additional questions, which may be asked throughout the cyber forensics investigation, are encouraged to review Appendix I, Questions that Every Cyber Investigator Should Ask, Before, During and After an Investigation.

Acknowledgment

The Information System Audit and Control Association (ISACA the "Owner") has designed and created this internal control questionnaire (ICQ), titled Cybercrime: Incident Response and Digital Forensics (the "Work"), primarily as an educational resource for control professionals. As owners of this ICQ, ISACA makes no claim that use of any of the Work will assure a successful outcome. The Work should not be considered inclusive of all proper information, procedures and tests or exclusive of other information, procedures and tests that are reasonably directed to obtaining the same results. In determining the propriety of any specific information, procedure or test, the control professionals should apply their own professional judgment to the specific circumstances presented by the particular systems or information technology environment.

References

1. ISACA, Internal Control Questionnaire, Source: Incident Response and Digital Forensics, Internal Control, Questionnaires, which is used by permission of ISACA. (c)2005 Information, Systems Audit and Control Association. www.isaca.org, All rights reserved, retrieved February 2007.
2. ——Good Practice Guide for Computer Based Electronic Evidence, Figure 7.1, March 2005, Association of Chief Police Officers, National High-Tech Crime Unit, www.nhtcu.org/ACPO%20Guide% 20v3.0.pdf, Used with permission, retrieved February 2007.

Chapter 8

Privacy and Cyber Forensics: An Australian Perspective

Introduction

Each day, a vast number of Australians are subject to surveillance and investigation. Corporations, employers, media organizations, attorneys, and private property owners, mainly through their privately contracted investigators, regularly engage in watching, filming and listening to others. Many have, at their fingertips, the tools of cyber forensics that can delve into the personal electronic databases upon which governments at all levels and many householders now store vast amounts of information.

Australian law does not often specifically empower such intrusive activities, but nor does it unduly restrict them. What legislative and common law restrictions there may be on personal "prying" still allow a fair degree of latitude to those who wish to engage in investigative activities.

In this chapter we focus on the variety of nongovernment personnel and private agencies in Australia that regularly delve into the private affairs of others. Indeed, the majority of invasions of individual privacy today emanate not from "Big Brother" (as the government sector was characterized in George Orwell's 1984), but from the modern technology available to thousands of little "brothers," such as commercial and corporate institutions, private investigators and marketing organizations, as they buy and sell information about people, their habits, movements and preferences.[1] The development of the techniques of data mining, for example, has the capacity to compromise privacy in ways not previously possible, an issue exacerbated by a lagging Legal Framework which struggles, at times, to keep up with technological innovations.[2]

Public opinion surveys show a raised level of concern about the use of private information, too.[3] There is some justification for this concern. A 2001 survey in *InfoWeek* found that over 20 percent

---

[1] Issues explored by writers such as Whitaker (1999) and Garfinkel (2001).
[2] Wahlstrom et al. (2007).
[3] Estivill–Castro et al. (1999).

of companies store data on their customers, including information about their medical pro-files. A similar percent store customer demographics with salary and credit information, and over 15 percent store information about their customers' legal history.[4]

To explore these issues in an Australian context, we need to begin with a review of the law of privacy as it has developed over the last century.

Law Relating to Privacy

The Australian Constitution (which, unlike the United States Constitution[5] and the Canadian Charter of Rights and Freedoms,[6] does not contain a Bill of Rights) provides some implied rights,[7] but they are limited, and they do not include rights related to privacy. This means that privacy law is found primarily in the common law and in some limited provisions of state and national legislation. It is to the former that we turn first of all.

Common Law Privacy

What does the common law say about privacy? Although many people would regard the right to privacy as a basic human right, no general right to privacy is recognized under Australian common law. Common law privacy protection depends upon a person being able to establish a claim in one of the existing torts, such as trespass to land, nuisance, defamation or breach of confidence.

The Australian High Court hinted at the possibility of a new tort of invasion of privacy in a significant decision in 2002.

Australian Broadcasting Corporation (ABC) vs. Lenah Game Meats Pty Ltd[8]

A video was filmed surreptitiously at Lenah Game Meats factory, Tasmania. It showed workers stunning brush–tailed possums that were being prepared for export to Hong Kong and China. The possums were then thrown through a chute to be slaughtered. Someone had trespassed onto private property to do the filming.[9] The ABC was successful in convincing a Tasmanian court that the piece should go to air, but they took the case to the High Court after an injunction banned them from showing the program again.[10] The High Court (Callinan J dissenting) lifted the injunction. Thus, the video could be screened, and the business proprietors of Lenah Meats could not protect their firm's interests from unwarranted electronic surveillance.

---

[4]Wahlstrom et al. (2007).

[5]Wacks (1995) at 10–14. Also Wartell and McEwen (2001). The First Amendment protection of freedom of speech has allowed the development of the tort of invasion of privacy in virtually all US jurisdictions.

[6]Section 5 of the Canadian Charter states that "every person has a right to respect for his private life." See *Aubry v Duclos* (1998) 157 DLR (4th) 577 at 595–599.

[7]Such as the implied right to freedom of political expression as defined in the High Court's decision in *Lange v ABC* (1997) 189 CLR 520.

[8](2002) 185 ALR 1.

[9]Who was responsible for the ten minutes tape was never revealed, but it was provided to the ABC's *7.30 Report* by a man named Mark Pearson, who was linked to the activist group Animal Liberation.

[10]For useful discussions of the *Lenah Meats* case see Norton et al. (2004) and Sarre (2003).

However, the High Court did not announce any new tort of invasion of privacy, which it was acknowledged, was well established in the United States[11] and Europe,[12] and had undergone strong development in New Zealand.[13] In the United Kingdom the development is somewhat in limbo.[14]

Although Lenah's legal action was ultimately unsuccessful, the majority of judges of the High Court were of the opinion that, in appropriate circumstances, an enforceable right of privacy may exist, although what form it would take is unclear.[15] Chief Justice Gleeson speculated that the right of privacy is not easily established. He cautioned against too broad a definition of "private act." "[An act does not] become private simply because the owner of land would prefer that it were unobserved," he wrote.[16]

How far will the common law go to protect privacy in the future? The High Court remains cautious. Will a limited "right" to privacy develop, or will the High Court's current scepticism of such a new tort prevail? Only time will tell.

Privacy: Legislative Intervention

The Australian parliament (often referred to as the "Commonwealth" parliament) has power to enact privacy–style laws, given the power found in the Australian Constitution[17] and Australia's accession, in September 1991, to the *First Optional Protocol to the International Covenant on Civil and Political Rights* (ICCPR), article 17 of which states:

No one shall be subjected to arbitrary or unlawful interference with his privacy, family, home or correspondence…
Everyone has the right to the protection of the law against such interference or attacks.

However, governments have been reluctant to enact specific privacy protection legislation. For example, the electoral platform of the Fraser government, which came to power in 1975, included a promise to initiate an investigation into Australian privacy laws.[18] The resulting Australian Law Reform Commission (ALRC) report, released in 1983,[19] was highly influenced by newly developed Organization for Economic Cooperation and Development (OECD) guidelines on the protection of privacy. In fact,

---

[11] An article published in 1890 in the *Harvard Law Review* is generally regarded as beginning the development of the tort: see Warren and Brandeis (1890).

[12] There is, generally speaking, a strong privacy ethic in European jurisprudence.

[13] *T v Attorney-General* (1988) 5 NZFLR 357; *Bradley v Wingnut Films Ltd* [1993] 1 NZLR 415 at 423; *Hosking v Runting and Ors* [2004] NZCA 34 (Court of Appeal).

[14] In *Wainwright v Home Office* [2004] UKHL 22, the House of Lords rejected a tort of invasion of privacy. In *Douglas v Hello! Ltd* (2001) QB 967, the plaintiffs, on appeal, succeeded in winning damages but they were awarded a nominal US$7,300 each, a far cry from the multi-million dollar claim. The "success" of the claim came not from the common law but under the UK *Data Protection Act*. Similarly, in *Campbell v Mirror Group Newspapers* [2004] UKHL 22, the plaintiff, supermodel Naomi Campbell, succeeded in her claim for breach of privacy, but only by linking it to the tort of breach of confidence.

[15] Greenleaf (2004) has referred to the post-Lenah climate on privacy generally as "indecipherable."

[16] Per Gleeson CJ at para 43.

[17] Section 51(xxix) of the Australian Constitution (the "external affairs" power).

[18] Kirby (1992) at 11.

[19] ALRC (1983) paras 1074–1081.

these guidelines were annexed in a schedule to the ALRC's draft legislation.[20] The ALRC rejected a general statutory right to privacy, but made a number of recommendations for changes to the law to deal with information privacy. Although these recommendations were never adopted formally, the OECD guidelines reemerged, in an altered form, as the Information Privacy Principles (IPPs), eventually enacted in the Commonwealth Privacy Act 1988.[21] In other words, the 1983 recommendations contributed in a major way to the final draft of the 1988 legislation, but the parliament stopped short of enacting legislation. The track record of the Australian States and Territories in attempting to introduce broadly–based privacy legislation is also decidedly chequered.[22]

Another weakness of enacting specific legislation to protect privacy is the fact that the jurisdictional boundaries that determine the limits of the Australian legal system were drawn up in ignorance of technological developments that render these boundaries virtually irrelevant, especially given the international structure of many organizations and ubiquity of the Internet. This is a legal dilemma not lost on international lawyers, and is one that does not readily admit of a simple solution.[23]

In the absence of a common law tort of invasion of privacy, and without clear privacy legislation, what other options does the law provide to protect information from being accessed illegitimately by those engaging in cyber forensics? At least two common law torts exist, which make sleuths potentially liable (through private civil legal action) if they engage in activities designed to breach privacy. Trespass to land and nuisance are useful in this regard, but they are designed to protect an individual only from physical interference or electronic surveillance. To find ways that society may be able to restrict cyber-forensic activity we need to move beyond the general laws relating to privacy to the realm of law that relates to information privacy specifically.

Law Relating to Access to Private Information

Increasingly advanced electronic information-gathering instruments are emerging almost on a daily basis in Australia,[24] allowing for the collection, storage, and retrieval of massive amounts of electronically based information.[25]

The storage and cross-matching of such data brings collective benefit in many contexts,[26] including combating tax evasion, and aiding in criminal investigations.[27] Moreover, government agencies regularly access public and private data sets containing information on Australian citizens and visitors to Australia to prevent fraud and to curtail suspected terrorist activities.[28] For example, the agency known as CrimTrac provides a significant data source in this respect. Since July 1, 2000,

---

[20]ALRC (1983) at 265.

[21]Parts III, IV, and V.

[22]See Queensland LCARC (1997), where failed attempts to introduce a statutory tort of invasion of privacy are listed in para 5.3.1. For the most part, State "privacy" legislation only deals with listening devices and optical surveillance devices.

[23] Wahlstrom et al. (2007).

[24]"On-selling" of electronic information has become an increasingly attractive business proposition: see Dearne (2001) at 43, John (1999), and Klang (2004).

[25]These include web-based prior convictions records, see Hickman (2000, 24). In relation to the vast array of biometric data currently stored in Canada, for example, see Canada (2004) at A2. See Sarre and Prenzler (2005) Chapter 6 generally.

[26]Gordon and Williams (1997).

[27]Berry and Linoff (1997).

[28]For information on private data laboratories collecting and storing DNA information, see Steadman (2002).

CrimTrac has operated as an agency under the *Public Service Act* (Commonwealth), and falls within the Commonwealth Attorney-General's portfolio. Its operatives are empowered to collect and collate data on DNA testing, fingerprinting, national police data and sex offender files. Few would doubt that this is an appropriate tool in the fight against crime or in defense of a nation.[29]

However, these activities pose a substantial potential risk to privacy, and thus we are presented with a two-edged sword. That is, an attack upon some social ills has the potential to become a simultaneous attack on our freedom to remain private. How has the law responded? In short, Australian policy-makers have moved very cautiously, preferring to investigate the issues and to advise parliaments to move after widespread consultation and public debate.

For example, in March 2002 the government of the Australian State of Victoria asked the Victorian Law Reform Commission (VLRC) to determine whether reforms were required to ensure that privacy was not jeopardized given current trends to video and audio surveillance of workers, e-mail and telephone monitoring, collecting, using and disclosing personal data, and scanning and searching workers and their possessions. The Terms of Reference required the Commission to have regard to:

> The interests of employers and other users of surveillance, including their interest in protecting property and assets, complying with laws and regulations, ensuring productivity and providing safe and secure places; the protection of the privacy, autonomy and dignity of workers and other individuals; the interaction between State and Commonwealth laws, and the jurisdictional limits imposed on the Victorian Parliament...[30]

On June 28, 2004, the Commission released a report recommending new privacy legislation, specifically to protect workers from covert surveillance, including checks on their e-mail and Internet use. The Legislative Framework does not, however, include a prohibition on the use of cyber forensic tools.

Access to Government-Held Information by Governments

Laws exist in Australia to restrict the way in which governments can store and use personal data in their databases. For example, under the *Privacy Act 1988*, Commonwealth agencies are only allowed to use information gathered for specific purposes. They are not permitted to use data for other purposes, and certainly cannot release information to members of the public. The law prevents the cross-matching of data, too—for example, tax records and social security files—in the hands of Commonwealth agencies unless there has been specific permission sought and received under the strict terms of the legislation. Even with these restrictions in place, data matching is widespread, with permissions granted regularly. For example, a report on matching done between the Australian Tax Office (ATO), the Department of Veteran's Affairs, and "Centrelink" (Australia's social security network) in the period 1998–2001 shows that the files of 277,092 customers were reviewed and were deemed to warrant further investigation; 210,921 customers had payments cancelled or reduced, and approximately US$350 million revenue was saved.[31]

The *Privacy Act* is overseen by a federal privacy commissioner who has power to enforce privacy protection in relation to government departments and agencies. Finally, there is a Commonwealth Australian Privacy Charter, but it is a voluntary code and has no penalty provisions.[32]

---

[29] Victoria (2004) at vii.
[30] *FindLaw* web site, 10 March 2002.
[31] Commonwealth (2002).
[32] See discussion in Dixon and Greenleaf (1995).

Access to Non-Government Information by the Private Sector

Invasion of individual privacy in the 21st century is more likely to result from the technology possessed by private entities who exchange information between themselves than by governments. For years, companies have been collecting detailed information about consumers, to allow them to track and interact with customers, suppliers and markets. The management of that data was often haphazard, and selling of information was rife. Collection, stockpiling and sale of information were largely unregulated, unless it involved credit references.[33] A survey in 1997 indicated that 70 percent of companies in Australia supported the introduction of privacy legislation that would cover the corporate sector.[34] The government finally acted in 1999. Interestingly, the legislation was introduced into parliament in December of that year, just two weeks after the media giant Publishing and Broadcasting Limited announced that it was joining with the United States company Acxiom to create a warehouse of information on up to 15 million Australians.[35] Four years in the making,[36] the Commonwealth *Privacy Amendment (Private Sector) Act 2000* was passed by the Australian parliament on December 6, 2000. The effect of this Act is to apply the provisions of the 1988 privacy legislation to the private sector. The Act came into effect on December 21, 2001.

It is now illegal for companies to collect or transfer sensitive personal information without an individual's permission.[37] Companies to which the legislation applies now need to be careful to ask clients only the basic information they need to carry on business, and they must tell customers how any information will be used, and to whom it will be disclosed. People must be given the choice to opt out of mailing lists when they provide personal data for business transactions. And the sale or disclosure of personal information collected by, or for, political parties is banned.

Significantly, the legislation does not, however, appear to restrict a person's prying into the data source or the information itself.

The *Privacy Act* amendments give the Privacy Commissioner the power to investigate privacy breaches by private sector bodies, to order compensation to aggrieved persons and to seek injunctions through the federal court. The Act sets out detailed guidelines in relation to the manner of collection, storage and use of personal information by private companies and organizations. The Act incorporates the National Principles for the Fair Handling of Personal Information, developed by the Privacy Commissioner after consulting with business and consumer groups. They are similar to the Information Privacy Principles discussed above but have been tailored towards the activities of private businesses and individuals, as opposed to governments.

Key Elements of the Privacy Act and the Principles for the Fair Handling of Personal Information.

Section 16A(1) of the Privacy Act 1988 (as amended) provides that an organization must not do an act, or engage in a practice, that breaches an "approved privacy code" which binds the

---

[33]Legislation in every jurisdiction in Australia now regulates the way in which credit referencing must be undertaken. See Sarre and Prenzler (2005) Chapter 7.

[34]Woolley (1998) at 11.

[35]Editorial (1999). See comments from the Acxiom CEO, Mr Andrew Robb in "The chance to get exactly what you want," *The Australian*, December 4, 1999, at 23. Concerns were nevertheless expressed by the Financial Services Consumer Policy Centre. See "Privacy laws a template for trust?" *The Australian* (*Media*), December 20, 2001, at 4, by Paul McIntyre.

[36]The reforms were first mooted by the House of Representatives Standing Committee on Legal and Constitutional Affairs (1995) paras 10.6–10.8.

[37]The legislation is not retrospective, so there can be continued trading in existing lists. Individuals can still check, however, on information on pre-existing lists, and correct it, where that information is used after December 21, 2001.

organization. An approved privacy code is a written code regulating acts and practices affecting privacy, approved by the Commissioner.[38]

Section 16A(2) provides that, to the extent (if any) that an organization is not bound by an approved privacy code, the organization must not do an act, or engage in a practice, that breaches one of the fair handling principles, mentioned above.[39]

Section 72(2) provides that if the Commissioner is satisfied that a practice of an organization breaches an approved privacy code or handling principle, but that the public interest in the practice outweighs the public interest in adhering to that code or principle, the Commissioner may exempt the organization from the operation of Section 16A.

Section 36(1) allows an individual to complain to the Commissioner about any act or practice that may be an "interference with the privacy of the individual."

Section 52(1) gives the Commissioner the power to perform any reasonable act to zedress any loss or damage suffered by the complainant. The complainant may be entitled to compensation for any loss or damage suffered due to the act or practice, which is the subject of the complaint. If a person ignores the Commissioner, enforcement proceedings can be instituted in the federal court or the federal magistrates court.[40]

There are many opponents of the new law, and much criticism that it is impossible to police.[41] Indeed, it may be impossible for legislation to remain relevant and to keep pace with information technology developments, such as Smart Cards.[42]

While there are uncertainties about the "reach" of the new law into commercial sales business, it may limit some of the activities of the larger private investigation firms. In November 2004, the Australian Institute of Private Detectives failed in its attempt in the federal court to seek a declaration that certain investigations by its members on behalf of their clients were not prohibited by the Act. This was only on the basis, however, of a technical finding that the court lacked jurisdiction to hear the matter, because there was not a dispute between the Institute and the Commissioner.[43] This is an unfortunate outcome, because we are left somewhat unsure about the reach of the legislation from a legal perspective. Certainly private detectives, for example, remain bound by the legislation in regards to the collection and storage and handling of personal data, but to what extent and in what circumstances does personal prying into data amount to an act that breach a privacy principle? We await some case law.

One can expect that there will emerge a growing number of sophisticated and relatively easy to use cyber forensic tools that will muddy the legal waters. Coupled with an increased interest by private companies and law enforcement in the utilization of cyber forensic investigative methods, we can only hope for a rapid development of case law that will address the issues and answer the legal uncertainties.

---

[38]See Section 6, Part IIIAA.

[39]See Schedule 3 of the Act.

[40]Section 55A(1).

[41]Bita (2001). According to an earlier *Australian* newspaper report, Privacy Foundation Chairman Tim Dixon claimed that 94 percent of Australian businesses are exempt. For example, small businesses, defined as those with a turnover of less than US$2 million, are exempt *unless* they collect or disclose information to third parties for a benefit or provide a health service or contract with the government.

[42]These cards have a microchip that is picked up by a sensor to deduct money from the deposit account. They allow a computer to keep track of every purchase and movement of a user, generating records of the date, time and location of transport, along with details of goods purchased, telephone use, car parking and so forth.

[43]See *Australian Institute of Private Detectives Ltd vs. Privacy Commissioner* (2004) FCA 1440 per Sackville J.

Legal Liability for Mistakes

In circumstances where personal data have been collected, the data is generally decontextualized and separated from the individual, improving privacy but making misuse and mistakes more likely.[44] When organizations trade the personal data, the possibility of legal liability is introduced.[45] A data mining exercise, for example, might erroneously declare an individual a poor credit risk, and decisions may be made prejudicial to that individual on that basis. Indeed, hundreds of millions of personal records are sold annually in the United States (by 200 "superbureaux") to direct marketers, private individuals, investigators, and government agencies.[46]

Compensation may be ordered against any organization that is found to have harmed (or failed to prevent harm to) an individual to whom it owed a duty of care. Once liability in the tort of negligence has been established, a plaintiff can claim financial compensation for any consequential losses caused by the negligent act.[47] The extent and exact nature of the losses is, for the most part, unique to each plaintiff, but the boundaries of negligence are never closed.

In some cases, algorithms may classify correctly, but such classification could be on the basis of controversial attributes such as gender, race, religion or sexual preference. This could run counter to antidiscrimination legislation. Individuals who suffer denial of credit or employment on the basis of race, gender, ethnic background and so forth are in a strong position to demonstrate harm simply by illustrating that the artificial classifiers are using such attributes. In the event that the person loses money or reputation as a result of this action, courts may award compensation. The potential for private legal suit thus remains significant.

This is an interesting legal landscape. The engineered, technological nature of electronic information dissemination suggests a greater liability for its disseminators.[48] Commonly, the conveyers of information are excused from liability if they are simply the carriers of the information from the publishers to the public. For example, a book-store selling a book that carries defamatory material will be excused from liability that might rightly attach to the author and the publisher. It is quite possible that a data mining exercise, particularly one that has mined inaccurate data, might be deemed by the courts to be an exercise in publishing, not just in dissemination. Again, we can do little but await relevant case law to emerge from the courts.

Conclusion

Australian common law is decidedly weak when it comes to the protection of privacy generally. Thus, state and national parliaments have enacted some legislation designed to stop the more egregious breaches of privacy that occur on a regular basis today. But whether this legislation is sufficient to dampen the enthusiasm of those who would regularly pry into private electronic databases remains to be seen.

The legislative rules which have applied since 1988 restricting access to private information held by governments have now been extended to the private sector, although the new regime is replete with exemptions and does not apply to a significant proportion of Australian businesses. Nor does it apply to information collected prior to the commencement of the Act.

---

[44] Gammack and Goulding (1999).
[45] Wahlstrom et al. (2007).
[46] Laudon (1996).
[47] Sarre and Prenzler (2005) Chapter 8.
[48] Samuelson (1993).

The Information Privacy Principles provide a welcome addition to the Privacy Framework in Australia. They apply to limit the amount of cyber forensic activity that can be employed. But their reach is yet to be tested in the courts.

What is the preferred form of legal regulation of cyber forensics? Legislative reform is probably unsuitable, as it is an unwieldy tool in a rapidly expanding technical environment. Common law can be creatively applied to novel situations but it requires the development of precedents, and litigation in this age of mediated dispute resolution and "in confidence" settlements are nowadays a rare phenomenon. Public awareness of the possibility of legal suits alleging negligence, breach of confidence and defamation may possibly have some prophylactic effect upon potential transgressions by those who would engage in unrestricted and unauthorized cyber forensics, but reliance upon private civil action is not an ideal way to provide consistency and deterrence on an issue of such great social importance.

The law endeavours to strike a balance between the legitimate needs of those who see a need to access information of a private nature and those who wish to remain protected from unwanted intrusions into their privacy. For the most part, the balancing act currently undertaken by governments does not cause overt public disquiet. But as cyber forensics continues to develop more powerful tools for the purpose of exposing more and more information of a private nature, so that public disquiet may begin to grow. We await developments with great interest.

Authors' Postscript

The authors wish to thank Dr. Sarre for his insights and contribution to this text. Dr. Sarre's examination into privacy and the lack of specific legislation in Australia aimed directly at protecting both individual and corporate privacy, provides an excellent foundation for companies, agencies and client operations to remind themselves of the importance of establishing solid policies and procedures to protect the confidentiality and privacy of data at rest, retained onsite or stored in third-party facilities or released to external investigators.

Company policies and procedures must ensure that only data directly related to an investigation are released. Rules regulating access to and collection of data, hardware, and physical records must be accurately drafted to identify specific data, and not, for example, the entire contents of a 100 GB drive, or to prevent wholesale data harvesting or collection.

When faced with the possibility or even when in direct compliance to a legally valid request for data, corporations have a responsibility to protect sensitive, confidential, and private data and to protect, within the full extent of the law, the privacy of those individuals that can or may be identified through those data which may be relinquished for investigatory purposes.

References

Australian Law Reform Commission (ALRC) (1983), Report No. 22, *Privacy,* Canberra: Australian Government Publishing Service.

Berry, M. and Linoff, G. (1997), *Data Mining Techniques for Marketing, Sales and Customer Support,* New York, NY: John Wiley.

Bita, N. (2001), Whose list are you on? *The Weekend Australian,* June 9–10, at 21, 24.

Canada (2004), Who's watching? Canada under surveillance, *Ottawa Citizen* Special Report, December 27, 2004, A2.

Commonwealth (2002), Office of the Minister for Family and Community Services, *Data-matching Program Report on Progress 1998–2001*, Canberra, January 9, 2002.

Dearne, K. (2001), Prescribing a privacy cure, *The Australian IT,* May 1, 2001, 43.

Dixon, T. and Greenleaf, G. (1995), Private Parts, *Privacy Law and Policy Reporter 2:* 20.

Editorial (1999), *The Australian*, December 1, 1999, p 12.

Estivill-Castro, V., Brankovic, L. and Dowe, D. (1999), Privacy in data mining, *Privacy, Law and Policy Reporter* 6(3), 33–35.

Gammack, J. and Goulding, P. (1999), Ethical responsibility and management of knowledge, *Australian Computer Journal* 31(3), 72–77.

Garfinkel, S. (2001), *Database Nation: The Death of Privacy in the 21st Century,* Sebastopol CA: O'Reilly and Associates.

Gordon, M. and Williams, M. (1997), Spatial data mining for health research, planning and education, *Proc. TEPR-97: Towards an Electronic Patient,* Newton, MA, 212–218.

Greenleaf, G. (2004), Australian Privacy Law Grows Up, *Privacy Law and Policy Reporter* (reprinted in CCH alerting service online, 16 August 2004), 1.

Hickman, B. (2000), Virtual Vigilantes *Weekend Australian,* 6 May, 24.

House of Representatives SCLCA (1995), *In Confidence: A report on the inquiry into the protection of confidential personal and commercial information held by the Commonwealth* (June 1995), Australian Government Publishing Service.

John, G. (1999), Behind-the-scenes data mining, *SIGKDD Explorations* 1(1), 9–11.

Klang, M. (2004), Spyware—the ethics of covert software, *Ethics and IT* 6(3), 193–202.

Kirby, M. (Justice) (1992), Human Rights—Emerging International Minimum Standards, unpublished paper presented to the 14th Annual National Conference of the Australian Society of Labor Lawyers, Melbourne, 23 May 1992.

Laudon, K. (1996), Markets and privacy, *CACM* 39(9), 92–104.

Norton, M., Clark, K. and Sainty, K. (2004), A Common Law Right to Privacy for Australia? *Information Bulletin,* Allens Arthur Robinson, October.

Queensland LCARC (1997), *Privacy in Queensland*, Report No. 9 of the Queensland Legal, Constitutional and Administrative Review Committee, Parliament of Queensland.

Samuelson, P. (1993), Liability for defective electronic information, *CACM* 36(1), 21–26.

Sarre, R. (2003), Journalists, invasion of privacy and the High Court decision in Lenah Game Meats, *Australian Journalism Review*, 25(1), 115–128.

Sarre, R. and Prenzler, T. (2005), *The Law of Private Security in Australia,* Pyrmont, New South Wales: Thomson LBC.

Steadman, G. (2002), Survey of DNA Crime Laboratories, 2001, Bureau of Justice Statistics, *January Bulletin,* Washington DC: US Department of Justice.

Victoria (2004), *Inquiry into Fraud and Electronic Commerce, Final Report,* Parliament of Victoria Drugs and Crime Prevention Committee, Melbourne: Government Printer for the State of Victoria.

Wacks, R. (1995), *Privacy and Press Freedom*, Oxford: Blackstone Press.

Wahlstrom, K., Roddick, J., Sarre, R., Estivill–Castro, V. and de Vries, D (2007), On the Ethical and Legal Implications of Data Mining, *Encyclopedia of Data Warehousing and Mining,* 2nd Edition.

Warren, S. and Brandeis, L. (1890), The Right to Privacy, 4 *Harvard Law Review*, 193.

Wartell, J. and McEwen, J.T. (2001), *Privacy in the Information Age: A Guide for Sharing Crime Maps and Spatial Data*, Institute for Law and Justice, Washington DC: US Department of Justice.

Whitaker, R. (1999), *The End of Privacy: How total surveillance is becoming a reality,* New York, NY: New Press.

Woolley, S. (1998), "The Yes case for Privacy," *The Australian*, March 5, 1998.

Chapter 9

Forensic Black Bag

Introduction

The phone rings, it is a call from the Director of Human Resources for ABC Incorporated. Someone, she believes it to be Employee "A," has been involved in selling company trade secrets. The Director informs you that she has received a phone call from her counterpart at the XYZ Corporation, whose manager of institutional research had been contacted by e-mail, by Employee A, asking if he would be interested in purchasing new development product schematics of ABC's innovative axle assembly. A small portion of the schematic had been attached to the e-mail sent by Employee A to substantiate his claim of having access to the actual product schematics.

Before any action (legal or otherwise) can be brought against the suspected Employee A, and to stop the potential loss of any further trade secrets, the Director wishes to determine conclusively the innocence or guilt of Employee A and the claim made by the XZY Corporation regarding Employee A's offer to sell trade secrets.

The Director's call launches an internal cyber forensic investigation into the activities of Employee A. As you plan your strategy, how will you conduct this cyber forensic investigation, and what necessary "tools" will you take with you, especially when at this moment you do not have a clear idea of exactly what type of IT environment you will encounter in Employee A's office?

Packing for Success

Exactly what should a cyber forensic investigator take to a potential e-crime scene? What tools of the trade should be standard equipment found in the mobile tool kit or "black bag" of the professional cyber forensic investigator?

To determine exactly what the contents of this multi-purpose, multi-functional, high-tech sleuth kit should contain, the authors sought the advice of a leading cyber forensic investigator, computer expert, and allaround technical guru John Minotti.

John is the Managing Director, at Acquisition Data, with an excess of ten years in the field of IT and cyber forensics. The authors asked John to provide them with a peek into his "black bag" and to explain the function and application of each "tool" that he carries with him, when called upon to conduct a cyber forensic investigation.

Several words of note to the reader, before, we take a more detailed look inside of John's cyber forensic black bag. First the tools described in this chapter are representative of the breadth of tools available to the cyber forensic investigator, they are not all inclusive. Outfitting your personal "black bag" should be guided by the type of investigations you are called upon to perform and the IT operating environment in which you or your clients operate. Realistically, a periodic review of the contents of your black bag is prudent and logical. As tools and technologies change, the cyber forensic investigator must remain abreast of these changes and arm themselves with the most appropriate technology or tools to conduct their investigations.

Secondly, any reference to commercial products contained in John's "Black Bag" and described in this chapter is for information only; it does not imply recommendation or endorsement by the authors, publisher, reviewers, contributors, or representatives nor does it imply that the products mentioned are necessarily the best available for the purpose. The reader is advised to receive proper and continued training in the correct use of these tools prior to undertaking either the use of the tools or their use as part of a cyber forensic investigation.

Finally, it is assumed that all the appropriate data cables and power cables for all of the components listed will be included in your Black Bag kit.

Take a comfortable seat, sit back, grab a pen and note pad, and start making your shopping list as John and our forensic colleagues open their field ready "forensic Black Bags" and we peek inside.

The following items were randomly pulled from these "Black Bags" and the order in which, they are discussed here does not constitute a level of importance, or criticality to conducting a successful cyber forensic investigation.

What's in Your Bag?

Laptop to IDE Hard Drive Adapter

The connector adaptor converts a laptop HDD 2.5-inch connector to a 3.5-inch HDD connector as used in the IDE bus system (see Figure 9.1). It is powered by, a 5V Molex plug.

This allows the use of a laptop hard drive with a 44-pin connector in a standard tower or desktop PC on the 40-pin IDE cable (see Figure 9.2). You will have to set the laptop hard drive as a Master or Slave depending on your Desktop configuration.

This adaptor will not work for plugging a standard IDE type hard drive into a laptop drive controller.

Note: It is important to properly connect both ends of the adapter to ensure functionality and prevent the possibility of shorts.

On the IDE interface end, the red wire on the ribbon represents pin 1.

On the HDD, pin 1 should be labeled by the drive's manufacturer. Pin 1 on the adapter is shown here in the graphic.

Adaptec SCSI Card 29160

The Adaptec SCSI Card 29160 (Figure 9.3) is tailored for entry to mid-range server environments. It delivers the maximum throughput for a single channel Ultra160 SCSI card by using a 64-bit PCI interface.

The Adaptec SCSI Card 29160 provides the ideal connection to Ultra160 SCSI (LVD) hard disks and devices (internally and externally) and legacy devices (internally).

Figure 9.1 Laptop to IDE hard drive adaptor.

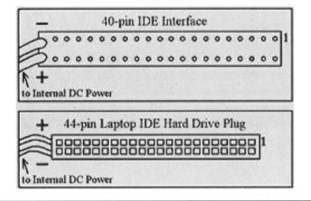

Figure 9.2 Shows the difference between a desktop (top) and a laptop (bottom) adaptors.

Figure 9.3 SCSI card.

Supported Operating Systems:

- Microsoft Windows
- Red Hat Linux
- SUSE Linux
- Novell NetWare
- Sun Solaris
- Unix
- IBM OS/2

Small Computer System Interface (SCSI) Adapter

Generic 540–106-np, SCSI SCA 80pin (Centronic) female to SCSI-3 68-pin female adapter converter, with pine header 20pin, ultra 4 320/m SCSI compliant.

A SCSI adapter is a card that has a 50-pin ribbon connector. It is used for connecting computers to peripheral devices (such as CD-ROM drives, scanners, hard drives, zip drives, jazz drives, or other removable drives). Peripheral devices are attached to a single SCSI port through a series of connections called a daisy chain.

Highlights

- 160 MByte/sec performance
- SpeedFlex technology ensures top performance of all connected devices, regardless of SCSI generation
- Seamless backwards compatibility protects legacy devices
- Industry-leading compatibility, reliability
- CRC (Cyclical Redundancy Checking) improves data integrity
- Domain Validation intelligently verifies system configuration for improved reliability
- RoHS Compliant

AEC-7720WP Ultra Wide SCSI-to-IDE Bridge, with Write Blocked Function

ACARD Ultra Wide SCSI-to-IDE Bridge, Supports IDE devices attached to SCSI bus, with write blocked function, for PC.

Features

- A general purpose SCSI-to-IDE device converter
- Higher system input and Output performance
- Creates new SCSI devices in economic cost
- Write Blocked function

Specifications

- Ultra Wide SCSI interface for up to 40 MB/sec data transfer rate
- Supports DMA 66/100/133 hard drives
- Onboard flash ROM for easy firmware upgrade

- Selectable SCS ID from 0 to 15
- Full Ultra Wide SCSI target features support

Devices Compatibility List

Support Hard Disk

Brand	Model
IBM HDD	DTLA series, DPTA series, DTTA series, DJNA series
QUANTUM HDD	FireBall LM series, LC series, LB series, LD series, FireBall KX series, KA series, FireBall CX series, CR series, EX series, FireBall EL series, AS series
MAXTOR HDD	54098U8, 52049U4, 91366U4, 94098U8, 91020U3, 98196H8 DiamondMax60 series
WD HDD	Expert 13BA, Caviar AC14300, WD 300BB
SEAGATE HDD	Barracuda IDE series; Barracuda ATA II/III 100 series; ST320430A, ST313620A, ST3240AT, ST38422A, ST36531A
FUJITSU HDD	MPF-3204AT, MPD-3173AT, MPD-3084

FireFly IDE and FireFly SATA

A deeper look inside John's tool kit and we find that John has elected to use the increasingly popular FireFly (available in IDE and SATA models), which has earned the reputation of the most widely respected write blocker in the computer forensic industry. The FireFly provides a hardware-based write-protected environment for the forensic imaging and processing of the attached IDE or SATA hard drive.

The FireFly is a significantly faster device which supports both FireWire 1394a (400 Mb/s) and 1394b (800 Mb/s). The FireFly is a more flexible device which can be selectively configured for either Read-Only or Read-Write functionality. The FireFly also provides increased diagnostic information, which includes Write Protect indication and Read and Write activity indication.

Because the FireFly operates as a 1394a/b mass storage device, support is provided directly from the Operating System itself. Full Operating System support provides complete device accessibility by all of the major Forensic Tools (including EnCase and FTK) and also any other tools, which can be run from within that environment. The Windows, Linux, and Mac Operating Systems all provide resident FireWire 1394 support.

You can daisy chain (cascade) multiple FireFly devices. To accomplish this connect your first FireFly to the PC using the appropriate cable. Then use a bilingual FireWire 800 (9-pin to 9-pin) cable to connect the first FireFly to the second FireFly. Additional FireWire devices can be daisy chained using this technique.

FireFly SATA

The new FireFly SATA adds native support for SATA devices. The FireFly SATA is also a flexible device, which can be selectively configured for either Read-Only or Read-Write functionality.

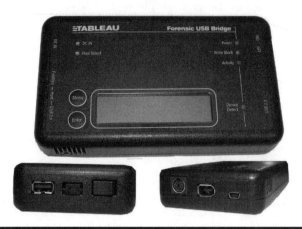

Figure 9.4   Tableau forensic USB bridge right blocker.

FireFly Read or Write

The FireFly IDE and SATA are also available in a read-write configuration to offer a FireWire 800 accessible destination for your files. Use your read-only FireFly to acquire the suspect data, and use your read-write FireFly to store your forensic images. A simple daisychain of read-only and read-write FireFly devices functions as a complete portable solution for most every forensic imaging needs.

Power can be supplied to the FireFly and the hard drive via a standard 4-pin Molex PC power connector or via the included external standalone power supply (110/220v). Simply connect the FireFly device to the back of the IDE or SATA drive, connect the power source, and the FireWire data cable.

In the field, forensic experts also utilize Tableau's Forensic USB Bridge (see Figure 9.4.), which brings secure, hardware-based write blocking to the world of USB mass storage devices. The T8 supports USB2.0 High-Speed (480 mbit/s), USB 1.1 Full-Speed (12 mbit/s) and Low-Speed (1.2 mbit/s) devices conforming to the USB Mass Storage "Bulk-only" class specification.

The T8 works with USB thumb drives, external USB disk drives, more exotic devices like Apple iPOD's(tm) with USB interfaces, even USB-based cameras with card-reader capability.

IDE Adapter

Convert 1.8″ HD Zero Insertion Force (ZIF) to IDE (44pin 5V) and 1.8″ ZIF drive converter (1.8″ hard disks are common in video or MP3-players).

Zero Insertion Force (ZIF) is a type of CPU socket on a computer motherboard that allows for the simple replacement or upgrade of the processor. Pulling a small release lever next to the processor and lifting it out can easily remove processors that use a ZIF socket. The replacement processor is then placed in the socket and secured by pushing the lever in the opposite direction—hence the phrase, "zero insertion force" (www.techterms.org/definition/zif, retrieved May 15, 2007).

This adapter makes a mechanical connection from connector device to the common connector version (44-pin, 2.00 mm pitch). 1.8″ devices need 3.3 V voltage feed. The facility for converting from 5 V to 3.3 V is integrated. Only use with 40-pin, Pitch = 0.50 mm ZIF connector 1.8″ Hard Disk Drives!

To go one step further, and connect it to a desktop machine, you will need to use an adapter to connect to data and power, such as IA40 IA40S or IDdj-a2. Make sure you connect the pins the right way round, or you may blow up both adapters.

Serial ATA (AT Bus Attachment)-to-IDE Drive Converter

This item allows you to acquire SATA (a computer bus technology for connecting hard disks and other devices) drives without changing your current imaging procedures.

You can:

- Attach to your existing write-blocker through the IDE ribbon
- Power the SATA drive from the converter
- Image using existing imaging software

Additional Miscellaneous and Crucial Supplies or Tools

While no one forensic investigator may lay claim to having all of the necessary tools at his or her fingertips for every case, it is the prudent investigator that has a growing inventory of specialized tools within easy reach, should the circumstances warrant.

In addition to some of the tools found in the forensic tool kit of our field expert, John Minotti, readers may also wish to investigate further, the following tools found in the kits of several cyber forensic investigators with whom the authors have contacted for expert insight for this text.

- Altra 160/m SCSI cables.
- Crossover Cables—A crossover cable directly connects two network devices of the same type to each other over Ethernet. Ethernet crossover cables are commonly used when temporarily networking two devices in situations where a network router, switch or hub is not present (see Figure 9.5).
- EnCase network acquisition CD (www.encase.com/support/downloads.aspx).
- Helix (www.e-fense.com/helix).
- PCMCIA Firewire Card (Using laptop with the FireFly). PCMCIA (Personal Computer Memory Card International Association) is an international standards body and trade

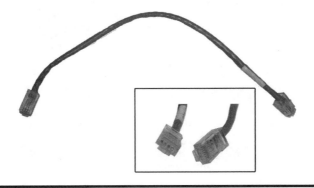

Figure 9.5   Ethernet crossover cables.

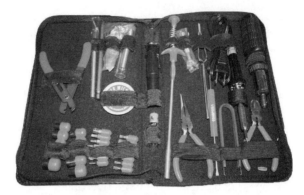

Figure 9.6   Advanced tool kit.

association with over 100 member companies that was founded in 1989 to establish standards for Integrated Circuit cards and to promote interchangeability among mobile computers where ruggedness, low power, and small size were critical. As the needs of mobile computer users have changed, so has PCMCIA. By 1991, PCMCIA had defined an I/O interface for the same 68-pin connector initially used for memory cards.

■ Laptop Tool Kit (Figures 9.6 and 9.7).
■ 12 volt Y-Adapters.
■ KVM Switch.
■ KVM (Figures 9.8 and 9.9) short for keyboard, video, mouse switch, a hardware device that enables a single keyboard, video monitor and mouse to control more than one computer one at a time.
■ Power Strips.

Other tools that will eventually be important to field investigators include but, are not limited to the following:

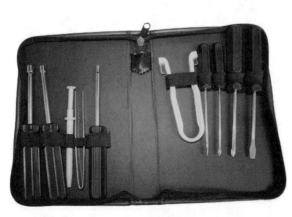

Figure 9.7   Small tool kit.

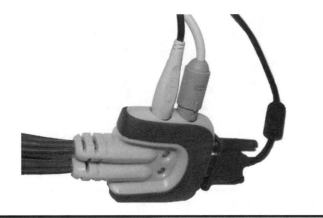

Figure 9.8   KVM switch.

ADP31 Adaptor SCSI 3 to SCSI 1 (Figure 9.10)

SCSI stands for "small computer systems interface. SCSI is a "parallel" interface. That means it sends an entire "chunk" (byte) of information at a time, rather than sending things one "bit" at a time. This can give it great speed, but also tends to cause problems with the length of the cables involved.

ADP32 Adaptor SCSI 3 to High Density

See Figure 9.11.

Figure 9.9   KVM switch.

Figure 9.10   ADP31 adaptor SCSI 3 to SCSI 1.

Figure 9.11   ADP32 adaptor SCSI 3 to high density.

Fastbloc Unit Blocker

Fastbloc is an IDE-IDE Write-Blocked Architecture allowing IDE media to be acquired quickly and safely in Windows (see Figure 9.12). These devices allow the investigator to conduct previews and acquisitions for desktop and laptop IDE hard drives, quickly, in Windows, without altering data on the suspect hard drive.

Logicube

These hard drive data capturing systems offer high-speed solutions for copying hard drives, drive formatting, data recovery, and disaster recovery (see Figures 9.13–9.15) (www.logicube.com).

Ultra Block Portable Device

The UltraBlock is used to acquire data from a hard drive in a forensically sound write-protected environment (www.digitalintelligence.com/products/ultrablock).

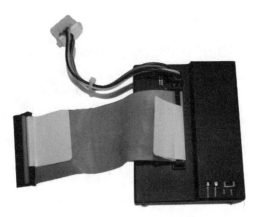

Figure 9.12   Fastbloc unit blocker.

Figure 9.13   Logicube.

Figure 9.14   Logicube.

Figure 9.15 Logicube.

Xbox 360 Adapters and Kit

If you want to prod the contents of the hard drive and instead of disassembling the drive unit, you can purchase the 360SATA, an adapter that simply plugs into the bottom of the drive, and via an internal SATA cable to one of your computer's SATA ports.

This Xbox 360 hard drive connector combines a SATA connector and a Mini USB connector into one plug. The Mini USB connector provides the power to the Xbox 360 hard drive. The hard drive inside Xbox 360 uses standard connectors, but this adapter will assist you by allowing a direct access without the need to open the case. You can use Xplorer360 to get full read or write access to the drive.

You can use a SATA cable and a USB cable from you digital camera or disk drive power to make the connections. Investigators may also wish to acquire the XBOX 360 DVD Drive Power Adapter V2 for the PC; it converts the XBOX 360 DVD Power input plug to a standard PC Molex Power plug (see Figure 9.17).

For further information on this product reference the URL at www.diygadget.com/store/xbox-360-adapters/xbox-360-dvd-and-hdd-adapter-combo-version-2/prod_27.html

Software

Forensic software (see Figure 9.18) was discussed in greater detail in Chapter 2.

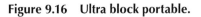

Figure 9.16 Ultra block portable.

Figure 9.17   Xbox 360 adapters and kit.

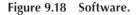

Figure 9.18   Software.

Conclusion

Chapter 9 has provided the reader with an overview of typical forensic tools, both hardware and software, which a forensic investigator should have in inventory, and ultimately on hand in his or her "forensics black bag" when conducting an investigation, whether that investigation be carried out in the field or the lab.

Chapter 10

Digital Multifunctional Devices: Forensic Value and Corporate Exposure

Introduction

The need to remain vendor neutral and to avoid the appearance of favoring any specific product, service or vendor is paramount when one undertakes a writing project, such as appears here in this text. To every rule, there is usually an exception, and as fate would have it, such is the case in the preparation of the material you are about to read in this chapter.

Considering the increasing complexity of technology and as a result, the devices, which may contain latent digital evidence, due to a migration from aged analog devices to state-of-the-art digital multifunctional devices (MFDs), the discussion of these MFDs and their importance or role in cyber forensic investigations necessitated the development of material in this chapter.

Assessment of Products

Our initial investigation centered on examining the potential, which photocopiers may have as a source for latent data and the potential necessity for the cyber forensic investigator to include these devices in the scope of his or her investigation. Additionally, we examined by default, the potential exposure to the confidentiality of data, which would befall organizations where data leakage occurred via an MFD.

A review of the major manufactures of photocopiers disclosed that the market although broad, is dominated by roughly 13 companies (Brother, Canon, Gestetner, IKON, Konica-Minolta, Okidata, Panasonic, Pitney Bowes, Ricoh, Savin, Sharp, Toshiba, and Xerox).

To investigate these photocopier brands as potential repositories of latent data, it is recommended that the investigator determine what, if any, potential exposures might exist with the overall security of the product.

One place to begin an assessment and to gather data on potential vulnerabilities is the National Vulnerability Database (NVD) (http://nvd.nist.gov). The NVD is a comprehensive cyber security vulnerability database that integrates all publicly available U.S. Government vulnerability, resources and provides references to industry resources. It is based on and synchronized with the common vulnerabilities and exposures (CVE) vulnerability naming standard. The NVD is a product of the NIST Computer Security Division and is sponsored by the Department of Homeland Security's National Cyber Security Division.

The NVD is the only database that is completely based upon the CVE standard vulnerability dictionary. It is the only database providing Common Vulnerability Scoring System (CVSS) scores for all CVE vulnerabilities. In addition it is the only vulnerability database that integrates Open Vulnerability Assessment Language (OVAL) queries.

CVE aspires to describe and name all publicly known facts about computer systems that could allow somebody, to violate a reasonable security policy for that system. Often, these things are referred to as vulnerabilities.

The NVD statistics engine allows one to generate statistics on vulnerability trends over time. One can track particular products or vendors. Alternately, one can track sets of vulnerabilities with particular attributes (such as remotely exploitable buffer overflows).

The most important usage of the statistics engine is, to look at the past history of a product as an indicator to see whether or not it is likely to be vulnerable in the future. For example, the statistics engine has revealed that some major software vendors have exponentially increasing numbers of vulnerabilities being discovered in their products every year, while the vulnerability discovery rate for other software vendors is staying steady or falling.

One should consider not purchasing products that are showing to continually be vulnerable (especially those that have many high severity vulnerabilities) (http://nvd.nist.gov/faq.cfm).

A "universal" vulnerability is one that is considered a vulnerability under any commonly used security policy, which includes at least some requirements for minimizing the threat from an attacker. (This excludes entirely "open" security policies in which all users are trusted, or where there is no consideration of risk to the system.) (http://cve.mitre.org/about/terminology.html.)

An examination of recent entries for photocopier products in the NVD provided the following information:

- CVE-2006-6439. Xerox WorkCentre and WorkCentre Pro before 12.050.03.000, 13.x before 13.050.03.000, and 14.x before 14.050.03.000 allows remote attackers to download the audit log and obtain potentially sensitive information via unspecified vectors (12/10/2006).
- CVE-2006-6433. Xerox WorkCentre and WorkCentre Pro before 12.060.17.000, 13.x before 13.060.17.000, and 14.x before 14.060.17.000 does not record accurate timestamps, which makes it easier for remote attackers to avoid detection when an audit tries to rely on these timestamps (12/10/206).
- CVE-2006-4680. The Remote UI in Canon imageRUNNER includes usernames and passwords when exporting an address book, which allows context-dependent attackers to obtain sensitive information (9/11/2006, http://nvd.nist.gov/nvd).

It would make little sense to base an investigation of potential latent data, residing on a photocopier, if it could be proven that the machine itself lacked basic security features that might render any potential evidence, which may have been collected from the machine, inadmissible or at least highly suspect with regards to its integrity. Checking with the NVD, prior to beginning a forensic examination of a MFD may provide additional useful information for the investigator.

While the authors endeavored and the publisher ensured, that the discussion of any products or services in this text remained free from specific vendor endorsement, the discussion of MFDs and their potential value (or exposure) in a cyber forensic investigation, led the authors to ask a simple, yet critical question: "Can a photocopy machine be a potential source for latent electronic, forensic evidence?" The short answer, most definitely "YES!"

Early in 2003, Sharp Electronics commissioned a survey of 1100 IT professionals to gauge their level of awareness about the security holes posed by common office equipment, such as copiers, printers, faxes, and scanners. The results were startling. The survey revealed that IT professionals are largely unaware or uncertain of the potential risk of the theft of documents from office equipment.

The survey revealed:

- Forty-seven percent of respondents erroneously believed that their copier or printer did not contain a hard drive.
- An additional 30 percent said they simply did not know whether the device contained a hard drive.
- Sixty-seven percent said copier or printers presented little or no risk to data security.
- Only five percent of survey respondents were aware of any data security breach in copiers or printers.

The results of the study underscore the convergence of several trends: The increased use of sophisticated, high-performance digital technology in office equipment, and the shift toward management of the increasingly connected devices by IT personnel who focus more on their computers than on peripheral devices [1].

Data Security and Latent Electronic Evidence

After a review of the information provided in the NVD, it is also very apparent that MFDs pose a significant, here-to-date, almost overlooked and underestimated security exposure for any organization in which MFDs are present. Although this chapter and text is not primarily focused on IT and data security, these issues and questions regarding controlling the potential exposure of MFDs will be addressed, albeit briefly, as appropriate throughout this chapter.

Our investigation led us to examine what methods organizations use to secure the varied MFDs operating within their many offices. Surprisingly, we found little awareness of the potential security exposure or legal liability, which faces an unprepared corporation. We also found little in the way of hard-, soft-, or firm-ware designed to protect data at rest. One vendor, however, which stood out from the crowd in providing a potential security solution for exposed MFDs are Sharp Electronics (Sharp).

A review of the market for similar products and vendors proved futile and we came away empty. In an effort to explore further and to bring to the reader's attention the connection and critical importance, which MFDs have to a cyber forensic investigation, we contacted Peter Cybuck, Associate Director Solution and Security Business Development at Sharp Electronics Corporation. Peter is acutely familiar with and deeply committed to securing content on MFDs. Peter is a member of The Software Assurance (SwA) Acquisition Working Group, NSA's High Tech crimes group, among other professional organizations.

In discussions and interviews with the authors, Peter has provided his insights, expertise, and comments regarding the varied vulnerabilities associated with MFDs. Peter's sage advice is worth reading and rereading by both the cyber forensics investigator and the professional charged with protecting his or her organization's data (e.g., internal auditors, IT security, etc.).

> The authors, the publisher, their estates and heirs yet to be born, oh you get the idea, are not endorsing products or services provided by this vendor. The vendor is referenced in an attempt to inform the reader and to call attention to a typically overlooked area, which may require potential forensic examination, as well as enhancing of existing security protocols.

Sharp offers clients a solution in the form of a product, which Sharp refers to as a Data Security Kit (DSK). This DSK is designed to protect document image data temporarily stored on the hard drive, or in other memory, and data processed by the MFD during copy, scan, print, or fax operations.

The DSK is an upgrade kit that not only adds security functions (e.g., encryption and overwrite), but also controls the major MFD systems and subsystems—print, copy, scan, fax jobs, network control, operating system, memory components (hard drive, RAM, ROM), local user interface, engine, and job controller (including postscript and PCL).

Sharp's DSK offers multiple layers of security. First, all latent image data within the MFD is encrypted (using an AES algorithm) before being written to the hard drive, RAM, or flash memory.

Peter noted, "that flash memory usually used in connection with fax applications can retain data as long as a hard drive. Your IPOD Nano does not lose your songs when you unplug it, thus, your copier also would not lose the documents in flash memory either. Copiers with RAM can be on a network plugged in for weeks holding document data in RAM, so clearing RAM is also an important security consideration."

When a document is printed, copied, scanned, or faxed, the temporary data stored or buffered in memory is overwritten up to seven times, rendering it unrecoverable [2].

"The Sharp DSK product overwrites encrypted data. The reason is that there is always the possibility that a power failure or even a machine mechanical failure (jam) might prevent the overwrites from executing. By storing the confidential data, as encrypted data it is protected even if the overwrites never execute (at the end of a "job").

Seven overwrites are used by Sharp to assure a statistically significant degradation of magnetic remnant data. One or two … even three overwrites used by some software can leave evidence on the magnetic surface of the drive sectors that very sophisticated labs might recover. In the case of the Sharp MFDs, the lab, after seven overwrites is very unlikely to recover anything beyond molecular noise and any fragments discovered would be fragments of a strongly encrypted file" [3].

This point is both important to the cyber investigator in that if a MFD is so protected, the potential of identifying and obtaining latent data is remote, and knowing this will help to initially limit the scope of the investigation as well as help determine the feasibility of pursuing this line of investigation to begin with.

For the internal controls professional, the existence of such technology at the source is a significant control point, however, lack of such control features exposes the organization to potential catastrophic risk, legally and financially.

Issues and Concerns

The risk of data theft or misuse in today's competitive marketplace is real—whether due to a malicious network attack, disgruntled employee, or electronic eavesdropping. Increasing this risk, as usually seen, is the threat from inside. The service agents that can swap drives and memory modules as they perform routine maintenance of corporate MFDs are a prime source of exposure. When was the last time you stood and watched as the service repairperson performed their job? Are you positive that he or she did not remove a hard drive full of potentially confidential data? You did stand there and watch while the service or repair work was performed, didn't you?

The resellers of MFDs removed from facilities when leases expire are also a major threat. They often mine used, decommissioned machines for confidential data. Does your photocopy lease agreement call for and guarantee the removal of the hard drive, prior to the machine being "turned"? Who receives this drive? What policies are in effect to wipe the drive (and certify that it no longer contains data) prior to its disposal? Should you wipe the drive? What if six months from now you need those data on the drive as evidence?

Every day, billions of pages of confidential information—medical records, legal documents, and financial data—are produced and distributed using sophisticated digital office systems—printers, copiers, facsimile, and MFDs. Many businesses and government agencies are unaware that whenever these devices are connected to a network, the risk of unauthorized access and data loss exists. Even as a standalone device, these "intelligent" systems retain latent document images, potentially exposing sensitive information.

When questioned about additional security exposures, both the cyber forensic investigator as well as the controls professional should consider, Peter responded "the often anonymous communication capabilities of today's MFD's deserves some attention. They can often be used to e-mail documents out of a facility without being logged to a sent mail folder. Documents (print, scan files) sent to or from the MFD over a network unencrypted can be sniffed by off-the-shelf software and captured by attackers. Sharp provides the option of sending encrypted PDFs and encrypted print files over the network to and from the MFD. The Sharp MFD firmware is capable of both encryption and decryption."

A review of the NVD discloses . . .

> CVE-2006-6430. Web services in Xerox WorkCentre and WorkCentre Pro before 12.060.17.000, 13.x before 13.060.17.000, and 14.x before 14.060.17.000 do not require HTTPS, which allows remote attackers to obtain sensitive information by sniffing the unencrypted HTTP traffic (12/10/2006, http://nvd.nist.gov/nvd).

This means that mission-critical data and documents are vulnerable to serious security breaches, yet organizations often focus attention and resources on securing their network, PCs and servers, not device input or output equipment. This leaves the back door open to anyone intent on undermining your business interests—attackers, employees, service agents, and competitors alike.

Failure to take steps to protect information assets has serious consequences, perhaps exposing an organization to liability claims, financial loss, and criminal penalties [4].

As part of a thorough investigation, the cyber forensic investigator must consider any device capable of storing data as a potential source of electronic evidence, important to his or her investigation. With this in mind, this chapter isolates and examines what in the day was simply called a photocopy machine, that is, the photocopier, and what is today referred to as an MFD. The once uni-task machine has grown up and grown into a multifunctional device hence the MFD, capable of not only photocopying an original document, but also scanning, faxing, creating a PDF file and e-mailing that original to anyone with a valid e-mail address, all from the same machine.

The technical growth and embellishment of the MFD has resulted in an internal reconfiguration of the machine now (and for some time) to be outfitted with a hard drive. Yes, a hard drive, the same type and almost the same capacity, as the hard drive, which sits inside your PC workstation on top of or beneath your desk, flash memory in both high and low end units without drives.

Stop and think for a moment, what are all of the access, security, and integrity concerns or issues you had (have) with controlling unauthorized access to data residing on your PC or laptop you now have (or should have) the same concerns or issues with the data, which resides on your photocopier's hard drive. In fact, you should probably be more concerned, be more worried, be more afraid the hard drive on your photocopier and the data residing on it, is completely exposed, unprotected, and accessible to anyone with the right tools and know how (which by the way IS NOT rocket science).

Unlike corporate desk and laptops, which over the past several years have received much attention when it comes to security, little if no attention has been afforded to securing data storage devices residing in corporate photocopiers, fax machines, and so on. Why should this lack of security consideration over photocopiers and MFDs in general, be of concern, of interest, to a cyber forensic investigator? Read on.

Technical Stuff

Most of the makes and models of today's photocopiers (aka MFDs) are outfitted with internal hard drives. These hard drives can range in size (storage capacity) from 40–80GB units. To put this in perspective, a 40MB hard drive is capable of storing and retaining:

- 43 billion characters
- 21 million pages of documents
- 374 feet of paper
- 838,000 pictures
- 16,384 songs

The same is true of the hard drive, which resides in an organization's photocopier. In fact, a rough estimate of the storage capabilities of photocopier hard drives indicates that at any one time, approximately 125,000 to a quarter million pages of text (of images of jobs, copied, scanned e-mailed, etc.) can remain or reside, on the hard drive of a corporate photocopier. Those data, those stored images represent a significant amount of potential electronic evidence, which may prove valuable in a cyber forensic investigation.

Most copiers do not sequentially store the documents copied. If they did they would quickly run out of memory. Many over write a temporary buffer memory used to capture the copied pages. Other MFD memory however such as a print spooler in the MFD or so called "secure print mail-boxes" used to store print jobs until the user walks up to the unit, enters a PIN or password and retrieves the documents, while at the copier cannot only indefinitely retain more page data, but retain it in a format (as PCL or Postscript files) that are easy for even amateurs to recover [3].

Not only do these data represent potential latent electronic evidence, they also represent a potential legal and financial exposure to the corporation.

Security is number one because legislation has put the focus on privacy, and the new initiatives and product capabilities needed to assure compliance. Privacy laws are having an impact everywhere, so security-conscious organizations now make Information Assurance a priority for all products that process sensitive information.

Left unprotected, however, MFD devices can create a breach in your Security Architecture and unauthorized parties can gain access to intellectual property and confidential information [4].

How the Process Works

Most MFDs in operation today, in almost every major organization around the globe, include a great deal of memory, even hard drives similar to those in desktop computers. The memory is used to buffer the documents that are copied, printed, scanned, and faxed. What most users do not realize is that the document information remains in the memory when they walk away from the machine.

Unlike previous generations of copiers, today's devices keep a copy of documents in memory, either on hard drives, random access memory (RAM) or flash memory. Just like a personal computer, the latent image data remains until that disk sector is overwritten. Documents could be accessed on the unit's hard drive from a PC and reprinted or the unit's hard drive could be replaced, moved or stolen [4].

The retained document data has unsettling ramifications for security-conscious organizations: It can expose confidential data to clever insiders and to enterprising cyber-thieves with enough savvy to hack into the machine's memory devices or penetrate its network interfaces.

Something as simple as moving your MFD to another department or selling it back to a broker after the lease expires, or taking it off site for repair or upgrade, all leave the hard disk, especially print mail boxes and controller hold and print queues exposed to data exposure and data theft. Fax data in flash memory is a similar concern. Residual confidential document data can remain in memory years after a print or copy job is completed.

Attackers are starting to see these devices and document processing devices as the weakest link in many networks and they are starting to draw unwanted attention. There is a high potential to retrieve and intercept confidential document data and they can be used to launch attacks on user networks [5].

Knowledge of how this procedure works is a critical asset to the cyber forensic investigator and to his or her efforts in conducting a thorough investigation and ensuring that all potential sources of electronic forensic evidence are examined.

Digital copiers store thousands of records in internal memory. At the end of a copier's lease period, thousands of records retained on the hard drive can fall into the wrong hands... this poses a privacy compliance risk.

Forensic Application

For most organizations, the more serious threat to data security does not come from external sources, but from internal sources, employees, contractors who come to work, have access to the building, systems, applications and ultimately sensitive, valuable, or critical data. Reports from the FBI point to internal threats as often being the greatest point of exposure for an organization.

Most incidents involve employees and their access to devices that process sensitive information—including the copiers, printers, scanners, and fax machines they use every day [4].

Ted, a mid-level manager supervises several engineers in his company's R&D department. Sally, a vendor's representative, and an entrepreneurial business woman, convinces Ted to sell her schematics and blueprints for a new hydraulic press Ted's company is developing. Excited by the potential for financial gain, Ted agrees, however, he does not want to get caught with paper or electronic copies of the documents either on his person or his desktop workstation.

Ted, staying late one evening, simply goes to the company's photocopier and selects the scan and e-mail options and in a matter of mere minutes, copies, scans, and e-mails the schematics and blueprints, saved as a PDF formatted file to Sally. Ted meets Sally, receives his payment and agrees to send Sally additional proprietary documents as they become available.

Alerted by a competitor to whom Sally attempted to sell the documents, Ted's company launches an investigation into the "leak." As part of the investigation, Ted's computer is seized and a cyber forensic examination is performed on Ted's computer. No incriminating evidence is uncovered as a result of the investigation.

It is at this point that the cyber forensic examiner may elect to expand the scope of the investigation to include an examination of other data storage devices to which Ted may have had access.

Enter the MFD

There are a multitude of factors, which must be considered before the investigator should begin an examination of a MFD. The first consideration is to determine the level of security (or lack thereof), which may be protecting access to and control over the MFD. If robust security (such as Sharp's DSK) is in place, and this is verifiable, the likelihood of uncovering any useable electronic evidence is highly unlikely, and the investigator would eliminate these MFDs as potential sources for review and examination.

If, on the other hand, there appears to be little or no security over the MFDs, then the investigator should proceed and forensically examine the hard drives of suspect MFDs.

It should be noted that even if the MFD has marginal security, or if it is very secure, it may be impossible for the investigator to obtain sufficient electronic evidence, which would proved, beyond question that Ted actually photocopied and e-mailed proprietary documents to an external third party.

Examination Process

Presented with the question, "How exactly would a cyber forensic investigator access stored images retained on the hard drive of a MFD and similarly, how would someone with less honorable or legal intentions acquire these data?" Peter Cybuck provided the following response...

> "Drives used in MFDs use PC-like interfaces and can easily be mounted using standard cables on PC's. If the MFD uses a Windows or Unix operating system it can be very easy to locate stored files. If proprietary disk control software is used (as is the case with the Sharp MFDs) the data may only appear as binary fields on undocumented drive sectors.
>
> The binary document data might also represent document images compressed using proprietary undocumented compression technology. Note that the copied documents are not stored as ASCII files. They are images, so if a small part of a document is recovered it might just be white space in a margin. If a small part of a word or text document is recovered it might provide a significant amount of information. Much more "data" must be recovered from a copier drive and much more analysis is necessary before it is understood.

That does not mean that it is not there and not recoverable. It does mean that depending on the architecture of the MFD and its operating system might or might not be vulnerable to low-level attackers. The use of off-the-shelf vulnerable mass market operating systems can make an MFD much more vulnerable.

Vendors who incorporate soft operating systems in their MFDs will most likely have potential security vulnerabilities associated with their MFDs. An examination of the NVD for the vendor's MFD under investigation (as discussed earlier) is a valuable exercise."

Step-by-Step Look at Examining an MFD's Hard Drive

1. Mount the drive using a compatible computer cable.
2. If a computer disk operating system was not used, search the Internet for software that permits you to examine drive sectors.
3. At a minimum, you will see binary arrays on the sectors that represent data.
4. Decoding it is possible, but can be nontrivial if the data is not in the form of traditional computer files, such as PCL or postscript print files or coded PDF files using ASCII characters.
5. Note that log files and audit files may be more easily decoded, because they will very likely be stored as ASCII files not compressed binary files.
6. If individual user access profiles were used to control MFD access, this can provide useful information if not document data.

There Are No Absolutes

After conducting such an examination, collecting and documenting electronic evidence, there is no guarantee that said evidence will be useable, lead to conviction, or justify the time and energy expended, nor the expense, for what evidence may have been obtained.

If the organization did not restrict access to or use of the MFD by even the simplest of measures, requiring a personal access code to operate the MFD, scan and transmit the schematics, then literally anyone could have had the opportunity to send the purloined PDF attached e-mail to Sally.

Consider for a moment, the example of someone printing confidential information from company records, because that information may be the easiest to recover. Stored fax pages and print files are usually the easiest to recover. The FBI report on Hansen, the convicted FBI spy, showed that he used the FBI's office copier to copy and print classified documents that he simply stuffed in his briefcase, and as a trusted, authorized insider, simply walked out of the building.

If the electronic evidence gathered by the investigator cannot place Ted at the MFD, as the individual who sent the scanned PDF e-mail to Sally, and is unable to obtain any additional corroborating evidence, which can be substantiated or forensically verified, the organization may never be able to prove, beyond a doubt, that Ted was the individual responsible for sending Sally the schematics.

Implementation of specific security features, such as Sharp's DSK, at the initial point of contact with the MFD, helps to establish the necessary security, date, time stamp, and audit trail required to ascertain with a greater degree of certainty, who is responsible for utilizing the MFD in question, and who leaked confidential, proprietary information to external third parties.

While there are many other MFD vulnerabilities most do not leave a data trail that can be mined for evidence. Most MFDs today can send documents to local computers as well as to e-mail servers and are often setup with customized "soft" buttons on the display that make it very easy to send to local desktops or network drives.

Simply looking at the list of scan destinations on the local copier might provide clues as to which computer was used to collect the scanned documents. It can also point toward possible network drives that might have been used to store even temporarily the scanned documents. It should be much easier to recover the documents from the desktop or network drives. The mail server address programmed into the MFD points toward another computer with a drive that could be mined for the document files [3].

Summary

The cyber forensic investigator should conduct an initial "inventory" of data storage devices accessible by the subject of the investigation, to establish a pool of potential devices, which may require detailed forensic examination.

Today's MFDs pose a considerable risk in the unsecured data, which may be accessible to unauthorized individuals, violating such legislation as FERPA, HIPAA, SoX, GLB, and so on, and exposing the organization to legal and financial sanctions. Some of these laws forbid the transmission of confidential files like health records across state or provincial borders through the public Internet unless they are encrypted. Cybuck states "Sharp's use of encrypted PDFs addresses this issue."

Today's MFDs add another source of potential electronic evidence, which should be considered as the cyber forensic investigator establishes the scope of his or her investigation.

Acknowledgments

The authors wish to personally recognize and to thank Peter Cybuck for giving his valuable time to discuss security issues related to uncontrolled MFDs and to provide his insights and expertise on the subject of MFDs and their role in a cyber forensic investigation. The authors would additionally like to thank Greg Gerritzen, also of Sharp Electronics, for his involvement in assisting the authors in providing data, which was analyzed for inclusion this chapter. Readers interested in obtaining further information regarding Sharp's DSK product may find additional information at www.sharpusa.com/security.

References

1. Cybuck. P. (2003), Machine Talk: What secrets are your office equipment passing along?, Security Products, page 34, March 2003, retrieved March 2007.
2. Sharp Electronics Corporation, (December 2006), Sharp Security Suite–Technical Questions & Answers, Sharp Electronics Corporation Sharp Plaza, Mahwah, NJ 07430-1163 1-800-BE-SHARP, www.sharpusa.com, www.sharpusa.com/security, documents provided to author.
3. Cybuck, P. (2007), Associate Director Solution and Security Business Development at Sharp Electronics Corporation, personal interview February 2007.

4. Sharp Electronics Corporation, (May 2005), Accountable for Security, Sharp Electronics of Canada, Ltd., www.ipac.ca, Sharp Electronics Corporation Sharp Plaza, Mahwah, NJ 07430-1163 1-800-BE-SHARP, www.sharpusa.com, documents provided to author.

5. Cybuck, P. (May 2005), Accountable for Security, Feature Interview, Sharp Electronics Corporation Sharp Plaza, Mahwah, NJ 07430-1163 1-800-BE-SHARP www.sharpusa.com, www.ipac.ca, documents provided to author.

Chapter 11

Cyber Forensics and the Law: Legal Considerations

Introduction

In perhaps the most important development in civil litigation in the past twenty years, the Federal Civil Rules of Civil Procedure (FRCP) are amended effective December 1, 2006 to specifically address the unique challenges of electronic discovery ("The eDiscovery Rules"). The amendments modify the rules in a manner intended to further highlight the importance of and provide a more established framework regarding electronic discovery. To comply with these rules, large organizations and their counsel must undergo significant procedural and operational changes [1].

For a detailed review and examination of the changes to FRCP, and the impact these changes will have on corporations in general and cyber forensic investigators specifically (see Chapter 13, Electronically Stored Information and Cyber Forensics).

This chapter will guide the reader through the various steps of basic cyber forensic investigations, with the objective of preparing the reader to participate with trained cyber forensic professionals, to forensically evaluate a suspect machine. The reader is cautioned against using this material as the sole source of education and training and not to attempt to seize or evaluate a suspect machine without undergoing extensive and certified forensic education and field-level training.

Readers are encouraged to read this chapter as presented, the organization of material presented here as a logical sequencing to the forensic process, and by following this logical approach, the reader will have a clear understanding of and a more complete picture of, the relationship between cyber forensics and the legal system or process.

Objectives

This chapter has several identifiable objectives, specifically designed to provide the reader with the following deliverables upon completing the chapter. Upon reading and absorbing the material presented here, you should be able to identify, establish and maintain a physical "chain of custody," recognize and pinpoint computer security risks and their associate remedies; determine incident responses and priorities in a cyber forensic investigation; as well as be able to develop policies for the preservation of computer evidence.

Lastly, by the conclusion of this chapter, the reader should be able to implement solid computer forensic processing methods and procedures, and develop the documentation necessary to communicate the findings of a computer forensics investigation to executive management for review and adjudication.

Cyber Forensics Defined

In attempting to define cyber forensics, one common problem is determining exactly what is and what *is not* or should not, be included in defining this extensive field.

At its broadest level, cyber forensics is defined as the use of scientifically derived and proven methods toward the preservation, collection, validation, identification, analysis, interpretation, documentation, and presentation of digital evidence derived from digital sources for the purpose of facilitating or furthering the reconstruction of events found to be criminal, or helping to anticipate unauthorized actions shown to be disruptive to planned operations [2].

At the grassroots level, this becomes the process of extracting information and data from computer storage media and guaranteeing its accuracy and reliability. In essence, cyber forensics is an archeological dig, designed to uncover (or discover) what happened on a specific hard drive, within a specific computer, during a specific period of time. Ultimately, cyber forensics is the combination of law and science (computer science).

The computer forensic expert or investigator knows how to extract evidence, based upon personal testing and validation of the findings, in accordance with the prescribed laws, for the extraction, collection and preservation of said evidence.

Digital Information

The amount of digital information generated by the technology, which exists in a single office, on a daily basis, is unfathomable. The impact on forensics is profound, and at times can be imposing and frightening. The likelihood that cases involving fraud, sexual harassment, inappropriate materials, or even intellectual property theft would involve digital information of some type is extremely high. In such cases, phone records, e-mail, transaction logs, voice-mail, accounting data, digital cameras, address books, temporary Internet logs, etc., all become potential sources of evidence.

Throughout the forensic process, digital data integrity must be maintained for effective analysis and the ultimate possibility that data, which represents evidence, will be acquired for eventual presentation in a court of law.

With respect to the success of an investigation, it all hinges upon the integrity of the data. Integrity can be defined as:

> "the property whereby digital data has not been altered in an unauthorized manner since the time it was created, transmitted, or stored by an authorized source. [3]"

The challenge becomes finding, collecting, preserving, and presenting data in a manner acceptable in a court of law, therefore, the necessity and critical importance of establishing and maintaining data integrity.

Identification and Analysis

In this chapter, we will focus much of our discussion on the digital forensic phases of identification and analysis. Using the previous definition, the goal of these phases can be expressed as:

> To identify digital evidence using scientifically derived and proven methods that can be used to facilitate or further the reconstruction of events in an investigation. [2]

All evidence that is needed for a successful investigation typically falls into one of the three categories:

1. Inculpatory Evidence, meaning evidence that is incriminating
2. Exculpatory Evidence, or evidence which clears one of guilt or blame
3. Evidence, which provides (or leaves behind) traces of tampering, unauthorized use, or theft

It is not a shocking revelation that computers can be involved in a crime, or be the instrument of a crime. There is a critical need for a proactive analysis and forensic investigation capability within most 21st century corporations today. A computer can be a victim; a weapon; a witness, an accomplice and a computer can also provide a record of all that has passed through its electronic memory.

Evidence is fragile and easily modified. Cyber thieves, criminals, dishonest and honest employees can manipulate electronic evidence in a multitude of ways. They can hide it, wipe it; disguise it; cloak it; encrypt it; and destroy it. Making the job of a cyber forensic investigator even more challenging (and rewarding), is finding this evidence once it has been hidden, wiped, disguised, cloaked, encrypted or destroyed.

Digital Forensics Complexity Problem

Data is typically acquired in its most raw format, and when in this raw form (generally streams of numbers or text, bits and pieces of character strings, incomplete words and sentences, etc.), it is generally difficult for investigators to make sense of or to put into terms understandable by management or judges. This problem has been solved by using specialized tools to translate data through one or more layers of abstraction until it can be understood.

It is proposed that the purpose of digital forensic analysis tools is to accurately present all data at a layer of abstraction and format that can be effectively used by an investigator to identify evidence. The needed layer of abstraction is dependent on the case and investigator [2].

Failure to use "blessed" software creates an unnecessary liability for any forensic investigator, and sets the investigator up for potential liability—the prosecuting attorney may accuse you of using uncertified, or out dated forensic tools or software.

The National Software Reference Library (NSRL) (www.nsrl.nist.gov) provides a repository of known software, file profiles, and file signatures for use by law enforcement and other organizations in computer forensics investigations.

Investigation of computer files requires a tremendous effort to review individual files. A typical desktop computer contains between 10,000 and 100,000 files, each of which may need to be reviewed. Investigators need to eliminate as many known files as possible from having to be reviewed.

An automated filter program can screen these files for specific profiles and signatures. If a specific file's profile and signature match the database of known files, then the file can be eliminated from review as a known file. Only those files that do not match would be subject to further investigation.

In addition, investigators can search for files that are not what they claim to be (e.g., the file has the same name, size, and date of a common file, but not the same contents) or files that match a profile (e.g., hacking tools).

The first release of Special Database 28, a "living" database of know file signatures, maintained by NSRL, was in October 2001, and it has been released quarterly since then. Subscriptions to receive approval to access Special Database 28, are available from NIST, and currently, policies and procedures are in place to support free redistribution of the database for authorized users. The September 2004 release of the database contained over 28 million file signatures.

Tool implementation errors are errors that are introduced by bugs in the tools used to perform the forensic analysis. Examples of such errors include general programming bugs; forensic tools which used an incorrect specification for design or analysis; and tools that used the correct specification, but the original source did not. Data extracted through the use of digital forensic analysis tools will have some margin of error associated with them. This does not include the errors associated with previous tampering, acquisition, or interpretation of the data however; it does include tool implementation error and abstraction error.

Programming consists of building successive "layers of abstraction," one on top of another. The process of going from one such layer to the next is abstraction. The goal of Abstraction Theory is to model this process mathematically, so that questions about abstraction—like, which of these two programming languages have more abstractive power—are objectively meaningful problems subject to formal investigation [4]. Therefore, errors introduced by the abstraction theory, exists in layers that were not part of the original design. Examples of abstraction errors may occur in areas such as log processing and IDS alerts [2].

All evidence must have an assumed margin of error associated with it and thus the output of any forensic tool must be verified, to ensure reliability, accuracy, completeness, and to sustain itself under the rigors of cross examination.

Proliferation of Digital Evidence

Digital devices are commonplace in society, and may contain information useful in developing a criminal case. Devices, which lend themselves to producing digital evidence for forensic investigators include but, are not limited to:

- PDAs
- Cell phones
- Computers
- USB flash cards
- FAX machines [5]

The forensic investigator should be cognizant that the crafty cyber criminal or the suspected employee may resort to hiding evidence of his or her lapses in discretion in places that the average investigator, auditor, and manager may overlook or fail to realize even exist. The astute forensic investigator will examine all possible data hiding places, such as slack space (or file slack) and swap files.

Slack Space

Slack space, is the term assigned to the unused space in a disk cluster. The DOS and Windows file systems use fixed-size clusters. Even if the actual data being stored requires less storage than the cluster size, an entire cluster is reserved for the file. The unused space is called the slack space. Rarely do file sizes exactly match the size of one or multiple clusters perfectly. The data storage space that exists from the end of the file to the end of the last cluster assigned to the file is called "file slack" [6].

DOS and older Windows systems use a 16-bit file allocation table (FAT), which results in very large cluster sizes for large partitions. For example, if the partition size is 2 GB, each cluster will be 32K. Even if a file requires only 4K, the entire 32K will be allocated, resulting in 28K of slack space. Windows 95 OSR 2 and Windows 98 resolve this problem by using a 32-bit FAT (FAT32) that supports cluster sizes smaller than 1K [7].

This slack space is simply space wasted as a result of the cluster system that FAT file system uses. Given that files are allocated entire clusters regardless of the file size, as drive sizes grow and along with them cluster sizes grow, the more space that will be wasted. As an example, if you had 200 files, each of which had a single byte of data occupying a cluster, the amount of wasted space, or slack, would be enormous. In essence, by doubling the cluster size of the disk, you're doubling the amount of disk space that is wasted. The space left at the end of the last cluster allocated to the file, is commonly called slack [8].

An example may serve best to illustrate this point. Think of this in terms of collecting rain water in quart-sized glass bottles. Even if you collect just one ounce of water, you have to use a whole bottle. Once the bottle is in use, however, you can fill it with 31 more ounces, until it is full. Then you'll need another whole bottle to hold the 33rd ounce [9].

RAM Slack

File slack potentially contains randomly selected bytes of data from computer memory. This happens because DOS or Windows normally writes in 512 byte blocks called sectors. Clusters are made up of blocks of sectors. If there is not enough data in the file to fill the last sector in a file, DOS or Windows makes up the difference by padding the remaining space with data from the memory buffers of the operating system. This randomly selected data from memory is called RAM Slack because it comes from the memory of the computer. RAM Slack can contain any information that may have been created, viewed, modified, downloaded or copied during work sessions that have occurred since the computer was last booted. Thus, if the computer has not been shut down for several days, the data stored in file slack can come from work sessions that occurred in the past.

Drive Slack

RAM slack pertains only to the last sector of a file. If additional sectors are needed to round out the block size for the last cluster assigned to the file, then a different type of slack is created. It is called drive slack and it is stored in the remaining sectors, which might be needed by the operating system to derive the size needed to create the last cluster assigned to the file. Unlike RAM slack, which comes from memory, drive slack is padded with what was stored on the storage device before. Such data could contain remnants of previously deleted files or data from the format pattern associated with disk storage space that has yet to be used by the computer.

It is important to understand the significance of file slack in computer-related investigations. Because file slack potentially contains data dumped randomly from the computer's memory, it is possible to identify network logon names, passwords and other sensitive information associated with computer usage. File slack can also be analyzed to identify prior uses of the subject computer and such legacy data can help the computer forensics investigator. File slack is not a trivial item. On large hard disk drives, file slack can involve several hundred megabytes of data. Fragments of prior e-mail messages and word processing documents can be found in file slack. From a computer forensic standpoint, file slack is very important as both a source of computer evidence and security risks [6].

For the forensic investigator, slack space represents another potential hiding place where the suspect or cyber criminal proceeds to split a pilfered document into smaller "segments" and hides these segments selectively into the slack spaces and the end of clusters.

Swap File

A swap file is an area on your hard disk used as virtual memory. It is called a swap file because virtual memory management software swaps data between it and main memory (RAM).

A swap file [or swap space] (Windows 95 and 98) (Windows NT, 2000 and XP the reference is to a page file) is a space on a hard disk used as the virtual memory extension of a computer's real memory (RAM), similar to a "scratch pad" to write data when additional random access memory is needed. Having a swap file allows your computer's operating system to pretend that you have more RAM than you actually do. The least recently used files in RAM can be "swapped out" to your hard disk until they are needed later so that new files can be "swapped in" to RAM. In larger operating systems (such as IBM's OS/390), the units that are moved are called pages and the swapping is called paging.

One advantage of a swap file is that it can be organized as a single contiguous space so that fewer I/O operations are required to read or write a complete file.

In general, Windows and Unix-based operating systems provide a default swap file of a certain size that the user or a system administrator can usually change.

Windows swap or page files are huge and most computer users are unaware of their existence. The size of these files can range from 100 million bytes to over a gigabyte and the potential exists for these huge files to contain remnants of word processing, e-mail messages, Internet browsing activity, database entries and almost any other work that may have occurred during past Windows work sessions. This situation creates a significant security problem because the potential exists for data to be transparently stored within the Windows swap file without the knowledge of the computer user. This can occur even if the work product was stored on a computer network server. The result is a significant computer security weakness that can be of benefit to the computer forensics specialist. Windows swap files can actually provide the computer forensics specialist with investigative leads that might not otherwise be discovered [10].

From Frye to FER

For the past 50 years or so, the Frye test of determining when evidence had reached the point where it was admissible, was to determine if the evidence collection technique had been generally accepted by the scientific community which was held to be the most knowledgeable regarding the rigors used to develop the technique.

According to Giannelli, The Admissibility of Novel Scientific Evidence: *Frye vs. United States*, A Half-Century Later, 80 Colum. L. Rev. 1197 (1980), the primary argument raised in favor of the Frye test is that it "assures that those most qualified to assess the general validity of a scientific method will have the determinative voice." *United States vs. Addison*, 498 F.2d 741, 743-744 (D.C. Cir. 1974). Thus, the Frye test assigns to experts the task of determining a test's reliability.

It is therefore best to adhere to a standard, which in effect permits the experts who know the most about a procedure to experiment and to study it. In effect, they form a kind of technical jury, which must first pass on the scientific status of a procedure before the lay jury utilizes it in making its findings of fact [11].

This evidence test stood the test of time, well at least 50 years anyway, when in 1973, Congress adopted the Federal Rules of Evidence (FRE).

For forensic investigators, the primary sections and sub-sections of this adoption, which most affect an investigator's work, are the following:

Article IV Relevancy and Its Limits

Rule 401. Definition of "Relevant Evidence"

"Relevant evidence" means evidence having any tendency to make the existence of any fact that is of consequence to the determination of the action more probable or less probable than it would be without the evidence.

Rule 402. Relevant Evidence Generally Admissible; Irrelevant Evidence Inadmissible

All relevant evidence is admissible, except as otherwise provided by the Constitution of the United States, by Act of Congress, by these rules, or by other rules prescribed by the Supreme Court pursuant to statutory authority. Evidence that is not relevant is not admissible.

Rule 403. Exclusion of Relevant Evidence on Grounds of Prejudice, Confusion, or Waste of Time

Although relevant, evidence may be excluded if its probative value is substantially outweighed by the danger of unfair prejudice, confusion of the issues, or misleading the jury, or by considerations of undue delay, waste of time, or needless presentation of cumulative evidence.

These rules govern the introduction of evidence in proceedings, both civil and criminal, in Federal courts. Although they do not apply to suits in state courts, the rules of many states have been closely modeled on these provisions.

Rule 104. Preliminary Questions (a) Questions of admissibility generally.

Preliminary questions concerning the qualification of a person to be a witness, the existence of a privilege, or the admissibility of evidence shall be determined by the court, subject to the provisions of subdivision (b). In making its determination it is not bound by the rules of evidence except those with respect to privileges [12].

Authentication

Before a party may move for admission of a computer record or any other evidence, the proponent must show that it is authentic. This includes laying a "foundation" or demonstrating a basis for why the evidence is relevant and useful. The government must offer evidence "sufficient to support a finding that the [computer record or other evidence] in question is what its proponent claims." Fed. R. Evid. 901(a). See *United States vs. Simpson*, 152 F.3d 1241, 1250 (10th Cir. 1998).

The standard for authenticating computer records is the same as for authenticating other records. The degree of authentication does not vary simply because a record happens to be (or has been at one point) in electronic form. See *United States vs. DeGeorgia*, 420 F.2d 889, 893 n.11 (9th Cir. 1969); *United States vs. Vela*, 673 F.2d 86, 90 (5th Cir. 1982).

But see *United States vs. Scholle*, 553 F.2d 1109, 1125 (8th Cir. 1977) (stating in dicta that "the complex nature of computer storage calls for a more comprehensive foundation").

For example, witnesses who testify to the authenticity of computer records need not have special qualifications. The witness does not need to have programmed the computer himself, or even need to understand the maintenance and technical operation of the computer. See *United States vs. Moore*, 923 F.2d 910, 915 (1st Cir. 1991). Instead, the witness simply must have first-hand knowledge of the relevant facts to which he or she testifies.

■ See generally *United States vs. Whitaker*, 127 F.3d 595, 601 (7th Cir. 1997) (FBI agent who was present when the defendant's computer was seized can authenticate seized files);
■ *United States vs. Miller*, 771 F.2d 1219, 1237 (9th Cir. 1985) (telephone company billing supervisor can authenticate phone company records);
■ Moore, 923 F.2d at 915 (head of bank's consumer loan department can authenticate computerized loan data [13].

Best Evidence Rule

The best evidence rule provides that the original of a "writing, recording, or photograph" is required to prove the contents thereof. Fed. R. Evid. 1002. A writing or recording includes a "mechanical or electronic recording" or "other form of data compilation." Fed. R. Evid. 1001(1). Photographs include "still photographs, x-ray films, video tapes, and motion pictures." Fed. R. Evid. 1001(2). An original is the writing or recording itself, a negative or print of a photograph or, "[i]f data are stored in a computer or similar device, any printout or other output readable by sight, shown to reflect the data accurately." Fed. R. Evid. 1001(3) [14].

Fed. R. Evid. 1001(3). Thus, an accurate printout of computer data always satisfies the best evidence rule. See *Doe vs. United States*, 805 F. Supp. 1513, 1517 (D. Hawaii. 1992). According to the Advisory Committee Notes that accompanied this rule when it was first proposed, this standard was adopted for reasons of practicality. Although strictly speaking the original of a photograph might be thought to be only the negative, practicality and common usage require that any print from the negative be regarded as an original. Similarly, practicality and usage confer the status of original upon any computer printout. Advisory Committee Notes, Proposed Federal Rule of Evidence 1001(3) (1972) [13].

In practice, this also includes "mirror imaged" drives or computer hard disk drives and peripherals, so long as the examiner can establish that the mirror image is an exact and precise duplicate and as well as substantiating the methods used to create the mirror image.

Article VII Opinions and Expert Testimony

Rule 702. Testimony by Experts

If scientific, technical, or other specialized knowledge will assist the trier of fact to understand the evidence or to determine a fact in issue, a witness qualified as an expert by knowledge, skill, experience, training, or education, may testify thereto in the form of an opinion or otherwise, if (1) the testimony is sufficiently based upon reliable facts or data, (2) the testimony is the product of reliable principles and methods, and (3) the witness has applied the principles and methods reliably to the facts of the case [15].

In *Daubert vs. Merrell* Dow Pharmaceuticals, 509 U.S. 579 (1993), the Supreme Court held that when expert evidence based upon "scientific knowledge" is offered at trial, the judge, upon proper motion by a litigant who challenges the admissibility of the testimony, should act as a gatekeeper and first determine whether the proffered evidence is "reliable"—whether it is evidence that can be trusted to be scientifically valid.

In the aftermath of Daubert, a number of courts had to address the unresolved issue whether the Daubert factors by which reliability was to be tested should also be applied to experts offering opinion testimony that was not based on clearly identified scientific principles, but which sprung from "technical or other specialized knowledge." Because the clear majority of informed opinion seemed to favor applying a Daubert-like standard to all expert opinion testimony, the Advisory Committee on the Rules of Evidence endorsed that requirement by including the above language in the amendment.

After the drafters first proposed this Amendment, the Supreme Court clarified its Daubert opinion in the case of *Kumho Tire Co. V. Carmichael*, 119 S.Ct. 1167 (1999) by mandating that the trial judges' duty to act as gatekeepers, charged with insuring that only reliable expert opinion evidence be admitted, apply to all forms of expert testimony.

In the Committee Note that follows the Amended language of Rule 702, the drafters emphasized again the nonexclusive checklist courts are to use in judging whether proffered scientific expert opinion testimony meets the Daubert criteria of reliability:

The specific factors explicated by the Daubert Court are:

1. Whether the expert's technique or theory can be or has been tested—that is, whether the expert's theory can be challenged in some objective sense, or whether it is instead simply a subjective, conclusory approach that cannot reasonably be assessed for reliability
2. Whether the technique or theory has been subject to peer review and publication
3. The known or potential rate of error of the technique or theory when applied
4. The existence and maintenance of standards and controls
5. Whether the technique or theory has been generally accepted in the scientific community

In Kumho Tire, the Court recognized that these same factors might not be applicable to all forms of expert opinion testimony, and stressed that these factors constituted not mandates but flexible guidelines, and that courts could look at other factors that, depending on the particular circumstances of a case, were likely to permit an assessment of the reliability of the nonscientific expert opinion testimony offered to the tribunal. The Court also specifically declared that the gatekeeping function of trial judges "applies not only to testimony based on 'scientific' knowledge, but also to knowledge based on 'technical' and 'other specialized' knowledge."

While in 1993 the Daubert Court was explicit in stating that the trial judge's focus in determining reliability was to be directed solely toward examining the "principles and methodology, not on the conclusions they generate," in the later case of *General Electric vs. Joiner*, 522 U.S. 136 (1997) the Court backpedaled from this announced position and recognized that "conclusions and methodology are not entirely distinct from one another." The problem of considering both methodology as well as the conclusion is also covered by the language of the proposed amendment to Rule 702, in that it directs a trial court to determine not only whether the methods used by an expert and the principles upon her analysis rests have been determined to be reliable, but also whether "the witness has applied the principles and methods reliably" to the facts that are in controversy in the particular case [16].

The Daubert decision changed the approach to admissibility in at least two significant aspects: (1) henceforth, the test for admissibility of evidence based upon "scientific knowledge" was not to be merely general acceptance in a particular field, but whether proof of "reliability" (validity) of a technique or scientific method could be established; and (2) this determination of reliability was to be made by the trial judge, upon whom the duty now falls to keep evidence based on unreliable "science" from breeching the gates of the edifice where justice is to be dispensed. Is it fair to equate "unreliable science" with "junk science"?

Daubert Test for Reliability

Rule 702 of the Federal Rules of Evidence states, in part:

- Witness qualified as an expert by knowledge, skill, experience, training, or education, may testify thereto in the form of an opinion or otherwise, if:
  - The testimony is based upon sufficient facts or data
  - The testimony is the product of reliable principles and methods
  - The witness has applied the principles and methods reliably to the facts of the case

The key for the Court in determining whether an expert may testify before a jury is therefore primarily one of "reliability of method." The court will not look at the actual opinion held by an expert, but merely examines his or her methodology to determine whether the procedures used would be expected to lead to trustworthy results. If an expert relies on unreliable foundational data or his methodology is not reliable, then his entire opinion is likewise unreliable and should be excluded from the jury.

Daubert Factors

The U.S. Supreme Court set out several specific factors that should be used by the courts in evaluating any proposed expert testimony. These factors are not exclusive and some or all may not apply in any given case, but they are always the place to start the reliability analysis. The factors are as follows:

1. Whether the theory or technique has been scientifically tested.
2. Whether the theory or technique has been subject to peer review or publication.
3. The (expected) error rate of the technique used.
4. Acceptance of the theory or technique in the relevant scientific community.

The test is meant to be a flexible one, with no single factor being dispositive. Likewise, the Supreme Court recognized that not all factors would be useful in all cases, and that other factors may be more important than any of the listed ones for a specific case.

Obviously, an opinion or type of analysis created specifically for use in a lawsuit is not given the same weight as a method of analysis that is widely accepted by the scientific community outside the litigation setting.

Although the Daubert test is certainly more liberal than the older, Frye standard, it still allows the exclusion of testimony where the court is convinced that the method used to support the opinion is simply too poorly designed to be trustworthy [17].

Keeping in mind that the "factors" of the Daubert opinion may not be appropriate for all forms of expert testimony, consider using the following criteria:

- Are the underlying premises upon which a technique or method rests empirically validated?
- Is there a professional literature that describes the purposes to be achieved and the methods whereby the aims of the field can be reliably realized?
- Are there professional associations or societies offering continuing education to which members with established credentials are eligible to belong?
- Does there exist a rigorous training program whereby one can achieve basic proficiency in the discipline under the supervision of persons with established credentials who can impart knowledge and experience to trainees seeking to qualify as examiners?
- Is there a meaningful certification program that attests to the competence and proficiency of workers in the discipline?
- Has an examination protocol been developed whereby investigations can be reliably carried out and which will yield reasonably consistent results when followed by properly credentialed examiners [18]?

Searching and Seizing Computers

Searching and Seizing Computers and Obtaining Electronic Evidence in Criminal Investigations, was newly revised and published in July 2002. This publication provides a comprehensive guide to the legal issues that arise when federal law enforcement agents search and seize computers and obtain electronic evidence in criminal investigations. The topics covered include the application of the Fourth Amendment to computers and the Internet, the Electronic Communications Privacy Act, workplace privacy, the law of electronic surveillance, and evidentiary issues.

This updated version includes discussion of significant changes to relevant Federal law arising from the USA PATRIOT Act of 2001, and supersedes the previous version of "Searching and Seizing Computers and Obtaining Electronic Evidence in Criminal Investigations," published January 2001, as well as "Federal Guidelines for Searching and Seizing Computers" (1994), and the Guidelines' 1997 and 1999 Supplements [19].

Readers interested in learning more about this updated version can find additional information at www.usdoj.gov/criminal/cybercrime/s&smanual2002.htm.

Junk Science Attack

Juries usually believe expert witnesses. Unfortunately, juries rarely understand the expert testimony they hear, and do not know what weight—if any—to give to terms like "consistent with" and "matching" and "virtually excluded." The lawyers and the judge rarely understand the science that is presented by these experts either. Our criminal justice system is adversarial and often dog-eat-dog. When the expert falls short of the minimum standards of the profession, or worse, is an outright fraud, it can spell disaster for the wrongly accused [20].

There are typically several tests, which the court may apply to determine relevancy, admissibility and reliability of an expert's testimony and methodologies and ultimately his or her opinion regarding the evidence in question. In cyber forensics, an effort by counsel to place into question the methods used by an investigator, to assail the reliability of the tools employed by the investigator, and to attempt to make suspect the investigator's competency, is generally referred to as a "junk science" attack.

Examples of junk science include: experts testifying about tests that were never conducted, suppression of evidence or exculpatory results of testing, falsified results, falsified credentials, misinterpretation of test results, and statistical exaggeration [21].

As the forensic investigator, you will need to be aware that the first level of attack by those seeking to discredit the validity of your findings and methods will be against YOU, the forensic examiner and against your credentials. You must have solid credentials that state that you know your stuff; and that you are well trained in cyber forensic techniques. Your resume must reflect your forensics training. Think about everything you say, do, and write from the very start of your investigation right through the completion of the investigation, because it could be admissible in a court of law, under a discovery motion.

The primary question, according to Steve Hailey, president of CyberSecurity Institute, that should be asked here is not whether a particular tool has been proven in court, but rather; "Does the examiner have the technical background to support the results of their investigation, and have they properly authenticated their results?"

"Think about this for a moment," states Hailey. "If the tools being used are the mechanism to find evidence on a computing device, and several different tools can replicate the process, then it does not matter what tools were used. The evidence is simply there and can be found by any competent forensic examiner using a variety of tools. Proper interpretation of the evidence however is another story—that's were the smarts of the forensic examiner come in to play" [22].

The second level of attack to be mounted against the forensic investigator will be against the tools that the investigator has used to conduct his or her investigation, and to perform his or her analysis. It is imperative to cross-validate the tools you used to conduct your investigation and analysis. This provides multiple layers of corroboration and reduces the potential of having your findings questioned.

Most all software is buggy to some degree thus; you MUST cross validate your findings. Depending on the criticality of the examination and case before you, it would be a prudent step to consider utilizing multiple software tools to reperform the same analysis. Proper documentation and retention of the results of these analyses will be critical should you be required to defend your tool selection or your methodologies, and the results you obtained.

You MUST therefore cross-validate your findings with several software tools, preferably with tools sold by major vendors, available through major distributor channels. Whenever possible, use the same types of tools that would be available to attorneys.

Any competent examiner knows that you do not use a single tool. Granted, we all have our favorite primary tools to use, but once the evidence has been extracted that is pertinent to the situation and will be used in some type of proceeding, the evidence needs to be authenticated using other tools as well. The key is to use different tools from different vendors and different sources. DO NOT rely solely on tools from a particular vendor or source [22].

Ask yourself, "Do I really understand what is going on behind the scenes with the tool I am using to collect the evidence? Or am I merely placing my trust in the technology and hoping that the technology is identifying and collecting the correct data?" If you truly do not understand the technology or the functional logic of the tool you are employing to gather the evidence, solely relying upon a technology which you are unable to explain if asked, will not only damage your reputation as a forensic investigator but, will seriously under mind the credibility of the evidence which you have collected, possibly causing that evidence to be inadmissible. Be 100 percent sure that you can fully explain HOW the tool you selected, identified AND retrieved the data which you have determined to be evidential matter. Failing to do so, may cost you more than your reputation.

Third level of attack leveled against the forensic investigator will be to target reliability, methodology, and credibility of the evidence, which you have gathered. Presently, this is the most common line of attack in criminal cyber cases. The first question that will be raised, is the evidence even admissible in court? Next, did you follow proper procedures for gathering and handling the evidence (i.e., chain of custody)? Do you even have established procedures and methods? Do your procedures and methods ensure the integrity of the collection and examination process? Did you follow the proper rules of evidence?

Understand that when you have evidence that is damning to the other side, opposing counsel will bring up arguments that your software tool is not "generally accepted in the computer forensics community" and so forth. If you have authenticated your results using several different tools and really understand the meaning of what the evidence shows, you will be fine [22].

Chain of Custody

The chain of custody begins when an item of evidence is collected, and the chain is maintained until the evidence is disposed of. The chain of custody assures continuous accountability. This accountability is important because, if not properly maintained, an item (of evidence) may be inadmissible in court.

The purpose of the chain of custody is that the proponent of a piece of evidence must demonstrate that it is what it purports to be. Said differently, there is reliable information to suggest that the party offering the evidence can demonstrate that the piece of evidence is actually in fact, what the party claims it to be, and can further demonstrate its origins and the handling of the evidence because it was acquired.

The chain of custody is a chronological written record of those individuals who have had custody of the evidence from its initial acquisition until its final disposition. These persons in the chain of custody must be identified on an appropriate and official "internal" Evidence or Property Custody Document, which is initiated when the evidence is acquired. Each individual in the chain of custody is responsible for an item of evidence to include its care, safekeeping, and preservation while it is under his or her control.

Because of the sensitive nature of evidence, an evidence custodian should be appointed to assume responsibility for the evidence when not in use by the cyber forensics investigator or other competent authority involved in the investigation. It is important to establish procedures for creating a "custody chain," to include a "running log" of who has had contact with (access to) an item of evidence, for how long, and for what reason(s) (why?).

The organizational representative directly responsible for "first response" to a cyber investigation and who will be the organization's immediate and single source point of contact with the cyber forensics investigator should begin immediately to determine and document a "backward" chain of custody before the investigator arrives.

Collecting information regarding the environment and use of the computer or machine under investigation, in an attempt to answer questions such as the following, prior to the arrival of the forensics investigator, should be of immediate importance:

- Who had access to the machine?
- What level of authorization did all of those individuals having access to the machine have?
- What was the machine used for?
- What external devices did the machine connect to or interact with?

- Which and how many servers did the machine "touch"?
- Where and how will you store and safeguard the machine and the evidence after seizure?
- Will you or an external third-party be responsible for the storage and safeguarding of the seized machine and associated evidence?

It is important to note regarding the above … establishing (obtaining) answers to these questions is cross applicable to establishing authenticity and a solid foundation for the organization's (or the investigator's) case, even more so than a chain of custody record or log.

At the very least, the evidence or property custody document should include the following information:

- Name or initials of the individual collecting the evidence
- Each person or entity subsequently having custody of it
- Dates the items were collected or transferred
- Department (or Agency or Unit or Team) name and case number
- Victim's or suspect's name
- A brief description of the item seized

Discredit the Witness (aka Refute the Cyber Forensic Expert)

If you screw up a case, due to your ineptness as a forensics investigator, lack of preparation, poor control over the chain of custody, or failure to provide, clear, accurate, and believable testimony, this failure will follow you and your career forever.

In subsequent cases, the prosecution, in pretrial preparation, will examine various forensic "lists" (e.g., professional societies, expert witness databases, online alt or chat sites, etc.) and look for evidence that your testimony was thrown out or did not uphold under cross examination.

Think twice about joining "lists" or seeking advice "in the open" with respect to forensic questions. These "lists," if public, can be a source for damming evidence that you are NOT the expert you claim to be, even if you are only seeking corroboration or clarification, these "questions" may be turned against you in an attempt to show that you really do not know your "stuff" and need to rely on the advice, input, opinions of others, who themselves may be even less knowledgeable.

At various times, in certain investigations, under certain circumstances, we all need the advice of or can benefit from the wisdom, experience and counseling of others, our peers, other industry professionals or experts, technical experts, etc., so operating in a void or attempting to "go it alone" is not a sound strategy either. Simply act judiciously and do not join "public" lists, instead, join industry or organization closed or restricted lists. If you need advice or seek input, ask general questions and then when you are sure of the person on the other end, ask your question off-line.

Not only are you more likely to receive more professionally "grounded" advice, the potential negative perception which a prosecutor *may* attempt to draw from your involvement with or inquiry of, these groups, may be minimal or negligible due to the professional standing and industry acceptance of these groups, and their membership.

As a witness, always use analogies when explaining technical terms or concepts. Your jury will likely not be technology literate or savvy. Try to use examples and analogies that an eighth grader could comprehend. Additionally, forensic examinations should be conducted by a team of at least two professionals. The presentation of your forensic evidence may not be immediate, and if over some time, you are not available or have moved on, there may be at least one other person familiar with the case who then can discuss the evidence and the collection methods employed at the time.

The integrity of witness testimony is always under question, and great care must be taken to ensure that your (the investigator's) testimony is presented based upon a solid foundation of truth. As the forensic investigator you must continually be aware of your personal integrity as this critical element will reflect both positively as well as negatively on your ability to convincingly argue the validity of the evidence that you are asked to present and defend.

Consider the potential liability to your case, and to your client, should under cross examination, your testimony become suspect, or is impeached as a result of past problems, personal or professional. Here your professional competencies as a cyber forensic or technical expert is not questioned or examined, however, your ability to be believed is, your credibility and integrity come under attack. Ever lie in a divorce proceeding? Ever have a problem with perjury in a previous case? Have your findings come under examination and the results blocked from admissibility? As a seasoned investigator once stated, "you could be the best forensic examiner know to man but, if you have ever had a problem with candor, forget about ever testifying."

Your integrity and credibility are pivotal to your success as a forensic investigator. The American College of Forensic Examiners International's Certified Forensic Consultant (CFC), for example, abides by Principles of Ethical Conduct. The forensic examiner's role is to serve justice by using his or her expertise to further the doctrine of fairness. By adhering to this Code of Ethics, the examiner pledges in part to:

1. To maintain the highest standards of professional practice.
2. To be forever vigilant of the importance of my role and to conduct myself only in the most professional manner at all times [23].

Internal auditing is an independent, objective assurance and consulting activity designed to add value and improve an organization's operations. It helps an organization accomplish its objectives by bringing a systematic, disciplined approach to evaluate and improve the effectiveness of risk management, control, and governance processes.

The Institute of Internal Auditors, the international governing body for internal auditors, in its Code of Ethics, states that a code of ethics is necessary and appropriate for the profession of internal auditing, founded as it is on the trust placed in its objective assurance about risk management, control, and governance. The Institute's Code of Ethics extends beyond the definition of internal auditing to include two essential components:

1. Principles that are relevant to the profession and practice of internal auditing
2. Rules of Conduct that describe behavior norms expected of internal auditors. These rules are an aid to interpreting the Principles into practical applications and are intended to guide the ethical conduct of internal auditors.

The list of principles which internal auditors are expected to apply and uphold is similar, in part, to principles of forensic investigators. In the course of performing their duties, internal auditors are expected to apply and uphold the principles of integrity and competency. The integrity of internal auditors establishes trust and thus provides the basis for reliance on their judgment. As to competency, internal auditors shall engage only in those services for which they have the necessary knowledge, skills, and experience [24].

These two organizations are representative examples of professional organizations with specific and defined Codes of Ethics and ethical practice. It would behoove the forensic investigator to be mindful of these codes of ethical practice when seeped in the daily toil of evidence gathering and report generation. Strive to ensure that your ability to testify, to be a credible witness is above reproach and is impeccable, not impeachable.

Outline of an Investigation

The first place to begin is by determining what is the goal of the investigation? Is the goal to enforce policy; bring legal action against a current or former employee or third-party contractor; participate in a civil investigation; or in support of an ongoing or pending criminal investigation?

In determining the ultimate goal of an investigation, the investigator may have to depend on a third party to provide that specific reason. Initially, there may not be a clear violation or indication of wrong doing, which would immediately indicate or signal that the investigation is headed for prosecution.

It is usually best to err on the conservative side, and always begin and carry out an investigation working under the pretext that the evidence you uncover and all of your actions will eventually be part of a litigation process. If your work never sees the inside of a courtroom, you can still rest easily knowing that your work would have withstood the legal scrutiny. Table 11.1 provides some guidance as to determining the goal of an investigation.

Table 11.1 Determining the Goal of an Investigation

Communities within Cyber Forensics	Primary Investigative Objective	Secondary Investigative Objective	Operating Environment
Law enforcement	Prosecution		After the fact Real time with appropriate warrants
Military operations	Ensure confidentiality and integrity of data systems Maintain Strategic Initiatives Preserve continuity of operations	Prosecution	Real time
Public and private business sectors	Adherence to the CIA Security model Information must not be disclosed to any unauthorized person (confidentiality) System must disallow unauthorized, malicious or accidental data changes (integrity) System must ensure the capacity to meet service needs (availability)	Prosecution	Real time
Academia	Expanding current knowledge base Research Publication	Critical thinking Life long learning Academic education Curriculum development	Laboratory and testing

Source: Adapted from Computer Forensics: Basics Lecture 1, The Context of Computer Forensics.

The basic steps in carrying out a cyber investigation are:

1. Obtain proper authorization
2. Secure the scene of the alleged e-crime
3. Seize evidence (Hard drives, floppies …)
4. Deliver evidence to the forensic lab
5. Make full backup image and second copy
6. Create duplicates for analysis
7. Analyze the duplicates
    - Exclude known benign files
    - Examine obvious files
    - Search for hidden evidence
8. Report results [26]

The reader is strongly recommended, to add a "Step 9" to the above list, and to repeat this step as often as necessary, as required, as prudent. Step 9—create clear and meaningful documentation for and of each and every step, action, process, communiqué and interaction you may have, as it relates to the investigation or case. Ensure the integrity and security of these documents and if the documentation is being produced and compiled in electronic format verses paper, provide for a viable backup schedule and secure storage of these electronic documents. If the documentation is in hardcopy form, the issues of security, integrity and retention remain the same.

The basis of an investigation will hinge upon the allegation leveled against a subject or suspect. Allegations surrounding technology and warranting a potential cyber investigation include but are not limited to:

- Internet and e-mail abuse
- Stealing company property
- Hacking
- Theft of intellectual property
- Inappropriate content resident on workstation
- Electronic tampering
- Theft for personal use or gain

Typically the cyber investigator has been called to the scene after the justification for a forensic search has been established. If this is NOT the case, you should first obtain authorization to conduct the forensic analysis.

Obtaining Proper Authorization

Obtaining authorization to begin an investigation is critical, especially if the investigation involves an internal company employee and organizational management initiates the investigation. If the investigation is initiated by law enforcement, they too must follow established procedures for obtaining authorization to begin an investigation. Failing to do so may result in legal liability to the investigator and the potential that the evidence gathered will not be admissible, the result being the potential termination or outright dismissal of your case.

If there is justification for a specific complaint or reason to investigate, there should also be rules or a baseline on which the complaint was filed. Establishing these rules or basis may come from; company policy or procedures, legal statute, mandatory statute, or regulatory statue. Company policy and procedures may be found in such areas as, but not limited to, human resources, security, employee manuals, external third-party contracts, service level, nondisclosure, and noncompete agreements, among other places.

Several basic questions which should be asked regarding company policies and procedures, which may effect a forensic investigation are:

- Are they published and available?
- Are they current?
- Available in hard or soft copy?
- Has mandatory training or orientation been provided to employees regarding these policies and procedures?
- Have company employees been advised that they have no privacy expectations in company workspace, property, and electronic systems?
- Are employee signatures obtained to verify review or receipt of policies and procedures?
- Have audits or reviews been conducted (timely) in an effort to verify compliance?

Determining the feasibility of conducting the cyber investigation, would entail assessing the benefits or risks to pursuing an investigation, examining the liabilities or risks of not pursuing an investigation, weighing the organization's obligation(s) to pursue further an investigation and ultimately, deciding if there are sufficient and knowledgeable internal resources available to conduct the investigation.

Once authorization has been obtained, and prior to engaging in a complete forensic analysis, a "presearch" should be undertaken to determine if there is justification; (a) to proceed further and (b) if so, whether the investigation is to move from an internal, company "matter" to one where external law enforcement officials will be called (i.e., the potential that the organization may wish to (or may be forced to) pursue legal action against an employee).

If this "presearch" produces data, which leads the investigator to suspect foul play, it is advisable now to determine:

If this is an internal investigation:

1. Does the organization desire to litigate, and if so against whom and on what grounds;
2. Does the examiner have the knowledge and cyber forensic training to continue, maintaining the integrity of the e-crime scene;
3. Whether the company will contact external law enforcement professionals.

Assessing the feasibility of continuing and proceeding further with the investigation will also involve:

- Obtaining a list of people to interview
- Gathering policies and procedures
- Collecting documentation or evidence
- Assessing the resources available
- Evaluating your skills. Are they appropriate?
- Determining which examination tools are available and appropriate for this particular investigation

Who Are You Going to Call?

Determining whom you will contact once you have elected to proceed with the investigation should be decided prior to the start of the investigation and should be routinely reviewed.

Operating units or departments that normally should consider when establishing a "call list" include but certainly are not limited to the following departments:

Internal Audit

- Network Operations
- Data Security
- Physical Security
- Human Resources
- Legal Department

External Consultants

If this is an external, law enforcement sanctioned investigation:

1. Does the preliminary "presearch" disclose sufficient data that allows the investigator to rely sufficiently upon the edict of probable cause, and depending upon the immediate circumstances:
   - continue with the investigation
   - obtain a search warrant
2. If the "presearch" does not warrant further continuance, terminate the investigation.

With respect to external law enforcement initiation, a search occurs when an expectation of privacy that society is prepared to consider reasonable is infringed upon by governmental action. *United States vs. Jacobsen*, 466 U.S. 109, 112 (1984). A search implies an invasion into private or hidden areas, including the body. *Coolidge vs. New Hampshire*, 403 U.S. 443 (1971). A person has been "seized" within the meaning of the Fourth Amendment if, in view of all of the circumstances surrounding the incident, a reasonable person would have believed that he was not free to leave. *United States vs. Mendenhall*, 446 U.S. 544, 554 (1980); *Michigan vs. Chesternut*, 486 U.S. 567 (1988).

Probable cause is the reasonable belief that a specific crime has been committed and that the defendant committed the crime. It does not require evidence of each element of the crime or evidence to the degree necessary to prove guilt beyond a reasonable doubt. Probable cause to issue a search warrant may be described as bits and pieces of information cobbled together until a picture is formed that leads a reasonable prudent person to believe a crime has been committed and to believe evidence of the crime may be found on a particular person or in a place or means of conveyance. *State vs. Grissom*, 251 Kan. 851, 910, 840 P.2d 1142 (1992).

The Warrant requirements are contained in the Fourth Amendment itself. Generally, there must be probable cause to believe a crime was committed and either the defendant committed it (for an arrest warrant) or that fruits or evidence of the crime can be found in a certain place (for a search warrant).

The warrant must particularly describe the person to be arrested or the place to be searched, and must specifically list the items that can be seized. Because most searches by law enforcement officers are carried out without a warrant, a detailed analysis of the warrant requirement is beyond the scope of this outline. Be advised, however, that a warrant is a strong preference, and is "good insurance" against a civil lawsuit against the officer.

If the police violate the defendant's rights, the evidence resulting from that violation is generally inadmissible in a criminal trial, and the violation subjects the officer to civil liability. However, sometimes the evidence collected as a result of a violation by the officer still gets admitted into evidence—generally when the officer acted in good faith, and no useful purpose would be served by application of the exclusionary rule [27].

Summarizing your investigative plan will include; estimating the time it will take to complete the investigation; the cost (including acquiring additional software tools, if necessary), the impact(s) to the organization (tangible and intangible), and the benefits (actual and perceived).

Secure the Scene of the Alleged E-Crime

After securing the scene and all persons at the scene, you should visually identify potential evidence, both conventional (physical) and electronic, and determine if perishable evidence exists.

A critical step in securing the scene involves ensuring that all persons are removed from the immediate area from which evidence is to be collected.

A valuable and critical step in maintaining physical control over the e-crime scene is to preserve the scene for future reference and verification. It is essential that the forensic investigator preserve the scene of any crime to his or her utmost ability. Beyond the arsenal of technological forensic tools, there is one tool which is equally valuable to the investigator and should be in all forensic toolkits—the camera, an SLR film camera, as opposed to digital cameras as their images can be more easily manipulated, thus making them less likely to hold up as evidence in a case.

Protect perishable data both physical and electrical, remembering that perishable data may be found on pagers, caller ID boxes, electronic organizers, cell phones, and other similar devices. You should always keep in mind that any device containing perishable data should be immediately secured, documented, or photographed.

Review the immediate area, identify and document any telephone lines attached to devices such as modems and caller ID boxes, etc. Document, disconnect, and label each telephone line from the wall rather than the device, when possible. Be advised that there may also be other communications lines present for LAN or Ethernet connections, document, disconnect, and label these as well.

Seizing Evidence

Evidence has to satisfy two tests: admissibility (i.e., it must conform to certain legal rules which are applied by a judge) and weight (i.e., it must be understood by, and be sufficiently convincing to the court—whether there is a jury or a judge acting as a trier of fact) [28].

Once obtaining management authority to proceed (internal company investigation, or via obtaining the appropriate warrant or in unnecessary via a warrantless search) the investigator should do the following:

- Isolate the suspect equipment and eventually identify, isolate, collect, secure and retain data resident within the suspect machine
- Do not alert Suspect (either distract or remove the suspect from the area)

Computer evidence, like all other evidence, must be handled carefully and in a manner that preserves its evidentiary value. This relates not just to the physical integrity of an item or device, but also to the electronic data it contains. Certain types of computer evidence, therefore, require special collection, packaging, and transportation.

Consideration should be given to protect data that may be susceptible to damage or alteration from electromagnetic fields such as those generated by static electricity, magnets, radio transmitters, and other devices.

When dealing with digital evidence, the following general forensic and procedural principles should be applied:

- Actions taken to secure and collect digital evidence should not affect the integrity of that evidence.
- Persons conducting an examination of digital evidence should be trained for that purpose.
- Activity relating to the seizure, examination, storage, or transfer of digital evidence should be documented, preserved, and available for review [29].

Managers have the responsibility of ensuring that personnel under their direction are adequately trained and equipped to properly handle electronic evidence. Actions that have the potential to alter, damage, or destroy original evidence may be closely scrutinized by the courts.

Electronic evidence is information and data of investigative value that is stored on or transmitted by an electronic device. As such, electronic evidence is latent evidence in the same sense that fingerprints or DNA (deoxyribonucleic acid) evidence are latent. In its natural state, we cannot "see" what is contained in the physical object that holds our evidence. Equipment and software are required to make the evidence visible. Testimony may be required to explain the examination process and any process limitations.

By its very nature, electronic evidence is fragile. It can be altered, damaged, or destroyed by improper handling or improper examination. For this reason, special precautions should be taken to document, collect, preserve, and examine this type of evidence. Failure to do so may render it unusable or lead to an inaccurate conclusion. The nature of electronic evidence is such that it poses special challenges for its admissibility in court.

Evidence can also be found in files and other data areas created as a routine function of the computer's operating system. In many cases, the user is not aware that data is being written to these areas. Passwords, Internet activity, and temporary backup files are examples of data that can often be recovered and examined. There are components of files that may have evidentiary value including the date and time of creation, modification, deletion, access, user name or identification, and file attributes. Even turning the system on can modify some of this information [30].

Isolating the suspect equipment, ensuring protection of the suspect equipment, and isolating and protecting the suspect equipment from tampering are critical steps in preserving the chain of evidence. Further securing the investigation scene entails taking pictures of the subject's workspace, addressing the issue of latent finger prints, and always being vigilant for the existence of finely crafted electronic booby traps. Booby traps designed to activate if certain sequential keystrokes are not entered properly and to destroy via erasure potentially critical data, hence the destruction of evidence.

STOP, LOOK, LISTEN… Keyboards, the computer mouse, diskettes, CDs, or other components may have latent fingerprints or other physical evidence that should be preserved. Chemicals used in processing latent prints can damage equipment and data. Therefore, latent prints should be collected after electronic evidence recovery is complete [30].

Documentation of the scene creates a permanent historical record of the scene. Documentation is an ongoing process throughout the investigation, thus it is important to accurately record the location and condition of computers, storage media, other electronic devices, and conventional evidence.

When dealing with electronic evidence, general forensic and procedural principles should be applied:

1. Actions taken to secure and collect electronic evidence should not change that evidence.
2. Persons conducting examination of electronic evidence should be trained for the purpose.
3. Activity relating to the seizure, examination, storage, or—transfer of electronic evidence should be fully documented—preserved, and available for review [30].

Chain of Evidence

The investigator has several tasks ahead of him or her and must follow certain procedures to ensure that the evidence is solid and will hold up in court. The basic criterions, which must exist in order for this to occur, are as follows:

1. No possible evidence is damaged, destroyed, or otherwise compromised by the procedures used to investigate the computer
2. Extracted and possibly relevant evidence is properly handled and protected from later mechanical or electromagnetic damage
3. A continuing chain of custody is established and maintained
4. All procedures and findings are thoroughly documented [31]

The identification of evidence and chain of evidence rules require that the proponent of the evidence show that the evidence has not been tampered with, and that there has not been any irregularity which altered its probative value. *State vs. Roszkowski*, 129 N.J. Super. 315, 323 A2d 531 (App.Div. 1974).

The gathering of evidence in the initial phase of an investigation hinges on proof of admissibility in court that unequivocally and without doubt the conclusions reached by the investigator, usually by way of induction, are sustainable, logical, and defensible.

Ensuring the chain of evidence requires that the forensic investigator log all actions performed on the equipment under review, document any access to the equipment, as well as documenting and identifying who retains control of equipment access log itself.

Additionally, the investigator must identify where the log is stored, document where and how the equipment is stored, and document how the equipment is secured from unauthorized access or use (tampering) (Figure 11.1).

The chain of evidence is designed to demonstrate, without a doubt:

■ Who obtained the evidence?
■ Where and when the evidence was obtained?
■ Who secured the evidence?
■ Who had control or possession of the evidence?

Industry standards and expert advice in the area of incident handling have traditionally limited the scope of the "crime scene" to the computer system itself. In a corporate intranet broadening the scope to include the immediate physical work environment around the computer system will significantly improve the context of computer-based evidence [32].

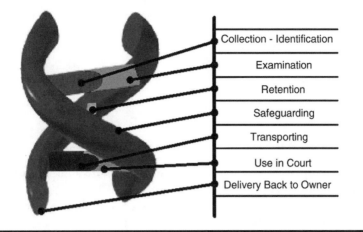

Figure 11.1   The "sequencing" of the chain of evidence.

Chain-of-Evidence Model

The Chain-of-Evidence Model illustrates the discrete sets of actions carried out by an insider attempting to inflict malicious damage in an intranet environment. One group of actions is separated from another, based on the level of authority required to execute them. Each group of actions has a different corresponding source of evidence that must be responsible for documenting activity for forensic purposes. However, each such source of evidence must be linked to the logs next to it (see Figure 11.2) to form a complete chain of evidence.

Figure 11.2 starts with physical access to computer systems, that must precede any malicious activity. It is in this stage that the crucial link between physical recognition and computer recognition take place. Following log-on procedures the user proceeds to invoke the services of a network application that must be used as a vehicle to inflict damage on a remote system. The network application issues the malicious network traffic that reaches a remote computer and executes the intended behavior.

As illustrated in Figure 11.2, the link between each log is crucial to the establishment of a complete chain of evidence. Across all of the links the crucial factor upon which the integrity of the entire chain rests is the authenticity of the time-line. If the accuracy of the time in any of the links is questionable then the entire chain is rendered useless [32].

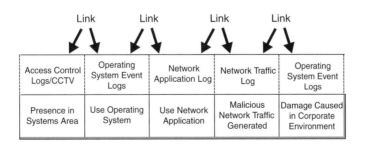

Figure 11.2   Chain-of-evidence model.

From an evidential point-of-view what we seek is something we can demonstrate to others long after the event itself is over: that tends to mean logs of various kinds. Potentially these can include:

- System logs
- Audit logs
- Application logs
- Network management logs
- Network traffic capture
- Contemporaneous manual entries

In addition it is also possible to process this primary data into a form in which it is easier to analyze and understand. We can call this "derived data."

Even before we get to the specific hurdles erected by the needs of the legal system these logs may be deficient in terms of their ability to persuade a third party:

- The logs may make little immediate sense without training in the operation of the IDS tool and an understanding of the principles upon which it operates.
- The logs may lack sufficient detail.
- The logs may not exist over a sufficient time period for comparisons of normal and abnormal activity to be made.
- The logs may be incomplete for the relevant period of time.
- In the case of real-time monitoring the monitoring tool may not be able to keep up with the stream of traffic with which it is expected to deal.
- In the case of real-time network monitoring the network location of the device hosting the monitoring tool may be such that it is unable to capture all relevant traffic, some of the packets using other routes.
- The logs may not sufficiently distinguish between a legitimate and an unwanted access.
- The logs may not identify the perpetrator in any useful way.
- The logs may have been compromised prior to collection as potential evidence.
- The logs may have been compromised during collection as potential evidence.
- The logs may have been compromised during postcollection analysis.
- In the case of derived data, the methods of analysis and subsequent presentation may lead to misleading results [28].

Establishing the link between the operating system logs and the invocation of a network application can be difficult if the operating system's event configuration did not require such events be recorded. In addition most network applications do not record user behavior within the boundaries of network application use making it difficult to record precisely how users used the network application.

Another weak link is the interaction between network applications and the traffic they generate. In general there is not enough information in operating systems event logs to determine whether network traffic was directly initiated by the user or was generated by some other source like a network application running in the background [32].

Seizing a Computer

The law does not authorize the government to seize items which do not have evidentiary value, and generally agents cannot take things from a search site when their nonevidentiary nature is apparent at the time of the search [33].

The following practices should be adhered to when involved in the seizure of electronic equipment:

1. Do not alert the suspect.
2. Isolate the suspect equipment and eventually identify, isolate, collect, secure and retain data resident within the suspect machine.
3. Ensure the protection of the seized equipment.
4. Isolate and protect the seized equipment from tampering.
5. Secure the scene and all persons on the scene.
6. DO NOT alter the condition of any electronic devices.
7. Protect perishable data both physical and electrical.
8. Document every aspect of the scene creating a permanent historical record of the scene.
9. Look at the computer before "pulling the plug."
10. Is there any drive activity?
11. Listen for drive activity (metal screw driver held against the case).
12. Make sure that NO drive writes are taking place prior to pulling the plug.

Pros and Cons of Pulling the Plug

On the positive side, the "pros" of pulling the plug are:

■ Keeps the SWAP files intact.
■ Isolates the machine from unauthorized access.
■ Protects unallocated space.

However, on the downside of this quandary, by pulling the plug…

■ The investigator might encounter drive problems, which may prevent restarting entire system at a later date.
■ There may be inadvertent corruption of data via "hot keys" preprogrammed by the suspect.
■ Any data held in TEMP files is lost.
■ The loss of the contents of dynamic RAM is to be expected.
■ Someone who may be monitoring the system remotely may initiate destructive sequences if there is any indication of system or network disconnect, port shut-down, etc. has occurred.

If the computer is running when seized, it should be powered down in a way that is least damaging to data currently in memory and that, which is on the hard disk. The method that should be used is dependent on the operating system that the computer is running.

The recommended methods for shutting down a seized computer are shown in the following table.

If the operating system cannot be determined, pulling the plug will suffice. When pulling the plug make sure that you pull the lead out from the computer unit itself. This is because if the computer has an uninterruptible power supply connected and the power to this is turned off, the power to the computer will remain powered.

Table 11.2   Recommended Shut Down Methods

Operating System	Shut Down Recommendation
DOS	Pull the plug
Windows 3.1	Pull the plug
Windows 95	Pull the plug
Windows 98	Pull the plug
Windows NT	Pull the plug
Windows NT Server	Shut down
Windows 2000	Pull the plug
Windows 2000 Server	Shut down
Windows XP	Pull the plug
Windows 2003	Shut down
Linux	Shut down
Unix	Shut down
Macintosh OS 9 and older	Pull the plug
Macintosh OS X	Shut down

Shutting the computer down by the correct method is critical if certain data is normally stored only in memory, to be committed back to disk when the machine is powered off. Shutting down computers, which do not normally store data in memory (such as Windows XP) by the usual method will result in possible changes to the data on the hard drive.

It is imperative, and worth repeating again, it is imperative, that at this point in the investigation you MUST NOT alter the condition of any electronic devices: If it is off, leave it off. If it is on, leave it on.

Once power to the machine has been shut off:

1. Open case and disconnect or remove hard drive(s) completely.
2. Place the hard drive(s) into antistatic collection bags to prevent data damage.
3. Wrap the unit with evidence tape, to clearly identify it as evidence in an investigation.
4. Identify via unique ID number the case from which the drive(s) was or were taken.
5. Take a picture of both the front and back of the case.
6. Take pictures of the serial numbers of both the case and the hard drive.
7. Cross-reference the serial numbers, and pictures to ensure that the hard drive to be examined came from the machine seized.
8. If the hard drive is left in the machine, insert a customized forensic disk into the floppy drive (if floppy drive is present).

DO NOT REMOVE any media until the entire system has been powered down. By opening drives, taking out CDs, etc., you could inadvertently set off a destructive sequence, and destroy evidence in the process.

When undertaking the collection of evidence and further upon conducting an examination of same, the investigator must be cognizant of the following legislation:

- 4th Amendment
- Privacy Protection Act
- Electronic Communications Privacy Act

and ensure that any action taken, is done so in accordance with enacted laws which protect individual rights.

In particular, under the Privacy Protection Act, with certain exceptions, it is unlawful for an agent to search for or seize certain materials possessed by a person reasonably believed to have a purpose of disseminating information to the public. For example, seizure of First Amendment materials such as drafts of newsletters or Web pages may implicate the Privacy Protection Act [30].

Warrantless workplace searches by private employers rarely violate the Fourth Amendment. So long as the employer is not acting as an instrument or agent of the government at the time of the search, the search is a private search and the Fourth Amendment does not apply. See *Skinner vs. Railway Labor Executives' Association*, 489 U.S. 602, 614 (1989).

Conclusion

This chapter presents the reader with a glimpse into the interplay and interaction, between cyber forensics and the legal system, a system designed to protect the innocent and prosecute the guilty. An unfortunate truism, however, "he who cannot produce the evidence or data—LOOSES," underscores the necessity for stringent adherence to appropriate procedures for the identification, collection and preservation of electronic evidence.

Should the evidence be deemed representative and crucial to an investigator's case, said evidence can, if required, be acceptable by and admissible into the courts and the legal system, and in as much as said evidence then can be utilized to protect the innocent and prosecute the guilty.

The discussion of the legal implications and ramifications of cyber forensic investigations and the relationship between these specific types of investigations or examinations as has been provided in this chapter, is not intended nor implied to be a substitute for professional legal advice and representation obtained through legal counsel.

The reader is advised to seek the advice and representation of either in-house or external legal counsel as may be appropriate for any matters to which the legal materials and information contained in this chapter may pertain and be applied to the reader's own cyber forensic investigation or to the reader's organization, agency, or department.

References

1. Guidance Software, (September 2006), Systemizing eDiscovery for Compliance with the New Federal Rules: A Practical Overview to Implementation of the New Rules, www.encase.com/downloads/Federal_Rules_Whitepaper.pdf, retrieved April 2007, Guidance Software, 215 North Marengo Avenue, Second Floor, Pasadena, California 91101, (626) 229–9191, www.guidancesoftware.com.

2. Carrier, B., (Winter 2003), Defining Digital Forensic Examination and Analysis Tools, *International Journal of Digital Evidence*, Volume 1, Issue 4, carrier@atstake.com.

3. Vanstone S., et al. (1997), *Handbook of Applied Cryptography*, CRC Press.

4. Shutt, J., (November 2004), Abstraction Theory, www.cs.wpi.edu/~jshutt/abstraction-theory.html, jshutt@cs.wpi.edu.

5. Harrison, W., (2002), Portland State University, Heuston, G., Hillsboro Police Department, Morrissey, M., Portland State University, Aucsmith, D., Intel Corporation, Mocas, S., Portland State University, Russelle, S., Portland Police Bureau, A Lessons Learned Repository for Computer Forensics, 2002 Digital Forensics Research Workshop, www.ijde.org/archives/02_fall_art1.html.

6. NTI, (2004), File Slack Defined, New Technologies, Inc., 2075 Northeast Division Street, Gresham, Oregon 97030 USA, 503-661-6912, www.forensics-intl.com/def6.html, info@forensics-intl.com. Slack Space, www.webopedia.com/TERM/S/slack_space.html. retrieved April 2007.

7. DEW Associates Corporation, (2002), Cutting the Slack (or maybe the Fat!), Drive Partition Efficiency: Controlling Slack, www.dewassoc.com/kbase/hard_drives/fat_slack.html, PO Box 841, Sparta, New Jersey 07871–0841, 973-702-0545, www.dewassoc.com/index.html.

8. Kozierok, C., (2004), The PC Guide, www.PCGuide.com, www.pcguide.com/ref/hdd/file/part Slack-c.html.

9. NTI, (2004a), Windows Swap/Page File Defined, New Technologies, Inc., 2075 Northeast Division Street, Gresham, Oregon 97030 USA, 503-661-6912, www.forensics-intl.com/def7.html, info@forensics-intl.com.

10. Nesson, C., Green, E., and Murray, P., (2005), Frye v. United States 293 F. 1013 (D.C. Cir. 1923), www.law.harvard.edu/publications/evidenceiii/cases/frye.htm, February 3, 2005.

11. IIA, (2005), The Institute of Internal Auditors, Code of Ethics, www.theiia.org/index.cfm?doc_id=604, The Institute of Internal Auditors, 247 Maitland Avenue, Altamonte Springs, Florida 32701–4201, +1-407-937-1100.

12. Kerr, O., (March 2001), Computer Records and the Federal Rules of Evidence, March 2001 Vol. 49, No.2. an excerpt of a larger DOJ manual entitled Searching and Seizing Computers and Obtaining Electronic Evidence in Criminal Investigations, which is available on the internet at www.cybercrime.gov/searchmanual.htm, Orin S. Kerr USA Bulletin, www.usdoj.gov/criminal/cybercrime/usamarch2001_4.htm, February 2, 2005.

13. United States Court of Appeals, (April 9, 2004), United States Court Of Appeals For The Ninth Circuit United States Of America, No. 02-50442 Plaintiff-Appellee, D.C. No. CR-00-00655, Mr Vincent Franklin Bennett, Opinion Defendant-Appellant. Appeal from the United States District Court for the Southern District of California Manuel L. Real, District Judge, Presiding, www.ca9.uscourts.gov/ca9/newopinions.nsf/0C0D511205B66BD688256E7000783A4B/$file/0250442.pdf?openelement, February 3, 2005.

14. Goldsholle, G., (2001), Federal Rules of Evidence, ExpertPages.com, http://expertpages.com/federal/federal.htm, February 3, 2005.

15. Moenssens, A., (1999a), Amendments of the Federal Rules of Evidence, www.forensic-evidence.com/site/EVID/EL00003_4.html, February 3, 2005.

16. Loomis, S., (November 2002), The Daubert Test of Reliability: Fighting Junk Science in the Courtrooms, Skeptic Report, www.skepticreport.com/mystics/dauberttest.htm, February 25, 2005.

17. Moenssens, A., (April 15, 1999b), Banning Junk Science from the Court Room … But How Can We Tell it's Junk?, Part of an Abstract for a discussion delivered at the National Conference on Science and the Law on April 15, l999, at San Diego. The Conference was cosponsored by the National Institute of Justice and several other organizations, www.forensic-evidence.com/site/EVID/EL00003_2.html, February 3, 2005.

18. United States Department of Justice, (February 2004a), Searching and Seizing Computers and Related Electronic Evidence Issues, Computer Crime and Intellectual Property Section (CCIPS), www.usdoj.gov/criminal/cybercrime/searching.html, (February 4, 2005).

19. Berry, D. and Berry, S., (February 2005), Junk Science in the Courtroom, www.truthinjustice.org/junk.htm, February 3, 2005.

20. Innocence Project, (February 2005), Junk Science, Innocence Project, 100 Fifth Avenue, 3rd Floor, New York, NY 10011, info@innocenceproject.org, 212.364.5340, www.innocenceproject.org/causes/junkscience.php, February 3, 2005.

21. Hailey, S., (2004), The Tools Proven in Court Question, Cyber Security Institute, www.cyber-securityinstitute.biz/tpicq.htm, February 3, 2005.

22. ACFEI, (2005), The American College of Forensic Examiners International, Principles of Ethical Conduct, www.acfei.com/certification_programs-cfc-ethics.php, The American College of Forensic Examiners International, 2750 East Sunshine, Springfield, MO 65804, (417) 881–3818.

23. LII, (2004), Federal Rules of Evidence, Legal Information Institute (LII), Cornell Law School, Myron Taylor Hall, Ithaca, NY 14853, lii@lii.law.cornell.edu, www.law.cornell.edu/rules/fre/rules.htm#Rule104, February 3, 2005.

24. Rogers, M., (October, 2005), Adapted from Computer Forensics: Basics Lecture 1, The Context of Computer Forensics, www.tech.purdue.edu/Cpt/Courses/CPT499S/lecture1.pdf, Purdue University, mkr@cerias.purdue.edu.

25. Lyle, J., (September 9, 2003), Computer Forensics: Tool Testing & National Software Reference Library, Information Technology Laboratory, www.cftt.nist.gov/documents/CFTTandNRSLat Moscow.pdf, February 13, 2005.

26. Knoll, J., (2001), Legal Aspects of Search & Seizure, Presented to the Topeka Police Department, Recruit Academy, May 22, & 23, 2001, John J. Knoll, Assistant City Attorney, City of Topeka, Kansas, originally compiled by Anthony W. Rues & James Brown, Assistant District Attorneys. Substantially revised & rearranged by John J. Knoll, Assistant City Attorney, January 3–6, 2000, www.kscoplaw.com/outlines/ssoutline.htm, February 13, 2005.

27. Sommer, P., (1998), Intrusion Detection Systems as Evidence, www.raid-symposium.org/raid98/Prog_RAID98/Full_Papers/Sommer_text.pdf, Computer Security Research Centre, London School of Economics & Political Science, P.M.Sommer@lse.ac.uk.

28. United States Department of Justice, (April, 2004b), Forensic Examination of Digital Evidence: A Guide for Law Enforcement, NCJ 199408, NIJ Guide, Office of Justice Programs, National Institute of Justice, www.ojp.usdoj.gov/nij, 810 Seventh Street N.W., Washington, DC 20531, February 16, 2005.

29. United States Department of Justice, (July 2001), Electronic Crime Scene Investigation: A Guide for First Responders, NCJ 187736, NIJ Guide, Office of Justice Programs, National Institute of Justice, www.ojp.usdoj.gov/nij, 810 Seventh Street N.W., Washington, DC 20531, February 16, 2005.

30. Tsoutsouris, D., (2001), Computer Forensic Legal Standards and Equipment, SANS Institute 2001, Information Security Reading Room, Version 1.2f (GSEC), www.sans.org/rr/whitepapers/incident/648.php.

31. Ahmad, A., (September 2002), The Forensic Chain-of-Evidence Model: Improving the Process of Evidence Collection in Incident Handling Procedures, Proceedings of the 6th Pacific Asia Conference on Information Systems, Tokyo, Japan, Department of Information Systems, University of Melbourne, Parkville, VIC 3010, Australia, www.dis.unimelb.edu.au/staff/atif/AhmadPACIS.pdf, atif@unimelb.edu.au, used with permission.

32. Federal Guidelines for Searching and Seizing Computers, US Department of Justice Criminal Division Office of Professional Development and Training, July1994, www.epic.org/security/computer_search_guidelines.txt, retrieved April 2007.

Chapter 12

Cyber Forensics and the Changing Face of Investigating Criminal Behavior

Introduction

To the people on the Internet, he was known simply as "NaughtyGrampa." He regularly came on line, offering to swap lurid sexual photos of very young children with others. None of the others in any of the online chat groups had ever met him. They probably did not know where he lived or even his true name.

In real life, "NaughtyGrampa" was Robert Earl Smith, a then 53-year-old resident of Eugene, Oregon. Smith used his digital camera to take explicit photos of his sexual abuse of infants including one of his own grandchildren. He used e-mail to encourage others to abuse young children and to send his photos to others. Smith was eventually apprehended. At his trial, his lawyer told a state court judge that it was the Internet that allowed him to exploit a life-long mental problem that caused him to be a pedophile (*Oregon vs. Smith*, Lane County Oregon Circuit Court case 20-03-23564, 2003).

In e-mail exchanges with an undercover investigator, Smith encouraged the investigator to abuse a young child. Smith also wrote that he only abused very young children because they could not report his actions to adults. Using computer forensics, the investigator identified Smith and, in conjunction with a prosecutor almost 3000 miles away, she built a case against the man that ultimately resulted in criminal convictions and a 50-year prison sentence.

The Smith case provides insight into how criminal investigations have changed with the advent of computer and Internet technology. Child pornography is not new. But even 20 years ago, Smith would neither have been able to distribute the pornographic images so readily, nor be apprehended by an undercover investigator working from the opposite side of the United States.

New technology provides opportunities for criminals in many areas other than pornography. Police now frequently chronicle criminals' use of the Internet and computer technology to commit a wide range of economic crimes and crimes involving malicious destruction of others' property.

Identity theft, a term almost unheard of 30 years ago, now makes up significant portions of the caseloads of police agencies and prosecutors in the United States [1]. The problem has become so pervasive that specific statutes designed to address the problem have been enacted in numerous jurisdictions including under federal law. See, for example, Identity Theft and Assumption Deterrence Act, Public Law 105–318, 112 Stat. 3007 (Oct. 30, 1998). Although identity theft does not require computers or the Internet, it does drive the use of these tools in countless scams ranging from e-mail fraud to systems intrusions, which allow the cyber–criminal to obtain information later used to engage in illegal activities (theft of financial, data and personnel assets).

In reality these identity theft cases present very little that is actually new in the realm of criminal behavior. But the emergence of new technology requires the law enforcement community—from police to prosecutors to judges—to utilize different strategies and different tools in addressing the new ways today's criminals commit these old crimes.

In addition to pornography and identity theft, the computer and the Internet allow malicious cyber-criminals to violate copyright protection, cause enormous damage to data and equipment and to lure children and even adults into situations where they can be sexually and physically assaulted.

Evidence in the 21st Century

Traditional evidence in criminal cases has substance, shape, and form. People can see it. In many cases they can touch it. Fingerprints, for example, are often visible on surfaces like tabletops. Even where they are latent, simple techniques exist for their retrieval. And fingerprints can last for years or even decades under the right conditions, as can trace evidence like hair and fibers. Computer evidence is entirely different. It cannot be seen, touched or smelled and it often lasts for only very short periods of time.

Computers typically store data in three ways, magnetic, semiconductor, and optical. Other less common data storage methods include magneto-optical disk storage, optical jukebox storage and ultra-density optical disk storage. Potentially significant new developments in technology suggest that techniques like phase-change storage [2], holographic storage [3], and use of molecular memory may become methods for data storage in the future [4]:

1. Magnetic storage—Using a magnetically coated surface, a computer can magnetically arrange that surface to create patterns that store information. This form of memory provides great flexibility because it allows relatively fast reading and writing of data, and it can be reused. This means that when the computer is no longer using a portion of the magnetically coated surface for a particular task, it is free to write over that surface with new data. Computer hard drives and removable floppy disks use magnetic storage.
2. Semiconductor or "chip" storage—This method of data storage utilizes integrated circuits or "chips" to uses semiconductor-based integrated circuits to keep information. The memory is designated as either volatile or nonvolatile. Most newer computers primarily rely on dynamic volatile memory, or what is known as dynamic random access memory. D–RAM and flash drives are examples of semiconductor storage. This memory is rapidly accessed by computers and, like magnetic media, it can easily be overwritten when no longer needed (nonvolatile

semiconductor memory is most often used for secondary storage in various advanced electronic devices and specialized computers and is not discussed in this chapter).

3. Optical storage—Optical storage utilizes tiny "pits" that are etched in the surface of the media. The computer uses a laser diode to read data stored on optical disks. CDs and DVDs are examples of the use of optical storage. Depending upon the nature of the hardware and media, optical storage may or may not be volatile.

Data stored on these devices, while potentially of tremendous value in the investigation, prosecution and prevention of crime, presents unique challenges to detectives and prosecutors because of its potentially volatile nature. Electronic data is fragile. It can easily be changed or eliminated. Thieves and other cyber criminals, along with dishonest and even honest employees can easily change the nature of this information—often unintentionally. Cyber forensics is the process of finding, extracting, preserving, and understanding electronic data while providing a guarantee that the data were not altered during the investigation.

Cyber Crime Defined

Without the Internet and the technology of his computer and digital camera, Robert Smith's "NaughtyGrampa" activities would probably not have come to the attention of investigators. However, his behavior in sexually abusing infants—regardless of any "cyber crime" aspects of his crime—would still have been criminal under the laws of all 50 U.S. states. In that context, *Oregon vs. Smith* is similar to most other so-called cyber crimes. Most of the time these adjudicated cases represent unlawful criminal behavior regardless of the suspect's use of computer or Internet technology.

For example, an undercover investigation resulted in the prosecution and conviction of Kenneth J. Flury for bank fraud. Flury fraudulently obtained CitiBank debit card account numbers and personal identification numbers (PINs). He then encoded the information onto counterfeit, blank ATM cards. Once in possession of the unauthorized cards, Flury used them in ATM machines to steal money from the bank and its account holders. Over a three-week period, he stole U.S. $384,000 from ATM machines located in Cleveland, Ohio (the *United States vs. Flury*, N.D. Ohio, February 18, 2006). Flury was convicted of bank fraud and conspiracy and sentenced to 32 months in prison and required to pay $300,748.64 in restitution [5]. Flury's actions were nothing more than old-fashioned theft. However, he used computers and computer technology to steal.

Other cyber crime cases bear somewhat less resemblance to old-style criminal behavior. In 2003, Patrick Angle logged into his employer's computer system and deleted the source code for software being developed for sale. This cost the company U.S. $26,455 to recover the data and restore the software [6].

Cyber crime is typically described as any criminal act dealing with computers or computer networks. It is also called by other names (e-crime, computer crime or Internet crime in different jurisdictions), which have roughly the equivalent meanings. In most cases cyber crime is a general—as opposed to a legal—term, although some jurisdictions have provided specific definitions for cyber crime behavior (e.g., Oregon Revised Statutes 164.377). Other jurisdictions take a somewhat more expansive approach by not trying to assign a specific definition, but rather by trying to address criminal behavior in the context of the use of computers [7].

Regardless of the definitions, the use of computers and the Internet in the commission of crimes require investigators applying cyber forensic techniques to extract data for those investigating these cases, prosecuting these cases and passing the ultimate judgment regarding the disposition of offenders and the redress of victims.

Economic Aspects of Cyber Forensics

The increasing globalization of the world's economy and infrastructure has dramatically influenced the logistics of criminal investigations at both local and international levels. With worldwide availability of the Internet, and with English language skills now taught in schools throughout the world, criminals no longer need to be physically present in a community or even a nation to violate the laws there. In fact, these perpetrators can identify targets, carry out their schemes and withdraw with all of the benefits of their illegal activities from literally anyplace on the globe with Internet connections. Their targets can reside in places where the criminals have never visited.

This reality prompted the U.S. Federal Bureau of Investigation (FBI) to make cyber security the third prong of its mission. Director Robert S. Mueller noted that

> The globalization of crime—whether terrorism, international trafficking of drugs, contraband, and people, or cyber crime—absolutely requires us to integrate law enforcement efforts around the world. And that means having our agents working directly with their counterparts overseas [8] …

The United States Secret Service took a similar approach in forming its Electronic Crimes Task Force in 2001, (HR 3162, 2001), as have agencies outside the United States including Interpol (www.interpol.com/Public/TechnologyCrime/default.asp) and the London Metropolitan Police (www.met.police.uk/computercrime).

The magnitude of the problem cannot be understated. The U.S. Federal Bureau of Investigation estimates that in the course of one year as many as 10 million Americans are the victims of identity theft alone [9]. Although definitive statistics regarding the location of perpetrators do not exist, the trend is undisputable: Cyber crime is increasing at a disproportionate rate as compared to more traditional crime.

The National White Collar Crime Center reported that in 2005, its Internet Crime Complaint Center received 231,493 complaint submissions. This reflected an 11.6 percent increase over 2004 when it received 207,449 complaints. These reports were both fraud and nonfraud cases with some nexus to the Internet [10]. The Center estimated that 75 percent of the perpetrators were male and that half resided in California, New York, Florida, Texas, Illinois, Pennsylvania, and Ohio. And while the majority of reported perpetrators resided in the United States, a significant number of perpetrators were also located overseas in countries including Nigeria, United Kingdom, Canada, Italy, and China. This boon to cyber criminals has become an almost overwhelming challenge for cyber enforcement agencies.

Denial presents another significant advantage for the criminal who would use the Internet or computers to ply his trade. The strong Islamic culture and traditions of the Arab countries in the Persian Gulf (Kuwait, Saudi Arabia, Qatar, Bahrain, United Arab Emirates, and Oman) have typically limited the occurrence of some types of criminal behavior there. Additionally, several of these nations typically employ strong software to block web sites deemed to be offensive or criminal [11].

Prosecutors in the Gulf region often indicate there is little or no cyber crime in their countries. The accuracy of this belief is undocumented and notably, inspite of anecdotal denials, at least some of the nations in the region like Saudi Arabia have adopted specific cyber crime statutes (www.itp.net/news/details.php?id=22318&category), or like Oman are in the process of adopting such laws (www.ibls.com/internet_law_news_portal_view.aspx?s=latestnews&id=1530).

Even so, because of the often-pervasive attitude that these crimes usually do not occur in their countries, investigators undoubtedly are not always looking for cyber criminals. Additionally, training and expertise is often not emphasized when agencies deny the existence of a problem. Given the international aspect of the Internet, cyber criminals of the future may well target areas where enforcement is lax.

Practical Issues

In both traditional and nontraditional investigations, detectives must have access to relevant evidence and to witnesses. They photograph and seize physical evidence. They create maps and diagrams of crime scenes. They document victims' injuries or economic losses. They interview witnesses and suspects. All of these components of a thorough investigation are required for a successful prosecution. Under the Fourth and Fourteenth Amendments to the U.S. Constitution, criminal suspects are afforded all the guarantees of due process including most importantly the presumption of innocence. Without sufficient proof, no conviction can be sustained. But cyber crimes present new challenges and tasks that change the tactics and economics of criminal investigations.

In *Oregon vs. Smith,* the defendant took pornographic photos of an infant in the Pacific Northwest. He engaged a police detective working almost 3000 miles away in Tennessee. The case abundantly illustrates the typical problems in Internet-related criminal behavior.

State and municipal statutes in the United States typically grant jurisdiction only for crimes occurring within their geographic boundaries. Although not automatically limiting, the jurisdiction rules do raise issues for investigators, prosecutors and judges handling Internet crimes. For example, if Robert Smith took the pornographic photos in Oregon and used the Internet to send them to Tennessee where a second person took possession of them, would Oregon or Tennessee have jurisdiction to prosecute Smith? The answer is often statute-specific and requires a careful analysis— preferably prior to the expenditure of substantial time and investigative resources. The analysis becomes much more difficult when the unlawful activities span international borders.

Any such investigation first begs the question of cost. Although the traditional criminal investigation requires a detective or police officer to drive or walk to the scene of the crime to seize evidence and interview the principles, the typical cyber crime can require air travel, great expenditures of time and confusing rules regarding both the logistics and legalities of evidence seizure.

Consider the investigation and prosecution of the common e-mail fraud scheme popularly known as the Nigerian or 419 scam, coined because, it originated in the West African nation some years ago. The solicitation was first delivered by letter, then by fax, and most recently by e-mail. In this scam, the potential victim receives a solicitation from someone purporting to need assistance moving money out of Nigeria or another West African nation. The perpetrator offers to share large sums of money with the victim in exchange for the victim's cooperation. Initially, the victim is asked to wire or otherwise provide money to the perpetrator to assist in paying costs like bribes, taxes, and government fees to transfer the money. Often the victim is asked to provide information about his or her bank accounts in the United States under the guise of needing the accounts for later money transfers. The scam continues until the victim stops sending money to the perpetrator, although the FBI has noted that at this point the perpetrator will sometimes take the victim's personal information and use it drain whatever is left in the bank accounts and credit card authorizations [12]. The schemes violate Section 419 of the Nigerian penal code, hence the name "419 scheme."

A detailed, technical investigation aimed at securing a conviction of a 419 scam, would be beyond the operational resources of nearly every police force in the world. For a successful prosecution, detectives and prosecutors would at a minimum need to take the following steps:

1. Identity of the perpetrators would need to be established. To establish identity, the detectives would need to trace their Internet access. This would require them to first obtain the IP address used for the e-mail. At this point they would need to determine, from the appropriate Internet service provider (ISP), who was assigned that IP address. Obtaining such information would depend not only upon great luck and speed, but also would depend upon following the rules of the jurisdiction of the ISP—which likely would require a subpoena or court order. If the ISP was in a foreign country, this task could be extraordinarily difficult.

2. Bank records and other financial documents would need to be obtained or seized. Money, when it moves, typically leaves a trail. If the victim sent a check to the perpetrator, bank records would document the negotiation of the check. This might provide a link to the perpetrators that would be essential in the ultimate prosecution of the case. As with obtaining IP and ISP information, detectives normally would need some type of court process to seize such data. Foreign jurisdiction complicates this process enormously.

3. Witnesses and suspects would need to be identified and interviewed. Detectives would need to talk with those who had communication with the perpetrators about their crimes. Additionally, bankers, wire transfer agents and other material witnesses would need to be interviewed. Of critical importance, most prosecutors will not proceed with charging anyone in such a case unless an attempt is made to interview the suspects. In a 419 scam, it is likely that every witness and all perpetrators are in West Africa, creating huge costs and difficulties—even assuming that they can be identified and located.

4. All evidence and all witnesses need to be brought to the jurisdiction. Assuming the detectives complete the first three steps, the prosecutor will still need to bring to the U.S. jurisdiction the witnesses and materials needed for a grand jury or preliminary hearing to charge the perpetrators. If that is successful, the same process will need to be repeated for the trial. Airfare and the associated costs with such travel can be extremely high.

5. The suspects will have to be extradited. Assuming the prosecutor is able to bring charges, extradition will be necessary to bring the suspects to the United States. This will require an arrest, with the cooperation of local authorities. Following the arrest, treaties with the foreign state will dictate the processes necessary to obtain the perpetrators, who will then need to be brought to the U.S.

The above example illustrates the extreme challenges posed in the investigation and prosecution of some cyber crime cases. In reality, the costs of these investigations are so high that virtually none are within the means of ordinary American law enforcement. Only where losses are extraordinary is enforcement generally viewed as justifiable—and then, only by very large agencies or federal agencies with budgets that can support such action.

Competence

The rules of evidence and sufficiency of proof in criminal prosecutions dictate the procedures for gathering evidence in cyber crime cases. Because they are complicated, investigators, prosecutors, and judges require specific knowledge to be competent in handling these matters. And because most of these individuals have little or no background in the field of information technology, they frequently fail to have a full appreciation for the way cyber crime differs from traditional criminal activity.

When a detective responds to a homicide scene, one of the first things she or he does is to make sure that the area is protected from anyone who would change or remove the evidence. Yellow crime scene tape goes up. Patrol officers are posted to enforce the boundary. Nobody enters the area inside the tape without specific authority and, even then, careful notes are made detailing exactly when the person came under the tape and what the person did. These precautions are critical because at trial the prosecutor will need to establish that the evidence was not contaminated. There may be trace evidence like fibers or hairs that link the suspect to the killing. Blood and fingerprint evidence will be gathered. Without crime scene integrity, a jury cannot properly draw conclusions about the crime because neither the investigators nor the evidence will have credibility.

Cyber crime evidence requires the same care and control—but because it exists in such a different form the precautions connected with its discovery, storage, and retrieval are much different. The investigator will be required to establish procedures or protocols, which guarantee that evidence from data storage media is unchanged from the time of its seizure or discovery. The cyber forensic investigator will need to put up the electronic equivalent of yellow crime scene tape to make sure that the data is not compromised.

This means that, at a minimum, forensic investigators must have adequate knowledge of computer hardware systems, cyber forensics software and the typical consumer software that will usually be seized. Additionally, investigators need a solid understanding of the requirements of the relevant constitutional law and evidentiary law. The legal knowledge enables them to conduct their investigations in a way that does not run afoul of suspects' rights—ensuring admissibility of evidence—and in a way that allows them to understand the procedural requirements of evidence seizure (e.g., how to legally obtain subscriber information from an ISP).

This expertise must be supplemented by adequate hardware and software resources to enable them to recover electronic data in a way that will allow its admissibility as evidence in the prosecution of criminals (cyber or otherwise). In reality, the competent investigator will become a regional resource for other investigators and prosecutors in cyber forensics investigations. This requires a very detailed and wide-ranging training scheme that includes continuing education, as technology changes both software and hardware.

Requirements for prosecutors, while not as technical, are never-the-less substantial. Prosecutors, at both the state and federal level, are the gate-keepers for all criminal cases in the United States. They operate at two basic levels: federal prosecutors, or assistant U.S. attorneys, are the lawyers in charge of investigation, charging and prosecuting criminal cases in U.S. District Court. State prosecutors, or deputy district attorneys or state attorneys, perform the same functions in state courts. Some cities and other small jurisdictions also employ prosecutors, although their roles tend to be limited to less serious misdemeanor and traffic prosecutions, so they will not be discussed here.

Prosecutors traditionally know little about cyber forensics. Although most are computer literate, their training has typically not included much of the technical information they need to successfully supervise cyber prosecutions. This deficiency arises in any number of contexts and calls for more thorough education in these essential areas:

■ *Use of computer-related data in traditional prosecutions*—In crimes involving fraud and in drug-related crimes, perpetrators increasingly use computer resources both to store data and to obtain data. Prosecutors need to be cognizant of the fact that a perpetrator's computer could provide significant evidence to establish criminal culpability. This evidence could include spreadsheets and financial data, e-mails and other communications, and Internet-based research.

■ *Use of computer-related information in cyber prosecutions*—Prosecutors handling these prosecutions need a sufficient understanding of the operation of the Internet, servers, networks, and similar systems.
■ *Use of hardware in traditional and cyber prosecutions*—Prosecutors need a basic understanding of how digital hardware functions to successfully supervise investigations and prosecutions. Hardware includes not only computers and their peripherals, but also equipment like digital cameras, photocopy machines and other devices that utilize computer-like technology, which may contain relevant data.
■ *Legal aspects of data and hardware seizure*—Prosecutors need a thorough understanding of the legal requirements for obtaining both data and hardware as evidence. Because data often resides in storage areas outside the prosecutor's jurisdiction, this legal knowledge must include an understanding of how to obtain evidence from nonlocal sources.

Specialized training exists in a multitude of venues for prosecutors. Organizations such as the National District Attorneys Association in Alexandria, Virginia (www.ndaa.org) and its main training arm, the National Advocacy Center in Columbia, South Carolina (www.ndaa.org/education/nac_index.html) regularly provide training designed to address the above areas. Much of this training is available to prosecutors at little or no cost to the local prosecution office.

Targeted Prosecutions

In the *United States vs. Maksym Vysochanskyy*, (N.D. California, 2005), the defendant sold counterfeit software programs included titles owned by Adobe, Autodesk, Borland and Microsoft on web sites including eBay. He stipulated to a profit of in excess of $400,000 and upon his extradition to the United States was sentenced to 35 months in federal prison. Authorities extradited Vysochanskyy from Thailand after he traveled to Asia from his home in Ukraine. Of the sentence, U.S. Attorney Kevin V. Ryan said it marked a ground-breaking resolve to bring foreign cyber criminals to justice and serve notice of the U.S. government resolve to protect intellectual property rights [13].

On a different scale, investigators and prosecutors targeted a University of Oregon student for similar behavior. Jeffrey Gerard Levy illegally posted computer software programs, musical recordings, entertainment software programs, and digitally-recorded movies on his Internet web site, allowing the general public to download and copy these copyrighted products (*United States vs. Levy Oregon*, 1999). Levy was the first person convicted under the No Electronic Theft ("NET") Act, enacted in 1997 to punish Internet copyright piracy. His activities came to authorities' attention after University systems administrators noticed large traffic on a web site on a University server. The FBI and Oregon State Police investigation confirmed Levy's unlawful activities [14].

Targeted investigations with high-profile arrests and dispositions, allow prosecutors to tout their diligence in cyber crime cases and, they hope, to discourage potential perpetrators from engaging in illegal activities.

Planning for and Prosecuting Cyber Crime

Because cyber crime will occur in the future, regardless of efforts to deter it, both private and public sector entities must plan to deal with on several levels.

Internally, both public and private entities must plan for the fact that at some time, their employees may use computers and the Internet to commit unlawful acts or acts that warrant discipline. This eventuality calls for internal policies governing the use of company or agency equipment for personal e-mail and Internet use. These policies should clearly and regularly be communicated to employees and should take into account relevant business practices of the entity. (A sample e-mail use policy is available from Electronic Frontiers Australia at www.efa.org.au/Publish/aup.html.)

The value of e-mail and Internet use policies is three-fold:

1. They provide the basis for employee discipline in the event of misuse of these resources
2. They deter inappropriate employee behavior
3. They simplify the resolution of any disputes over ownership of equipment or information in the event of a criminal investigation.

In addition to appropriate policies, both public and private entities must decide whether it is fitting to utilize any level of auditing or viewing of employee e-mail or Internet accounts. Software for monitoring Internet use is readily available, but its use should be consistent with business practices of the agency or corporation. Again, its use should be accompanied by clear policies that are communicated to employees.

Depending upon the nature of the business, the entity may be required to have its own internal cyber investigation team in place. This may be necessary for business reasons and it also would allow the entity to substantiate any claims it needs to make about internal controls and adherence to good corporate governance.

Cooperative Efforts

Officials in Eugene, Oregon would never have been able to prosecute "NaughtyGrampa" Robert Earl Smith without substantial cooperation from other agencies. The case illustrates the need for collaboration that transcends both jurisdictions and organizations.

In 1984, very early in the days of cyber crimes, the National Center for Missing and Exploited Children (NCMEC) [www.missingkids.com] was established to operate as a clearinghouse for information on missing and exploited children (42 U.S.C. § 5771 et seq.; 42 U.S.C. § 11606; 22 C.F.R. § 94.6.). The Center's assistance was crucial in assisting in the investigation of Smith and plays a central role in assisting local agencies in cyber investigations related to children. It does so by bringing together investigators from a number of federal agencies and coordinating their work with local agencies on this type of case. It also provides cyber forensics training both in the United States and abroad.

Centralization and coordination of investigations provides significant advantages over smaller police departments. First, entities like NCMEC can maintain a group of experts that is highly trained and well-equipped with appropriate hardware and software for cyber investigations; second, such entities draw from a wide geographical area and can act as a database for both information and evidence related to cyber crime; and third, such entities typically have the financial resources that are not present for local agencies.

Successful investigative cooperation is required in many international cases. When Oleg Zezev was brought to trial in U.S. District Court in New York in 2003, it was only after detectives from three nations concluded a lengthy systems intrusion investigation. Zezev, a resident of Kazakhstan, was sentenced to 51 months in U.S. custody after being convicted of hacking into a corporate computer system and attempting to extort money from the firm upon threat of revealing confidential information.

From his home in Almaty, Kazakhstan, Zezev manipulated the software of a New York-based multinational corporation allowing him to access various accounts including the personal account of the chief corporate officer. He then copied information from those accounts including credit card numbers and internal corporate data. Following some of his unlawful intrusions, Zezev demanded money from the corporation.

According to evidence at trial, investigators from the U.S. FBI, the Kazakhstan National Bureau of Special Services, the Kazakhstan General Prosecutor's Office and the London Metropolitan Police worked cooperatively to piece together the case [15].

Successful legal cooperation must also occur to deal with the international aspects of cyber-crime. The Council of Europe's Convention on Cybercrime represents one attempt to address Internet crimes on an international level. The U.S. Senate ratified the convention in August of 2006 [16].

Recommendations

Proliferation of both Internet connectivity and of criminals who exploit the new technology will drive significant changes in law enforcement efforts. Old-style criminal investigations and, more significantly, old-style thinking about crime will fail to effectively address Internet crime. This is true for several practical reasons:

Cost—Only the largest and best-funded investigative agencies have the financial resources to investigate most cyber crimes. Although cyber forensics permits some aspects of investigations to occur without travel, the technology does not eliminate the need to put detectives in the place where the crime originated. When any of those locations are across the country or on the other side of the world, costs simply prevent the investigation from going forward most of the time.

Jurisdiction—Particularly in the United States, jurisdictional issues in old-style crime are rare. Liberal extradition between states and interstate cooperation, both formal and informal, expedite investigations in the uncommon cases where criminal activity crosses state borders. Moreover, federal criminal jurisdiction typically resolves any such issues in many significant multi-state prosecutions. All of these advantages evaporate in many cyber crimes, however, because cases with victims in the United States—as an example—may well involve suspects in Eastern Europe or Asia. Even if cost issues are overcome, investigators will have no juris-diction outside of the U.S. to seize evidence, make arrests and compel attendance in court proceedings. Returning suspects to face trial, and even determining the appropriate venue for such trial, becomes difficult or impossible.

Education and training—Investigators, prosecutors, criminal defense attorneys and judges typically have adequate training in the law. They typically have little or no training in the technology related to cyber crime. Sometimes this training can be expensive and hard to obtain. And because technology continues to evolve, today's education may become irrelevant tomorrow.

These three issues will force new approaches to cyber crime. Any analysis underlying recommen-dations must begin with two assumptions: (1) Most cyber crimes will never be investigated or prosecuted because of resource or jurisdiction issues; and (2) Technology is too complex for any one person or even an agency to master. In this context, decision makers with wisdom and foresight will consider policies, which take into account deterrence and prevention, cooperative efforts and training to meet the paradigm created by the new technology.

> *Prevention*—Although controversial, policy makers will quickly understand that their agencies cannot address every instance of cyber crime. This makes a consideration of prevention important.

Selective investigation and prosecution of cyber criminals who perpetrate particular forms of cyber crime may have a prophylactic effect. In fact, this activity can be in the criminal system—but it can also take place in civil court. Targeted and high-profile prosecution may well encourage would-be cyber criminals to abandon their plans to engage in similar behavior.

As noted above, another form of deterrence or prevention can occur at the level of corporate human resources policies. Appropriate policies on computer use, including the use of corporate resources for e-mail and other personal activities, should be adequately communicated to employees.

Finally, software and hardware such as firewalls and data encryption can make cyber crime much more difficult for the would-be cyber criminals.

> *Cooperative efforts*—The very nature of cyber crime and cyber forensics investigations dictate the strong need for cooperative efforts. Cooperation in the area of cyber forensics fits into two general categories: inter-agency cooperation and cooperation between law enforcement and nonlaw enforcement entities.

The National Center for Missing and Exploited Children, by bringing together representatives from multiple federal agencies, represents a good example of formal cooperation in cyber investigations. But such formal, permanent organizations are not required for multi-jurisdictional cooperation. Informally, local police departments with trained cyber investigators often make their facilities and experts available for departments without the resources, and on a case-by-case basis, departments frequently work together to investigate and prosecute cyber criminals. These cooperative efforts predate cyber investigations and represent business as usual in the law enforcement community. However, the U.S. Justice Department's centralized reporting of cyber crime using the Internet represents a newer technology-based example of inter-agency cooperation that simplifies the processes for victims and may serve as a model for the future [17].

Cooperation with nonpolice entities is somewhat different and can take several different forms. Some investigations cannot occur without cooperation with corporate systems administrators. As an example, large systems intrusions at major corporations require close cooperation between the company and the investigators. This is true mainly because detectives can never have adequate training to understand proprietary software and network systems. Without the technical expertise provided by the company's experts, the investigation will fail. Additionally, many large corporations providing computers, software and Internet access actively participate in training for law enforcement specific to their operations.

As an example, Microsoft, America Online and Yahoo! regularly provide training both independently and in conjunction with others. These corporations frequently maintain significant security departments. In addition to internal issues that sometimes result in criminal investigations, these departments set procedures for law enforcement to use to easily obtain information about products and subscribers. The presence of these procedures and practices provides protection for the corporations in addition to benefiting cyber investigators' investigations.

Finally, international legal cooperation is required. Specific treaties and conventions recognizing the benefits of cooperative investigations and prosecutions can facilitate international cyber crime enforcement. These agreements should pave the way for procedures that recognize and accommodate the transnational nature of cyber crime. They must also take into account the need for speed in some phases of these investigations by limiting the bureaucratic steps needed to obtain information and evidence in investigations. For example, digital evidence such as e-mails and subscriber IP information is often retained by Internet service providers for a very short time—often only days or weeks. These international agreements must make it possible to either preserve this volatile digital evidence or to grant prompt access to the investigating agency without the undue procedural hurdles so common to international dealings.

> *Training*—Education relating to cyber crime and cyber forensics must occur at all levels of the judicial system.

At the investigatory level, solving cyber crime cases requires dedicated and trained experts with adequate forensic tools to examine the relevant evidence and protect the rights of suspects. In large police departments, subspecialization can result in a more dynamic and successful capacity by creating a collectively higher level of expertise throughout the agency. It will also allow more targeted and successful continuing education of the expert forensic examiners. Whether or not there is subspecialization, continuing education is crucial because of the changing nature of the technology. No law enforcement-training program can succeed, however, without attention to the training of supervisors in at least the basic levels of cyber forensics. Sergeants, captains, and chiefs must have this knowledge to appropriately staff, train, fund, and lead their departments' cyber investigations.

At the legal level, an attorney cannot adequately represent a cyber crime suspect without at least a basic level of computer understanding. Although it is true that the attorney can hire experts to aid and assist with criminal defense, the attorney remains in charge of any such process and cannot function successfully without knowledge of the relevant technology. This rationale applies equally to prosecutors who will direct cyber investigations, make charging decisions and lead the cases through the courts.

Any discussion of the training of legal professionals that does not include mention of judicial training falls short. Judges must possess a strong basic knowledge of computers, the Internet and cyber forensics. They must make decisions regarding probable cause in the issuance of search warrants and in preliminary hearings, the admissibility of cyber evidence, the appropriateness of expert testimony and many other significant legal issues. The analysis of old-style evidence does not intuitively carry forward to cyber evidence without an understanding of the nature of such evidence. Larger courts may well wish to designate some judges as "cyber judges" who specialize in these types of cases and who have the necessary training to be successful in this context.

Finally, adequate training should result in the development and implementation of protocols that set standard procedures for cyber forensics investigations. Such protocols, which must consider legal requirements for admissibility of evidence, successfully direct the course of investigations to ensure that they are both thorough and constitutional.

Conclusion

The role which cyber forensics has and will continue to play in the successful prosecution of 21st century criminals is at an embryonic stage. The union of computer technology, cyber forensics and law enforcement is poised for rapid and exciting growth as both technology and the exploitation of technology provide continued opportunities for illegal activities to be perpetrated in a matter of milliseconds from remote geographical distances.

Professionals (law enforcement, attorneys, judges), tasked with prosecuting those who elect to utilize technology to undermine the social rules of acceptable use, can no longer accept the status quo and must strive to elevate their level of technical expertise in hopes of remaining at least at par with those whom they pursue and prosecute.

Technology will continue to change, making cyber crime an ever present, evolving and changing reality, one not destined to go away. By being proactive, remaining abreast of technological changes, obtaining on-going training in the theories and techniques that define the field of cyber forensics, today's professionals will be better prepared for the challenges of prosecuting tomorrow's cyber criminals.

References

1. United States Department of Justice. Bureau of Justice Statistics 2006. Identity Theft from www.ojp. usdoj.gov/bjs/abstract/it04.htm
2. Lai, S., Current Status of the Phase Change Memory and its Future, retrieved March 1, 2007 from http://www.intel.com/research/documents/Stefan-IEDM-1203-paper.pdf
3. Knight, W., (2005), Holographic Memory Discs May Put DVDs to Shame, NewScientist.com, retrieved March 1, 2007 from http://www.newscientist.com/article.ns?id=dn8370
4. Bullis, K. (2007), Ultradense Molecular Memory, MIT Technology Review, retrieved March 1, 2007 from http://www.technologyreview.com/Nanotech/18100/
5. United States Department of Justice, Eastern District of Pennsylvania (2006). Cleveland, Ohio Man Sentenced to Prison for Bank Fraud and Conspiracy from www.cybercrime.gov/flurySent.htm
6. United States Department of Justice, District of Massachusetts (2004). Former Employee of a Massachusetts High-Technology Firm Charged with Computer Hacking from www.cybercrime.gov/ angleCharged.htm
7. Council of Europe, Convention on Cybercrime (2001), http://conventions.coe.int/Treaty/EN/ Treaties/Html/185.htm
8. Mueller, Robert S., Statement to Senate Judiciary Committee, December 6, 2006, retrieved March 3, 2007 from http://www.fbi.gov/congress/congress06/mueller120606.htm
9. Martinez, S. M., (September 22, 2004), Testimony Before House Government Reform Committee's Subcommittee on Technology, Information Policy, Intergovernmental Relations and the Census, retrieved March 3, 2007 from www.fbi.gov/congress/congress04/martinez092204.htm
10. National White Collar Crime Center and Federal Bureau of Investigation, IC3 2005 Internet Crime Report, retrieved March 3, 2007 from http://www.ic3.gov/media/annualreport/2005_ IC3Report.pdf
11. Zittrain, Jonathan and Edelman, Benjamin (2002), Documentation of Internet Filtering in Saudi Arabia, retrieved March 28, 2007 from cyber.law.harvard.edu/filtering/saudiarabia/
12. Federal Bureau of Investigation, Common Fraud Schemes, retrieved March 4, 2007, http://www.fbi. gov/majcases/fraud/fraudschemes.htm
13. United States Department of Justice, Northern District of California (2006). Ukrainian Software Pirate Sentenced To 35 Months from www.usdoj.gov/usao/can/press/2006/2006_05_09_vysochan-skyy_sentence.press.htm
14. United States Department of Justice, District of Oregon (1999). First Criminal Copyright Conviction Under the 'No Electronic Theft' (NET) Act for Unlawful Distribution of Software on the Internet from http://www.usdoj.gov/opa/pr/1999/August/371crm.htm

15. United States Department of Justice, Southern District of New York (2003). Kazakhstan Hacker Sentenced to Four Years Prison for Breaking into Bloomberg Systems and Attempting Extortion from www.cybercrime.gov/zezevSent.htm

16. United States Department of Justice, (August 2006), Computer Crime & Intellectual Property Section, Council of Europe Convention on Cybercrime, retrieved March 4, 2007 from www.justice.gov/criminal/cybercrime/COEFAQs.htm

17. United States Department of Justice, Computer Crime & Intellectual Property Section. Reporting Computer, Internet-Related, or Intellectual Property Crime from www.usdoj.gov/criminal/cyber crime/reporting.htm

Chapter 13

Electronically Stored Information and Cyber Forensics

Record keeping: Managing the life cycle of the record by appraising the record's values and setting the standards by which records are retained and disposed of.

There are three distinct phases in a record's life cycle:

1. The time at which a record is created or received and is of immediate administrative, fiscal or legal value and use to the office of origin in conducting university activities.
2. The second phase is the point at which records have ongoing value and use but are no longer referred to on a regular basis.
3. The last phase in the life cycle is the point in time at which records have no further operational value to the office of record and are disposed of either by destroying them or transferring them [to the Archives] where they are preserved for their archival value [1].

New Age of Discovery

Sarbanes–Oxley, HIPAA, GLB, Basel II, ISO 17799, ISO 27000, thought you were struggling to meet compliance guidelines and internal control standards—you have not seen anything yet. Your worst nightmares may just have come true.

Though we were all thinking that noncompete, nondisclosure, acceptable use, and rights management policies were difficult to articulate and then implement, those may become the halcyon days. Your next set of policies will be even tougher to define and then implement. In addition, failure to do so will no longer be looked at as an outstanding noncompliance item in an audit report.

On December 1, 2006, the world of records retention and content management as most industry professionals knew it, was re-tooled with the official enactment of the new amendments to the

U.S. court system's FRCP [Committee on Rules of Practice and Procedure, Report of the Judicial Conference: Committee on Rules of Practice and Procedure FRCP, Agenda E-18 Rules, Appendix C-1 (US Courts, Federal Judiciary), (www.uscourts.gov/rules/), September 2005, pp. C18–C109], which now require any business which may find itself involved in litigation in federal court to retain and manage electronic records. Yes, broadly just simply electronic records.

Let us see, that would be, e-mail, instant messaging (IM), text, and blog traffic, just to scratch the surface.

Soon to be effectively known by everyone responsible for establishing retention procedures and those responsible for attesting to controls over those procedures as electronically stored information (ESI).

One of the Judicial Conference Committee's key findings was that the discovery of ESI differs markedly from that in paper form, which naturally has been the focus of conventional discovery procedures. A few of the differences it (the Committee) cited include:

1. Exponentially greater volumes exist than with hardcopy documents.
2. Unlike paper, the information is dynamic, being affected by the turning on and off of the computer itself, or by the computer deleting or overwriting information without the operator's intervention or direct knowledge.
3. ESI, unlike words on paper, might be incomprehensible when separated from the system that created it (loss of context, structure, and other problems). It also found that the discovery of electronic information is becoming more costly, time-consuming and burdensome than for hardcopy information [2].

As a result of the Committee's findings, as of December 1, we must educate ourselves as to the mandated rules and the new requirements for the proper care and feeding of corporate electronic records.

Federal Rules of Civil Procedure—Proposed Amendments

The Civil Rules Advisory Committee "began intensive work on this subject in 2000 .... Study of the issues included several conferences that brought together lawyers, academics, judges, litigants, and experts in information technology with a variety of experiences and viewpoints" [3]. Arguably the most noteworthy, The Sedona Conference Working Group came together in October 2002.

The group consisted of attorneys and others experienced in matters of e-discovery (e-discovery) with "the premise that electronic document production standards arising out of [their] practical experiences would bring needed predictability to litigants and guidance to courts" [4]. They recognized that e-discovery should be "a tool to help resolve [disputes] and should not be viewed as a strategic weapon to coerce unjust, delayed, or expensive results." The fruits of their labor were "intended to complement the Federal Rules of Civil Procedure," and The Sedona Principles were first published in January 2004. These 14 principles are listed in Appendix O of this text.

In July 2005, The Sedona Conference published The Sedona Principles: Best Practices Recommendations & Principles for Addressing Electronic Document Production as part of their working group series (WG1). This was followed in September 2005 with The Sedona Guidelines: Best Practice Guidelines & Commentary for Managing Information & Records in the Electronic Age [5].

The first of these documents goes into great detail regarding proposed amendments to the Federal Rules of Civil Procedure (FRCP) that are involved with e-discovery. A summary and recap of those rules can be found in Appendix P of this text.

As can be seen in Appendix O, there are several amendments to the FRCP regarding e-discovery, and they begin with a change in terminology. Federal Rule of Civil Procedure 34, which defines and gives examples of "documents" and "electronically stored information," has been updated to include:

> … writings, drawings, graphs, charts, photographs, sound recordings, images, and other data or data compilations stored in any medium from which information can be obtained, translated, if necessary, by the respondent into reasonably usable form. [6]

Federal Rules of Civil Procedure: December 1, 2006

E-discovery in legal matters is a complex issue, which cannot be ignored. Consider the massive volume of enterprise data located in file systems, applications, preprimary storage and archives, and then recognize that it may be, at any time, discoverable. The new rules merely underline what was already known: as ESI has become the norm, these records must be made available in the course of litigation. The new rules make this mandatory, and require redesigning organizational discovery processes. Information technology (IT) will require innovation to locate information, and in some cases to restore it, prior to review and production. General counsel must be able to comprehend the categories of information stored and how it may be located. Critical is the recognition that this insight will inform negotiations of the conditions of discovery and will be essential in preparing strategies in support of that litigation.

Organizations will need to alter discovery processes to rely more on IT as information needs to be located and, in some cases, restored before it is reviewed.

An overarching theme in the FRCP changes is the need for organizations, especially general counsel for those organizations, to comprehend what information it has and where it is located. This insight can prove invaluable as parties negotiate conditions of discovery and prepare strategies in support of litigation [7].

Specifically, the new rules require that company attorneys and IT managers must be able to demonstrate how ESI are actually stored, the procedures established to manage, control, protect, and retrieve them under court order, and the policies governing their retention. In addition, the new rules will require evidence of an established history and implemented routine for the deletion of corporate ESI. No longer will midnight deletion and shredding parties excuse noncompliance. Feigned ignorance and plausible denial are matters that may have satisfied judicial inquiry in the past, but will no longer be tolerated by the courts. Noncompliance risks the most serious of consequences.

- The National Association of Securities Dealers (NASD) has accused Morgan Stanley of failing to provide e-mails requested by investors with complaints against its retail brokerage unit, falsely claiming they were lost in the September 11, 2001, attacks.
- Morgan Stanley said in a statement that once its previous management realized that there were backup e-mails for those destroyed in the attacks, it made a big effort to produce them and provide them to plaintiffs and regulators.
- The NASD said Morgan Stanley's actions meant hundreds of retail investors may have been denied their right to obtain e-mail evidence during arbitration procedures against Dean Witter, the retail brokerage's former name [8].

■ In a high-profile case between Morgan Stanley and Ron Perelman (*Morgan Stanley & Co. vs. Coleman Holdings Inc.*, No. 4D05-2606), Fourth District Court of Appeal, Palm Beach, Florida, concerning the sale of Sunbeam to Coleman graphically illustrates the perils of failing to employ a defensible electronic data collection and preservation approach.

■ In this fraud case, Morgan Stanley collected electronic documents itself, using software it had developed in-house, with dire consequences: (A Morgan Stanley employee)s reported that … she and her team had discovered that a flaw in the software they had written had prevented (Morgan Stanley) from locating all responsive e-mail attachments. [She also] reported that (Morgan Stanley) discovered … that the date-range searches for e-mail users who had a Lotus Notes platform were flawed, so there were at least 7000 additional e-mail messages that appeared to fall within the scope of (existing orders).

■ The judge viewed Morgan Stanley's failures as intentional. As described on the front page of *The Wall Street Journal*: As a result of what she described as Morgan Stanley's bad faith' actions, Judge Elizabeth Mass made an extraordinary legal decision: She told the jury it should simply assume the firm helped defraud Mr. Perelman.

■ Morgan Stanley is in serious trouble because of the way it mishandled an increasingly critical matter for companies: handing over e-mail and other documents in legal battles. Lawsuits these days require companies to comb through electronic archives and are sometimes won or lost based on how the litigants perform these tasks [9].

■ The jury decided in Perelman's favor awarding the plaintiff over $600 million of compensatory damages, and over $800 million of punitive damages.

■ As of June 2006, attorneys for Morgan Stanley have petitioned the Florida Fourth District Court of Appeal to overturn, what is in their opinion is a "disproportionate" award.

Morgan Stanley has repeatedly gotten into trouble over how it stores and turns over documents.

■ November 2002: Is one of five firms that together paid regulators $8.3 million for violating rules about retaining e-mail.

■ July 13, 2004: Averts a sex-discrimination trial by agreeing to pay $54 million to settle claims; case features a dispute about e-mail.

■ July 21, 2004: Is fined $250,000 for failing to hand over documents in investor-complaint cases.

■ July 30, 2004: Agrees to pay $2.2 million to regulators to resolve allegations it delayed disclosing 1800 customer complaints involving stockbrokers.

■ March 2005: Is chastised by a Florida state judge for "bad faith" toward its discovery obligations in a suit by financier Ronald Perelman [10].

■ In June 2006, Morgan Stanley also agreed to pay $10 million to settle SEC charges that it failed to maintain proper procedures against possible insider trading.

■ In a separate case, Morgan Stanley in February 2006, agreed in principle to pay the SEC $15 million in civic penalties. The payment is intended to settle the regulator's investigation into a potential violation of e-mail retention rules. If the SEC accepts the payment, it will be the largest fee ever paid for failure to comply with regulations regarding e-mail retention (www.wallstreetandtech.com/news/compliance/showArticle.jhtml?articleID= 180203215).

- October 10, 1999, the Court issued an order…requiring preservation of "all documents and other records containing information which could be potentially relevant to the subject matter of this litigation." Despite this order, Defendants Philip Morris and Altria Group mail, which was over sixty days old, on a monthly system wide basis for a period of at least two years after October 19, 1999.
- The Court found that the defendants' noncompliance with its order warranted the imposition of a sanction precluding all individuals who had failed to comply with the document retention program from testifying in any capacity at trial, as well as a monetary sanction of $2,750,000 [9].
- In 2005, the Alabama Circuit Court of Appeals fined General Motors $700,000 for delaying a discovery process by 98 days.

Ready or Not … It's the Law

Surveys completed by several organizations show clearly that the large percentage of corporations are either unaware of this new federal ruling and its impact on their day-to-day operations or if they are aware, they are under-prepared to comply should they be compelled to do so.

- An Enterprise Strategy Group recent survey showed that 91 percent of organizations with more than 20,000 employees have experienced an e-discovery involving e-mail in the past 12 months.
- Of 75 company attorneys surveyed by LexisNexis Applied Discovery, more than half were unaware of the December 1, 2006 compliance deadline. Only 7 percent indicated that their companies have procedures in place enabling them to comply with the new rules.
- In a Cohasset Associates survey nearly 50 percent of respondent organizations have no e-mail retention policy in place [11].
- A survey conducted by *Computerworld* magazine, reported that roughly 32 percent of 170 IT managers and staffers polled indicated that their organizations were unprepared to meet the requirements of the federal pronouncement, 11 percent indicated that they are somewhat prepared, while what seems to be an alarming 42 percent responded by saying that they do not know what the current status is of their companies' preparation.
- The ability to handle difficult e-discovery matters is a source of concern for most organizations surveyed by law firm Fulbright and Jaworski. Just 19 percent of respondents consider their companies to be well-prepared for e-discovery issues while the vast majority (81 percent) report is being not at all prepared to only somewhat prepared.
- More than a third of the United Kingdom contingent (35 percent) felt "not at all" or "poorly prepared," while 23 percent of the United States respondents fell into this category. Even the largest companies demonstrated little confidence in their preparedness with just 19 percent feeling well-prepared. No one feels completely prepared [12].

The rules, described in a 300-plus-page document compiled by the Judicial Conference of the U.S. Supreme Court's Committee on Rules of Practice and Procedure, require that companies involved in civil litigation meet within 30 days of the filing to decide how to handle electronic data. The firms must agree on what records are shared and on which electronic format [13].

Cost Shifting

It is generally understood and accepted that the responding party should bear the cost of production of ESI, if the data is "reasonably accessible." If it is not reasonably accessible, however, a cost-shifting analysis will most likely be conducted, as per the precedent set by Judge Shira A. Scheindlin of the U.S. District Court in Zubulake vs. UBS Warburg LLC.

In this landmark case, Judge Scheindlin noted that, "whether production of electronic evidence is unduly burdensome or expensive turns primarily on whether it is kept in an accessible or inaccessible format. And whether electronic data is accessible or inaccessible depends on which of five types of media it is stored on."

As further defined in Judge Scheindlin's ruling data which is:

1. "Online" or archived on current computer systems, such as hard drives,
2. "Near-line," such as that stored on optical disks or magnetic tape stored in a robotic storage library form which records can be retrieved in two minutes or less, or
3. "Off-line," but in storage or archives, such as removable optical disks or magnetic tape media are readily accessible using standard search engines because the data is retained in machine readable format.

On the other hand,

4. Routine disaster recovery backup tapes that save information in compressed, sequential, and nonindexed format, and
5. Erased, fragmented, or damaged data is generally inaccessible, because a time-consuming, expensive restoration process is required to obtain the information [14].

Judge Scheindlin went on to craft a three-step analysis process to be considered in the cost-shifting decision. In the first step, it is necessary that the court be knowledgeable about the responding party's computer system to be able to assess whether the data is or is not accessible.

Second, because the cost shifting analysis is so fact-intensive, it is necessary to determine what data may be found on the inaccessible media. And finally, Judge Scheindlin concluded that seven factors should be considered in making the final determination:

1. The extent to which the request is specifically tailored to discover relevant information
2. The availability of such information from other sources
3. The total cost of production, compared with the amount in controversy
4. The total cost of production compared to the resources available to each party
5. The relative ability of each party to control costs and its incentive to do so
6. The importance of the issues at stake in the litigation
7. The relative benefits to the parties of obtaining the information [14].

The corresponding amendments to the federal rule 37 have adopted and continue to follow these guidelines. It should be noted here, however, that "Rule 37 in no way suggests that cost sharing should be considered with regard to the preservation of ESI … [though]. The Committee Notes accompanying Rule 26(b)(2) … hint that cost allocation can be considered in circumstances requiring extraordinary production of such information" [15].

How Likely Are You to Face a Need to Produce ESI?

A significant difference exists between the criminal and civil court systems. The chief difference is that in a civil case, the victim controls essential decisions shaping the case. It is the victim who decides whether to sue, accept a settlement offer, or go to trial.

In the civil justice system, liability must be proven by a preponderance of the evidence, which simply means that one side's evidence is more persuasive than the other's. In other words, the plaintiff must prove there is a 51 percent or greater chance that the defendant committed all the elements of the particular wrong. This standard is far lower than the "proof beyond a reasonable doubt" required for a conviction in the criminal justice system.

It may not be a case of "if" but more realistically "when" that will compel organizations to take a hard look at their ability to identify, retrieve, and produce requisite ESI.

What is the potential or probability of your organization facing exposure arising from litigation brought against it, for:

- Wrongful termination
- Employee discrimination (e.g., age, gender, sexual orientation, race, creed, etc.)
- Wrongful death
- Assault
- Battery (intentional physical contact with a person without that person's consent. Battery includes such crimes as sexual battery, fondling, and malicious wounding)
- Intentional or negligent infliction of emotional distress (causing a victim emotional distress or anxiety through extreme and offensive conduct)
- Fraud—an intentional misrepresentation of facts made to deceive the victim, resulting in damages. This is often seen in white collar or economic crimes such as criminal fraud, telemarketing schemes, or racketeering
- Negligence (the failure to use such care as a reasonably prudent person would use under similar circumstances, when such failure is the cause of the plaintiff's injury. Examples include negligent security and negligent hiring)
- Conversion (the theft or destruction of personal property or money). This includes larceny, concealment, and embezzlement [16]

Now ask yourself, or better yet ask your organization's C-level positions CEO, CFO, CSO, CIO, how likely are you to face a need to produce ESI?

In some civil cases, a "third-party" defendant may be held liable. Third-party defendants are not the persons who actually commit the crimes, but instead are those parties who may have contributed to or facilitated the crimes. A few examples of possible third-party defendants in a victim's case include:

- Landlords who do not provide adequate security measures, such as locks on doors and windows and adequate lighting;
- Colleges that fail to provide adequate security for students or fail to notify students of campus assaults, leaving students vulnerable to victimization;
- Shopping malls that do not employ security guards or other necessary measures, despite a likelihood of criminal attacks on customers;
- People who allow children access to firearms or other dangerous instruments when the children, in turn, use the weapons to injure other people;
- Child-care centers, schools, and churches that do not properly check the backgrounds of their employees, or simply transfer employees to other locations following allegations of abuse; or
- Tavern owners or social hosts who continue to serve alcohol to inebriated persons who subsequently injure other people in drunk driving crashes [16]

Is your organization capable of acting in the role or being perceived as a third-party? Once again, time to ask yourself, or better yet ask your organization's senior management, how likely are you to face a need to produce ESI and is your organization prepared to respond within mandated timeframes?

Additional findings from the Fulbright & Jaworski survey indicate that large companies (more than $1 billion) face an average of 556 lawsuits worldwide and spend an average of $34 million on legal costs. The survey of 422 members of in-house counsels also found that 89 percent of respondents reported at least one new suit filed against their company in the past year [12].

Today's reality is that "93 percent of all business documents are created electronically" [17]. When coupled with the decreasing cost of storage, this allows "[to]day's 'digital packrat' [to] hoard astronomical quantities of electronic information" [17]. According to a recent article in the Wall Street Journal, 'We went through a belief that storage was cheap so we could save everything' … [and] although storage may be cheap or free, … it is not necessarily the wisest decision for an organization to make. Cautions Bandrowsky, who is COO of Wescott Technology Services, LLC, "The volume of data that must be managed or handled for litigation directly affects the cost of discovery" [18]. And in the eventuality of e-discovery, cost containment is the challenge.

What Is Document Management Anyway?

Document management is basically the ability to store and retrieve documents in a centralized facility that is accessible to all. It is the managing of electronic files, graphics, images, and other data types used in document creation. A single document's files may contain text, charts, voice and video clips, process steps, fonts, and more. More importantly, document management is a systematic method for storing, locating, and keeping track of information that is valuable to a business. The key characteristics of a document management system are the ability to manage information, to collaborate when creating information, to distribute the information, and to allow secure access to the greatest number of people [19].

With increasing societal dependence on technology, there are almost daily changes in the growth of that same technology. Global corporations have been affected by these changes. The variety of types and the expanding quantity of documents and records such corporations generate in all forms are staggering. However, increased dependence on electronic storage for such volumes of documents has become an essential business process. These data are now made subject to requests for production in the course of litigation.

Consider the enormous number of electronic records and documents created each business day. Taking into account the use of e-mail, instant messaging, blogging and all other forms of 21st century personal communications, modern business must be prepared to meet the new duties created by the rule. Compliance must come from organizations whose business activities cross state borders and international boundaries, firms involved in Sarbanes–Oxley, HIPAA, GLB, Basel II, ISO compliance activities, as well as companies facing or initiating civil litigation.

Managing these records in conformity with the new FRCP is essential. Documented policies, explicitly directed at assuring integrity, accessibility, retention, and destruction are no longer merely a suggested business practice. It has now become imperative that organizations of all sizes develop a sustainable, viable, and proactive document management program. Failing to do so will risk substantial legal and financial consequences.

Document Management: The Basics

While the concept of document management has routinely been part of good business practice, the use of electronic means of generation and storage of documents has dramatically altered the universe. Answers to what constitutes reasonable policy in this area will differ depending upon the party you address, as well as the perspective from which they respond.

The growing profession of document management (yet another area of professional specialization, made even more important by the new federal rules) has developed its own operational terms. If you are not a member of this professional group, these terms may not yet be part of your vocabulary. Terms such as:

- Versioning
- Metadata
- Indexing and
- Retrieval

Briefly, these terms provide us with additional insight into the mechanics of a viable, functional document management system.

To say that information changes over time is to state the obvious. However, consider the forms that must now be examined to document such changes, such as documents, spreadsheets, web pages, and source code, to name a few. Tracking changes of a document over time is what a versioning system does. It will identify who made a specific change, allow for backing-out undesirable changes, and gives the ability to record why a specific change was made, showing the document contents at a specific point in time. Versioning content is basically archiving important alterations to documents. It will track the changes over time that may be at issue in litigation.

Document versioning allows you to keep multiple versions of a document. If a change needs to be reversed, you can restore the previous version and continue working. When versioning is enabled, versions are automatically created whenever a user updates a document in a document library. Versions are created in the following situations:

- When a user checks out a file, makes changes, and checks the file back in.
- When a user opens a file, makes changes, and then saves the file for the first time.
- When a user restores an old version of a file (and does not check it out).
- When a user uploads a file that already exists, in which case the current file becomes an old version [20].

Metadata is a component of data, which describes the data. It is "data about data." Imagine trying to find a book in the library without the help of a card catalog or computerized search interface. The information contained in these types of systems is essentially metadata about the books housed at that library or other libraries. The metadata describes the who, what, when, where, why, and how about a data set. Without proper documentation, a data set is incomplete.

Metadata is critical to preserving the usefulness of data over time. For instance, metadata captures important information on how the data were collected or processed so that future users of that data understand these details. Another vital function metadata serves is as a record in search systems so that users can locate data sets of interest (www.csc.noaa.gov/metadata/).

Indexing records is similar to what is done with data records residing on your computer. It is a technical term for the process by which specialized application software scans the files on your computer and makes a distinctive list of them to help you easily find them later. As you save or add new documents to your hard drive, or send and receive e-mails, this application software will automatically index these items. In essence, indexing then is the process of establishing and applying terms or codes to records, to be used to retrieve them and to search for and analyze information in records across classifications or categories.

Retrieval is the search for, and presentation of, archival material in response to a specific user request.

Hold Everything—or Not!

Two additional, and very important concepts related to ESI, document management and the ever related and associated legal issues, include hold management and spoliation.

Hold Management refers to the ability to respond to a legal action. Once an organization is notified of a legal action, all records that may relate to that action are placed on legal hold. They may not be destroyed and their profile information may not be modified. They must then be prevented from destruction until the hold is lifted. The ability to hold records may also be applied to audit situations when required (www.cmswatch.com/GlossaryTerm/137).

Once a legal action has begun or there is reason to believe an action will begin, the organization's normal retention policies should be made subordinate to a policy of "hold everything" for information that is deemed likely to be relevant to the action. Those interested in more information about what constitutes a credible "good faith" effort to assure the availability of all relevant records should examine the Fifth Principle in Sedona's Best Practices, Recommendations and Principles for Addressing Electronic Document Production (www.thesedonaconference.org/dlt), which explores the "good faith" test and what constitutes reasonable efforts in retaining relevant information for threatened or pending litigation.

The specific actions to be taken by organizations will vary from one action to another and one organization to another. Each instance should be examined on an individual basis to make the best determination (in conjunction with counsel) about what the appropriate hold and preserve steps should be [21].

Spoliation of evidence refers to the willful destruction of evidence that is germane to the case in litigation. This would include destruction of ESI. However, given the volume of electronic documents created in virtually every business, today, it is usually necessary to delete, archive, or overwrite documents in the routine and normal course of business. Accordingly, many companies have data management systems or data retention policies in place, which include deletion of ESI on a regular basis.

Preservation of discoverable information is further addressed by FRCP 26(f) in terms of the "litigation hold" process. As Judge Scheindlin stated in Zubukake IV, "Once a party reasonably anticipates litigation, it must suspend its routine document retention or destruction policy and put in place a 'litigation hold' to ensure the preservation of relevant documents" [22].

Safe Harbor

FRCP 36(f) provides for a safe harbor against sanctions being imposed in the event of electronic information that might be lost under the "routine, good faith operation" of such a data management system or data retention policy. It's important to remember, however, that this amendment does not provide a shield for any party "that intentionally destroys specific information due to its relationship to litigation or for a party that allows such information to be destroyed to make it unavailable in discovery by exploiting the routine operation of an information system" [3].

Planning a Shredding Party?

Spoliation's legal definition is the intentional destruction of a document or an alteration of it that destroys its value as evidence. Loss or destruction of evidence exposes litigants to drastic monetary, evidentiary, criminal and other sanctions, including in some jurisdictions liability for the tort of spoliation [23].

A spoliator of evidence in a legal action is an individual who neglects to produce evidence that is in her possession or control. In such a situation, any inferences that might be drawn against the party are permitted, and the withholding of the evidence is attributed to the person's presumed knowledge that it would have served to operate against her ("Spoliation" West's Encyclopedia of American Law. The Gale Group, Inc, 1998. Answers.com 07 Jan. 2007. www.answers.com/topic/spoliation).

In *ABC Home Health Servc., Inc. vs. Int'l Bus. Machs. Corp.*, 158 F.R.D. 180 (S.D. Ga. 1994), this case involved the destruction of personal files on an AS/400, a computer used by IBM to work on a software project for ABC entitled "Medical Operations Management System" (MOMS). When ABC terminated IBM's involvement in the MOMS project, IBM returned the computer to ABC as they had initially received it, that is, without any of the personal files created by the IBM or ABC team during the duration of their work on the project. The files were "both project-related documents and purely personal documents." ABC, which believed that the files were critical of IBM, alleged IBM destroyed the files in anticipation of litigation and requested that the court rule in favor of its motion to dismiss IBM's counterclaims as a sanction and, thereby, effectively enter default judgment in favor of ABC.

The court denied ABC's motion for dismissal of IBM's counterclaims under rule 37 of the FRCP, because the destruction of files was not in response to a specific discovery request. (The erasure of files occurred prior to the filing of the case.) The court did leave open the possibility for a jury instruction on the matter, however, stating that "ABC may be entitled to a jury instruction explaining that destroyed documents are presumed to be damaging to the party responsible for the destruction."

However, in *Linnen vs. A.H. Robins Co., Inc.*, 10 Mass.L.Rptr. 189 (Mass. Super. Ct. 1999), the Court held that "a discovery request aimed at the production of records retained in some electronic form is no different, in principle, from a request for documents contained in an office file cabinet .... There is nothing about the technological aspects involved which renders documents stored in an electronic media 'undiscoverable'."

In response to the defendant drug company's reluctance and delays to submit to the plaintiff key e-mails stored on back-up tapes, the court ordered a sample of said e-mails to be provided to plaintiff, with the potential for further e-mails to be furnished—at the expense of the defendant—if the initial e-mails proved valuable to the plaintiff's case. Furthermore, the court (*i*) sanctioned the defendant by ordering it to pay costs and fees associated with the plaintiff's efforts to pursue this line of discovery; and (*ii*) ordered sanctions that the jury be instructed on the "spoliation inference" at the time of the trial [24].

Document Management—Flavor of the Month

To both implement and then assess the effectiveness of an organization's document or records management program, one first needs to establish a base of knowledge regarding the various ways in which document or records management can be viewed. Armed with this information, you now know how the records or documents are stored, accessed, and archived. This information is important in establishing control metrics as well identify weaknesses in an organization's document management program, which may lead to financial as well as legal liabilities.

Given the mandated requirements of the new federal rules, and the serious implications of failure to comply, establishing solid, defensible document or records management policies, procedures and systems are not only a compliance issue but one which touches almost every operating unit within an organization—IT, legal, internal audit, information security, human resources, finances, etc.

Therefore, professionals charged with assessing the internal control structure and risk exposure brought about by the new federal rules must, at the very least, understand the process of establishing a document management program before it can be assessed with any degree of quality and before any effective recommendations for improvement can be presented to management.

The reader would be well advised to explore further the various document management approaches identified below, of which a detailed examination is beyond the scope of this text.

- Integrated Content Management
- EDRMS (Electronic Document and Records Management System)
- Enterprise and Web content management system
- Document imaging
- Digital archives

Paying Special Attention to Daily Document Flow

Organizations, which generate communications, both internally, externally, will be required to comply with the federal rules. Thus, that pretty much identifies almost every public and private company doing business today. If you generate communiqué, which in any way, shape or form ultimately ends up being identified as ESI, then you must have policies, procedures and internal controls in place, to be in compliance with the United States FRCP.

Your decision to invest in a document or records management philosophy and requisite applications and technologies will ultimately be based upon your calculation of perceived risk of not having such policies, procedures, and technologies in place, when they are needed.

This risk perception will be determined by answering these three simple questions:

1. What is the impact to the business? This includes not only the potential effects on financial results but also those to reputation and legislative liability.
2. What is the likelihood of occurrence? Here one may also wish to factor in frequency of occurrence.
3. What is the cost of addressing the risk? This should factor in level of effort, required investment and organizational capabilities. What is the real cost of avoiding the risk and being unprepared?

Types of communiqué that qualify include, however, are not limited to:

Briefing papers	Proposals
Business plans (for a project or start-up company)	Feasibility studies
Consultant's report to a client	Status reports, trip and sales reports
Expert witness's report	Organization information memos
Test plan (or design of experiment)	Requests for information and proposals
Metacode and postscript page description languages (pdl)	Work assignments
Portable document format or PDF	Business plans
Business-to-consumer (B2C) communications	Memos
Letters	Executive summaries
Telephone calls	Cover letter for a report or proposal
Instant messages	Web pages
	Etc.

Therefore, when examining the risk of improper records management, several key questions must be raised. Using e-mail as an example, consider the following: Is e-mail a business record? If so, which category of e-mail is included? What is our legal exposure if we were to retain e-mail for long periods of time, with no business justification?

These questions can easily be expanded to include any of the communiqué types listed above, when assessing an organization's potential under preparedness in its ability to meet the new federal rules.

Establishing a Proactive Document Management Program

Where critical documents may reside can vary greatly by organization. However, most organizations can look to the following as sources of potential document management concern:

Desktop pc	Voice mail database system
Laptops	Instant messaging logs
E-mail servers	Network system logs
File and print servers	Backup tapes
Fax servers	Archival CDs
Pdas	Zip drives
Blackberries	Floppy disks
Internet repositories	Home PCs
Home directory	Etc.

Although not all organizations' e-mail retention policies will be the same, there are three elements that are essential to make such policies litigation ready:

1. A clearly written records and information management policy
2. A legal hold-and-lift process to secure all information that will be relevant to an action
3. An e-mail archiving process that includes services and software

Systems, which intrinsically have these attributes, provide "enabled discovery" because, once information is stored in the archiving system, best practices in archiving can be leveraged to facilitate the organization's response to inquire and investigations [21].

One critical point to both consider and to remember, is that the law does allow for the destruction of ESI, if and only if, the organization has a well articulated policy which defines what ESI is to be destroyed, according to what timeline, when, and how, AND, (and this is a critical and), the policy has been in effect for a period of time far exceeding the receipt of legal hold and retention order from the courts (meaning you cannot begin to implement your long outdated document destruction policy once you get wind or word of potential civil litigation being brought against your organization). According to an October 2006 White Paper [2], the growing volumes of e-mail and other forms of ESI add enormous difficulty to the implementation of consistent destruction policies.

For those who have not yet made the leap into e-mail archiving, here are some of the items that should be considered:

1. Frequency: When, how often must data be archived?
2. Retention: How long will the data be kept?
3. Retrievability: How often and in what ways will archived data be accessed or searched?
4. Taxonomy: What is the methodology by which archived data will be identified and indexed?
5. Ingestion: Does preexisting or historical data need to be entered into the archive?
6. Security: What are the physical (site) and logical (encryption) security requirements?
7. Authentication: What levels of access control are required?
8. Immutability: Is there a requirement to prove that data is unchanged?
9. Render options: Is it acceptable for the data to be transformed for rendering purposes?
10. Future proofing: Does the data need to be retained in a common format (e.g., PDF, XML) to ensure future readability?
11. Refresh criteria: What considerations need to be given to expiration of media life?
12. Purge: When is archived data no longer required, and how will it be destroyed?

Formulating answers to these questions will go a long way toward ensuring that the right technology is selected [25].

Effects of FRCP Amendments on Organizational IT Policies and Practices

Table 13.1 summarizes the impact the new amendments will have on an organization's IT policies and procedures. The reader is advised to asses these changes with respect to the impact which they may have on the reader's own internal IT practices and policies.

Table 13.1 New Amendments' Impact on IT Policies

Amendment	Effect on IT
Rule 16(b): A description of all ESI must be presented within 99 days of the beginning of a legal case.	E-mail archiving and retention software and policies should be put in place.
Rule 26(a): ESI, including e-mail, must be searched without waiting for a discovery request.	IT should put in place e-mail archiving and retention policies so information can be discovered rapidly.
Rule 26(b): A party need not provide discovery of ESI if there is an undue burden or cost.	Requires the organization to prove that putting in e-mail archiving software is an onerous expense.
Rule 26(f): Requires litigants to discuss any issues relating to preserving discoverable information.	Requires legal counsel to know how e-mails are being retained and how they can be searched and retrieved.
Rule 34(b): Requires requesting party to designate the form in which it wants ESI to be produced; requires the responding party to identify the form in which records will be produced.	IT must be aware of how e-mails are stored—on disk or tape, for example—and how they will be retrieved.
Rule 37: Establishes a safe harbor provision for deleting records.	Lets IT establish policies for the deletion of e-mail.

Assessing Corporate Readiness: Are You Prepared for E-Discovery?

The following points, actions, and activities should be examined as potential recommendations to management and best practices implemented in an effort to establish an enterprise wide, proactive document management program, which addresses the issues of compliance, governance and assists in mitigating potential legal culpability.

1. Have a plan and a process for discovery of ESI that you can improve over time.
2. Understand your end-to-end process from discovery to production and the implementation of "holds." This encompasses methods and practices that make sense for your organization, understanding where technology is needed to facilitate or improve process efficiencies or quality of results, and identifying which specific technology capabilities are required to make your end-to-end process effective. It is best accomplished through a cooperative effort among legal, IT, and the line of business (LOB) organizations.
3. Consider technology capabilities such as dedicated computer storage and processing resources with robust security, inventory, and identification of sources of ESI potentially relevant to the request.
4. Examine search and retrieval tools that can be responsive to the request and are robust enough to deliver results in tight time frames and with the appropriate degree of precision, among others.

5. Consider integrated content management, which provides "middleware" to link multiple sources of ESI for search, retrieval and possible collection, if there are multiple content sources.

6. Conduct benchmarks to test and establish estimating parameters for various e-discovery scenarios. Repeatable processes that have been tested to provide evidence of results sought after records production for a given set of metrics can be a significant key to negotiating e-discovery requests, to effectively plan the response activities and timeframe, and to prudently applying resources and budget. Develop repeatable processes that have the flexibility to accommodate a variety of discovery and regulatory requests.

7. Develop and implement records management and retention policies that can effectively preclude retaining nonmaterial information. Formal guidance to promote the appropriate and prompt disposal of unneeded ESI is an important component of records management.

8. Maintain an inventory of ESI sources that documents system descriptions and characterizations such as computing system and location, software product and version, business purpose and scope, data storage (active drives or archives), retention location and periods for backup data, estimated volume of data being retained, native capabilities for search and data formats, and so forth. This inventory provides auditors and legal counsel with data needed to estimate e-discovery time and costs and to determine an efficient and reasonable approach to develop the body of material for legal review.

9. Implement an ESI records management program that controls the volume of information through appropriate and regular destruction of ESI in the normal course of business.

10. In addition to establishing and implementing destruction policies, the records management program also should provide the mechanisms and protocols to suspend destruction for specific ESI required to comply with discovery and preservation orders.

11. Keep pace with changing regulations, new requirements and trends in enforcement.

12. Have a process whereby compliance or regulatory affairs, or whatever organization has the responsibility to monitor regulatory initiatives and implement compliance measures for new regulations, communicates the requirements across the enterprise. These communications would include, for example, legal, technologies, risk management, records management, audit and relevant LOB management.

13. Potential impact of legislation such as SoX and Basel II (financial services) on requirements for controls and audit trails across intra-organizational boundaries should be understood.

14. Records management mechanisms, technologies, and protocols for retention and destruction should be reviewed and appropriately updated in a timely manner.

15. To avoid increasing risk and costs of noncompliance, it is probably advisable not to just update the records retention and management program, but to completely overhaul it. This requires knowledge of electronic records, records management, and ESI technology issues and characteristics, an understanding of the total information fabric of the business encompassing information in all forms.

16. A concerted effort to create an effective records management program for ESI might reduce volumes of physical material held in storage considerably and significantly decrease discovery efforts and production of physical records.

17. Effective use of e-discovery and search tools is often influenced by the amount of experience with the process and the tools. Establish a consistent team with appropriate skills in e-discovery and knowledge of your company's ESI sources, technology platforms and tools.

18. Establish a set of tools that can provide predictable results based on established protocols.

19. Conduct benchmarking exercises periodically against a variety of ESI sources to establish metrics using your tools of choice. These metrics will help to establish the time frames and costs of searching various electronic source systems using various scenarios and parameters. For example, how long does it take to search and report results on 20 named individuals in your e-mail system regarding one matter over a period of three years?

20. Understand the metrics and time requirements for simple search, de-duping and creation of "collection" stage files, separate from the time and effort required for legal or other reviews, advanced searching, and culling of irrelevant or privileged information. Conduct the benchmarking on current systems, retired systems, and archive systems.

21. Hold management rules (prelitigation identification of potentially material information and ongoing implementation of document preservation orders) requires special attention and tools for ESI. The "rules" that will determine which ESI are to be held (beyond their scheduled retention period) require careful crafting (by legal counsel, perhaps with assistance from IT and LOB managers) and an analysis of holdings in the context of ESI and business systems. A lack of a clearly defined "registry" for records (such as can be provided by a document management or records management system) to which the rules can then be applied, constrains adoption of automated techniques and can lead to an outcome that all ESI is "on hold forever."

22. Consider the information fabric of your organization and create policy-based rules for managing ESI that will not only facilitate discovery and document production activities, but will yield business benefits as well. Defining and incorporating records life-cycle-based controls and retrieval protocols will also facilitate meeting trustworthiness and authenticity requirements.

23. Make retention decisions in the context of what the data represents, where it resides, longevity of preservation, and vitality of systems.

24. Evaluate systems (sources of ESI) and determine how older information might reasonably be accessed—and if it cannot reasonably be accessed, examine critically why it is being retained.

25. Implement policies and records-destruction practices in accordance with documented protocols that become part of the normal course of business.

26. Update IT governance practices to include identification of retention requirements (based on legal, regulatory, or other factors) in the design requirements for new systems.

27. Consider the impact of encryption policies on search and retrieval capabilities. With the increasing adoption of encryption for e-mail and attachments, there are concerns that e-mail will not be searchable because of "loss" of the appropriate encryption keys, introducing further complexity to maintain accessibility of aging ESI. ESI that is subject to production but cannot be decrypted could result in raising suspicions of spoliation.

28. Consider the impact of destruction methods and available technology.

29. Multiple regulatory requirements can pertain to any particular class of ESI. Therefore, when there are changes in any particular regulation affecting records, the impact of that change on the retention policy must be evaluated in consideration of other requirements that might apply.

30. Establish standard practices (automated where feasible) for regular destruction of ESI (for example, on a monthly or quarterly basis) that are not unduly burdensome on employees. Establish communications and oversight practices that reinforce awareness and promote compliance. Destroy ESI as soon as is possible, on a regular, consistent basis and use methods that promote security and privacy for the information being destroyed.

31. Because many retention periods are triggered by an event, an event notification to the records management system to trigger the start of a defined retention time period is critical. Any ESI

that is on hold would have the retention period trigger set "on" when the event has occurred, but would not be destroyed until two conditions are met: the "hold" was lifted and the retention period has expired.

32. Establish basic metadata that will be maintained as part of the record for each class of ESI and implement metadata standards.

33. Identify audit-trail requirements when developing metadata standards. If there are requirements for traceability and chain of custody, for example, capturing (as metadata) who did what and when they did it (who created, who updated, and so forth) should be part of the metadata standard.

34. The legal team should be armed with an understanding of what ESI is accessible and what is not before entering e-discovery negotiations [2].

Remember ... "It Is Not Going to Be *If* But, *When*!!"

Given the volume and variety of communications that pass through an organization on any given day, the absolute necessity for a viable, well-thought out, well-planned, and well-tested document management program is essential to the very survival of the 21st century corporation. Add to that, the legislatively mandated requirement, that any business, which may find itself involved in litigation in federal court now must have procedures in place to retain and manage electronic records, and the need for a document management program goes from a necessity to a business requirement.

Identification first of exactly which corporate communiqué must be retained and then establishing appropriate procedures to do so, will take time, effort, energy, and financial resources. Assessment by the organization's internal audit function or review by an external third party must be built into the overall program to ensure compliance and corporate readiness.

Weaknesses in the organization's document management program must be corrected and appropriate controls implemented, that endeavor to maintain a compliant document management program and provide management with the information resources necessary to respond effectively, appropriately and in a timely manner to a court order requiring the organization to produce ESI.

Although the FRCP and their application to ESI as discussed here is agreeably U.S.–centric in its application, these principles along with the recommendations presented for implementing vigilant internal controls are truly global in their implication and application. Organizations which may never anticipate stepping foot into a U.S. federal court will benefit greatly from an assessment of their current document management procedures and subsequent implementation of a well designed strategy to control organizational ESI.

As regulators and courts increasingly recognize the enhanced and richer information value of electronic data compared with physical documents, companies should strengthen their ability to safeguard their rights and respond appropriately [2].

Fail to establish appropriate polices, procedures, retention methodologies, and internal controls to properly manage ESI, and we'll see you in court!

References

1. Allsen, N. and Wieland, D. (2002). Practicum in the Park, Simon Fraser University Archives and Records Management Department, http://slim.emporia.edu/park/glossary.htm, retrieved December 2006.

2. Churchill, B. et al. (October 2006). The impact of ESI on corporate legal and compliance management: An IBM point of view, IBM Corporation, IBM Raleigh (RTP), Building 500, 4205 S Miami Blvd, RTP, North Carolina 27709-2195, (919) 543-0091, www-03.ibm.com/industries/financialservices/doc/content/bin/fss_the_impact_of_eletronically.pdf, retrieved December 2006, used with permission.

3. Cortese, A. W. Jr. (October 2005). Proposed Amendments to the Federal Civil Rules Strike a Healthy Balance. *Defense Counsel Journal*, October 2005, Volume 72, Issue 4, pp. 354–361. Retrieved January 25, 2007, from EBSCOHost database.

4. The Sedona Conference Working Group Series (July 2005). The Sedona Principles: Best Practices Recommendations & Principles for Addressing Electronic Document Production, July 2005 Version. Retrieved February 10, 2007, from www.thesedonaconference.org/dltForm? did=7_05TSP.pdf

5. The Sedona Conference Working Group Series (September 2005). The Sedona Guidelines: Best Practice Guidelines & Commentary for Managing Information & Records in the Electronic Age. Retrieved February 10, 2007, from www.thesedonaconference.org/dltForm?did=TSG9_05.pdf

6. Shelton, G. D. (October 2006). Dont Let the Terabyte You: New E-Discovery Amendments to the FRCP. *Defense Counsel Journal*, October 2006, Volume 73, Issue 4, pp. 324-331. Retrieved February 4, 2007, from EBSCOHost database.

7. Enterprise Strategy Group (October 2006). Leveraging IT and E-discovery Technology to Meet the Expected Challenges Posed by Recent Changes to the FRCP, Index Engines Inc., 960 Holmdel Road, Building One, First Floor, Holmdel, NJ 07733, (732) 817-1060, www.indexengines.com, retrieved December 2006.

8. Plumb, C. (December 20, 2006). NASD: Morgan Stanley falsely said it lost e-mails, Computerworld, www.computerworld.com/action/article.do?command=viewArticleBasic&articleId=9006398&source=NLT_AM&nlid=1, retrieved December 2006.

9. EnCase Legal Journal (November 2005). John Patzakis, Victor Limongelli, Guidance Software, Inc., Guidance Software, Inc., 215 North Marengo Ave., Pasadena, CA 91101, (626) 229–9191, www.guidancesoftware.com/corporate/downloads/whitepapers/legaljournalnovember2005.pdf, retrieved, December 2006.

10. Craig, S. (May 16, 2005). How Morgan Stanley botched a big case by fumbling e-mails, The Wall Street Journal, www.post-gazette.com/pg/05136/505304.stm, retrieved, December 2006.

11. Connor, D., (December, 2006). New E-Records Rules: Whos Complying? Network World, December 4, 2006, Volume 23, Issue 47, p. 16.

12. Fulbright and Jaworski (October 2006). Third Annual Litigation Trends Survey Findings, Fulbright & Jaworski, Fulbright Tower, 1301 McKinney, Suite 5100, Houston, TX 77010–3095, (713) 651 5151, www.fullbright.com, retrieved October 2006, used with permission.

13. Fisher, S. (November 27, 2006). IT Unready for New Rules on Electronic Evidence, Computerworld, www.computerworld.com/action/article.do?command=viewArticleBasic&articleId=274762,retrieved December 2006.

14. Barkett, J. M. (October 2004). Bytes, Bits and Bucks: Cost Shifting and Sanctions in E-Discovery. Defense Counsel Journal, October 2004, Volume 70, Issue 4, pp. 334–356. Retrieved February 4, 2007, from EBSCOHost database.

15. Rice, T. E., Sterchi, T. N., and Boschert, T. M. (Winter 2005). Proposed FRCP Amendments Concerning E-discovery: Will They Be Enough? FDCC Quarterly, Winter/2005, Volume 55, Issue 2, pp. 155–174. Retrieved February 4, 2007, form EBSCOHost database.

16. NCVBA (2001). Civil Justice for Victims of Crime, The National Crime Victim Bar Association, 2000 M Street, NW Suite 480, Washington, DC 20036, 1-800-FYI-CALL, victimbar@ncvc.org, www.victimbar.org, www.ncvc.org/vb/AGP.Net/Components/documentViewer/Download.aspxnz?DocumentID=33494, retrieved December 2006.

17. Lange, M. C. S. (June 2003). E is for Evidence: Using an Online Repository to Review and Produce Electronic Data. *Journal of Internet Law*, Jun/2003, Volume 6, Issue 12, pp. 18–21. Retrieved February 4, 2007, from EBSCOHost database.

18. Garretson, R. (December 2006). A Lifecycle of Its Own. CIO Insight, December/2006, Issue 76, pp. 81–89. Retrieved February 4, 2007, from EBSCOHost database.

19. DataCore (2006). Glossary of Terms, DataCore Technology, www.data-core.com/glossary-of-terms.htm, 436 Creamery Way, Suite 100, Exton, PA 19341, (800) 531–2287, retrieved December 2006.

20. IBM, 2006. Managing Versions and Checking Documents In and Out, Administrators Guide for Windows Sharepoint Services, www.microsoft.com/resources/documentation/wss/2/all/adminguide/en-us/stsaindx.mspx?mfr=true, retrieved December 2006.

21. Cohasset Associates (July 2006). Making the Case for E-mail Archiving and Litigation Readiness, Cohasset Associates, Inc., 3806 Lake Point Tower, 505 North Lake Shore Drive, Chicago, IL 60644 USA, www.cohasset.com, 312-527-1550, retrieved January 2007.

22. Allman, T. Y. (January 2005). Proposed National E-Discovery Standards and the Sedona Principles. *Defense Counsel Journal*, January 2005, Volume 72, Issue 1, pp. 47–55. Retrieved January 25, 2007, from EBSCOHost database.

23. Collins, C. (July 21, 1999). California Eliminates Intentional Spoliation Tort, Thelen Reid & Priest LLP, (415) 369.7306, www.thelenreid.com/index.cfm?section=articles&function=ViewArticle&articleID=1088, retrieved January 2007.

24. Berkman Center for Internet and Society (January 2007), Spoliation Case Reviews, Harvard Law School, 23 Everett Street, Second Floor, Cambridge, MA 02138, (617) 495–7547, http://cyber.law.harvard.edu/digitaldiscovery/casereviews.html.

25. Damoulakis, J. (August 09, 2006). Opinion: Twelve questions to answer before buying e-mail archiving, Computerworld, www.computerworld.com/action/article.do?command=viewArticleBasic&articleId=9002294&intsrc=article_more_bot, retrieved December 2006.

Chapter 14

Cyber Forensic Awareness: Management Survey

Introduction

Over the course of several months, a series of global workshops were held (subject matter ranged from IT audit, security and control topics, to IT management, ethics, privacy and cyber forensics), which were attended by internal and external auditors (financial, operational, and IT), security professionals, and IT managers. These workshops were held in Budapest, Lithuania, Croatia, Prague, Dubai, Oman, Jordan, Toronto, Jakarta, Idaho, Florida, California, and Michigan.

At the conclusion of these workshops, a questionnaire was distributed in an effort to assess the overall state of cyber forensics awareness and response readiness that existed among firms represented at the workshops. The number of surveys distributed totaled 455.

Of the 455 surveys distributed, a total of 118 surveys were returned of which three were unusable (incomplete), resulting in a useable sample of 115 surveys. This return yielded a survey response rate of 25 percent. The high rate of return can be attributed to the personal plea and request of the author to the workshop attendees to complete and return the survey, to the ability for workshop attendees to comply with the author's request without incurring any additional costs. Workshop attendees completed the survey prior to departing the workshop venue.

The questionnaire (see Appendix Z), consisting of 13 yes or no questions followed by two open-ended questions, was designed such that a "yes" response implied some measure of preparedness in a given area.

To encourage a maximum response, the questionnaire was designed so as not to disclose or reveal any demographic information of the respondent and to preclude bias on the part of the respondents, the survey questions were not presented in any sort of weighted order.

Sample Integrity

A survey of this type, one that yields a sample of respondents whose answers to specific questions are then analyzed and from which conclusions are drawn, is typically designed under strict guidelines for the practice and implementation of social research. The survey and the results discussed in this chapter followed these guidelines—but neither to the strictest letter nor under the pretext that the survey methodology used would withstand the strongest scrutiny from social science practitioners.

The sample of 115 surveys collected via this distribution method, is best described as being a sample collected because of its convenience (the convenience of obtaining responses to survey questions), not one of strictest or purest probability.

A pure probability sample is a sample drawn from a population using a random mechanism so that every element of the population has a known chance of ending up in the sample. Samples of convenience are not typically representative, and it is not typically possible to quantify how unrepresentative results based on samples of convenience will be [1]. A sample drawn because of its convenience is therefore not a probability sample.

The hard fast rules of social science research tell us to use a sample of convenience only when it is not feasible to draw a random sample. Convenience samples and voluntary response samples are common but do not produce trustworthy, representative results because they are usually biased [2].

True, Clark's statement taken to heart cannot be ignored. However, the research conducted for this chapter, and the data gathered and analyzed as a result are not intended to replace stringent, academic social science research but rather to provide the reader with an unscientific analysis of the state of preparedness and cyber forensic awareness of a sample of practitioners. And while small in size and scope, the survey comes fairly close to representing a broader professional population.

Bias is the systematic favoring of one part of the population (and their opinions) over other parts of the population. In this chapter, we were not interested in collecting or analyzing responses from individuals who do not come into contact with the subject matter of the survey (cyber forensics), for example, mill workers, department store clerks, airline pilots, stevedores, etc.

Thus a population that would have a more direct exposure and potentially more direct knowledge of the subject being surveyed would provide us a deeper and clearer insight into just how well-prepared and aware the respondents are to the larger picture that is cyber forensics. This objective and scope naturally led to convenience sampling.

The analysis that you are about to read while broad in its potential application, certainly speaks volumes to the fact that as a discipline, the application of cyber forensics and the implementation of cyber forensic investigation techniques are in their infancy and organizational awareness to establishing and implementing policies and procedures dealing with the various elements of cyber forensics, almost nonexistent.

As can be seen in Figure 14.1, only 24 percent of the respondents were able to answer "yes" to more than half of the questions posed; and if we were to consider an academic score of 70 percent to represent a passing grade of preparedness, less than 13 percent of respondents would have made the mark.

Survey Analysis and Findings

The following is a discussion and examination of the detailed survey responses, corresponding to the order of the questions presented on the original survey instrument (see Appendix Z).

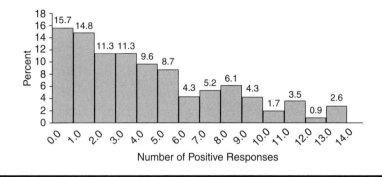

Cyber Forensics Questionnaire Responses

Figure 14.1 Positive responses to cyber forensics questionnaire.

Question 1: Does your firm have a cyber forensics response team in place?

The first question is a very basic one with surprising results. More than 80 percent of respondents noted that their firms either did not have a cyber forensics response team in place, or if they did, the respondent was unaware of its existence (Figure 14.2).

Question 2: Has your staff received formal training in cyber forensic investigations?

Given that most of the respondents noted their firms had no formal response teams in place, the response to this next question was not surprising. In more than 85 percent of the firms represented, there had been no formal training in cyber forensic investigations (Figure 14.3).

Question 3: Within the past 12 months, have you met with your legal counsel to discuss internal methods and procedures your staff should follow for engagements that may lead to litigation?

In spite of the growing number of litigation cases, less than 24 percent of respondents noted that they had met with legal counsel to begin discussing methods and procedures to be followed for engagements that seemed likely to lead to litigation.

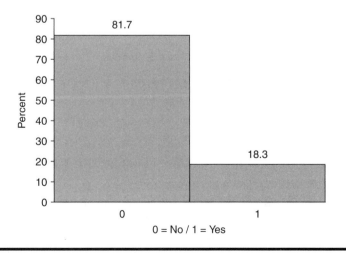

Figure 14.2 Does your firm have a cyber forensics response team in place?

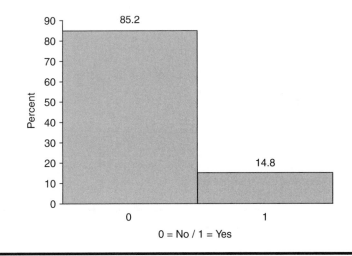

Figure 14.3   Has your staff received formal training in cyber froensic investigations?

More than 75 percent of the respondents have not met with their organization's legal counsel.

If you consider the growing cost of preparing for e-discovery in litigation cases today, not to mention the size of potential awards that might be involved, these results not only support the premise of lack of preparedness—they suggest lack of awareness regarding today's litigious climate and significantly increase risk exposure (Figure 14.4).

Question 4: Do you have written procedures in place for handling digital evidence?

As more and more of the literature is showing, it is imperative that organizations have formal, written procedures in place for handling electronic data, and particularly for the handling of data that falls under the auspices of "digital evidence."

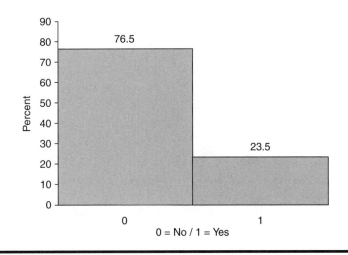

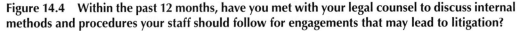

Figure 14.4   Within the past 12 months, have you met with your legal counsel to discuss internal methods and procedures your staff should follow for engagements that may lead to litigation?

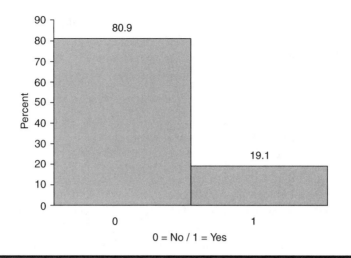

Figure 14.5   Do you have written procedures in place for handling digital evidence?

The survey shows that nearly 81 percent of the respondents have no such written procedures in place (Figure 14.5).

Question 5: Do procedures exist that direct staff on how to conduct a forensic investigation involving digital media?

As landmark cases have shown us, doing the wrong thing can be even more costly than doing nothing at all (e.g., Perleman vs. Morgan Stanley: award $604.3 million; punitive damages $850 million).

Yet nearly 90 percent of firms represented in the survey have no procedures in place directing staff on appropriate methodologies to follow when conducting forensic investigations involving electronic data (Figure 14.6).

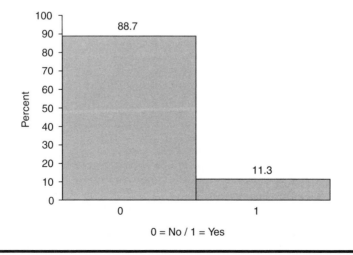

Figure 14.6   Do procedures exist that direct staff on how to conduct a forensic investigation involving digital media?

Question 6: Does staff know the proper procedure(s) to follow if field audit work results in the disclosure of inappropriate material on an employee's computer?

Make no mistake—litigation involving staff can be just as costly to the firm in terms of time and money.

If the organization becomes involved in issues such as wrongful termination, harassment, or discrimination, the case can easily turn on whether or not the firm followed proper procedures. Even more importantly, when there is internal staff involved, they are far more likely to be aware of your policies (or lack thereof) than an outside litigant.

Unfortunately, in 56.5 percent of the firms represented in this survey, staff working for these firms does not seem to know what those procedures are (Figure 14.7).

Question 7: Are these procedures written and distributed to all field auditors?

If your procedures are not written, they are far more subject to interpretation—and misinterpretation—both by employees (whether they are auditors, managers, or laborers) and by the courts.

What good are procedures if they are not distributed to employees, to an organization's "first responders;" that is, the organization's audit professionals?

In 78 percent of firms responding, either there are no such written procedures, or they have not been distributed or made available to the firm's internal auditors (Figure 14.8).

Question 8: Does your organization have a policy regarding the disclosure of sensitive internal information, which may become public, as a result of a legal deposition?

Although it may not necessarily be in terms of information that falls under the umbrella of electronically discoverable data, more than 65 percent of respondents indicated that their respective firms do have policies in place regarding disclosure of sensitive internal information (Figure 14.9).

Question 9: Do policies and procedures exist which address exactly what data your organization will (or can) release, when a plaintiff's attorney requests such data?

This question involves not only internally sensitive information, but may also include privileged information or work products involving the organization's clients. Still, more than half of the organizations represented have no detailed policies or procedures in place addressing this issue (Figure 14.10).

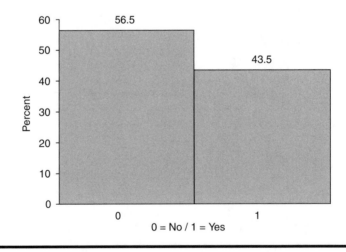

Figure 14.7   Does staff know the proper procedure(s) to follow if field audit work result in the disclosure of inappropriate material on an employee's computer?

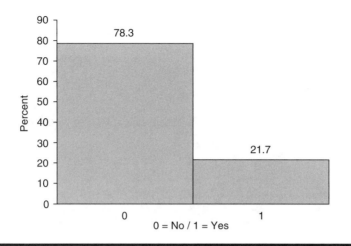

Figure 14.8   Are these procedures written and distributed to all field auditors?

Question 10: Are procedures in place to prevent nonrelevant data, data unrelated to a cyber forensic investigation, from being released or disclosed as part of a larger examination of an employee's suspect activities?

Taking the issue a step further, 68.7 percent of individuals responding to the survey have no procedures in place to prevent the release or disclosure of nonrelevant data in the course of a larger examination of suspect activities.

This may be an even larger issue if the nonrelevant data is sensitive or considered intellectual property or whose disclosure may violate corporate, government or even customer privacy policies. By not having specific procedures in place that allow for the separation of unrelated, nonrelevant data, the organization risks the potential of having to turn over all of its data, due to an inability to separate out just the data requested by a plaintiff's attorney (Figure 14.11).

Question 11: Are policies in place within your organization that address preservation of data integrity and the archiving of a terminated employee's workstation (e.g., hard drive), in the event that those data may need to be examined after the fact?

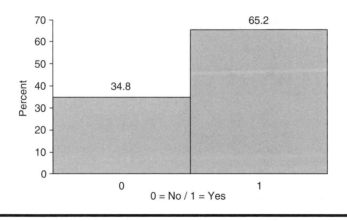

Figure 14.9   Does your organization have a policy regarding the disclosure of sensitive internal information, which may become public, as a result of a legal deposition?

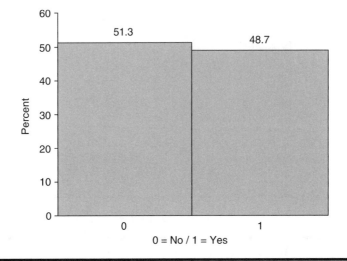

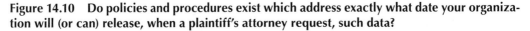

Figure 14.10   Do policies and procedures exist which address exactly what date your organization will (or can) release, when a plaintiff's attorney request, such data?

From a security standpoint, it is certainly important to ensure that access rights are immediately disabled upon the termination or resignation of an employee. It is important to remember however, that terminating an employee has a greater likelihood of resulting in some sort of litigation, either relating to the termination itself, or to the cause of that termination.

That being said, it is even more important that your organization ensure any and all pertinent data is preserved and data integrity remain intact. Should related issues go to litigation, it will be very important that the firm be able to show that established policy was followed.

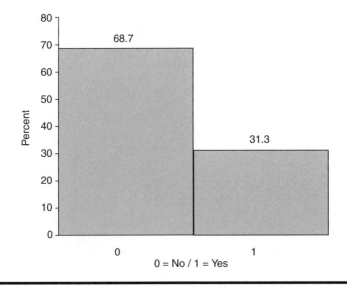

Figure 14.11   Are procedures in place to prevant nonrelevant data, data unrelated to a cyber forensic investigation, from being released or disclosed as part of a larger examination of an employee's suspect activities?

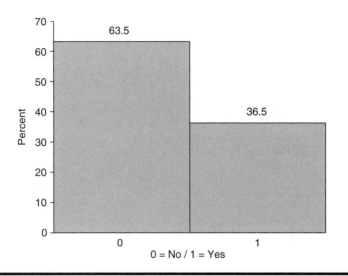

Figure 14.12 Are policies in place within your organization that address preservation of data integrity and the archiring of a terminated employee's work station (eg., hard drive), in the event that those data may to be examined after the fact?

However, of the firms represented in this survey, 63.5 percent do not have any such policies in place (Figure 14.12).

Question 12: Is there a retention policy for such preserved and archived data?

It's not only important that data be preserved and integrity be maintained, it is also important that the investigator ensures that any data be retained in accordance with all applicable regulatory guidelines.

The majority of firms represented in this survey, 57.4 percent have no retention policy in place at this time (Figure 14.13).

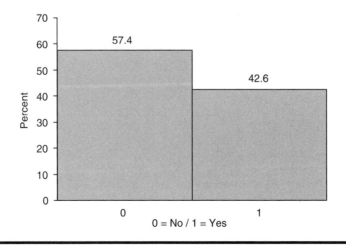

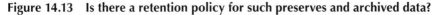

Figure 14.13   Is there a retention policy for such preserves and archived data?

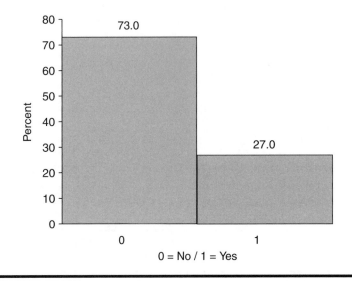

Figure 14.14 Would you be able to demonstrate that controls are in place that would prevent any unauthorized access to there archieved data that could result in the manipulation or destruction of these archived data?

Question 13: Would you be able to demonstrate that controls are in place that would prevent any unauthorized access to these archived data that could result in the manipulation or destruction of these archived data?

As previously seen, without the requisite policies and procedures in place, 73 percent of the firms represented fully acknowledge they would not be able to demonstrate that proper controls are in place to ensure data integrity! (Figure 14.14).

Conclusions

After reviewing the responses to each of the survey questions, a weighting was applied whereby the five items most frequently addressed by the firms (i.e., those with the greatest number of "yes"

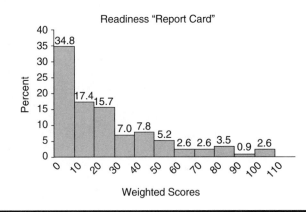

Figure 14.15 Forensic response readiness "report cards."

responses) were given the least amount of weight (one point); those least frequently addressed were given the greatest amount of weight (three points); and the remainder were given an intermediate weight of two points.

This resulted in a 25 points basis from which we produced "report cards." These resultant scores represent both the comparative forensic response readiness and the commensurate level of risk management being practiced by the firms represented in this survey.

The representation of those results are shown in Figure 14.15.

These results are somewhat more pronounced than those of the original, not weighted response data, but the overall message is generally the same.

Given our sample size of 115 respondents and as previously noted, there are limits to the global and broad applicability of the results revealed from this research, in terms of overall cyber forensic readiness and risk management in practice, today.

However, the basic findings clearly indicate that more work—and more research in this area— is warranted. Litigation adjudicated and pending supports this final analysis.

Remember, it will not be a matter of "if" but "when." How well organized and how well prepared will you be? Your Organization? Your clients?

References

1. Stark, P., Glossary of Statistical Terms, http://stat-www.berkeley.edu/~stark/SticiGui/Text/gloss. htm#c, Professor of Statistics, University of California, Berkeley, 403 Evans Hall, Berkeley, CA, stark@stat.berkeley.edu, (510) 642–1430, retrieved April 2007.
2. Clark, S. (January 9, 2007). Samples, Good and Bad, Department of Sociology, University of Washington, Institute of Behavioral Science, University of Colorado at Boulder, Agincourt Health and Population Unit, University of the Witwatersrand, http://faculty.washington.edu/ samclark/Soc220/Lectures/2/1/Samples,%20Good%20and%20Bad%20-%20Chapter%202.ppt, retrieved April 2007.

Appendix A

Computer Forensic Web Sites

Computer Forensic Analysis
www.porcupine.org/forensics

DoD Cyber Crime Center
www.dcfl.gov/dc3/home.htm

Computer Forensics Online is a web magazine that conveys information pertaining to computer
law from a technical expert's viewpoint
www.shk-dplc.com/cfo/

Computer Forensics & Security Training
www.forensics-intl.com/training.html

Forensic Computing & Analysis
www.fish.com/forensics/

The Computer Forensic Community
www.computerforensicscommunity.com

Digital Investigation
www.compseconline.com/digitalinvestigation/welcome.htm

The Digital Forensic Research Workshop
www.dfrws.org

Communications Law & Ethics
http://excellent.com.utk.edu/~bowles/C400list.html

CompLaw
www.complaw.com/

344 ■ *Appendix A*

Computer and Internet Law
www.sosig.ac.uk/roads/subject-listing/World-cat/compintlaw.html

Computer Crime Laws by [US] State
http://nsi.org/Library/Compsec/computerlaw/statelaws.html

Computer Crime Laws in 44 Countries
www.mosstingrett.no/info/legal.html

Cyberlaw Encyclopedia
www.gahtan.com/cyberlaw/

Cyberspace Law Institute
www.cli.org/papers.html

Law Enforcement Cybercrime Resources
www.vaonline.org/internet_LEO.html

Legislation Affecting the Internet
www.cdt.org/legislation/106th/privacy/

US Code (Complete) Online
www.law.cornell.edu/uscode/

Computer Crime and Intellectual
Property Section of the U.S.
Department of Justice
202–514–1026,
www.cybercrime.gov

National Cybercrime Training Partnership,
877–628–7674
www.nctp.org

www.forensicsweb.com/downloads/cfid/isplist/isplist.htm

Appendix B

Cyber Crime and Forensic Organizations

National Cybercrime Training Partnership
877–628–7674
Technical Resources List
National Computer Analysis Response Team
FBI Laboratory
935 Pennsylvania Avenue N.W.
Washington, DC 20535
Phone: 202-324-9307

High Tech Crime Consortium
International Headquarters
1506 North Stevens Street
Tacoma, Washington 98406–3826
Phone: 253-752-2427
Fax: 253-752-2430
E-mail: admin@hightechcrimecops.org

Internal Revenue Service
Criminal Investigation Division
Rich Mendrop
Computer Investigative Specialist Program Manager
2433 South Kirkwood Court
Denver, Colorado 80222
Phone: 303-756-0646
E-mail: richard.mendrop@ci.irs.gov

National Aeronautics and Space Administration
Cheri Carr
Computer Forensic Lab Chief
NASA Office of the Inspector General
Network and Advanced Technology Protections Office
300 E Street S.W.
Washington, DC 20546
Phone: 202-358-4298

National Center for Forensic Science
University of Central Florida
P.O. Box 162367
Orlando, Florida 32816
Phone: 407-823-6469
Fax: 407-823-3162

National Law Enforcement and Corrections Technology Center (NLECTC)–Northeast
26 Electronic Parkway
Rome, New Jersey 13441
Phone: 888-338-0584
Fax: 315-330-4315

National Law Enforcement and Corrections Technology Center (NLECTC)–West
c/o The Aerospace Corporation
2350 East El Segundo Boulevard
El Segundo, California 90245
Phone: 888-548-1618
Fax: 310-336-2227

National Criminal Justice Computer Laboratory and Training Center
SEARCH Group, Inc.
7311 Greenhaven Drive, Suite 145
Sacramento, California 95831
Phone: 916-392-2550

National White Collar Crime Center
7401 Beaufont Springs Drive
Richmond, Virginia 23225
Phone: 800-221-4424

National Railroad Passenger Corporation (NRPC) (AMTRAK)
Office of Inspector General
Office of Investigations
William D. Purdy
Senior Special Agent
10 G Street NE, Suite 3E–400
Washington, DC 20002
Phone: 202-906-4318
E-mail: oigagent@aol.com

Scientific Working Group on Digital Evidence
Social Security Administration
Office of Inspector General
Electronic Crime Team
4–S–1 Operations Building
6401 Security Boulevard
Baltimore, Maryland 21235
Phone: 410-965-7421
Fax: 410-965-5705

U.S. Customs Service's Cyber Smuggling Center
11320 Random Hills, Suite 400
Fairfax, Virginia 22030
Phone: 703-293-8005
Fax: 703-293-9127

U.S. Department of Defense
DoD Computer Forensics Laboratory
911 Elkridge Landing Road, Suite 300
Linthicum, Maryland 21090
Phone: 410-981-0100 or 877-981-3235

U.S. Department of Defense
Office of Inspector General
Defense Criminal Investigative Service
David E. Trosch
Special Agent
Program Manager, Computer Forensics Program
400 Army Navy Drive
Arlington, Virginia 22202
Phone: 703-604-8733
E-mail: dtrosch@dodig.osd.mil

U.S. Department of Energy
Office of the Inspector General
Technology Crimes Section
1000 Independence Avenue, 5A–235
Washington, DC 20585
Phone: 202-586-9939
Fax: 202-586-0754
E-mail: tech.crime@hq.doe.gov

U.S. Department of Justice
Computer Crime Intellectual Property Section (CCIPS)
1301 New York Avenue N.W.
Washington, DC 20530
Phone: 202-514-1026

U.S. Department of Justice
Drug Enforcement Administration
Michael J. Phelan
Group Supervisor
Computer Forensics
Special Testing and Research Lab
10555 Furnace Road
Lorton, Virginia 22079
Phone: 703-495-6787
Fax: 703-495-6794
E-mail: mphelan@erols.com

U.S. Department of Transportation
Office of Inspector General
Jacquie Wente
Special Agent
111 North Canal, Suite 677
Chicago, Illinois 60606
Phone: 312-353-0106
E-mail: wentej@oig.dot.gov

U.S. Department of the Treasury
Bureau of Alcohol, Tobacco and Firearms
Technical Support Division
Visual Information Branch
Jack L. Hunter, Jr.
Audio and Video Forensic Enhancement Specialist
650 Massachusetts Avenue N.W., Room 3220
Washington, DC 20226-0013
Phone: 202-927-8037
Fax: 202-927-8682
E-mail: jlhunter@atfhq.atf.treas.gov

U.S. Postal Inspection Service
Digital Evidence
22433 Randolph Drive
Dulles, Virginia 20104-1000
Phone: 703-406-7927

U.S. Secret Service
Electronic Crimes Branch
950 H Street N.W.
Washington, DC 20223
Phone: 202-406-5850
Fax: 202-406-9233

Veterans Affairs
Office of the Inspector General
Robert Friel
Program Director, Computer Crimes and Forensics
801 I Street N.W., Suite 1064
Washington, DC 20001
Phone: 202-565-5701
E-mail: robert.friel@mail.va.gov

Appendix C

Cyber Forensic Training Resources List

AccessData
384 South 400 West
Suite 200
Lindon, Utah 84042, U.S.A.
Phone: 801-377-5410

Acquisition Data
P.O. Box 1511
Cypress, Texas 77410-1511, U.S.A.
Phone: 281-256-4470

Canadian Police College
P.O. Box 8900
Ottawa, Ontario
K1G 3J2, Canada
Phone: 613-993-9500

DoD Computer Investigations Training Program
911 Elkridge Landing Road
Airport Square 11 Building, Suite 200
Linthicum, Maryland 21090, U.S.A.
Phone: 410-981-1604

FBI Academy at Quantico
U.S. Marine Corps Base
Quantico, Virginia 22135, U.S.A.
Phone: 703-640-6131

Federal Law Enforcement Training Center
Headquarters Facility
Glynco, Georgia 31524, U.S.A.
Phone: 912-267-2100

Federal Law Enforcement Training Center
Artesia Facility
1300 W. Richey Avenue
Artesia, New Mexico 88210, U.S.A.
Phone: 505-748-8000

Federal Law Enforcement Training Center
Charleston Facility
2000 Bainbridge Avenue
Charleston, South Carolina 29405-2607, U.S.A.
Phone: 843-743-8858

Florida Association of Computer Crime Investigators, Inc.
P.O. Box 1503
Bartow, Florida 33831-1503, U.S.A.
Phone: 352-357-0500

Forensic Association of Computer Technologists
P.O. Box 703
Des Moines, Iowa 50303, U.S.A.
Phone: 515-281-7671

Guidance Software, Inc.
215 North Marengo Avenue
Pasadena, California 91101, U.S.A.
Phone: 626-229-9191

High Technology Crime Investigation Association (International)
1474 Freeman Drive
Amissville, Virginia 20106, U.S.A.
Phone: 540-937-5019

Institute of Police Technology and Management
University of North Florida
12000 Alumni Drive
Jacksonville, Florida 32224-2678, U.S.A.
Phone: 904-620-4786

International Association of Computer Investigative Specialists (IACIS)
P.O. Box 21688
Keizer, Oregon 97307-1688, U.S.A.
Phone: 503-557-1506

International System Security Association (ISSA)
7044 South 13th Street
Oak Creek, Wisconsin 53154, U.S.A.
Phone: 800-370-4772

Information Security University
149 New Montgomery Street, Second Floor
San Francisco, California 94105, U.S.A.

National Center for Forensic Science
University of Central Florida
P.O. Box 162367
Orlando, Florida, U.S.A.
Phone: 407-823-6469

National Cybercrime Training Partnership (NCTP)
1000 Technology Drive, Suite 2130
Fairmont, West Virginia 26554, U.S.A.
Phone: 877-628-7674

National Criminal Justice Computer Laboratory and Training Center
SEARCH Group, Inc.
7311 Greenhaven Drive, Suite 145
Sacramento, California 95831, U.S.A.
Phone: 916-392-2550

National White Collar Crime Center
1000 Technology Drive, Suite 2130
Fairmont, West Virginia 26554, U.S.A.
Phone: 877-628-7674

New Technologies, Inc.
2075 N.E. Division Street
Gresham, Oregon 97030, U.S.A.
Phone: 503-661-6912

Purdue University
CERIAS (Center for Education and Research in Information and Assurance Security)
Recitation Building
Purdue University
West Lafayette, Indiana 47907-1315, U.S.A.
Phone: 765-494-7806

SpearTip Technologies
1415 Elbridge Payne Road, Suite 180
St. Louis, Missouri 63017, U.S.A.
Phone: 636-532-5055

Redlands Community College
Criminal Justice and Forensic Computer Science
1300 South Country Club Road
El Reno, Oklahoma 73036-5304, U.S.A.
Phone: 405-262-2552, ext. 2517

University of New Haven
School of Public Safety and Professional Studies
300 Orange Avenue
West Haven, Connecticut 06516, U.S.A.

University of New Haven–California Campus
Forensic Computer Investigation Program
6060 Sunrise Vista Drive
Citrus Heights, California 95610, U.S.A.

Utica College
Economic Crime Programs
1600 Burrstone Road
Utica, New York 13502, U.S.A.

Appendix D

Pertinent Legislation

Electronic Communications Privacy Act, (ECPA). 18 USC 2510 et seq.; 18 USC, 2701 et seq.; 18 USC 3121 et seq.

Privacy Protection Act (PPA), 42 USC 2000aa et seq.

USA PATRIOT ACT of 2001, Public Law 107-56, amended statutes relevant to computer investigations. Statutes amended include 18 USC 1030; 18 USC 2510 et, seq.; 18 USC 2701 et seq.; 18 USC 3121, et seq.; and 47 USC 551.

The Economic Espionage Act 8 U.S.C. §§ 1831–9.

California Online Privacy Protection Act of 2003—Business and Professions Code Section 22575–22579.

Appendix E

Recommended Readings

Searching and Seizing Computers and Obtaining Electronic Evidence in Criminal Investigations. Washington, D.C.: U.S. Department of Justice, Computer Crime and Intellectual Property Section, July 2002, (www.cybercrime.gov/searching.html#A)

Prosecuting Cases That Involve Computers: A Resource for State and Local Prosecutors (CD-ROM), National White Collar Crime Center, 2001. (www.nctp.org and www.training.nw3c.org)

Forward Edge: Computer Training on Seizing Electronic Evidence (CD-ROM), U.S. Secret Service, 2001. (Contact your local U.S. Secret Service office)

Federal Rules of Evidence, www.law.cornell.edu/rules/fre/overview.html

Computer Records and the Federal Rules of Evidence, Orin S. Kerr, USA Bulletin, (March 2001) www.usdoj.gov/criminal/cybercrime/usamarch2001_4.htm

How IDE Controllers Work, Jeff Tyson, Ed Grabianowski, http://computer.howstuffworks.com/pci.htm

Defining Digital Forensic Examination and Analysis Tools, Brian Carrier, carrier@atstake.com

A Lessons Learned Repository for Computer Forensics, 2002 Digital Forensics Research Workshop, Warren Harrison, Portland State University, George Heuston, Hillsboro Police Department, Mark Morrissey, Portland State University, David Aucsmith, Intel Corporation, Sarah Mocas, Portland State University, Steve Russelle, Portland Police Bureau, www.ijde.org/archives/02_fall_art1.html

Time and Computer Forensics, Digital Forensics Research Workshop (DFRWS), 8 August 2002, Mike Duren, Olivier de Vel, Jason Burke, John Faust, Shiu-Kai Chin, www.dfrws.org

Can Digital Evidence Endure the Test of Time?, Digital Forensics Research Workshop (DFRWS), August 7, 2002, Michael Duren, WetStone Technologies, Inc., www.dfrws.org

Vanstone Scott A., Oorschot Paul C. van, Menezes, Alfred J. (1997) *Handbook of Applied Cryptography*, CRC Press.

United States Department of Justice, (July 2001), *"Electronic Crime Scene Investigation: A Guide for First Responders,"* NCJ 187736, NIJ Guide, Office of Justice Programs, National Institute of Justice, www.ojp.usdoj.gov/nij, 810 Seventh Street N.W., Washington, DC 20531.

Larry Leibrock, Ph.D., eForensics, October 18, 2004, "Systems Auditing, Forensics, and Digital Discovery: The Good, The Bad, The Ugly," Security Conference, Leadership Series, Arlington, Texas, www.eforensics.com/assets/SecLeadership.pdf, (512) 479–5959.

Christiaan Best & Bill Kirby, eForensics, "Digital Media: Where to Look for Evidence of a Crime," Texas District and County Attorneys Association, 2004 Annual Criminal & Civil Law Update, www.eforensics.com/assets/TDCAA.pdf, (512) 479–5959.

James, S., (2002), "Computer Forensics A White Paper," http://docs.ibas.com/cf/CF_white_paper. pdf, Ibas UK Limited, Stone Castle, London Road Stone, Kent DA9 9JG, Tel: +44 (0) 1322 388900.

United States Department of Justice, (April 2004), "Forensic Examination of Digital Evidence: A Guide for Law Enforcement," NCJ 199408, NIJ, Office of Justice Programs, National Institute of Justice, www.ojp.usdoj.gov/nij, 810 Seventh Street N.W., Washington, DC 20531.

Computer Forensics: Tool Testing & National Software Reference Library, Jim Lyle Information Technology Laboratory, 9 September 2003, www.cftt.nist.gov/documents/CFTTandNRSLat Moscow.pdf

Systems Auditing, Forensics, and Digital Discovery: The Good, The Bad, The Ugly, Security Conference, Leadership Series, Arlington, Texas, Larry Leibrock, Ph.D., eForensics, October 18, 2004, www.eforensics.com/assets/SecLeadership.pdf

Berry, D., and Berry, S., (February 2005), "Junk Science in the Courtroom," www.truthinjustice .org/junk.htm, February 3, 2005.

Carrier, B., (Winter 2003), "Defining Digital Forensic Examination and Analysis Tools," *International Journal of Digital Evidence*, Volume 1, Issue 4, carrier@atstake.com.

DEW Associates Corporation, (2002), "Cutting the Slack (or maybe the Fat!), Drive Partition Efficiency: Controlling Slack," www.dewassoc.com/kbase/hard_drives/fat_slack.html, PO Box 841, Sparta, New Jersey 07871-0841, 973-702-0545, www.dewassoc.com/index.html

Goldsholle, G., (2001), Federal Rules of Evidence, ExpertPages.com, http://expertpages.com/federal/federal.htm, February 3, 2005.

Hailey, S., (2004), "The Tools Proven in Court Question," Cyber Security Institute, www.cyber-securityinstitute.biz/tpicq.htm

Harrison, W., (2002) Portland State University, Heuston, G., Hillsboro Police Department, Morrissey, M., Portland State University, Aucsmith, D., Intel Corporation, Mocas, S., Portland State University, Russelle, S., Portland Police Bureau, "A Lessons Learned Repository for Computer Forensics," 2002 Digital Forensics Research Workshop, www.ijde.org/archives/02_fall_art1.html

Innocence Project, (February 2005), "Junk Science," Innocence Project, 100 Fifth Avenue, 3rd Floor, New York, NY 10011, info@innocenceproject.org, 212.364.5340, www.innocenceproject.org/causes/junkscience.php

Kerr, O., (March 2001), "Computer Records and the Federal Rules of Evidence," March 2001 Vol. 49, No.2 an excerpt of a larger DOJ manual entitled "Searching and Seizing Computers and Obtaining Electronic Evidence in Criminal Investigations," which is available on the Internet at www.cybercrime.gov/searchmanual.htm, Orin S. Kerr USA Bulletin, www.usdoj.gov/criminal/cybercrime/usamarch 2001_4.htm

Knoll, J., (2001), "Legal Aspects of Search and Seizure," Presented to the Topeka Police Department, Recruit Academy, May 22, and 23, 2001, John J. Knoll, Assistant City Attorney, City of Topeka, Kansas, originally compiled by Anthony W. Rues and James Brown, Assistant District Attorneys. Substantially revised & rearranged by John J. Knoll, Assistant City Attorney, January 3–6, 2000, www.kscoplaw.com/outlines/ssoutline.htm

Loomis, S., (November 2002), "The Daubert Test of Reliability: Fighting 'Junk Science' in the Courtrooms," Skeptic Report, www.skepticreport.com/mystics/dauberttest.htm

Lyle, J. (September 9, 2003) "Computer Forensics: Tool Testing and National Software Reference Library," Information Technology Laboratory, www.cftt.nist.gov/documents/CFTTandNRSLat Moscow.pdf

Moenssens, A., (April 15, 1999b), Banning Junk Science from the Court Room... But How Can We Tell it's "Junk"? Part of an Abstract for a discussion delivered at the National Conference on Science and the Law on April 15, 1999, at San Diego. The Conference was co-sponsored by the National Institute of Justice and several other organizations, www.forensic-evidence.com/site/EVID/EL00003_2.html

Management Assessment: 20 Questions

Is My Organization Prepared to Conduct a Cyber Forensic Investigation?

1. Does your firm have a cyber forensics response team in place?
2. Has your staff received formal training in cyber forensic investigations?
3. Within the past 12 months, have you met with your legal counsel to discuss internal methods and procedures your staff should follow for engagements that may lead to litigation?
4. Do you have written procedures in place for handling digital evidence?
5. Do procedures exist that direct staff on how to conduct a forensic investigation involving digital media?
6. Does staff know the proper procedure to follow if field audit work results in the disclosure of inappropriate material on an employee's computer?
7. Are these procedures written and distributed to all field auditors?
8. Do you and your staff carry personal E&O insurance?
9. Is such coverage provided you and your staff through your organization?
10. Will your organization indemnify you and hold you blameless should the organization be sued as a result of an improperly conducted cyber forensic investigation?
11. Prior to attending this presentation, where you aware of the broad implications of the concept of chain of custody?
12. Have you ever been deposed as a result of your role as an auditor or in the performance of your job in examining internal controls?
13. What is your organization's policy regarding the disclosure of sensitive internal information, which may become public, as a result of a legal deposition?
14. Do policies and procedures exist, which address exactly what data your organization will (or can) release, when such data is requested by a plaintiff's attorney?

15. What procedures are in place to prevent non-relevant data, data unrelated to a cyber forensic investigation, from being released or disclosed as part of a larger examination of an employee's suspect activities?

16. Are policies in place within your organization that addresses preservation of data integrity and the archiving of a terminated employee's workstation (e.g., hard drive), in the event that those data may need to be examined after the fact?

17. What is the retention policy for such data preserved and archived data?

18. Would you be able to demonstrate that controls are in place that would prevent any unauthorized access to these archived data that could result in the manipulation or destruction of these archived data?

19. What cyber forensics best practices does your firm employ?

20. What is your greatest fear with respect to the emerging importance and impact of cyber forensics to the corporate enterprise?

Appendix G

Flowchart for the Seizure of a Personal Digital Assistant

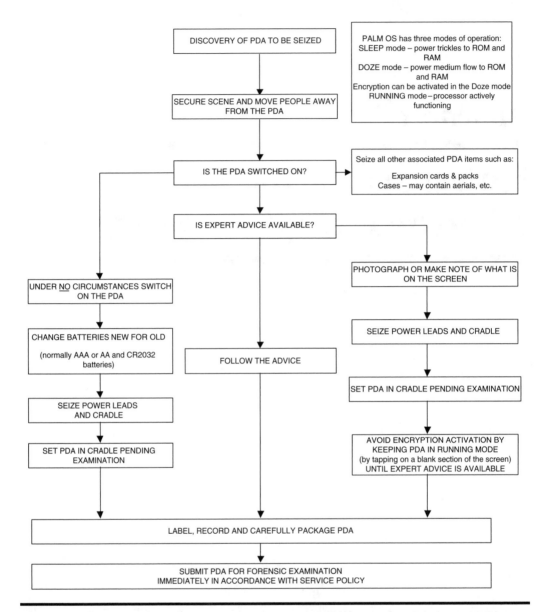

Figure G.1 **Flowchart for the seizure of a personal digital assistant. (From "Good Practice Guide for Computer Based Electronic Evidence," Association of Chief Police Officers, National High-Tech Crime Unit, www.nhtcu.org/ACPO%20Guide%20v3.0.pdf, March 2005. With permission.)**

Appendix H

Additional Information: Computer Hardware

NIC Cards

Network interface controller (NIC) cards are devices that are used to allow computers to communicate with each other over a network. Network interface controller cards can be found in the expansion slot of the motherboard as a peripheral component interconnect (PCI) card or they may be built into the many of the newer motherboards found in today's computers.

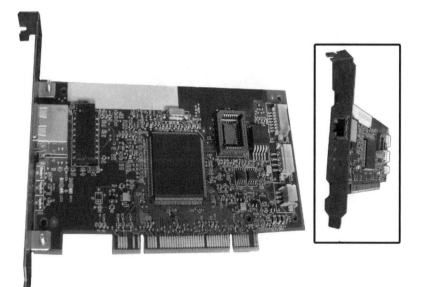

Sound Cards

Sound cards are devices that give the computer the ability to transmit sounds to the user. Sound cards can be found in the expansion slot of the motherboard as a PCI card just as network card. Similar to the network card, sound cards are frequently preinstalled on the motherboard. If the motherboard has onboard sound, the sound cable running from the CD-ROM or DVD-ROM drive will plug directly into the motherboard. Otherwise, the cable will be found running to the sound card installed in one of the expansion slots in the motherboard.

Video Cards

Video cards are the devices used to output graphics to the computer monitor. Video cards can be installed in a few different ways. Video cards can be preinstalled onto the motherboard, installed into one of the PCI expansion slots on the motherboard, or placed in the accelerated graphics port, AGP, of the motherboard. The evolution of the accelerated graphics port on the motherboard has occurred through the need of the video card to communicate more quickly with the motherboard, the CPU, and the system's memory or RAM.

Appendix I

Questions That Every Cyber Investigator Should Ask; before, during, and after an Investigation

Following the Best Practice for the Seizure of Electronic Evidence as set forth by the National High Tech Crime Unit, published by the Association of Chief Police Officers.

In a preliminary stage that should precede the "Discovery of Computer or Digital Equipment to be Seized," several items need to be determined before launching the investigation. These preliminary steps should include:

1. The computer that will become evidence, what is the role in this case?
2. Is it the suspect's computer? Is it a victim's computer?
3. Is it a computer that is used as an intermediate tool to commit a crime?
4. Because the lead investigator of a case is often not the individual that actually performs the forensic analysis of the computer, what is it that the investigator is looking for?
5. What evidence is being sought? Besides simple cases of possession of child pornography, where an investigator can easily find evidence with today's tools, the forensic analyst must have a thorough understanding of what the lead investigator is seeking.

A good interview of the suspect—this is probably the most important part of the investigation beside the actual analysis of the electronic evidence. Computer crime investigators have indicated that this is an important fact finding opportunity if you have a cooperative suspect.

This interview, coupled with a thorough background check, can give you insight to the technical skills of your suspect. By using a variety of interview techniques, a skilled investigator may get a suspect to reveal passwords, tips to unusual system configurations, and identify the potential for unusual circumstances like logic bombs or booby traps.

Review of Search Warrant or Consent

1. If it is consent, will it be considered valid in court?
2. Are you sure that the person giving consent is authorized to do so?
3. Is the computer that you are going to analyze the computer that you think it is?
4. Could someone have switched computers?
5. Determining the situation that will be encountered at the scene—is the computer that is to be seized at the incarcerated suspect's apartment, where no one else lives? Or is it a workstation in a business.
6. If it is at a business, is the network or system administrator considered friendly and reliable? They may be able to assist in identifying important information about their configuration. It may be that a suspect's betrayed spouse may give you information such as where passwords are written down or where evidence may be hidden.

Preparation

Do not plan to image a desktop computer and show up to find a server farm. Again, proper preliminary investigations will prevent this. Make sure you have the proper tools in order, that policies are followed, investigative tools checked and validated, proper crime scene processing equipment is available (camera, gloves, paper bags, anti-static bags, logs, labels).

Another important consideration is the availability of expert advice. It is doubtful that most agencies have an efficient communication system set up where there are contact people for unusual situations. The time to set up those lines of communications is not in the mist of a raid or an emergency.

Most municipal police departments do not have the expertise on staff to handle computer crime. They rely on county or state police agencies, or regional task forces and those resources are often thin as well. The depth of available computer expertise for some law enforcement agencies is only one layer deep.

Where Is Seized Equipment Stored? Heat Humidity, CMOS Battery Life, or PDA—Keep Devices Charged

Consideration of how to move and store seized equipment is an important part of both the preliminary stage and transportation stage of a computer crime investigation and seizure. Police often encounter a single personal computer tower or desktop unit. But what if the seizure ends up being dozens of computers, or large rack mounted computer equipment?

1. Where will numerous computer hardware units be stored and how can they be safely transported? Many local police departments have limited space for evidence and that space is not always conducive to housing electronic equipment long term.

Fingerprinting: Must Tie the Evidence to a Person, Do Forensic First, Then Fingerprints

1. What other crime scene processing is going to be done for this case?

Fingerprinting can severely damage a computer and should be done after the computer forensic analysis is completed. But the same protections used on other crime scene items should be afforded to computer crime scenes.

Seize All Peripherals. Smart Keyboards, Other Devices May Have Fingerprints

Many departments seize only the CPU (tower or desktop unit), leaving monitors, keyboards, and printers behind. Each case will have to be evaluated on its own. If you are working a forgery case, then it would be appropriate to seize the printer.

Technology keeps changing and investigators must keep up on new devices and trends. A popular computer enthusiast magazine recently demonstrated how some USB keyboards can be modified to fit a USB hub inside. With the addition of high capacity USB thumb drives, the modified keyboard could conceal several gigabytes of storage.

Look for Media in the Area of Computer, Passwords, ISP Info

The Investigator must make a thorough search for passwords and other documentation that will help with the investigation. Obviously this could be a very difficult task. Although many people will write passwords down on the back of the keyboard or on a post it stuck to the monitor. Other people may have concealed their passwords reasonably well, intentionally, or unintentionally in mounds of paper and clutter on their desk.

Other things to consider are manuals and documentation for the computer, software disks, software manuals, and retail software boxes. If you cannot seize those items, make sure they are documented in your crime scene report. This becomes important when dealing with a suspect that uses proprietary software (like some accounting system) or evidence cleansing programs.

The fact that a particular piece of software was at the scene may save your computer forensic analyst a few hours of trying to figure out what those unusual files are or why usual files are not there.

Other considerations include how the computer is connected to the outside world.

1. Is the computer hooked up to a modem, if so what is the number?
2. Is in attached to a broadband connection, if so, who is the ISP?
3. Could there be backups of the computer you are investigating?
4. Could your suspect be technically advanced enough to use hidden networked storage devices, control a remote system, use IPods or X boxes as a storage device?

Photograph Scene, Computer, Monitor, Screen. Work with Digital Photos to Make Sure You Have "Evidence Grade" Pictures

Treat this computer crime scene as any other crime scene. Do not be intimidated because it is a computer. Get general computer experience or training until you feel comfortable with seizing computers for evidence. This scene is no different than other crime scenes.

The e-crime scene will be secured for unauthorized access, it will be photographed, every procedure documented and, a diagram of the setup will be made.

The cables will be labeled in respect of how they were connected. Be sure to photograph the computer screen making sure that the time is displayed and if there were any visibly identifiable programs are running. Note if there is a difference in the time displayed on the computer and the actual time.

Digital photos are suggested because it is easy to review the quality of the pictures because some of the necessary angles may be close up shots or have reflectivity off of the monitor.

Also, treat the chain of custody of these items the same as you would for other evidence. That may be stating the obvious, but better very safe and sure than sorry after the fact.

If Off, Leave Off. If On, Pull Plug

Serious consideration needs to be made for a networked server. If there are business applications running, a sudden power down may cause data corruption and loss. This could have serious liability issues for an agency, auditor or cyber forensics investigator.

Questions That Every Cyber Investigator Should Ask, before, during, and after an Investigation…

1. Have I learned everything that I can from the suspect?
2. Do I have a sense of his or her technical skills?
3. Did he or she reveal anything about his or her set up that may help my investigation?
4. Based on his or her background and interview, do I have to be concerned with booby traps?
5. Does he or she use passwords in protecting the computer?
6. Is the computer networked, and if so, could he or she be using unusual devices to store data?
7. If the computer is in a work environment, is there someone there that will be in a position to assist me?
8. Is the search warrant accurate?
9. Is the consent valid and does it everything check out (computer ownership can be validated, the person giving consent is who they claim to be and they have the right to give consent)?
10. Have I prepared for unusual circumstances by setting up lines of communications in advanced?
11. Do I have MOU (Memos of Understanding) with agencies that can assist me?
12. Have I prepared for physically transporting any evidence collected at the scene, and do I have the ability to maintain secured storage of that evidence?
13. If I am doing an onsite image, have I properly prepared my tools (performed checks and validations)? Do I have "clean" media to image to? Am I prepared for things like using different adapters? Do I have items such as anti-static bags or other appropriate storage materials?
14. Does my investigation follow my department's policy for computer forensic investigations?

15. Does my investigation follow good forensic methodologies that are widely accepted and will it stand up to judicial review?

At the Scene ...

1. Did I take photographs of the scene, both general shots of the layout , and specific shots like how the peripherals are hooked up to the computer in back and the screen to include the time and any visibly identifiable programs running?
2. Did I document who was on scene and anyone else who had access to the computer?
3. Have I properly documented and logged activities?
4. Did I document and label the configuration of peripheral connections?
5. Did I search for and document other items of interest in the area, such as the actual time, program manuals, program disks, and potential passwords?
6. Will I need to take extra care to preserve fingerprint or other trace evidence?
7. Will I need to take just the CPU, or does the case dictate that the monitor, keyboard, printer, and other equipment be seized as well?
8. Are there others available to interview to determine unusual circumstances, passwords, or potentially hidden evidence?

Upon Transport ...

1. If I have a large number of CPU's or rack mounted equipment, where will these items be stored and how will they be securely transported?
2. Has a defensible chain of custody for the evidence been maintained?

This appendix was prepared for this text by Brian O'Neil, president of Confidential Computers, 857 Carriage Hills Drive, St. Peters, MO 63304, (314) 210-4400, Brianoneil@charter.net, brian@ confidentialcomputers.com, used with permission.

Appendix J

Cyber Forensic Best Practice Recommendations

The following recommendations may be looked at as best practices in the performance of a cyber forensic investigation. The term best practice generally refers to the best possible way of doing something; it is commonly used in the fields of business management, software engineering, medicine, and government. Now we can add cyber forensics to this list.

These recommendations have been taken from the National Institute of Standards and Technology (www.nist.gov), Special Publication 800-86, Guide to Integrating Forensic Techniques into Incident Response, [www.csrc.nist.gov/publications/nistpubs/800-86/SP800-86.pdf], Karen Kent, Suzanne Chevalier, Tim Grance, and Hung Dang (August 2006).

The first group of recommendations applies to organizing a forensics capability. The remaining recommendations have been grouped by the phases of the forensics process: collection, examination, analysis, and reporting.

Organizing a Forensics Capability

1. Organizations should have a capability to perform computer and network forensics. Forensics is needed for various tasks within an organization, including investigating crimes and inappropriate behavior, reconstructing computer security incidents, troubleshooting operational problems, supporting due diligence for audit record maintenance, and recovering from accidental system damage. Without such a capability, an organization will have difficulty determining what events have occurred within its systems and networks, such as exposures of protected, sensitive data. Also, handling evidence in a forensically sound manner puts decision makers in a position where they can confidently take the necessary actions.

Forensic Participants

1. Organizations should determine which parties should handle each aspect of forensics. Most organizations rely on a combination of their own staff and external parties to perform forensic tasks. Organizations should decide which parties should take care of which tasks based on skills and abilities, cost, response time, and data sensitivity.

2. Analysts should have reasonably comprehensive technical knowledge. Because current tools have rather limited analysis abilities, analysts should be well-trained, experienced, and knowledgeable in networking principles, common network and application protocols, network and application security products, and network-based threats and attack methods.

3. Incident handling teams should have robust forensic capabilities. More than one team member should be able to perform each typical forensic activity. Hands-on exercises and IT and forensic training courses can be helpful in building and maintaining skills, as can demonstrations of new tools and technologies.

4. Many teams within an organization should participate in forensics. Individuals performing forensic actions should be able to reach out to other teams and individuals within an organization, as needed, for additional assistance. Examples of teams that may provide assistance in these efforts include IT professionals, management, legal advisors, human resources personnel, auditors, and physical security staff. Members of these teams should understand their roles and responsibilities in forensics, receive training and education on forensic-related policies, guidelines, and procedures, and be prepared to cooperate with and assist others on forensic actions.

Forensic Policies, Guidelines, and Procedures

1. Forensic considerations should be clearly addressed in policies. At a high level, policies should allow authorized personnel to monitor systems and networks and perform investigations for legitimate reasons under appropriate circumstances. Organizations may also have a separate forensic policy for incident handlers and others with forensic roles that provides more detailed rules for appropriate behavior. Everyone who may be called upon to assist with any forensic efforts should be familiar with and understand the forensic policy. Additional policy considerations are as follows:
   - Forensic policy should clearly define the roles and responsibilities of all people performing or assisting with the organization's forensic activities. The policy should include all internal and external parties that may be involved and should clearly indicate who should contact which parties under different circumstances.
   - The organization's policies, guidelines, and procedures should clearly explain what forensic actions should and should not be performed under normal and special circumstances and should address the use of anti-forensic tools and techniques. Policies, guidelines, and procedures should also address the handling of inadvertent exposures of sensitive information.
   - Incorporating forensic considerations into the information system life cycle can lead to more efficient and effective handling of many incidents.
   - The organization's policies should address inadvertent disclosures and long-term storage of sensitive information captured by forensic tools, and should ensure that this does not violate the organization's privacy or data retention policies.

- The organization's policies should also address the monitoring of networks, as well as requiring warning banners on systems that indicate that activity might be monitored. The policies should take into account reasonable expectations of user privacy.

2. Organizations should create and maintain guidelines and procedures for performing forensic tasks. The guidelines should include general methodologies for investigating an incident using forensic techniques, and step-by-step procedures should explain how to perform routine tasks. The guidelines and procedures should support the admissibility of evidence into legal proceedings. Because electronic logs and other records can be altered or otherwise manipulated, organizations should be prepared, through their policies, guidelines, and procedures, to demonstrate the reliability and integrity of such records. The guidelines and procedures should also be reviewed regularly and maintained so that they are accurate.

Technical Preparation

1. Analysts should have a forensic toolkit for data collection, examination, and analysis. It should contain various tools that provide the ability to collect and examine volatile and non-volatile data and to perform quick reviews of data as well as in-depth analysis. The toolkit should allow its applications to be run quickly and efficiently from removable media (e.g., floppy disk, CD) or a forensic workstation.
2. Organizations should provide adequate storage for network activity-related logs. Organizations should estimate typical and peak log usage, determine how many hours or days' worth of data should be retained based on the organization's policies, and ensure that systems and applications have sufficient storage available. Logs related to computer security incidents might need to be kept for a substantially longer period of time than other logs.

Performing the Forensics Process

1. Organizations should perform forensics using a consistent process. This guide presents a four-phase forensics process, with collection, examination, analysis, and reporting phases. The exact details of the phases may vary based on the need for forensics.

Data Collection

1. Organizations should be proactive in collecting useful data. Configuring auditing on OSs, implementing centralized logging, performing regular system backups, and using security monitoring controls can all generate sources of data for future forensic efforts.
2. Analysts should be aware of the range of possible data sources. Analysts should be able to survey a physical area and recognize possible sources of data. Analysts should also think of possible data sources located elsewhere within an organization and outside the organization. Analysts should be prepared to use alternate data sources if it is not feasible to collect data from a primary source.

3. Analysts should consider all possible application data sources. Application events might be recorded by many different data sources. In addition, applications might be used through multiple mechanisms, such as multiple client programs installed on a system and Web-based client interfaces. In such situations, analysts should identify all application components, decide which are most likely to be of interest, find the location of each component of interest, and acquire the data.

4. Analysts should perform data collection using a standard process. The recommended steps are identifying sources of data, developing a plan to acquire the data, acquiring the data, and verifying the integrity of the data. The plan should prioritize the data sources, establishing the order in which the data should be acquired, based on the likely value of the data, the volatility of the data, and the amount of effort required. Before data collection begins, a decision should be made by the analyst or management regarding the need to collect and preserve evidence in a manner that supports its use in future legal or internal disciplinary proceedings. In such situations, a clearly defined chain of custody should be followed to avoid allegations of mishandling or tampering of evidence.

5. Analysts should act appropriately to preserve volatile OS data. The criteria for determining whether volatile OS data must be preserved should be documented in advance so that analysts can make informed decisions as quickly as possible. To determine whether the effort required to collect volatile OS data are warranted, the risks associated with such collection should be weighed against the potential for recovering important information.

6. Analysts should use a forensic toolkit for collecting volatile OS data. Use of a forensic toolkit enables accurate OS data to be collected while minimizing disturbance to the system and protecting the tools from changes. The analyst should know how each tool is likely to affect or alter the system during collection of data.

7. Analysts should choose the appropriate shutdown method for each system. Each way of shutting down a particular OS can cause different types of data to be preserved or corrupted; analysts should be aware of the typical shutdown behavior of each OS.

8. Analysts should preserve and verify file integrity. Using a write-blocker during backups and imaging prevents a computer from writing to its storage media. The integrity of copied data should be verified by computing and comparing the message digests of files. Backups and images should be accessed as read-only whenever possible; write-blockers can also be used to prevent writes to the backup or image file or restored backup or image.

Examination and Analysis

1. Analysts should use a methodical approach to studying the data. The foundation of forensics is using a methodical approach in analyzing the available data so that analysts can either draw appropriate conclusions based on the available data, or determine that no conclusion can yet be drawn. If evidence might be needed for legal or internal disciplinary actions, analysts should carefully document the findings and the steps that were taken.

2. Analysts should examine copies of files, not the original files. During the collection phase, the analyst should make multiple copies of the desired files or filesystems, typically a master copy and a working copy. The analyst can then work with the working copy of the files without affecting the original files or the master copy. A bit stream image should be performed if evidence may be needed for prosecution or disciplinary actions, or if preserving file times is important.

3. Analysts should consider the fidelity and value of each data source. Analysts should have more confidence in original data sources than in data sources that receive normalized data from other sources. Analysts should validate any unusual or unexpected data that is based on interpreting data, such as IDS and SEM alerts.

4. Analysts should rely on file headers, not file extensions, to identify file content types. Because users can assign any file extension to a file, analysts should not assume that file extensions are accurate. Analysts can identify the type of data stored in many files by examining their file headers. Although people can alter file headers to conceal actual file types, this is much less common than altering file extensions.

5. Analysts should generally focus on the characteristics and impact of the event. Determining the identity of an attacker and other similar actions are typically time-intensive and difficult to accomplish, and do not aid the organization in correcting operational issues or security weaknesses. Establishing the identity and intent of an attacker may be important, especially if a criminal investigation will ensue, but it should be weighed against other important goals.

6. Organizations should be aware of the technical and logistical complexity of analysis. A single event can generate records on many different data sources and produce more information than analysts can feasibly review. Tools such as SEM can assist analysts by bringing information from many data sources together in a single place.

7. Analysts should bring together data from various sources. The analyst should review the results of the examination and analysis of individual data sources, such as data files, OSs, and network traffic, and determine how the information fits together, to perform a detailed analysis of application-related events and event reconstruction.

Reporting

1. Analysts should review their processes and practices. Reviews of current and recent forensic actions can help identify policy shortcomings, procedural errors, and other issues that might need to be remedied, as well as ensuring that the organization stays current with trends in technology and changes in law.

Appendix K

Steganography Tools

Steganography Tool	URL	Description
CameraShy	www.sourceforge.net/ projects/camerashy	This freeware will automatically scan the Internet looking for content on Web sites that has hidden data. It can then download and extract the information.
CryptoBola	www.cryptobola.com/	JPG (JFIF)-based stego. Unique in that the unstegoing extraction process delivers some result with almost any key. Consequently, a brute attack would have to try to extract data with each possible key from an image and the resulted data would have to be analyzed before determining, that the attempt was futile.
Gifshuffle	www.darkside.com.au/ gifshuffle/	This command-line tool helps hide information in .gif files.
Hermetic Stego	www.hermetic.ch/hst/hst.htm	Easy-to-use program which hides data in BMP images. Includes a stego key, which the authors claim makes detecting the presence of the hidden file is undetectable (even by forensic software using statistical methods). Unique to Hermetic Stego is that there is no limit on the size of the file to be hidden because Hermetic Stego can hide a message file, not just in a single BMP image file, but in a set of them—as many images as needed to contain the message file.

Steganography Tool	URL	Description
Hydan	www.crazyboy.com/hydan/	Hides data in executables!
Invisible Secrets	www.invisiblesecrets.com	This Windows-based commercial suite of stego tools offers step-by-step wizards for embedding data in .jpg, .png, .bmp, .html and .wav files.
JSteg	www.stegoarchive.com	This free Windows 95/98/NT program hides information in .jpg files.
Jsteg		Amiga version of the popular command line DOS program to hide files in JPGs.
MP3Stego	www.petitcolas.net/ fabien/steganography/ mp3stego/	MP3Stego is a command-line program that runs in a Windows-DOS box and hides information in MP3 files, which are WAV file sound tracks that are compressed using the MPEG Audio Layer III format. They offer near-CD quality sound at a compression ratio of 11 to 1 (128 kilobits per second). This gives a very good opportunity for information hiding. A GUI for Windows is also available.
Paranoid		Paranoid is primarily an encryption program that allows you to encrypt files with IDEA, triple DES, and an algorithm written by the author Nathan Mariels. It is a steganography program in that it allows you to hide files in sounds. Comes with built-in file wiping function.
Pretty Good Envelope v1.0		Pretty Good Envelope (PGE) is a DOS-based program that hides a message in another file by the very simple method of appending the message to the file, and then appending a 4 byte little endian number which points to the start of the message. A companion program UNPGE retrieves the message. PGE can be used with graphic files (GIF and JPG) or any other binary files, including .COM and .EXE files.
Puff	www.freeonline.it/pr/ pr-902/puff	It hides data in a variety of image formats and supports several different types of encryption. The primary language is Italian, with English help files.

Steganography Tool	URL	Description
Scramdisk	www.scramdisk.clara.net	Scramdisk is a Win 95/98 based disk encryption program that allows the creation and use of virtual encrypted drives. These can be created in a container file on a FAT formatted hard disk, on an empty partition, or stored in the low bits of a WAV audio file (which makes it steganography). It has a slick interface and comes with a number of 'industry standard' encryption algorithms, including Triple-DES, IDEA, MISTY1, Blowfish, TEA, and Square. Also available as French-based exe.
Stealth		Stealth is a simple filter for PGP which strips off all identifying header information to leave only the encrypted data in a format suitable for steganographic use. That is, the data can be hidden in images, audio files, text files, CAD files, or any other file type that may contain random data, then sent to another person who can retrieve the data from the file, attach headers, and PGP decrypt it.
Steganos Security Suite 2006	www.steganos.com	This comprehensive commercial suite of cyrpto and stego tools allow you to hide information and cover your tracks on the system.
Steganosaurus		Text-based stego program
Stego		Stego is a steganography tool that enables you to embed data in Macintosh PICT format files, without changing the appearance or size. Thus, Stego can be used as an "envelope" to hide a previously encrypted data file in a PICT file, making it much less likely to be detected.
StegoVideo	http://compression.ru/video/stego_video/index_en.html	MSU StegoVideo allows you to hide any file in a video sequence. When the program was created, different popular codes were analyzed and an algorithm was chosen which provides small data loss after video compression. You can use MSU StegoVideo as a VirtualDub filter or as standalone .exe program, independent from VirtualDub.

Steganography Tool	*URL*	*Description*
S-Tools		Perhaps the most popular free steganography tool, it features an easy-to-use Windows-based GUI that hides information in .bmp, .gif, and .wav files. It is available from numerous sites.
wbStego4open	http://wbstego.wbailer.com/	Hides data in BMP/TXT/HTML/PDF files.
Wnstorm		Wnstorm (White Noise Storm) is a cryptography and steganography software package which you can use to encrypt and hide files within PCX images.

Appendix L

Forensic Resources— Literature and Selected Readings

Allman, T. Y., E-Discovery in the State Courts: Uniform Rulemaking (or Lack Thereof) and the Ongoing Role of the Sedona Principles. *The Computer & Internet Lawyer*, February 2007, Volume 24, Number 2, pp. 10–13.

Allman, T. Y., Proposed National E-Discovery Standards and the Sedona Principles. *Defense Counsel Journal*, January 2005, Volume 72, Issue 1, pp. 47–55.

Allman, T. Y., The Case for a Preservation Safe Harbor in Requests for E-Discovery. *Defense Counsel Journal*, October 2003, Volume 70, Issue 4, pp. 417–423.

Amendments to the Federal Rules of Civil Procedure. (2006). U.S. Courts: The Federal Judiciary Web Site www.uscourts.gov/rules/Ediscovery_w_Notes.pdf

Andrade, L. and Firestone, W., *Foundations to Computer Forensics and Online Crime Investigations*, Outskirts Press, 2006.

Barkett, J. M., Bytes, Bits and Bucks: Cost Shifting and Sanctions in E-Discovery. *Defense Counsel Journal*, October 2004, Volume 70, Issue 4, pp. 334–356.

Bejtlich, R., The Tao of Network Security Monitoring: Beyond Intrusion Detection, Addison-Wesley, 2004.

Benton, D. and Grindstaff, F., *Practical Guide to Computer Forensics: For Accountants, Forensic Examiners, and Legal Professionals*, BookSurge Publishing, 2006.

Boehning, H. C. and Twiste, E., New Rules for Electronic Discovery. *Risk Management Magazine*, November 2006, Volume 53, Issue 11, p. 58.

Bosch, W., New Discovery Rules Offer Operators Increased Transparency. *Hotel & Motel Management Magazine*, Volume 221, Issue 20, p. 11.

Caloyannides, M., *Computer Forensics and Privacy*, Artech House, 2001.

Carrier, B., *File System Forensic Analysis*, Addison-Wesley, 2005.

Casey, E., *Digital Evidence and Computer Crime*, Academic Press, 2004.

Casey, E., *Handbook of Computer Crime Investigation: Forensic Tools & Technology*, Academic Press, 2001.

Connor, D., New E-Records Rules: Who's Complying? *Network World*, December 4, 2006, Volume 23, Issue 47, p. 16.

Cortese, A. W., Jr., Proposed Amendments to the Federal Civil Rules Strike a Healthy Balance. *Defense Counsel Journal*, October 2005, Volume 72, Issue 4, pp. 354–361.

Curtis, C. E., The E-discovery Awakening. *Securities Industry News*, December 4, 2006, Volume 18, Issue 41, pp. 1, 30.

Davis, Chris, et al., *Hacking Exposed: Computer Forensics Secrets & Solutions*, McGraw-Hill Osborne Media, 2004.

E-Discovery Amendments. Secured Lender, Jan/Feb 2007, Volume 63, Issue 1, p. 100.

E-discovery Amendments to FRCP Approved. (July/August, 2006). *The Information Management Journal*, Volume 40, Issue 4, p. 15.

Edwards, J., Follow the E-Mail Trail. CFO Magazine, January 2007, Volume 23, Issue 1, pp. 25–27.

Farmer, D. and Wietse, V., *Forensic Discovery*, Addison-Wesley, 2004.

Farrell, G., If There Could be a Case, Then Don't Delete That E-Mail. USA Today, December 1, 2006.

Ferguson, N. and Schneier, B., *Practical Cryptography*, John Wiley, 2003.

Garretson, R., A Lifecycle of Its Own. CIO Insight, December 2006, Issue 76, pp. 81–89.

Gassler, F. H., Dealing with Discovery in the Too Much Information Age. *FDCC Defense Quarterly*, Spring 2002, pp. 513–528.

Gibson, S., The Urgent Need for E-Data Management at the Enterprise Level: The Impending implosion of Electronic Stored Information. *The Computer & Internet Lawyer*, August 2006, Volume 23, Number 8, pp. 5–8.

Greenemeier, L., Study Shows IT Security Holds the Key to Compliance. Information Week, December 4, 2006. www.informationweek.com/management/showArticle.jhtml?article ID=196601378&subSection=Compliance

Greenwald, J., Electronic Discovery Rules Revised. Business Insurance, December 18, 2006, Volume 40, Issue 51, pp. 4–6.

Hoglund, G. and Butler, J., *Rootkits: Subverting the Windows Kernel*, Addison-Wesley, 2005.

Honeynet Project. *Know Your Enemy: Learning about Security Threats*, Addison-Wesley, 2004.

Jones, K., et al., *Real Digital Forensics: Computer Security and Incident Response*, Addison-Wesley, 2005.

Kruse, W. and Heiser, J., *Computer Forensics: Incident Response Essentials*, Addison-Wesley, 2001.

Lange, M. C. S., E is for Evidence: Using an Online Repository to Review and Produce Electronic Data. *Journal of Internet Law*, June 2003, Volume 6, Issue 12, pp. 18–21.

Lofton, L., With New Electronic Discovery Rules, Technology Targeted. *Mississippi Business Journal*, January 1, 2007, Volume 29, Issue 1, pp. 19–21.

Lucas, J. and Moeller, B., *The Effective Incident Response Team*, Addison-Wesley, 2004.

McMillan, R., Ready to Produce IMs in Court? CIO Magazine, December 15, 2006, Volume 20, Issue 6, p. 34.

McNamara, J., *Secrets of Computer Espionage: Tactics and Countermeasures*, John Wiley, 2003.

Marcella, A. and Greenfield, R., *Cyber Forensics: A Field Manual for Collecting, Examining, and Preserving Evidence of Computer Crimes*, Auerbach Publishers and CRC Press, 2002.

Marcus, R. L., E-Discovery & Beyond: Toward Brave New World or 1984? *Review of Litigation, Symposium 2006*, Volume 25, Issue 4, pp. 635–689.

Matthews, J., *Computer Networks: Internet Protocols in Action*, John Wiley, 2005.

Mohay, G., et al., Computer and Intrusion Forensics, Artech House Publishers, 2006.

Myler, E., The ABCs of Records Retention Schedule Development. *AIIM E-DOC*, May/June 2006, Volume 20, Issue 3, pp. 52–56.

Nelson, S. and Simek, J., The New Federal Rules of Civil Procedure: An ESI Primer. ABA Law Practice Magazine, December 2006, Volume 32, Number 8, p. www.abanet.org/lpm/magazine/articles/v32/is8/an7.shtml.

Newman, R., *Computer Forensics: Evidence Collection and Management*, Auerbach Publishers, 2007.

Orebaugh, A., Ethereal Packet Sniffing, *Syngress*, 2004.

Oseles, L., Computer Forensics: The Key to Solving the Crime, October 2001. http://faculty.ed.umuc.edu/~meinkej/inss690/oseles_2.pdf.

Phillips, A., Nelson, B., et al., Guide to Computer Forensics and Investigations, Course Technology, 2005.

Preimesberger, C., Saving the Data. eWeek, November 27, 2006, Volume 23, Issue 47, pp. 11–12.

Prosise, Chris, et al., *Incident Response and Computer Forensics*, McGraw-Hill Osborne Media, 2003.

Ramsland, K., The C.S.I. Effect, Berkley Boulevard Books, 2006.

Rhinehart, C., E-mail Management for SOX: More than Meets the Eye. Compliance Pipeline. www.informationweek.com/177103858.

Rice, T. E., Sterchi, T. N., and Boschert, T. M., Proposed Federal Rules of Civil Procedure Amendments Concerning Electronic Discovery: Will They Be Enough? FDCC Quarterly, Winter/2005, Volume 55, Issue 2, pp. 155–174.

Ropple, L. M. and Wolkoff, H. J., Amended Federal Rules of Civil Procedure Focus on E-Discovery, Ropes & Gray LLP, www.ropesgray.com.

Sanders, R. L., Personal Business Records in an Electronic Environment. *The Information Management Journal*, October 1999, Volume 33, Issue 4, pp. 60–63.

Schiffman, M., et al., Hacker's Challenge 2: Test Your Network Security & Forensic Skills, McGraw-Hill Osborne Media, 2002.

Schwartz, E., Regulation Watch: IT's Day in Court. InfoWorld, November 20, 2006, Volume 28, Issue 47, pp. 29–33.

Schweitzer, D., Incident Response: Computer Forensics Toolkit, Wiley, 2003.

Sheetz, M., *Computer Forensics: An Essential Guide for Accountants, Lawyers, and Managers*, John Wiley, 2007.

Shelton, G. D., Don't Let the Terabyte You: New E-Discovery Amendments to the Federal Rules of Civil Procedure. *Defense Counsel Journal*, October 2006, Volume 73, Issue 4, pp. 324–331.

Soat, J., IT Confidential: Supreme Court Says, Show Me the Data. Information Week, November 13, 2006. www.informationweek.com/management/showArticle.jhtml?articleID=193700356&subSection=Compliance

Solnik, C., E-discovery Pushes Limits as Law's Digital Dynamo. Long Island Business News, September 28-October 5, 2006, Volume 53, Issue 41, p. 38.

Solnik, C., In Law, Electronic Information Becomes the Brave New World. Long Island Business News, December 22–28, 2006, Volume 53, Issue 60, p. 4B, 14B.

Solomon, M., Broom, N., and Barrett, D., Computer Forensics JumpStart, Sybex, 2004.

Spira, J., Electronic Content—a Federal Case. KMWorld, January 2007, pp. 1–3.

Steel, C., Windows Forensics: The Field Guide for Corporate Computer Investigations, John Wiley, 2006.

Stephenson, P., *Investigating Computer-Related Crime*, CRC Press, 1999.

Swann, J., E-mail Becomes Fair Game in Federal Court. Community Banker, January 2007, Volume 16, Issue 1, p. 58.

The Sedona Conference Working Group Series. The Sedona Principles: Best Practices Recommendations & Principles for Addressing Electronic Document Production, July 2005, www.thesedonaconference.org/dltForm?did=7_05TSP.pdf.

The Sedona Conference Working Group Series. The Sedona Guidelines: Best Practice Guidelines & Commentary for Managing Information & Records in the Electronic Age. www.thesedonaconference.org/dltForm?did=TSG9_05.pdf.

Vacca, John, Computer Forensics: Computer Crime Scene Investigation, Charles River Media; 2005.

Volonino, L., Anzaldua, R., and Godwin, J., *Computer Forensics: Principles and Practices*, Prentice Hall Security Series, 2006.

Zalewski, M., Silence on the Wire: A Field Guide to Passive Reconnaissance and Indirect Attacks, No Starch, 2005.

Zeidner, R., Employees Don't "Get" Electronic Storage. HR Magazine, January 2007, Volume 52, Issue 1, pp. 28.

These forensic literature resources have been collected from several repositories and are compiled here for the reader who may desire to obtain additional insight into the topic of cyber forensics, beyond the information provided in this text.

Appendix M

Forensic Online Resources

Organizations	URL
Computer Crime and Intellectual Property Section (CCIPS), U.S. Department of Justice	www.cybercrime.gov
Federal Bureau of Investigation (FBI)	www.fbi.gov
Florida Association of Computer Crime Investigators (FACCI)	www.facci.org
High Technology Crime Investigation Association (HTCIA)	www.htcia.org
International Association of Computer Investigative Specialists (IACIS)	www.cops.org
National Law Enforcement and Corrections Technology Center North East (NLECTC-NE)	www.nlectc.org/nlectcne
National White Collar Crime Center (NW3C)	www.nw3c.org
Regional Computer Forensics Laboratory (RCFL)	www.rcfl.gov
SEARCH: National Consortium for Justice Information and Statistics	www.search.org

Technical Resource Sites	URL
Computer Crime Research Center	www.crime-research.org
Computer Forensics Links and Whitepapers	www.forensics.nl/links
Computer Forensics Tool Testing Project	www.cftt.nist.gov
Digital Mountain Technical and Legal Resources	www.digitalmountain.com/technical_resources

Technical Resource Sites	*URL*
The Electronic Evidence Information Center	www.e-evidence.info
Forensic Focus Billboard and Links	www.forensicfocus.com
National Institute of Justice (NIJ) Electronic Crime Program	www.ojp.usdoj.gov/nij/topics/ecrime/ welcome.html
National Software Reference Library (NSRL)	www.nsrl.nist.gov
Wotsit's Format	www.wotsit.org

Training Resource Name	*URL*
CompuForensics	www.compuforensics.com/training.htm
Computer Forensic Services	www.computer-forensic.com/training.html
Computer Forensics Training Center Online	www.cftco.com
Federal Law Enforcement Training Center (FLETC), Computer and Financial Investigations (CFI) Division	www.fletc.gov/cfi/index.htm
Foundstone	www.foundstone.com
IACIS	www.iacis.info/iacisv2/pages/training.php
InfoSec Institute	www.infosecinstitute.com/courses/ computer_forensics_training.html
New Technologies, Inc.	www.forensics-intl.com/training.html
NW3C	www.nw3c.org/ocr/courses_desc.cfm
SANS Institute	www.sans.org

Technical Resource Documents	*URL*
Computer Forensics: Introduction to Incident Response and Investigation of Windows NT/2000, by Norman Haase	www.sans.org/rr/whitepapers/ incident/647.php
Digital Investigation: The International Journal of Digital Forensics and Incident Response	www.compseconline.com/ digitalinvestigation

Technical Resource Documents	URL
Electronic Crime Scene Investigation: A Guide for First Responders	www.ncjrs.gov
Evidence Seizure Methodology for Computer Forensics, by Thomas Rude	www.crazytrain.com/seizure.html
Forensic Analysis of a Live Linux System, by Mariusz Burdach	www.securityfocus.com/infocus/ 1769 (part one) www.securityfocus.com/infocus/ 1773 (part two)
How to Bypass BIOS Passwords	http://labmice.techtarget.com/articles/ BIOS_hack.htm
International Journal of Digital Evidence	www.utica.edu/academic/institutes/ecii/ijde

Resource Name	URL
NIST Interagency Report (IR) 7100, PDA Forensic Tools: An Overview and Analysis	http://csrc.nist.gov/publications/nistir/ index.html
NIST IR 7250, Cell Phone Forensic Tools: An Overview and Analysis	http://csrc.nist.gov/publications/nistir/ index.html
NIST SP 800-31, Intrusion Detection Systems	http://csrc.nist.gov/publications/nistpubs/ index.html
NIST SP 800-44, Guidelines on Securing Public Web Servers	http://csrc.nist.gov/publications/nistpubs/ index.html
NIST SP 800-45, Guidelines on Electronic Mail Security	http://csrc.nist.gov/publications/nistpubs/ index.html
NIST SP 800-61, Computer Security Incident Handling Guide	http://csrc.nist.gov/publications/nistpubs/ index.html
NIST SP 800-72, Guidelines on PDA Forensics	http://csrc.nist.gov/publications/nistpubs/ index.html
NIST SP 800-83, Guide to Malware Incident Prevention and Handling	http://csrc.nist.gov/publications/nistpubs/ index.html
An Overview of Steganography for the Computer Forensic Examiner, by Gary Kessler	www.fbi.gov/hq/lab/fsc/backissu/july 2004/research/2004_03_research01.htm
RFC 3164: The BSD Syslog Protocol	www.ietf.org/rfc/rfc3164.txt
RFC 3227: Guidelines for Evidence Collection and Archiving	www.ietf.org/rfc/rfc3227.txt

Software Type	Web Site Name	URL
Intrusion detection and prevention systems	Honeypots.net	www.honeypots.net/ids/products
Network packet sniffers and protocol analyzers	Packet Storm	http://packetstormsecurity.org/defense/sniff
Network protocol analyzers	Softpedia	www.softpedia.com/get/Network-Tools/Protocol-Analyzers-Sniffers
Various computer and network tools	Foundstone	www.foundstone.com/index.htm?subnav=resources/navigation.htm&subcontent=/resources/freetools.htm
	Forensic and Incident Response Environment (F.I.R.E.)	http://fire.dmzs.com/?section=tools
	Freshmeat	http://freshmeat.net/search/?q=forensic&section=projects
	Helix	www.e-fense.com/helix/
	Open Source Digital Forensics Analysis Tool Categories	www.opensourceforensics.org/tools/categories.html
	Penguin Sleuth Kit	www.linux-forensics.com/forensics/pensleuth.html
	Talisker Security Wizardry Portal	www.networkintrusion.co.uk
	The Sleuth Kit	www.sleuthkit.org/sleuthkit/tools.php
	The Ultimate Collection of Forensic Software (TUCOFS)	www.tucofs.com/tucofs.htm
	Top 75 Security Tools	www.insecure.org/tools.html
	Trinux	http://trinux.sourceforge.net/
Various computer tools	Checksum Tools	http://lists.thedatalist.com/pages/Checksum_Tools.htm
	Computer Forensics Tools, Software, Utilities	http://lists.thedatalist.com/pages/Checksum_Tools.htm
	Funduc Software	www.funduc.com
Various network tools	Common Vulnerabilities and Exposures (CVE)	www.cve.mitre.org/compatible/product.html

The information for Appendix M has been taken from the National Institute of Standards and Technology (www.nist.gov), Special Publication 800-86, Guide to Integrating Forensic Techniques into Incident Response, [www.csrc.nist.gov/publications/nistpubs/800-86/SP800-86.pdf], Karen Kent, Suzanne Chevalier, Tim Grance, and Hung Dang (August 2006).

Appendix N

Locating Forensic Data in Windows Registries

Information	File	Location	Description	When Updated
AOL Instant Messenger				
Away Messages	NTUSER.DAT	\Software\America Online\AOL Instant Messenger™\CurrentVersion\Users\ screen name\IAmGoneList	Shows default and customized Away messages.	Immediately
File Transfers and Sharing	NTUSER.DAT	\Software\America Online\AOL Instant Messenger™\CurrentVersion\Users\ screen name\Xfer	Shows settings for file transfers and sharing.	Immediately
Last User	NTUSER.DAT	\Software\America Online\AOL Instant Messenger™\CurrentVersion\Login— Screen Name	Shows the screen name of the last logged-in user.	At login
Profile Info	NTUSER.DAT	\Software\America Online\AOL Instant Messenger™\CurrentVersion\Users\ screen name\DirEntry	Shows user profile information (optional).	Immediately
Recent Contacts	NTUSER.DAT	Software\America Online\AOL Instant Messenger\CurrentVersion\users\ username\recent IM ScreenNames	Shows a list of recently contacted buddies.	When the application closes
Registered Users	NTUSER.DAT	\Software\America Online\AOL Instant Messenger™\CurrentVersion\Users	Shows registered AIM users on the machine.	At sign-on
Saved Buddy List	NTUSER.DAT	\Software\America Online\AOL Instant Messenger™\CurrentVersion\Users\ username\ConfigTransport	Shows the directory path of a saved Buddy List, a BLT file.	Immediately
ICQ				
ICQ	NTUSER.DAT	\Software\Mirabilis\ICQ*	Lists IM contacts, file transfer information, etc.	Not applicable
ICQ Information	SOFTWARE	\Software\Mirabilis\ICQ\Owner	Stores the User Identification Number (UIN).	At logon

Last User	NTUSER.DAT	\Software\Mirabilis\ICQ\Owners—LastOwner	Shows the last logged-in user.	At login
Nickname	NTUSER.DAT	\Software\Mirabilis\ICQ\Owners\UIN—Name	Nickname of user (optional value).	At login
Registered Users	NTUSER.DAT	\Software\Mirabilis\ICQ\Owners\UIN	UIN folder is named for the user.	At login
Internet Explorer				
IE Auto Logon and Password	NTUSER.DAT	\Software\Microsoft\Protected Storage System Provider\SID\Internet Explorer\Internet Explorer—URL: StringData	Stores IE auto logon IDs and passwords with date and time stamp.	Immediately
IE Search Terms	NTUSER.DAT	\Software\Miscrosoft\Protected Storage System Provider\SID\Internet Explorer\Internet Explorer—q:StringIndex	Stores IE search terms with date and time stamp.	Immediately
IE Settings	NTUSER.DAT	\Software\Microsoft\Internet Explorer\Main	Stores IE settings such as start page, save directory, home page, and download location.	Immediately
IE URL History—Days Saved	NTUSER.DAT	\Software\Microsoft\Windows\CurrentVersion\Internet Settings\URL History—DaysToKeep	The number of days the system stores URLs visited in IE. The default is 20 days.	Immediately
Typed URLs	NTUSER.DAT	\Software\Microsoft\Internet Explorer\Typed URLs	Stores data entered into the URL address bar.	When the application closes
Web Form Data	NTUSER.DAT	\Software\Microsoft\Protected Storage System Provider\SID\Internet Explorer\Internet Explorer—q:StringIndex	Stores form data provided within IE.	Immediately
IE Auto—Complete Passwords	NTUSER.DAT	\Software\Microsoft\Internet Explorer\IntelliForms	Stores Web page auto complete passwords. These are encrypted values.	Immediately

Information	File	Location	Description	When Updated
IE Auto—Complete Web Addresses	NTUSER.DAT	\Software\Microsoft\Protected Storage System Provider	Lists web pages wherein autocomplete was utilized.	Immediately
IE Default Download Directory	NTUSER.DAT	\Software\Microsoft\Internet Explorer	Identifies the default download directory when utilizing Internet Explorer.	Immediately
MSN Messenger				
MSN Messenger	NTUSER.DAT	\Software\Microsoft Messenger Service\ListCache\.NET Messngr Service*	Contains IM groups, contacts, file transfer information, etc. for MSN Messenger.	Most on signoff; however, FTReceive is immediate
File Sharing	NTUSER.DAT	\Software\Microsoft\MSNMessenger\FileSharing—Autoshare	Shows if file sharing is turned on.	Immediately
File Transfers	NTUSER.DAT	\Software\Microsoft\MSNMessenger\—FTReceiveFolder	Shows the location of the Received Files folder.	Immediately
Logging Enabled	NTUSER.DAT	\Software\Microsoft\MSNMessenger\PerPass portSettings\######\—MessageLogging Enabled	Shown if message logging is turned on.	Immediately
Message History	NTUSER.DAT	MSNMessenger\PerPass portSettings\######\—MessageLog Path	Shows the location of message history files.	Immediately
Saved Contact List	NTUSER.DAT	\Software\Microsoft\Messenger Service—ContactListPath	Shows the location of a saved Contact List (CTT) file.	Immediately
Outlook and Outlook Express				
Passwords	NTUSER.DAT	\Software\Microsoft\Protected Storage SystemProvider\SID\Identification\INETCOMM Server Passwords	Stores Outlook and Outlook Express account passwords.	Immediately

Outlook Temporary Attachment Directory	NTUSER.DAT	\Software\Microsoft\Office\version\ Outlook\Security	Identifies the location where attachments are stored when they are opened from Outlook.	Immediately

Window Messenger

Contact List	NTUSER.DAT	\Software\Microsoft\MessengerService\ ListCache\.NET Messenger Service	Contains Contact, Allow, Block, and Reverse entries.	At sign-off
File Transfers	NTUSER.DAT	\Software\Microsoft\Messenger Service—FtReceiveFolder	Shows the location of the Received Files folder.	Immediately
Last User	NTUSER.DAT	\Software\Microsoft\MessengerService\ ListCache\.NET Messenger Service— IdentityName	Screen name of last logged-in user.	At sign-off

YAHOO *Messenger*

Chat Rooms	NTUSER.DAT	\Software\Yahoo\Pager\profiles\ screen name\Chat	Shows information for chat rooms visited or created.	Immediately
File Transfers	NTUSER.DAT	\Software\Yahoo\Pager\File Transfer (global value)	Shows number of transfers in and out.	Immediately
File Transfers	NTUSER.DAT	Software\Yahoo\Pager\profiles\ screen name\FileTransfer (user specific)	Shows settings for file transfers.	Immediately
Identities	NTUSER.DAT	\Software\Yahoo\Pager\profiles\ screen name—All Identities, Selected Identities	Shows alternate user identities.	Unknown
IMVs MRU List	NTUSER.DAT	Software\Yahoo\Pager\profiles\screen name\IMVironments (user-specific value)	Shows usage of IMVironments.	Immediately
IMV Usage	NTUSER.DAT	\Software\Yahoo\Pager\IMVironments (global value)	Shows usage of IMVironments.	Immediately
Last User	NTUSER.DAT	\Software\Yahoo\Pager—Yahoo! User ID	Last logged-in user.	Immediately
Message Archiving	NTUSER.DAT	\Software\Yahoo\Pager\profiles\screen name\Archive	Shows settings for message archiving.	Immediately

Information	File	Location	Description	When Updated
Password	NTUSER.DAT	\Software\Yahoo\Pager—EOptions string	Encrypted password.	Immediately
Recent Contacts	NTUSER.DAT	Software\Yahoo\Pager\profiles\screen name\IMVironments\Recent	Shows recent contacts and which IMV was used.	Immediately
Saved Password	NTUSER.DAT	\Software\Yahoo\Pager—Save Password	Shows if the password is saved.	Immediately
Screen Names	NTUSER.DAT	\Software\Yahoo\Pager\profiles\screen name	Shows registered screen names and identities.	Immediately
Yserver	NTUSER.DAT	\Software\Yahoo\Yserver	Points to a directory location for file transfer information.	Not applicable
System Information				
Computer Name	SYSTEM	\ControlSet###\Control\ComputerName\ComputerName	Identifies the computer's name defined in System Properties.	Not applicable
Current Control Set	SYSTEM	\Select	Identifies which control set is current.	Not applicable
Current Control Set	SYSTEM	\SelectCurrent	Contains information about the system's configuration settings.	Not applicable
Dynamic Disk	SYSTEM	\ControlSetXXX\Services\DMIO\Boot Info\Primary Disk Group	Identifies the most recent dynamic disk mounted in the system.	Not applicable
Event Logs	SYSTEM	\ControlSetXXX\Services\Eventlog	Identifies the location of Event logs.	Not applicable
Install Date	SOFTWARE	\Microsoft\Windows NT\CurrentVersion	Lists the date the operating system was installed.	Not applicable
Last User Logged In	SOFTWARE	\Microsoft\Windows NT\CurrentVersion\Winlogon	Lists the last user that logged in to the system. This can be local or domain account.	Not applicable

Logon Banner Message	SOFTWARE	\Microsoft\Windows\CurrentVersion\Policies\System\LegalNoticeText	Contains the banner that appear at boot time. Users must click through the logon banner to logon to a system.	Not applicable
Logon Banner Message	SOFTWARE	\Microsoft\Windows\CurrentVersion\Policies\System\LegalNoticeText	Contains user-defined data.	Not applicable
Logon Banner Title	SOFTWARE	\Microsoft\Windows\CurrentVersion\Policies\System\LegalNotice Caption	Contains user-defined data.	Not applicable
Logon Info—Default User and Domain Name	SOFTWARE	\Microsoft\Windows NT\CurrentVersion\Winlogon	Identifies the default user and the associated domain name.	Not applicable
Logon Info—Legal Notices on Bootup	SOFTWARE	\Microsoft\Windows NT\CurrentVersion\Winlogon	Contains legal notices that appear at boot time. Users must click through the logon banner to logon to a system.	Not applicable
Mounted Devices	SYSTEM	\MountedDevices	Lists current and prior mounted devices that use a drive letter.	Immediately
O\S Version	SOFTWARE	\Microsoft\Windows NT\CurrentVersion	Identifies the currently installed OS version and Service Pack release.	Not applicable
Pagefile	SYSTEM	\ControlSetXXX\Control\Session Manager\Memory Management	Contains the page file settings such as location, size, set to wipe, etc.	View updates immediately; however, not effective until reboot
PDA Information	SYSTEM	\ControlSet###\Enum\ USB	Contains PDA information.	Not applicable
Product ID	SOFTWARE	\Microsoft\Windows NT\CurrentVersion	Lists the Windows OS product key.	Not applicable

Information	File	Location	Description	When Updated
Product Name	SOFTWARE	\Microsoft\Windows NT\CurrentVersion	Lists the name of the operating system.	Not applicable
Registered Organization	SOFTWARE	\Microsoft\Windows NT\CurrentVersion	Identifies the registered organization entered during installation. Note this information may be modified after installation.	Not applicable
Registered Owner	SOFTWARE	\Microsoft\Windows NT\CurrentVersion	Identifies the registered owner entered during installation. Note this information may be modified after installation.	Not applicable
Restricted Access to Removable Media	SOFTWARE	\Microsoft\WindowsNT\CurrentVersion\Winlogon	Lists allocated CD-ROMS and floppies that are set to 0 (restricted).	Not applicable
Run	SOFTWARE	\Microsoft\Windows\CurrentVersion\Run	Lists programs that run automatically when the system boots.	Not applicable
Shutdown Time	SYSTEM	\ControlSetXXX\Control\Windows	Lists the system shutdown time.	Not applicable
Time Zone	SYSTEM	\ControlSet001(or002)\Control\TimeZoneInformation\StandardName	Identifies the time zone entered during installation. Note this information may be modified after installation.	Immediately
USB Devices	SYSTEM	\Enum\USBSTOR	Lists the system's USB devices.	Immediately
Networking				
Local Groups	SAM	\Domains\Builtin\Aliases\Names	Lists local account security identifiers.	Not applicable

Local Users	SAM	\Domains\Account\Users\Names	Lists local account security identifiers.	Not applicable
Map Network Drive MRU	NTUSER.DAT	\Software\Microsoft\Windows\CurrentVersion\Explorer\Map Network Drive MRU	Contains a most recently used list of mapped network drives.	Not applicable
Printers—Currently Defined	SYSTEM	\ControlSet###\Control\Print\Printers	Lists all printers that are configured on the current system.	Immediately
Printer—Default	NTUSER.DAT	\Software\Microsoft\WindowsNT\CurrentVersion\Windows	Identifies the current default printer.	Immediately
	NTUSER.DAT	\printers	Identifies the current default printer.	On shutdown
Printer Information	SYSTEM	\ControlSet###\Control\Print\Environments\WindowsNTx86\Drivers\Version…	Contains information about the current printer.	Immediately
Profile List	SOFTWARE	\Microsoft\Windows NT\CurrentVersion\ProfileList	Contains the user security identifier for users with a profile on the system.	Not applicable
TCPIP Data	SYSTEM	\ControlSetXXX\Services\TCPIP\Parameters	Lists the current system's domain and hostname data.	Not applicable
TCPIP Settings of a Network Adapter	SYSTEM	\ControlSetXXX\Services\adapter\Parameters\TCPIP	Lists the current system's IP address and gateway information.	Immediately
User Data				
EFS	NTUSER.DAT	Software\Microsoft\WindowsNT\CurrentVersion\EFS\CurrentKeys	Lists the current user's certificate thumbprint. (Each user has a unique certificate thumbprint.) The same certificate thumbprint is contained in the $EFS alternate data stream for every EFS file encrypted by the current user.	Not applicable

Information	*File*	*Location*	*Description*	*When Updated*
Event Log Restrictions	SYSTEM	\ControlSet###\Services\EventLog\ Application	Identifies who can read your event logs. A value of 1 restricts access; 0 permits access for guest and mull users.	Not applicable
	SECURITY	\ControlSet###\Services\EventLog\ Application	Identifies who can read your event logs. A value of 1 restricts access; 0 permits access for guest and mull users.	Not applicable
File Extensions\ Program Association	NTUSER.DAT	\Software\Microsoft\Windows\ CurrentVersion\Explorer\FileExts	Identifies associated programs with file extensions.	Immediately
Last Logon Time	SAM	\SAM\Domains\Account\Users\F Key	Bytes 9–16 store the last logon time.	Not applicable
Last Time Password Changed	SAM	\SAM\Domains\Account\Users\F Key	Bytes 25–32 store the last time the password was changed.	Not applicable
Account Expiration	SAM	\SAM\Domains\Account\Users\F Key	Bytes 33–40 store the account expiration. If no expiration is set, FF FF FF FF will show.	Not applicable
Last Failed Login	SAM	\SAM\Domains\Account\Users\F Key	Bytes 41–48 store the last unsuccessful logon.	Not applicable
MRU — Last Visited	NTUSER.DAT	\Software\Microsoft\Windows\ CurrentVersion\Explorer\ComDlg 32\	Lists the application and filename of the most recent files opened in Windows.	Immediately
MRU — Open Saved	NTUSER.DAT	\Software\Microsoft\Windows\ CurrentVersion\Explorer\ComDlg32\ OpenSaveMRU	Lists the filename and path of the most recent files saved or copied to a specific location in Windows.	Immediately

Name	File	Registry Path	Description	Timing
MRU—Recent Documents	NTUSER.DAT	\Software\Microsoft\Windows\CurrentVersion\Explorer\RecentDocs\	Identifies the documents in the Recent Documents list available from the Windows Start menu.	Immediately
MRU—Run MRU	NTUSER.DAT	\Software\Microsoft\Windows\CurrentVersion\Explorer\RunMR U	Lists the most recent commands entered in the Windows Run box.	Immediately
POP3 Passwords	NTUSER.DAT	\Software\Microsoft\Internet Account Manager \Accounts\0000000#	Stores the user's POP3 passwords. # is a digit identifying that particular account.	Immediately
Run	NTUSER.DAT	\Software\Microsoft\Windows\CurrentVersion\Run	Lists programs that run automatically when the user logs on.	Not applicable
Screen Savers and Wallpaper	NTUSER.DAT	\Control Panel\Desktop\	Identifies the system's screen saver and wallpaper.	Immediately
Theme—Current Theme	NTUSER.DAT	\Software\Microsoft\Windows\CurrentVersion\Themes	Identifies the desktop theme and wallpaper.	Unknown
Theme—Last Theme	NTUSER.DAT	\Software\Microsoft\Windows\CurrentVersion\Themes\Last Theme	Identifies the desktop theme and wallpaper.	Immediately
Converted Wallpaper	NTUSER.DAT	\Control Panel\Desktop	Identifies converted graphic to wallpaper.	Immediately
Converted Wallpaper	NTUSER.DAT	\Control Panel\Desktop	Identifies date and time of converted wallpaper.	Immediately
User Name and SID	SAM	\SAM\Domains\Account\Users\VKey	Contains the user name and SID in Hex. You must convert the last three hex numbers to decimal to determine the decimal version the SID that is used of in the Recycler and System Volume Information folder.	Not applicable

Information	File	Location	Description	When Updated
	SOFTWARE	\Microsoft\WindowsNT\CurrentVersion\ProfileList\	Contains the user name and SID in Hex. You must convert the last three hex numbers to decimal to determine the decimal version of the SID that is used in the Recycler and System Volume Information folder.	Not applicable
User Application Data				
Adobe	NTUSER.DAT	\Software\Adobe*	Lists Adobe products such as Acrobat and FrameMaker.	
AIM	NTUSER.DAT	\Software\America Online\AOL InstantMessenger\CurrentVersion\Users\username	Lists IM contacts, file transfer information, etc.	Immediately
Google Client History	NTUSER.DAT	\Software\Google\NavClient\1.1\History	Contains a list of search terms with date and time stamps if Google is included in the Internet Explorer task bar.	Immediately
Individual Application Information	NTUSER.DAT	\Software\%Application Name%	This class of registry keys contains the information each application stores in the registry.	Not applicable
Kazaa	NTUSER.DAT	\Software\Kazaa*	Stores configuration, search, download, IM data, etc. for Kazaa.	Not applicable
Media Player Recent List	NTUSER.DAT	\Software\Microsoft\MediaPlayer\Player\RecentFileList	Contains the user's most recently used list for Windows Media Player.	Immediately

Startup Software	NTUSER.DAT	\Software\Microsoft\Windows\CurrentVersion\Run	Stores the applications automatically launched at boot time. This key is a good place to look for Trojans.	Not applicable
	NTUSER.DAT	\Software\Microsoft\Windows\CurrentVersion\RunOnce	Stores the applications automatically launched at boot time. This key is a good place to look for Trojans.	Not applicable
	SOFTWARE	\Microsoft\Windows\CurrentVersion\Run	Stores the applications automatically launched at boot time. This key is a good place to look for Trojans.	Not applicable
	SOFTWARE	\Microsoft\Windows\CurrentVersion\RunOnce	Stores the applications automatically launched.	Not applicable
			launched at boot time. This key is a good place to look for Trojans.	
WinZip Information	NTUSER.DAT	\Software\Nico Mak Computing\FileMenu	Stores the list of files extracted from WinZip archives.	Immediately
	SOFTWARE	\Nico Mak Computing	Contains WinZip information.	
Word—Recent Docs	NTUSER.DAT	\Software\Microsoft\office\version\Common\Open Find\Microsoft Office\Word\Settings\Save As\File Name MRU	Microsoft Word recent documents in the "value" value.	Unknown
Word—User Info	NTUSER.DAT	\Software\Microsoft\office\version\Common\UserInfo	Identifies the user information entered when installing Microsoft Office. Note this information may be modified after installation.	Unknown

Information	File	Location	Description	When Updated
Access—Recent Databases	NTUSER.DAT	\Software\Microsoft\office\version\ Common\Open Find\Microsoft Office Access\Settings\File New Database\File Name MRU	Microsoft Access recent databases in the "value" value.	Immediately
Excel—Recent Spreadsheets	NTUSER.DAT	\Software\Microsoft\office\version\ Common\Open Find\Microsoft Office Excel\Settings\Save As\File Name MRU	Microsoft Excel recent spreadsheets in the "value" value.	Immediately
Outlook—Recent Attachments	NTUSER.DAT	\Software\Microsoft\office\version\ Common\Open Find\Microsoft	Microsoft Outlook recent documents.	Immediately
		Office Outlook\Settings\Save Attachment\File Name MRU		
PowerPoint—Recent PPT's	NTUSER.DAT	\Software\Microsoft\office\version\ Common\Open Find\Microsoft Office PowerPoint\Settings\Save As\File Name MRU	Microsoft PowerPoint recent documents.	Unknown

Publisher—Recent Documents	NTUSER.DAT	\Software\Microsoft\office\version\ Common\Open Find\Microsoft Office Publisher\Settings\Save As\File Name MRU	Microsoft Publisher recent documents.	Unknown
Yahoo	NTUSER.DAT	\Software\Yahoo\Pager\Profiles*	Stores IM contacts, file transfer information, etc. for Yahoo.	Not applicable
File Extension Associations	NTUSER.DAT	\Software\Microsoft\Windows\ CurrentVersion\Explorer\FileExts\.EXT Type	Lists file extension associations and files that have been opened with the Open With command.	Immediately
User Assist	NTUSER.DAT	\Software\Microsoft\Windows\ CurrentVersion\ Explorer\UserAssist	Windows history logged with path and time stamp information.	Not applicable
ShellBags	NTUSER.DAT	\Software\Microsoft\Windows\Shell\ BagMRU	Pointers to link history and other file/folder information.	Not applicable

Registry Quick Find Chart (2005), AccessData Corporation. www.accessdata.com/media/en_US/print/papers/wp.Registry_Quick_Find_ Chart.en_us.pdf, All Rights Reserved, retrieved March 2007, used with permission.

Appendix O

Sedona Principles for Electronic Document Production

1. Electronic data and documents are potentially discoverable under Fed. R. Civ. P. 34 or its state law equivalents. Organizations must properly preserve electronic data and documents that can reasonably be anticipated to be relevant to litigation.
2. When balancing the cost, burden, and need for electronic data and documents, courts and parties should apply the balancing standard embodied in Fed. R. Civ. P. 26(b)(2) and its state law equivalents, which require considering the technological feasibility and realistic costs of preserving, retrieving, producing, and reviewing electronic data, as well as the nature of the litigation and the amount in controversy.
3. Parties should confer early in discovery regarding the preservation and production of electronic data and documents when these matters are at issue in the litigation, and seek to agree on the scope of each party's rights and responsibilities.
4. Discovery requests should make as clear as possible what electronic documents and data are being asked for, while responses and objections to discovery should disclose the scope and limits of what is being produced.
5. The obligation to preserve electronic data and documents requires reasonable and good faith efforts to retain information that may be relevant to pending or threatened litigation. However, it is unreasonable to expect parties to take every conceivable step to preserve all potentially relevant data.
6. Responding parties are best situated to evaluate the procedures, methodologies, and technologies appropriate for preserving and producing their own electronic data and documents.
7. The requesting party has the burden on a motion to compel to show that the responding party's steps to preserve and produce relevant electronic data and documents were inadequate.
8. The primary source of electronic data and documents for production should be active data and information purposely stored in a manner that anticipates future business use and permits efficient searching and retrieval. Resort to disaster recovery backup tapes and other

sources of data and documents requires the requesting party to demonstrate need and relevance that outweigh the cost, burden, and disruption of retrieving and processing the data from such sources.

9. Absent a showing of special need and relevance a responding party should not be required to preserve, review, or produce deleted, shadowed, fragmented, or residual data or documents.

10. A responding party should follow reasonable procedures to protect privileges and objections to production of electronic data and documents.

11. A responding party may satisfy its good faith obligation to preserve and produce potentially responsive electronic data and documents by using electronic tools and processes, such as data sampling, searching, or the use of selection criteria, to identify data most likely to contain responsive information.

12. Unless it is material to resolving the dispute, there is no obligation to preserve and produce metadata absent agreement of the parties or order of the court.

13. Absent a specific objection, agreement of the parties or order of the court, the reasonable costs of retrieving and reviewing electronic information for production should be borne by the responding party, unless the information sought is not reasonably available to the responding party in the ordinary course of business. If the data or formatting of the information sought is not reasonably available to the responding party in the ordinary course of business, then, absent special circumstances, the costs of retrieving and reviewing such electronic information should be shifted to the requesting party.

14. Sanctions, including spoliation findings, should only be considered by the court if, upon a showing of a clear duty to preserve, the court finds that there was an intentional or reckless failure to preserve and produce relevant electronic data and that there is a reasonable probability that the loss of the evidence has materially prejudiced the adverse party.

The following principles were taken directly from The Sedona Principles: Best Practices Recommendations and Principles for Addressing Electronic Document Production (July, 2005, pp. 12–13), used with permission.

Appendix P

Recap of Federal Rules of Civil Procedure Involving E-Discovery Amendments

Rule 1

"Rule 1 provides that the Federal Rules be administered to secure the just, speedy, and inexpensive determination of every action."

Rule 16(b)

"Counsel should also be prepared to discuss electronic discovery issues during the Rule 16(b) pretrial conference with the court, whether required by local rule or not."

"[T]he scheduling order entered under this rule may now include provisions for disclosure or discovery of electronically stored information and may now include any agreements the parties reach for asserting claims of privilege or protection as trial-preparation material after production."

Rule 26

"Rule 26 requires that any requested discovery be relevant."

Under Rule 26(a)(1)(B), the rule would be amended "to add that a party must, without awaiting a discovery request, provide to other parties a copy of, or description by category and location of, electronically stored information."

Rule 26(a)(2)(B)

"The obligation to preserve and produce electronic data may apply to exert witness testimony. The 1993 amendments to Rule 26(a)(2)(B) require the disclosure of all information considered by the [expert] in forming the [expert's] opinion."

Rule 26(b)

"Rule 26(b) allows a court to weigh the potential relevance of requested documents against the burden on the party that would have to produce the documents."
"Among the factors that must be addressed in electronic discovery are:

a) Large volumes of data,
b) Data being stored in multiple repositories,
c) Complex internal structures of collections of data and the relationships of one document to another,
d) Data in different formats and coding schemes that may need to be converted into text to be understood by humans, and
e) Frequent changes in information technology."

It should also be noted that "[t]he ordinary and predictable costs of discovery are fairly borne by the producing party." However, Rule 26(b) empowers courts to shift costs where the demand is unduly burdensome because of the nature of the effort involved to comply.

Rule 26(b)(2)(B)

"The amendment to this rule [provides] that a party need not provide discovery of electronically stored information form sources that the party identifies as not reasonably accessible because of undue burden or cost. On both a motion to compel discovery or for a protective order, the burden would be on the responding party to show that the information is not reasonably accessible because of undue burden or cost. Even if that showing is made, the court may nonetheless order discovery from that party if the requesting party shows good cause."

Rule 26(b)(2)(i)

Rule 26(b)(2)(i) provides that discovery may be limited if "the discovery sought is unreasonably cumulative or duplicative, or is obtainable from some other source that is more convenient, less burdensome, or less expensive."

Rule 26(b)(2)(iii)

"Rule 26(b)(2)(iii) provides for limiting discovery when the burden or expense of the proposed discovery outweighs its likely benefit, taking into account the needs of the case, the amount in controversy, the parties resources, the importance of the issues at stake in the litigation, and the importance of the proposed discovery in resolving the issues."

Rule 26(b)(5)

"[W]hen a party withholds information otherwise discoverable under these rules by claiming that it is privileged or subject to protection as trial preparation material, the party shall make the claim expressly and shall describe the nature of the documents, communications, or things not produced or disclosed in a manner that, without revealing information itself privileged or protected, will enable other parties to assess the applicability of the privilege or protection. … The rule does not attempt to define for each case what information must be provided when a party asserts a claim of privilege or work product protection. Details concerning time, persons, general subject matter, etc., may be appropriate if only a few items are withheld, but may be unduly burdensome when voluminous documents are claimed to be privileged or protected, particularly if the items can be described by categories."

Rule 26(c)

"Allows a court to enter a protective order against burdensome discovery." "These broad powers enable a court to limit discovery of electronic documents or condition their production on cost-shifting if the court concludes that the burden of discovery outweighs its ultimate benefit."

Rule 26(f)

"Requires parties to confer early in litigation to attempt to develop a discovery plan." Rule 26(f)(3) & (4) requires that "when the parties confer pursuant to this rule they discuss any issues relating to preserving discoverable information and any issues related to disclosure or discovery of electronically stored information. This would include the form or forms in which electronically stored information should be produced, and any issues relating to claims of privilege or protection as trial-preparation material. If the parties agree on a procedure to assert such claims after production, the parties should discuss whether to ask the court to include this agreement in an order."

Rule 33(d)

"This rule would … provide that where the answer to an interrogatory may be derived form electronically stored information, and the burden of deriving the answer is substantially the same for the responding party and the requesting party, it is a sufficient answer to the interrogatory to specify the records form which the answer may be derived or ascertained. The responding party would be required to allow the requesting party reasonable opportunity to examine, audit of inspect such records and make copies, compilations, abstracts or summaries."

It should also be noted that under this rule, "wholesale dumping of documents is not allowed."

Rule 34

"Permits the service by one party upon another of a request for documents of any type."

Rule 34(a) & (b)

"The inclusive description of documents is revised to accord with changing technology. It makes clear that Rule 34 applies to electronics [sic] data compilations from which information can be obtained only with the use of detection devices." The rule also provides that "the request may specify the form or forms in which electronically stored information is to be produced. The producing party may object to the requested form or forms for producing electronically stored information stating the reason for the objection. If an objection is made to the form or forms for producing electronically stored information—or no form was made in the request—the responding party would be required to state the form or forms it intends to use. If a request does not specify the form or forms for producing electronically stored information, a responding party must produce the information in a form or forms in which it is ordinarily maintained or in a form or forms that are reasonably usable."

Rule 37

Sets forth guidelines for resolving discovery disputes … A party that receives a request for production of electronic documents may object to some or all of the request. If such objections are filed and the requesting party opts not to accept the objections, the requesting party must file a motion to compel pursuant to Rule 37.

Rule 37(f)

"Absent exceptional circumstances, a court may not impose sanctions under the rules on a party for failing to provide electronically stored information lost as a result of the routine, good faith operation of an electronic information system."

Rule 45

"The 1991 amendment to Rule 45 … requires persons issuing subpoenas to take reasonable steps to avoid imposing undue burdens or expense on the requested part, and, if objection is made, any order to compel production shall protect [the requested party] from significant expense."

Rule 45(c)(1)

"Under a 1991 amendment … Rule 45(c)(1) requires a party or attorney responsible for the issuance of a subpoena to take reasonable steps to avoid imposing undue burden or expense on a person subject to the subpoena."

Rule 45(c)(2)(B)

"Provides that, if objection is made to a subpoena, an order to compel production shall protect any person who is not a party or an officer of a party from significant expense resulting from the inspection and copying commanded."

Rule 53(a)(1)(C)

"Use of special masters and court appointed experts to preserve privilege" … "One immediate benefit of using such a court appointed 'neutral' third party is the probable elimination of privilege waiver concerns with respect to the review of information by that person. In addition, the 'neutral' may be able to speed the resolution of disputes by fashioning fair and reasonable discovery plans based upon specialized knowledge of electronic discovery or technical issues with access to specific facts of the case."

Material for this Appendix was extrapolated and synthesized from the following sources:

Court Rules. (2006). LexisNexis Applied Discovery: Court Rules. Retrieved February 11, 2007, from: www.lexisnexis.com/applieddiscovery/lawLibrary/courtRules.asp

Gassler, F. H. (Spring, 2002). "Dealing with Discovery in the Too Much Information Age." FDCC Defense Quarterly, Spring/2002, pp. 513–528. Retrieved January 25, 2007, from EBSCOHost database.

The Sedona Conference Working Group Series. (July, 2005). "The Sedona Principles: Best Practices Recommendations and Principles for Addressing Electronic Document Production," July 2005 Version [pages 1, 2, 17, 19, 20, 21, 34, 40, 49, 51]. Retrieved February 10, 2007, from www.thesedonaconference.org/dltForm?did=7_05TSP.pdf, used with permission.

Appendix Q

Selected Acronyms

ADS	Alternate Data Stream
ARIN	American Registry for Internet Numbers
ARP	Address Resolution Protocol
ASCII	American Standard Code for Information Interchange
ATA	Advanced Technology Attachment
BIOS	Basic Input/Output System
CCIPS	Computer Crime and Intellectual Property Section
CD	Compact Disc
CD-R	CD-Recordable
CD-ROM	CD-Read Only Memory
CD-RW	CD-Rewritable
CDFS	CD File System
CFI	Computer and Financial Investigations
CFRDC	Computer Forensics Research and Development Center
CFTT	Computer Forensics Tool Testing
CMOS	Complementary Metal Oxide Semiconductor
CVE	Common Vulnerabilities and Exposures
DDoS	Distributed Denial of Service
DHCP	Dynamic Host Configuration Protocol
DLL	Dynamic Link Library
DNS	Domain Name System
DoD	Department of Defense
DVD	Digital Video Disc or Digital Versatile Disc
DVD-R	DVD-Recordable
DVD-ROM	DVD-Read Only Memory
DVD-RW	DVD-Rewritable
ESP	Encapsulating Security Payload
ext2fs	Second Extended Filesystem
ext3fs	Third Extended Filesystem
FAT	File Allocation Table

FBI	Federal Bureau of Investigation
FIPS	Federal Information Processing Standards
F.I.R.E.	Forensic and Incident Response Environment
FISMA	Federal Information Security Management Act
FTP	File Transfer Protocol
GB	Gigabyte
GUI	Graphical User Interface
HFS	Hierarchical File System
HPA	Host Protected Area
HPFS	High-Performance File System
HTCIA	High Technology Crime Investigation Association
HTTP	Hypertext Transfer Protocol
IACIS	International Association of Computer Investigative Specialists
ICMP	Internet Control Message Protocol
ID	Identification
IDE	Integrated Drive Electronics
IDS	Intrusion Detection System
IGMP	Internet Group Management Protocol
IM	Instant Messaging
IMAP	Internet Message Access Protocol
IOS	Internetwork Operating System
IP	Internet Protocol
IPsec	Internet Protocol Security
IR	Interagency Report
IRC	Internet Relay Chat
IRQ	Interrupt Request Line
ISO	International Organization for Standardization
ISP	Internet Service Provider
IT	Information Technology
ITL	Information Technology Laboratory
JPEG	Joint Photographic Experts Group
KB	Kilobyte
MAC	Media Access Control
MAC	Modification, Access, and Creation
MB	Megabyte
MD	Message Digest
MMC	Multimedia Card
MO	Magneto Optical
MS-DOS	Microsoft Disk Operating System
NAT	Network Address Translation
NFAT	Network Forensic Analysis Tool
NFS	Network File Sharing
NIC	Network Interface Card
NIJ	National Institute of Justice
NIST	National Institute of Standards and Technology
NSRL	National Software Reference Library
NTFS	Windows NT File System

NTP	Network Time Protocol
NW3C	National White Collar Crime Center
OEM	Original Equipment Manufacturer
OMB	Office of Management and Budget
OS	Operating System
OSR2	OEM Service Release 2
PCMCIA	Personal Computer Memory Card International Association
PDA	Personal Digital Assistant
POP3	Post Office Protocol 3
RAID	Redundant Arrays of Inexpensive Disks
RAM	Random Access Memory
RCFL	Regional Computer Forensics Laboratory
RFC	Request for Comment
SAM	Security Account Manager
SCSI	Small Computer System Interface
SD	Secure Digital
SDMI	Secure Digital Music Initiative
SEM	Security Event Management
SFTP	Secure FTP
SHA-1	Secure Hash Algorithm 1
SIP	Session Initiation Protocol
SMB	Server Message Block
SMTP	Simple Mail Transfer Protocol
SNMP	Simple Network Management Protocol
SP	Special Publication
SSH	Secure Shell
SSL	Secure Sockets Layer
TB	Terabytes
TCP	Transmission Control Protocol
TCP/IP	Transmission Control Protocol/Internet Protocol
UDF	Universal Disk Format
UDP	User Datagram Protocol
UFS	UNIX File System
UPS	Uninterruptible Power Supply
URL	Uniform Resource Locator
USB	Universal Serial Bus
VoIP	Voice Over IP
VPN	Virtual Private Network

These acronyms have been taken from the National Institute of Standards and Technology (www.nist.gov), Special Publication 800-86, Guide to Integrating Forensic Techniques into Incident Response, [www.csrc.nist.gov/publications/nistpubs/800-86/SP800-86.pdf], Karen Kent, Suzanne Chevalier, Tim Grance, and Hung Dang (August 2006).

Appendix R

Generic Cellular Telephone Search Warrants

SEARCH WARRANT

THE STATE OF _____

COUNTY OF _____

To any Peace Officer of the State of _____, GREETINGS:

WHEREAS, the Affiant whose name appears on the affidavit is a Peace Officer under the laws of _____ and did heretofore this day subscribe and swear to said Affidavit before me and whereas I find that the verified facts stated by Affiant in said Affidavit show that Affiant has probable cause for the belief expressed therein and establish the existence of proper grounds for issuance of this Warrant.

Now, therefore, you are commanded to search the property described as:

1. (Brand of Phone) cellular telephone bearing serial number XXXXXXXXX.

You are further commanded to seize and bring before me the property described below.

1. Any media or software which can collect, analyze, create, display, convert, store, conceal, or transmit electronic, magnetic, optical, or computer impulses or data contained within said (Brand of Phone) cellular phone (S/N XXXXXXXXX) or any of its component parts.
2. Any records, files or fields of stored data contained within said (Brand of Phone) cellular phone (S/N XXXXXXXXX) or any of its component parts.
3. Any transmission and termination of communications data contained within said (Brand of Phone) cellular phone (S/N XXXXXXXXX) or any of its component parts.

To facilitate this search you are AUTHORIZED to seize all computer hardware, software, to include cellular telephones, which can collect, analyze, create, display, convert, store, conceal, or transmit electronic, magnetic, optical, or similar computer impulses or data. You are further AUTHORIZED to remove such electromagnetic media from the premises described above and conduct a detailed forensic analysis and search of the media in a sterile laboratory environment.

Further, you are ORDERED, pursuant to the provisions of Article 18.10, _____ Code of Criminal Procedure, to retain custody of any property seized pursuant to this Warrant, until further order of this Court or any other court of appropriate jurisdiction shall otherwise direct the manner of safekeeping of said property. This Court grants you leave and authority to remove such seized property from this county, if and only if such removal is necessary for the safekeeping of such seized property by you, or if the provisions of Article <applicable reference here>. Otherwise authorize such removal. You are further ORDERED to give notice to this Court, as a part of the inventory to be filed subsequent to the execution of this Warrant, and as required by Article <applicable reference here>, of the place where the property seized hereunder is kept, stored and held.

HEREIN FAIL NOT, but have you then and there this Warrant within three days, exclusive of the day of its issuance and exclusive of the day of its execution, with your return thereon, showing how you executed the same, file in this court.

ISSUED THIS THE _____ DAY OF _____, A.D., 2007, AT _____O'CLOCK _____.M. TO CERTIFY WHICH WITNESS MY HAND THIS DAY.

MAGISTRATE

SEARCH WARRANT RETURN

THE STATE OF _____

COUNTY OF _____

Each of the undersigned Affiants, being a Peace Officer under the laws of _____ and being duly sworn, on oath certified that the foregoing Warrant came to hand on the day it was issued and that it was executed on the _____ day of _____, A.D., 2007, by making the search directed therein and by seizing during such search the following described property, retained by such Peace Officer, and kept, stored and held as hereinafter set out:

1. (Brand of Phone) Cellular Telephone (S/N XXXXXXXXX). This item was relinquished to the U.S. Secret Service Hi-Tech Crimes Taskforce for forensic analysis.

_____

AFFIANT

SUBSCRIBED AND SWORN TO BEFORE ME by each of said Affiants whose name

is signed above on this the _____ day of _____, 2007.

MAGISTRATE   _____

SEARCH WARRANT AFFIDAVIT

THE STATE OF _____

COUNTY OF _____

THE UNDERSIGNED AFFIANT, BEING A PEACE OFFICER UNDER THE LAWS OF _____ AND BEING DULY SWORN, ON OATH MAKES THE FOLLOWING STATEMENTS AND ACCUSATIONS.

1. THERE IS IN _____ COUNTY, _____, AN OBJECT DESCRIBED AND LOCATED AS FOLLOWS:

An (Brand of Phone) cellular telephone bearing the serial number XXXXXXXXX, now in the custody of the Police Agency in <applicable County reference here>, _____.

2. IT IS THE BELIEF OF AFFIANT THAT AT THE CELLULAR TELEPHONE DESCRIBED ABOVE CONTAINS CRIMINAL EVIDENCE WITHIN ITS ELECTRONIC DATA STORAGE DEVICE(S) AS FOLLOWS:
    1. Any media or software which can collect, analyze, create, display, convert, store, conceal, or transmit electronic, magnetic, optical, or computer impulses or data contained within said (Brand of Phone) cellular phone (S/N XXXXXXXXX) or any of its component parts.
    2. Any records, files or fields of stored data contained within said (Brand of Phone) cellular phone (S/N XXXXXXXXX) or any of its component parts
    3. Any transmission and termination of communication data contained within said (Brand of Phone) cellular phone (S/N XXXXXXXXX) or any of its component parts.

3. AFFIANT HAS PROBABLE CAUSE FOR THE SAID BELIEF BY REASON OF THE FOLLOWING FACTS, TO WIT:
    1. Investigator Name, Badge Number, is a certified and licensed _____ Peace Officer with (X) years of law enforcement experience. Investigator Name. # Badge Number is currently assigned to the Police Agency.

(Probable Cause Statement)

4. THE FOLLOWING CONSIDERATIONS AND PRACTICALITIES GOVERN THE MANNER OF THE EXECUTION OF THE SEARCH WARRANT:

Based upon Affiant's knowledge, training, and experience, and experience of other law enforcement personnel, Affiant knows that to completely and accurately retrieve data maintained in computer hardware or on computer software, (to include cellular telephones); all computer equipment, related instructions in the form of manuals and notes, as well as the software utilized to operate such a computer, must be seized and subsequently processed by a qualified computer specialist in an appropriate setting. Accordingly, it is very often necessary to take all computer hardware and software found at the suspected location to have it examined in a qualified forensic environment. Such will sometimes be the only way that items such as previously sent and received e mails can be effectively recovered from a computer or its password, can be encrypted, or could have been previously "deleted". In light of these concerns, Affiant requests the Court's permission to transport all such seized computer materials to a qualified forensic facility for imaging and analysis by experts.

WHEREFORE, AFFIANT ASKS FOR ISSUANCE OF A WARRANT THAT WILL AUTHORIZE THE SEARCH OF SAID OBJECT FOR SAID PROPERTY AND SEIZURE OF THE SAME (INCLUDING THE COMPUTER HARDWARE HOUSING IT) AND TO TAKE CUSTODY OF ALL SEIZED PROPERTY AND SAFE KEEP SUCH PROPERTY AS PROVIDED BY STATUTE.

_____

AFFIANT

SUBSCRIBED AND SWORN TO BEFORE ME BY SAID AFFIANT ON THIS THE

_____ day of _____, A.D., 2007.

_____

MAGISTRATE

Appendix S

Generic Computer Search Warrant

SEARCH WARRANT

THE STATE OF (STATE)

COUNTY OF (COUNTY)

To any Peace Officer of the State of (State), GREETINGS:

WHEREAS, the Affiant whose name appears on the affidavit is a Peace Officer under the laws of (State) and did heretofore this day subscribe and swear to said Affidavit before me and whereas I find that the verified facts stated by Affiant in said Affidavit show that Affiant has probable cause for the belief expressed therein and establish the existence of proper grounds for issuance of this Warrant.

Now, therefore, you are commanded to search the premises described as:

Street Address, (City), (State) (Zip) (description of property here); and any electromagnetic media contained therein.

You are further commanded to seize and bring before me the personal property described below.

1. Computer hardware, software, and peripherals, which can collect, analyze, create, display, convert, store, conceal, or transmit electronic, magnetic, optical, or similar computer impulses or data.

2. Any computer files, fragments of files, or image files containing references to E-mail Address, Name of business and its subsidiaries, properties, and holdings to include but not limited to computer equipment and peripherals.
3. Business records, correspondence, notes, papers, ledgers, personal telephone and address books, memoranda, telexes, facsimiles, documents, or maps which reference Business Name, (City) URLs, or other representatives of Business Name.

To facilitate this search you are AUTHORIZED to seize all computer hardware, software, and peripherals, which can collect, analyze, create, display, convert, store, conceal, or transmit electronic, magnetic, optical, or similar computer impulses or data. You are further AUTHORIZED to remove such electromagnetic media from the premises described above and conduct a detailed forensic analysis and search of the media in a sterile laboratory environment.

Hardware includes, but is not limited to, any data processing devices (such as central processing units and self contained laptop or notebook computers and digital cameras); internal and peripheral storage devices such as computer disks, magnetic media, floppy disks, tape systems, hard drives, disk drives, USB drives, tape drives, transistor like binary devices, zip cartridges/drives and other memory storage devices; and any externally attached peripheral input/output devices such as keyboards, printers, scanners, plotters, video display monitors, and optical readers; and related communications devices such as modems, cables and connections, RAM or ROM units, acoustic couplers, automatic dialers, programmable telephone dialing or signaling devices, and electronic tone generating devices; as well as any devises, mechanisms, or parts that can be used to restrict access to computer hardware (such as physical keys and locks).

Computer software includes, but is not limited to, digital information, which can be interpreted by a computer and any of its related components, which may be stored in electronic, magnetic, optical, or other digital form. Computer software commonly includes programs to run operating systems, applications (such as word processing, graphics, or spreadsheet programs), utilities, compilers, interpreters, and communications programs; computer related documentation, that is, written recorded, printed, or electronically stored material which explains or illustrates how to configure or use computer hardware, software, or other related items.

Further, you are ORDERED, pursuant to the provisions of <applicable statute, code here>, (State) Code of Criminal Procedure, to retain custody of any property seized pursuant to this Warrant, until further order of this Court or any other court of appropriate jurisdiction shall otherwise direct the manner of safekeeping of said property. This Court grants you leave and authority to remove such seized property from this county, if and only if such removal is necessary for the safekeeping of such seized property by you, or if the provisions of <applicable reference to statute here>. otherwise authorize such removal. You are further ORDERED to give notice to this Court, as a part of the inventory to be filed subsequent to the execution of this Warrant, and as required by <applicable reference to statute here>, of the place where the property seized hereunder is kept, stored and held.

HEREIN FAIL NOT, but have you then and there this Warrant within three days, exclusive of the day of its issuance and exclusive of the day of its execution, with your return thereon, showing how you executed the same, file in this court.

ISSUED THIS THE _____ day of _____, A.D., 2007, at
_____ o'clock ____.M. to certify which witness my hand this day.

_____

MAGISTRATE

SEARCH WARRANT RETURN

THE STATE OF (STATE)

COUNTY OF (COUNTY)

Each of the undersigned Affiants, being a Peace Officer under the laws of (State) and being duly sworn, on oath certified that the foregoing Warrant came to hand on the day it was issued and that it was executed on the _____ day of _____, A.D., 2007, by making the search directed therein and by seizing during such search the following described property, retained by such Peace Officer, and kept, stored and held as hereinafter set out:

<detailed description of seized equipment here, including disposition of same or transfer to other legal entity, agency or enforcement officer – here>

_____

AFFIANT

SUBSCRIBED AND SWORN TO BEFORE ME by each of said Affiants whose name

is signed above on this the _____ day of _____, 2007.

_____

MAGISTRATE

SEARCH WARRANT AFFIDAVIT

THE STATE OF (STATE)

COUNTY OF (COUNTY)

THE UNDERSIGNED AFFIANT, BEING A PEACE OFFICER UNDER THE LAWS OF (STATE) AND BEING DULY SWORN, ON OATH MAKES THE FOLLOWING STATEMENTS AND ACCUSATIONS.

1. THERE IS IN (COUNTY) COUNTY, (STATE), A SUSPECTED PLACE DESCRIBED AND LOCATED AS FOLLOWS:
<Describe equipment here> SN XXXXXXXXX, and any electro-magnetic media contained their-in (Description same herein)

2. THIS SUSPECTED PLACE IS IN CHARGE OF AND CONTROLLED BY EACH OF THE FOLLOWING NAMED PARTIES, TO WIT:
Subject Name
Subject Address

3. IT IS THE BELIEF OF AFFIANT THAT AT THE SUSPECTED PLACE THERE WILL BE FOUND PROPERTY AND ITEMS CONSTITUTING CONTRABAND AND INSTRUMENTS USED TO COMMIT CRIMINAL ACTS IN VIOLATION OF THE LAWS OF (STATE). SUCH PROPERTY AND ITEMS WILL CONSIST OF THE FOLLOWING:
1. Computer hardware, software, and peripherals, which can collect, analyze, create, display, convert, store, conceal, or transmit electronic, magnetic, optical, or similar computer impulses or data.
2. Any computer files, fragments of files, or image files containing references to E-mail Address, Business Name and its subsidiaries, properties, and holdings to include but not limited to computer equipment and peripherals.
3. Business records, correspondence, notes, papers, ledgers, personal telephone and address books, memoranda, telexes, facsimiles, documents, or maps which reference Business Name, (City) URLS, or other representatives of Business Name.

4. AFFIANT HAS PROBABLE CAUSE FOR THE SAID BELIEF BY REASON OF THE FOLLOWING FACTS, TO WIT:
1. (Probable Cause Statement)

5. THE FOLLOWING CONSIDERATIONS AND PRACTICALITIES GOVERN THE MANNER OF THE EXECUTION OF THE SEARCH WARRANT:
Based upon Affiant's knowledge, training, and experience, and experience of other law enforcement personnel, Affiant knows that to completely and accurately retrieve data maintained in computer hardware or on computer software, all computer equipment, peripherals, related instructions in the form of manuals and notes, as well as the software utilized to operate such a computer, must be seized and subsequently processed by a qualified computer specialist in an appropriate

setting. Accordingly, it is very often necessary to take all computer hardware and software found at the suspected location to have it examined in a qualified forensic environment. Such will sometimes be the only way that items such as previously sent and received e mails can be effectively recovered from a computer or its password, can be encrypted, or could have been previously "deleted." In light of these concerns, Affiant requests the Court's permission to transport all such seized computer materials to a qualified forensic facility for imaging and analysis by experts.

WHEREFORE, AFFIANT ASKS FOR ISSUANCE OF A WARRANT THAT WILL AUTHORIZE THE SEARCH OF SAID SUSPECTED PLACE FOR SAID PERSONAL PROPERTY AND SEIZURE OF THE SAME (INCLUDING THE COMPUTER HARDWARE HOUSING IT) AND TO TAKE CUSTODY OF ALL SEIZED PROPERTY AND SAFE KEEP SUCH PROPERTY AS PROVIDED BY STATUTE.

_____

AFFIANT

SUBSCRIBED AND SWORN TO BEFORE ME BY SAID AFFIANT ON THIS THE

_____ day of _____, A.D., 2007.

_____

MAGISTRATE

Appendix T

Generic Affidavit for Search Warrant

AFFIDAVIT FOR SEARCH WARRANT

STATE OF _____
COUNTY OF _____

Before me this day personally appeared before me, the undersigned judicial of said county, OFFI
CERS, and, , known to me to be
(a) credible person (s), and who, after having been first duly sworn, on oath says (s) that the property described hereinafter falls within those grounds indicated below by "X" (s) in that it:

1. That affiant(s) have good reason to believe and do believe that certain things hereafter
   described are now being concealed in or about the following place in this County:

   A house located at:

   <SEARCH WARRANT LOCATION>

together with all approached and appurtenances thereto and surrounding curtilage thereon, in
particular, any computers or electronic storage media devices which may contain evidence of the
crime of receipt or possession of child pornography.

2. That the place described above is occupied and controlled by :
SUSPECT NAME

3. That said things are particularly described as follows:

1. Computer and Electronic Equipment:
   a. Any and all information or data stored in the form of magnetic or electronic coding on computer media or on media capable of being read by a computer or with the aid of computer related equipment. This media includes network servers, back-up tapes and diskettes, hard drives, floppy diskettes, fixed hard disks, removable hard disk cartridges, tapes, laser disks, video cassettes and other media which is capable of storing magnetic coding.
   b. Any and all electronic devices which are capable of analyzing, creating, displaying, converting or transmitting electronic or magnetic computer impulses or data. These devices to computers, computer components, computer peripherals, work processing equipment, modems, monitors, printers, plotters, encryption circuit boards, optical scanners, external hard drives and other computer related devices.
   c. Any and all instruction or programs stored in the form of electronic or magnetic media which are capable of being interpreted by a computer or related components. The items to be seized could include operating systems, application software, utility program, compilers, interpreters, and other programs or software used to communicate with computer hardware peripherals whether directly or indirectly via telephone lines, radio, or other means of transmission.
2. The search procedure of the electronic data contained in computers or operating software or memory devices, whether performed on site or in a laboratory, or other controlled environment, may include the following techniques:
   a. Surveying various file "directories" and the individual files they contain (analogous to looking at the outside of a file cabinet for the markings it contains and opening a drawer believed to contain pertinent files); or
   b. "Opening" or cursorily reading the first few "pages" of such files to determine their precise contents; or
   c. "Scanning" storage areas to discover and possibly recover recently deleted data; or
   d. "Scanning" storage areas for deliberately hidden, encrypted, or password protected files; or
   e. Performing key word searches through all electronic storage areas in existence that are intimately related to the subject matter of the investigation.
3. Documents, books, magazines, letters, pamphlets, photographs, drawings, videos, or any sexually related paraphernalia which in any way relate to the sexual abuse of minors, including the depiction of minors in a nude/semi-nude state or engaged in sexual activity.
4. That possession of the above described things is in itself unlawful, in that said things are:
Part of an ongoing investigation centered in <County>, <State>, into <description of investigation here>
5. The facts tending to establish the foregoing grounds for a Search Warrant are shown on a sheet headed "Underlying Facts and Circumstances" which is attached hereto, made a part hereof and adopted herein by reference.

6. WHEREFORE, affiant requests that a search warrant issue directing a search of the above described place and seizure of the above described things.

_____   _____

Affiant   Affiant

Sworn to and Subscribed before me, the   day of   , 2007.

                                        Official Title
                                       _____ County Judge

Appendix U

Configuring the Investigator's Forensic Analysis Machine

How does one go about configuring a computer (desktop or laptop) to serve as the cyber forensic investigator's "forensic analysis machine?"

If you were to begin an internal cyber forensic investigation, what would be the recommended hardware configuration for your personal "analysis machine" and what basic software would you expect to find installed on this machine?

This Appendix provides a suggested approach to configuring the cyber forensic investigator's "analysis machine." The "analysis machine" is the primary machine which will be used to carry out the actual investigation, run the forensic software tools and analyze the electronic evidence seized from suspected electronic devices.

Any reference to commercial products and described in this Appendix is for information only; it does not imply recommendation or endorsement by the authors, publisher, reviewers, contributors, or representatives nor does it imply that the products mentioned are necessarily the best available for the purpose. The reader is advised to independently assess and verify that the products identified in this Appendix will meet the investigator's individual and sometimes unique investigative needs.

Basic Hardware Configuration

Note: You can choose to upgrade some of these components such as the extreme quad core 2, and RAM.

Shuttle SD39P2 http://hq1.shuttle.com/products_page03.jsp?PLLI=503&PI=536

Intel u320 SCSI RAID Controller SRCU42E

www.intel.com/design/servers/RAID/srcu42e/

Core 2 Duo E6600 (or Core 2 Quad Q6600)

2GB OCZ PC2-8500 RAM
2*Seagate Barracuda ES 750GB or 2*Hitachi 7K1000 (1TB) – just released, not for sale on sites

MSI low profile GeForce 7100GS PCI-E video
www.newegg.com/Product/Product.aspx?Item=N82E16814127243

Logitech V100 Optical Mouse for Notebooks
www.logitech.com/index.cfm/products/details/CA/EN,CRID=686,CONTENTID=11823

Mini Keyboard with laptop style keys:
www.fentek-ind.com/kbmsm.htm or

ASK-3100/SU www.directron.com/psk3100u.html

Lite-On 20x DVD+-R
www.newegg.com/Product/Product.aspx?Item=N82E16827106045

Philips 15″ LCD monitor
www.newegg.com/Product/Product.aspx?Item=N82E16824133012 or

Samsung SyncMaster 711t 17″ LCD
http://reviews.cnet.com/Samsung_SyncMaster_711t/4505-3174_7-31116462.html?tag=txt
(supports 2 pc inputs, has a switch button)

As for OS software, WinXP, MS Office, Access Data UTK software suite, EnCase and BackTrack. Eventually add Vista to this list.

Additional software could include:

BXDR
www.sandersonforensics.co.uk/html/bxdr.html

Stego Suite 4.1
www.wetstonetech.com/catalog/item/1104418/619451.htm

Steganography Application Fingerprint Database (SAFDB)
www.sarc-wv.com/products.aspx

Cache Reader for Internet Explorer
www.talknet.de/~wolfgbaudisch/CR5.exe

Encase (current release)
www.guidancesoftware.com/

Gargoyle (current release)
www.wetstonetech.com

StegAlyzerAS
www.backbonesecurity.com

Byte Back
www.toolsthatwork.com/

FTK (current release)
www.accessdata.com

Appendix V

Generic Search Warrant

SEARCH WARRANT

STATE OF <State name here>

COUNTY OF _____

To any lawful officer of _____ County, State

    Whereas, OFFICERS NAME, known to me to be a credible person, who after have this day made complaint on oath before me as follows:

1. That affiant has good reason to believe and does believe that certain things described herein are now being concealed in or about the following place in this County:

      A house located at:

LOCATION OF HOUSE

together with all approached and appurtenances thereto and surrounding curtilage thereon, in particular, any computers or electronic storage media devices which may contain evidence of the crime of receipt or possession of <state crime here>.

2. That the place described above or the equipment described above is occupied or controlled by:

John Doe
2222 No Such Place
Some City, State. 36111

3. That said things are particularly described as follows:
   1. Computer and Electronic Equipment:

   a. Any and all information or data stored in the form of magnetic or electronic coding on computer media or on media capable of being read by a computer or with the aid of computer related equipment. This media includes network, servers, back-up tapes and diskettes, hard drives, floppy diskettes, fixed hard disks, removable hard disk cartridges, tapes, laser disks, video cassettes and other media which is capable of storing magnetic coding.
   b. Any and all electronic devices which are capable of analyzing, creating displaying, converting or transmitting electronic or magnetic computer impulses or data. These devices include computers, computer components, computer peripherals, word processing equipment, modems, monitors, printers, plotters, encryption circuit boards, optical scanners, external hard drives and other computer related devices.
   c. Any and all instruction or programs stored in the form of electronic or magnetic media which are capable of being interpreted by a computer or related components. The items to be seized could include operating systems, application software, utility program, compilers, interpreters, and other programs or software used to communicate with computer hardware peripherals whether directly or indirectly via telephone lines, radio, or other means of transmission.

2. The search procedure of the electronic data contained in computers or operating software or memory devices, whether performed on site or in a laboratory, or other controlled environment, may include the following techniques:

   a. Surveying various file "directories" and the individual files they contain which are analogous to looking at the outside of a file cabinet for the markings it contains and opening a drawer believed to contain pertinent files;
   b. "Opening" or cursorily reading the first few "pages" of such files to determine their precise contents;
   c. "Scanning" storage areas to discover and possibly recover recently deleted data;
   d. "Scanning" storage areas for deliberately hidden, encrypted, or password-protected files; or
   e. Performing key word searches through all electronic storage areas in existence that are intimately related to the subject matter of the investigation.

3. Books, magazines, letters, financial records or other documents which in any way relate to the crime of exploitation of children.
4. That possession of the above described things is in itself unlawful (or the public has a primary interest in, or primary right to possession of, the above described things), in that said things are:

IN VIOLATION OF <state violation here>

5. The facts tending to establish the foregoing grounds of issuance of a Search Warrant are shown on a sheet headed "Underlying Facts and Circumstances" which is attached hereto as Exhibit "A," made a part hereof and adopted herein by reference.
6. This Court, having examined and considered said affidavit, and also having heard and considered evidence in support thereof from the affiant named therein does find that probable cause for the issuance of a search warrant does exist. THEREFORE, you are commanded to proceed at any time in the day or night to the place described above and to search forthwith said place for the things specified above, making known to the person or persons occupying or controlling said

place, if any, your purpose and authority for so doing, and if the things specified above be found there to seize them, leaving a copy of this warrant and a receipt for the things taken: and to bring the things seized before this Court instanter; and prepare a written inventory of the items seized, and have then and there this writ, with your proceedings noted thereon.

7. Do not interpret this writ as limiting your authority to seize all contraband and things the possession of which in itself is unlawful which you find incident to your search, or as limiting your authority to make otherwise valid arrest at the place described above.

WITNESS MY HAND, THIS THE _____ DAY OF _____, 2007.

_____

SIGNATURE

_____

OFFICIAL TITLE

RETURN

I received this warrant on the _____ day of _____, 2007 and have executed as follows:

On the _____ day of _____, 2007, at _____ am/pm, I searched the place described in said warrant and I left a copy of the warrant with _____, the person occupying and controlling said place, together with a receipt of the items seized.

The following is an inventory of the things taken pursuant to the warrant:

<include detailed description here>

This inventory was made in the presence of _____,
and _____. I swear that this inventory is a true and detailed account of all things taken by me on the warrant.

OFFICER

Subscribed and Sworn to and returned before me this _____ day of _____, 2007.

_____

SIGNATURE

_____

OFFICIAL TITLE

Appendix W

Statement of Underlying Facts and Circumstances

Based on information and belief, I, OFFICERS NAME, criminal investigator with the AGENCY, having been duly sworn, do hereby state and depose as follows:

Officers Qualifications

Underlying Facts and Circumstances

(INSERT FACTS AND CIRCUMSTANCES OR BASIS OF SEARCH WARRANT)

The Role of the Computer

Computer hardware, software and electronic files may be important to a criminal investigation in two distinct ways: (1) the objects themselves may be contraband, evidence, instrumentalities, or fruits of crime, or (2) the objects may be used as storage devices that contain contraband, evidence, instrumentalities, or fruits of crime in the form of electronic data. In the instant case, the warrant application requests permission to search the described items for *<insert specific search request here>* including those that may be stored on a computer.

Your affiant knows that when an individual uses a computer to obtain *<state item here>*, the individual's computer will generally serve both as an instrumentality for committing the crime and also a storage device for evidence of the crime. Your affiant believes that, in this case, the computer hardware is a container for evidence, a container for contraband, and is also itself an instrumentality of the crime under investigation.

In the instant case, your affiant believes that the subject computer was the primary means used by SUSPECT'S NAME for accessing the Internet, and ultimately *<state infraction and violation of law here>*. The subject computer is also a likely storage device for evidence of such crime because criminals generally maintain records and evidence relating to their crimes on their computers or diskettes. In addition, such records and evidence may also include files that recorded access, downloading and the saving of *<description here>* on the subject computer or diskettes. The subject computer and diskettes may also contain the individual's notes as to how the access was achieved, records of Internet chat discussions about the crime and other records that indicate the scope of the individual's illegal activity.

Child Porn and Obscenity

Computer as Storage Device

Child pornographers generally prefer to store images of child pornography in an electronic form such as the computer may be used to connect to the Internet to download, receive, or share media or data depicting children in sexually explicit poses which may constitute child pornography. The computer's ability to store images in digital form makes a computer an ideal repository for such pornography. A small portable disk can contain hundreds or thousands of images of child pornography, and a computer hard drive can contain tens of thousands of such images at very high resolution. The images can be easily sent to or received from other computer users over the Internet. Further, both individual files of child pornography and the disks that contain the files can be mislabeled or hidden to evade detection.

Computer as Instrumentality

It is common for child pornographers to use personal computers to produce both still and moving images. For example, a computer can be connected to a common video camera using a device called a video capture board; the device turns the video output into a form that is usable by computer programs. Alternatively, the pornographer can use a digital camera to take photographs or videos and load them directly onto the computer. The output of the camera can be stored, transferred or printed out directly from the computer. The producers of child pornography can also use a device known as a scanner to transfer photographs into a computer-readable format. All of these devices, as well as the computer, constitute instrumentalities of the crime.

Seizing Hardware & Conducting Subsequent Offsite Search

Based upon your affiant's knowledge, training and experience, your affiant knows that searching and seizing information from computers often requires agents to seize most or all electronic storage devices (along with related peripherals) to be searched later by a qualified computer expert in a controlled environment. This is true because of the following:

Volume of Evidence

Computer storage devices or electronic media storage devices (like hard disks, diskettes, etc.) can store millions of documents. Additionally, a suspect may try to conceal criminal evidence; he or she might store it in random order with deceptive file names. This may require searching authorities to examine all the stored data to determine which particular files are evidence or instrumentalities of crime. This sorting process can take weeks or months, depending on the volume of data stored, and it would be impractical and invasive to attempt this kind of data search onsite.

Technical Requirements

Searching computer systems for criminal evidence is a highly technical process requiring expert skill and a properly controlled environment. The vast array of computer hardware and software available requires even computer experts to specialize in some systems and applications, so it is difficult to know before a search which expert is qualified to analyze the system and its data. In any event, data search protocols are exacting scientific procedures designed to protect the integrity of the evidence and to recover even "hidden", erased, compressed, password-protected, or encrypted files. Because computer evidence is vulnerable to inadvertent or intentional modification or destruction (both from external sources or from destructive code imbedded in the system as a "booby trap"), a controlled environment may be necessary to complete and accurate analysis. Further, such searches often require the seizure of most or all of a computer system's input/output peripheral devices, related software, documentation, and data security devices (including passwords) so that a qualified computer expert can accurately retrieve the system's data in a controlled environment.

In light of these concerns, your affiant hereby requests the Court's permission to seize the computer and peripherals to search the computer hardware (and associated peripherals) that are believed to contain some or all of the evidence described in the warrant and to conduct an offsite search of the hardware for the evidence described, if, upon arriving at the scene, the agents executing the search conclude that it would be impractical to search the computer hardware and software onsite for this evidence.

Use of Comprehensive Data Analysis Techniques

Searching (the suspect's) computer system for the evidence of child pornography or illicit obscenity may require a range of data analysis techniques. In some cases, it is possible for agents to conduct carefully targeted searches that can locate evidence without requiring a time-consuming manual search through unrelated materials that may be commingled with criminal evidence. For example, agents may be able to execute a "keyword" search that searches through the files stored in a computer for special words that are likely to appear only in the materials covered by a warrant. Similarly, agents may be able to locate the materials covered in the warrant by looking for a particular directory or file names. In other cases, however, such techniques may not yield the evidence described in the warrant, criminals can mislabel or hide files and directories; encode communications to avoid using key words; attempt to delete files to evade detection; or take other steps designed to frustrate law enforcement searches for information. These steps may require agents to conduct more extensive searches such as scanning areas of the disk not allocated to listed files, or opening every file and scanning its contents briefly to determine whether it falls within the scope of the warrant. In light of these difficulties, your affiant request permission to use whatever data analysis techniques appears necessary to locate and retrieve the evidence of child pornography or exploitation of children.

In Conclusion

OFFICERS NAME of the AGENCY NAME comes now on information and belief that a search warrant be issued for computers and other related media at SEARCH WARRANT ADDRESS the residence being owned or occupied by SUSPECT'S NAME.

SWORN AND SUBSCRIBED to by me, this the _____ day of _____, 2007.

_____

OFFICER'S NAME

AFFIANT

WITNESS MY SIGNATURE, this the _____ day of _____, 2007.

_____

COURT OFFICIAL

Appendix X

Generic State Court Order— Seizure of Electronic Hardware and Records

IN THE MATTER OF THE § THE STATE OF _____ APPLICATION OF THE STATE OF _____ FOR AN ORDER AUTHORIZING THE RELEASE OF CELLULAR RECORDS, § WITH CALL DETAIL, INCLUDING CALLER IDENTIFICATION RECORDS, CELLULAR SITE INFORMATION, AND, STORED VOICE/DATA INFORMATION § THE COUNTY OF _____.

APPLICATION

COMES NOW, the State of _____, by and through <enter name here>, _____, and hereby requests that an Order be signed, pursuant to <enter specific and relative State's code here> _____ Code of Criminal Procedure, and, in accordance with, 18 United States Code (U.S.C.), 2703(d.); requiring the herein named utility to furnish all cellular phone records; including call detail(incoming and outgoing), caller identification(s), and cellular site information, for the listed phone number. And, to furnish to the AGENCY Name through the below named officer or his or her designee(s), as soon as practical and at reasonable interval(s) during regular business hours, or, during non-business hours during emergency/exigent situation(s), for the duration of the order.

I.

The utility is _____; cellular provider.

II.

The subscriber is unknown and the cellular telephone number is **(XXX) XXX – XXXX**.

III.

The location of the cellular telephone instrument is unknown in _____ County, _____.

IV.

The release of said cellular phone records are material to the investigation of a criminal offense; supporting information/"specific and articulatable fact(s)" follows:

INCLUDE DETAILED STATEMENT HERE

The release of the records is likely to assist investigators in Goal of Investigation as the records are likely to reveal cellular site information as well as call detail information. This information is likely to lead investigators to the complainant's whereabouts and, thereby, the suspects. Case Number Here.

It is also requested that subscriber information, with call detail and cell site information, be provided, upon the specific request(s) of the investigator(s), for the listed number for the dates of xx/xx/xx (or the beginning of the account/which ever is latest) through the present, and, extending sixty days into the future as necessary and at the specific request(s) of investigators; as efforts are being made to confirm investigative leads related to the homicide investigation. Investigator(s), or their representative(s), will advise as to what exact information is needed.

WHEREFORE, PREMISES CONSIDERED, Your Applicant respectfully requests that an order, consistent with this Application, be granted. Further, that the utility be ordered not to reveal to anyone that this order exists.

_____
ADA NAME
ASSISTANT DISTRICT ATTORNEY
_____ COUNTY, _____

On this the _____ day of _____, 200x, appeared before me the above named applicant, who stated under oath, that the above Application is true and correct to the best of his knowledge.

_____

NOTARY PUBLIC in and for

_____ County, _____

My commission expires:_____

IN THE MATTER OF THE   §   THE   STATE   OF   _____
APPLICATION OF THE STATE OF _____ FOR AN ORDER AUTHORIZING
THE RELEASE OF CELLULAR RECORDS,   §   WITH CALL DETAIL, INCLUDING
CALLER IDENTIFICATION RECORDS, CELLULAR SITE INFORMATION, AND,
STORED VOICE/DATA INFORMATION   §   THE COUNTY OF _____

ORDER

On this the _____ day of _____, 200x, upon proper Application by ADA Name, Assistant District Attorney of _____ County, _____, attached and incorporated for all purposes, the following is hereby ORDERED pursuant to specific articulatable fact(s), to-wit:

That, in as much as _____ will furnish all information, records, and technical assistance necessary to release cellular phone records on the telephone number contained in the attached and incorporated Application. It is hereby ordered that _____ be provided with a copy of this order ordering and ratifying compliance with <enter specific and relative State's code her> of the _____ Code of Criminal Procedure, and, in accordance with, 18 United States Code (U.S.C.), 2703(d.)

That _____ provide all subscriber information, call detail records, with cellular site information, for the provided cellular phone number for the dates of xx/xx/xx (or the beginning of account/which ever is latest) through the present, and, extending sixty days into the future as necessary.

That _____ provide to agent(s)/officer(s)/designee(s) upon their specific request(s), the following; call detail(s), caller identification(s), and cellular site records for the listed dates, and, extending sixty (60) days from the date of the order pertaining to cellular phone number (XXX) XXX–XXXX, or, any telephone/pager/telecommunications device number(s) revealed from these record(s):

1. Cell site(s) activation(s).
2. Number(s) dialed.
3. Incoming number(s), if identified.
4. Subscriber(s), Electronic Serial Number (E.S.N.), and billing information for the specified cellular/wireless telephone, or, any telephone number(s) revealed from these record(s.)
5. An engineering map; showing all cell-site tower locations, sectors, and orientations.
6. Subscriber(s), E.S.N., and billing information for any other cellular/wireless telephone(s) on this account, or, that may be identified from these record(s.)
7. Should this cellular/wireless, Mobile Identification Number (M.I.N.)/E.S.N., or combination, be changed by the subscriber(s) during the course of this order, this order will apply to any new M.I.N./E.S.N.
8. That, upon the specific request from agent(s)/officer(s)/designee(s), that this cellular/wireless number, or any other number(s) identified through these records, shall be activated in compliance with the Communications Assistance to Law Enforcement Act (C.A.L.E.A.); upon the specific request of agent(s)/officer(s)/designee(s.)
9. Further, that said utility provide, as requested within the time period(s) confined by this order, officer(s)/agent(s)/designee(s) access to all stored or non-live recorded voice mail message(s), text message(s), numeric message(s), alpha-numeric message(s), electronic mail(s)[e-mail(s)],

picture(s), file(s), data, etc., for said number(s)/account(s) for said time period(s). And, if required, that said account(s)' personal identification number(s) (P.I.N.)'s or other code(s)/accessing method(s) be provided or reset, as necessary, so that officer(s)/agent(s)/designee(s) be allowed access to said stored or recorded voice mail message(s), text message(s), numeric message(s), alpha-numeric message(s), electronic mail(s)[e-mail(s)], picture(s), file(s), data, etc. This shall be done only upon the specific request(s), and as directed, by investigator(s)/designee(s). Also, that officer(s)/agent(s)/designee(s) be provided with instruction/documentation, as necessary, on the procedure(s) to access said stored or non-live recorded voice mail message(s), text message(s), numeric message(s), alpha-numeric message(s), electronic mail(s)[e-mail(s)], picture(s), file(s), data, etc., for said number(s)/account(s) for said time period(s). And, that access to said information/data be kept confidential from user(s) of the number(s)/account(s).

10. That all call detail, subscriber, stored or non-live recorded voice mail message(s), text message(s), numeric message(s), alpha-numeric message(s), electronic mail(s)[e-mail(s)], picture(s), file(s), data, etc., and any related record(s) or access be provided, upon the specific request of officer(s)/agent(s)/designee(s) of specific data from specific time period(s) within the confines of this order, in an electronic format/e-mail(s)[if possible] specified by agent(s)/officer(s)/designee(s). Also, that the record(s)/data/recording(s), be forwarded, upon the specific request of agent(s)/officer(s)/designee(s), to the listed officer or his/her designee(s). These designee(s) may include, but are not limited to, officer(s)/agent(s)/designee(s) or representative(s) of the <enter city name here> Police Department (P.D.), _____ County, _____ District Attorney's Office, <enter county name here> [list multiple counties if required] County, _____ District Attorney's Office, _____ Department of Public Safety (D.P.S.), United States Attorney's Office, Federal Bureau of Investigation (F.B.I.), United States Secret Service (U.S.S.S.), United States Marshal's Service (U.S.M.S.), United States Immigration and Naturalization Service (I.N.S.), United States Customs Service (U.S.C.S.), United States Drug Enforcement Agency (D.E.A.), etc.

11. Finally, that this order will apply to the actual physical analysis by agent(s)/officer(s)/designee(s), as necessary for the collection of said data, stored voice mail(s), or information, of the actual telecommunications device (cellular phone, pager, etc.), itself, associated with the number(s), account(s), etc. which is the target of this order.

Also, that _____ keep confidential the existence of this order, unless and until, this order is superseded by a court of competent jurisdiction.

IT IS FURTHER ORDERED, that any other telecommunications provider such as; Southwestern Bell Telephone Company, AT&T telephone Company, Verizon Telephone Company, Alltel Communications, AT&T Wireless, T-Mobile, Cingular Wireless, Nextel Communications, Verizon Wireless, Sprint Spectrum/Wireless, L.L.P., Voicestream Wireless, Virgin Mobile, and any other telecommunications related carrier(s); shall provide officer(s), or his/her designee, of the Agency Name with telephone/cellular/wireless records for any number(s) which are derived from record(s) pertaining to the initial number, (XXX) XXX–XXXX that this order will apply to any such number(s). These records are to include customer and subscriber information (listed and unlisted), including customer(s)' service and credit record(s), and, the name(s) and address(es) of all subscriber(s) to the telephone number(s) revealed by the initial cellular record(s), caller identification record(s), cellular site list(s), or cellular site information for any listed call(s).

SIGNED AND ENTERED on this the _____day of _____, 2007.

_____

JUDGE

DISTRICT COURT

_____

COUNTY,

_____

Appendix Y

Consent to Search

(Adapted from Maine Computer Crimes Task Force Consent-to-Search Form)

I hereby give my consent and permission for the items described below to be searched by law enforcement officer _____, and by any law enforcement officer of the _____ [insert name of task force or agency].

I hereby state that I myself have the authority and the ability to gain access to, possess, inspect, examine, and search the items described below.

I understand that I have the right to refuse to give my consent to search the items described below. I give my consent to this search voluntarily and as an act of my own free will, and not because of any threats, compulsion, promises, or inducements. I further state that no threats or promises have been made to compel or induce me to sign this consent form.

I understand that any items, images, documents, or other evidence discovered pursuant to a search of the items described below may be used as evidence in a court of law.

Items to be searched (description, serial numbers, etc.):

<List all detail and information here>

By signing this form, I hereby declare that I have read and understood its contents entirely.

_____   _____

Signature   Date

Witnessed by:

_____   _____

Witness/Law Enforcement Officer   Date

Supplemental Consent to Search

To assist agents of the _____ [insert name of task force or agency], or other local, State, or Federal law enforcement personnel with their search of computers, hard drives, and other electronic storage media seized with my consent, I am providing the following information:

Screen Saver/BIOS Password

Other Passwords/Usernames

Program/Service	Username	Password

Encryption Keys

Public Key	Private Key

_____

Initials

Supplemental Consent to Search
(Internet Service Provider/Web-Based E-Mail)

I, _____, hereby consent to agents of _____ [insert name of task force or agency], or other local, State, or Federal law enforcement personnel who are accessing, viewing, downloading, printing, or copying the contents of any electronic mail in all folders (sent, received, trash, etc.) stored offsite by my Internet service provider or Web based e-mail provider. In cooperation with this search, I am freely and voluntarily providing the following account names, user names, and passwords:

Internet Service Provider (e.g., AOL, Yahoo, Hotmail, etc.)	Username	Password

This consent is limited to a one-time only access for purposes of viewing, downloading, copying, or printing and expires 48 hours after the listed date and time.

_____ _____ _____

Signature   Date   Time

_____ _____ _____

Witness/Law Enforcement Officer   Date   Time

Stipulation Regarding Evidence Returned to the Defendant

_____, in the interest of expediting the searching and seizing of
            [Suspect]

records and other evidence as authorized by Search Warrant #_____, signed by

_____, Judge, on _____, so as to minimize interruption of
                                                            [date]

the normal computing activities of _____, stipulate
                                                    [suspect or suspect's company]
to the [suspect or suspect's company] following terms applicable to the records, equipment, and
evidence itemized in the attached inventory, incorporated by reference:
_____, is satisfied that the backup or forensic copies made
            [Suspect]

on _____, are complete and accurate copies of the entire contents of the systems
        [date]

searched as of that date. _____, will not contest the
                                        [Suspect]

accuracy, reliability, or source of any record copied, printed out, or derived from those

backups/forensic copies. _____ waives any objection
[Suspect]

as to best evidence, authenticity, or foundation as to any record copied, printed out, or

derived from those backups/forensic copies.

> Material in Appendix Y was taken from:
> Digital Evidence in the Courtroom: A Guide for Law Enforcement and Prosecutors, U.S. Department of Justice, Office of Justice Programs, National Institute of Justice, 810 Seventh Street N.W., Washington, DC 20531, NCJ 211314, January 2007, www. ojp.usdoj.gov/nij, retrieved April 2007.

Appendix Z

Confidential Cyber Forensics Questionnaire

	Y	N

1. Does your firm have a cyber forensics response team in place?		

2. Has your staff received formal training in cyber forensic investigations?		

3. Within the past 12 months, have you met with your legal counsel to discuss internal methods and procedures your staff should follow for engagements that may lead to litigation?		

4. Do you have written procedures in place for handling digital evidence?		

5. Do procedures exist that direct staff on how to conduct a forensic investigation involving digital media?		

6. Does staff know the proper procedure to follow if field audit work results in the disclosure of inappropriate material on an employee's computer?		

7. Are these procedures written and distributed to all field auditors?		

8. Does your organization have a policy regarding the disclosure of sensitive internal information, which may become public, as a result of a legal deposition?		

9. Do policies and procedures exist, which address exactly what data your organization will (or can) release, when such data is requested by a plaintiff's attorney?		

10. Are procedures in place to prevent non-relevant data, data unrelated to a cyber forensic investigation, from being released or disclosed as part of a larger examination of an employee's suspect activities?		

11. Are policies in place within your organization that addresses preservation of data integrity and the archiving of a terminated employee's workstation (e.g., hard drive), in the event that those data may need to be examined after the fact?		

12. Is there a retention policy for such preserved and archived data?		

13. Would you be able to demonstrate that controls are in place that would prevent any unauthorized access to these archived data that could result in the manipulation or destruction of these archived data?		

14. What cyber forensics best practices does your firm employ?

15. What is your greatest fear with respect to the emerging importance and impact of cyber forensics to the corporate enterprise?

Thank you for completing the Cyber Forensics Questionnaire. All results will remain strictly confidential and only summary data will be utilized for upcoming research publication.

Appendix AA

Forensic Case Study: Files from the Field

Introduction

This field case involved an alleged sexual assault, torrid exchanges of instant messages and an overwhelming amount of initial evidence, which pointed to the potential guilt of the suspect. Uncovering the truth required old school investigative acumen and 21st century cyber forensic analysis. Read on...

Lead-up

He was working the evening shift; it was spring, the year 2006.

The phone rings, fracturing the detective's concentration. A patrol officer on the line; there has been a reported sexual assault. The patrol officer has traveled out of his jurisdiction to contact the victim, and has conducted an initial interview ... the victim was very emotional, but did a good job in relating the circumstances of the incident. It is the detective's turn now; he's needed for a follow up investigation.

Just the Facts

Arriving at the victim's residence, the detective, experienced in gathering initial evidence relative to such a case, knew very well that as with most sexual assaults, keeping an open mind is critical to obtaining the exact facts and circumstances surrounding the assault. Preconceptions of guilt or innocence, is both unprofessional and dangerous.

The facts support the reality, a majority of reported sexual assaults are indeed legitimate, from time to time however, false reports are filed. Objectivity, the detective knows, is an essential quality in getting to the truth.

The victim, unfortunately typical—young, female, well spoken, polite, and visibly upset, the neighborhood, unfortunately typical—upscale, trendy, affluent.

She Said...

Contact with the male suspect was initiated by the victim through a popular instant messenger program. Conversations consisted of casual talk generally about their lives and interests. Over a period of several weeks, they had frequently sent each other instant messages and often spoke directly over the phone, eventually agreeing to meet in person.

She arranged for him to come to her residence to pick her up. They had planned to go to a nearby mall for shopping and lunch. On the way to the mall the victim stated that he needed to stop by his apartment to pick something up. The victim reluctantly decided to go into the suspect's apartment, where she eventually entered his room to listen to music which they had discussed through previous instant messages.

It was at this time and location that the suspect then forced himself on the victim and sexually assaulted her. The victim, the detective wrote in his notes, was visibly upset although appeared consistent in her story. The victim provided the suspect's name, phone number, and place of employment, and repeatedly denied any talk of sex or desiring a sexual encounter during either their exchange of instant messages or phone conversations.

Satisfied that he had enough information to take the suspect into custody and to interview the suspect, the detective discussed the case with the victim's parents, and at the request of the victim, the detective went to the suspect's place of employment.

Prior to leaving the victim's residence, the victim signed a consent form and granted the detective permission to seize the computer, which the victim had used to communicate with the suspect.

He Said...

The detective went to the suspect's place of employment where he made contact with the suspect. The suspect appeared very nervous as the detective approached. As the suspect began walking toward the detective, the suspect appeared to almost pass out. The suspect's reaction to the detective's presence appeared as an initial sign of guilt, as was the suspect's failure to question why was he being taken to the police station for questioning. The suspect cooperated and agreed to accompany the detective for further questioning.

Immediately upon entering the interview room, the suspect started talking about a girl he met on the Internet. He said he knew it would eventually catch up to him. After having a conversation with the victim for just a few hours, the suspect commented that the victim had invited him to her house to pick her up. The suspect stated that almost the entire conversation which they had via instant messenger revolved around sex, and the victim specifically had discussed a fantasy of being raped.

The suspect disclosed that he had told the victim that he would consider having sex with her, but was not sure about the rape fantasy. According to the suspect, the victim was very aggressive in her conversation about sex and had expressed a desire to meet him for sex as soon as possible.

The suspect drove to the victim's residence, where he picked her up as she had directed. They then drove to the suspect's apartment where they engaged in sexual intercourse. The suspect denied that he had forced the victim to engage in sexual intercourse, and further stated that after they had sex, the victim even used his computer to show him a few of her favorite web sites. He later drove her home.

Innocent or Guilty?

Stepping outside of the interview room, the detective discussed the case with his partner. Both detectives agreed that the victim was much more convincing in her version of the story. While the suspect had some threads of believability to his version of the events, he may have been trying to cover for the presence of trace evidence, including DNA, which would link him to the crime.

At the conclusion of the interview and prior to his release, the suspect granted permission to the detective to seize and search the suspect's personal computer.

The prosecutor would determine whether to charge the suspect with the crime, once the field investigation was complete.

Digital Investigation

A cyber forensic examination was performed on both the victim's and suspect's seized computers. The detective, following procedure, photographed both computers and removed their respective hard drives.

A forensic image of the data on both hard drives was created by the detective using Encase and a hardware based write blocker. Having conducted cyber forensic examinations for several years, the detective was well aware not to get his hopes up and knew not to expect much when it came to examining instant message programs, as the instant message programs often turn off their archiving function by default.

When the imaging was complete, using Encase, the detective reviewed the results of the forensic image from the victim's hard drive and immediately noticed several hundred archived files associated with the instant message program.

Utilizing Encase's Enscript function, the detective identified and decoded the archived instant messages. The detective was very surprised as he began reading the contents of the archived conversations. The archives included over one hundred conversations between the victim and various men. During the various instant message conversations, the victim had discussed the topic of sex almost immediately and detailed her rape fantasy, just as had been described by the suspect, during his interview with the detective.

Upon further analysis and examination, the detective isolated specific instant message conversations relevant to this case. Details of the instant messages sent between the victim and the suspect, matched exactly the sequence of events as communicated to the detective, by the suspect. Evidence in the form of hard copy printouts of instant message conversations between the victim and various men along with specific conversations between the victim and the suspect, were collected by the detective.

This was a turning point in the investigation, as the detective knew with a fair degree of certainty that he had an answer the question—who was lying and who was telling the truth.

Moment of Truth

The detective contacted the victim and asked he back to the police station for a second interview.

Following procedure, the detective asked the victim to re-tell her account of the incident. The victim told the identical story which she had told during her initial interview, including her denial of any discussion about sex.

The detective discussed the basics of computer forensic investigation and its relationship to an ability to examine the contents of instant messages. The victim appeared unimpressed and outright bored by the entire conversation on cyber forensics.

At the conclusion of his short discussion on cyber forensics, the detective presented the victim with hard copy printouts of her conversations, which she was asked to read out loud. The victim refused to do so and she began to cry.

It was only then that the victim admitted to fabricating the sexual assault story.

The victim was charged with filing a false police report and released into the custody of her mother. The detective immediately called the suspect and informed him that the victim had recanted her story, and in doing so vindicated the suspect, confirming his innocence in this incident. The suspect was elated and thankful, indicating that he had been unable to sleep because his arrest and was unsure how he was going to prove his innocence.

Summary

Technology has infiltrated almost every aspect, every facet and every corner of our 21st century world. The art and science of cyber forensic investigation is at its infancy, we are barely scratching the surface with the implementation and application of cyber forensics as a means to serve and protect.

The application of cyber forensics as a tool, as a control over the advances in technology remains to be seen. As society grows in its dependence upon technology, there will always be individuals attempting to abuse this technology. We will need a means and a method with which to peek under the hood, wipe away the veneer, to look behind the curtain and strip away the mysteries of the black box—cyber forensics will be one means to accomplish this—its time has yet to come.

Case Post Script

Four months after the incident described in the above case, the lead detective was off duty, shopping at an electronics store, waiting in line to pay for merchandise. He was approached by a man who hugged him and said "thank you!" Momentarily stunned, it was only after regaining his composure that the detective recognized the man who had hugged him as the exonerated suspect from the closed, instant message case.

This case was submitted to the authors by Detective Brian Mize of the Chesterfield (MO) Police Department. Brian is a forensic investigator assigned to the Regional Computer Crimes Education and Enforcement Group.

Glossary of Terms

AccessData: A leading provider of computer forensic software tools such as FTK and UTK. www.accessdata.com

Access Token: In Windows NT, an internal security card that is generated when users log on. It contains the security IDs (SIDs) for the user and all the groups to which the user belongs. A copy of the access token is assigned to every process launched by the user.

Active Data: Data existing on the data and file storage media of computer systems. Active data are easily viewed on the operating system or application software that were used to create it and is directly available to users without un-deletion, alteration, or restoration.

Active Records: Those records related to current, ongoing or in-process activities and are referred to on a regular basis to respond to day-to-day operational requirements. An active record resides in native application format and is accessible for purposes of business processing with no restrictions on alteration beyond normal business rules.

Acquisition: A process by which digital evidence is duplicated, copied, or imaged.

AES: Advanced Encryption Standard.

Affine Transformation: A transformation consisting of multiplication by a matrix followed by the addition of a vector.

Ambient Data (see also Latent data): Ambient data are data stored in non-traditional computer storage areas and formats, such as Windows swap files, unallocated space, and file slack.

Analysis: The third phase of the computer and network forensic process, which involves using legally justifiable methods and techniques, to derive useful information that addresses the questions that were the impetus for performing the collection and examination.

Anti-Forensic: A technique for concealing or destroying data so that others cannot access it.

Archival Data: Data that is not immediately available to the computer user but that the organization preserves for storage and record keeping purposes, often stored on CD-ROMs, tapes, or other electronic storage devices.

Array: An enumerated collection of identical entities (e.g., an array of bytes).

ASCII (American Standard Code for Information Interchange): Pronounced "ask-ee," ASCII is a nonproprietary text format built on a set of 128 (or 255 for extended ASCII) alphanumeric and control characters. Documents in ASCII format consist of only text with no formatting and can be read by most computer systems.

Attribute: In NTFS, the principal file system for Windows NT, exist as entries in the Master File Table and some number of attributes, which are characteristics of the file. Some of the attributes include the file's name, the date it was created, and the data within the file itself.

Audit Trail: In computer security systems, a chronological record of when users logged in, how long they were engaged in various activities, what they were doing, and whether any actual or attempted security violations occurred.

An audit trail is an automated or manual set of chronological records of system activities that may enable the reconstruction and examination of a sequence of events or changes in an event.

AVI (Audio-Video Interleave): A Microsoft standard for Windows animation files that interleaves audio and video to provide medium quality multimedia.

B+ Tree: A data structure used by NTFS to store files within a directory. The information in the tree is in sorted order and indexed at various points so that NTFS can find a file within a directory by examining relatively little data in the directory.

Bates Number: Sequential numbering used to track documents and images in production data sets, where each page is identified by a unique production number. Often used in conjunction with a suffix or prefix to identify the producing party, the litigation, or other relevant information.

BIOS: Basic Input Output System. The set of routines stored in read-only memory that enable a computer to start the operating system and to communicate with the various devices in the system such as disk drives, keyboard, monitor, printer, and communication ports.

Bit: A binary digit having a value of 0 or 1.

Bit Map: Provides information on the placement and color of individual bits and allows the creation of characters or images by creating a picture composed of individual bits (pixels).

Bit Stream Backup: Bit stream backups (also referred to as mirror image backups) involve the backup of all areas of a computer hard disk drive or another type of storage media (e.g., Zip disks, floppy disks, Jazz disks, etc.).

Such backups exactly replicate all sectors on a given storage device. Thus, all files and ambient data storage areas are copied.

Bit stream backups are sometimes also referred to as "evidence grade" backups and they differ substantially from traditional computer file backups and network server backups.

Bit Stream Imaging: A bit-for-bit copy of the original media, including free space and slack space. Also known as disk imaging.

Bit String: A finite, ordered sequence of bits.

Block: A sequence of binary bits that comprise the input, output, State, and Round Key. The length of a sequence is the number of bits it contains. Blocks are also interpreted as arrays of bytes.

Block Cipher: An algorithm for a parameterized family of permutations on bit strings of a fixed length.

Block Size: For a given block cipher, the fixed length of the input (or output) bit strings.

Buffer: An area of memory often referred to as a "cache," used to speed up access to devices. It is used for temporary storage of data read from or waiting to be sent to a device such as a hard disk, CD-ROM, printer, or tape drive.

Byte: A group of eight bits that is treated either as a single entity or as an array of 8 individual bits.

Case Records: All notes, reports, custody records, charts, analytical data, and any correspondence generate in the laboratory pertaining to a particular case.

Cache: A dedicated, high speed storage location which can be used for the temporary storage of frequently used data. As data may be retrieved more quickly from cache than the original storage location, cache allows applications to run more quickly. Web site contents often reside in cached storage locations on a hard drive.

Cache Manager: Under Windows NT, caching is an integral part of the operating system, called the Cache Manager. The Windows NT Cache Manager is a self tuning cache, with no user configurable parameters, that can, and does, use all available free memory.

The Cache Manager does write behind caching on all three currently supported file systems (FAT, HPFS, NTFS), and can be used by all processes without any special considerations.

CBC: Cipher Block Chaining.

CDPD (Cellular Digital Packet Data): A data communication standard utilizing the unused capacity of cellular voice providers to transfer data.

CD-R: Compact disk-recordable. A disk to which data can be written but not erased.

CD-RW: Compact disk-rewritable. A disk to which data can be written and erased.

Chain of Custody: A process used to maintain and document the chronological history of electronic evidence. A chain of custody ensures that the data presented is "as originally acquired" and has not been altered prior to admission into evidence.

An electronic chain of custody link should be maintained between all electronic data and its original physical media throughout the production process.

Chain of Evidence: The "sequencing" of the chain of evidence follows this order:

1. Collection & Identification
2. Analysis
3. Storage
4. Preservation
5. Transportation
6. Presentation in Court
7. Return to Owner.

The chain of evidence shows:

1. Who obtained the evidence
2. Where and when the evidence was obtained
3. Who secured the evidence
4. Who had control or possession of the evidence.

Check Digit: One digit, usually the last, of an identifying field is a mathematical function of all of the other digits in the field. This value can be calculated from the other digits in the field and compared with the check digit to verify the validity of the whole field.

Cipher: A way to make a word or message secret by changing or rearranging the letters in the message.

Cipher Key: Secret, cryptographic key that is used by the Key Expansion routine to generate a set of Round Keys; can be pictured as a rectangular array of bytes, having four rows and Nk columns.

Ciphertext: Data output from the Cipher or input to the Inverse Cipher.

Clear Message: Is called a plaintext message, which is transformed by cryptography into a ciphertext message.

Cluster: All Microsoft operating systems rely upon the storage of data in fixed length blocks of bytes called clusters. Clusters are essentially groupings of sectors which are used to allocate the data storage area in all Microsoft operating systems, i.e., DOS, Windows, Windows 95, Windows 98, Windows NT, Windows 2000 and Windows XP.

Clusters can be one sector in size to 128 sectors in size and cluster sizes vary depending on the size of the logical storage volume and the operating system involved.

Collection: The first phase of the computer and network forensics process, which involves identifying, labeling, recording, and acquiring data from the possible sources of relevant data, while following guidelines and procedures that preserve the integrity of the data.

Collision: For a given function, a pair of distinct input values that yield the same output value.

CMOS: Series of transformations that converts plaintext to ciphertext using the Cipher Key.

Compression: Compression algorithms such as Zip and RLE reduce the size of files saving both storage space and reducing bandwidth required for access and transmission. Data compression is widely used in backup utilities, spreadsheet applications and database management systems. Compression generally eliminates redundant information or predicts where changes will occur. "Lossless" compression techniques such as Zip and RLE preserve the integrity of the input. Coding standards such as JPEG and MPEG employ "lossy" methods which do not preserve all of the original information, and are most commonly used for photographs, audio, and video.

Compressed File: A file that has been reduced in size through a compression algorithm to save disk space. The act of compressing a file will make it unreadable to most programs until the file is uncompressed.

Computer Evidence: Computer evidence is rather unique when compared to other forms of more traditional documentary evidence. Unlike paper documentation, computer evidence is extremely fragile and it occurs in the form of an identical copy of a specific document that is stored in a computer file. In addition, the legal "best evidence" rules differ for the processing of computer evidence.

However, there is the potential for unauthorized copies to be made of important computer files without leaving behind a trace that the copy was made.

Computer evidence is not limited to data stored in computer files, rather most relevant computer evidence is uncovered in uncommonly known locations. For example, on Microsoft Windows and Windows NT-based computer systems, large quantities of evidence can be found in the Windows swap files or Page Files. In addition, computer evidence can also be uncovered in file slack and unallocated file space.

Computer Investigations: Computer crimes are specifically defined by federal or state statutes and any computer documentary evidence utilized during a computer investigation may include computer data stored on floppy diskettes, zip disks, CDs and computer hard disk drives.

The evidence necessary to prove computer-related crimes can potentially be located on one or more computer hard disk drives in various geographic locations. This evidence can reside on computer storage media as bytes of data in the form of computer files and ambient data; however, ambient data are usually unknown to most computer users and is therefore often very useful to computer forensics investigators.

Computer investigations rely upon evidence stored as data and the timeline of dates and times that files were created, modified, or last accessed by a computer user. Timelines of activities can be essential when multiple computers and individuals are involved in the commission of a crime.

In addition, computer investigations generally involve the review of Internet log files to determine Internet account abuses and analysis of the Windows swap file.

Using computer forensics procedures, processes, and tools, computer forensics investigators can identify passwords, network logons, Internet activity, and fragments of email messages that were dumped from computer memory during past Windows work sessions.

Concept Search: Searching electronic documents to determine relevance by analyzing the words and putting search requests in conceptual groupings so the true meaning of the request is considered. Concept searching considers both the word and the context in which it appears to differentiate between concepts such as diamond (baseball) and diamond (jewelry).

CRC (Cyclical Redundancy Checking): Used in data communications to create a checksum character at the end of a data block to ensure integrity of data transmission and receipt.

Cryptology: Includes making authentication or digital signature schemes that use an algorithm and a key. A crypto system is an implementation of an encryption scheme or algorithm. The making of crypto systems is called cryptography, the breaking of them is called cryptanalysis.

Cyber Forensics: To collect, preserve, and search computer media without changing or harming the original evidence. To find all relevant facts involved in the criminal investigations that now or ever have existed on the computer media.

Considered to be the use of analytical and investigative techniques to identify, collect, examine and preserve evidence or information which is magnetically stored or encoded.

Data Mapping: Going beyond basic search capabilities, data mapping is also called keyless searching. It finds or suggests associations between files within a large body of data, which may not be apparent using other techniques.

Data Mining: Refers to techniques for extracting summaries and reports from an organization's databases and data sets. In the context of electronic discovery, this term often refers to the processes used to cull through a collection of electronic data to extract evidence for production or presentation in an investigation or in litigation.

Data Streams: In DOS and Microsoft Windows 9x, a file contains just one type of data, i.e., data are stored in the form of files. The files can be programs, graphic files, databases, word processing documents, spreadsheets or other file types. Files also are used to store these types of data with Microsoft Windows NT on an NTFS partition. However, starting with Windows NT version 3.51, Microsoft introduced a data storage concept called data streams. Data streams allow multiple forms of data to be associated with a file. This means there can be any number of program files, graphics files, word processing documents, databases, spreadsheets, or any other types of data associated with a given file. This changes some of the rules concerning computer security issues and computer forensics investigations.

Daubert (challenge) *Daubert v. Merrell Dow Pharmaceuticals*, **509 U.S. 579 (1993):** Addresses the admission of scientific expert testimony to ensure that the testimony is reliable before considered for admission pursuant to Rule 702. The court assesses the testimony by analyzing the methodology and applicability of the expert's approach.

Faced with a proffer of expert scientific testimony, the trial judge must determine first, pursuant to Rule 104(a), whether the expert is proposing to testify to (1) scientific knowledge that (2) will assist the trier of fact to understand or determine a fact at issue. This involves preliminary assessment of whether the reasoning or methodology is scientifically valid and whether it can be applied to the facts at issue.

Daubert suggests a open approach and provides a list of four potential factors: (1) whether the theory can be or has been tested; (2) whether the theory has been subjected to peer review or publication; (3) known or potential rate of error of that particular technique and the existence and maintenance of standards controlling the technique's operation; and (4) consideration of general acceptance within the scientific community (509 U.S. at 593-94).

Daubert Test for Reliability: See Rule 702.

Daubert Factors: The U.S. Supreme Court set out several specific factors that should be used by the courts in evaluating any proposed expert testimony. These factors are not exclusive and some or all may not apply in any given case, but they are always the place to start the reliability analysis. The factors are as follows:

1. Whether the theory or technique has been scientifically tested;
2. Whether the theory or technique has been subject to peer review or publication;
3. The (expected) error rate of the technique used;
4. Acceptance of the theory or technique in the relevant scientific community.

While the Daubert test is certainly more liberal than the older, Frye standard, it still allows the exclusion of testimony where the court is convinced that the method used to support the opinion is simply too poorly designed to be trustworthy.

Digital Forensics: The application of science to the identification, collection, examination, and analysis, of data while preserving the integrity of the information and maintaining a strict chain of custody for the data.

Discovery: Discovery is the process of identifying, locating, securing and producing information and materials for the purpose of obtaining evidence for utilization in the legal process. The term is also used to describe the process of reviewing all materials which may be potentially relevant to the issues at hand or which may need to be disclosed to other parties, and of evaluating evidence to prove or disprove facts, theories or allegations. There are several ways to conduct discovery, the most common of which are interrogatories, requests for production of documents and depositions.

Discwipe: Utility that overwrites existing data. Various utilities exist with varying degrees of efficiency—some wipe only named files or unallocated space of residual data, thus unsophisticated users who try to wipe evidence may leave behind files of which they are unaware.

Disk Imaging: Generating a bit-for-bit copy of the original media, including free space and slack space. Also known as a bit stream image.

Disk Mirroring: When files are stored on a computer system's hard disk, a "mirror" copy is made on an additional hard disk or a separate part of the same disk to safeguard information in the case of a disaster.

Documentation: Written notes, audio/videotapes, printed forms, sketches, or photographs that form a detailed record of the scene, evidence recovered, and actions taken during the search of the scene.

Document Metadata: Data about the document stored in the document, as opposed to document content. Often this data are not immediately viewable in the software application used to create or edit the document but often can be accessed via a "Properties" view. Examples include document author and company, and create and revision dates. Contrast with File System Metadata and Email Metadata.

Dongle: Also called a hardware key, a dongle is a copy protection device supplied with software that plugs into a computer port, often the parallel port on a PC. The software sends a code to that port and the key responds by reading out its serial number, which verifies its presence to the program.

The key hinders software duplication because each copy of the program is tied to a unique number, which is difficult to obtain, and the key has to be programmed with that number.

Duplicate Digital Evidence: A duplicate is an accurate digital reproduction of all data objects contained on the original physical item.

Electronic Evidence: According to Black's law dictionary, evidence is "any species of proof, or probative matter, legally presented at the trial of an issue, by the act of parties and through the medium of witnesses, records, documents, exhibits, concrete objects, etc. for the purpose of inducing belief in the minds of the court or jury as their contention."

Electronic information generally is admissible into evidence in a legal proceeding.

Encase: A leading industry standard in computer forensic investigation technology.

Encase allows investigators to acquire data in a forensically sound manner, and to analyze multiple platforms—Windows, Linux, AIX, OS X, Solaris, etc., using a single tool. www. guidancesoftware.com.

Encryption: The automated process of hiding data so that no unauthorized people can access them; this is done by means of a procedure (algorithm) and a key. Decryption is the reverse process.

ESDI (Enhanced Small Device Interface): A defined, common electronic interface for transferring data between computers and peripherals, particularly disc drives.

Evidence: Testimony—whether oral, documentary or real, which may legally be received to prove or disprove some fact in dispute.

Examination: The second phase of the computer and network forensics process, which involves forensically processing large amounts of collected data using a combination of automated and manual methods to assess and extract data of particular interest, while preserving the integrity of the data.

Extended Partitions: If a computer hard drive has been divided into more than four partitions, extended partitions are created. Under such circumstances each extended partition contains a partition table in the first sector that describes how it is further subdivided.

Extrinsic Data: Information about the file, such as file signature, author, size, name, path, and creation and modification dates.

This data are the accumulation of what is in the file, on the media label, discovered by the operator, and contributed by the user. Collectively, it represents the real value of examining an electronic file as opposed to the printed version.

File Allocation Table (FAT): All Microsoft operating systems rely upon the storage of data in fixed length blocks of bytes called clusters. The size of these blocks is dependant upon the type of storage device and the size of the storage device.

For Microsoft DOS, Windows, Windows 95 and Windows 98, a File Location Table (FAT) is used to track which clusters have been allocated to a specific file. The FAT is relied upon by the operating system much like a road map to locate the data associated with a specific file.

References in the FAT act as pointers and they point to clusters by numeric reference. The top four bits of the cluster number in FAT 32 are reserved and are not available for cluster enumeration. Thus, FAT 32 systems can have at most $2**28-1$ or 268,435,455 clusters.

The same rule of thumb applies for FAT 12 and FAT 16 systems. FAT 12 systems can have up to 4079 clusters and FAT 16 systems can have up to 65519 clusters.

The four reserved bits are reserved to identify values meaning things like "empty," "bad sector" and "End of file" in the referenced cluster.

The FAT on a floppy diskette will typically rely upon 12-bit numbers (FAT 12). When hard disk drives are involved, Microsoft Windows and Windows 95a rely upon a 16-bit FAT. Microsoft Windows 95b and Windows 98 were designed to deal with more data and huge hard disk drives. The FAT on these newer operating systems relies upon 32-bit numbers.

File Name Anomaly: Header or extension mismatch; file name inconsistent with the content of the file.

File Slack Space: File slack potentially contains randomly selected bytes of data from computer memory because DOS or Windows normally writes in 512 byte blocks called sectors.

Clusters are made up of blocks of sectors. However, if there is not enough data in the file to fill the last sector in a file, DOS or Windows makes up the difference by padding the remaining space with data from the memory buffers of the operating system.

This randomly selected data from memory is called "RAM Slack" because it comes from the memory of the computer. RAM Slack can contain any information that may have been created, viewed, modified, downloaded, or copied during work sessions that have occurred because the computer was last booted.

Thus, if the computer has not been shut down for several days, the data stored in file slack can come from work sessions that occurred in the past.

FIPS: Federal Information Processing Standard.

File Extension: Many systems, including DOS and UNIX, allow a filename extension that consists of one or more characters following the proper filename. For example, image files are usually stored as .bmp, .gif, .jpg, or .tiff. Audio files are often stored as .aud or .wav. There are a multitude of file extensions identifying file formats. The filename extension should indicate what type of file it is; however, users may change filename extensions to evade firewall restrictions or for other reasons.

Therefore, file types should be identified at a binary level rather than relying on file extensions. To research file types, see (http://www.filext.com). Different applications can often recognize only a predetermined selection of file types.

File Level Binary Comparison: Method of de-duplication using the digital fingerprint (hash) of a file. File Level Binary comparison ignores metadata, and can determine that "SHOPPING LIST.DOC" and "TOP SECRET.DOC" are actually the same document.

Forensics: Computer forensics is the scientific examination and analysis of data held on, or retrieved from, computer storage media in such a way that the information can be used as evidence in a court of law. It may include the secure collection of computer data; the examination of suspect data to determine details such as origin and content; the presentation of computer based information to courts of law; and the application of a country's laws to computer practice.

Forensics may involve recreating "deleted" or missing files from hard drives, validating dates and logged in authors or editors of documents, and certifying key elements of documents or hardware for legal purposes.

Forensically Clean: Digital media that are completely wiped of nonessential and residual data, scanned for viruses, and verified before use.

Forensic Copy: A precise bit-by-bit copy of a computer system's hard drive, including slack and unallocated space.

Forensically Sound Procedures: Procedures used for acquiring electronic information in a manner that ensures it is "as originally discovered" and is reliable enough to be admitted into evidence.

Forward Cipher Function: A permutation on blocks that is determined by the choice of a key for a given block cipher.

Fragmented: In the course of normal computer operations when files are saved, deleted or moved, the files or parts thereof may be broken into pieces, or fragmented, and scattered in various locations on the computer's hard drive or other storage medium, such as removable discs.

Data saved in contiguous clusters may be larger than contiguous free space, and it is broken up and randomly placed throughout the available storage space.

Free Space: An area on media or within memory that is not allocated.

Frye Test: Originally envisioned a process whereby the admissibility of a scientific technique would be decided by reference to the stages of its evolution. The technique, after being invented or discovered within a particular field, would be first subjected to rigorous analysis by the scientific community during its "experimental stage."

Only after this community "agreed" that the technique was valid ("demonstrable") would evidence of its use be admissible in court. Thus, the way in which the Frye test determined when evidence had reached the point of admissibility was to see if the technique was generally accepted by the relevant scientific community.

In the last half century the Frye test was used for determining the admissibility of many types of scientific evidence besides the polygraph.

Fuzzy Search: Subjective content searching (as compared to word searching of objective data). Fuzzy Searching lets the user find documents where word matching does not have to be exact, even if the words searched are misspelled due to optical character recognition (OCR) errors.

GAL: A Microsoft Outlook global address list—directory of all Microsoft Exchange users and distribution lists to whom messages can be addressed. The administrator creates and maintains this list.

The global address list may also contain public folder names. Entries from this list can be added to a user's personal address book.

Gargoyle Investigator: A software tool for digital investigations. When performing incident response, field investigations, digital forensic analysis, threat management, or compliance audits.

Gargoyle Investigator performs a quick search on a stand-alone system for known contraband, hostile, or "bad" programs, and provides significant clues regarding the activities, motives and the intent of suspects or potential suspects. Made by Wetstone Technologies www.wetstonetech.com.

Gigabyte (GB): A unit of consisting of either 1,000 or 1,024 megabytes. In terms of image storage capacity, one gigabyte equals approximately 17,000 81/2" x 11" pages scanned at 300 dpi, stored as TIFF Group IV images.

Harvesting: The process of retrieving or collecting electronic data from storage media or devices; an EDiscovery vendor "harvests" electronic data from computer hard drives, file servers, CDs, and backup tapes for processing and load to storage media or a database management system.

Hash: An algorithm that creates a value to verify duplicate electronic documents. A hash mark serves as a digital thumb print.

Hash Coding: To create a digital fingerprint that represents the binary content of a file unique to every electronically-generated document; assists in subsequently ensuring that data has not been modified.

Hash Function: A function used to create a hash value from binary input. The hash is substantially smaller than the text itself, and is generated by the hash function in such a way that it is extremely unlikely that some other input will produce the same hash value.

Hidden Data: Many computer systems include an option to protect information from the casual user by hiding it. A cursory examination may not display hidden files, directories, or partitions to the untrained viewer. A forensic examination will document the presence of this type of information.

Host Protected Area: An area that can be defined on IDE drives that meets the technical specifications as defined by ATA4 and later. If a Max Address has been set that is less than a Native Max Address, then a host protected area is present.

ICR (Intelligent Character Recognition): The conversion of scanned images (bar codes or patterns of bits) to computer recognizable codes (ASCII characters and files) by means of software or programs which define the rules of and algorithms for conversion.

IDE: Integrated drive electronics. A type of data communications interface generally associated with storage devices.

Imaging: Is the process used to obtain all of the data present on a storage media (e.g., hard disk) whether it is active data or data in free space, in such a way as to allow it to be examined as if it were the original data.

Instant Messaging ("IM"): A form of electronic communication involving immediate correspondence between two or more online users. Peer-to-peer IM communications may not be stored on servers after receipt; logging of peer-to-peer IM messages is typically done on the client computer, and may be optionally enabled or disabled on each client.

Interlaced: TV & CRT pictures must constantly be "refreshed". Interlace is to refresh every other line once or refresh cycle. Because only half the information displayed is updated each cycle, interlaced displays are less expensive than "non-interlaced".

However, interlaced displays are subject to jitters. The human eye/brain can usually detect displayed images, which are completely refreshed at less than 30 times per second.

Interleave: To arrange data in a noncontiguous way to increase performance. When used to describe disc drives, it refers to the way sectors on a disc are organized. In one-to-one interleaving, the sectors are placed sequentially around each track.

In two-to-one interleaving, sectors are staggered so that consecutively numbered sectors are separated by an intervening sector. The purpose of interleaving is to make the disc drive more efficient. The disc drive can access only one sector at a time, and the disc is constantly spinning beneath.

Inter-Partition Space: Unused sectors on a track located between the start of the partition and the partition boot record. This space is important because it is possible for a user to hide information here.

Inverse Cipher: Series of transformations that converts ciphertext to plaintext using the Cipher Key.

IP address (Internet Protocol Address): A string of four numbers separated by periods used to represent a computer on the Internet—a unique identifier for the physical location of the server containing the data.

Journaling: A function of e-mail systems (such as Microsoft Exchange and Lotus Notes) that copies sent and received items into a second information store for retention or preservation.

Because Journaling takes place at the information store (server) level when the items are sent or received, rather than at the mailbox (client) level, some message-related metadata, such as user foldering (what folder the item is stored in within the recipient's mailbox) and the status of the "read" flag, is not retained in the journaled copy.

The Journaling function stores items in the system's native format, unlike e-mail archiving solutions, which use proprietary storage formats that are designed to reduce the amount of storage space required. Journaling systems also lack the sophisticated search and retrieval capabilities contained in email archiving solutions.

JPEG (Joint Photographic Experts Group): A compression format used to store photographs.

Junk Science Legal Challenge: Computer forensics is a relatively new forensic science and it is different from most of the other forensic sciences, e.g., peer reviews are limited and very few universities offer courses or degrees in computer forensic science.

Another aspect of computer forensics that makes it unique is that computer technology is continually changing with the times. These technology changes mandate that computer forensic software tools and processes must change frequently.

For these reasons some criminal and civil defense lawyers have challenged the expertise of computer forensics practitioners in U.S. courts and have sought to exclude computer related evidence claiming that computer forensics is a "Junk Science" and therefore cannot be relied upon to produce accurate and reliable results.

Sometimes the junk science argument is referred to as the Daubert–Frye argument.

Key Drive: A small removable data storage device that uses flash memory and connects via a USB port. Keydrives are also known as keychain drive, thumb drive, jump drive, USB flash drive. Can be imaged and may contain residual data.

Key Expansion: Routine used to generate a series of Round Keys from the Cipher Key.

Keystroke Monitoring: A form of user surveillance in which the actual character-by-character traffic (that user's keystrokes) are monitored, analyzed, or logged for future reference.

Latent: Present, although not visible, but capable of becoming visible.

Latent (also called ambient) Data: The information that one typically needs specialized tools to get at. An example would be information that has been deleted or partially overwritten.

Least Significant Bit(s): The rightmost bit(s) of a bit string.

Legacy Data: Information in the development process that may have significant resources invested into it that has been produced or stored on software or hardware that has become obsolete.

Legal Hold: A legal hold is a communication issued as a result of current or anticipated litigation, audit, government investigation or other such matter that suspends the normal disposition or processing of records.

Legal holds can encompass business procedures affecting active data, including, but not limited to, backup tape recycling. The specific communication to business or IT organizations may also be called a "hold," "preservation order," "suspension order," "freeze notice," "hold order," or "hold notice."

LiveWire: A "law enforcement only" computer forensics software product by WetStone Technologies. www.wetstonetech.com.

Load File: A file that relates to a set of scanned images and indicates where individual pages belong together as documents. A load file may also contain data relevant to the individual documents, such as metadata, coded data and the like. Load files must be obtained and provided in prearranged formats to ensure transfer of accurate and usable images and data.

Log File—$logfile: This file's Data attribute is used by NTFS and the Log File Service to make the file system recoverable. The Log File is a system file so that it can be found early in the boot process and used to recover the volume, if necessary.

The Microsoft Windows NT Logfile, officially designated as $Logfile, is a special system file used by Microsoft Windows NT to keep track of what it is doing.

If the system fails, NT uses the information stored in the Logfile to stabilize itself. The Logfile is similar to the Windows NT Page File because user information can pass through the Logfile unbeknownst to the user.

Like the NT Page file, the Logfile should be analyzed for security leaks and investigative leads.

Logical Cluster Number (Lcn): The number of a cluster in a file as an index into the complete list of clusters on that whole volume. NTFS uses LCNs to determine the physical location of a cluster.

Logical File Space: The actual amount of space occupied by a file on a hard drive. The amount of logical file space differs from the physical file space because when a file is created on a computer, a sufficient number of clusters (physical file space) are assigned to contain the file.

If the file (logical file space) is not large enough to completely fill the assigned clusters (physical file space) then some unused space will exist within the physical file space.

Logical Volume: A partition or a collection of partitions acting as a single entity that has been formatted with a filesystem.

LTO (Linear Tape-Open): A type of backup tape which can hold as much as 400 GB of data, or 600 CDs depending on the data file format.

MAC Generation (Generation): An algorithm that computes a MAC from a message and a key.

MAC Verification (Verification): An algorithm that verifies if a purported MAC is valid for a given message and key.

MAPI (Mail Application Program Interface): A Windows software standard that has become a popular email interface used by MS Exchange, GroupWise, and other email packages.

Master File Table (MFT)—$mft: The Master File Table contains one record for every file on an NTFS volume in its Data attribute, including one for itself. The first 16 records are reserved for NTFS system files, with only the first nine currently in use.

A unique system file that essentially acts as a database, containing information on all the files and subdirectories located within the NTFS logical volume (partition).

There is at least one record for every file and subdirectory on the NTFS logical volume and each one is 1024 bytes in length and contains information, known as attributes, that tell the system how to deal with the file or directory associated with the record.

If the full 1024 bytes are not used, the record can contain information from previous files, which is known as MFT slack. Knowledge of this MFT slack is vital to investigators because a computer forensics utility that captures file slack does not capture MFT slack.

In addition, the MFT sometimes stores the actual file data along with all the system data relating to the file, which is known as resident data. Resident data can have significant meaning concerning computer security issues regarding the potential leakage of sensitive data.

MD5 Hash: An algorithm created in 1991 by Professor Ronald Rivest that is used to create digital signatures (i.e., fingerprints) of storage media such as a computer hard drive.

When this algorithm is applied to a hard drive then it creates a unique value. Changing the data on the disk in any way will change the MD5 value.

Message Authentication Code (MAC): A bit string of fixed length, computed by a MAC generation algorithm, that is used to establish the authenticity and, hence, the integrity of a message.

Message Digest: A hash that uniquely identifies data. Changing a single bit in the data stream used to generate the message digest will yield a completely different message digest.

Metadata: Metadata are information about a particular data set or document which describes how, when and by whom it was collected, created, accessed, modified and how it is formatted. Can be altered intentionally or inadvertently. Can be extracted when native files are converted to image. Some metadata, such as file dates and sizes, can easily be seen by users; other metadata can be hidden or embedded and unavailable to computer users who are not technically adept. Metadata are generally not reproduced in full form when a document is printed.

MFT (Master File Table): Index to files on a computer. If corrupt, a drive may be unusable, yet data may be retrievable using forensic methods.

Misnamed Files and Files with Altered Extensions: One simple way to disguise a file's contents is to change the file's name to something innocuous. For example, if an investigator was looking for spreadsheets by searching for a particular file extension, such as ".XLS," a file whose extension had been changed by the user to ".DOC" would not appear as a result of the search.

Forensic examiners use special techniques to determine if this has occurred, which the casual user would not normally be aware of.

Mirror-Image Backup: This copy of a hard drive, or other storage device, exactly replicates every sector of the original. It is accepted as a substitute for the original in a court of law.

Mode of Operation (Mode): An algorithm for the cryptographic transformation of data that features a symmetric key block cipher.

Most Significant Bit(s): The leftmost bit(s) of a bit string.

Native Format: Electronic documents have an associated file structure defined by the original creating application. This file structure is referred to as the "native format" of the document. Because viewing or searching documents in the native format may require the original application (e.g., viewing a Microsoft Word document may require the Microsoft Word application), documents are often converted to a vendor-neutral format as part of the record acquisition or archive process. "Static" formats (often called "imaged formats"), such as TIFF or PDF, are designed to retain an image of the document as it would look viewed in the original creating application but do not allow metadata to be viewed or the document information to be manipulated.

NIST: National Institute of Standards and Technology.

NTFS Boot Sector: The NTFS Boot Sector is located at the beginning of the volume, with a duplicate located in the middle of the volume.

   The NTFS Boot Sector contains the standard BIOS Parameter Block (BPB), the number of sectors in the volume, and the starting Logical cluster numbers (Lcns) of the Master File Table (MFT) and the Master File Table Mirror (MFT2).

NTFS Volume Structure: When a drive is formatted with the NTFS file system, the partition is initialized to contain an NTFS volume. More accurately, each instance of a Master File Table (MFT) is a volume. Unlike a FAT or HPFS partition, all space which is allocated and in use on an NTFS volume is part of a file, including the bootstrap and system files which are used to implement the volume structure.

   The heart of the NTFS volume structure is the Master File Table (MFT) which contains at least one record for each file on the volume, including one for itself, with each record being 2K in size. This makes NTFS appear very much like a relational database.

   On an NTFS volume all files are identified by a file number, which is created from the position of the file in the MFT and a sequence number. Each file, and directory, on an NTFS volume is made up of a set of attributes.

OLE: Object Linking and Embedding. A feature in Microsoft's Windows which allows each section of a compound document to call up its own editing tools or special display features. This allows for combining diverse elements in compound documents.

Operating System (OS): An Operating system provides the software platform which directs the overall activity of a computer, network or system, and on which all other software programs and applications can run. In many ways, choice of an operating system will effect which applications can be run.

   Operating systems perform basic tasks, such as recognizing input from the keyboard, sending output to the display screen, keeping track of files and directories on the disc and controlling peripheral devices such as disc drives and printers. For large systems, the operating system has even greater responsibilities and powers—becoming a traffic cop to makes sure different programs and users running at the same time do not interfere with each other.

   The operating system is also responsible for security, ensuring that unauthorized users do not access the system. Examples of operating systems are UNIX, DOS, Windows, LINUX, Macintosh, and IBM's VM. Operating systems can be classified in a number of ways, including:

■ Multi-user (allows two or more users to run programs at the same time—some operating systems permit hundreds or even thousands of concurrent users);

- Multiprocessing (supports running a program on more than one CPU);
- Multitasking (allows more than one program to run concurrently);
- Multithreading (allows different parts of a single program to run concurrently); and
- Real time (instantly responds to input—general-purpose operating systems, such as DOS and UNIX, are not real-time).

ORB: A high-capacity removable hard disk system. ORB drives use magnetoresistive (MR) read/write head technology.

Original Electronic Evidence: Physical items and those data objects that are associated with those items at the time of seizure.

Partition Gap: One physical hard disk drive can be partitioned to contain one or more logical drives when computer users utilize programs such as FDisk or Partition Magic.

On large hard disk drives it is not uncommon to have multiple partitions that can be used to store data in different logical drives, like drives C or D.

When multiple partitions are involved it is possible for gaps to exist between the partitions, which are referred to as partition gaps because they can be used for covert data storage.

Partition gaps can contain legacy data in sectors that were previously associated with data files stored on prior partitions, which can occur when physical hard disk drives are repartitioned during the upgrade of a computer.

For these reasons, partition gaps can be a source of computer security risks and data hiding.

Partition Waste Space: After the boot sector of each volume or partition is written to a track, it is customary for the system to skip the rest of that track and begin the actual useable area of the volume on the next track.

This results in unused or "wasted" space on that track where information can be hidden. This "wasted space" can only be viewed with a low level disc viewer.

However, forensic techniques can be used to search these "wasted space" areas for hidden information.

PDF (Portable Document Format): An imaging file format technology developed by Adobe Systems. PDF captures formatting information from a variety of applications in such a way that they can be viewed and printed as they were intended in their original application by practically any computer, on multiple platforms, regardless of the specific application in which the original was created.

PDF files may be text-searchable or image-only. Adobe® Reader, a free application distributed by Adobe Systems, is required to view a file in PDF format. Adobe® Acrobat, an application marketed by Adobe Systems, is required to edit, capture text, or otherwise manipulate a file in PDF format.

Phreaking: Telephone hacking.

Physical File Space: When a file is created on a computer, a sufficient number of clusters (physical file space) are assigned to contain the file. If the file (logical file space) is not large enough to completely fill the assigned clusters (physical file space) then some unused space will exist within the physical file space.

This unused space is referred to as file slack and can contain unused space, previously deleted or overwritten files or fragments thereof.

PKI Digital Signature: A document or file may be digitally signed using a party's private signature key, creating a "digital signature" that is stored with the document.

Anyone can validate the signature on the document using the public key from the digital certificate issued to the signer.

Validating the digital signature confirms who signed it, and ensures that no alterations have been made to the document because it was signed.

Similarly, an email message may be digitally signed using commonly available client software that implements an open standard for this purpose, such as Secure Multipurpose Internet Mail Extensions (S/MIME). Validating the signature on the email can help the recipient know with confidence who sent it, and that it was not altered during transmission.

Plaintext Data: Input to the Cipher or output from the Inverse Cipher.

Port: An interface by which a computer communicates with another device or system. Personal computers have various types of ports.

Internally, there are several ports for connecting disk drives, display screens, and keyboards. Externally, personal computers have ports for connecting modems, printers, mice, and other peripheral devices.

Port Replicator: A device containing common PC ports such as serial, parallel, and network ports that plugs into a notebook computer.

A port replicator is similar to a docking station but docking stations normally provide capability for additional expansion boards.

Preservation Order: A document ordering a person or company to preserve potential evidence. The authority for preservation letters to ISPs is in 18 USC 2703(f).

Proficiency Tests : Tests to evaluate the competence of analysts and the quality performance of a laboratory; in open tests, the analysts are aware that they are being tested; in blind tests, they are not aware.

Internal proficiency tests are conducted by the laboratory itself; external proficiency tests are conducted by an agency independent of the laboratory being tested.

Protocol: A directive listing the procedures to be followed in performing a particular laboratory examination or operation—the overall plan for analysis of a particular type of evidence.

PST: A Microsoft Outlook email store. Multiple .pst files may exist and contain archived email.

Quality Audit : A management tool used to evaluate and confirm activities related to quality. Its primary purpose is to verify compliance with the operational requirements of the quality system.

RAM (Random Access Memory): Hardware inside a computer that retains memory on a short-term basis and stores information while the computer is in use. It is the "working memory" of the computer into which the operating system, startup applications and drivers are loaded when a computer is turned on, or where a program subsequently started up is loaded, and where thereafter, these applications are executed.

RAM can be read or written in any section with one instruction sequence. It helps to have more of this "working space" installed when running advanced operating systems and applications. RAM content is erased each time a computer is turned off.

Relevant Evidence: Is defined as that which has "any tendency to make the existence of any fact that is of consequence to the determination of the action more probable or less probable than it would be without the evidence."

Rule 401. The Rule's basic standard of relevance thus is a liberal one.

Reliable Scientific Evidence: The Supreme Court provided four non-definitive factors to consider in making a determination (a fifth has been added by the Seventh Circuit court.) A judge must take into account the following:

1. Whether the theory or technique can be and has been tested
2. Whether it has been subjected to peer review and publication
3. The known or potential error

4. The general acceptance of the theory in the scientific community

5. Whether the proffered testimony is based upon the expert's special skill

Reporting: The final phase of the computer and network forensic process, which involves reporting the results of the analysis; this may include describing the actions used, explaining how tools and procedures were selected, determining what other actions need to be performed (e.g., forensic examination of additional data sources, securing identified vulnerabilities, improving existing security controls), and providing recommendations for improvement to policies, guidelines, procedures, tools, and other aspects of the forensic process.

The formality of the reporting step varies greatly depending on the situation.

Residual Data: Data that is not currently live on the computer system, including data found in file slack space, data found on media free space, and data from deleted files. Also known as Ambient Data.

Rijndael: Cryptographic algorithm specified in the Advanced Encryption Standard (AES).

ROM (Read Only Memory): Random memory which can be read but not written or changed. Also, hardware, usually a chip, within a computer containing programming necessary for starting up the computer, and essential system programs that neither the user nor the computer can alter or erase.

Information in the computer's ROM is permanently maintained even when the computer is turned off.

Round Key: Round keys are values derived from the Cipher Key using the Key Expansion routine; they are applied to the State in the Cipher and Inverse Cipher.

Rules of Evidence: There are various tests that courts can apply to the methodology and testimony of an expert to determine admissibility, reliability, and relevancy. The particular test(s) used will vary from state to state and even from court to court within the same state.

Commonly, you will hear about the Frye test and the Daubert test. You need to be aware of the Rules of Evidence for your locale and situation. Your best bet is to ask legal counsel about any Rules of Evidence that you need to be aware of pertinent to the situation, and familiarize yourself with this information early on.

Rule 702 (Governing Expert Testimony): If scientific, technical, or other specialized knowledge will assist the trier of fact to understand the evidence or to determine a fact in issue,

A witness qualified as an expert by knowledge, skill, experience, training, or education, may testify thereto in the form of an opinion or otherwise if:

1. The testimony is based upon sufficient facts or data

2. The testimony is the product of reliable principles and methods

3. The witness has applied the principles and methods reliably to the facts of the case

S-box: Non-linear substitution table used in several byte substitution transformations and in the Key Expansion routine to perform a one-for-one substitution of a byte value.

SAN (Storage Area Network): A high-speed subnetwork of shared storage devices. A storage device is a machine that contains nothing but a disc or discs for storing data.

A SAN's architecture works in a way that makes all storage devices available to all servers on a LAN or WAN. As more storage devices are added to a SAN, they too will be accessible from any server in the larger network. In this case, the server merely acts as a pathway between the end user and the stored data.

Because stored data does not reside directly on any of a network's servers, server power is utilized for business applications, and network capacity is released to the end user.

SCSI: Small Computer System Interface. A type of data communications interface.

Sector: The smallest unit of storage on a computer. Sectors are composed of bits, and are generally a power of 2 bytes in size. A "regular" disk sector is 512 bytes.

Sector Gap: Sectors consist of fixed blocks of storage space that usually contain 512 bytes of data. An equal number of sectors are written to each track on a floppy diskette, hard disk drive, and most storage devices, however, the circumference of the outside tracks is much larger than the circumference of the inside tracks.

For this reason, much of the storage space is wasted on some storage devices, however, modern hard disk drives have eliminated much of this waste through the use of advanced data storage mapping techniques.

In addition, on some storage devices the area between sectors on the larger tracks can be used for covert data storage and this area is referred to as sector gap.

Seizure Disk: A specially prepared floppy disk designed to protect the computer system from accidental alteration of data.

SHA-1: Secure Hash Algorithm, for computing a condensed representation of a message or a data file specified by FIPS PUB 180-1.

Slack Space: The unused space in a disk cluster. The DOS and Windows file systems use fixed-size clusters. Even if the actual data being stored requires less storage than the cluster size, an entire cluster is reserved for the file. The unused space is called the slack space.

Spoliation: Generally, the intentional or negligent destruction or alteration of evidence when there is current litigation or an investigation or there is reasonable anticipation that either may occur in the near future. Some jurisdictions also define it as a failure to preserve information that may become evidence.

State: Intermediate Cipher result that can be pictured as a rectangular array of bytes, having four rows and Nb columns.

Steganography: The art and science of communicating in a way that hides the existence of the communication. It is used to hide a file inside another.

For example, a child pornography image can be hidden inside another graphic image file, audio file, or other file format.

Symmetric Crypto Systems: Both sender and receiver use the same key. In asymmetric or public-key cryptography, they use different keys.

Symmetric Keys: Are called secret keys, whereas public-key encryption uses pairs consisting of one private and one public key.

Subkey: A secret string that is derived from the key.

Subkey Generation: An algorithm that derives subkeys from a key.

Swap File: A file used to temporarily store code and data for programs that are currently running. This information is left in the swap file after the programs are terminated, and may be retrieved using forensic techniques. Also referred to as a page file or paging file.

Temporary and Swap Files: Many computers use operating systems and applications that store data temporarily on the hard drive.

These files, which are generally hidden and inaccessible, may contain information that the investigator finds useful.

TDEA: Triple Data Encryption Algorithm.

Thumbnail: A miniature representation of a page or item for quick overviews to provide a general idea of the structure, content and appearance of a document. A thumbnail program may be standalone or part of a desktop publishing or graphics program.

Thumbnails take considerable time to generate, but provide a convenient way to browse through multiple images before retrieving the one needed. Programs often allow clicking on the thumbnail to retrieve it.

Unallocated Space: The area of computer media, such as a hard drive, that does not contain normally accessible data. Unallocated space is usually the result of a file being deleted. When a file is deleted, it is not actually erased, but is simply no longer accessible through normal means.

The space that it occupied becomes unallocated space, that is, space on the drive that can be reused to store new information. Until portions of the unallocated space are used for new data storage, in most instances, the old data remains and can be retrieved using forensic techniques. The only way to clean this space is with cleansing devices known as scrubbers.

Virtual Cluster Number (VCN): The number of a cluster in a file relative to other clusters in that file. The first VCN in a file is 0, the next 1, and so on. NTFS uses VCNs to determine the logical positioning of a cluster within a file.

WAV: File extension name for Windows sound files. ".WAV" files can reach 5 Megabytes for one minute of audio.

Windows 95 (or 98): Operating system marketed by Microsoft. In use on desktop PCs the system automatically loads into the computer's memory in the act of switching the computer on. MS-DOS, Windows, Windows 3.0, Windows 95, Windows 98, .NET, Office XP, Windows XP and Windows Server are registered trademarks of Microsoft Corporation.

Windows NT: Operating system marketed by Microsoft primarily aimed at the business market. Multiple layers of security are available with this system.

Windows NT Log File: Almost every Web server worth its salt has some sort of system that stores information about which pages, images, and files are requested, who requests them, and how many bytes are transferred. All of this information is dumped into a log file that is stored in a specific location on your server.

Windows Swap/Page File: Microsoft Windows-based computer operating systems utilize a special file as a "scratch pad" to write data when additional random access memory is needed, called Windows Swap Files or Windows Page Files.

Windows Swap and Page Files are potentially very large and most computer users are unaware of their existence and the potential exists for these huge files to contain remnants of word processing, email messages, Internet browsing activity, database entries, and almost any other work that may have occurred during past Windows work sessions.

This situation creates a significant security problem because the potential exists for data to be transparently stored within the Windows Swap File without the knowledge of the computer user, which can occur even if the work product was stored on a computer network server.

The result is a significant computer security weakness that can be of benefit to the computer forensics specialist.

Word: A group of 32 bits that is treated either as a single entity or as an array of 4 bytes.

Write-Blocker: A tool that prevents all computer storage media connected to a computer from being written to or modified.

Definitions for this glossary were compiled from various sources including but, not limited to the following.

1. The PC911 web site
2. www.pcnineoneone.com/index.html
3. www.littleharbor.com/ntfs-details.htm

4. NSTL White Paper, "System Performance and File Fragmentation In Windows NT," October, 1999, Testing And Distribution Center, 625 Ridge Pike, Conshohocken, PA 19428-1180, http://64.233.167.104/search?q=cache:aUaRd1I5Kp0J:networking.ittoolbox.com/browse.asp%3Fc%3DNetworkingPeerPublishing%26r%3Dhttp://www.executive.com%252Fwhats-new%252Fdkwp-1.doc+%22NT+Log+File%22&hl=en

5. Villano, M. (May 1, 2001) "Say What? So You're New To The World Of Computer Forensics?" CIO Magazine, www.cio.com/archive/030101/autopsy_sidebar1.html

6. www.computerforensicsworld.com/

7. New Technologies, Inc. (NTI), www.forensics-intl.com/aboutus.html, 2075 Northeast Division Street, Gresham, Oregon 97030 USA, (503) 661-6912, info@forensics-intl.com

8. United States Department of Justice, (July 2001), "Electronic Crime Scene Investigation: A Guide for First Responders," NCJ 187736, NIJ Guide, Office of Justice Programs, National Institute of Justice, www.ojp.usdoj.gov/nij, 810 Seventh Street N.W., Washington, DC 20531.

9. Frye v. United States 293 F. 1013 (D.C. Cir. 1923), www.law.harvard.edu/publications/evidenceiii/cases/frye.htm

10. Hailey, S., (September 19, 2003), "What is Computer Forensics?), steve@cybersecurityinstitute.biz, SP Hailey Enterprises, www.cybersecurityinstitute.biz/forensics.htm

11. Good Practice Guide for Computer based Electronic Evidence, National Hi-tech Crime Unit, Association of Chief Police Officers, www.nhtcu.org/ACPO%20Guide%20v3.0.pdf

12. Setec Investigations, www.setecinvestigations.com/aboutus/index.php, 8391 Beverly Blvd. # 167, Los Angeles, CA 90048, (800) 748-5440, info@setecinvestigations.com

13. United States Department of Justice, (April 2004), "Forensic Examination of Digital Evidence: A Guide for Law Enforcement," NCJ 199408, NIJ, Office of Justice Programs, National Institute of Justice, www.ojp.usdoj.gov/nij, 810 Seventh Street N.W., Washington, DC 20531.

14. Federal Information Processing Standards Publication 197, November 26, 2001, Announcing the ADVANCED ENCRYPTION STANDARD (AES), http://csrc.nist.gov/publications/fips/fips197/fips-197.pdf

15. Recommendation for Block Cipher Modes of Operation: The CMAC Mode for Authentication, Morris Dworkin, NIST Special Publication 800-38B, Computer Security Division Information Technology Laboratory, National Institute of Standards and Technology, Gaithersburg, MD 20899-8930, May 2005, http://csrc.nist.gov/publications/nistpubs/800-38B/SP_800-38B.pdf

16. The Sedona Conference Glossary: E-Discovery & Digital Information Management, A Project of The Sedona Conference, Working Group on Electronic Document, Retention & Production (WG1) RFP+ Group, May 2005.

17. Guide to Integrating Forensic Techniques into Incident Response Recommendations of the National Institute of Standards and Technology, Karen Kent, Suzanne Chevalier, Tim Grance, Hung Dang, National Institute of Standards and Technology Special Publication 800-86, Computer Security Division, Information Technology Laboratory, National Institute of Standards and Technology, Gaithersburg, MD 20899-8930, August 2006.

Index

O

P